기출의 파급효과

영어 영역

영어(하)

orbibooks

영어(하)
기출의 파급효과

영어(하)

이 책을 펴내며

기나긴 상권을 넘어 기출의 파급효과 영어 하권으로 넘어오신 수험생 여러분들에게 먼저 대견함이 느껴지고, 응원의 박수를 보내면서 시작하고 싶습니다. 상권이 20번(주장), 22번(요지), 23번(주제), 24번(제목), 31~34번(빈칸)과 21번(함축 의미 추론), 40번(요약) 유형을 다뤘다면, 이번 하권에서는 35번(흐름 무관), 30번(어휘), 41~42번(단문 독해), 36~37번(순서), 38~39번(문장 삽입) 유형, 또한 29번(문법)을 Chapter 6에서 다루어 수능에서 문제를 포기하는 일이 없이 대비할 수 있도록 합니다.

상권은 빈칸과 그 빈칸을 응용한 문제 풀이가 중심이 되었다면, 이번 하권은 상대적으로 좀 더 다양한 수능 유형의 접근 방법에 대해 알아볼 것입니다. 그리고 마지막에는 여러분들이 어려워하고 양이 많은 문법에 대해서 효율적으로 대비할 수 있도록 제시하고 있습니다.

항상 올바른 영어 공부란 무엇인지, 수험생들에게 가장 도움이 되는 영어 공부에 대해서 생각해왔습니다. 단순한 문제, 단순한 해설만 제공하는 기존의 문제집에서 벗어나, 많은 종류의 수능 문제들을 푸는 방법을, 풀이 과정을 이해할 수 있고, 명쾌한 해설을 작성하기 위해 노력했습니다.

파급효과 영어는 단순한 풀이를 지양하는 문제집이라고 생각합니다. 문제 하나 풀고, 답지 보고 고개만 끄덕거리면서 넘어가는 영어 문제집으로는 남지 않을 것이라 자신합니다. 하권 역시 최고의 영어 준비 교재로 거듭나기 위해, 모의고사와 수능 문제들을 철저하게 분석했고 교육청 모의고사를 면밀하게 선별했습니다.

그렇기 때문에 이 책을 풀면서 해설을 그저 답을 찾는 도구로만 이용하는 것을 지양하셨으면 좋겠습니다. 본인이 문제를 풀고, 그 답이 옳다면, 그 답이 옳은 근거를 지문에서 찾아보고, 틀렸다면 본인이 오답을 생각한 근거, 그 근거가 잘못된 근거, 올바른 해답에 대한 근거를 모두 지문에서 파악을 하는 연습을 하시는 것을 추천합니다. 한 문장씩 분석한 해설은 그 근거 파악을 돕는 방식으로 양보다는 질을 염두에 두고 자세하게 학습한다면 좀 더 빠르고 정확하게 영어 문제를 풀 수 있을 것이라 자신합니다.

여러분들의 도전은 이제 시작입니다. 이 책이 그 도전을 매듭지을 첫 번째 단추가 되기를 기원합니다.

영어 학습방법 소개

1. 가장 중요한 것은 어휘입니다! **기출에서 제시된 어휘들은 반드시 습득하셔야 합니다.** 아무리 뛰어난 독해능력을 갖고 있더라고 문장에 사용된 단어를 알지 못한다면 확실한 이해를 할 수 없습니다. 어휘가 구성되는 원리에 대한 이해와 더불어 이 교재로 공부하시면서 모르는 어휘가 나올 때마다 따로 정리하여 외우시길 바랍니다.

2. **평가원 기출의 모든 문장이 해석되셔야 합니다.** 어려운 구문들은 분석해드리지만 이해가 잘 안되시거나 다른 문장에서 해석이 안 되시는 경우 질문 게시판을 적극적으로 활용하시길 바랍니다.

3. **풀이법을 체화하시길 바랍니다.** 풀어보셨던 문제들이더라도 책에서 보여드리는 풀이법으로 근거를 찾아서 풀어보시길 바랍니다. 책에 제시된 풀이법은 모든 문제들을 풀 수 있는 풀이법으로 수능에서 어떤 문제가 출제되든 간에 풀이하실 수 있습니다. 책에서 제시된 풀이법으로 많이 풀어보셔야 합니다.

책 소개

저희 교재는
'Ⅰ. 설명 듣기 ⇒ Ⅱ. 같이하기 ⇒ Ⅲ. 혼자 하기'의 틀을 반영하여 학습 과정을 구성했습니다.

1. 평가원이 제시한 유형

평가원이 수능 영어에 대해서 제시한 2018학년도 수능 영어 절대평가 학습안내와 2021~2025학년도 대학수학능력 시험 학습 방법안내를 통해서 평가원이 각 유형에 대해서 학생들에게 무엇을 요구하는 지를 같이 확인하고 이를 바탕으로 각 유형에 대한 풀이법을 정립하고 유형별로 학습합니다.

2. 본문

본문에서는 1. 평가원이 제시한 유형을 통해 정립한 풀이법을 구체적으로 학습하는 과정입니다. 절대평가 이전 평가원 기출을 예시로 하여 풀이법을 세부적으로 정립하며 해당 유형을 학습합니다.

3. 체화

2. 본문에서 학습한 풀이법의 중요 사고 과정을 절대평가 이전 평가원 기출에 적용하는 과정입니다. 체화의 과정을 통해서 2.본문에서 배운 풀이법과 각 유형별 접근법을 본인의 것으로 만들게 됩니다.

4. 중. 최. 평. (중요 최신 평가원 기출)

2. 본문에서 배우고 3. 체화에서 본인의 것으로 만든 풀이법과 접근법을 최근 평가원 중요 기출에 적용하여 같이 풀어보는 과정입니다. 중요 기출을 본책에서 같이 풀어보며 해당 유형에 대한 최근 평가원 기조를 파악하고 풀이법을 최근 평가원에도 적용하는 연습을 합니다.

5. 절. 모. 평. (절대평가 이후 모든 평가원 기출)

2. 본문에서 배우고 3. 체화에서 연습하며 4. 중. 최. 평.에서 최근 평가원 기출에 적용한 것을 연습한 방법을 21학년도 6월 평가원부터 2025학년도 수능까지의 모든 평가원 기출 문제에 실현하는 과정입니다.

책 기호

구▶ 문장의 구문 해설과 문장의 해석을 제시합니다.
독▶ 문장에 대한 독해입니다. 지문 속 문장의 역할과 사고과정에 대한 해설입니다.
* - 단어나 주의 사항을 표시합니다.
Q & A 학생들이 자주하는 질문을 제시하고 그에 대한 답변을 제시합니다.

문장 부호

S (주어), V (동사), O (목적어), C (보어), O.C (목적격 보어), I.O (간접 목적어), D.O (직접목적어), 관부 (관계부사), 관대 (관계대명사)

파급의 기출효과

cafe.naver.com/spreadeffect
파급의 기출효과 NAVER 카페

기출의 파급효과 시리즈는 기출 분석서입니다. 기출의 파급효과 시리즈는 국어, 수학, 영어, 물리학 1, 화학 1, 생명과학 1, 지구과학 1, 사회·문화가 예정되어 있습니다.

준킬러 이상 기출에서 얻어갈 수 있는 '꼭 필요한 도구와 태도'를 정리합니다.

'꼭 필요한 도구와 태도' 체화를 위해 관련도가 높은 준킬러 이상 기출을 바로바로 보여주며 체화 속도를 높입니다. 단시간 내에 점수를 극대화할 수 있도록 교재가 설계되었습니다.

학습하시다 질문이 생기신다면 '파급의 기출효과' 카페에서 질문을 할 수 있습니다.

교재 인증을 하시면 질문 게시판을 이용하실 수 있습니다.

기출의 파급효과 팀 소속 오르비 저자분들이 올리시는 학습자료를 받아보실 수 있습니다.
위 저자 분들의 컨텐츠 질문 답변도 교재 인승 시 가능합니다.

더 궁금하시다면 https://cafe.naver.com/spreadeffect/15에서 확인하시면 됩니다.

▌평가원이 제시한 전개상 흐름 파악

[2018학년도 수능 영어 절대평가 학습안내 18p]

글의 흐름과 무관한 문장을 찾기 위해서는 전체 글의 중심 내용을 정확하게 파악하는 것이 중요합니다. 흐름에 무관한 문장은 전체 글의 중심 내용과 상관없이 추가로 포함된 문장이기 때문입니다. **그러므로 흐름과 무관한 문장인지를 판단할 때에는 한 두 개의 어휘보다는 글 전체의 내용적, 논리적 흐름에 근거하는 것이 필요합니다.**

- 평가원은 무관한 문장을 판단하기 위해서는 내용적, 논리적 흐름에 근거해야 한다고 합니다. 평가원이 흐름 무관의 정답을 출제하는 출제 패턴 역시 한 두 개의 어휘보다는 내용적, 논리적 흐름의 단절이 발생할 것입니다. 우리는 Chapter 4-1에서 최근 7년간 흐름 무관 정답의 패턴은 세 가지로 나누어 흐름무관 유형을 분석할 것입니다.

[2018학년도 수능 영어 절대평가 학습안내 21p]

어휘 능력을 기르기 위해서는 다양한 소재의 글을 읽고 글의 전체적 흐름을 빠르게 파악하고 문맥을 활용하여 어휘의 의미를 유추해 보는 연습이 필요합니다. 단순히 어휘의 사전적인 의미를 암기하는 것에 그치지 않고, **글의 중심 내용과 흐름을 고려하여 문맥에 어울리는 적절한 의미를 생각해야 합니다. 또한 어휘의 1차적 의미뿐만 아니라 2차적, 3차적 의미까지 고려해서 문맥에 가장 적절한 의미가 무엇인지 생각해 보는 것도 도움을 줄 수 있습니다.**

- 평가원이 어휘 문제에서는 글의 중심 내용과 흐름을 고려해야 하며, 문맥에 적합한 의미를 찾아야 한다고 합니다. 어휘 역시 첫 번째 뜻만을 출제하는 것이 아니고 다른 뜻도 출제할 수 있다고 합니다.

[2018학년도 수능 영어 절대평가 학습안내 22p]

글을 읽고 네모 안에 주어진 두 개의 어휘 중에서 문맥에 가장 적절한 어휘를 찾는 문항입니다. 문맥상 적절한 의미의 어휘인지를 판단하기 위해서는 우선 글의 요지나 주제와 같은 중심 내용과 논지의 전개 방식을 파악하고, **해당 어휘가 포함된 문장과 전후 문장의 내용을 고려하여 두 어휘 중 글의 흐름과 가장 자연스러운 의미를 지닌 어휘를 찾아야 합니다.**

- 박스형 어휘 문제에 대한 평가원의 설명입니다. 어휘가 포함된 문장과 전후 문장의 내용 즉 흐름을 고려하여 어휘를 찾아야 한다고 합니다. 우리는 Chapter 4-2를 포함한 모든 어휘 문제에서 한 문장씩 살펴보며 흐름을 파악하는 훈련을 하게 될 것입니다.

[2024학년도 대학수학 능력시험 학습방법 안내 122p]

본 문항의 정답을 찾기 위해서는 제시된 어휘의 개별적 의미와 함께 글의 맥락 속에서 낱말의 의미를 이해하는 것이 중요하다.

[2024학년도 대학수학 능력시험 학습방법 안내 123p]

동의어, 반의어, 파생어, 철자 혼동 어휘에 대한 기본적인 학습이 필요하다. 어휘의 의미를 많이 암기하는 것에만 그치지 말고 글의 전체적인 흐름, 다시 말해 글의 논지를 염두에 두고 문맥에 적절한 어휘의 의미를 추론하는 연습이 중요하다. 문맥 속에서 적절한 어휘를 추론할 때 앞뒤 문장의 논리적인 관계에 주목하여 단서를 찾아내야 한다는 점을 명심해야 한다.

- 밑줄형 어휘와 박스형 어휘 문제를 포괄하는 설명입니다. 2018학년도에 이어서 2021학년도에서도 평가원은 어휘 문제에서 문맥 즉 흐름 속에서 어휘를 추론하는 능력을 강조하고 있습니다. 또한 동의어, 반의어, 파생어, 철자 혼동 어휘에 대한 학습이 필요하다고 합니다. Chapter 3-2에서 평가원이 출제하는 어휘 문제의 패턴을 보여드리고 우리가 이러한 패턴을 어떻게 해결할 수 있는 지를 제시합니다.

4-1 무관하다의 기준을 알아야 한다.

▌다른 소재

소재가 다르다는 것은, 지문의 내용과 완전히 다른 소재에 대한 문장을 출제하거나 혹은 중심 내용이 아닌 예시로 제시된 내용을 중심 소재로 하는 문장을 출제하는 것입니다. 다음 기출 문제를 풀어봅시다.

16학년도 수능 39번

다음 글에서 전체 흐름과 관계 <u>없는</u> 문장은?

  Food intake is essential for the survival of every living organism. The failure to detect spoiled or toxic food can have deadly consequences. Therefore, it is not surprising that humans use all their five senses to analyze food quality. ① A first judgment about the value of a food source is made on its appearance and smell. ② Food that looks and smells attractive is taken into the mouth. ③ The value of a particular food is an estimation of how good it is, based on its level of vitamins, minerals, or calories. ④ Here, based on a complex sensory analysis that is not only restricted to the sense of taste but also includes smell, touch, and hearing, the final decision whether to swallow or reject food is made. ⑤ Frequently, this complex interaction between different senses is inappropriately referred to as 'taste' although it should be better called flavor perception, because it uses multiple senses.

다음 글에서 전체 흐름과 관계 <u>없는</u> 문장은?

Food intake is essential for the survival of every living organism. The failure to detect spoiled or toxic food can have deadly consequences. **Therefore,** it is not surprising that humans use all their five senses to analyze food quality. ① A first judgment about the value of a food source is made on its appearance and smell. ② Food that looks and smells attractive is taken into the mouth. ③ The value of a particular food is an estimation of how good it is, based on its level of vitamins, minerals, or calories. ④ Here, based on a complex sensory analysis that is not only restricted to the sense of taste **but** also includes smell, touch, and hearing, the final decision whether to swallow or reject food is made. ⑤ Frequently, this complex interaction between different senses is inappropriately referred to as 'taste' **although** it **should** be better called flavor perception, **because** it uses multiple senses.

🔖 해설 [정답 : ③]

이 지문은 사람이 음식의 질을 분석하는데 오감을 사용한다는 것을 보여줍니다. 하지만 ③번에서는 오감이 아닌 비타민, 미네랄, 칼로리의 수준에 기반을 두어 음식의 질을 평가하므로 다른 소재가 제시된 무관한 문장이 됩니다.

즉, 다른 소재란 'A라는 소재 ⇒ B라는 내용' 글에서 'C라는 소재 ⇒ B라는 내용' 혹은 'C라는 소재 ⇒ D라는 내용'이 출제된 것을 이야기합니다.

🔖 해석

음식 섭취는 모든 생물의 생존을 위해 필수적이다. 상했거나 독이 있는 음식을 감지하지 못하면 치명적인 결과가 생길 수 있다. 따라서 인간이 음식의 질을 분석하기 위해 자신의 모든 오감을 사용하는 것은 놀랍지 않다. 음식 재료의 가치에 대한 최초의 판단은 그것의 외관과 냄새를 바탕으로 이뤄진다. 매력적으로 보이고 냄새도 매혹적인 음식은 입속으로 들어가게 된다. (특정한 음식의 가치는 비타민, 미네랄, 칼로리의 수준에 근거하여 그것이 얼마나 좋으냐에 대한 평가이다.) 여기에서 단지 미각에만 국한되지 않고, 후각, 촉각, 그리고 청각도 포함하는 복합적인 감각 분석을 토대로, 음식의 섭취나 거부에 대한 최종 결정이 이뤄진다. 빈번히, 이러한 서로 다른 감각 간의 복합적 상호작용은 여러 가지 감각을 사용하기 때문에 향미 지각으로 불리는 편이 더 낫겠지만, 부적절하게도 '맛'이라 불린다.

같은 소재, 다른 내용

같은 소재이지만 다른 내용이 전개될 경우 무관한 문장입니다. 즉 'A ⇒ B'라는 글에서
'A ⇒ C'라는 문장을 출제합니다. 다음 기출 문제를 봅시다.

16학년도 9월 평가원 39번

다음 글에서 전체 흐름과 관계 <u>없는</u> 문장은?

Scientific experiments should be designed to show that your hypothesis is wrong and should be conducted completely objectively with no possible subjective influence on the outcome. ① Unfortunately few, if any, scientists are truly objective as they have often decided long before the experiment is begun what they would like the result to be. ② This means that very often bias is (unintentionally) introduced into the experiment, the experimental procedure or the interpretation of results. ③ It is all too easy to justify to yourself why an experiment which does not fit with your expectations should be ignored, and why one which provides the results you 'hoped for' is the right one. ④ It is important to draw a meaningful result from the experiment on peer group activities. ⑤ This can be partly avoided by conducting experiments 'blinded' and by asking others to check your data or repeat experiments.

다음 글에서 전체 흐름과 관계 <u>없는</u> 문장은?

Scientific experiments **should** be designed to show that your hypothesis is wrong and **should** be conducted completely objectively with no possible subjective influence on the outcome. ① Unfortunately few, if any, scientists are truly objective as they have often decided long before the experiment is begun what they would like the result to be. ② This means that very often bias is (unintentionally) introduced into the experiment, the experimental procedure or the interpretation of results. ③ It is all too easy to justify to yourself why an experiment which does not fit with your expectations **should** be ignored, and why one which provides the results you 'hoped for' is the right one. ④ It is important to draw a meaningful result from the experiment on peer group activities. ⑤ This can be partly avoided by conducting experiments 'blinded' and by asking others to check your data or repeat experiments.

☞ 해설 [정답 : ④]

이 지문은 과학 실험이 객관적으로 수행되어야 한다는 내용입니다. 하지만 ④번 문장에서 실험으로부터 중요한 결과를 이끌어내는 것이 중요하다고 하므로 ④번 문장이 무관합니다. 즉 '과학 실험 ⇒ 객관적 수행'이란 글에서 '과학 실험 ⇒ 중요한 결과를 이끎'이라는 '같은 소재, 다른 내용'이 출제되었습니다.

☞ 해석

과학 실험은 자신의 가설이 틀렸다는 것을 보여 주도록 설계되어야 하고, 결과에 대해 있을 법한 그 어떤 주관적 영향도 없이 완벽하게 객관적으로 수행되어야 한다. 유감스럽게도 있다 하더라도 진정으로 객관적인 과학자는 거의 없는데 이는 그들이 흔히 실험이 시작되기 오래전에 어떤 결과가 나왔으면 좋겠는지 결정했기 때문이다. 이것은 매우 빈번히 편견이 실험, 실험 절차 혹은 결과의 해석에 (무심코) 더해진다는 것을 의미한다. 자신의 기대와 어긋나는 실험이 왜 무시되어야 하는지, 그리고 자신이 '기대했던' 결과를 가져다주는 실험이 왜 옳은 것인지를 자신에게 정당화하기는 너무나 쉽다. (또래 집단 활동에 관한 실험에서 의미 있는 결과를 도출하는 것이 중요하다.) 이것은 여러분이 '앞을 예측하지 않고서' 실험을 하고 다른 사람들에게 여러분의 데이터를 점검하거나 실험을 되풀이해 보라고 요청함으로써 어느 정도 피할 수 있다.

반대 내용

반대 내용 전개란 지문에서 'A ⇒ B'를 전개할 때, 'A ⇒ not B'인 문장을 출제하는 것입니다. 즉 A라는 소재에 대해서 (+)를 지문에서 제시할 때 한 문장만 A에 대하여 (-)를 제시하는 것입니다.

다음 기출 문제를 봅시다.

17학년도 6월 평가원 35번

다음 글에서 전체 흐름과 관계 <u>없는</u> 문장은?

Roles are like a fence. They allow us a certain amount of freedom, but for most of us that freedom doesn't go very far. Suppose that a woman decides that she is not going to wear dresses-or a man that he will not wear suits and ties-regardless of what anyone says. ① In most situations, they'll stick to their decision. ② When a formal occasion comes along, however, such as a family wedding or a funeral, they are likely to cave in to norms that they find overwhelming. ③ The increasing social pressure discourages us from fulfilling the social norms and committing ourselves to shared social conventions of behaviour. ④ Almost all of us follow the guidelines for what is "appropriate" for our roles. ⑤ Few of us are bothered by such restrictions, for our socialization is so thorough that we usually want to do what our roles indicate is appropriate.

다음 글에서 전체 흐름과 관계 <u>없는</u> 문장은?

Roles are like a fence. They allow us a certain amount of freedom, **but** for most of us that freedom doesn't go very far. Suppose that a woman decides that she is not going to wear dresses-or a man that he will not wear suits and ties-regardless of what anyone says. ① In most situations, they'll stick to their decision. ② When a formal occasion comes along, **however**, such as a family wedding or a funeral, they are likely to cave in to norms that they find overwhelming. ③ The increasing social pressure discourages us from fulfilling the social norms and committing ourselves to shared social conventions of behaviour. ④ Almost all of us follow the guidelines for what is "appropriate" for our roles. ⑤ Few of us are bothered by such restrictions, for our socialization is so thorough that we usually want to do what our roles indicate is appropriate.

⊙ 해설 ㅣ 정답 : ③ ㅣ

이 지문에서 우리는 우리에게 적절한 것을 알려주는 규범을 따른다고 합니다. 하지만 ③번에서 사회적 압력이 우리가 규범을 이행하는 것을 낙담시킨다고 하므로 반대 내용이 전개되어 무관한 문장이 됩니다. 즉 '우리 ⇒ 사회적 규범을 따름' 지문에서 '우리 ⇒ 사회적 규범 이행 못함'이라는 문장으로 반대 내용을 출제했습니다.

⊙ 해석

역할은 울타리와 같다. 역할은 우리에게 일정 정도의 자유를 부여하지만 우리들 대부분에게 있어서 그 자유는 멀리까지 확장되지는 않는다. 가령 어떤 여자가, 누가 뭐라고 하든 상관없이, 자신은 드레스를 입지 않을 것이라고, 혹은 어떤 남자가 자신은 정장을 차려입지 않을 것이라고 결심한다고 하자. 대부분의 상황에서, 그들은 자신들의 결정을 고수할 것이다. 하지만 가족 결혼식이나 장례식과 같은 공식적인 행사가 생길 때, 그들은 저항하기 힘들다고 느껴지는 규범에 어쩔 수 없이 따르기 쉽다. (늘어나는 사회적 압박으로 인해 우리는 사회적 규범을 이행하고 행동에 대한 공유된 사회적 관습에 따르는 것을 포기하게 된다.) 우리들은 거의 모두 우리의 역할에 '적절한' 것이 무엇인가에 대한 지침을 따른다. 우리들 중 그러한 구속을 귀찮아하는 사람은 거의 없는데, 우리의 사회화가 너무 철저해서 우리는 대게 우리의 역할이 적절하다고 말해주는 것을 하기 '원하기' 때문이다. 역할의 사회학적 중요성은 그것이 사람들에게 기대되는 것을 제시한다는 것이다.

▌체화

다음 기출 문제를 풀어보며 정답 선지가 1. 다른 소재, 2. 같은 소재, 다른 내용, 3. 반대 내용 중 어떤 선지에 해당하는지 판단해 봅시다.

01

다음 글에서 전체 흐름과 관계 <u>없는</u> 문장은?

The pull effect of a destination can be positively influenced by the introduction and reinforcement of pro-tourism policies that make a destination more accessible. ① Governments, for example, can and often do employ awareness campaigns among the resident population to promote a welcoming attitude towards visitors, in order to foster a positive market image. ② However, because such campaigns depend on widespread social engineering, and because their effects can be counteracted by random acts of violence, positive outcomes cannot be guaranteed. ③ Most governments in developing countries encourage international tourism because tourists from wealthy countries usually spend more. ④ Furthermore, it is the behaviour of some tourists, and the structure and development of tourism itself, that often generate negative attitudes within the host community. ⑤ This implies that major structural changes to tourism itself, rather than awareness campaigns, may be required to foster a welcoming attitude.

1. 다른 소재
2. 같은 소재, 다른 내용
3. 반대 내용

02

다음 글에서 전체 흐름과 관계 <u>없는</u> 문장은?

Most often, you will find or meet people who introduce themselves in terms of their work or by what they spend time on. These people introduce themselves as a salesman or an executive. ① There is nothing criminal in doing this, but psychologically, we become what we believe. ② Identifying what we can do in the workplace serves to enhance the quality of our professional career. ③ People who follow this practice tend to lose their individuality and begin to live with the notion that they are recognized by the job they do. ④ However, jobs may not be permanent, and you may lose your job for countless reasons, some of which you may not even be responsible for. ⑤ In such a case, these people suffer from an inevitable social and mental trauma, leading to emotional stress and a feeling that all of a sudden they have been disassociated from what once was their identity.

1. 다른 소재
2. 같은 소재, 다른 내용
3. 반대 내용

03

다음 글에서 전체 흐름과 관계 <u>없는</u> 문장은?

School physical education programs should offer a balanced variety of activities that allow young people to develop ability in lifetime activities that are personally meaningful and enjoyable. A balance should exist in any physical education program among team, dual, and individual (lifetime) sports. ① Team sports such as basketball and soccer provide an opportunity for students to develop skills and to enjoy working and competing together as a team. ② However, in many school physical education programs, team sports dominate the curriculum at the expense of various individual and dual sports, like tennis, swimming, badminton, and golf. ③ In such cases, the students lose the opportunity to develop skills in activities that they can participate in throughout their adult lives. ④ Baseball, in particular, is one of the most popular sports frequently broadcast on TV. ⑤ Only through a balanced program of team, dual, and individual sports is it possible to develop well-rounded individuals.

* dual: 둘의

1. 다른 소재
2. 같은 소재, 다른 내용
3. 반대 내용

04

다음 글에서 전체 흐름과 관계 <u>없는</u> 문장은?

It is difficult to appreciate what a temperature of 20,000,000℃ means. ① If the solar surface, not the center, were as hot as this, the radiation emitted into space would be so great that the whole Earth would be vaporized within a few minutes. ② Indeed, this is just what would happen if some cosmic giant were to peel off the outer layers of the Sun like skinning an orange, for the tremendously hot inner regions would then be exposed. ③ It is believed that the brightness of the Sun can be predicted theoretically. ④ Fortunately, no such circumstance is possible, and the outer layers of the Sun provide a sort of blanket that protects us from its inner fires. ⑤ Yet in spite of these blanketing layers, some energy must leak through from the Sun's center to its outer regions, and this leakage is of just the right amount to compensate for the radiation emitted by the surface into surrounding space.

1. 다른 소재
2. 같은 소재, 다른 내용
3. 반대 내용

체화 해설

01

다음 글에서 전체 흐름과 관계 <u>없는</u> 문장은?

The pull effect of a destination can be positively influenced by the introduction and reinforcement of pro-tourism policies that make a destination more accessible. ① Governments, **for example**, can and often do employ awareness campaigns among the resident population to promote a welcoming attitude towards visitors, in order to foster a positive market image. ② **However**, because such campaigns depend on widespread social engineering, and because their effects can be counteracted by random acts of violence, positive outcomes cannot be guaranteed. ③ Most governments in developing countries encourage international tourism because tourists from wealthy countries usually spend more. ④ Furthermore, it is the behaviour of some tourists, and the structure and development of tourism itself, that often generate negative attitudes within the host community. ⑤ This implies that major structural changes to tourism itself, rather than awareness campaigns, may be required to foster a welcoming attitude.

1. 다른 소재
2. 같은 소재, 다른 내용
3. 반대 내용

⚙ 해설 [정답 : ③]

이 지문은 여행지에 대한 선호도를 높이기 위한 관광산업 정책의 하나로 주민 대상 인식 제고 운동을 벌이는 것은 한계가 있으므로, 긍정적 결과를 얻기 위해서는 관광 산업 자체의 구조적 변화가 필요하다는 내용입니다. 하지만 ③번 문장은 개발도상국들의 정부들이 국제 관광산업을 장려하는 이유를 언급하여 ③번은 ①번에서 제시된 예시인 정부를 중심 소재로 사용하므로 1. 다른 소재에 해당합니다.

⚙ 해석

여행지의 유인 효과는 여행지의 접근성을 더욱 높여 주는 친관광산업 정책의 도입 및 강화로 긍정적으로 영향을 받을 수 있다. 예를 들어, 정부는 긍정적 시장 이미지를 증진하기 위해 주민들 사이에서 방문객에 대한 우호적인 태도를 촉진하는 인식 제고 운동을 벌일 수 있고 실제로 흔히 하고 있다. 하지만 그러한 운동은 광범위한 사회공학에 의존하고, 그 효과는 무작위적 폭력 행위로 상쇄될 수 있으므로 긍정적 결과가 보장될 수는 없다. [개발도상국들의 대부분의 정부는 국제 관광산업을 장려하는데, 이는 부유한 국가에서 온 관광객들이 일반적으로 돈을 더 많이 쓰기 때문이다.] 게다가, 그 관광지 지역 사회 내에서 자주 부정적인 태도를 만들어 내는 것은 일부 여행객들의 행동과 관광산업 자체의 구조와 발전이다. 이것은 아마도 우호적 태도를 촉진하기 위해서는 인식 제고 운동보다는 오히려 관광산업 자체에 주된 구조적 변화가 필요할 수 있다는 것을 의미한다.

02

다음 글에서 전체 흐름과 관계 <u>없는</u> 문장은?

Most often, you will find or meet people who introduce themselves in terms of their work or by what they spend time on. These people introduce themselves as a salesman or an executive. ① There is nothing criminal in doing this, **but** psychologically, we become what we believe. ② Identifying what we can do in the workplace serves to enhance the quality of our professional career. ③ People who follow this practice tend to lose their individuality and begin to live with the notion that they are recognized by the job they do. ④ **However**, jobs may not be permanent, and you may lose your job for countless reasons, some of which you may not even be responsible for. ⑤ In such a case, these people suffer from an inevitable social and mental trauma, **leading to** emotional stress and a feeling that all of a sudden they have been disassociated from what once was their identity.

1. 다른 소재
2. 같은 소재, 다른 내용
3. 반대 내용

▾ 해설 [정답 : ②]

이 지문은 사람들이 자신이 하는 일을 통해 정체성을 확인하는데, 이로 인해 자신의 개성을 잃어 스트레스와 혼란이 일어날 수 있다는 (-) 부정적 내용입니다. 하지만 ②번에서 직장에서 우리가 할 수 있는 것을 확인하는 것은 일의 질을 높이는 데 도움이 된다는 (+) 반대 내용이 전개되었습니다. 그러므로 3. 반대 내용에 해당합니다.

▾ 해석

아주 자주 여러분은 자신이 하는 일로 혹은 자신이 시간을 보내는 일에 의해 자기 자신을 소개하는 사람들을 발견하거나 만날 것이다. 이러한 사람들은 자기 자신을 판매원이나 경영 간부로서 소개한다. 이렇게 할 때 죄가 되는 것은 없지만, 정신적으로 우리는 우리가 (그렇다고) 믿는 존재가 된다. [직장에서 우리가 할 수 있는 것을 확인하는 것은 우리가 하는 전문적 일의 질을 높이는 데 도움이 된다.] 이러한 관행을 따르는 사람들은 자신들의 개성을 잃어버리고 자신들이 하는 일에 의해 인식된다는 개념을 가지고 살기 시작하는 경향이 있다. 그러나 일은 영구적이지 못할 수 있으며 여러분은 무수하게 많은 이유로 인해 일자리를 잃을지도 모르는데, 여러분은 그 이유 중 몇몇에 대해서는 아무런 책임도 없을 수 있다. 그러한 경우에 이러한 사람들은 피할 수 없는 사회적, 정신적 외상 때문에 고통을 받고 이것은 감정적 스트레스와 한때 그들의 정체성이었던 것과 자신들이 갑자기 단절되어왔다는 느낌을 유발한다.

03

다음 글에서 전체 흐름과 관계 <u>없는</u> 문장은?

 School physical education programs should offer a balanced variety of activities that allow young people to develop ability in lifetime activities that are personally meaningful and enjoyable. A balance **should** exist in any physical education program among team, dual, and individual (lifetime) sports. ① Team sports such as basketball and soccer provide an opportunity for students to develop skills and to enjoy working and competing together as a team. ② **However**, in many school physical education programs, team sports dominate the curriculum at the expense of various individual and dual sports, like tennis, swimming, badminton, and golf. ③ In such cases, the students lose the opportunity to develop skills in activities that they can participate in throughout their adult lives. ④ Baseball, in particular, is one of the most popular sports frequently broadcast on TV. ⑤ Only through a balanced program of team, dual, and individual sports is it possible to develop well-rounded individuals.

* dual: 둘의

---

1. 다른 소재
2. 같은 소재, 다른 내용
3. 반대 내용

🔎 해설 [정답 : ④]

이 지문은 학교 체육 프로그램은 균형 있고 다양한 활동을 제공해야 하지만 교육 과정에는 한 명 혹은 짝을 지어 할 수 있는 스포츠에 비해 단체 스포츠가 대부분이라는 내용입니다. 하지만 ④번은 단체 스포츠의 예시이기도 한 야구를 중심 소재로 하는 문장입니다. 그러므로 전혀 다른 소재가 언급되고 있어 1. 다른 소재가 됩니다.

🔎 해석

학교 체육 프로그램은 어린 학생들이 개인적으로 의미 있고 즐길만한 평생 활동의 능력을 계발하게 해 주는 균형 있는 다양한 활동을 제공해야 한다. 균형은 단체 스포츠, 듀얼 스포츠, 개인(평생)스포츠 중의 어떠한 체육 프로그램에서라도 존재해야 한다. 농구와 축구 같은 단체스포츠는 학생들이 기술을 계발하고 팀으로서 함께 활동하고 경쟁하는 것을 즐길 수 있는 기회를 제공한다. 그러나 많은 학교 체육 프로그램에서는 팀 스포츠가 테니스, 수영, 베드민턴, 골프와 같은 다양한 개인 스포츠와 듀얼 스포츠를 희생시키며 교육과정을 지배하고 있다. 그러한 경우에 학생들은 성인 시절 내내 자신들이 참여할 수 있는 활동의 기술을 계발할 기회를 박탈당한다. [특히, 야구는 TV에서 빈번하게 방송되는 가장 인기 있는 스포츠중의 하나이다.] 단체 스포츠, 듀얼 스포츠, 개인 스포츠의 균형있는 프로그램을 통해서만 고르게 균형을 갖춘 개인의 성장이 가능하다.

04

다음 글에서 전체 흐름과 관계 <u>없는</u> 문장은?

It is difficult to appreciate what a temperature of 20,000,000℃ means. ① If the solar surface, not the center, were as hot as this, the radiation emitted into space would be so great that the whole Earth would be vaporized within a few minutes. ② **Indeed**, this is just what would happen if some cosmic giant were to peel off the outer layers of the Sun like skinning an orange, for the tremendously hot inner regions would then be exposed. ③ It is believed that the brightness of the Sun can be predicted theoretically. ④ Fortunately, no such circumstance is possible, and the outer layers of the Sun provide a sort of blanket that protects us from its inner fires. ⑤ **Yet** in spite of these blanketing layers, some energy must leak through from the Sun's center to its outer regions, and this leakage is of just the right amount to compensate for the radiation emitted by the surface into surrounding space.

1. 다른 소재
2. 같은 소재, 다른 내용
3. 반대 내용

⚓ 해설 [정답 : ③]

이 지문은 태양 중심부의 열을 덮어주는 외층의 역할을 설명하는 내용입니다. 하지만 ③번에서는 태양 밝기의 예측이 가능하다고 하므로 2. 태양이라는 같은 소재이지만 다른 내용을 전개하고 있습니다.

⚓ 해석

섭씨 2천만 도의 온도가 무엇을 의미하는지를 이해하는 것은 어렵다. 태양의 중심부가 아니라 표면이 이만큼 뜨겁다면, 우주로 방사되는 방사에너지는 지구 전체가 몇 분 내로 증발될 정도로 그렇게 엄청날 것이다. 사실, 이것은 어떤 우주의 거인이 오렌지의 껍질을 벗겨내는 것처럼 태양의 외층을 떼어낸다면 일어날 바로 그런 일인데, 왜냐하면 엄청나게 뜨거운 내부가 그럴 경우 노출이 될 것이기 때문이다. [태양의 밝기는 이론상으로 예측될 수 있다고 여겨진다.] 다행히도, 그런 상황은 가능하지 않고, 태양의 외층은 내부의 불로부터 우리를 보호하는 일종의 담요를 제공한다. 그러나 이 덮어주는 층이 있음에도 불구하고, 얼마간의 에너지가 태양의 중심부에서 외부로 새어 나오는 것이 틀림없는데, 이 유출량은 표면에 의해 주위의 우주로 방사되는 방사 에너지를 보충하기에 꼭 적당한 양에 해당한다.

01 25학년도 수능 35번

다음 글에서 전체 흐름과 관계 <u>없는</u> 문장은?

The expansion of sports tourism in the twentieth century has been influenced by further developments in transportation. Just as the railways revolutionized travel in the nineteenth century, so the automobile produced even more dramatic changes in the twentieth. ① The significance of the car in the development of sport and tourism generally has attracted considerable coverage and it has had no less an impact on sports tourism specifically. ② Although originally invented towards the end of the nineteenth century, it started to become a mass form of transport in the 1920s in the USA and rather later in Britain. ③ Apart from its convenience and flexibility, the car has the additional advantages of affording access to many areas not served by public transport, as well as allowing the easy transport of luggage and equipment. ④ The expansion of reasonably priced, good quality accommodation associated with tourism growth has also facilitated the growth of locally based restaurants. ⑤ As a result, it was invaluable for the development of many forms of sports tourism but especially those which require the transportation of people and equipment to relatively remote locations.

02 24학년도 수능 35번

다음 글에서 전체 흐름과 관계 <u>없는</u> 문장은?

Speaking fast is a high-risk proposition. It's nearly impossible to maintain the ideal conditions to be persuasive, well-spoken, and effective when the mouth is traveling well over the speed limit. ① Although we'd like to think that our minds are sharp enough to always make good decisions with the greatest efficiency, they just aren't. ② In reality, the brain arrives at an intersection of four or five possible things to say and sits idling for a couple of seconds, considering the options. ③ Making a good decision helps you speak faster because it provides you with more time to come up with your responses. ④ When the brain stops sending navigational instructions back to the mouth and the mouth is moving too fast to pause, that's when you get a verbal fender bender, otherwise known as filler. ⑤ *Um*, *ah*, *you know*, and *like* are what your mouth does when it has nowhere to go.

중. 최. 평. 해설

01 25학년도 수능 35번 (정답률 66%)

다음 글에서 전체 흐름과 관계 <u>없는</u> 문장은?

> The expansion of sports tourism in the twentieth century has been influenced by further developments in transportation. Just as the railways revolutionized travel in the nineteenth century, **so** the automobile produced even more dramatic changes in the twentieth. ① The significance of the car in the development of sport and tourism generally has attracted considerable coverage and it has had no less an impact on sports tourism specifically. ② Although originally invented towards the end of the nineteenth century, it started to become a mass form of transport in the 1920s in the USA and rather later in Britain. ③ Apart from its convenience and flexibility, the car has the additional advantages of affording access to many areas not served by public transport, as well as allowing the easy transport of luggage and equipment. ④ The expansion of reasonably priced, good quality accommodation associated with tourism growth has also facilitated the growth of locally based restaurants. ⑤ **As a result**, it was invaluable for the development of many forms of sports tourism **but** especially those which require the transportation of people and equipment to relatively remote locations.

해설 [정답 : ④]

④번 선지는 관광업의 성장에 따른 질 좋은 숙박 시설의 증가와 이로 인한 식당이 성장은 자동차이 발전과 자동차로 인한 스포츠 관광이라는 앞 내용과 소재나 내용에서 아예 관련이 없습니다. 다른 소재에 해당합니다.

* 18%의 수험생이 ③번 선지를 골랐습니다. ③번 선지는 ②번 선지에서 제시된 자동차의 발명과 대중성에 더불어 자동차의 장점을 제시하고 이는 ⑤번 선지의 자동차의 장점이 스포츠 관광에 끼친 영향을 구체적으로 설명하는 내용으로 이어져 적합한 내용입니다. 그러므로 ③번은 정답이 될 수 없습니다.

Ⅰ. The expansion of sports tourism (in the twentieth century) / has been influenced (by further developments in transportation).

　구▶ 20세기의 스포츠 관광의 확대는 교통수단이 더욱 발전되는 것에 영향을 받았다고 합니다.

　독▶ 교통수단의 발달이 스포츠 관광에 영향을 끼쳤다고 합니다.

Ⅱ. Just as the railways / revolutionized / travel (in the nineteenth century), **so** the automobile / produced / even more dramatic changes (in the twentieth).

　구▶ 철도가 19세기 여행에 혁신을 일으켰던 것처럼, 자동차가 20세기에 훨씬 더 극적인 변화를 만들어 냈다고 합니다.

　독▶ 'so'가 제시되었으므로 중심 문장
　- 철도가 여행에 혁신을 일으킨 것처럼 자동차도 20세기에 혁신을 일으켰다고 합니다.

① . The significance (of the car) (in the development of sport and tourism) / generally has attracted / considerable coverage and it / has had no less an impact on / sports tourism specifically.

> **구** 스포츠와 관광의 발달에서 자동차의 중요성은 일반적으로 상당한 주목을 끌었으며, 그것은 (= 자동차의 중요성은) 구체적으로 스포츠 관광에 적지 않은 (= 못지 않은) 영향을 끼쳤다고 합니다.

> **독** Ⅰ, Ⅱ번 문장에 이어 교통수단인 자동차가 스포츠와 관광 그리고 스포츠 관광에 영향을 끼쳤다고 합니다.

② . Although originally invented (towards the end of the nineteenth century), it / started to become / a mass form of transport (in the 1920s in the USA) and rather later in Britain.

> **구** 자동차는 원래 19세기 말에 발명되었지만, 그것은 (= 자동차는) 1920년대에 미국에서, 그리고 다소 늦게 영국에서 대중적인 교통수단이 되기 시작했다고 합니다.

> **독** 자동차는 19세기 말에 (= 1800년대 말에) 발명되었지만 비교적 빠른 1920년대에 미국과 그 이후 영국에서 대중적인 교통수단이 되었다고 합니다.

③ . (Apart from its convenience and flexibility), the car / has / the additional advantages of affording access to many areas (not served by public transport), as well as allowing / the easy transport of luggage and equipment.

> **구** 'A as well as B'는 'B뿐만 아니라 A도'를 의미합니다.
> - 자동차는 편리함과 유연성 외에도 짐과 장비를 쉽게 운송해 준다는 것뿐만 아니라 대중교통이 제공되지 않는 많은 지역에 접근하게 해준다는 추가적인 장점이 있다고 합니다.

> **독** 자동차의 발명과 대중성을 제시한 ②번 문장에 이어서 ③번 문장에서는 자동차의 장점을 설명하고 있습니다.

④ . The expansion of reasonably priced, good quality accommodation (associated with tourism growth) / has also facilitated / the growth of locally based restaurants.

> **구** 관광업 성장과 연관된 가격이 합리적이고 질이 좋은 숙박 시설의 확대는 또한 현지에 기반을 둔 식당의 성장을 촉진했다고 합니다.

> **독** 관광업의 성장에 따른 질 좋은 숙박 시설의 증가와 이로 인한 식당의 성장은 자동차의 발전과 자동차로 인한 스포츠 관광이라는 앞 내용과 소재나 내용에서 아예 관련이 없습니다.

⑤ . **As a result**, it / was / invaluable (for the development of many forms of sports tourism) **but** especially those (which require / the transportation of people and equipment to relatively remote locations).

> **구** 결과적으로, 그것은 (= ③번 문장에서 자동차의 장점은) 스포츠 관광의 다양한 형태의 발전에 매우 귀중했고, 그러나 특히 사람과 장비를 비교적 먼 곳으로 운송해야 하는 그것들에 (= 스포츠 관광들에) 매우 유용했다고 합니다.

> **독** 'As a result'와 'but'이 제시되었으므로 중심 문장
> - 자동차의 장점이 특히 사람과 비교적 먼 곳으로 운송해야 하는 스포츠 관광에 매우 귀중했으며, 스포츠 관광의 다양한 형태의 발전을 이끌었다고 합니다.

> * invaluable - 매우 귀중한, 매우 유용한

다음 글에서 전체 흐름과 관계 <u>없는</u> 문장은?

Speaking fast is a high-risk proposition. It's nearly impossible to maintain the ideal conditions to be persuasive, well-spoken, and effective when the mouth is traveling well over the speed limit. ① Although we'd like to think that our minds are sharp enough to always make good decisions with the greatest efficiency, they just aren't. ② In reality, the brain arrives at an intersection of four or five possible things to say and sits idling for a couple of seconds, considering the options. ③ Making a good decision helps you speak faster **because** it provides you with more time to come up with your responses. ④ When the brain stops sending navigational instructions back to the mouth and the mouth is moving too fast to pause, that's when you get a verbal fender bender, otherwise known as filler. ⑤ *Um, ah, you know,* and *like* are what your mouth does when it has nowhere to go.

해설 [정답 : ③]

첫 번째 문장에서부터 지문의 주제는 'Speaking fast is a high-risk proposition', 빨리 말하는 것의 위험 부담으로 정하고 글이 전개되지만, ③번 문장에서는 'Making a good decision helps you speak faster' 좋은 결정을 내리면 응답해 낼 시간이 많아지므로 더 빠르게 말할 수 있다는 내용이 언급됩니다. 이것은 ②번 문장의 뇌가 말할 가능성이 있는 것들 사이에서 몇 초 동안 선택지를 고려하는 것과, ④번 문장의 그로 인한 결과로 뇌가 지시를 멈췄지만, 우리의 입이 말을 멈추지 못할 때 겪는 언어적 장애와 관련된 내용과 관련이 없는 내용이므로 정답은 ③번이 됩니다.

Ⅰ. Speaking fast / is / a high-risk proposition.

> 구 빨리 말하는 것은 위험 부담이 큰일이라고 합니다.

> 독 빨리 말하는 것의 단점을 언급합니다.

Ⅱ. It's / nearly impossible / to maintain the ideal conditions to be persuasive, well-spoken, and effective / when / the mouth / is traveling well over the speed limit.

> 구 'It + be 동사 + 형용사 + to-V'는 가주어/진주어입니다.
> - 입이 속도 제한을 훨씬 초과하여 움직일 때 설득력 있고, 말을 잘하며, 효과적인 이상적 조건을 유지하는 것은 거의 불가능하다고 합니다.

> 독 Ⅰ번 문장을 구체화한 문장입니다.

①. Although we'd like to think / that / our minds / are sharp enough to always make good decisions (with the greatest efficiency), they / just aren't.

> **구** 우리는 우리의 정신이 항상 최고의 효율로 좋은 결정을 내릴 수 있을 정도로 예리하다고 생각하고 싶겠지만, 그것은 정말 그렇지 않다고 합니다.

> **독** 효율적으로 빠르게 말하는 것이 불가능한 이유에 대해서 설명하고 있습니다.

②. In reality, the brain / arrives at an intersection (of four or five possible things to say) / and sits idling for a couple of seconds, considering the options.

> **구** 실제로 뇌는 말할 가능성이 있는 것들 4~5가지가 교차하는 지점에 도달하면 몇 초 동안 빈둥거리며 선택지를 고려한다고 합니다.

③. Making a good decision / helps / you / speak faster **because** / it / provides / you with more time to come up with your responses.

> **구** provide A with B – A에게 B를 제공하다
> - 좋은 결정을 내리면 응답을 생각해 낼 시간이 더 많아지기 때문에, 여러분은 더 빨리 말할 수 있다고 합니다.

> **독** 'because'가 제시되었으므로 중심 문장
> - 빨리 말할 수 있는 조건으로 내용이 전환됩니다.

④. When / the brain / stops / sending navigational instructions back to the mouth / and the mouth / is moving too fast to pause, that's when you / get / a verbal fender bender, otherwise known as filler.

> **구** 뇌가 입에 항해 지시를 다시 보내는 것을 멈추었는데 입은 너무 빨리 움직여 멈출 수 없을 때, 이때가 바로 여러분이 가벼운 언어적 장애, 또는 필러라고도 하는 것을 겪게 되는 시간이라고 합니다.

> **독** Ⅳ번 문장에서 뇌가 선택지를 고려하는 것이 본 문장의 뇌가 지시를 보내지 않는 것으로 이어지며, 그와 동시에 계속해서 빠르게 말할 때 겪는 언어적 장애에 관한 설명은 역시 빠르게 말하는 것의 단점에 관한 내용임을 알 수 있습니다.

⑤. *Um, ah, you know, and like* / are / what / your mouth / does / when / it / has nowhere to go.

> **구** '음, 아, 알다시피, 그러니까'는 입이 갈 곳이 없을 때 하는 행동이라고 합니다.

> **독** 필러의 예시에 대해서 설명하고 있습니다.

절. 모. 평. (절대평가 모든 평가원 기출)

01 25학년도 6월 평가원 35번

[정답과 해설 6page]

다음 글에서 전체 흐름과 관계 <u>없는</u> 문장은?

Avian song learning occurs in two stages: first, songs must be memorized and, second, they must be practiced. In some species these two events overlap, but in others memorization can occur before practice by several months, providing an impressive example of long-term memory storage. ① The young bird's initial efforts to reproduce the memorized song are usually not successful. ② These early songs may have uneven pitch, irregular tempo, and notes that are out of order or poorly reproduced. ③ However, sound graphs of songs recorded over several weeks or months reveal that during this practice period the bird fine-tunes his efforts until he produces an accurate copy of the memorized template. ④ An important idea to emerge from the study of birdsong is that song learning is shaped by preferences and limitations. ⑤ This process requires hearing oneself sing; birds are unable to reproduce memorized songs if they are deafened after memorization but before the practice period.

* avian: 조류의

---

02 22학년노 6월 평가원 35번

[정답과 해설 9page]

다음 글에서 전체 흐름과 관계 <u>없는</u> 문장은?

Kinship ties continue to be important today. In modern societies such as the United States people frequently have family get-togethers, they telephone their relatives regularly, and they provide their kin with a wide variety of services. ① Eugene Litwak has referred to this pattern of behaviour as the 'modified extended family'. ② It is an extended family structure because multigenerational ties are maintained, but it is modified because it does not usually rest on co-residence between the generations and most extended families do not act as corporate groups. ③ Although modified extended family members often live close by, the modified extended family does not require geographical proximity and ties are maintained even when kin are separated by considerable distances. ④ The oldest member of the family makes the decisions on important issues, no matter how far away family members live from each other. ⑤ In contrast to the traditional extended family where kin always live in close proximity, the members of modified extended families may freely move away from kin to seek opportunities for occupational advancement.

* kin: 친족 ** proximity: 근접

다음 글에서 전체 흐름과 관계 <u>없는</u> 문장은?

　Interestingly, experts do not suffer as much as beginners when performing complex tasks or combining multiple tasks. Because experts have extensive practice within a limited domain, the key component skills in their domain tend to be highly practiced and more automated. ① Each of these highly practiced skills then demands relatively few cognitive resources, effectively lowering the total cognitive load that experts experience. ② Thus, experts can perform complex tasks and combine multiple tasks relatively easily. ③ Furthermore, beginners are excellent at processing the tasks when the tasks are divided and isolated. ④ This is not because they necessarily have more cognitive resources than beginners; rather, because of the high level of fluency they have achieved in performing key skills, they can do more with what they have. ⑤ Beginners, on the other hand, have not achieved the same degree of fluency and automaticity in each of the component skills, and thus they struggle to combine skills that experts combine with relative ease and efficiency.

다음 글에서 전체 흐름과 관계 <u>없는</u> 문장은?

　The animal in a conflict between attacking a rival and fleeing may initially not have sufficient information to enable it to make a decision straight away. ① If the rival is likely to win the fight, then the optimal decision would be to give up immediately and not risk getting injured. ② But if the rival is weak and easily defeatable, then there could be considerable benefit in going ahead and obtaining the territory, females, food or whatever is at stake. ③ Animals under normal circumstances maintain a very constant body weight and they eat and drink enough for their needs at regular intervals. ④ By taking a little extra time to collect information about the opponent, the animal is more likely to reach a decision that maximizes its chances of winning than if it takes a decision without such information. ⑤ Many signals are now seen as having this information gathering or 'assessment' function, directly contributing to the mechanism of the decision-making process by supplying vital information about the likely outcomes of the various options.

다음 글에서 전체 흐름과 관계 <u>없는</u> 문장은?

Actors, singers, politicians and countless others recognise the power of the human voice as a means of communication beyond the simple decoding of the words that are used. Learning to control your voice and use it for different purposes is, therefore, one of the most important skills to develop as an early career teacher. ① The more confidently you give instructions, the higher the chance of a positive class response. ② There are times when being able to project your voice loudly will be very useful when working in school, and knowing that you can cut through a noisy classroom, dinner hall or playground is a great skill to have. ③ In order to address serious noise issues in school, students, parents and teachers should search for a solution together. ④ However, I would always advise that you use your loudest voice incredibly sparingly and avoid shouting as much as possible. ⑤ A quiet, authoritative and measured tone has so much more impact than slightly panicked shouting.

다음 글에서 전체 흐름과 관계 <u>없는</u> 문장은?

In a highly commercialized setting such as the United States, it is not surprising that many landscapes are seen as commodities. In other words, they are valued because of their market potential. Residents develop an identity in part based on how the landscape can generate income for the community. ① This process involves more than the conversion of the natural elements into commodities. ② The landscape itself, including the people and their sense of self, takes on the form of a commodity. ③ Landscape protection in the US traditionally focuses on protecting areas of wilderness, typically in mountainous regions. ④ Over time, the landscape identity can evolve into a sort of "logo" that can be used to sell the stories of the landscape. ⑤ Thus, California's "Wine Country," Florida's "Sun Coast," or South Dakota's "Badlands" shape how both outsiders and residents perceive a place, and these labels build a set of expectations associated with the culture of those who live there.

다음 글에서 전체 흐름과 관계 <u>없는</u> 문장은?

Because plants tend to recover from disasters more quickly than animals, they are essential to the revitalization of damaged environments. Why do plants have this preferential ability to recover from disaster? It is largely because, unlike animals, they can generate new organs and tissues throughout their life cycle. ① This ability is due to the activity of plant meristems — regions of undifferentiated tissue in roots and shoots that can, in response to specific cues, differentiate into new tissues and organs. ② If meristems are not damaged during disasters, plants can recover and ultimately transform the destroyed or barren environment. ③ You can see this phenomenon on a smaller scale when a tree struck by lightning forms new branches that grow from the old scar. ④ In the form of forests and grasslands, plants regulate the cycling of water and adjust the chemical composition of the atmosphere. ⑤ In addition to regeneration or resprouting of plants, disturbed areas can also recover through reseeding.

* revitalization: 소생

다음 글에서 전체 흐름과 관계 <u>없는</u> 문장은?

Workers are united by laughing at shared events, even ones that may initially spark anger or conflict. Humor reframes potentially divisive events into merely "laughable" ones which are put in perspective as subservient to unifying values held by organization members. Repeatedly recounting humorous incidents reinforces unity based on key organizational values. ① One team told repeated stories about a dumpster fire, something that does not seem funny on its face, but the reactions of workers motivated to preserve safety sparked laughter as the stories were shared multiple times by multiple parties in the workplace. ② Shared events that cause laughter can indicate a sense of belonging since "you had to be there" to see the humor in them, and non-members were not and do not. ③ Since humor can easily capture people's attention, commercials tend to contain humorous elements, such as funny faces and gestures. ④ Instances of humor serve to enact bonds among organization members. ⑤ Understanding the humor may even be required as an informal badge of membership in the organization.

* subservient: 도움이 되는

다음 글에서 전체 흐름과 관계 <u>없는</u> 문장은?

Since their introduction, information systems have substantially changed the way business is conducted. ① This is particularly true for business in the shape and form of cooperation between firms that involves an integration of value chains across multiple units. ② The resulting networks do not only cover the business units of a single firm but typically also include multiple units from different firms. ③ As a consequence, firms do not only need to consider their internal organization in order to ensure sustainable business performance; they also need to take into account the entire ecosystem of units surrounding them. ④ Many major companies are fundamentally changing their business models by focusing on profitable units and cutting off less profitable ones. ⑤ In order to allow these different units to cooperate successfully, the existence of a common platform is crucial.

다음 글에서 전체 흐름과 관계 <u>없는</u> 문장은?

The best dealers offer a much broader service than merely having their goods on display and 'selling from stock'. Once they know the needs of a particular collector they can actively seek specific items to fill gaps in the collection. ① Because it is their business, to which they devote themselves full-time, they will inevitably have a much wider network than any non-professional collector can ever develop. ② As a matter of course they can enquire about the availability of pieces from dealers in other cities and, most crucially in some categories, from overseas. ③ They will be routinely informed of news of all auctions and important private sales, and should be well-enough connected to hear occasionally of items which are not yet quite on sale but might be available for a certain price. ④ The main advantage of buying from a dealer is getting personalised service on your purchases. ⑤ In turn, they can circulate their own contacts with 'want-lists' of desired items or subjects, multiplying their client collectors' chances of expanding their collections.

다음 글에서 전체 흐름과 관계 <u>없는</u> 문장은?

A variety of theoretical perspectives provide insight into immigration. Economics, which assumes that actors engage in utility maximization, represents one framework. ① From this perspective, it is assumed that individuals are rational actors, i.e., that they make migration decisions based on their assessment of the costs as well as benefits of remaining in a given area versus the costs and benefits of leaving. ② Benefits may include but are not limited to short-term and long-term monetary gains, safety, and greater freedom of cultural expression. ③ People with greater financial benefits tend to use their money to show off their social status by purchasing luxurious items. ④ Individual costs include but are not limited to the expense of travel, uncertainty of living in a foreign land, difficulty of adapting to a different language, uncertainty about a different culture, and the great concern about living in a new land. ⑤ Psychic costs associated with separation from family, friends, and the fear of the unknown also should be taken into account in cost-benefit assessments.

* psychic: 심적인

다음 글에서 전체 흐름과 관계 <u>없는</u> 문장은?

Although organizations are offering telecommuting programs in greater numbers than ever before, acceptance and use of these programs are still limited by a number of factors. ① These factors include manager reliance on face-to-face management practices, lack of telecommuting training within an organization, misperceptions of and discomfort with flexible workplace programs, and a lack of information about the effects of telecommuting on an organization's bottom line. ② Despite these limitations, at the beginning of the 21st century, a new "anytime, anywhere" work culture is emerging. ③ Care must be taken to select employees whose personal and working characteristics are best suited for telecommuting. ④ Continuing advances in information technology, the expansion of a global workforce, and increased desire to balance work and family are only three of the many factors that will gradually reduce the current barriers to telecommuting as a dominant workforce development. ⑤ With implications for organizational cost savings, especially with regard to lower facility costs, increased employee flexibility, and productivity, telecommuting is increasingly of interest to many organizations.

* telecommute: (컴퓨터로) 집에서 근무하다

다음 글에서 전체 흐름과 관계 <u>없는</u> 문장은?

One of the most widespread, and sadly mistaken, environmental myths is that living "close to nature" out in the country or in a leafy suburb is the best "green" lifestyle. Cities, on the other hand, are often blamed as a major cause of ecological destruction—artificial, crowded places that suck up precious resources. Yet, when you look at the facts, nothing could be farther from the truth. ① The pattern of life in the country and most suburbs involves long hours in the automobile each week, burning fuel and pumping out exhaust to get to work, buy groceries, and take kids to school and activities. ② City dwellers, on the other hand, have the option of walking or taking transit to work, shops, and school. ③ The larger yards and houses found outside cities also create an environmental cost in terms of energy use, water use, and land use. ④ This illustrates the tendency that most city dwellers get tired of urban lives and decide to settle in the countryside. ⑤ It's clear that the future of the Earth depends on more people gathering together in compact communities.

* compact: 밀집한

4-2 어휘 문제의 정답은 흐름상 반댓말이다.

우리는 Chapter 1과 Chapter 2를 통해서 Paraphrasing을 배웠습니다. Paraphrasing이 뭐였죠? 바로 하나의 내용을 다르게 표현하는 것이었습니다. 재진술을 파악하는 방법은 바로 문맥을 통해서 파악하는 것이었습니다. 어휘 문제는 흐름을 통해서 잘못 표현된 어휘를 고르는 것입니다. 즉 흐름을 통해서 잘못 쓰인 어휘를 찾는 것입니다. 그렇다면 중복 정답이 무조건 없어야 하는 수능 영어에서 확실히 어휘를 잘못 쓰여 답이 1개가 되게 하는 방법은 반대말을 사용하는 것입니다. 왜냐하면 비슷한 어휘를 사용할 경우 문맥상 재진술을 통해서 잘못 쓰인 것이 아닐 수 있기 때문입니다. 그리고 평가원은 실제로 반대말로 출제합니다.

이는 박스형 어휘 문제를 통해서 파악할 수 있습니다.

16학년도 수능 29번

The Atitlán Giant Grebe was a large, flightless bird that had evolved from the much more widespread and smaller Pied-billed Grebe. By 1965 there were only around 80 birds left on Lake Atitlán. One immediate reason was easy enough to spot: the local human population was cutting down the reed beds at a furious rate. This **(A) [accommodation / destruction]** was driven by the needs of a fast growing mat-making industry. But there were other problems. An American airline was intent on developing the lake as a tourist destination for fishermen. However, there was a major problem with this idea: the lake **(B) [lacked / supported]** any suitable sporting fish! To compensate for this rather obvious defect, a specially selected species of fish called the Large-mouthed Bass was introduced. The introduced individuals immediately turned their attentions to the crabs and small fish that lived in the lake, thus **(C) [competing / cooperating]** with the few remaining grebes for food. There is also little doubt that they sometimes gobbled up the zebra-striped Atitlán Giant Grebe's chicks.

* reed: 갈대   ** gobble up: 게걸스럽게 먹다

(A) [accommodation / destruction]

'accommodation'은 '수용' ⇔ 'destruction'은 '파괴'

(B) [lacked / supported]

'lacked'는 '부족하다, 잃다' ⇔ 'supported'는 '지지하다, 도와주다'

(C) [competing / cooperating]

'competing'은 '경쟁하다' ⇔ 'cooperating'은 '협동하다'

(A), (B), (C) 모두 반대말로 출제되었습니다.
최근에는 스펠링이 비슷한 어휘로 출제하지 않고 의미상 반대말이 되는 어휘로 출제하고 있습니다.
밑줄형 어휘 문제는 어떨까요?
밑줄형 어휘로 나왔던 문제를 풀어봅시다.

An Egyptian executive, after entertaining his Canadian guest, offered him joint partnership in a new business venture. The Canadian, delighted with the offer, suggested that they meet again the next morning with their ① respective lawyers to finalize the details. The Egyptian never showed up. The surprised and disappointed Canadian tried to understand what had gone wrong: Did Egyptians ② lack punctuality? Was the Egyptian expecting a counter-offer? Were lawyers unavailable in Cairo? None of these explanations proved to be correct; rather, the problem was ③ caused by the different meaning Canadians and Egyptians attach to inviting lawyers. The Canadian regarded the lawyers' ④ absence as facilitating the successful completion of the negotiation; the Egyptian interpreted it as signaling the Canadian's mistrust of his verbal commitment. Canadians often use the impersonal formality of a lawyer's services to finalize ⑤ agreements.

주어진 지문의 세 번째 문장에서 캐나다인이 변호사 서비스를 이용한다고 하므로 두 번째 문장에서 캐나다인은 변호사의 부재를 협상의 성공적인 마무리를 용이하게 하는 것으로 간주하는 것이 흐름상 반대가 됩니다. 즉 'absence', '부재'가 아니라 'presence', '존재'가 되어야합니다.

이와 같이 밑줄형 어휘 또한 정답이 원래 의미의 반댓말로 출제됩니다.

그럼 우리는 어휘 문제를 어떻게 풀어야 할까요?

Ⅰ. 밑줄 친 어휘가 다 올바르게 사용되었다고 가정하고 지문을 읽는다.
Ⅱ. 지문을 읽으며 흐름상 반대 내용을 찾는다. (흐름 무관 3. 반대 내용과 동일하게)로 풀이하시면 됩니다.

하지만 시험장에서 어휘 문제 특성상 반대 내용이 보이지 않을 경우가 있습니다.

이때만 박스형 어휘는 이미 반대말로 제시되었으므로 우리는 밑줄 친 어휘를 다음처럼 반대말과 비교해보며 풀어야 합니다.

16학년도 9월 평가원 29번

An Egyptian executive, after entertaining his Canadian guest, offered him joint partnership in a new business venture. The Canadian, delighted with the offer, suggested that they meet again the next morning with their ① [**respective** / **common**] lawyers to finalize the details. The Egyptian never showed up. The surprised and disappointed Canadian tried to understand what had gone wrong: Did Egyptians ② [**lack** / **have**] punctuality? Was the Egyptian expecting a counter-offer? Were lawyers unavailable in Cairo? None of these explanations proved to be correct; rather, the problem was ③ [**caused** / **solved**] by the different meaning Canadians and Egyptians attach to inviting lawyers. The Canadian regarded the lawyers' ④ [**absence** / **presence**] as facilitating the successful completion of the negotiation; the Egyptian interpreted it as signaling the Canadian's mistrust of his verbal commitment. Canadians often use the impersonal formality of a lawyer's services to finalize ⑤ [**agreements** / **disagreements**].

반대 내용이 적절하지 않다면 올바르게 사용된 것이고 반대 내용이 흐름상 올바르다면 그 밑줄친 어휘가 정답이 됩니다.

체화에서 박스형 어휘 문제를 통해 반댓말을 고려하며 푸는 것을 연습해 봅시다.

01

(A), (B), (C)의 각 네모 안에서 문맥에 맞는 낱말로 가장 적절한 것은?

Although children watch television at various times, the programming that they view alone tends to be specifically aimed at children. In the United States particularly, most of the advertising during this segment consists of ads for food, particularly sugared food. During the run-up to Christmas, **(A) [increasing / decreasing]** numbers of ads concern toys and games. Such practices are believed to put pressure on parents to yield to what the media have dubbed "pester power." This has led to calls for legislation to **(B) [promote / regulate]** advertising in Europe and the United States. Indeed, the Swedish government has outlawed television advertising of products aimed at children under 12, and recently in the United States, 50 psychologists **(C) [rejected / signed]** a petition calling for a ban on the advertising of children's goods.

* pester power: 부모에게 떼를 써서 물건을 구매하게 하는 힘

** petition: 탄원(서)

	(A)	(B)	(C)
①	increasing	promote	rejected
②	increasing	regulate	signed
③	increasing	regulate	rejected
④	decreasing	promote	signed
⑤	decreasing	regulate	signed

02

(A), (B), (C)의 각 네모 안에서 문맥에 맞는 낱말로 가장 적절한 것은?

In 2001, researchers at Wayne State University asked a group of college volunteers to exercise for twenty minutes at a **(A) [preset / self-selected]** pace on each of three machines: a treadmill, a stationary bike, and a stair climber. Measurements of heart rate, oxygen consumption, and perceived effort were taken throughout all three workouts. The researchers expected to find that the subjects unconsciously targeted the same relative physiological intensity in each activity. Perhaps they would **(B) [automatically / intentionally]** exercise at 65 percent of their maximum heart rate regardless of which machine they were using. Or maybe they would instinctively settle into rhythm at 70 percent of their maximum rate of oxygen consumption in all three workouts. But that's not what happened. There was, in fact, no **(C) [consistency / variation]** in measurements of heart rate and oxygen consumption across the three disciplines. Instead, the subjects were found to have chosen the same level of perceived effort on the treadmill, the bike, and the stair climber.

* treadmill: 러닝머신 ** physiological: 생리학적인

	(A)	(B)	(C)
①	preset	intentionally	consistency
②	preset	automatically	variation
③	self-selected	intentionally	variation
④	self-selected	intentionally	consistency
⑤	self-selected	automatically	consistency

03

(A), (B), (C)의 각 네모 안에서 문맥에 맞는 낱말로 가장 적절한 것은?

You can't have a democracy if you can't talk with your neighbors about matters of mutual interest or concern. Thomas Jefferson, who had an enduring interest in democracy, came to a similar conclusion. He was prescient in understanding the dangers of **(A) [concentrated / limited]** power, whether in corporations or in political leaders or exclusionary political institutions. Direct involvement of citizens was what had made the American Revolution possible and given the new republic vitality and hope for the future. Without that involvement, the republic would die. Eventually, he saw a need for the nation to be **(B) [blended / subdivided]** into "wards" — political units so small that everyone living there could participate directly in the political process. The representatives for each ward in the capital would have to be **(C) [resistant / responsive]** to citizens organized in this way. A vibrant democracy conducted locally would then provide the active basic unit for the democratic life of the republic. With that kind of involvement, the republic might survive and prosper.

* prescient: 선견지명이 있는

** vibrant: 활력이 넘치는

	(A)		(B)		(C)
①	concentrated	⋯⋯	blended	⋯⋯	resistant
②	concentrated	⋯⋯	subdivided	⋯⋯	responsive
③	concentrated	⋯⋯	subdivided	⋯⋯	resistant
④	limited	⋯⋯	subdivided	⋯⋯	resistant
⑤	limited	⋯⋯	blended	⋯⋯	responsive

04

(A), (B), (C)의 각 네모 안에서 문맥에 맞는 낱말로 가장 적절한 것은?

When teachers work in isolation, they tend to see the world through one set of eyes — their own. The fact that there might be someone somewhere *in the same building or district* who may be more successful at teaching this or that subject or lesson is **(A) [based / lost]** on teachers who close the door and work their way through the school calendar virtually alone. In the absence of a process that **(B) [allows / forbids]** them to benchmark those who do things better or at least differently, teachers are left with that one perspective — their own. I taught various subjects under the social studies umbrella and had very little idea of how my peers who taught the same subject did what they did. The idea of meeting regularly to compare notes, plan common assessments, and share what we did well **(C) [mostly / never]** occurred to us. Rather, we spent much time in the social studies office complaining about a lack of time and playing the blame game.

	(A)	(B)	(C)
①	based	allows	never
②	based	forbids	mostly
③	lost	allows	mostly
④	lost	allows	never
⑤	lost	forbids	never

체화 해설

01

(A), (B), (C)의 각 네모 안에서 문맥에 맞는 낱말로 가장 적절한 것은?

Although children watch television at various times, the programming that they view alone tends to be specifically aimed at children. In the United States particularly, most of the advertising during this segment consists of ads for food, particularly sugared food. During the run-up to Christmas, **(A) [increasing / decreasing]** numbers of ads concern toys and games. Such practices are believed to put pressure on parents to yield to what the media have dubbed "pester power." This has **led to** calls for legislation to **(B) [promote / regulate]** advertising in Europe and the United States. **Indeed**, the Swedish government has outlawed television advertising of products aimed at children under 12, and recently in the United States, 50 psychologists **(C) [rejected / signed]** a petition calling for a ban on the advertising of children's goods.

* pester power: 부모에게 떼를 써서 물건을 구매하게 하는 힘

** petition: 탄원(서)

♾ 해설 [정답 : ②]

(A) 뒷 문장에서 그러한 관행은 부모에게 압력을 준다고 하므로 아이들이 좋아하는 날콤한 음식과 장난감, 게임에 대한 광고는 증가해야 합니다. 그러므로 (A)는 'increasing'이 들어가야 합니다.

(B) 뒷 문장에서 스웨덴 정부는 12세 미만 아이들을 겨냥하는 제품의 티비 광고를 금지했다고 하므로 (B)에는 'regulate', '규제하다'가 들어가야 합니다.

(C)에서는 스웨덴 정부가 금지한 것과 같이 광고를 규제하는 것이 들어가야 하므로 아동 상품의 광고에 대한 금지를 요구하는 탄원서에 서명했다고 합니다. (C)에는 'signed'가 들어가야 합니다.

♾ 해석

아이들이 다양한 시간에 텔레비전을 시청하지만, 그들만이 보는 프로그램은 특정적으로 아이들을 겨냥하는 경향이 있다. 특히 미국에서는, 이러한 편성 마디에서 대부분의 광고가 식품, 특히 설탕이 첨가된 식품을 위한 광고로 구성되어 있다. 크리스마스 준비 기간에는, 점점 더 많은 수의 광고가 장난감 및 게임용품과 관련된다. 그러한 관행이 매스컴이 칭해온 '부모를 졸라 구매하게 하는 힘'에 굴복하라고 부모들에게 압력을 가한다고 여겨진다. 이 때문에 유럽과 미국에서 광고를 규제하는 법률 제정 요구가 이어졌다. 실제로, 스웨덴 정부는 12세 미만 아이들을 겨냥하는 제품의 텔레비전 광고를 금지했고, 최근 미국에서는 50명의 심리학자가 아동 상품의 광고에 대한 금지를 요구하는 청원서에 서명했다.

02

(A), (B), (C)의 각 네모 안에서 문맥에 맞는 낱말로 가장 적절한 것은?

In 2001, researchers at Wayne State University asked a group of college volunteers to exercise for twenty minutes at a **(A) [preset / self-selected]** pace on each of three machines: a treadmill, a stationary bike, and a stair climber. Measurements of heart rate, oxygen consumption, and perceived effort were taken throughout all three workouts. The researchers expected to find that the subjects unconsciously targeted the same relative physiological intensity in each activity. Perhaps they would **(B) [automatically / intentionally]** exercise at 65 percent of their maximum heart rate regardless of which machine they were using. Or maybe they would instinctively settle into rhythm at 70 percent of their maximum rate of oxygen consumption in all three workouts. **But** that's not what happened. There was, **in fact**, no **(C) [consistency / variation]** in measurements of heart rate and oxygen consumption across the three disciplines. **Instead**, the subjects were found to have chosen the same level of perceived effort on the treadmill, the bike, and the stair climber.

* treadmill: 러닝머신
** physiological: 생리학적인

⚓ 해설 ┃ 정답 : ⑤ ┃

(A)는 마지막 문장에서 실험 대상자들이 같은 수준의 운동 강도를 선택했다고 하므로 'self-selected'가 들어가야 합니다.

(B)의 앞 뒷 문장에서 'unconsciously', '무의식적으로 동일한 생리학적 강도를 목표를 할 것을 예상한다'고 하였고, 'instinctively', '본능적으로 70% 리듬에 자리 잡을 것을 예상한다'고 합니다. 그러므로 (B)는 'unconsciously', 'instinctively'와 비슷한 뜻인 'automatically'가 들어가야 합니다.

(C)의 앞에 나온 내용에서 동일한 강도와 비슷한 리듬에 자리 잡을 것이라고 예상했지만 (C)의 앞 문장에서 이 예상이 발생하지 않았다고 합니다. 이를 통해 동일한 강도와 비슷한 리듬이 보이지 않았음을 알 수 있으므로 (C) 문장의 'no'를 고려하여 (C)에서는 'consistency'가 들어가야 합니다.

⚓ 해석

2001년에 Wayne 주립대학의 연구자들은 한 무리의 대학생 지원자들에게 20분간 러닝머신, 고정 자전거, 스테퍼의 세 가지 운동 기구에서 각각 자신이 선택한 속도로 운동할 것을 요청했다. 심박 수, 산소 소모량과 인지된 운동 강도가 세 가지 운동이 이루어지는 내내 측정되었다. 연구자들은 실험 대상자들이 세 가지 활동 모두에서 무의식적으로 상대적으로 동일한 생리학적 강도를 목표로 할 것으로 예상했다. 어쩌면 그들은 어떤 기계를 사용하는지와 관계없이 무의식적으로 최대 심박 수의 65퍼센트로 운동할 것이었다. 혹은 어쩌면 그들은 세 가지 운동 모두에서 최대 산소 소모 속도의 70퍼센트라는 리듬에 본능적으로 자리 잡을 것이었다. 그러나 일어난 일은 그렇지 않았다. 사실, 세 가지 종목에서 심박 수와 산소 소모량 측정에서 일관성이 없었다. 대신, 실험 대상자들이 러닝머신, 자전거, 그리고 스테퍼에서 같은 수준의 인지된 운동 강도를 선택했다는 것이 밝혀졌다.

(A), (B), (C)의 각 네모 안에서 문맥에 맞는 낱말로 가장 적절한 것은?

You can't have a democracy if you can't talk with your neighbors about matters of mutual interest or concern. Thomas Jefferson, who had an enduring interest in democracy, came to a similar conclusion. He was prescient in understanding the dangers of **(A) [concentrated / limited]** power, whether in corporations or in political leaders or exclusionary political institutions. Direct involvement of citizens was what had made the American Revolution possible and given the new republic vitality and hope for the future. Without that involvement, the republic would die. **Eventually**, he saw a need for the nation to be **(B) [blended / subdivided]** into "wards" — political units so small that everyone living there could participate directly in the political process. The representatives for each ward in the capital would **have to** be **(C) [resistant / responsive]** to citizens organized in this way. A vibrant democracy conducted locally would then provide the active basic unit for the democratic life of the republic. With that kind of involvement, the republic might survive and prosper.

* prescient: 선견지명이 있는

** vibrant: 활력이 넘치는

⚓ 해설 ㅣ 정답 : ② ㅣ

(A)의 뒷 문장에서 시민의 직접직인 침어가 미국 혁명을 가능하게 하고 새로운 공화국에 활력과 미래에 대한 희망을 부여했다고 합니다. (A)는 'danger'로 고려하여 'Thomas Jefferson'이 (-), 부정적으로 인식하는 것이 들어가야 하므로 시민 참여와 반대인 'concentrated'가 들어가야 합니다.

(B)의 문장에서 정치 단위가 너무 작아서 모든 사람들이 참여할 수 있다고 하므로 'subdivided', '세분화된'이 들어가야 합니다.

(C)는 지문에서 참여 없이는 공화국이 죽는다는 내용을 통해 시민이 참여해야 한다고 하므로 'responsive'가 들어가야 합니다.

⚓ 해석

서로의 흥미나 관심거리에 대해 이웃과 이야기할 수 없다면 민주주의 체제를 가질 수 없다. 민주주의에 대해 지속적인 관심이 있었던 Thomas Jefferson은 이와 유사한 결론에 이르렀다. 그는 기업에서든, 정치적 지도자들에게서든, 혹은 배타적인 정치 제도에서든 집중된 권력의 위험성을 이해하는 데 있어서 선견지명이 있었다. 시민의 직접적인 참여는 미국 혁명을 가능하게 하고 새로운 공화국에 활력과 미래에 대한 희망을 부여했던 존재였다. 그러한 참여가 없다면 그 공화국은 멸망할 것이다. 결국, 그는 국가가 '(지방 의회 구성단위가 되는) 구'로 세분되어야 할 필요성을 인식했는데, '구'는 그곳에 사는 모든 사람들이 정치적인 과정에 직접 참여할 수 있을 정도로 작은 정치 단위였다. 수도에 있는 각 구의 대표들은 이런 방식으로 조직된 시민들에게 반응해야 할 것이다. 그런 다음 지역적으로 운영되는 활기찬 민주주의 체제는 공화국의 민주적인 삶을 위한 활발한 기본적 단위를 제공할 것이다. 그런 유형의 참여가 있으면, 공화국은 생존하고 번영할 것이다.

17학년도 수능 29번

(A), (B), (C)의 각 네모 안에서 문맥에 맞는 낱말로 가장 적절한 것은?

When teachers work in isolation, they tend to see the world through one set of eyes — their own. The fact that there might be someone somewhere in the same building or district who may be more successful at teaching this or that subject or lesson is **(A)** **[based** / **lost]** on teachers who close the door and work their way through the school calendar virtually alone. In the absence of a process that **(B)** **[allows** / **forbids]** them to benchmark those who do things better or at least differently, teachers are left with that one perspective — their own. I taught various subjects under the social studies umbrella and had very little idea of how my peers who taught the same subject did what they did. The idea of meeting regularly to compare notes, plan common assessments, and share what we did well **(C)** **[mostly** / **never]** occurred to us. **Rather**, we spent much time in the social studies office complaining about a lack of time and playing the blame game.

☞ 해설 **| 정답 : ④ |**

(A)의 앞 문장에서 선생님들이 고립되어 일을 할 때, 그들은 오직 자신의 눈으로만 세상을 본다고 합니다. 즉, 문을 닫고 혼자 일하는 선생님은 '같은 건물 혹은 같은 지역'에 더 성공적인 누군가가 있다는 것을 인지하지 못해야 합니다. 그러므로 (A)에는 'lost'가 들어가야 합니다.

(B) 문장은 고립된 선생님을 제시하므로 더 잘하는 사람을 벤치마킹하는 것을 하지 않아야 합니다.

(B) 앞의 'absence'를 고려하여 'allow'가 들어가야 합니다.

(C)의 앞 문장에서 다른 사람들이 어떻게 가르치는지 모른다고 했으므로 의견이나 정보를 교환하고, 공통 평가를 계획하고, 무엇을 잘하는 지 공유하는 것은 일어나지 않아야 합니다. 그러므로 (C)에는 'never'가 들어가야 합니다.

☞ 해석

교사가 홀로 일을 할 때 그들은 오직 한 쌍의 눈, 즉 자기 자신의 눈으로 세상을 보는 경향이 있다. 이런저런 과목이나 혹은 수업을 가르치는 데 있어서 더 성공적일 수 있는 누군가가 '같은 건물 혹은 같은 지역' 어딘가에 있을 수 있다는 사실을, 문을 닫고 거의 혼자서 학교의 연간 행사 계획표를 실천해 나가는 교사는 이해하지 못한다. 일을 더 잘하거나 최소한 다르게 하는 사람들을 벤치마킹할 수 있게 해주는 과정이 없는 상태에서, 교사들은 하나의 시각, 즉 자신의 시각만을 갖게 된다. 나는 사회 과학 분야에 속한 다양한 과목을 가르쳤는데 동일한 과목을 가르치는 나의 동료들이 어떻게 가르치는지에 대해 아는 것이 거의 없었다. 의견이나 정보를 교환하고, 공동 평가를 계획하고, 자신이 잘한 것을 공유하기 위해서 정기적으로 만난다는 생각을 우리는 전혀 해보지 않았다. 오히려 우리는 사회 교과 교무실에서 시간이 부족한 것에 대해 불평하면서 그리고 서로 비난하고 책임 전가를 하면서 많은 시간을 보냈다.

01 25학년도 수능 30번

다음 글의 밑줄 친 부분 중, 문맥상 낱말의 쓰임이 적절하지 <u>않은</u> 것은?

Studies in psychology have reported cases in which competitive incentives resulted in lower task effort, and their focus was on the psychological underpinnings of the reduction in motivation. For example, competition presents an inevitable conflict between the motivation to achieve one's personal goal and the ① <u>desire</u> to maintain good relationships with others. When the maintenance of interpersonal relationships is important, with their counterparts in particular or with others generally, competitors experience an ② <u>internal</u> conflict that can harm their desire to achieve their goal and taint the good feeling brought about by winning. Exline and Lobel found that the perception of oneself as a target for upward social comparison often makes people ③ <u>uncomfortable</u>. When they believe that others are making envious comparisons with them, people feel uneasiness, distress, or sorrow. Feelings of guilt, an emotion generally associated with high motivation for goal-achievement, lead to ④ <u>stronger</u> motivation and performance in the pursuit of competitive goals. Consequences of this emotional state include lower task motivation in a competition and preferences for more cooperative and altruistic outcomes, such as ⑤ <u>diminishing</u> the significance of the outcome or sharing the winner's reward.

* taint: 더럽히다 ** altruistic: 이타주의의

02 24학년도 수능 30번

다음 글의 밑줄 친 부분 중, 문맥상 낱말의 쓰임이 적절하지 <u>않은</u> 것은?

Bazaar economies feature an apparently flexible price-setting mechanism that sits atop more enduring ties of shared culture. Both the buyer and seller are aware of each other's ① <u>restrictions</u>. In Delhi's bazaars, buyers and sellers can ② <u>assess</u> to a large extent the financial constraints that other actors have in their everyday life. Each actor belonging to a specific economic class understands what the other sees as a necessity and a luxury. In the case of electronic products like video games, they are not a ③ <u>necessity</u> at the same level as other household purchases such as food items. So, the seller in Delhi's bazaars is careful not to directly ask for very ④ <u>low</u> prices for video games because at no point will the buyer see possession of them as an absolute necessity. Access to this type of knowledge establishes a price consensus by relating to each other's preferences and limitations of belonging to a ⑤ <u>similar</u> cultural and economic universe.

* constraint: 압박 ** consensus: 일치

중. 최. 평. 해설

01 25학년도 수능 30번   (정답률 57%)

다음 글의 밑줄 친 부분 중, 문맥상 낱말의 쓰임이 적절하지 <u>않은</u> 것은?

Studies in psychology have reported cases in which competitive incentives **resulted in** lower task effort, and their focus was on the psychological underpinnings of the reduction in motivation. **For example**, competition presents an inevitable conflict between the motivation to achieve one's personal goal and the ① <u>desire</u> to maintain good relationships with others. When the maintenance of interpersonal relationships is important, with their counterparts in particular or with others generally, competitors experience an ② <u>internal</u> conflict that can harm their desire to achieve their goal and taint the good feeling **brought about** by winning. Exline and Lobel found that the perception of oneself as a target for upward social comparison often makes people ③ <u>uncomfortable</u>. When they believe that others are making envious comparisons with them, people feel uneasiness, distress, or sorrow. Feelings of guilt, an emotion generally associated with high motivation for goal-achievement, **lead to** ④ <u>stronger</u> motivation and performance in the pursuit of competitive goals. **Consequences** of this emotional state include lower task motivation in a competition and preferences for more cooperative and altruistic outcomes, such as ⑤ <u>diminishing</u> the significance of the outcome or sharing the winner's reward.

* taint: 더럽히다 ** altruistic: 이타주의의

해설 [정답 : ④]

I번 문장에서 경쟁적 인센티브는 업무 효율을 낮춘다고 합니다. 또한 Ⅶ번 문장에서 경쟁 목표를 성취하는 것에 죄책감을 느끼는 상태의 결과는 업무 동기를 포함한다고 하므로 'stronger'이 아닌 'weaker', '더 약하게'가 와야 합니다.

* ⑤번을 27%의 학생들이 골랐습니다. ⑤번 문장인 Ⅶ번 문장은 대인 관계를 좀 더 중시하게 되는 상황을 제시하며 이로 인해 업무 동기가 낮아지게 된다고 합니다. 이어서 ⑤번에서는 결과의 중요성을 낮추는 즉, 업무 동기가 낮아지게 되는 것을 재진술하므로 ⑤번의 'diminishing'은 적절한 어휘 사용에 해당합니다.

I. Studies (in psychology) / have reported / cases (in which competitive incentives / **resulted in** / lower task effort), and their focus / was (on the psychological underpinnings of the reduction in motivation).

> 구▶ 심리학 연구에서는 경쟁적 인센티브가 (= 유인책이) 업무 노력의 감소를 유발한 사례들을 보고했으며, 그들의 초점은 (= 연구들의 초점은) 동기 감소의 심리적 기반에 두었다고 합니다.

> 독▶ 'result in'이 제시되었으므로 중심 문장.
> - 경쟁적 인센티브가 업무 노력을 감소시키는 연구를 제시하며, 그 연구는 동기 감소의 심리적 기반을 집중적으로 보고했다고 합니다.

* under (아래) + pin (고정하다) = underpin - 뒷받침하다, 기반을 두다.

Ⅱ. **For example,** competition / presents / an inevitable conflict (between the motivation (to achieve one's personal goal) and the ① desire (to maintain good relationships with others)).

> 구▶ 'between A and B'는 'A와 B 사이'를 의미합니다.
> - 예를 들어, 경쟁은 개인의 목표를 달성하려는 동기와 다른 사람들과 좋은 관계를 유지하려는 욕구 사이에 피할 수 없는 갈등을 제시한다고 합니다.

> 독▶ 'For example'이 제시되었으므로 앞 문장 중심 문장.
> - Ⅰ번 문장의 예시로 경쟁이 개인의 목표를 위한 동기와 다른 사람과의 좋은 관계 사이 갈등을 유발한다고 합니다.

Ⅲ. When the maintenance of interpersonal relationships / is / important, (with their counterparts in particular or with others generally), competitors / experience / an ② internal conflict (that can harm / their desire (to achieve their goal) and taint / the good feeling (**brought about** by winning)).

* taint: 더럽히다

> 구▶ 자신의 상대와 혹은 일반적으로는 타인과의 대인 관계 유지가 중요할 때, 경쟁하는 이들은 자신의 목표를 달성하려는 욕구에 손상을 주고 승리로 인해 생기는 좋은 기분을 더럽힐 수 있는 내적 갈등을 경험한다고 합니다.

> 독▶ 'bring about'이 제시되었으므로 중심 문장.
> - Ⅱ번 문장의 예시를 좀 더 구체화하여, 인간 관계가 중요할 때, 즉 인간 관계를 선택하게 되면, 본인의 목표를 달성할 수 없고 경쟁에서의 승리로 인해 생기는 좋은 기분을 더럽힌다는 갈등이 생기게 된다고 합니다.

Ⅳ. Exline and Lobel / found / that the perception of oneself (as a target for upward social comparison) often makes / people / ③ uncomfortable.

> 구▶ 'make + O + O.C'는 'O가 O.C하게 만들다'를 의미합니다.
> - Exlinc과 Lobel은 상향 사회적 비교의 대상으로 자신을 인식하는 것이 흔히 사람들을 불편하게 만든다는 것을 발견했다고 합니다.

> 독▶ 사람들이 스스로를 비교의 대상으로 생각하면 불편하게 느끼게 된다고 합니다.

Ⅴ. When they / believe / that others / are making / envious comparisons with them, people / feel / uneasiness, distress, or sorrow.

> 구▶ 그들은 (= 사람들은) 다른 사람들이 질투하며 자신과 비교하고 있다고 생각하면 불안, 괴로움, 혹은 슬픔을 느낀다고 합니다.

> 독▶ Ⅳ번 문장을 재진술하여 다른 사람들이 자신을 비교의 대상으로 생각한다면, 그 비교의 대상이 되는 사람들은 불편하다고 느낀다고 합니다.

Ⅵ. Feelings of guilt, (an emotion (generally associated with high motivation for goal-achievement)), / lead to / ④ stronger motivation and performance (in the pursuit of competitive goals).

구 일반적으로 목표 달성에 대한 높은 동기와 연관된 감정인 죄책감은 경쟁 목표를 추구할 때의 동기와 성과를 더 강하게 만든다고 합니다.

독 'lead to'가 제시되었으므로 중심 문장.
- Ⅰ번 문장에서 경쟁적 인센티브는 업무 효율을 낮춘다고 합니다. 또한 뒤에 나올 Ⅷ번 문장에서 그러한 감정적 상태는 (= 죄책감을 느끼는 상태는) 낮은 업무 동기를 포함한다고 하므로 'stronger'이 아닌 'weaker', '더 약하게'가 와야 합니다.

Ⅶ. **Consequences** of this emotional state / include / lower task motivation (in a competition and preferences) (for more cooperative and altruistic outcomes), (such as ⑤ diminishing the significance of the outcome or sharing the winner's reward).

** altruistic: 이타주의의

구 이러한 감정 상태의 (= 죄책감을 느끼는 상태의) 결과는 경쟁에서 업무 동기의 감소, 그리고 결과의 중요성을 줄이거나 승자의 보상을 나누는 것과 같은 더 협력적이고 이타주의의 결과에 대한 선호가 포함된다고 합니다.

독 'Consequences', 결과가 제시되었으므로 중심 문장
- Ⅲ번 문장의 내용을 좀 더 구체화하여 경쟁 목표를 추구하는 것에 죄책감을 느낀 결과, 즉, 대인 관계를 더 중시하게 되면 업무 동기의 감소와 승자의 보상을 나누는 것과 같은 행동을 하게 된다고 합니다.

다음 글의 밑줄 친 부분 중, 문맥상 낱말의 쓰임이 적절하지 <u>않은</u> 것은?

Bazaar economies feature an apparently flexible price-setting mechanism that sits atop more enduring ties of shared culture. Both the buyer and seller are aware of each other's ① <u>restrictions</u>. In Delhi's bazaars, buyers and sellers can ② <u>assess</u> to a large extent the financial constraints that other actors have in their everyday life. Each actor belonging to a specific economic class understands what the other sees as a necessity and a luxury. In the case of electronic products like video games, they are not a ③ <u>necessity</u> at the same level as other household purchases such as food items. <u>**So**</u>, the seller in Delhi's bazaars is careful not to directly ask for very ④ <u>low</u> prices for video games <u>**because**</u> at no point will the buyer see possession of them as an absolute necessity. Access to this type of knowledge establishes a price consensus by relating to each other's preferences and limitations of belonging to a ⑤ <u>similar</u> cultural and economic universe.

* constraint: 압박 ** consensus: 일치

해설 [정답 : ④]

③번 앞 문장에서부터 내용을 정리하며 전체적인 지문의 맥락을 추론해야 합니다.

③번 앞 문장 : 'actor belonging to a specific economic class understands what the other sees as a necessity and a luxury' - 특정 경제 계층에 속하는 행위자는 상대방이 무엇을 필수품, 사치품으로 여기는지를 이해한다,

③번 문장 : 'video games, they are not a necessity' 비디오 게임은 필수품이 아니다 (사치품이다)

④번 문장 : 'seller in Delhi's bazaars is careful not to directly ask for very low prices for video games' - 델리의 상점가에서 판매자는 비디오 게임에 대해 낮은 가격을 요구하지 않으려고 한다.

④번 문장 : 'at no point will the buyer see possession of them as an absolute necessity' - 구매자가 게임의 소유를 절대적인 필수 사항으로 볼 이유가 없다.

여기서 지문의 맥락을 추론해 볼 경우, 비디오 게임은 필수품이 아니다 - 구매자는 비디오 게임을 필수 사항으로 원하지 않는다

　- 비디오 게임을 원하지 않는 구매자는 비디오 게임에 낮은 가치를 부여한다

　- 그 경우, 판매자는 비디오 게임을 높은 가격으로 판매할 수 없게 된다 - 그러므로 판매자는 구매자의 성향을 알 수 없으므로 비디오 게임에 높은 가격을 요구하지 않는다

다음과 같은 맥락을 볼 때, 판매자가 비디오 게임에 대해 낮은 가격을 요구하는 것은 문맥상 적절하지 않으므로, 'low'를 'high' '높은'과 같은 단어로 바꾸어야 합니다.

Ⅰ. Bazaar economies / feature / an apparently flexible price-setting mechanism / that / sits atop more enduring ties of shared culture.

> 구▶ 상점가 경제는 공유되는 문화라는 더 지속적인 유대 위에 자리 잡은, 겉으로 보기에 유연한 가격 설정 메커니즘을 특징으로 한다고 합니다.

> 독▶ 일반적인 가격 구매 경제(편의점, 마트)가 아닌, 상점가 경제(마을시장, 길거리 시장)의 특징을 언급하고 있습니다.

Ⅱ. Both the buyer and seller / are aware of each other's ① restrictions.

> 구▶ 구매자와 판매자 둘 다 서로의 제약을 알고 있다고 합니다.

> 독▶ 상점가 경제의 특징을 언급하고 있습니다.

Ⅲ. In Delhi's bazaars, buyers and sellers / can ② assess to a large extent the financial constraints / that / other actors / have (in their everyday life).

* constraint: 압박

> 구▶ 델리의 상점가에서, 구매자와 판매자는 대체로 다른 행위자들이 그들의 일상생활에서 가지는 재정적인 제약을 평가할 수 있다고 합니다.

> 독▶ 예시 문장에서 Ⅱ번 문장의 'restriction'이 'constraints', 일상생활에서의 재정적인 제약으로 확대되어 재언급되었습니다.

Ⅳ. Each actor / belonging to a specific economic class / understands / what / the other / sees / as a necessity and a luxury.

> 구▶ 특정 경제 계층에 속하는 각 행위자는 상대방이 무엇을 필수품으로 여기고 무엇을 사치품으로 여기는지를 이해한다고 합니다.

> 독▶ 상대방의 필수품과 사치품을 알고 있는 것 역시 Ⅱ번 문장의 제약을 알고 있다는 것을 말하고 있습니다.

Ⅴ. In the case of electronic products like video games, they / are not / a ③ necessity at the same level as other household purchases (such as food items).

> 구▶ 비디오 게임과 같은 전자 제품의 경우, 그것들은 식품과 같은 다른 가정 구매품과 동일한 수준의 필수품이 아니라고 합니다.

> 독▶ 식품은 필수품, 비디오 게임은 사치품이라는 것을 알 수 있습니다.

VI. **So**, the seller (in Delhi's bazaars) / is / careful not to directly ask for very ④ <u>low</u> prices for video games **because** at no point / will / the buyer / see possession of them as an absolute necessity.

> 구 ▶ 부사구 'at no point'가 because 접속사절 앞으로 나오면서 주어와 동사가 도치된 문장입니다.
> - 따라서 델리의 상점가에서 판매자는 비디오 게임에 대해 직접적으로 매우 낮은 가격을 요구하지 않으려 주의하는데, 구매자가 비디오 게임의 소유를 절대적인 필수 사항으로 볼 이유가 전혀 없기 때문이라고 합니다.

> 독 ▶ 'so', 'because'가 제시되었으므로 중심 문장
> - 구매자에게 있어서 필수품이 중요하므로 가치가 상대적으로 사치품보다 높다는 것을 이해한다면, 판매자는 사치품보다 필수품을 우선적으로 구매하려고 하는 것을 이해할 수 있고,
> 이 제약을 알고 있는 판매자는 사치품(비디오 게임)에 대해 필수품(식품)보다 높은 가격을 요구하지 않는다는 것을 이해할 수 있습니다.

VII. Access (to this type of knowledge) / establishes / a price consensus by relating to each other's preferences and limitations of belonging to a ⑤ <u>similar</u> cultural and economic universe.

** consensus: 일치

> 구 ▶ 이러한 유형의 지식에 대한 접근은 비슷한 문화적이고 경제적인 세상의 소속에서 비롯한 서로의 선호와 한계를 관련지어 가격 일치를 형성한다고 합니다.

> 독 ▶ 이렇게 문화적, 소속감에 따라 가격이 형성되는 상점가 경제는 가격 설정과 판매로 이어지는 일반적인 시장 경제 구조와 다르다는 것을 언급하고 있습니다.

01 21학년도 6월 평가원 30번 [정답과 해설 36page]

다음 글의 밑줄 친 부분 중, 문맥상 낱말의 쓰임이 적절하지 <u>않은</u> 것은?

Chunking is vital for cognition of music. If we had to encode it in our brains note by note, we'd ① <u>struggle</u> to make sense of anything more complex than the simplest children's songs. Of course, most accomplished musicians can play compositions containing many thousands of notes entirely from ② <u>memory</u>, without a note out of place. But this seemingly awesome accomplishment of recall is made ③ <u>improbable</u> by remembering the musical process, not the individual notes as such. If you ask a pianist to start a Mozart sonata from bar forty-one, she'll probably have to ④ <u>mentally</u> replay the music from the start until reaching that bar— the score is not simply laid out in her mind, to be read from any random point. It's rather like describing how you drive to work: you don't simply recite the names of roads as an abstract list, but have to construct your route by mentally retracing it. When musicians make a mistake during rehearsal, they wind back to the ⑤ <u>start</u> of a musical phrase ('let's take it from the second verse') before restarting.

* chunking: 덩어리로 나누기 ** bar: (악보의) 마디

02 22학년도 6월 평가원 30번 [정답과 해설 39page]

다음 글의 밑줄 친 부분 중, 문맥상 낱말의 쓰임이 적절하지 <u>않은</u> 것은?

Sport can trigger an emotional response in its consumers of the kind rarely brought forth by other products. Imagine bank customers buying memorabilia to show loyalty to their bank, or consumers ① <u>identifying</u> so strongly with their car insurance company that they get a tattoo with its logo. We know that some sport followers are so ② <u>passionate</u> about players, teams and the sport itself that their interest borders on obsession. This addiction provides the emotional glue that binds fans to teams, and maintains loyalty even in the face of on-field ③ <u>failure</u>. While most managers can only dream of having customers that are as passionate about their products as sport fans, the emotion triggered by sport can also have a negative impact. Sport's emotional intensity can mean that organisations have strong attachments to the past through nostalgia and club tradition. As a result, they may ④ <u>increase</u> efficiency, productivity and the need to respond quickly to changing market conditions. For example, a proposal to change club colours in order to project a more attractive image may be ⑤ <u>defeated</u> because it breaks a link with tradition.

* memorabilia: 기념품 ** obsession: 집착

다음 글의 밑줄 친 부분 중, 문맥상 낱말의 쓰임이 적절하지 <u>않은</u> 것은?

How the bandwagon effect occurs is demonstrated by the history of measurements of the speed of light. Because this speed is the basis of the theory of relativity, it's one of the most frequently and carefully measured ① <u>quantities</u> in science. As far as we know, the speed hasn't changed over time. However, from 1870 to 1900, all the experiments found speeds that were too high. Then, from 1900 to 1950, the ② <u>opposite</u> happened—all the experiments found speeds that were too low! This kind of error, where results are always on one side of the real value, is called "bias." It probably happened because over time, experimenters subconsciously adjusted their results to ③ <u>match</u> what they expected to find. If a result fit what they expected, they kept it. If a result didn't fit, they threw it out. They weren't being intentionally dishonest, just ④ <u>influenced</u> by the conventional wisdom. The pattern only changed when someone ⑤ <u>lacked</u> the courage to report what was actually measured instead of what was expected.

* bandwagon effect: 편승 효과

다음 글의 밑줄 친 부분 중, 문맥상 낱말의 쓰임이 적절하지 <u>않은</u> 것은?

Although the wonders of modern technology have provided people with opportunities beyond the wildest dreams of our ancestors, the good, as usual, is weakened by a downside. One of those downsides is that anyone who so chooses can pick up the virtual megaphone that is the Internet and put in their two cents on any of an infinite number of topics, regardless of their ① <u>qualifications</u>. After all, on the Internet, there are no regulations ② <u>preventing</u> a kindergarten teacher from offering medical advice or a physician from suggesting ways to safely make structural changes to your home. As a result, misinformation gets disseminated as information, and it is not always easy to ③ <u>differentiate</u> the two. This can be particularly frustrating for scientists, who spend their lives learning how to understand the intricacies of the world around them, only to have their work summarily ④ <u>challenged</u> by people whose experience with the topic can be measured in minutes. This frustration is then ⑤ <u>diminished</u> by the fact that, to the general public, both the scientist and the challenger are awarded equal credibility.

* put in one's two cents: 의견을 말하다 ** disseminate: 퍼뜨리다 *** intricacy: 복잡성

다음 글의 밑줄 친 부분 중, 문맥상 낱말의 쓰임이 적절하지 <u>않은</u> 것은?

Why is the value of place so important? From a historical perspective, until the 1700s textile production was a hand process using the fibers available within a ① <u>particular</u> geographic region, for example, cotton, wool, silk, and flax. Trade among regions ② <u>increased</u> the availability of these fibers and associated textiles made from the fibers. The First Industrial Revolution and subsequent technological advancementsin manufactured fibers ③ <u>added</u> to the fact that fibers and textiles were no longer "place-bound." Fashion companies created and consumers could acquire textiles and products made from textiles with little or no connection to where, how, or by whom the products were made. This ④ <u>countered</u> a disconnect between consumers and the products they use on a daily basis, a loss of understanding and appreciation in the skills and resources necessary to create these products, and an associated disregard for the human and natural resources necessary for the products' creation. Therefore, renewing a value on place ⑤ <u>reconnects</u> the company and the consumer with the people, geography, and culture of a particular location.

* textile: 직물

다음 글의 밑줄 친 부분 중, 문맥상 낱말의 쓰임이 적절하지 <u>않은</u> 것은?

It has been suggested that "organic" methods, defined as those in which only natural products can be used as inputs, would be less damaging to the biosphere. Large-scale adoption of "organic" farming methods, however, would ① <u>reduce</u> yields and increase production costs for many major crops. Inorganic nitrogen supplies are ② <u>essential</u> for maintaining moderate to high levels of productivity for many of the non-leguminous crop species, because organic supplies of nitrogenous materials often are either limited or more expensive than inorganic nitrogen fertilizers. In addition, there are ③ <u>benefits</u> to the extensive use of either manure or legumes as "green manure" crops. In many cases, weed control can be very difficult or require much hand labor if chemicals cannot be used, and ④ <u>fewer</u> people are willing to do this work as societies become wealthier. Some methods used in "organic" farming, however, such as the sensible use of crop rotations and specific combinations of cropping and livestock enterprises, can make important ⑤ <u>contributions</u> to the sustainability of rural ecosystems.

* nitrogen fertilizer: 질소 비료 ** manure: 거름
*** legume: 콩과(科) 식물

다음 글의 밑줄 친 부분 중, 문맥상 낱말의 쓰임이 적절하지 <u>않은</u> 것은?

Everywhere we turn we hear about almighty "cyberspace"! The hype promises that we will leave our boring lives, put on goggles and body suits, and enter some metallic, three-dimensional, multimedia otherworld. When the Industrial Revolution arrived with its great innovation, the motor, we didn't leave our world to go to some ① <u>remote</u> motorspace! On the contrary, we brought the motors into our lives, as automobiles, refrigerators, drill presses, and pencil sharpeners. This ② <u>absorption</u> has been so complete that we refer to all these tools with names that declare their usage, not their "motorness." These innovations led to a major socioeconomic movement precisely because they entered and ③ <u>affected</u> profoundly our everyday lives. People have not changed fundamentally in thousands of years. Technology changes constantly. It's the one that must ④ <u>adapt</u> to us. That's exactly what will happen with information technology and its devices under human-centric computing. The longer we continue to believe that computers will take us to a magical new world, the longer we will ⑤ <u>maintain</u> their natural fusion with our lives, the hallmark of every major movement that aspires to be called a socioeconomic revolution.

* hype: 과대광고 ** hallmark: 특징

다음 글의 밑줄 친 부분 중, 문맥상 낱말의 쓰임이 적절하지 <u>않은</u> 것은?

Internalization depends on supports for autonomy. Contexts that use controlling strategies such as salient rewards and punishments or evaluative, selfesteem-hooking pressures are ① <u>least</u> likely to lead people to value activities as their own. This is not to say that controls don't ② <u>work</u> to produce behavior — decades of operant psychology prove that they can. It is rather that the more salient the external control over a person's behavior, the more the person is likely to be merely externally regulated or introjected in his or her actions. Consequently, the person does not ③ <u>develop</u> a value or investment in the behaviors, but instead remains dependent on external controls. Thus, parents who reward, force, or cajole their child to do homework are more likely to have a child who does so only when rewarded, cajoled, or forced. The salience of external controls ④ <u>drives</u> the acquisition of self-responsibility. Alternatively, parents who supply reasons, show an emotional understanding of difficulties overcoming problems, and use a ⑤ <u>minimum</u> of external incentives are more likely to cultivate a sense of willingness and value for work in their child.

* autonomy: 자율성 ** salient: 두드러진 *** introject: 투입하다

다음 글의 밑줄 친 부분 중, 문맥상 낱말의 쓰임이 적절하지 <u>않은</u> 것은?

In recent years urban transport professionals globally have largely acquiesced to the view that automobile demand in cities needs to be managed rather than accommodated. Rising incomes inevitably lead to increases in motorization. Even without the imperative of climate change, the physical constraints of densely inhabited cities and the corresponding demands of accessibility, mobility, safety, air pollution, and urban livability all ① <u>limit</u> the option of expanding road networks purely to accommodate this rising demand. As a result, as cities develop and their residents become more prosperous, ② <u>persuading</u> people to choose *not* to use cars becomes an increasingly key focus of city managers and planners. Improving the quality of ③ <u>alternative</u> options, such as walking, cycling, and public transport, is a central element of this strategy. However, the most direct approach to ④ <u>accommodating</u> automobile demand is making motorized travel more expensive or restricting it with administrative rules. The contribution of motorized travel to climate change ⑤ <u>reinforces</u> this imperative.

* acquiesce: 따르다 ** imperative: 불가피한 것 *** constraint: 압박

다음 글의 밑줄 친 부분 중, 문맥상 낱말의 쓰임이 적절하지 <u>않은</u> 것은?

If I say to you, 'Don't think of a white bear', you will find it difficult not to think of a white bear. In this way, 'thought suppression can actually increase the thoughts one wishes to suppress instead of calming them'. One common example of this is that people on a diet who try not to think about food often begin to think much ① <u>more</u> about food. This process is therefore also known as the rebound effect. The ② <u>ironic</u> effect seems to be caused by the interplay of two related cognitive processes. This dual-process system involves, first, an intentional operating process, which consciously attempts to locate thoughts ③ <u>unrelated</u> to the suppressed ones. Second, and simultaneously, an unconscious monitoring process tests whether the operating system is functioning effectively. If the monitoring system encounters thoughts inconsistent with the intended ones, it prompts the intentional operating process to ensure that these are replaced by ④ <u>inappropriate</u> thoughts. However, it is argued, the intentional operating system can fail due to increased cognitive load caused by fatigue, stress and emotional factors, and so the monitoring process filters the inappropriate thoughts into consciousness, making them highly ⑤ <u>accessible</u>.

(A), (B), (C)의 각 네모 안에서 문맥에 맞는 낱말로 가장 적절한 것은?

> To the extent that an agent relies on the prior knowledge of its designer rather than on its own percepts, we say that the agent lacks autonomy. A rational agent should be autonomous — it should learn what it can to (A) compensate / prepare for partial or incorrect prior knowledge. For example, a vacuum-cleaning agent that learns to foresee where and when additional dirt will appear will do better than one that does not. As a practical matter, one seldom requires complete autonomy from the start: when the agent has had little or no experience, it would have to act (B) purposefully / randomly unless the designer gave some assistance. So, just as evolution provides animals with enough built-in reflexes to survive long enough to learn for themselves, it would be reasonable to provide an artificial intelligent agent with some initial knowledge as well as an ability to learn. After sufficient experience of its environment, the behavior of a rational agent can become effectively (C) independent / protective of its prior knowledge. Hence, the incorporation of learning allows one to design a single rational agent that will succeed in a vast variety of environments.

	(A)	(B)	(C)
①	compensate	randomly	protective
②	compensate	purposefully	protective
③	prepare	randomly	protective
④	compensate	randomly	independent
⑤	prepare	purposefully	independent

12 22학년도 9월 평가원 30번

[정답과 해설 67page]

다음 글의 밑줄 친 부분 중, 문맥상 낱말의 쓰임이 적절하지 <u>않은</u> 것은?

In economic systems what takes place in one sector has impacts on another; demand for a good or service in one sector is derived from another. For instance, a consumer buying a good in a store will likely trigger the replacement of this product, which will generate ① <u>demands</u> for activities such as manufacturing, resource extraction and, of course, transport. What is different about transport is that it cannot exist alone and a movement cannot be ② <u>stored</u>. An unsold product can remain on the shelf of a store until bought (often with discount incentives), but an unsold seat on a flight or unused cargo capacity in the same flight remains unsold and cannot be brought back as additional capacity ③ <u>later</u>. In this case an opportunity has been ④ <u>seized</u>, since the amount of transport being offered has exceeded the demand for it. The derived demand of transportation is often very difficult to reconcile with an equivalent supply, and actually transport companies would prefer to have some additional capacity to accommodate ⑤ <u>unforeseen</u> demand (often at much higher prices).

13 25학년도 9월 평가원 30번

[정답과 해설 69page]

다음 글의 밑줄 친 부분 중, 문맥상 낱말의 쓰임이 적절하지 <u>않은</u> 것은?

We all like to think of ourselves as rational actors, careful and considered in our thinking, capable of sound and reliable judgments. We might believe that we generally consider different points of view and make ① <u>informed</u> decisions. We are, in fact, "predictably irrational," as psychologist Dan Ariely titled his book on the topic. All of us engage in automatic, reflexive thinking, typically taking the ② <u>easier</u> path and conserving mental effort. Although we each may have the subjective impression that we are careful thinkers, we often make snap judgments or no real judgments at all. In addition, numerous biases inhibit or override reflective, deliberative thought; intuitive theories can also interfere with ③ <u>acceptance</u> of accurate scientific explanations. Understanding more about how our minds work and how biases may operate can make us each ④ <u>less</u> subject to fallacious reasoning, more rational, and more aware of the problems in others' thinking. Learning to understand the built-in ⑤ <u>rationality</u> of our mental processes can also help us improve our ability to inform others more effectively.

* intuitive: 직관적인 ** fallacious: 오류가 있는

41~42번 단문의 경우 우리가 Chapter 1-2에서 배운 제목/주제 유형과 Chapter 4-2에서 배운 어휘가 합쳐진 것으로 생각하시면 됩니다. 우리가 배운 내용에 대해서 간략히 설명하고 바로 문제를 풀어보겠습니다.

41번 Road Map

평가원 오답선지 Pattern

- **모호한 선지**
  : 객관적 이해가 어려운 선지
  - **비유적 선지**
    : 지문과 대응하여 해석
  - **질문 선지**
    : 질문에 대한 답이 주제

- **언급되지 않은 선지**
  : 우리의 통념과 비슷하여 그럴듯 하지만 지문에서 언급되지 않은 선지

- **포괄하지 않는 선지**
  : 지문 전체 내용이 아닌 일부 내용에 대하여 일치하는 선지

- **방향 바꾸기**
  : A ⇒ B 를 제시하는 지문에서 B ⇒ A라는 선지를 구성하여 원인을 결과로 결과를 원인으로 제시하는 선지

42번 Road Map

1. 어휘 유형 풀이법

Ⅰ. 밑줄형 어휘는 모든 밑줄친 어휘가 문맥상 적절하다고 가정하고 풀이한다.

Ⅱ. 밑줄형 어휘의 모두 첫 문장부터 한 문장씩 해석하며 지문의 문맥을 파악한다.

Ⅲ. 밑줄형 어휘는 역접의 표현없이 문맥과 반대되는 밑줄 친 어휘를 찾는다.

2. 어휘 유형 Tip

(1). 모르는 어휘가 출제되었을 경우 일단 넘어가고 (긍정, 부정과 같은) 방향성만 추론한다.

(2). 밑줄 친 어휘의 앞 뒷 문장에서 근거를 파악하지 못했다고 하더라도 되돌아가지 말고 그 다음 문장을 읽는다.
(평가원 기출 중 어휘에 대한 근거가 근처에 존재하지 않고 첫 부분이나 마지막 부분에 위치하는 등 어휘와 멀리
존재하는 경우가 있습니다.)

[01~02] 다음 글을 읽고, 물음에 답하시오.

People are correct when they feel that the written poetry of literate societies and the oral poetry of non-literate ones differ considerably from the everyday language spoken in the community. Listeners not only accept the (a) <u>strange</u> use of words, rearrangement of word order, assonance, alliteration, rhythm, rhyme, compression of thought, and so on — they actually expect to find these things in poetry and they are disappointed when poetry does not sound "poetic." But those who regard poetry as a (b) <u>different</u> category of language altogether are deaf to the true achievements of the poet. Rather, the poet artfully manipulates the same raw materials of his language as are used in everyday speech; his skill is to find new possibilities in the resources already in the language. In much the same way that people living at the seashore become so accustomed to the sound of waves that they no longer hear it, most of us have become (c) <u>sensitive</u> to the flood tide of words, millions of them every day, that hit our eardrums. One function of poetry is to depict the world with a (d) <u>fresh</u> perception — to make it strange — so that we will listen to language once again. But the successful poet never departs so far into the strange world of language that none of his listeners can (e) <u>follow</u> him. He still remains the communicator, the man of speech.

* assonance: 유운(類韻) ** alliteration: 두운(頭韻) *** depict: 묘사하다

01 25학년도 9월 평가원 41번

윗글의 제목으로 가장 적절한 것은?

① Make It New: How Poetry Refreshes Everyday Language
② Why Do Poets No Longer Seek Inspiration from Nature?
③ The Influence of Natural Sounds on Poetic Expression
④ Ways to Cite Poetic Expressions in Everyday Speech
⑤ Beauty Rediscovered: The Return of Oral Poetry

02 25학년도 9월 평가원 42번

밑줄 친 (a) ~ (e) 중에서 문맥상 낱말의 쓰임이 적절하지 <u>않은</u> 것은?

① (a)　　　② (b)　　　③ (c)　　　④ (d)　　　⑤ (e)

중. 최. 평. 해설

[01~02] 다음 글을 읽고, 물음에 답하시오.

People are correct when they feel that the written poetry of literate societies and the oral poetry of non-literate ones differ considerably from the everyday language spoken in the community. Listeners not only accept the (a) <u>strange</u> use of words, rearrangement of word order, assonance, alliteration, rhythm, rhyme, compression of thought, and so on — they actually expect to find these things in poetry and they are disappointed when poetry does not sound "poetic." But those who regard poetry as a (b) <u>different</u> category of language altogether are deaf to the true achievements of the poet. Rather, the poet artfully manipulates the same raw materials of his language as are used in everyday speech; his skill is to find new possibilities in the resources already in the language. In much the same way that people living at the seashore become so accustomed to the sound of waves that they no longer hear it, most of us have become (c) <u>sensitive</u> to the flood tide of words, millions of them every day, that hit our eardrums. One function of poetry is to depict the world with a (d) <u>fresh</u> perception — to make it strange — so that we will listen to language once again. But the successful poet never departs so far into the strange world of language that none of his listeners can (e) <u>follow</u> him. He still remains the communicator, the man of speech.

* assonance: 유운(類韻) ** alliteration: 두운(頭韻) *** depict: 묘사하다

01 25학년도 9월 평가원 41번

(정답률 69%)

윗글의 제목으로 가장 적절한 것은?

해설 [정답 : ①]

시는 시인이 새로운 언어를 사용하는 것이 아니라 일상의 언어를 새롭게 사용하여 세상을 신선하게 묘사하는 것이라고 합니다.

①번 선지 : 새롭게 만들기 : 시가 일상의 언어를 새롭게 하는 방법
　　- 정답 선지입니다.
②번 선지 : 시인은 왜 더 이상 자연에서 영감을 구하지 않는가?
　　- 자연에 대해서 제시되지 않았습니다. 언급되지 않은 선지입니다.
③번 선지 : 자연에서의 소리가 시적 표현에 끼치는 영향
　　- 자연이 제시되지 않았고 자연이 시에 영향을 끼친다는 내용도 제시되지 않았습니다. 언급되지 않은 선지입니다.
④번 선지 : 일상적인 연설에서 시적 표현을 인용하는 방법
　　- 일상적인 연설, 즉 일상적인 언어와 시에 대해서는 제시되었습니다. 하지만 일상적인 언어가 시에 영향을 끼치는 것이지, 시가 일상적인 언어에 끼치는 영향은 제시되지 않았습니다. 인과관계를 바꾸는 방향 바꾸기 선지에 해당합니다. 또한 인용에 대해서는 제시되지 않았습니다.
⑤번 선지 : 재발견된 아름다움 : 구전 시의 귀환
　　- 입으로 전달되는 시에 대해서는 첫 문장에서 제시되었지만 입으로 전달된 시들이 잊혔다가 다시 사용된다는 내용은 제시되지 않았습니다.

밑줄 친 (a) ~ (e) 중에서 문맥상 낱말의 쓰임이 적절하지 <u>않은</u> 것은?

해설 [정답 : ③]

③번 선지의 문장에서 'In much the same way'로 비슷한 내용이 나와야 하는데, 바닷가에 사는 사람들이 파도 소리에 익숙해진 것은 매일 수백만 단어가 홍수처럼 쏟아지는 것과 대응됩니다. 하지만 바닷가에 사는 사람들은 익숙해져서 파도 소리를 더 이상 듣지 못하는 것과는 달리 우리는 매일 수백만 단어를 들으면서 그 단어들에 감각적인, 즉, 들리는 것은 'In much the same way'의 논리와 맞지 않으므로 'sensitive'가 아닌 'insensitive'가 와야 합니다.

Ⅰ. People / are / correct (when they / feel / that the written poetry of literate societies and the oral poetry of non-literate ones / differ considerably from / the everyday language (spoken in the community).

> [구] 그들이 (= 사람들이) 글자 그대로의 (= 문자 기반의) 사회에서 쓰인 시와 글자 그대로가 아닌 (문자 기반이 아닌) 사회에서 말로만 있는 시가 공동체에서 사용되는 일상 언어와 상당히 다르다고 느낄 때, 사람들은 옳은 것이라고 합니다.

> [독] 시에서 쓰인 언어와 공동체에서 사용되는 일상 언어가 상당히 다르다고 느끼는 것이 옳다고 합니다.

Ⅱ. Listeners / not only accept / the (a) <u>strange</u> use of words, rearrangement of word order, assonance, alliteration, rhythm, rhyme, compression of thought, and so on — they / actually expect to find / these things (in poetry) and they / are disappointed (when poetry / does not sound / "poetic.")

* assonance: 유운(類韻) ** alliteration: 두운(頭韻)

> [구] 'not only A but (also) B'는 'A뿐만 아니라 B도'를 의미합니다. 이 문장에서 'but'은 '-'으로 대체되었으며, 'also'는 생략되었습니다. 'not only'가 제시되었다면, 'but'이 없더라도 '-', ';' 등 기호로 대체될 수 있다는 것을 기억하셔야 합니다.
> - 감상자는 단어의 낯선 사용, 어순의 재배열, 유운, 두운, 리듬, 라임, 사고의 압축 등을 받아들일 뿐만 아니라, 실제로 시에서 이러한 요소들을 발견하기를 기대하며, 시가 '시적으로' 들리지 않을 때는 실망한다고 합니다.

> [독] 독자들은 단어의 낯선 사용, 어순의 재배열 등을 기대하며, 이러한 특징들을 시의 특징, 즉, 시적으로 생각하며 시에서 나타나기를 기대한다고 합니다.

Ⅲ. But those (who regard / poetry as a (b) <u>different</u> category of language altogether) / are / deaf (to the true achievements of the poet).

구▶ 'regard A as B'는 'A를 B로 간주하다'를 의미합니다.
- 그러나 시를 완전히 다른 범주의 언어로 간주하는 사람들은 시인의 진정한 업적에 귀머거리가 된다고 합니다.

독▶ 'But'이 제시되었으므로 앞 뒷 문장 중심 문장
- Ⅱ번 문장의 독자들은 시에서 단어의 낯선 쓰임 등 시의 특징들을 원한다는 내용에서 역접을 이루어 Ⅲ번 문장에서는 독자들이 시의 특이함을 좋아하더라도 시를 완전히 다른 범주의 언어로 간주하는 사람들은 시인의 업적에 귀를 기울이지 않는 것이라고 합니다.

Ⅳ. Rather, the poet / artfully manipulates / the same raw materials of his language (as are used in everyday speech); his skill / is to find / new possibilities (in the resources already in the language).

구▶ 오히려, 시를 쓰는 사람은 (= 시인은) 예술적으로 일상의 언어에서 사용되는 것과 동일한 언어의 원료를 조작하는데, 그의 (= 시인의) 기술은 이미 언어에 있는 자원에서 새로운 가능성을 찾아내는 것이라고 합니다.

독▶ 'Rather'이 제시되었으므로 중심 문장
- Ⅲ번 문장에서 제시된 것처럼 시는 완전히 다른 범주의 언어로 간주하는 것이 아니고, Ⅳ번 문장에서 제시되었듯이, 시인이 일상에서 사용되는 것과 동일한 언어를 예술적으로 조작한 것이라고 합니다.

Ⅴ. (In much the same way (that people (living at the seashore) / become so accustomed to the sound of waves that they / no longer hear / it)), most of us / have become / (c) <u>sensitive</u> (to the flood tide of words, millions of them every day), (that hit / our eardrums).

구▶ 'so + 형용사 (과거분사도 형용사 중 하나입니다) + that S + V'는 '너무 형용사해서 S가 V하다'를 의미합니다.
- 바닷가에 사는 사람들이 파도 소리에 너무 익숙해져서 더 이상 그것을 (= 파도 소리를) 듣지 못하는 것과 같은 방식으로, 우리 대부분은 고막을 때리는 매일 수백만 단어로 홍수처럼 쏟아지는 말에 민감하게 (⇒ 무감각하게) 된다고 합니다.

독▶ 바닷가에 사는 사람들은 파도 소리를 많이 듣게 되니 파도 소리를 신경쓰지 않는 것처럼 우리도 일상적인 언어를 많이 사용하고 듣게 되니 일상적인 언어를 신경쓰지 않게 된다고 합니다.
- 'In much the same way'로 비슷한 내용이 나와야 하는데, 바닷가에 사는 사람들이 파도 소리에 익숙해진 것은 매일 수백만 단어가 홍수처럼 쏟아지는 것과 대응됩니다. 하지만 바닷가에 사는 사람들은 익숙해져서 파도 소리를 더 이상 듣지 못하는 것과는 달리 우리는 매일 수백만 단어를 들으면서 그 단어들에 민감한 것은, 즉, 들리는 것은 'In much the same way'의 논리와 맞지 않으므로 'sensitive'가 아닌 'insensitive'가 와야 합니다.

Ⅵ. One function of poetry / is to depict / the world (with a (d) <u>fresh</u> perception) — to make / it / strange — so that we / will listen (to language once again).

*** depict: 묘사하다

> **구** 'make + O + O.C'는 'O가 O.C하게 만들다'를 의미합니다.
> - 시의 한 가지 기능은 신선한 인식으로 세상을 묘사하여, 즉 그것을 (= 시를) 낯설게 만들어서, 우리가 다시 한번 언어에 귀를 기울이게 하는 것이라고 합니다.

> **독** 'so that'이 제시되었으므로 중심 문장
> - Ⅳ번과 Ⅴ번 문장에서 제시되었듯이 언어는 세상을 새로운 인식으로 묘사하는 것이라고 합니다.

Ⅶ. But the successful poet / never departs / so far (into the strange world of language) that none of his listeners / can (e) <u>follow</u> / him.

> **구** 'so + 형용사 + that S + V'는 '너무 형용사해서 S가 V하다'를 의미합니다.
> - 그러나 성공을 이룬 시인은 낯선 언어의 세계로 결코 자신의 청취자 중 누구도 자신을 따라가지 못할 만큼 멀리 떨어지지 않는다고 합니다.

> **독** 'But'이 제시되었으므로 앞 뒷 문장 중심 문장 'so'가 제시되었으므로 중심 문장
> - Ⅴ번 문장에서처럼 시는 세상에 대한 신선한 인식을 주지만, 독자들이 이해하지 못할 정도로 낯선 언어를 사용하는 것은 아니라고 합니다.

Ⅷ. He / still remains / the communicator, the man of speech.

> **구** 그는 (= 시인은) 여전히 전달자, 즉 사람의 언어로 남아있다고 합니다.

> **독** Ⅳ번 문장에서 제시되었듯이 시인들은 사람의 언어 즉, 일상의 언어를 사용하여 시를 전달한다고 합니다.

▎절. 모. 평. (절대평가 모든 평가원 기출)

[01~02] 다음 글을 읽고, 물음에 답하시오.

Imagine grabbing a piece of paper between your thumb and index finger. Maybe you already are, as you turn this page. We use this type of forceful, pad-to-pad precision gripping without thinking about it, and literally in a snap. Yet it was a breakthrough in human evolution. Other primates exhibit some kinds of precision grips in the handling and use of objects, but not with the kind of (a) underlined efficient opposition that our hand anatomy allows. In a single hand, humans can easily hold and manipulate objects, even small and delicate ones, while adjusting our fingers to their shape and reorienting them with (b) displacements of our fingertip pads. Our relatively long, powerful thumb and other anatomical attributes, including our flat nails (which nearly all primates possess), make this (c) possible. Just picture trying — and failing — to dog-ear this page with pointy, curved claws.

With a unique combination of traits, the human hand shaped our history. No question, stone tools couldn't have become a keystone of human technology and subsistence (d) without hands that could do the job, along with a nervous system that could regulate and coordinate the necessary signals. Anybody who's ever attempted to make a spear tip or arrowhead from a rock knows that it (e) excludes strong grips, constant rotation and repositioning, and forceful, careful strikes with another hard object. And even with a fair amount of know-how, it can be a bloody business.

* primate: 영장류 ** anatomy: 해부학 *** subsistence: 생계

01 25학년도 수능 41번
[정답과 해설 72page]

윗글의 제목으로 가장 적절한 것은?

① Anatomical Distance Between Humans and Other Primates
② Human Hands: A Decisive Leap in the Evolutionary Path
③ Our Hands: An Unexpected Outcome of Evolution
④ Human Grip: The Dilemma of Human Survival
⑤ Hidden Power of the Daily Use of Tools

02 25학년도 수능 42번
[정답과 해설 73page]

밑줄 친 (a) ~ (e) 중에서 문맥상 낱말의 쓰임이 적절하지 <u>않은</u> 것은?

① (a)   ② (b)   ③ (c)   ④ (d)   ⑤ (e)

[03~04] 다음 글을 읽고, 물음에 답하시오.

Classifying things together into groups is something we do all the time, and it isn't hard to see why. Imagine trying to shop in a supermarket where the food was arranged in random order on the shelves: tomato soup next to the white bread in one aisle, chicken soup in the back next to the 60-watt light bulbs, one brand of cream cheese in front and another in aisle 8 near the cookies. The task of finding what you want would be (a) time-consuming and extremely difficult, if not impossible.

In the case of a supermarket, someone had to (b) design the system of classification. But there is also a ready-made system of classification embodied in our language. The word "dog," for example, groups together a certain class of animals and distinguishes them from other animals. Such a grouping may seem too (c) abstract to be called a classification, but this is only because you have already mastered the word. As a child learning to speak, you had to work hard to (d) learn the system of classification your parents were trying to teach you. Before you got the hang of it, you probably made mistakes, like calling the cat a dog. If you hadn't learned to speak, the whole world would seem like the (e) unorganized supermarket; you would be in the position of an infant, for whom every object is new and unfamiliar. In learning the principles of classification, therefore, we'll be learning about the structure that lies at the core of our language.

03 22학년도 수능 41번

[정답과 해설 76page]

윗글의 제목으로 가장 적절한 것은?

① Similarities of Strategies in Sales and Language Learning

② Classification: An Inherent Characteristic of Language

③ Exploring Linguistic Issues Through Categorization

④ Is a Ready-Made Classification System Truly Better?

⑤ Dilemmas of Using Classification in Language Education

04 22학년도 수능 42번

[정답과 해설 77page]

밑줄 친 (a) ~ (e) 중에서 문맥상 낱말의 쓰임이 적절하지 <u>않은</u> 것은?

① (a) 　② (b) 　③ (c) 　④ (d) 　⑤ (e)

[05~06] 다음 글을 읽고, 물음에 답하시오.

Our irresistible tendency to see things in human terms—that we are often mistaken in attributing complex human motives and processing abilities to other species—does not mean that an animal's behavior is not, in fact, complex. Rather, it means that the complexity of the animal's behavior is not purely a (a) <u>product</u> of its internal complexity. Herbert Simon's "parable of the ant" makes this point very clearly. Imagine an ant walking along a beach, and (b) <u>visualize</u> tracking the trajectory of the ant as it moves. The trajectory would show a lot of twists and turns, and would be very irregular and complicated. One could then suppose that the ant had equally complicated (c) <u>internal</u> navigational abilities, and work out what these were likely to be by analyzing the trajectory to infer the rules and mechanisms that could produce such a complex navigational path. The complexity of the trajectory, however, "is really a complexity in the surface of the beach, not a complexity in the ant." In reality, the ant may be using a set of very (d) <u>complex</u> rules: it is the interaction of these rules with the environment that actually produces the complex trajectory, not the ant alone. Put more generally, the parable of the ant illustrates that there is no necessary correlation between the complexity of an (e) <u>observed</u> behavior and the complexity of the mechanism that produces it.

* parable: 우화 ** trajectory: 이동 경로

05 21학년도 수능 41번

[정답과 해설 80page]

윗글의 제목으로 가장 적절한 것은?

① Open the Mysterious Door to Environmental Complexity!

② Peaceful Coexistence of Human Beings and Animals

③ What Makes the Complexity of Animal Behavior?

④ Animals' Dilemma: Finding Their Way in a Human World

⑤ Environmental Influences on Human Behavior Complexity

06 21학년도 수능 42번

[정답과 해설 81page]

밑줄 친 (a) ~ (e) 중에서 문맥상 낱말의 쓰임이 적절하지 <u>않은</u> 것은?

① (a) ② (b) ③ (c) ④ (d) ⑤ (e)

[07~08] 다음 글을 읽고, 물음에 답하시오.

The right to privacy may extend only to the point where it does not restrict someone else's right to freedom of expression or right to information. The scope of the right to privacy is (a) <u>similarly</u> restricted by the general interest in preventing crime or in promoting public health. However, when we move away from the property-based notion of a right (where the right to privacy would protect, for example, images and personality), to modern notions of private and family life, we find it (b) <u>easier</u> to establish the limits of the right. This is, of course, the strength of the notion of privacy, in that it can adapt to meet changing expectations and technological advances.

In sum, *what* is privacy today? The concept includes a claim that we should be unobserved, and that certain information and images about us should not be (c) <u>circulated</u> without our permission. *Why* did these privacy claims arise? They arose because powerful people took offence at such observation. Furthermore, privacy incorporated the need to protect the family, home, and correspondence from arbitrary (d) <u>interference</u> and, in addition, there has been a determination to protect honour and reputation. *How* is privacy protected? Historically, privacy was protected by restricting circulation of the damaging material. But if the concept of privacy first became interesting legally as a response to reproductions of images through photography and newspapers, more recent technological advances, such as data storage, digital images, and the Internet, (e) <u>pose</u> new threats to privacy. The right to privacy is now being reinterpreted to meet those challenges.

* arbitrary: 임의의

---

07 22학년도 6월 모평 41번

[정답과 해설 83page]

윗글의 제목으로 가장 적절한 것은?

① Side Effects of Privacy Protection Technologies

② The Legal Domain of Privacy Claims and Conflicts

③ The Right to Privacy: Evolving Concepts and Practices

④ Who Really Benefits from Looser Privacy Regulations?

⑤ Less Is More: Reduce State Intervention in Privacy!

08 22학년도 6월 모평 42번

[정답과 해설 84page]

밑줄 친 (a) ~ (e) 중에서 문맥상 낱말의 쓰임이 적절하지 <u>않은</u> 것은?

① (a)　　　② (b)　　　③ (c)　　　④ (d)　　　⑤ (e)

In many mountain regions, rights of access to water are associated with the possession of land—until recently in the Andes, for example, land and water rights were (a) <u>combined</u> so water rights were transferred with the land. However, through state land reforms and the development of additional sources of supply, water rights have become separated from land, and may be sold at auction. This therefore (b) <u>favours</u> those who can pay, rather than ensuring access to all in the community. The situation arises, therefore, where individuals may hold land with no water. In Peru, the government grants water to communities separately from land, and it is up to the community to allocate it. Likewise in Yemen, the traditional allocation was one measure (tasah) of water to one hundred 'libnah' of land. This applied only to traditional irrigation supplies—from runoff, wells, etc., where a supply was (c) <u>guaranteed.</u> Water derived from the capture of flash floods is not subject to Islamic law as this constitutes an uncertain source, and is therefore free for those able to collect and use it. However, this traditional allocation per unit of land has been bypassed, partly by the development of new supplies, but also by the (d) <u>decrease</u> in cultivation of a crop of substantial economic importance. This crop is harvested throughout the year and thus requires more than its fair share of water. The economic status of the crop (e) <u>ensures</u> that water rights can be bought or bribed away from subsistence crops.

* irrigation: 관개(灌漑) ** bribe: 매수하다
*** subsistence crop: 생계용 작물

09 21학년도 6월 평가원 41번

[정답과 해설 87page]

윗글의 제목으로 가장 적절한 것은?

① Water Rights No Longer Tied to Land

② Strategies for Trading Water Rights

③ Water Storage Methods: Mountain vs. Desert

④ Water Supplies Not Stable in Mountain Regions

⑤ Unending Debates: Which Crop We Should Grow

10 21학년도 6월 평가원 42번

[정답과 해설 88page]

밑줄 친 (a) ~ (e) 중에서 문맥상 낱말의 쓰임이 적절하지 <u>않은</u> 것은?

① (a) ② (b) ③ (c) ④ (d) ⑤ (e)

Climate change experts and environmental humanists alike agree that the climate crisis is, at its core, a crisis of the imagination and much of the popular imagination is shaped by fiction. In his 2016 book *The Great Derangement*, anthropologist and novelist Amitav Ghosh takes on this relationship between imagination and environmental management, arguing that humans have failed to respond to climate change at least in part because fiction (a) <u>fails</u> to believably represent it. Ghosh explains that climate change is largely absent from contemporary fiction because the cyclones, floods, and other catastrophes it brings to mind simply seem too "improbable" to belong in stories about everyday life. But climate change does not only reveal itself as a series of (b) <u>extraordinary</u> events. In fact, as environmentalists and ecocritics from Rachel Carson to Rob Nixon have pointed out, environmental change can be "imperceptible"; it proceeds (c) <u>rapidly</u>, only occasionally producing "explosive and spectacular" events. Most climate change impacts cannot be observed day-to-day, but they become (d) <u>visible</u> when we are confronted with their accumulated impacts.

Climate change evades our imagination because it poses significant representational challenges. It cannot be observed in "human time," which is why documentary filmmaker Jeff Orlowski, who tracks climate change effects on glaciers and coral reefs, uses "before and after" photographs taken several months apart in the same place to (e) <u>highlight</u> changes that occurred gradually.

* anthropologist: 인류학자 ** catastrophe: 큰 재해 *** evade: 피하다

11 23학년도 9월 평가원 41번 [정답과 해설 91page]

윗글의 제목으로 가장 적절한 것은?

① Differing Attitudes Towards Current Climate Issues

② Slow but Significant: The History of Ecological Movements

③ The Silence of Imagination in Representing Climate Change

④ Vivid Threats: Climate Disasters Spreading in Local Areas

⑤ The Rise and Fall of Environmentalism and Ecocriticism

12 23학년도 9월 평가원 42번 [정답과 해설 92page]

밑줄 친 (a) ~ (e) 중에서 문맥상 낱말의 쓰임이 적절하지 <u>않은</u> 것은?

① (a)   ② (b)   ③ (c)   ④ (d)   ⑤ (e)

Once an event is noticed, an onlooker must decide if it is truly an emergency. Emergencies are not always clearly (a) <u>labeled</u> as such; "smoke" pouring into a waiting room may be caused by fire, or it may merely indicate a leak in a steam pipe. Screams in the street may signal an attack or a family quarrel. A man lying in a doorway may be having a coronary — or he may simply be sleeping off a drunk.

A person trying to interpret a situation often looks at those around him to see how he should react. If everyone else is calm and indifferent, he will tend to remain so; if everyone else is reacting strongly, he is likely to become alert. This tendency is not merely blind conformity; ordinarily we derive much valuable information about new situations from how others around us behave. It's a (b) <u>rare</u> traveler who, in picking a roadside restaurant, chooses to stop at one where no other cars appear in the parking lot.

But occasionally the reactions of others provide (c) <u>accurate</u> information. The studied nonchalance of patients in a dentist's waiting room is a poor indication of their inner anxiety. It is considered embarrassing to "lose your cool" in public. In a potentially acute situation, then, everyone present will appear more (d) <u>unconcerned</u> than he is in fact. A crowd can thus force (e) <u>inaction</u> on its members by implying, through its passivity, that an event is not an emergency. Any individual in such a crowd fears that he may appear a fool if he behaves as though it were.

* coronary: 관상동맥증 ** nonchalance: 무관심, 냉담

13 23학년도 6월 평가원 41번

[정답과 해설 95page]

윗글의 제목으로 가장 적절한 것은?

① Do We Judge Independently? The Effect of Crowds

② Winning Strategy: How Not to Be Fooled by Others

③ Do Emergencies Affect the Way of Our Thinking?

④ Stepping Towards Harmony with Your Neighbors

⑤ Ways of Helping Others in Emergent Situations

14 23학년도 6월 평가원 42번

[정답과 해설 96page]

밑줄 친 (a) ~ (e) 중에서 문맥상 낱말의 쓰임이 적절하지 <u>않은</u> 것은?

① (a) ② (b) ③ (c) ④ (d) ⑤ (e)

One way to avoid contributing to overhyping a story would be to say nothing. However, that is not a realistic option for scientists who feel a strong sense of responsibility to inform the public and policymakers and/or to offer suggestions. Speaking with members of the media has (a) <u>advantages</u> in getting a message out and perhaps receiving favorable recognition, but it runs the risk of misinterpretations, the need for repeated clarifications, and entanglement in never-ending controversy. Hence, the decision of whether to speak with the media tends to be highly individualized. Decades ago, it was (b) <u>unusual</u> for Earth scientists to have results that were of interest to the media, and consequently few media contacts were expected or encouraged. In the 1970s, the few scientists who spoke frequently with the media were often (c) <u>criticized</u> by their fellow scientists for having done so. The situation now is quite different, as many scientists feel a responsibility to speak out because of the importance of global warming and related issues, and many reporters share these feelings. In addition, many scientists are finding that they (d) <u>enjoy</u> the media attention and the public recognition that comes with it. At the same time, other scientists continue to resist speaking with reporters, thereby preserving more time for their science and (e) <u>running</u> the risk of being misquoted and the other unpleasantries associated with media coverage.

* overhype: 과대광고하다 ** entanglement: 얽힘

15 24학년도 수능 41번　　　　　　　　　　　　　　　　　[정답과 해설 100page]

윗글의 제목으로 가장 적절한 것은?

① The Troubling Relationship Between Scientists and the Media

② A Scientist's Choice: To Be Exposed to the Media or Not?

③ Scientists! Be Cautious When Talking to the Media

④ The Dilemma over Scientific Truth and Media Attention

⑤ Who Are Responsible for Climate Issues, Scientists or the Media?

16 24학년도 수능 42번　　　　　　　　　　　　　　　　　[정답과 해설 101page]

밑줄 친 (a) ~ (e) 중에서 문맥상 낱말의 쓰임이 적절하지 <u>않은</u> 것은?

① (a)　　　　　② (b)　　　　　③ (c)　　　　　④ (d)　　　　　⑤ (e)

If we understand critical thinking as: 'the identification and evaluation of evidence to guide decision-making', then ethical thinking is about identifying ethical issues and evaluating these issues from different perspectives to guide how to respond. This form of ethics is distinct from higher levels of conceptual ethics or theory. The nature of an ethical issue or problem from this perspective is that there is no clear right or wrong response. It is therefore (a) <u>essential</u> that students learn to think through ethical issues rather than follow a prescribed set of ethical codes or rules. There is a need to (b) <u>encourage</u> recognition that, although being ethical is defined as acting 'in accordance with the principles of conduct that are considered correct', these principles vary both between and within individuals. What a person (c) <u>values</u> relates to their social, religious, or civic beliefs influenced by their formal and informal learning experiences. Individual perspectives may also be context (d) <u>dependent</u>, meaning that under different circumstances, at a different time, when they are feeling a different way, the same individual may make different choices. Therefore, in order to analyse ethical issues and think ethically it is necessary to understand the personal factors that influence your own 'code of behaviour' and how these may (e) <u>coincide</u>, alongside recognizing and accepting that the factors that drive other people's codes and decision making may be different.

17 25학년도 6월 평가원 41번

[정답과 해설 104page]

윗글의 제목으로 가장 적절한 것은?

① Critical Reasoning: A Road to Ethical Decision-making
② Far-reaching Impacts of Ethics on Behavioural Codes
③ Ethical Thinking: A Walk Through Individual Minds
④ Exploring Ethical Theory in the Eyes of the Others
⑤ Do Ethical Choices Always Take Priority?

18 25학년도 6월 평가원 42번

[정답과 해설 105page]

밑줄 친 (a) ~ (e) 중에서 문맥상 낱말의 쓰임이 적절하지 <u>않은</u> 것은?

① (a)　　　② (b)　　　③ (c)　　　④ (d)　　　⑤ (e)

There is evidence that even very simple algorithms can outperform expert judgement on simple prediction problems. For example, algorithms have proved more (a) <u>accurate</u> than humans in predicting whether a prisoner released on parole will go on to commit another crime, or in predicting whether a potential candidate will perform well in a job in future. In over 100 studies across many different domains, half of all cases show simple formulas make (b) <u>better</u> significant predictions than human experts, and the remainder (except a very small handful), show a tie between the two. When there are a lot of different factors involved and a situation is very uncertain, simple formulas can win out by focusing on the most important factors and being consistent, while human judgement is too easily influenced by particularly salient and perhaps (c) <u>irrelevant</u> considerations. A similar idea is supported by further evidence that 'checklists' can improve the quality of expert decisions in a range of domains by ensuring that important steps or considerations aren't missed when people are feeling (d) <u>relaxed</u>. For example, treating patients in intensive care can require hundreds of small actions per day, and one small error could cost a life. Using checklists to ensure that no crucial steps are missed has proved to be remarkably (e) <u>effective</u> in a range of medical contexts, from preventing live infections to reducing pneumonia.

* parole: 가석방 ** salient: 두드러진 *** pneumonia: 폐렴

19 23학년도 수능 41번

[정답과 해설 108page]

윗글의 제목으로 가장 적절한 것은?

① The Power of Simple Formulas in Decision Making

② Always Prioritise: Tips for Managing Big Data

③ Algorithms' Mistakes: The Myth of Simplicity

④ Be Prepared! Make a Checklist Just in Case

⑤ How Human Judgement Beats Algorithms

20 23학년도 수능 42번

[정답과 해설 109page]

밑줄 친 (a) ~ (e) 중에서 문맥상 낱말의 쓰임이 적절하지 <u>않은</u> 것은?

① (a)　　　② (b)　　　③ (c)　　　④ (d)　　　⑤ (e)

To the extent that sufficient context has been provided, the reader can come to a well-crafted text with no expert knowledge and come away with a good approximation of what has been intended by the author. The text has become a public document and the reader can read it with a (a) <u>minimum</u> of effort and struggle; his experience comes close to what Freud has described as the deployment of "evenly-hovering attention." He puts himself in the author's hands (some have had this experience with great novelists such as Dickens or Tolstoy) and he (b) <u>follows</u> where the author leads. The real world has vanished and the fictive world has taken its place. Now consider the other extreme. When we come to a badly crafted text in which context and content are not happily joined, we must struggle to understand, and our sense of what the author intended probably bears (c) <u>close</u> correspondence to his original intention. An out-of-date translation will give us this experience; as we read, we must bring the language up to date, and understanding comes only at the price of a fairly intense struggle with the text. Badly presented content with no frame of reference can provide (d) <u>the same</u> experience; we see the words but have no sense of how they are to be taken. The author who fails to provide the context has (e) <u>mistakenly</u> assumed that his picture of the world is shared by all his readers and fails to realize that supplying the right frame of reference is a critical part of the task of writing.

* deployment: (전략적) 배치

** evenly-hovering attention: 고르게 주의를 기울이는 것

21 21학년도 9월 평가원 41번

[정답과 해설 112page]

윗글의 제목으로 가장 적절한 것은?

① Building a Wall Between Reality and the Fictive World

② Creative Reading: Going Beyond the Writer's Intentions

③ Usefulness of Readers' Experiences for Effective Writing

④ Context in Writing: A Lighthouse for Understanding Texts

⑤ Trapped in Their Own Words: The Narrow Outlook of Authors

22 21학년도 9월 평가원 42번

[정답과 해설 113page]

밑줄 친 (a) ~ (e) 중에서 문맥상 낱말의 쓰임이 적절하지 <u>않은</u> 것은?

① (a)　　　② (b)　　　③ (c)　　　④ (d)　　　⑤ (e)

In studies examining the effectiveness of vitamin C, researchers typically divide the subjects into two groups. One group (the experimental group) receives a vitamin C supplement, and the other (the control group) does not. Researchers observe both groups to determine whether one group has fewer or shorter colds than the other. The following discussion describes some of the pitfalls inherent in an experiment of this kind and ways to (a) <u>avoid</u> them. In sorting subjects into two groups, researchers must ensure that each person has an (b) <u>equal</u> chance of being assigned to either the experimental group or the control group. This is accomplished by randomization; that is, the subjects are chosen randomly from the same population by flipping a coin or some other method involving chance. Randomization helps to ensure that results reflect the treatment and not factors that might influence the grouping of subjects. Importantly, the two groups of people must be similar and must have the same track record with respect to colds to (c) <u>rule out</u> the possibility that observed differences in the rate, severity, or duration of colds might have occurred anyway. If, for example, the control group would normally catch twice as many colds as the experimental group, then the findings prove (d) <u>nothing</u>. In experiments involving a nutrient, the diets of both groups must also be (e) <u>different</u>, especially with respect to the nutrient being studied. If those in the experimental group were receiving less vitamin C from their usual diet, then any effects of the supplement may not be apparent.

* pitfall: 함정

23 22학년도 9월 평가원 41번

[정답과 해설 116page]

윗글의 제목으로 가장 적절한 것은?

① Perfect Planning and Faulty Results: A Sad Reality in Research

② Don't Let Irrelevant Factors Influence the Results!

③ Protect Human Subjects Involved in Experimental Research!

④ What Nutrients Could Better Defend Against Colds?

⑤ In-depth Analysis of Nutrition: A Key Player for Human Health

24 22학년도 9월 평가원 42번

[정답과 해설 117page]

밑줄 친 (a) ~ (e) 중에서 문맥상 낱말의 쓰임이 적절하지 <u>않은</u> 것은?

① (a)　② (b)　③ (c)　④ (d)　⑤ (e)

One reason we think we forget most of what we learned in school is that we underestimate what we actually remember. Other times, we know we remember something, but we don't recognize that we learned it in school. Knowing where and when you learned something is usually called context information, and context is handled by (a) <u>different</u> memory processes than memory for the content. Thus, it's quite possible to retain content without remembering the context. For example, if someone mentions a movie and you think to yourself that you heard it was terrible but can't remember (b) <u>where</u> you heard that, you're recalling the content, but you've lost the context. Context information is frequently (c) <u>easier</u> to forget than content, and it's the source of a variety of memory illusions. For instance, people are (d) <u>unconvinced</u> by a persuasive argument if it's written by someone who is not very credible (e.g., someone with a clear financial interest in the topic). But in time, readers' attitudes, on average, change in the direction of the persuasive argument. Why? Because readers are likely to remember the content of the argument but forget the source — someone who is not credible. If remembering the source of knowledge is difficult, you can see how it would be (e) <u>challenging</u> to conclude you don't remember much from school.

* illusion: 착각

25 24학년도 9월 평가원 41번

[정답과 해설 120page]

윗글의 제목으로 가장 적절한 것은?

① Learned Nothing in School?: How Memory Tricks You

② Why We Forget Selectively: Credibility of Content

③ The Constant Battle Between Content and Context

④ How Students Can Learn More and Better in School

⑤ Shift Your Focus from Who to What for Memory Building

26 24학년도 9월 평가원 42번

[정답과 해설 121page]

밑줄 친 (a) ~ (e) 중에서 문맥상 낱말의 쓰임이 적절하지 <u>않은</u> 것은?

① (a)　　　② (b)　　　③ (c)　　　④ (d)　　　⑤ (e)

Many negotiators assume that all negotiations involve a fixed pie. Negotiators often approach integrative negotiation opportunities as zero-sum situations or win-lose exchanges. Those who believe in the mythical fixed pie assume that parties' interests stand in opposition, with no possibility forintegrative settlements and mutually beneficial trade-offs, so they (a) <u>suppress</u> efforts to search for them. In a hiring negotiation, a job applicant who assumes that salary is the only issue may insist on $75,000 when the employer is offering $70,000. Only when the two parties discuss the possibilities further do they discover that moving expenses and starting date can also be negotiated, which may (b) <u>block</u> resolution of the salary issue.

The tendency to see negotiation in fixed-pie terms (c) <u>varies</u> depending on how people view the nature of a given conflict situation. This was shown in a clever experiment by Harinck, de Dreu, and Van Vianen involving a simulated negotiation between prosecutors and defense lawyers over jail sentences. Some participants were told to view their goals in terms of personal gain (e.g., arranging a particular jail sentence will help your career), others were told to view their goals in terms of effectiveness (a particular sentence is most likely to prevent recidivism), and still others were told to focus on values (a particular jail sentence is fair and just). Negotiators focusing on personal gain were most likely to come under the influence of fixed-pie beliefs and approach the situation (d) <u>competitively</u>. Negotiators focusing on values were least likely to see the problem in fixed-pie terms and more inclined to approach the situation cooperatively. Stressful conditions such as time constraints contribute to this common misperception, which in turn may lead to (e) <u>less</u> integrative agreements.

* prosecutor: 검사 ** recidivism: 상습적 범행

27 24학년도 6월 평가원 41번   [정답과 해설 124page]

윗글의 제목으로 가장 적절한 것은?

① Fixed Pie: A Key to Success in a Zero-sum Game

② Fixed Pie Tells You How to Get the Biggest Salary

③ Negotiators, Wake Up from the Myth of the Fixed Pie!

④ Want a Fairer Jail Sentence? Stick to the Fixed Pie

⑤ What Alternatives Maximize Fixed-pie Effects?

28 24학년도 6월 평가원 42번   [정답과 해설 125page]

밑줄 친 (a) ~ (e) 중에서 문맥상 낱말의 쓰임이 적절하지 <u>않은</u> 것은?

① (a)   ② (b)   ③ (c)   ④ (d)   ⑤ (e)

Chapter

05

간접 쓰기

▎평가원이 제시한 간접쓰기

[2025학년도 대학수학 능력시험 학습방법 안내 125p]

본 유형은 쓰기 능력을 간접적으로 평가하기 위한 유형으로, 좋은 글쓰기를 위해 필요한 **통일성, 일관성, 응집성에 대한 이해도를 평가하여.** 단락이나 문장 간의 관계를 정확히 파악하여 글의 논리적 흐름을 완성하는 능력을 요구하고 있다.

- 우리는 통일성, 일관성, 응집성이 무엇인지 기출 문제를 통해서 파악해야 합니다.

[2025학년도 대학수학 능력시험 학습방법 안내 125p]

본 유형은 출제되는 문항의 정답을 찾기 위해서는 주어진 글을 신속히 읽고 글의 소재 및 중심 내용을 파악한 후, **문장 간의 논리적 관계와 단서들(세부 정보, 연결사, 지시사등)을 활용하여** 전체 흐름을 종합적으로 파악하는 능력이 무엇보다 중요하다. 특히, **예시, 나열, 비교와 대조, 원인과 결과 등 글쓰기에서 사용되는 보편적 글의 구조를 이해하는 능력**이 필요하다.

[2025학년도 대학수학 능력시험 학습방법 안내 126p]

교육 과정의 쓰기 성취기준 달성 여부를 평가하기 위한 간접 쓰기 유형은 글의 종합적 이해 능력을 요구하는 비교적 어려운 유형이다. 이 유형에 대비하기 위해서는 글의 중심 내용 파악뿐만 아니라 **문장 간의 논리적 관계, 글의 통일성과 일관성, 그리고 응집성을 이해하는 학습**과 더불어 이를 바탕으로 평상시 한 단락 이상의 영어 글쓰기 연습을 충실히 하는 것이 중요하다.

이를 위한 몇 가지 학습 방법을 소개하면 다음과 같다. **우선 비교, 예시, 대조, 열거, 인과 등의 전개 구조로 이루어진 다양한 학술적 내용의 글을 평소 자주 접하고 이해하는 학습이 필요하다.** 이와 같은 구조로 이루어진 **좋은 글을 읽으면서 하나의 중심 내용에 대해 글의 통일성과 일관성이 어떻게 전개되어 가는지에 대해 확인하는 습관을 길러야** 한다.

더불어 글의 논리적 구성을 위해 사용되는 **대명사, 지시사, 연결사 등의 언어 장치들의 쓰임에 대해 학습해야 한다.**

마지막으로 **독해의 기본은 어휘력에서 시작된다는 점을 잊지 말고** 평상시 기초 학술문에서 자주 쓰이는 **어휘의 다양한 쓰임을 깊이 있게 학습**해 두는 것도 중요하다.

- 문장 간의 논리적 관계와 단서들이 중요하다고 합니다. 우리는 이를 명시적 단서 (연결사, 지시사), 내용적 단서 (문장 간의 논리적 관계)를 종합하여 두 단서를 파악하는 연습을 하게 됩니다. 또한 평가원은 문장 간의 논리적 관계를 예시, 나열, 비교와 대조, 원인과 결과 등으로 제시해주었습니다. 이를 위해 우리는 접속사를 정리하여 각 접속사가 의미하는 구조를 배우게 될 것입니다.

- 단어를 중요성은 평가원도 강조합니다. 다의어 역시 마찬가지입니다. 외웁시다.

접속사 정리

1. 역접 표현/ 접속사 정리

But, However	하지만	(Al/Even) though	그럼에도 불구하고
Still	하지만	Despite	그럼에도 불구하고
Yet	하지만	In spite of	그럼에도 불구하고
Conversely	반면에	Even so	그럼에도 불구하고
In contrast	반면에	Nevertheless	그럼에도 불구하고
On the contrary	반면에	Nonetheless	그럼에도 불구하고
On the other hand	반면에	Regardless	상관없이
While	반면에	Even if	비록 ~일지라도
Even if it is ture	비록 사실 일지라도	Rather/Instead	(앞 내용이 부정을 제시해야함) 오히려/대신에

2. 예시 표현/ 접속사 정리

For example	예를 들어	In + 연도	처음부터 제시X 갑작스러우 제시
For instance	예를 들어	In + 나라	처음부터 제시X 갑작스러운 제시
Consider	~을 고려하면	Suppose	~을 가정하면
Given	~을 고려하면	To name a few	몇 가지 예를 들면

3. 인과관계 표현/ 접속사 정리

Because	~ 때문에 (접속사)	As	~ 때문에
Because of	~ 때문에 (전치사)	Since	~ 때문에
Therefore	그러므로	Thus	그러므로
So	그러므로	As a result	결과적으로
In turn	결과적으로	As a consequence	결과적으로
Contribute to	~에 기여하다	Cause	~를 야기하다
Lead to	~를 야기하다	Result from	~로부터 야기되다
In the end	결국	Eventually	결국

In other words	다시 말해서	That is to say	다시 말해서
In brief	간단히 말해서	To sum up	간단히 말해서
Namely	즉	That is	즉
In essence	즉	In short	요컨대
Indeed	사실상	Put more generally	더 일반적으로

5. 나열 표현/ 접속사 정리

In this way	이러한 방식으로	Further	게다가
Likewise	마찬가지로	Moreover	게다가
Similarly	비슷하게	Alternatively	대안으로

꼼꼼히 외웁시다.

Chapter 5-2 시작하기 전에 뜻을 비워둔 시험지를 배치하겠습니다!

모두 기출에서 출제되었던 것이니 꼭 외웁시다.

평가원이 제시한 것처럼 순서에서 글이 연결되기 위해서는 통일성, 일관성, 응집성의 조건을 충족시켜야 합니다. 기출에서 제시하는 통일성, 일관성, 응집성의 조건에 대해서 알아보도록 합시다.

재진술

즉, 같은 내용을 다르게 표현하여 반복하는 경우를 이야기합니다.

다음 문제를 풀어봅시다.

16학년도 9월 평가원 35번

If you walk into a store looking for a new computer and the first salesperson you meet immediately points to a group of computers and says, "Any of those are good," and then walks away, there is a good chance you will walk away, too, and with good reason

(A) That is, the reader is the writer's "customer" and one whose business or approval is one we need to seek. The more you know about your reader, the greater the chances you will meet his or her needs and expectations.

(B) Why? You were never asked what you were seeking, how much you could spend, or if the computer would be used for business or pleasure or your child's homework assignments.

(C) In brief, the salesperson never considered or asked about your needs and preferences. Just as it would come as no surprise to learn the salesperson who was indifferent to a potential customer's needs was soon out of a job, the same holds true for writers who ignore their readers..

If you walk into a store looking for a new computer and the first salesperson you meet immediately points to a group of computers and says, "Any of those are good," and then walks away, there is a good chance you will walk away, too, and with good reason.

(A)

① **That is**, the reader is the writer's "customer" and one whose business or approval is one we need to seek.

② The more you know about your reader, the greater the chances you will meet his or her needs and expectations.

(B)

① Why? You were never asked what you were seeking, how much you could spend, or if the computer would be used for business or pleasure or your child's homework assignments.

(C)

① **In brief**, the salesperson never considered or asked about your needs and preferences.

② Just as it would come as no surprise to learn the salesperson who was indifferent to a potential customer's needs was soon out of a job, the same holds true for writers who ignore their readers.

주어진 문장에서 네가 새 컴퓨터를 찾아 가게로 들어갔는데 만나는 첫 번째 판매원이 즉시 한 무더기의 컴퓨터를 가리키면서 "저것들 다 좋아요."라고 말한 뒤가 버린다면, 너도 가버릴 가능성이 크며, 그것도 그럴만한 충분한 이유가 있다고 합니다.

(A)에서 'That is'를 통해 앞 내용을 재진술하여 독자는 필자의 '고객'이며 그 고객의 관심사나 인정은 우리가 추구할 필요가 있는 것이라고 합니다. 이를 통해서 (A) 앞 내용에서는 독자에 대한 설명이 제시되어야 하고 고객의 관심사나 인정을 추구해야 한다는 내용이 제시되어야 합니다.

(B)에서는 왜 그럴까? 무엇을 찾고 있는지, 얼마나 돈을 쓸 수 있는지, 또는 컴퓨터가 사업용으로 오락용으로 아니면 아이의 숙제용으로 사용될 것인지, 너는 한 번도 질문을 받지 않았다고 합니다. 이는 (B)에 대한 상황을 제시하고 있기 때문에 (C)에서 주어진 문장에 대한 추가적인 내용이 제시되지 않는다면 (B)가 주어진 문장 다음에 와야 합니다.

(C)에서 'In brief'를 통해서 앞 내용을 재진술하여 간단히 말해, 그 판매원은 너의 필요와 선호도에 대해 전혀 고려하거나 묻지 않았다고 합니다. 이를 통해서 (C)에 앞에는 판매원이 너의 필요와 선호도를 고려하지 않았다는 내용이 재진술되어야 합니다.

(C) 앞에 제시되어야 하는 내용이 (B)-①번에서 제시되고 있습니다. 또한 (C)-②번에서 독자가 제시되고 (A) ①번과 같은 내용이므로 (B) - (C) - (A)가 정답이 됩니다.

굳이 'That is'나 'In brief'와 같은 재진술의 표현이 제시되지 않았더라도, 같은 내용 즉, 재진술된 내용은 이어져야 합니다.

다음 지문에서 (A) 뒤에 와야할 것이 (B)인지, (C)인지 판단해봅시다.

(A) The psychological effects of warm and cool hues seem to be used effectively by the coaches of the Notre Dame football team. The locker rooms used for half-time breaks were reportedly painted to take advantage of the emotional impact of certain hues.

(B) The home-team room was painted a bright red, which kept team members excited or even angered. The visiting-team room was painted a blue-green, which had a calming effect on the team members. The success of this application of color can be noted in the records set by Notre Dame football teams.

(C) The temperature was maintained at the same level, but the walls were painted a warm coral. The employees stopped complaining about the temperature and reported they were quite comfortable.

판단하셨나요? 어렵지 않으실 겁니다.

(A)에서는 따뜻하고 차가운 색조의 심리적 효과는 Notre Dame 미식축구 팀 코치들에 의해서 이용된다고 합니다. 이것이 이용된 구체적인 사례로 보여주는 것은 (B)에서 홈 팀은 빨간색으로 칠해서, 팀원들을 흥분하거나 분노에 찬 상태로 있게 했고 원정팀은 청록색으로 칠해서 차분하게 하는 효과를 나타냈다고 합니다. 그러므로 (A) - (B)가 정답입니다.

이 지문은 재진술의 표현이 제시되지 않았지만 같은 내용이 재진술되거나 구체화되는 것을 연결해 주어야 합니다.

▌접속사에 의한 논리적 결함이 없음.

'but'이 제시되었을 때, 전환이 발생해야만 합니다.
예를 들어, (+) 내용이 전개되었는데, 'but' 이후 똑같은 (+) 내용이면 안 됩니다.

다음 지문에서 (A)의 앞부분으로 연결되어야 할 부분이 (B)인지, (C)인지 파악해봅시다.

16학년도 수능 36번

(A) Avoidance training, however, doesn't always work in our favor. For instance, a child who has been repeatedly criticized for poor performance on math may learn to dodge difficult math problems in order to avoid further punishment.

(B) Unfortunately, because of this avoidance, the child fails to develop his math skills and therefore improve the capabilities he has, and so a vicious cycle has set in. The avoidance must be unlearned through some positive experiences with math in order for this cycle to be broken.

(C) Psychologists call this avoidance training because the person is learning to avoid the possibility of a punishing consequence. Avoidance training is responsible for many everyday behaviors. It has taught you to carry an umbrella when it looks like rain to avoid the punishment of getting wet, and to keep your hand away from a hot iron to avoid the punishment of a burn.

이번에도 잘 판단하셨나요? 어렵지 않습니다.

(A)에서는 'However' 뒷부분으로 회피 훈련이 항상 우리에게 유리하게 작용하는 것은 아니라고 합니다.
그렇다면 (A)의 앞부분은 회피 훈련이 우리에게 주는 이점이 제시됩니다.
그러므로 (C)가 (A) 앞에서 제시되어야 합니다.

그렇다면 왜 (B)는 (A) 앞에 올 수 없을까요?

그 이유는 (B)는 (A)와 같이 회피 훈련의 단점을 제시하고 있습니다.
'회피 훈련의 단점 but 회피 훈련의 단점'으로 제시될 경우 논리적 결함이 생기기 때문에 (B)는 (A) 앞에 올 수 없습니다.

* 'moreover' 혹은 'Similarly'처럼 나열의 접속사가 제시되었을 때, A. moreover A'이 아닌
  'B. moreover A'이 제시되었다면, 논리적으로 결함이 생깁니다.

다음 지문에서 (A) 앞에 와야 할 것이 (B)인지 (C)인지 판단해봅시다.

13학년도 6월 평가원 43번

(A) Similarly, human societies in contact affect each other's development. World historians, recognizing this, seek to understand human history through studying both developments within societies and the way in which societies relate to each other.

(B) Bacteria, however, fundamentally shape each other as they interact. Because the membranes covering bacteria are full of pores, bacteria can exchange genetic information and can even fundamentally alter each other's basic make-up when they touch.

(C) Billiard balls rolling around the table may collide and affect each other's trajectories, but they do not actually change each other: The eight ball is an eight ball even after it is struck by the cue ball.

* membrane: 얇은 막 ** trajectory: 궤도

(A)에서는 서로 접촉하고 있는 인간 사회도 서로의 발전에 영향을 준다고 합니다.

(B)에서 박테리아가 상호작용 하면서 근본적으로 서로의 모양을 형성해가는 것을 통해서 (B)가 (A) 앞에 와야 함을 알 수 있습니다.

그런데 (C)는 왜 안 될까요? (C)에서 당구공이 돌아다니면서 충돌하여 서로의 궤도에 영향을 주지만, 서로에게 변화를 야기하지 않는다고 합니다.

즉 (A)와 (B)의 내용과 반대 내용이 'Similarly'를 통해서 나열이 될 수 없습니다.

그러므로 정답은 (B)가 됩니다.

이처럼 'Similarly'와 같은 나열의 표현이 논리적 결함이 없기 위해서는 'A 나열 A'의 형태를 가져야합니다.

지시사가 지칭하는 대상이 앞 쪽에 존재

지시사는 어떠한 내용을 대신해서 쓰이는 단어입니다. 그러므로 지시사가 지칭하는 대상이 앞 문장이나
앞 내용에 존재하지 않는다면 논리적 오류가 생깁니다. (가주어/진주어, It that 강조 구문 제외)

다음 지문에서 (A)의 앞부분으로 연결되어야 할 부분이 (B)인지, (C)인지 파악해봅시다.

16학년도 6월 평가원 36번

(A) Like those infectious diseases, cultural habits such as pop music preferences and clothing fashions may spread very quickly nowadays, especially through the media of radio and television.

(B) So some cultural changes may be adopted quite quickly by a whole population. Transmission of culture is rather like transmission of an infection. Flu and colds spread very quickly, especially with the large amount of contact that people now have with each other.

(C) However, other deep-rooted cultural characteristics of races and racial subgroups are much more difficult to change. These are the cultural patterns that are so resistant to alteration that they have the appearance of being inherent.

'those infectious disease', '그러한 전염병'이 지칭하는 대상이 (A) 앞에 제시되어야 합니다.
전염병은 (B)에서 'Flu'와 'colds', '감기'로 제시되므로 (B)가 (A)의 앞으로 와야 합니다.

이렇듯 지시사가 지칭하는 대상이 앞에 제시되어야 합니다.

체화를 통해서 좀 더 연습해 봅시다.

체화

다음 (A), (B), (C)의 알맞은 순서를 찾아봅시다.

01

Interestingly, being observed has two quite distinct effects on performance. In some cases, performance is decreased, even to the point of non-existence. The extreme of this is stage fright, the sudden fear of public performance.

(A) So, if you are learning to play a new sport, it is better to begin it alone, but when you become skilled at it, then you will probably perform better with an audience.

(B) There are many instances of well-known actors who, in mid-career, develop stage fright and simply cannot perform. The other extreme is that being observed enhances performance, people doing whatever it might be better when they know that others are watching.

(C) The general rule seems to be that if one is doing something new or for the first time, then being observed while doing it decreases performance. On the other hand, being observed while doing some task or engaging in some activity that is well known or well practiced tends to enhance performance.

02

Evolution works to maximize the number of descendants that an animal leaves behind. Where the risk of death from fishing increases as an animal grows, evolution favors those that grow slowly, mature younger and smaller, and reproduce earlier.

(A) Surely these adaptations are good news for species hard-pressed by excessive fishing? Not exactly. Young fish produce many fewer eggs than large-bodied animals, and many industrial fisheries are now so intensive that few animals survive more than a couple of years beyond the age of maturity.

(B) This is exactly what we now see in the wild. Cod in Canada's Gulf of St. Lawrence begin to reproduce at around four today; forty years ago they had to wait until six or seven to reach maturity. Sole in the North Sea mature at half the body weight they did in 1950.

(C) Together this means there are fewer eggs and larvae to secure future generations. In some cases the amount of young produced today is a hundred or even a thousand times less than in the past, putting the survival of species, and the fisheries dependent on them, at grave risk.

03

The ancient Greeks sought to improve memory through brain training methods such as memory palaces and the method of loci. At the same time, they and the Egyptians became experts at externalizing information, inventing the modern library, a grand storehouse for externalized knowledge.

(A) This need isn't simply learned; it is a biological imperative-animals organize their environments instinctively. Most mammals are biologically programmed to put their digestive waste away from where they eat and sleep.

(B) We don't know why these simultaneous explosions of intellectual activity occurred when they did (perhaps daily human experience had hit a certain level of complexity). But the human need to organize our lives, our environment, even our thoughts, remains strong.

(C) Dogs have been known to collect their toys and put them in baskets; ants carry off dead members of the colony to burial grounds; certain birds and rodents create barriers around their nests in order to more easily detect invaders.

* method of loci: 장소를 활용한 기억법
** rodent: 설치류 동물

04

Some people make few intentional changes in life. Sure, over time they may get fatter, gather lines, and go gray.

(A) They train for marathons, quit smoking, switch fields, write plays, take up the guitar, or learn to tango even if they never danced before in their lives. What is the difference between these two groups of people?

(B) But they wear their hair the same way, buy the same brand of shoes, eat the same breakfast, and stick to routines for no reason other than the ease of a comfortable, predictable life. Yet as both research and real life show, many others do make important changes.

(C) It's their perspective. People who change do not question whether change is possible or look for reasons they cannot change. They simply decide on a change they want and do what is necessary to accomplish it. Changing, which always stems from a firm decision, becomes job number one.

체화 해설

01

① Interestingly, being observed has two quite distinct effects on performance.
② In some cases, performance is decreased, even to the point of non-existence.
③ The extreme of this is stage fright, the sudden fear of public performance.

(A)
① **So**, if you are learning to play a new sport, it is better to begin it alone, but when you become skilled at it, then you will probably perform better with an audience.

(B)
① There are many instances of well-known actors who, in mid-career, develop stage fright and simply cannot perform.
② The other extreme is that being observed enhances performance, people doing whatever it might be better when they know that others are watching.

(C)
① The general rule seems to be that if one is doing something new or for the first time, then being observed while doing it decreases performance.
② **On the other hand**, being observed while doing some task or engaging in some activity that is well known or well practiced tends to enhance performance.

⚓ 해설 [정답 : B - C - A]

주어진 지문 ③번 문장에서 무대 공포증이 제시되고 이에 대한 무대 공포증에 대한 예시를 제시하며 (B)의 ①번 문장이 이 내용을 재진술하고 있으므로 주어진 지문 다음에는 (B)가 와야 합니다. (B)의 ②번 문장에서 다른 극단으로 다른 누군가가 지켜보고 있을 때 수행하는 능력이 높아지는 것인데, 사람들은 다른 사람들이 보고 있다는 것을 알 때 그 일을 잘한다고 합니다. (A)에서는 'So'가 제시되며 앞 내용을 이어받아 새로운 운동을 할 때는 혼자 하는 것이 능숙한 운동을 할 때는 남들이 지켜보는 것이 더 잘한다고 합니다. 'So'는 인과관계이므로 앞 내용이 이와 비슷하게 처음 운동할 때는 혼자, 능숙한 것은 남들이 지켜보는 것이 잘한다는 내용이 제시되어야 하지만 (B)에서는 그러한 언급이 없으므로 (B) - (A)의 연결을 할 수 없습니다. (A)의 앞에서 제시되어야 하는 내용은 (C)에서 제시하고 있으므로 (C) - (A)가 됩니다. 그러므로 정답은 (B) - (C) - (A)가 됩니다.

02

> ① Evolution works to maximize the number of descendants that an animal leaves behind.
> ② Where the risk of death from fishing increases as an animal grows, evolution favors those that grow slowly, mature younger and smaller, and reproduce earlier.

(A)

① Surely **these adaptations** are good news for species hard-pressed by excessive fishing? Not exactly.

② Young fish produce many fewer eggs than large-bodied animals, and many industrial fisheries are now so intensive that few animals survive more than a couple of years beyond the age of maturity.

(B)

① **This** is exactly what we now see in the wild.

② Cod in Canada's Gulf of St. Lawrence begin to reproduce at around four today; forty years ago they had to wait until six or seven to reach maturity.

③ Sole in the North Sea mature at half the body weight they did in 1950.

(C)

① **Together** this means there are fewer eggs and larvae to secure future generations.

② In some cases the amount of young produced today is a hundred or even a thousand times less than in the past, putting the survival of species, and the fisheries dependent on them, at grave risk.

해설 [정답 : B - A - C]

주어진 지문 ②번 문장에서 낚시로 인해 죽을 위험이 증가하는 상황에서 진화는 천천히 성장하고, 더 어린 나이에 그리고 더 작을 때 성숙하고, 더 일찍 번식하는 것들을 선호한다고 합니다. (B)에서 ②번 문장이 40년 전에 성숙기에 도달하려면 6세 혹은 7세여야 했지만 현재는 4세만에 번식을 시작한다는 것을 통해서 (B)가 주어진 지문의 ②번 문장을 구체화하여 재진술함을 알 수 있습니다. (A)에서 'these adaptations'은 (B)의 ②번, ③번 문장에서 적응을 지칭하므로 (B) - (A)가 됩니다. (C)의 ①번 문장의 'Together'은 나열의 표현이고 그것은 미래 세대를 보장하는 알이나 유충이 더 적어진다는 의미라고 하므로 (C) 앞에는 알이 적거나 유충이 적다는 내용이 제시되어야 합니다. 이는 (A)의 ②번 문장에서 제시하고 있으므로 정답은 (B) - (A) - (C)가 됩니다.

* (A)도 주어진 지문에 연결될 수 있으나 (A)가 연결될 경우 (A) - (C) - (B)가 되어야 하는데 (B)가 (C)에서 제시된 적은 알이나 적은 유충에 대한 설명이 아니므로 오답이 됩니다. 정답은 1개인데, 만약 한 지문에 두 개가 된다면 뒤의 연결도 고려하셔야 합니다.

03

① The ancient Greeks sought to improve memory through brain training methods such as memory palaces and the method of loci.

② At the same time, they and the Egyptians became experts at <u>externalizing information, inventing the modern library, a grand storehouse for externalized knowledge.</u>

(A)

① **This need** isn't simply learned; it is a biological imperative-animals organize their environments instinctively.

② Most mammals are biologically programmed to put their digestive waste away from where they eat and sleep.

(B)

① We don't know why **these simultaneous explosions of intellectual activity** occurred when they did (perhaps daily human experience had hit a certain level of complexity).

② **But** the human need to organize our lives, our environment, even our thoughts, remains strong.

(C)

① Dogs have been known to collect their toys and put them in baskets; ants carry off dead members of the colony to burial grounds; certain birds and rodents create barriers around their nests in order to more easily detect invaders.

* method of loci: 장소를 활용한 기억법
** rodent: 설치류 동물

해설 [정답 : B - A - C]

주어진 지문에서 고대 그리스인들은 기억의 궁전과 장소법과 같은 두뇌 훈련 방법을 통해 기억을 상승시키기 위해 노력했고 외면화된 지식의 저장소인 도서관을 만들면서 정보를 외면화하는 일에 전문가들이 되었다고 합니다. (B)의 ①번 문장 'these simultaneous explosions of intellectual activity'는 주어진 지문의 외면화하는 일에 전문가가 된 것을 지칭합니다. 그러므로 주어진 지문 다음에 (B)가 와야 합니다. (A)의 ①번 문장에서 제시된 'this need'는 (B)의 ②번 문장에서 제시된 우리의 삶과 우리의 환경과 우리의 사고까지도 정리하려는 인간의 욕구를 지칭합니다. (A)의 ②번 문장에서 대부분의 포유류 동물은 자신의 소화 배설물을 자신이 먹고 자는 곳으로부터 치우는 성향을 타고났다고 합니다. 이는 (C)의 ①번 문장에서 개, 개미, 새, 설치류 동물을 제시하며 구체화하므로 정답은 (B) - (A) - (C)가 됩니다.

04

① Some people make few intentional changes in life.
② Sure, over time they may get fatter, gather lines, and go gray.

(A)

① **They** train for marathons, quit smoking, switch fields, write plays, take up the guitar, or learn to tango even if they never danced before in their lives.
② What is the difference between these two groups of people?

(B)

① **But they** wear their hair the same way, buy the same brand of shoes, eat the same breakfast, and stick to routines for no reason other than the ease of a comfortable, predictable life.
② **Yet** as both research and real life show, many others do make important changes.

(C)

① It's their perspective.
② People who change do not question whether change is possible or look for reasons they cannot change.
③ They simply decide on a change they want and do what is necessary to accomplish it.
④ Changing, which always stems from a firm decision, becomes job number one.

해설 [정답 : B - A - C]

주어진 지문에서 살면서 의도적인 변화를 거의 하지 않는 사람들이 있지만 물론 그들도 시간이 지나면서 더 뚱뚱해지고, 주름살이 늘어나고 머리가 하얗게 될 것이라고 합니다. (B)의 ①번 문장에서 'But'을 통해 이를 뒤집으며 그들은 편안하고 예측 가능한 삶이 쉽다는 이유로 똑같이 행동한다고 합니다. (B)의 ①번 문장에서 'they'는 주어진 지문에서 의도적인 변화를 거의 하지 않는 사람을 지칭하므로 주어진 지문 다음에 (B)가 와야 합니다. (B)의 ②번 문장에서 'Yet'을 통해 이를 뒤집으며 다른 많은 사람들은 중요한 변화를 한다고 합니다. (A)의 ①번 문장에서 이를 훈련을 하고, 담배를 끊는 것 등으로 구체화하여 제시하고 (A)의 ①번 문장의 'they'가 변화하는 사람을 지칭하므로 (A)가 (B) 뒤에 와야 합니다. (A)의 ②번 문장에서 두 집단의 사람들의 차이를 묻고 (C)의 ①번 문장에서 이 질문에 대한 답으로 관점을 제시하므로 정답은 (B) - (A) - (C)가 됩니다.

심화 (1) 예시 대응 훈련

평가원은 주어진 예시가 어떠한 내용에 대한 예시인지 사고하는 과정을 출제합니다.
예를 들어

주어진 지문 - 1에 대한 내용
(A) - 2에 대한 내용
(B) - 1에 대한 내용
(C) - 예시 ⓐ

혹은

주어진 지문 - 1에 대한 내용
(A) - 예시 ⓐ
(B) - 2에 대한 내용
(C) - 예시 ⓑ

를 제시합니다.
위와 같이 예시 ⓐ가 1에 대한 예시인지 2에 대한 예시인지 판단하도록 하거나
예시 ⓐ, ⓑ가 각각 1,2 중 어떠한 내용에 대한 예시인지 판단시킵니다.
비기출 문제를 풀어보며 패턴에 적응해 봅시다.

01

> Many traditional sports remain important elements of contemporary national sporting cultures.

(A) In many cases, however, what are commonly assumed to be traditional sporting practices actually represent hybrid amalgamations of traditional games and imported sporting values and practices. Judo, for instance, dates from only 1882 and was developed as a modernization of traditional styles of jujitsu.

(B) Similarly, muay thai adopted the ring, system of rounds, gloves, and weight divisions after concerns about thigh levels of death and injuries during the early 20th century, while sepak takraw took its current form in the 1930s, with the addition of a net and court adopted from badminton to the traditional pastime of kicking a rattan ball.

(C) Sumo, despite recent image problems, remains immensely popular and important in Japan. Similarly, sepak takraw and combat sports like muay thai, silat, and arnis remain permanent fixtures of Southeast Asia′s sporting landscape.

* amalgamation: 융합체 ** rattan: 등나무

① (A) – (C) – (B) ② (B) – (A) – (C)
③ (B) – (C) – (A) ④ (C) – (A) – (B)
⑤ (C) – (B) – (A)

02

> With so many people sharing the most intimate details of their lives with the world, something was bound to disrupt the trajectory of online sharing.

(A) For example, app developers have created a photo messaging app that enables users to send a photo or video with text to a specific group of people and control the time limit for how long they can view the sent message from one to ten seconds.

(B) When the time limit ends, the message is no longer available and is deleted from the app's servers. In this way users can control their digital footprints.

(C) The year 2013 saw NSA (National Security Agency) leaks, hackers targeting consumer credit cards, and blanket inquiries into individuals' personal lives through their online connections, to name a few. These invasions of privacy and more have inspired whole new platforms based on giving the user a digital experience that can be anonymous, deleted, and secure.

* trajectory: 진행 과정 ** anonymous: 익명의

① (A) – (C) – (B) ② (B) – (A) – (C)
③ (B) – (C) – (A) ④ (C) – (A) – (B)
⑤ (C) – (B) – (A)

03

Given our unique life-scripted beliefs about how things should be: our expectations — differences in preferences, attitudes, and beliefs are inevitable, and not all of them need to be resolved. Many, in fact, add the spice to relationships.

(A) You and your partner may need to decide where you will live and whether to rent or purchase a home. A decision must be made, or you may find yourselves living in the backseat of your car. Often you can't have things both ways, so a choice must be made.

(B) But sometimes you cannot just agree to disagree. Some issues impact each of you and perhaps others (your children or coworkers) in ways that require a clear, unambiguous resolution.

(C) For example, you can't practically visit your mother in Florida and your father in Connecticut on Thanksgiving Day. So coping with conflicts as we traverse the ups and downs of daily life is not just a useful tool; it is absolutely necessary for the kinds of successful relationships and outcomes we most desire.

* traverse: 가로지르다, 횡단하다

① (A) – (C) – (B)
② (B) – (A) – (C)
③ (B) – (C) – (A)
④ (C) – (A) – (B)
⑤ (C) – (B) – (A)

04

Music tourism sites and attractions generally attract two kinds of visitors: those particularly drawn for whatever reason to the memory or music of a particular performer, composer or genre (most obvious for festivals), and those who are there because the place fits into an itinerary devised for other reasons or because the visit is likely to be enjoyable.

(A) New Orleans and the Cajun region are popular with French tourists. For French tourists, travel to New Orleans in part allows an experience of Francophone identities in the New World, just as it is more likely to be Americans who visit Jim Morrison's grave in Paris.

(B) Particular links to music sites are, however, much more idiosyncratic and dependent on personal musical taste. Wider cultural and national links may also be evident.

(C) Thus, at Abbey Road, a place identified in many general guidebooks, most visitors were there because they had some appreciation of the Beatles' music, but others were there simply because it was part of an agenda that included a range of obvious London landmarks.

* idiosyncratic: (개인에게)특유한 ** Francophone: 프랑스어를 주 언어로 사용하는

① (A) – (C) – (B)
② (B) – (A) – (C)
③ (B) – (C) – (A)
④ (C) – (A) – (B)
⑤ (C) – (B) – (A)

01

Many traditional sports remain important elements of contemporary national sporting cultures.

(A) In many cases, **however**, what are commonly assumed to be traditional sporting practices actually represent hybrid amalgamations of traditional games and imported sporting values and practices. Judo, **for instance**, dates from only 1882 and was developed as a modernization of traditional styles of jujitsu.

(B) Similarly, muay thai adopted the ring, system of rounds, gloves, and weight divisions after concerns about thigh levels of death and injuries during the early 20th century, while sepak takraw took its current form in the 1930s, with the addition of a net and court adopted from badminton to the traditional pastime of kicking a rattan ball.

(C) Sumo, **despite** recent image problems, remains immensely popular and important in Japan. Similarly, sepak takraw and combat sports like muay thai, silat, and arnis remain permanent fixtures of Southeast Asia′s sporting landscape.

* amalgamation: 융합체 ** rattan: 등나무

⑧ 해석 [정답 : ④]

많은 전통 스포츠는 현대의 국가적인 스포츠 문화의 중요한 요소로 남아있다.

(C) 스모는 최근의 이미지 문제에도 불구하고 여전히 일본에서 엄청나게 인기 있는 상태로 중요하게 남아있다. 이와 비슷하게 세팍타크로와 무에타이, 실랏, 그리고 아르니스와 같은 격투 스포츠는 동남아시아의 스포츠 분야에서 영구적으로 정착된 것으로 남아 있다.

(A) 그러나 많은 경우, 전통적인 스포츠의 관행으로 흔히 추정되는 것이 사실상 전통 스포츠와 들여온 스포츠의 가치와 관행의 혼성 융합체를 나타낸다. 예를 들어, 유도는 고작 1882년으로 거슬러 올라가며 주짓수의 전통적인 양식을 현대화한 것으로 개발되었다.

(B) 이와 유사하게, 무에타이는 20세기 초반에 높은 수준의 사망과 부상에 대한 우려가 있은 후, 링, 라운드 체계, 글러브, 그리고 체중에 따른 구분을 채택했고, 한편 세팍타크로는 1930년대에 그것의 현재 형태를 채택했는데 그것은 배드민턴으로부터 채택된 네트와 코트를 등나무 공을 발로 차는 전통적인 오락에 추가했다.

⑧ 해설

주어진 지문에서 많은 전통 스포츠들은 여전히 스포츠 문화의 중요한 요소로 남아있다고 합니다. (C)의 ①번 문장에서 'Sumo'가 최근 이미지 문제에도 불구하고, 일본에서 엄청나게 인기 있고 중요한 상태로 남아있다고 합니다. (C)의 'remains immensely popular and important'는 주어진 지문의 'remain important elements'를 재진술하므로 'Sumo'는 주어진 지문의 예시에 해당합니다. 그러므로 주어진 지문 다음에 (C)가 와야 합니다.

(B)의 ①번 문장에서 'muay thai'는 20세기 초반에 사망과 부상에 대한 높은 수준의 우려가 있은 후, 링, 라운드 체계, 체중에 따른 구분을 채택하며 변화를 선택하였다고 합니다. 이 내용은 (C)의 ①번 문장과 ②번 문장에서 제시된 'remain important elements'에 대한 내용이 아닌 전통적인 부분에 새롭게 추가되는 부분을 제시하므로 (B)는 (C) 뒤에 올 수 없습니다. (A)의 ①번 문장에서 'however'을 통해서 내용을 전환하여 전통적인 스포츠 관행으로 흔히 가정되는 것이 사실상 전통 스포츠와 주입된 스포츠 가치와 관행의 융합체라고 합니다. 즉 전통적 스포츠에 추가적인 스포츠 가치와 관행이 주입된다고 합니다. (C)의 ①번, ②번 문장에서 제시된 전통 스포츠가 중요한 요소로 유지되는 것과 (A)의 ①번 문장에서 전통 스포츠에 스포츠 가치와 관행을 주입하는 것은 서로 역접을 이루고 소재가 전환되므로 (C) 뒤에는 (A)가 와야 합니다.

(B)의 ①번 문장에서 'Similarly'가 제시되며 전통적인 부분에 새롭게 추가되는 부분을 제시하고 (A)의 ②번 문장에서 (A)의 ①번 문장에서 제시된 전통적 스포츠에 스포츠 가치와 관행이 주입된 것에 대한 예시를 제시합니다. (B)의 ①번 문장에서 제시된 'muay thai'가 (A)의 ①번 문장에 대한 예시이고 (A)의 ②번 문장과 'Similarly'로 나열되므로 (A) 뒤에는 (B)가 와야합니다.

그러므로 정답은 (C) - (A) - (B)가 됩니다.

With so many people sharing the most intimate details of their lives with the world, something was bound to disrupt the trajectory of online sharing.

(A) **For example**, app developers have created a photo messaging app that enables users to send a photo or video with text to a specific group of people and control **the time limit** for how long they can view the sent message from one to ten seconds.

(B) When **the time limit ends**, the message is no longer available and is deleted from the app's servers. In this way users can control their digital footprints.

(C) The year 2013 saw NSA (National Security Agency) leaks, hackers targeting consumer credit cards, and blanket inquiries into individuals' personal lives through their online connections, **to name a few.** These invasions of privacy and more have inspired whole new platforms based on giving the user a digital experience that can be anonymous, deleted, and secure.

* trajectory: 진행 과정 ** anonymous: 익명의

§ 해석 [정답 : ④]

아주 많은 사람이 자신들 삶의 가장 사적인 세부 내용들을 세상과 공유하는 상황에서, 무언가 온라인 공유의 진행 과정에 지장을 줄 가능성이 컸다.

(C) 몇 가지를 예로 들자면, 2013년 (미국) 국가안보국의 기밀 유출, 소비자의 신용카드를 목표로 하는 해커들, 그리고 개인들의 온라인 관계를 통한 그들의 사생활에 대한 전면 조사가 있었다. 이러한 사생활 침해와 더 많은 사건은 사용자에게 익명이고, 삭제되며, 그리고 안전할 수 있는 디지털 경험을 제공하는 것을 기반으로 하는, 완전히 새로운 플랫폼이 생겨나게 했다.

(A) 예를 들면, 애플리케이션 개발자들은 사용자들이 특정 집단의 사람들에게 텍스트와 함께 사진이나 비디오를 보내고 상대방이 그 보낸 메시지를 얼마나 오랫동안 볼 수 있는지 1초에서 10초까지의 시간제한을 둘 수 있는 포토 메시지 애플리케이션을 개발했다.

(B) 시간제한이 끝날 때, 그 메시지는 더 이상 볼 수 없고 그 애플리케이션의 서버에서 삭제된다. 이런 식으로, 사용자들은 자신들이 남긴 디지털 사용 흔적을 통제할 수 있다.

§ 해설

주어진 지문에서 많은 사람들이 자신들의 사적인 세부 내용들을 세상과 공유하는 상황에서 어떠한 것이 온라인 공유의 진행 과정에 지장을 줄 수 있다고 합니다. (C)의 ①번 문장에서 'to name a few'를 통해 2013년 'NSA'의 기밀 유출, 소비자의 신용카드를 목표로 하는 해커들, 그리고 개인들의 온라인 관계를 통한 그들의 사생활에 대한 조사가 있었다고 합니다. 이는 주어진 지문에서 제시한 온라인 공유 진행 과정에 지장을 줄 가능성이 있는 어떠한 것에 대한 예시이므로 주어진 지문 뒤에 (C)가 와야 합니다.

(C)의 ②번 문장에서 이러한 사생활 침해를 대비하기 위한 새로운 플랫폼이 생겨났다고 합니다. (A)의 ①번 문장에서 애플리케이션 개발자들은 상대방이 보낸 메시지를 볼 수 있는 시간제한이 있는 포토 메시지 어플리케이션을 개발했다고 합니다. 이는 (C)의 ②번 문장에서 제시한 사생활 침해를 대비하기 위한 새로운 플랫폼에 예시에 해당하고 (A)의 ①번 문장의 'For example'로 연결되므로 (C) 뒤에는 (A)가 와야 합니다.

(B)의 ①번 문장에서 'the time limit'가 (A)의 ①번 문장에서 제시된 시간제한을 지칭하므로 정답은 (C) - (A) - (B)가 됩니다.

03

Given our unique life-scripted beliefs about how things should be: our expectations — differences in preferences, attitudes, and beliefs are inevitable, and not all of them need to be resolved. Many, **in fact**, add the spice to relationships.

(A) You and your partner may need to decide where you will live and whether to rent or purchase a home. A decision **must** be made, or you may find yourselves living in the backseat of your car. Often you can't have things both ways, so a choice **must** be made.

(B) **But** sometimes you cannot just agree to disagree. Some issues impact each of you and perhaps others (your children or coworkers) in ways that require a clear, unambiguous resolution.

(C) **For example**, you can't practically visit your mother in Florida and your father in Connecticut on Thanksgiving Day. **So** coping with conflicts as we traverse the ups and downs of daily life is not just a useful tool; it is absolutely necessary for the kinds of successful relationships and outcomes we most desire.

* traverse: 가로지르다, 횡단하다

⍟ 해석 | 정답 : ② |

만사가 어떤 모습이어야 하는가에 대한 고유하고 살면서 얻게 된 우리의 믿음, 즉 우리의 기대를 고려해볼 때, 선호, 태도, 믿음에서의 차이는 필연적이며, 그것이 모두 다 해결될 필요는 없다. 사실, 많은 것들이 관계에 풍미를 더해 준다.

(B) 하지만 여러분은 가끔식 의견 불일치에 동의할 수 없게 된다. 몇몇 문제는 분명하고 확실한 해결책을 요구하는 방식으로 여러분 각자에게 그리고 아마도 다른 사람들 (자녀나 동료들)에게 영향을 미친다.

(A) 여러분과 여러분의 배우자는 어디서 거주할 것인지와 집을 빌릴 것인지 아니면 (집을) 구매할 것인지를 결정할 필요가 있을지도 모른다. 결정이 내려져야 하며, 그렇지 않으면 여러분은 자동차 뒷좌석에서 살게 될지도 모른다. 많은 경우 두 가지를 취할 수는 없으며, 따라서 선택을 해야한다.

(C) 예를 들어, 현실적으로 추수감사절에 Florida 주에 사는 어머니와 Connecticut 주에 사는 아버지를 다 방문할 수는 없다. 그래서 일상의 우여곡절을 가로지를 때 갈등을 처리하는 것은 쓸모 있는 도구일 뿐만 아니라 우리가 가장 바라는 종류의 성공적인 관계와 결과에 절대적으로 필요한 것이다.

⍟ 해설

주어진 지문의 ①번 문장에서 선호, 태도, 믿음에서의 차이는 필연적이며, 그것이 모두 다 해결될 필요가 없다고 합니다. (A)의 ①번 문장에서 너와 너의 배우자는 어디서 거주할 것인지와 집을 빌릴 것인지 아니면 구매할 것인지를 결정할 필요가 있으며 (A)의 ②번 문장에서 그 결정은 반드시 이루어져야만 한다고 합니다. 이러한 내용은 주어진 지문의 ①번 문장에서 모두 다 해결될 필요가 없다는 내용과 반대되는 내용이 제시되므로 (A)는 주어진 지문 뒤에 올 수 없습니다.

(C)의 ①번 문장에서 추수감사절에 Florida 주에 사는 어머니와 Connecticut 주에 사는 아버지를 다 방문할 수는 없다고 하며 (C)의 ②번 문장에서 갈등을 처리하는 것이 성공적인 관계와 결과에 절대적으로 필요하다고 합니다. 주어진 지문에서 갈등을 처리해야만 한다는 내용이 제시되지 않았고 오히려 모두 다 해결될 필요가 없는 갈등이 없다고 볼 수 있는 상황을 제시하므로 (C)는 주어진 지문 뒤에 올 수 없습니다.

(B)의 ①번 문장에서 ‘But’으로 전환되며 너는 가끔식 의견 불일치에 동의 할 수 없으며, (B)의 ②번 문장에서는 몇몇 문제는 분명하고 확실한 해결책을 요구한다고 합니다. 이는 주어진 지문의 ①번, ②번 문장에서 모두 해결될 필요가 없다는 내용과 ‘But’으로 전환되므로 주어진 지문 뒤에는 (B)가 와야 합니다.

(B)의 ②번 문장에서 확실한 해결책을 요구하는 방식으로 너와 그리고 다른 사람들에게 영향을 미친다고 합니다. (A)의 ①번 문장에서 너와 너의 배우자가 결정을 내려야만 하는 상황이 제시되므로 (A)의 ①번 문장은 (B)의 ②번 문장에 대한 예시이자 재진술에 해당합니다. 그러므로 (B) 뒤에 (A)가 와야 합니다.

(A)의 ③번 문장에서 많은 경우 모두 취할 수 없으며, 선택을 해야 한다고 합니다. (C)의 ①번 문장에서 추수감사절에 Florida 주에 사는 어머니와 Connecticut 주에 사는 아버지를 다 방문할 수는 없다는 예시가 제시되며 (C)의 ②번 문장에서 갈등을 처리하는 것은 둘 중 선택을 하는 것을 재진술하므로 (A) 뒤에 (C)가 와야 합니다. 그러므로 정답은 (B) - (A) - (C)가 되야 합니다.

04

Music tourism sites and attractions generally attract two kinds of visitors: those particularly drawn for whatever reason to the memory or music of a particular performer, composer or genre (most obvious for festivals), and those who are there because the place fits into an itinerary devised for other reasons or **because** the visit is likely to be enjoyable.

(A) New Orleans and the Cajun region are popular with French tourists. For French tourists, travel to New Orleans in part allows an experience of Francophone identities in the New World, just as it is more likely to be Americans who visit Jim Morrison's grave in Paris.

(B) Particular links to music sites are, **however**, much more idiosyncratic and dependent on personal musical taste. Wider cultural and national links may also be evident.

(C) **Thus**, at Abbey Road, a place identified in many general guidebooks, most visitors were there **because** they had some appreciation of the Beatles' music, **but** others were there simply **because** it was part of an agenda that included a range of obvious London landmarks.

* idiosyncratic: (개인에게)특유한

** Francophone: 프랑스어를 주 언어로 사용하는

🔖 해석 ｜ 정답 : ⑤ ｜

음악 관광지와 명소들은 일반적으로 두 종류의 방문객들을 끌어들이는데, 그것은 (가장 두드러지게는 축제에서의) 특정 연주자, 작곡가 또는 장르에 대한 기억이나 음악에 어떤 이유로든 특별히 끌리는 사람들과 그 장소가 다른 이유로 계획된 여행 일정표와 맞아떨어지거나 혹은 그 방문이 즐거울 것 같아서 그곳에 있는 사람들이다.

(C) 따라서 많은 일반 여행 안내서에서 발견되는 장소인 Abbey Road에서는 대부분의 방문객들이 Beatles의 음악 가치를 조금 알기 때문에 그곳에 있었지만, 다른 방문객들은 단순히 여러 확실한 London의 명소들을 포함하는 예정된 일정의 일부였기 때문에 그곳에 있었다.

(B) 하지만 음악 관광지와의 특별한 연관성은 훨씬 더 개인 특유의 것이고 개인적인 음악적 취향에 의존한다. 더 넓은 문화적, 국가적 연관성 또한 명백할 수 있다.

(A) New Orleans와 Cajun 지역은 프랑스 관광객들에게 인기가 있다. 프랑스 관광객에게 있어 New Orleans 여행은, 마치 파리에 있는 Jim Morrison의 묘를 방문하는 것이 미국인일 가능성이 더 높듯이, 부분적으로 신세계 (아메리카)에서 프랑스어를 쓰는 정체성 경험을 가능하게 한다.

🔖 해설

주어진 지문에서 음악 관광지나 명소는 음악적인 기억이나 음악에 어떤 이유로든 특별히 끌리는 사람들과 그 장소가 다른 이유로 계획된 여행 일정표와 맞아떨어지거나 혹은 그 방문이 즐거울 것 같아서 방문하는 사람들, 즉 음악적인 이유로 방문하거나 비음악적인 이유로 방문하는 사람들 모두 끌어들인다고 합니다. (C)의 ①번 문장에서 'Abbey Road'를 제시하며 몇몇 사람들은 'Beatles'의 음악 가치를 알기 때문에 'Abbey Road'를 방문하지만 다른 사람들은 London의 명소들을 포함하는 예정된 일정의 일부였기 때문에 'Abbey Road'를 방문한다고 합니다. 음악의 가치를 아는 사람은 주어진 지문에서 음악적인 이유로 방문하는 사람과 대응되고 일정에 포함되었기 때문에 방문하는 사람은 비음악적인 이유로 방문하는 사람에 대응하므로 (C)의 ①번 문장은 주어진 지문의 예시이자 결과에 해당하며 'Thus'를 통해서 연결될 수 있습니다. 그러므로 주어진 지문 뒤에 (C)가 와야 합니다.

(A)의 ①번 문장에서 'New Orleans'와 'Cajun' 지역은 프랑스 관광객들에게 인기가 있다고 하며, (A)의 ②번 문장에서는 프랑스 인들에게 'New Orleans'를 방문하는 것이 신세계 (아메리카)에서 프랑스어를 쓰는 정체성을 경험하는 것을 가능하게 한다고 합니다. 정체성과 관련된 내용은 주어진 지문과 (C)의 ①번 문장에서 제시된 음악적인 이유와 비음악적인 이유로 방문하는 관광객과는 무관한 내용에 대한 예시이므로 (C) 뒤에 (A)가 올 수 없습니다.

(B)의 ①번 문장에서 음악 관광지와의 특별한 연관성은 개인적인 것이라고 하며 (B)의 ②번 문장에서 더 넓은 문화적, 국가적 연관성 또한 명백하다고 합니다. 즉 음악 관광지가 개인적인 차원이 아닌 집단적 차원에서 제시될 수 있다고 합니다. 개인적 차원에서의 음악 관광지와의 특별한 연관성은 주어진 지문과 (C)의 ①번 문장에서 제시된 개인의 음악적인 선호와 개인의 일정에 의해서 음악 관광지를 방문하는 것을 재진술한 것이고 (B)의 ①번, ②번 문장에서 개인적 차원에서 'But'으로 전환하여 집단적 차원에서 음악 관광지와의 연관성을 제시하므로 (C) 뒤에는 (B)가 와야 합니다.

(A)의 ①번, ②번 문장에서 제시된 프랑스 인들이 신세계에서 프랑스어를 쓰는 정체성 경험을 하기 위해 'New Orleans'를 방문하는 것은 (B)의 ②번 문장에서 제시된 문화적 국가적 연관성에 대한 예시이므로 (B) 뒤에는 (A)가 와야하며 정답은 (C) - (B) - (A)가 되야 합니다.

심화 (2) 전환 대응 훈련

평가원은 정답인 순서가 1개만 확정될 수 있도록 출제하기 위해서 전환의 표현을 이용한 ⓐ but ⓑ 구조의 지문을 사용합니다. 예를 들어

주어진 지문 - ⓐ에 대한 내용

(A) - ⓑ에 대한 내용

(B) - ⓐ에 대한 내용 but ⓑ에 대한 내용

(C) - ⓐ에 대한 내용

일 경우 정답은 (C) - (B) - (A)로 확정됩니다.

또한 평가원이 혼란을 주기 위해서 A and A'으로 내용이 살짝 바뀌는 구조의 지문을 사용하기도 합니다. 예를 들어

주어진 지문 - A에 대한 내용

(A) - A'에 대한 내용

(B) - A에 대한 내용

(C) - A에 대한 내용 (Similarly) A'에 대한 내용

일 경우 정답은 (B) - (C) - (A)로 확정됩니다. 비기출 문제를 통해서 이 패턴에 적응해봅시다.

01

One stance to approach literary production is one that completely ignores taste and hence is a purely scientific approach. Using this approach, we never say something is well or badly done.

(A) We must also accept that such a stance is permissible in discussing literary works. In fact, leaving aside an analysis of a single work, this approach becomes especially useful in comparing two or more works, or comparing a series of works.

(B) Moreover, people generally do not fancy such an approach. They say that it lacks taste or that it is incomprehensible. But this is a different stance, and we must accept the fact that it features an objective attitude that precludes taste.

(C) If we are to evaluate a script, we say that the structure is such and such, the plot is such and such — but we never praise or criticize based on our taste. This is the polar opposite of the appreciative stance and is an approach that very few critics have adopted. In the rare cases it has been adopted, it seems to have been limited to dull people.

① (A) − (C) − (B)   ② (B) − (A) − (C)
③ (B) − (C) − (A)   ④ (C) − (A) − (B)
⑤ (C) − (B) − (A)

02

Whereas nineteenth-century dietary reformers worried that we'd stopped baking our own bread, today's food evangelists worry that we've stopped cooking altogether. It's true that families eat out more than in the past.

(A) And women spend less time cooking than they did a few generations ago. But oversimplified comparisons of today's families with those of previous generations fail to acknowledge the fact that Americans have long depended on the labor of others to get dinner on the table.

(B) At the peak, almost two million domestic workers were employed in American households. Anthropologist Amy Trubek notes that idealized visions of home cooking persistently neglect "the many generations of paid cooks who first worked in homes and then in commercial settings to make these meals possible."

(C) Poor white women and women of color prepared many people's meals a century ago, just as they do today. The difference is that these women previously worked inside the home, as domestic laborers, rather than in restaurants.

* evangelist: 전도사

① (A) – (C) – (B) ② (B) – (A) – (C)
③ (B) – (C) – (A) ④ (C) – (A) – (B)
⑤ (C) – (B) – (A)

03

Unlike conventional marketing activities, like advertising and promotions, that are planned and scripted, sports events are inherently unpredictable. Fans, athletes, teams, and companies do not know outcomes.

(A) Fans have an emotional attachment to their favorite teams and athletes, irrespective (mostly) of their recent performances. If sports were scripted then they would lose credibility, spontaneity would be lost, and they would be no different than a conventional company-directed ad campaign.

(B) Indeed, many business managers find this prospect of uncertainty distinctly uncomfortable and consequently shy away from using sports as a marketing platform. Yet sports fans follow sports partly because outcomes are not guaranteed.

(C) Despite even the most formidable track records of success, one cannot know for certain whether past sport performances will continue or whether expectations will be turned upside down. This very unpredictability separates sports from almost all other corporate marketing activities.

① (A) − (C) − (B) ② (B) − (A) − (C)
③ (B) − (C) − (A) ④ (C) − (A) − (B)
⑤ (C) − (B) − (A)

04

A lichen is an organism consisting of a fungus and an alga living together, usually in an interdependent relationship.

(A) In contrast, areas with clean air can support larger varieties of lichens. Some lichen species are sensitive to specific air-polluting chemicals. Old man's beard and yellow Evernia lichens, for example, can sicken and die in the presence of excessive sulfur dioxide (SO_2), even if the pollutant originates far away.

(B) These hardy species are good biological indicators of air pollution because they continually absorb air as a source of nourishment. A highly polluted area around an industrial plant might have only gray-green crusty lichens or none at all. An area with moderate air pollution might support only orange crusty lichens.

(C) For this reason, scientists discovered SO_2 pollution on Isle Royale, Michigan, in Lake Superior, an island where no car or tall factory chimney has ever existed. They used Evernia lichens to point the finger northwest toward coal-burning facilities in and around the Canadian city of Thunder Bay, Ontario.

* lichen: 이끼, 지의류 ** alga: 조류, 말

① (A) − (C) − (B) 　　② (B) − (A) − (C)
③ (B) − (C) − (A) 　　④ (C) − (A) − (B)
⑤ (C) − (B) − (A)

심화 (2) 전환 대응 훈련 해설

01

One stance to approach literary production is one that completely ignores taste and **hence** is a purely scientific approach. Using this approach, we never say something is well or badly done.

(A) We **must** also accept that such a stance is permissible in discussing literary works. **In fact**, leaving aside an analysis of a single work, this approach becomes especially useful in comparing two or more works, or comparing a series of works.

(B) Moreover, people generally do not fancy such an approach. They say that it lacks taste or that it is incomprehensible. **But** this is a different stance, and we **must** accept the fact that it features an objective attitude that precludes taste.

(C) If we are to evaluate a script, we say that the structure is such and such, the plot is such and such — but we never praise or criticize based on our taste. This is the polar opposite of the appreciative stance and is an approach that very few critics have adopted. In the rare cases it has been adopted, it seems to have been limited to dull people.

ꝑ 해석 [정답 : ⑤]

문학 작품에 접근하는 한 가지 입장은 취향을 완전히 무시하는, 따라서 순전히 과학적인 접근인 입장이다.
이런 접근 방법을 이용할 때, 우리는 결코 어떤 것이 잘 되었다거나 잘못되었다고 말하지 않는다.

(C) 우리가 어떤 원고를 평가하려고 하면, 우리는 구조가 이러이러하고, 줄거리가 이러이러하다고
    말하지만, 결코 우리의 취향에 근거하여 칭찬하거나 비판하지 않는다. 이것은 (문학 작품을) 감상하는
    입장과 완전히 반대인 것이며 아주 극소수의 비평가가 채택한 접근 방법이다. 그것이 채택된 드문
    경우에, 그것은 따분한 사람들에게 국한되었던 것처럼 보인다.
(B) 더욱이, 사람들은 일반적으로 그렇나 접근 방법을 좋아하지 않는다. 그것은 취향이 없거나 이해할 수
    없다고 그들은 말한다. 그러나 이것은 다른 입장이며, 그것이 취향을 배제하는 객관적인 태도를
    특징으로 한다는 사실을 우리는 인정해야 한다.
(A) 우리는 또한 문학 작품을 논하는데 있어서 그러한 입장이 허용된다는 것을 받아들여야 한다. 실제로,
    단일 작품을 분석하는 것 말고도, 이 접근 방법은 두 개 이상의 작품을 비교하거나, 일련의 작품들을
    비교할 때 특히 유용해진다.

ꝑ 해설

주어진 지문 ①번 문장에서 문학 작품에 접근할 때, 취향을 무시하고 순전히 과학적인 접근인 입장을
제시합니다. 주어진 지문 ②번 문장에서 이러한 접근의 특징은 어떤 것이 잘 되었거나 잘못되었다고
판단할 수 없다고 합니다. (C)의 ①번 문장에서 우리는 구조가 어떠하고 줄거리가 어떠하다고 판단할 수
있지만, 우리는 우리의 취향에 근거하여 칭찬하거나 비판하지 않는다고 합니다. 이는 주어진 지문의 ②번
문장을 재진술하므로 (C)는 주어진 지문 뒤에 와야 합니다.

(C)의 ③번 문장에서 극소수 비평기기 채택한 과학적인 접근 방법은 그 방법이 따분한 사람들에게
국한되었던 것처럼 보인다고 제시하며 과학적인 접근 방법의 단점에 대해서 제시합니다. (B)의 ①번
문장에서 사람들은 'such an approach'인 과학적인 접근 방법을 좋아하지 않는다고 하며 과학적인 접근
방법의 단점을 제시합니다. 이는 (C)의 ③번 문장과 'Moreover'로 나열되므로 (C) 뒤에는 (B)가 와야
합니다.

(B)의 ③번 문장에서 (B)의 ①번, ②번 문장까지 제시된 과학적인 접근 방법의 단점을 전환하여 과학적인
접근 방법은 다른 입장이며, 객관적인 태도를 특징으로 한다는 것을 인정해야 한다고 합니다.
이는 (A)의 ①번 문장에서 우리는 'such a stance'인 과학적인 접근 방법이 인정되어야 한다는 내용으로
재진술되므로 (B) 뒤에는 (A)가 와야합니다. 그러므로 정답은 (C) - (B) - (A)가 되어야 합니다.

02

  <u>**Whereas**</u> nineteenth-century dietary reformers worried that we'd stopped baking our own bread, today's food evangelists worry that we've stopped cooking altogether. It's true that families eat out more than in the past.

(A) And women spend less time cooking than they did a few generations ago. **But** oversimplified comparisons of today's families with those of previous generations fail to acknowledge the fact that Americans have long depended on the labor of others to get dinner on the table.

(B) At the peak, almost two million domestic workers were employed in American households. Anthropologist Amy Trubek notes that idealized visions of home cooking persistently neglect "the many generations of paid cooks who first worked in homes and then in commercial settings to make these meals possible."

(C) Poor white women and women of color prepared many people's meals a century ago, just as they do today. The difference is that these women previously worked inside the home, as domestic laborers, rather than in restaurants.

* evangelist: 전도사

⚓ 해석 [정답 : ①]

9세기 음식 개량가들은 우리가 우리 자신의 빵을 굽는 것을 중지해 버렸다고 걱정했지만, 오늘날의 음식 전도사들은 우리가 요리를 완전히 중지해 버렸다고 걱정한다. 가족이 과거보다 더 많이 외식한다는 것은 사실이다.

(A) 그리고 여성은 몇 세대 전에 그랬던 것보다 더 적은 시간을 요리하면서 보낸다. 그러나 오늘날의 가족을 이전 세대의 가족과 지나치게 단순화하여 비교하는 것은 미국인들이 식사를 식탁에 올리기 위해 오랫동안 다른 사람들의 노동에 의지해 왔다는 사실을 받아들이지 않는 것이다.

(C) 가난한 백인 여성과 유색 인종 여성은, 마치 오늘날 그들이 그러하듯이, 한 세기 전에 많은 사람들의 식사를 준비했다. 차이는 이 여성들이 전에는 식당에서보다는 가사 노동자로서 집 안에서 일했다는 것이다.

(B) 절정에 이르렀을 때 거의 2백만 명의 가사 근로자가 미국 가정에 고용되었다. 인류학자인 Amy Trubek은 가정 요리에 대해 이상적으로 보는 시각은 '이런 식사가 가능하게 하도록 처음에 가정에서, 그리고 나서 상업적 환경에서 일했던 여러 세대의 유급 요리사들'을 지속적으로 무시한다는 점에 주목한다.

⚓ 해설

주어진 지문 ①번 문장에서 오늘날의 음식 전도사들은 우리가 요리를 완전히 중지해 버렸다고 걱정한다고 하며 주어진 지문 ②번 문장에서는 가족이 과거보다 더 많은 외식을 한다는 것은 사실이라고 합니다. 즉 우리는 가정에서 요리하는 것을 중지하고 외식을 한다고 합니다. (A)의 ①번 문장에서는 여성은 몇 세대 전보다 더 적은 시간을 요리하면서 보낸다고 합니다. 이는 주어진 지문의 ②번 문장에서 제시된 가정에서 요리하는 것이 적어지는 것과 (A) ①번 문장의 'And'로 나열되므로 주어진 지문 뒤에는 (A)가 와아 합니다.

(A)의 ②번 문장에서 'But'을 통해 (A)의 ①번 문장까지 제시된 오늘날 스스로 요리를 적게한다는 관점을 전환하여 오늘날의 가족을 이전 세대의 가족과 지나치게 단순화하여 비교하는 것이며, 미국인들이 식사를 식탁에 올리기 위해 오랫동안 나른 사람들의 노동에 의지해 왔다는 것을 빋아들이지 않는다고 합니다. (C)의 ①번 문장에서 가난한 백인 여성과 유색 인종 여성은 오늘날 그러하듯이, 한 세기 전에도 많은 사람들의 식사를 준비했다고 합니다. 이는 (A)의 ②번 문장에서 제시된 식사를 식탁에 올리기 위해 오랫동안 다른 사람들에게 의지한 것에 대한 예시에 해당하므로 (A) 뒤에는 (C)가 와야 합니다.

(C)의 ①번, ②번 문장에서 제시된 가난한 백인 여성과 유색 인종 여성이 오랫동안 가사 노동자로 고용되었다는 것은 (B)의 ①번 문장에서 절정에 이르렀을 때, 거의 2백만 명의 가사 근로자가 고용되었다는 내용으로 이어지므로 (C) 뒤에는 (B)가 와야 합니다. 그러므로 정답은 (A) - (C) - (B)가 되야 합니다.

03

> Unlike conventional marketing activities, like advertising and promotions, that are planned and scripted, sports events are inherently unpredictable. Fans, athletes, teams, and companies do not know outcomes.

(A) Fans have an emotional attachment to their favorite teams and athletes, irrespective (mostly) of their recent performances. If sports were scripted then they would lose credibility, spontaneity would be lost, and they would be no different than a conventional company-directed ad campaign.

(B) **Indeed**, many business managers find <u>this prospect of uncertainty</u> distinctly uncomfortable and consequently shy away from using sports as a marketing platform. **Yet** sports fans follow sports partly because outcomes are not guaranteed.

(C) **Despite** even the most formidable track records of success, one cannot know for certain whether past sport performances will continue or whether expectations will be turned upside down. <u>This very unpredictability</u> separates sports from almost all other corporate marketing activities.

♪ 해석 [정답 : ⑤]

계획되고 대본이 있는 광고나 홍보와 같은 전통적인 마케팅 활동과는 달리, 스포츠 경기는 본질적으로 예측할 수 없다. 팬, 운동선수, 팀, 회사는 결과를 모른다.

(C) 심지어 성공한 트랙 경기의 가장 뛰어난 기록일지라도, 과거의 스포츠 성과가 계속될 것인지 아니면 기대가 거꾸로 뒤집힐지 확실히 알 수 없다. 바로 이러한 예측 불가능성이 스포츠를 거의 모든 다른 기업 마케팅 활동과 구분 짓는다.

(B) 실제로, 많은 업체의 관리자들이 이러한 불확실성에 대한 전망을 명백히 불편하다고 느끼고 결과적으로 스포츠를 마케팅 플랫폼으로 사용하기를 꺼린다. 그러나 스포츠팬들은 부분적으로 결과가 확실하지 않기 때문에 스포츠에 흥미를 갖는다.

(A) 팬들은 (대체로) 최근의 경기 성과와 상관없이 자신이 좋아하는 팀과 선수들에 대해 감정적인 애착을 갖고 있다. 만약 스포츠가 대본을 갖는다면, 신뢰를 잃을 것이고, 자발성은 사라질 것이며, 전통적인 회사 주도의 광고 캠페인과 다를 바가 없을 것이다.

♪ 해설

주어진 지문의 ①번 문장에서 계획된 광고나 홍보와 같은 전통적인 마케팅 활동과는 달리, 스포츠 경기는 예측할 수 없다고 합니다. 주어진 지문의 ②번 문장에서는 아무도 결과를 알 수 없다고 하며 주어진 지문의 ①번 문장을 구체화합니다. 주어진 지문의 ②번 문장에서 'Fans'가 제시되었고 (A)의 ①번 문장에서도 'Fans'가 제시되었습니다. 또한 (A)의 ①번 문장에서 팬들은 경기 성과와 상관없이 팀과 선수들에게 애착을 갖는다는 내용은 주어진 지문의 ②번 문장의 스포츠 경기는 결과를 알 수 없다는 내용과 연관되어 있습니다. 하지만 (C)의 ①번 문장에서 심지어 성공한 트랙 경기이 가장 뛰어난 기록일지라도 과거 성과가 계속될지 아니면 기대가 뒤집힐지 알 수 없다는 내용은 주어진 지문의 ①번, ②빈 문장의 결과를 알 수 없디는 내용을 예시를 통해서 재진술하므로 주어진 지문 뒤에 (C)가 연결될지 (A)가 연결될지 알 수 없습니다.

(C)의 ②번 문장에서 스포츠의 예측 불가능성이 다른 기업 마케팅 활동과 구분 짓는다고 합니다. (B)의 ①번 분상에서 많은 업체의 관리자들이 'this prospect of uncertainty'에 불편하다고 느낀디고 합니다. (B)-①번 문장의 'this prospect of uncertainty'는 (C)-②번 문장의 'this very unpredictability'를 지칭하므로 (C) 뒤에는 (B)가 와야 합니다.

(B)의 ②번 문장에서 'But'을 통해 업체 관리자들이 스포츠의 불확실성에 의해서 불편하다고 느끼고 스포츠를 마케팅 플랫폼으로 사용하기를 꺼린다는 내용을 전환하여, 스포츠팬들은 결과가 확실하지 않기 때문에 스포츠에 흥미를 갖는다고 합니다. (A)의 ①번 문장에서 팬들이 경기 성과와 상관없이 팀과 선수들에 대해 애착을 갖고 있다고 하는 것은 (B)의 ②번 문장에서 팬들이 결과가 확실하지 않아서 스포츠에 흥미를 갖는 것을 재진술하므로 (B) 뒤에는 (A)가 와야 합니다.

04

> A lichen is an organism consisting of a fungus and an alga living together, usually in an interdependent relationship.

(A) **In contrast**, areas with clean air can support larger varieties of lichens. Some lichen species are sensitive to specific air-polluting chemicals. Old man's beard and yellow Evernia lichens, **for example**, can sicken and die in the presence of excessive sulfur dioxide (SO_2), even if the pollutant originates far away.

(B) These hardy species are good biological indicators of air pollution **because** they continually absorb air as a source of nourishment. A highly polluted area around an industrial plant might have only gray-green crusty lichens or none at all. An area with moderate air pollution might support only orange crusty lichens.

(C) For this reason, scientists discovered SO_2 pollution on Isle Royale, Michigan, in Lake Superior, an island where no car or tall factory chimney has ever existed. They used Evernia lichens to point the finger northwest toward coal-burning facilities in and around the Canadian city of Thunder Bay, Ontario.

* lichen: 이끼, 지의류   ** alga: 조류, 말

§ 해석 | 정답 : ② |
이끼는 대개 상호 의존적인 관계에서 함께 살아가는 균류와 조류로 구성된 생물이다.

(B) 이 강인한 종은 대기 오염의 좋은 생물학적 지표인데 왜냐하면 그것들은 자양분의 원천으로 끊임없이 공기를 흡수하기 때문이다. 산업 공장 주변의 매우 오염된 지역은 단지 회녹색의 껍질이 딱딱한 이끼들만 있거나 아니면 이끼들이 전혀 없을 수 있다. 중간 정도로 공기가 오염된 지역은 오렌지 빛깔의 껍질이 딱딱한 이끼들만 살게 할 수 있다.

(A) 이와는 대조적으로 공기가 깨끗한 지역은 더 다양한 이끼들을 살게 할 수 있다. 어떤 이끼 종들은 공기를 오염시키는 특정한 화학 물질에 민감하다. 예를 들어 Old man's beard 이끼와 yellow Evernia 이끼는 과도한 SO_2가 존재하면 그 오염 물질이 아주 멀리서 비롯된 경우라도 병이나서 죽을 수 있다.

(C) 이런 이유 때문에 과학자들은 Superior 호에 있는 Michigan 주의 Isle Royale에서, 즉 자동차나 높은 공장 굴뚝이 존재한 적이 없는 섬에서 SO_2 오염을 발견했다. 그들은 Everia 이끼를 이용하여 북서쪽에 있는 Ontario 주의 Thunder Bay라는 캐나다 도시 안과 그 도시 주변에 있는 석탄을 태우는 시설을 (그 원인으로) 지목했다.

§ 해설
주어진 지문의 ①번 문장에서 이끼는 상호 의존적인 관계에서 함께 살아가는 균류와 조류로 구성된 생물이라고 합니다. (B)의 ①번 문장에서 'These hardy species'는 공기 오염의 좋은 생물학적 지표라고 하며 (B)의 ②번, ③번 문장에서 높은 공기 오염 지역에서는 회녹색의 껍질이 딱딱한 이끼들만 있거나 이니면 이끼들이 전혀 없을 수 있으며 중간 정도로 오염된 지역에서는 오렌지 빛깔이 껍질이 딱딱한 이끼들만 산다고 하며 공기 오염정도에 따라 서식하는 이끼의 종류가 다르다는 것을 제시하고 있습니다. (A)의 ①빈 문장에시 깨끗한 공기의 지역에서는 다양한 종류의 이끼들이 산다는 것은 (B)의 ②번, ③번 문장에서 공기 오염 정도에 따라 서식하는 이끼의 종류가 다르다는 것을 제시하는 것과 이어지며 (B)의 ③번 문장에서 제시된 중간 정도의 공기 오염과 (A)의 ①번 문장에서 제시된 깨끗한 공기 지역이 'In contrast'로 전환되므로 (B) 뒤에는 (A)가 와야 합니다.

(A)의 ②번 문장에서는 (A)의 ①번 문장까지 이어진 공기 오염 정도에 따라 서식하는 이끼의 종류에 대한 내용에서 전환하여 어떤 이끼 종들은 공기를 오염시키는 특정한 화학 물질에 민감하다고 합니다. (A)의 ③번 문장에서 이에 대한 예시로 SO_2에 민감한 Old man's beard 이끼와 yellow Evernia를 제시하며 (C)의 ①번 문장에서 SO_2에 대한 내용이 이어지고 (C)의 ②번 문장에서 Evernia 이끼를 이용하여 과학자들이 SO_2 오염을 발견했다고 하므로 (A) 뒤에는 (C)가 와야 합니다.
그러므로 정답은 (B) - (A) - (C)가 됩니다.

중. 최. 평. (중요 최신 평가원 기출)

01 25학년도 9월 평가원 37번

주어진 글 다음에 이어질 글의 순서로 가장 적절한 것을 고르시오.

> The generally close connection between health and what animals want exists because wanting to obtain the right things and wanting to avoid the wrong ones are major ways in which animals keep themselves healthy.

(A) They can take pre-emptive action so that the worst never happens. They start to want things that will be necessary for their health and survival not for now but for some time in the future.

(B) Animals have evolved many different ways of maintaining their health and then regaining it again once it has been damaged, such as an ability to heal wounds when they are injured and an amazingly complex immune system for warding off infection.

(C) Animals are equally good, however, at dealing with injury and disease before they even happen. They have evolved a complex set of mechanisms for anticipating and avoiding danger altogether.

* pre-emptive: 선제의 ** ward off: 막다

① (A) – (C) – (B)　　② (B) – (A) – (C)　　③ (B) – (C) – (A)
④ (C) – (A) – (B)　　⑤ (C) – (B) – (A)

02 25학년도 수능 36번

주어진 글 다음에 이어질 글의 순서로 가장 적절한 것을 고르시오.

> The potential for market enforcement is greater when contracting parties have developed reputational capital that can be devalued when contracts are violated.

(A) Similarly, a landowner can undermaintain fences, ditches, and irrigation systems. Accurate assessments of farmer and landowner behavior will be made over time, and those farmers and landowners who attempt to gain at each other's expense will find that others may refuse to deal with them in the future.

(B) Over time landowners indirectly monitor farmers by observing the reported output, the general quality of the soil, and any unusual or extreme behavior. Farmer and landowner reputations act as a bond. In any growing season a farmer can reduce effort, overuse soil, or underreport the crop.

(C) Farmers and landowners develop reputations for honesty, fairness, producing high yields, and consistently demonstrating that they are good at what they do. In small, close-knit farming communities, reputations are well known.

* ditch: 개천 ** irrigation: 물을 댐

① (A) – (C) – (B)　　② (B) – (A) – (C)　　③ (B) – (C) – (A)
④ (C) – (A) – (B)　　⑤ (C) – (B) – (A)

03 24학년도 6월 평가원 37번

주어진 글 다음에 이어질 글의 순서로 가장 적절한 것을 고르시오.

> Darwin saw blushing as uniquely human, representing an involuntary physical reaction caused by embarrassment and self-consciousness in a social environment.

(A) Maybe our brief loss of face benefits the long-term cohesion of the group. Interestingly, if someone blushes after making a social mistake, they are viewed in a more favourable light than those who don't blush.

(B) If we feel awkward, embarrassed or ashamed when we are alone, we don't blush; it seems to be caused by our concern about what others are thinking of us. Studies have confirmed that simply being told you are blushing brings it on. We feel as though others can see through our skin and into our mind.

(C) However, while we sometimes want to disappear when we involuntarily go bright red, psychologists argue that blushing actually serves a positive social purpose. When we blush, it's a signal to others that we recognize that a social norm has been broken; it is an apology for a faux pas.

* faux pas: 실수

① (A) − (C) − (B)　　　② (B) − (A) − (C)　　　③ (B) − (C) − (A)

④ (C) − (A) − (B)　　　⑤ (C) − (B) − (A)

04 24학년도 수능 37번

주어진 글 다음에 이어질 글의 순서로 가장 적절한 것을 고르시오.

> Norms emerge in groups as a result of people conforming to the behavior of others. Thus, the start of a norm occurs when one person acts in a particular manner in a particular situation because she thinks she ought to.

(A) Thus, she may prescribe the behavior to them by uttering the norm statement in a prescriptive manner. Alternately, she may communicate that conformity is desired in other ways, such as by gesturing. In addition, she may threaten to sanction them for not behaving as she wishes. This will cause some to conform to her wishes and act as she acts.

(B) But some others will not need to have the behavior prescribed to them. They will observe the regularity of behavior and decide on their own that they ought to conform. They may do so for either rational or moral reasons.

(C) Others may then conform to this behavior for a number of reasons. The person who performed the initial action may think that others ought to behave as she behaves in situations of this sort.

* sanction: 제재를 가하다

① (A) − (C) − (B)　　　② (B) − (A) − (C)　　　③ (B) − (C) − (A)

④ (C) − (A) − (B)　　　⑤ (C) − (B) − (A)

중. 최. 평. 해설

01 25학년도 9월 평가원 37번 (정답률 60%)

주어진 글 다음에 이어질 글의 순서로 가장 적절한 것을 고르시오.

> ① The generally close connection between health and what animals want exists **because** wanting to obtain the right things and wanting to avoid the wrong ones are major ways in which animals keep themselves healthy.

(A)
① They can take pre-emptive action **so that** the worst never happens.
② They start to want things that will be necessary for their health and survival not for now **but** for some time in the future.

(B)
① Animals have evolved many different ways of maintaining their health and then regaining it again once it has been damaged, such as an ability to heal wounds when they are injured and an amazingly complex immune system for warding off infection.

(C)
① Animals are equally good, **however**, at dealing with injury and disease before they even happen.
② They have evolved a complex set of mechanisms for anticipating and avoiding danger altogether.

* pre-emptive: 선제의 ** ward off: 막다

해설 [정답 : ③]

주어진 지문에서 건강과 동물이 원하는 것 사이에 일반적으로 밀접한 관계가 존재하는데, 올바른 것을 원하는 것과 잘못된 것을 피하고자 하는 것은 동물이 그들 스스로 건강을 유지하는 주요한 방법이기 때문이라고 합니다.

심화 (2) 전환 대응 훈련을 통해서 쉽게 풀 수 있습니다. (B)-①번 문장은 현재에 다쳤을 때 상처를 치료하거나 감염을 막기 위한 복잡한 면역 체계 등 위험에 노출되었을 때 이를 대비하기 위한 방법들이 제시되었습니다. (A)와 (C)는 현재 위험이 닥친 것이 아니고 미래의 위험을 대비하기 위해 예상하고 피하는 것에 대해서 제시되었습니다. (C)-①번 문장에 'however'가 제시되었고 같은 내용은 붙어 있어야 하는 통일성을 고려하면 (B)-(C)-(A)가 유일한 정답임을 알 수 있습니다.

* 다른 방법으로는 (C)-①번 문장에서 'they'는 (B)-①번 문장에서 제시된 손상이 되었을 때, 혹은 다쳤을 때를 의미합니다. 그러므로 (B)-(C)가 됩니다. (A)-(B)-(C)가 선지에 없기도 하고 (A)의 내용은 최악의 상황 즉, 다쳤을 상황을 대비하는 것에 대한 것이므로 (C)-②번 문장에서 제시된 위험을 예측하고 위험을 완전히 피하기 위한 복잡한 메커니즘의 구체화된 내용에 해당합니다. 그러므로 (C)-(A)가 되어야 합니다. 그러므로 정답은 (B)-(C)-(A)가 됩니다.

주 ①. The generally close connection (between health and what animals / want) / exists **because** wanting to obtain the right things and wanting to avoid the wrong ones / are / major ways (in which animals / keep / themselves / healthy).

> 구▶ 'between A and B'는 'A와 B 사이'를 의미합니다.
> - 'keep + O + O.C'는 'O가 O.C하도록 유지시키다'를 뜻합니다.
> - 건강과 동물이 원하는 것 사이에 일반적으로 밀접한 관계가 존재하는데, 올바른 것을 얻기를 원하는 것과 잘못된 것을 피하고자 하는 것은 동물이 그들 스스로 건강을 유지하는 주요한 방법이기 때문이라고 합니다.

> 독▶ 'because'가 제시되었으므로 중심 문장
> - 동물들은 건강을 스스로 유지하고자 하기 때문에, 올바른 것을 원하고 잘못된 것을 피하는 것과 같은 동물들이 원하는 것과 건강 사이의 밀접한 관계가 있다고 합니다.

(A) ①. They / can take / pre-emptive action **so that** the worst / never happens.

* pre-emptive: 선제의

> 구▶ 'so that'은 '~하기 위해서'로 해석하시면 됩니다.
> - 그들은 최악의 상황이 발생하지 않도록 선제 행동을 취할 수 있다고 합니다.

> 독▶ 'so that'이 제시되었으므로 중심 문장
> - 그들은 최악이 발생하지 않도록 먼저 행동을 할 수도 있다고 합니다.

(A) ②. They / start to want / things (that will be / necessary (for their health and survival not for now **but** for some time in the future)).

> 구▶ 그들은 지금이 아니라 미래 어느 때의 건강과 생존에 필요할 것들을 원하기 시작한다고 합니다.

> 독▶ (A)-①번 문장에서 최악의 상황이 발생하지 않도록 선제 행동을 취하는 것에 대한 구체화된 내용으로 그들은 현재가 아닌 미래에 건강과 생존을 위해서 필요한 것들을 원할 것이라고 합니다.

(B) ①. Animals / have evolved / many different ways (of maintaining their health and then regaining it again) (once it / has been damaged), (such as an ability (to heal wounds) (when they / are injured) and an amazingly complex immune system for warding off infection).

** ward off: 막다

> 구▶ 동물들은 그들의 (= 동물들의) 건강을 유지하고 그것을 (= 건강을) 다시 얻기 위한 다양한 방법들을 진화시켜왔는데, 이는 그들이 (= 동물들이) 다쳤을 때 상처를 치료하는 능력이나 감염을 막기 위한 놀랍도록 복잡한 면역 체계와 같은 것들이라고 합니다.

> 독▶ 동물들은 건강을 유지하고 건강을 다시 얻기 위해서 상처를 치료하는 능력과 감염을 막는 면역 체계 등 다양한 방법들을 진화시켜 왔다고 합니다.

(C) ①. Animals / are / equally good, **however**, (at dealing with injury and disease before they even happen).

> 구 그러나 동물들은 그것들이 일어나기 전에 부상과 질병을 다루는 능력도 똑같이 뛰어나다고 합니다.

> 독 'however'이 제시되었으므로 중심 문장
> - 동물들은 그것들이 일어나기 전에 부상과 질병을 다루는 능력도 뛰어나다고 합니다.

(C) ②. They / have evolved / a complex set of mechanisms (for anticipating and avoiding danger altogether).

> 구 그들은 (= 동물들은) 위험을 예측하고 완전하게 피하기 위해서 복잡한 메커니즘을 발달시켜 왔다고 합니다.

> 독 동물들은 미래의 위험을 예측하고 피할 수 있도록 진화되어 왔다고 합니다.

주어진 글 다음에 이어질 글의 순서로 가장 적절한 것을 고르시오.

> ① The potential for market enforcement is greater when contracting parties have developed reputational capital that can be devalued when contracts are violated.

(A)

① **<u>Similarly</u>**, a landowner can undermaintain fences, ditches, and irrigation systems.

② Accurate assessments of farmer and landowner behavior will be made over time, and those farmers and landowners who attempt to gain at each other's expense will find that others may refuse to deal with them in the future.

(B)

① Over time landowners indirectly monitor farmers by observing the reported output, the general quality of the soil, and any unusual or extreme behavior.

② Farmer and landowner reputations act as a bond.

③ In any growing season a farmer can reduce effort, overuse soil, or underreport the crop.

(C)

① Farmers and landowners develop reputations for honesty, fairness, producing high yields, and consistently demonstrating that they are good at what they do.

② In small, close-knit farming communities, reputations are well known.

* ditch: 개천 ** irrigation: 물을 댐

해설 [정답 : ⑤]

순서 삽입과 같은 유형은 지문의 접속사와 표현들에 집중해야 합니다. 우리가 지문을 보았을 때 가장 직접적인 근거이기 때문입니다. 이 문제에서는 (A)의 'Similarly'와 (B)의 'Over time'이 우리에게 직접적인 근거가 될 수 있습니다.

(A)-①번 문장에서 제시된 지주가 제대로 관리하지 않는 것에 이어서 (A)-②번 문장에서는 농부와 지주들의 행동에 대한 평가에 대해서 제시됩니다. 즉, 'Similarly'가 있는 (A)-①번 문장 앞에서는 지주의 행동과 나열이 될 수 있는 농부의 행동에 대해서 제시되어야 함을 알 수 있습니다. 이는 (B)-③번 문장에서 농부들이 재배 철에 일을 안 하거나, 토양을 과도하게 사용하거나 작물을 실제 재배한 작물보다 작게 보고할 수 있다는 내용과 일치하므로 (B)-(A)의 연결을 확정할 수 있습니다.

(B)-(A)의 연결이 확정되었으니 우리는 (B)-(A)-(C)와 (C)-(B)-(A) 중 하나를 결정해야 합니다. 즉, (C)의 내용이 주어진 지문 뒤, (B) 앞에 와야 하는지 아니면 (A) 뒤에 와야 하는지를 결정해야 합니다. (B)-①번 문장에 'Over time'을 통해 시간이 지났다고 합니다. 즉 (B)의 앞 내용에서는 농부와 지주에 대한 내용이 제시되어야 '그 이후 시간이 지나면서'라는 표현이 제시될 수 있습니다. 하지만 주어진 지문에서는 농부와 지주에 대한 내용이 제시되지 않으므로 주어진 지문 뒤에는 (B)가 올 수 없습니다. (C)에서는 농부와 지주들에 대한 내용이 제시되므로 (C)-(B)-(A)가 되어야 합니다.

* 추가적으로 (A)-②번 문장은 농부들과 지주들이 태업을 한 결과 부정적인 평판이 쌓이는 것을 제시합니다. 하지만 (C)-①번 문장은 생산량을 증가시키거나 잘하는 것을 입증하는 등 긍정적인 평판이 제시되므로 'But'과 같은 역접의 접속사 없이는 (A)-(C)의 연결은 불가능합니다. 그러므로 (C)-(B)-(A)가 됩니다.

주 ①. The potential (for market enforcement) / is / greater when contracting parties / have developed / reputational capital (that can be devalued when contracts / are violated).

구 시장 규제의 가능성은 계약 당사자들이 계약 위반 시 가치가 떨어질 수 있는 평판적인 자본을 발달시켜왔을 때 커진다고 합니다.

독 시장 규제의 가능성은 계약이 위반되었을 때 가치가 떨어질 평판적인 자본이라는 것이 크면 커진다고 합니다.

* de (감소) + value (가치) = devalue – 가치가 감소하다.

(A) ①. **Similarly**, a landowner / can undermaintain / fences, ditches, and irrigation systems.

* ditch: 개천 ** irrigation: 물을 댐

구 비슷하게, 땅주인은 울타리, 도랑, 물을 대는 시스템을 덜 유지할 수 있다고 합니다. (= 제대로 관리하지 않을 수 있다고 합니다.)

독 순서와 삽입 같은 유형에서 접속사는 상당히 중요하게 봐야합니다. 'Similarly'는 나열 접속사로 앞에 누가 무엇인가를 제대로 관리하지 않는 등의 부정적인 내용이 나와야 합니다.
- 지주들이 땅을 제대로 관리하지 않는다고 합니다.

(A) ②. Accurate assessments (of farmer and landowner behavior) / will be made (over time), and those farmers and landowners (who attempt to gain at each other's expense) will find / that others / may refuse to deal with / them (in the future).

구 농부와 지주의 행동에 대한 정확한 평가는 시간이 지남에 따라 이루어질 것이고, 상대방의 비용으로 이익을 얻으려고 한 농부와 지주들은 미래에 다른 사람들이 거래를 거부할 수도 있다는 것을 알게 된다고 합니다.

독 (A)-①번 문장에서 제시된 지주가 제대로 관리하지 않는 것에 이어서 (A)-②번 문장에서는 농부와 지주들의 행동에 대한 평가에 대해서 제시됩니다. 즉, (A)-①번 문장 앞에서는 농부의 행동에 대해서 제시되어야 함을 알 수 있습니다.

(B) ①. Over time landowners / indirectly monitor / farmers (by observing the reported output, the general quality of the soil, and any unusual or extreme behavior).

구 'by V-ing'는 'V-ing함으로써'를 의미합니다.
- 시간이 지나면서 지주들은 보고된 생산량, 토양의 전반적인 질, 어떤 평범하지 않거나 극단적인 행동을 관찰함으로써 농부들을 간접적으로 관찰한다고 합니다.

독 어떠한 시점에서 시간이 지나고 지주들이 농부들을 간접적으로 감시한다고 합니다.

(B) ②. Farmer and landowner reputations / act as / a bond.
^s ^v ^o

구▶ 농부와 지주의 평판은 결속으로써의 역할을 한다고 합니다.

독▶ 농부와 지주의 평판을 통해서 결속, 즉 주어진 지문에서 제시된 계약의 역할을 한다고 합니다.

(B) ③. (In any growing season) a farmer / can reduce / effort, overuse / soil, or underreport / the crop.

구▶ 어떤 재배 시절에 농부는 노력을 줄이거나 토양을 과하게 사용하거나 혹은 작물을 축소 보고할 수 있다고 합니다.

독▶ 농부들이 재배철에 일을 안하거나, 토양을 과도하게 사용하거나 작물을 실제 재배한 작물보다 작게 보고할 수 있다고 합니다. 이는 (A)-①번 문장에서 지주들이 땅을 제대로 관리하지 않는 것과 나열되어 (B)-(A)의 연결을 확정할 수 있습니다.

* over (넘어가는 이미지) + use (사용하다) = overuse (넘어가서 사용하다 즉, 과도하게 사용하다)

* under (아래에 있는 이미지) + report (보고하다) = underreport (아래로 보고하다 즉, 축소 보고하다)

(C) ①. Farmers and landowners / develop / reputations (for honesty, fairness), (producing high yields, and consistently demonstrating that they are good at what they do).

구▶ 농부들과 지주들은 높은 수확량을 생산하고, 자신이 하는 일을 잘한다는 것을 지속적으로 입증하면서 정직함과 공정함에 대한 평판을 발전시킨다고 합니다.

독▶ 농부들과 지주들은 높은 수확량 즉, 결과와 자신이 하는 일에 대해서 잘한다는 것을 지속적으로 입증 즉, 행동을 통해서 평판을 높인다고 합니다. (한마디로 Show and Prove)

(C) ②. In small, close-knit farming communities, reputations / are well known.

구▶ 작은, 긴밀히 맺어진 농업 사회에서, 평판들은 잘 알려진다고 합니다.

독▶ 작은 농업 사회에서는 평판들에 대해서 서로 잘 알게 된다고 합니다.

주어진 글 다음에 이어질 글의 순서로 가장 적절한 것을 고르시오.

> ① Darwin saw blushing as uniquely human, representing an involuntary physical reaction <u>caused by embarrassment and self-consciousness in a social environment</u>.

(A)
① Maybe our brief <u>loss of face benefits the long-term cohesion of the group</u>.
② Interestingly, if someone blushes after making a social mistake, they are viewed in a more favourable light than those who don't blush.

(B)
① If we feel awkward, embarrassed or ashamed <u>when we are alone, we don't blush</u>; it seems to be caused by our concern about what others are thinking of us.
② Studies have confirmed that simply being told you are blushing brings it on.
③ We feel as though <u>others can see through our skin and into our mind</u>.

(C)
① **However**, while <u>we sometimes want to disappear</u> when we involuntarily go bright red, psychologists argue that blushing actually serves a positive social purpose.
② When we blush, it's a signal to others that we recognize that a social norm has been broken; it is an <u>apology for a faux pas</u>.

* faux pas: 실수

해설 [정답 : ③]

주어진 문장에서는 'caused by embarrassment and self-consciousness in a social environment.', 얼굴이 붉어지는 것은 사회적 환경에서의 당혹감과 자의식에 의해 발생한다고 했습니다. (B)의 ①번 문장에서는 'ashamed when we are alone, we don't blush.' 우리가 혼자 있을 때에는 창피할 때도 얼굴이 붉어지지 않는다고 했는데, 이것은 주어진 문장의 사회적 환경에서 부끄러움을 느낄 때 얼굴이 붉어지는 것과 대조되는 내용으로 언급되어야 하므로 (B)는 주어진 지문 뒤에 와야 합니다.

(B)의 ③번 문장에서는 'We feel as though others can see through', 우리는 다른 사람들이 우리의 마음을 들여다볼 수 있는 것처럼 느낀다고 했습니다. (C)-①번 문장에서는 'while we sometimes want to disappear', 우리가 얼굴이 붉어질 때 사라지고 싶어 한다고 했는데, 이것은 (B)의 타인이 자신을 들여다보는 원인과, (C)의 사라지고 싶어하는 결과로 이어져야 하므로 (C)는 (B)의 뒤에 와야 합니다.

(C)의 ②번 문장에서는 'it is an apology for a faux pas', 얼굴이 붉어지는 것은 실수에 대한 사과라고 합니다. (A)-①번 문장에서는 'loss of face benefits the long-term cohesion of the group', 우리가 체면을 잃는 것이 집단의 장기적인 결속에 도움이 된다고 했습니다. 얼굴이 붉어지는 것으로 실수에 대한 사과를 하는 것은 (A)의 사회에서 장기적인 결속이라는 장점으로 이어진다는 내용으로 이어져야 하므로 (A)는 (C)의 뒤에 와야 합니다. 그러므로 정답은 (B) - (C) - (A)가 됩니다.

주 ①. Darwin / saw / blushing as uniquely human, representing an involuntary physical reaction /
caused by embarrassment and self-consciousness in a social environment.

> 구 'see A as B' - A를 B로 여기다
> - 다윈은 얼굴이 붉어지는 것을 특별나게 인간적인 것으로, 사회적 환경에서 당혹감과 자의식에 의한 무의식적인 신체 반응을 나타내는 것으로 여겼다고 합니다.

> 독 얼굴이 붉어지는 것은 인간만의 고유한 특징이며, 사회 환경에서 창피함에 의한 무의식적인 반응이라고 합니다.

(A) ①. Maybe our brief loss of face / benefits / the long-term cohesion of the group.

> 구 아마도 우리가 잠시 체면을 잃는 것이 집단의 장기적인 결속에 도움이 될 수 있을 것이라고 합니다.

> 독 자신의 창피함이 집단의 결속에 이득이 된다는 내용입니다.

(A) ②. Interestingly, if someone / blushes (after making a social mistake), they / are viewed in a more
favourable light than those / who / don't blush.

> 구 흥미롭게도 누군가가 사회적 실수를 저지른 후 얼굴을 붉히면, 우리는 그 사람을 얼굴을 붉히지 않는 사람보다 더 호의적인 시각으로 바라보게 된다고 합니다.

> 독 사회적 실수를 저지르고 얼굴을 붉히는 것은 (A)-①번 문장의 체면을 잃는 것의 예시이며, 그로 인해 얼굴을 붉히는 사람을 호의적으로 바라보게 되므로 집단 결속으로 이어진다고 볼 수 있습니다.

(B) ①. If we / feel awkward, embarrassed or ashamed when we / are / alone, we / don't blush; it /
seems / to be caused by our concern about / what / others / are thinking of us.

> 구 우리가 혼자 있을 때는 어색하거나 부끄럽거나 창피하다고 느끼더라도 얼굴이 붉어지지 않는데, 얼굴이 붉어지는 것은 우리가 다른 사람들이 우리를 어떻게 생각할지에 대해 염려하기 때문인 것으로 보인다고 합니다.

> 독 혼자 있는 것은 사회에 속한 것이 아니며, 이 경우에는 창피하더라도 얼굴이 붉어지지 않는다고 합니다. 이것은 주어진 문장의 사회적인 환경이 얼굴이 붉어지는 것의 조건임을 알 수 있습니다.

(B) ②. Studies / have confirmed / that / simply being told / you / are blushing / brings it on.

> 구 연구에 따르면 단지 얼굴이 붉어진다는 말을 듣는 것만으로도 얼굴이 붉어진다는 것이 확인되었다고 합니다.

(B) ③. We / feel / as though others can see through our skin and into our mind.

> 구 우리는 다른 사람들이 우리의 피부를 꿰뚫어 우리의 마음을 들여다볼 수 있는 것처럼 느낀다고 합니다.

> 독 다른 사람들이 마음을 들여다보는 것 역시 창피함의 감정을 유발하는 원인인데, 이 역시 얼굴이 붉어지기 위해서는 사회적 환경에 존재해야 한다는 것을 보여줍니다.

(C) ①. **However**, while we / sometimes want / to disappear when / we / involuntarily go bright red, psychologists / argue / that / blushing / actually serves / a positive social purpose.

구▶ 그러나 우리가 때로 자신도 모르는 사이에 얼굴이 새빨개질 때 사라지고 싶어 하지만, 심리학자들은 얼굴이 붉어지는 것이 실제로는 긍정적인 사회적 목적에 부합한다고 주장한다고 합니다.

독▶ 'however'가 제시되었으므로 중심 문장
- 얼굴이 붉어지는 것이 오히려 긍정적인 사회적 목적과 맞는다는 내용으로 전환됩니다.

(C) ②. When we / blush, it's / a signal / to others that / we / recognize / that / a social norm / has been broken; it / is / an apology for a faux pas.

* faux pas: 실수

구▶ 얼굴이 붉어질 때, 그것은 사회적 규범을 어겼다는 것을 우리가 인정한다는 것을 다른 사람에게 알리는 신호이자 실수에 대한 사과라고 합니다.

독▶ (C)-①번 문장의 원인이 되는 문장입니다. 다른 사람에게 잘못에 대한 인정과 사과를 얼굴이 붉어지는 것으로 대신하므로 사회에서 오히려 긍정적인 인상을 갖게 해준다는 것을 알 수 있습니다.

주어진 글 다음에 이어질 글의 순서로 가장 적절한 것을 고르시오.

> ① Norms emerge in groups as a result of people conforming to the behavior of others.
>
> ② **Thus**, the start of a norm occurs when one person acts in a particular manner in a particular situation **because** she thinks she ought to.

(A)

① **Thus, she may prescribe the behavior to them** by uttering the norm statement in a prescriptive manner.

② Alternately, she may communicate that conformity is desired in other ways, such as by gesturing.

③ In addition, she may threaten to sanction them for not behaving as she wishes.

④ This will cause some to conform to her wishes and act as she acts.

(B)

① **But some others will not need to have the behavior prescribed to them.**

② They will observe the regularity of behavior and decide on their own that they ought to conform.

③ They may do so for either rational or moral reasons.

(C)

① Others may then conform to **this behavior** for a number of reasons.

② **The person who performed the initial action** may think that **others ought to behave as she behaves** in situations of this sort.

* sanction: 제재를 가하다

해설 [정답 : ④]

주어진 지문에서는 'start of a norm occurs when one person acts in a particular manner in a particular situation', 규범의 시작은 한 사람이 특정 상황에서 자신이 그래야 한다고 생각하여 특정 방식으로 행동할 때 발생한다고 합니다.

(C)-①번 문장에서는 'Others may then conform to this behavior for a number of reasons', 그 다음 다른 사람들은 여러 가지 이유로 이 행동에 순응할 수도 있다고 하는데, 한 사람이 특정 방식으로 시작한다는 주어진 지문 뒤에, 그에 관한 결과 다른 사람들이 이 행동에 순응하는 과정으로 전개되고, (C)-①번 문장의 'this behavior'은 주어진 지문 ②번 문장의 한 사람이 특정 방식으로 행동하는 것을 지칭하므로 (C)는 주어진 지문 뒤에 와야 합니다.

또한 (C)-②번 문장의 'person who performed the initial action' 최초의 행동을 한 사람 역시 주어진 지문의 사람을 지칭하므로 더더욱 (C)가 주어진 지문 뒤에 위치하는 근거가 됩니다.

(C)-②번 문장에서는 'person who performed the initial action may think that others ought to behave as she behaves', 최초의 행동을 한 사람은 다른 사람들이 자신이 행동하는 것처럼 행동해야 한다고 생각할 수도 있다고 했습니다.

다음 (A)-①번 문장에서는 'Thus, she may prescribe the behavior to them by uttering the norm statement', 따라서 그 사람은 지시하는 방식으로 규범 진술을 말함으로써 그들에게 행동을 지시한다고 했는데, 이것은 (C)의 최초의 사람의 생각에 대한 결과를 진술하며, 최초의 사람을 지칭하는 대명사도 일치하므로 (A)는 (C) 뒤에 와야 합니다.

(A)-④번 문장에서는 'This will cause some to conform to her wishes and act as she acts', 제재의 위협을 통해 일부 사람들이 그 사람(최초의 행동자)의 바람에 순응한다고 했습니다. (B)-①번 문장에서는 'But some others will not need to have the behavior prescribed to them.', 그러나 다른 일부 사람들은 그 행동이 지시되게 할 필요가 없다고 했습니다. 이것은 최초의 행동을 순응하게 하는 (A)의 내용으로부터 순응할 필요가 없다는 (B)의 내용으로 전환됩니다. 또한 (B)-①번 문장의 'some others', 스스로 결정하는 사람들은 (A)-④번 문장의 'some', 순응하는 사람들과 대조되는 내용이므로 (B)는 (A) 뒤에 와야 합니다. 그러므로 정답은 (C)-(A)-(B)가 됩니다.

* 처음 행동을 한 사람을 she, 그 행동을 따라 하는 사람들을 'they'로 잡고 특징을 정리한다면 순응하는 과정을 수월하게 정리할 수 있을 것입니다.

주 ①. Norms / emerge in groups (as a result of people conforming (to the behavior of others)).

> 규범은 사람들이 다른 사람들의 행동에 순응하는 결과로 집단에서 생겨난다고 합니다.

> 규범의 조건으로 타인의 행동에 대한 순응, 집단에서 발생하는 점이 언급됩니다.

주 ②. **Thus**, the start (of a norm) / occurs / when / one person / acts in a particular manner in a particular situation **because** / she / thinks / she / ought to.

> 따라서 규범의 시작은 한 사람이 특정 상황에서 자신이 그래야 한다고 생각하여 특정 방식으로 행동할 때 발생한다고 합니다.

> 'thus', 'because'가 제시되었으므로 중심 문장
> - 규범이 시작하는 조건에 대한 문장이며, 한 명의 사람이 특정한 방식으로 행동하는 것이 그 특징이 됩니다.

(A) ①. **Thus**, she / may prescribe / the behavior to them by uttering the norm statement (in a prescriptive manner).

> by V-ing - V함으로써
> - 따라서 그 사람은 지시하는 방식으로 규범 진술을 말함으로써 그들에게 행동을 지시할 수도 있다고 합니다.

> 'thus'가 제시되었으므로 중심 문장
> - 타인이 특정 방식으로 행동하는 것이 아닌, 타인의 행동을 지시하는 사람에 대한 설명이 언급됩니다.

(A) ②. Alternately, she may communicate that conformity is desired in other ways, such as by gesturing.

> 다른 방식으로는 몸짓과 같은 것으로 순응이 요망된다는 것을 전달할 수도 있다고 합니다.

> 그러한 타인의 순응을 몸짓과 같은 신호로 암시를 주는 내용이 언급됩니다.

(A) ③. In addition, she / may threaten to sanction them for not behaving as she / wishes.

* sanction: 제재를 가하다

> 게다가 자신이 원하는 대로 행동하지 않으면 그들에게 제재를 가하겠다고 위협할 수도 있다고 합니다.

> 타인이 자신에게 순응하지 않는 경우에 취할 수 있는 하는 행동을 설명하고 있습니다.

(A) ④. This / will cause / some to conform to her wishes and act as she acts.
_S _V _A _{to-V (1)} _{to-V (2)}

구▶ 이렇게 하면 일부 사람들은 그 사람의 바람에 순응하고 그 사람이 행동하는 대로 행동할 것이라고 합니다.

독▶ (A)-①~③번 내용을 종합하여 타인이 자신에게 순응하도록 유도하는 조건을 정리합니다.
(A)-①: 규범을 지시하는 방식으로 언급한다
(A)-②: 몸짓을 사용하여 규범을 전달한다
(A)-③: 순응하지 않을 경우 제재를 가하겠다고 위협한다

(B) ①. **But** some others / will not need to have the behavior prescribed to them.
_S _V _O

구▶ 그러나 다른 일부 사람들에게는 그 행동이 자신에게 지시되게 할 필요가 없을 것이라고 합니다.

독▶ 'but'이 제시되었으므로 중심 문장
- (A)가 타인을 자신에게 따르도록 하는 상황이었다면, (B)에서는 따르도록 설정할 필요가 없는 사람들의 관한 설명으로 내용이 전환됩니다.

(B) ②. They / will observe / the regularity of behavior / and decide (on their own) / that / they ought
_S _{V-1} _O _{V-2} _{명사절} _S _V
to conform.

구▶ 그들은 행동의 규칙성을 관찰하고 자신이 순응해야 할 것을 스스로 결정할 것이라고 합니다.

독▶ 자신을 따를 필요가 없는 사람들의 조건에 대해서 설명하고 있습니다.

(B) ③. They / may do so (for either rational or moral reasons).
_S _V

구▶ 그들은 이성적 또는 도덕적 이유로 그렇게 할 수도 있다고 합니다.

독▶ 또 다른 원인으로 이성적, 도덕적 이유가 언급됩니다.

(C) ①. Others / may then conform to this behavior (for a number of reasons).
_S _V

구▶ 그런 다음 다른 사람들은 여러 가지 이유로 이 행동에 순응할 수도 있다고 합니다.

독▶ 주어진 문장이 규범, 맨 처음 일어난 행동에 관한 내용이었다면, (C)는 그 행동에 순응하는 타인들에 관한 설명이 언급됩니다.

(C) ②. The person (who / performed / the initial action) may think / that / others / ought to behave as
_S _{관대} _V _O _V _{명사절} _S _V
she / behaves in situations of this sort.
_S _V

구▶ 최초의 행동을 한 사람은 다른 사람들이 이런 종류의 상황에서 자신이 행동하는 것처럼 행동해야 한다고 생각할 수도 있다고 합니다.

독▶ 최초의 행동을 한 사람이 타인을 자신에게 순응시키려는 원인이 언급되는 문장입니다.

절. 모. 평. (절대평가 모든 평가원 기출)

01 22학년도 수능 36번

[정답과 해설 130page]

주어진 글 다음에 이어질 글의 순서로 가장 적절한 것을 고르시오.

According to the market response model, it is increasing prices that drive providers to search for new sources, innovators to substitute, consumers to conserve, and alternatives to emerge.

(A) Many examples of such "green taxes" exist. Facing landfill costs, labor expenses, and related costs in the provision of garbage disposal, for example, some cities have required households to dispose of all waste in special trash bags, purchased by consumers themselves, and often costing a dollar or more each.

(B) Taxing certain goods or services, and so increasing prices, should result in either decreased use of these resources or creative innovation of new sources or options. The money raised through the tax can be used directly by the government either to supply services or to search for alternatives.

(C) The results have been greatly increased recycling and more careful attention by consumers to packaging and waste. By internalizing the costs of trash to consumers, there has been an observed decrease in the flow of garbage from households.

① (A) − (C) − (B)　　② (B) − (A) − (C)　　③ (B) − (C) − (A)
④ (C) − (A) − (B)　　⑤ (C) − (B) − (A)

02 21학년도 수능 36번

[정답과 해설 133page]

주어진 글 다음에 이어질 글의 순서로 가장 적절한 것을 고르시오.

The objective of battle, to "throw" the enemy and to make him defenseless, may temporarily blind commanders and even strategists to the larger purpose of war. War is never an isolated act, nor is it ever only one decision.

(A) To be political, a political entity or a representative of a political entity, whatever its constitutional form, has to have an intention, a will. That intention has to be clearly expressed.

(B) In the real world, war's larger purpose is always a political purpose. It transcends the use of force. This insight was famously captured by Clausewitz's most famous phrase, "War is a mere continuation of politics by other means."

(C) And one side's will has to be transmitted to the enemy at some point during the confrontation (it does not have to be publicly communicated). A violent act and its larger political intention must also be attributed to one side at some point during the confrontation. History does not know of acts of war without eventual attribution.

* entity: 실체 ** transcend: 초월하다

① (A) − (C) − (B)　　② (B) − (A) − (C)　　③ (B) − (C) − (A)
④ (C) − (A) − (B)　　⑤ (C) − (B) − (A)

주어진 글 다음에 이어질 글의 순서로 가장 적절한 것을 고르시오.

> In spite of the likeness between the fictional and real world, the fictional world deviates from the real one in one important respect.

(A) The author has selected the content according to his own worldview and his own conception of relevance, in an attempt to be neutral and objective or convey a subjective view on the world. Whatever the motives, the author's subjective conception of the world stands between the reader and the original, untouched world on which the story is based.

(B) Because of the inner qualities with which the individual is endowed through heritage and environment, the mind functions as a filter; every outside impression that passes through it is filtered and interpreted. However, the world the reader encounters in literature is already processed and filtered by another consciousness.

(C) The existing world faced by the individual is in principle an infinite chaos of events and details before it is organized by a human mind. This chaos only gets processed and modified when perceived by a human mind.

* deviate: 벗어나다 ** endow: 부여하다 *** heritage: 유산

① (A) − (C) − (B) ② (B) − (A) − (C) ③ (B) − (C) − (A)
④ (C) − (A) − (B) ⑤ (C) − (B) − (A)

주어진 글 다음에 이어질 글의 순서로 가장 적절한 것을 고르시오.

> When two natural bodies of water stand at different levels, building a canal between them presents a complicated engineering problem.

(A) Then the upper gates open and the ship passes through. For downstream passage, the process works the opposite way. The ship enters the lock from the upper level, and water is pumped from the lock until the ship is in line with the lower level.

(B) When a vessel is going upstream, the upper gates stay closed as the ship enters the lock at the lower water level. The downstream gates are then closed and more water is pumped into the basin. The rising water lifts the vessel to the level of the upper body of water.

(C) To make up for the difference in level, engineers build one or more water "steps," called locks, that carry ships or boats up or down between the two levels. A lock is an artificial water basin. It has a long rectangular shape with concrete walls and a pair of gates at each end.

* rectangular: 직사각형의

① (A) − (C) − (B) ② (B) − (A) − (C) ③ (B) − (C) − (A)
④ (C) − (A) − (B) ⑤ (C) − (B) − (A)

[정답과 해설 142page]

주어진 글 다음에 이어질 글의 순서로 가장 적절한 것을 고르시오.

> Studies of people struggling with major health problems show that the majority of respondents report they derived benefits from their adversity. Stressful events sometimes force people to develop new skills, reevaluate priorities, learn new insights, and acquire new strengths.

(A) High levels of adversity predicted poor mental health, as expected, but people who had faced intermediate levels of adversity were healthier than those who experienced little adversity, suggesting that moderate amounts of stress can foster resilience. A follow-up study found a similar link between the amount of lifetime adversity and subjects' responses to laboratory stressors.

(B) Intermediate levels of adversity were predictive of the greatest resilience. Thus, having to deal with a moderate amount of stress may build resilience in the face of future stress.

(C) In other words, the adaptation process initiated by stress can lead to personal changes for the better. One study that measured participants' exposure to thirty-seven major negative events found a curvilinear relationship between lifetime adversity and mental health.

* resilience: 회복력

① (A) – (C) – (B)　　　② (B) – (A) – (C)　　　③ (B) – (C) – (A)
④ (C) – (A) – (B)　　　⑤ (C) – (B) – (A)

[정답과 해설 145page]

주어진 글 다음에 이어질 글의 순서로 가장 적절한 것을 고르시오.

> The growing complexity of computer software has direct implications for our global safety and security, particularly as the physical objects upon which we depend — things like cars, airplanes, bridges, tunnels, and implantable medical devices — transform themselves into computer code.

(A) As all this code grows in size and complexity, so too do the number of errors and software bugs. According to a study by Carnegie Mellon University, commercial software typically has twenty to thirty bugs for every thousand lines of code — 50 million lines of code means 1 million to 1.5 million potential errors to be exploited.

(B) This is the basis for all malware attacks that take advantage of these computer bugs to get the code to do something it was not originally intended to do. As computer code grows more elaborate, software bugs flourish and security suffers, with increasing consequences for society at large.

(C) Physical things are increasingly becoming information technologies. Cars are "computers we ride in," and airplanes are nothing more than "flying Solaris boxes attached to bucketfuls of industrial control systems."

* exploit: 활용하다

① (A) – (C) – (B)　　　② (B) – (A) – (C)　　　③ (B) – (C) – (A)
④ (C) – (A) – (B)　　　⑤ (C) – (B) – (A)

주어진 글 다음에 이어질 글의 순서로 가장 적절한 것을 고르시오.

> A fascinating species of water flea exhibits a kind of flexibility that evolutionary biologists call adaptive plasticity.

(A) That's a clever trick, because producing spines and a helmet is costly, in terms of energy, and conserving energy is essential for an organism's ability to survive and reproduce. The water flea only expends the energy needed to produce spines and a helmet when it needs to.

(B) If the baby water flea is developing into an adult in water that includes the chemical signatures of creatures that prey on water fleas, it develops a helmet and spines to defend itself against predators. If the water around it doesn't include the chemical signatures of predators, the water flea doesn't develop these protective devices.

(C) So it may well be that this plasticity is an adaptation: a trait that came to exist in a species because it contributed to reproductive fitness. There are many cases, across many species, of adaptive plasticity. Plasticity is conducive to fitness if there is sufficient variation in the environment.

* spine: 가시 돌기 ** conducive: 도움되는

① (A) − (C) − (B) ② (B) − (A) − (C) ③ (B) − (C) − (A)
④ (C) − (A) − (B) ⑤ (C) − (B) − (A)

주어진 글 다음에 이어질 글의 순서로 가장 적절한 것을 고르시오.

> Culture operates in ways we can consciously consider and discuss but also in ways of which we are far less cognizant.

(A) In some cases, however, we are far less aware of why we believe a certain claim to be true, or how we are to explain why certain social realities exist. Ideas about the social world become part of our worldview without our necessarily being aware of the source of the particular idea or that we even hold the idea at all.

(B) When we have to offer an account of our actions, we consciously understand which excuses might prove acceptable, given the particular circumstances we find ourselves in. In such situations, we use cultural ideas as we would use a particular tool.

(C) We select the cultural notion as we would select a screwdriver: certain jobs call for a Phillips head while others require an Allen wrench. Whichever idea we insert into the conversation to justify our actions, the point is that our motives are discursively available to us. They are not hidden.

* cognizant: 인식하는 ** discursively: 만연하게

① (A) − (C) − (B) ② (B) − (A) − (C) ③ (B) − (C) − (A)
④ (C) − (A) − (B) ⑤ (C) − (B) − (A)

09 24학년도 9월 평가원 36번　　　　　　　　　　　　　　[정답과 해설 154page]

주어진 글 다음에 이어질 글의 순서로 가장 적절한 것을 고르시오.

> The intuitive ability to classify and generalize is undoubtedly a useful feature of life and research, but it carries a high cost, such as in our tendency to stereotype generalizations about people and situations.

(A) Intuitively and quickly, we mentally sort things into groups based on what we perceive the differences between them to be, and that is the basis for stereotyping. Only afterwards do we examine (or not examine) more evidence of how things are differentiated, and the degree and significance of the variations.

(B) Our brain performs these tasks efficiently and automatically, usually without our awareness. The real danger of stereotypes is not their inaccuracy, but their lack of flexibility and their tendency to be preserved, even when we have enough time to stop and consider.

(C) For most people, the word stereotype arouses negative connotations: it implies a negative bias. But, in fact, stereotypes do not differ in principle from all other generalizations; generalizations about groups of people are not necessarily always negative.

* intuitive: 직관적인 ** connotation: 함축

① (A) − (C) − (B)　　　② (B) − (A) − (C)　　　③ (B) − (C) − (A)
④ (C) − (A) − (B)　　　⑤ (C) − (B) − (A)

10 23학년도 6월 평가원 36번　　　　　　　　　　　　　　[정답과 해설 157page]

주어진 글 다음에 이어질 글의 순서로 가장 적절한 것을 고르시오.

> The fossil record provides evidence of evolution. The story the fossils tell is one of change. Creatures existed in the past that are no longer with us. Sequential changes are found in many fossils showing the change of certain features over time from a common ancestor, as in the case of the horse.

(A) If multicelled organisms were indeed found to have evolved before single-celled organisms, then the theory of evolution would be rejected. A good scientific theory always allows for the possibility of rejection. The fact that we have not found such a case in countless examinations of the fossil record strengthens the case for evolutionary theory.

(B) The fossil record supports this prediction — multicelled organisms are found in layers of earth millions of years after the first appearance of single-celled organisms. Note that the possibility always remains that the opposite could be found.

(C) Apart from demonstrating that evolution did occur, the fossil record also provides tests of the predictions made from evolutionary theory. For example, the theory predicts that single-celled organisms evolved before multicelled organisms.

① (A) − (C) − (B)　　　② (B) − (A) − (C)　　　③ (B) − (C) − (A)
④ (C) − (A) − (B)　　　⑤ (C) − (B) − (A)

주어진 글 다음에 이어질 글의 순서로 가장 적절한 것을 고르시오.

> In the fifth century B.C.E., the Greek philosopher Protagoras pronounced, "Man is the measure of all things." In other words, we feel entitled to ask the world, "What good are you?"

(A) Abilities said to "make us human" — empathy, communication, grief, toolmaking, and so on — all exist to varying degrees among other minds sharing the world with us. Animals with backbones (fishes, amphibians, reptiles, birds, and mammals) all share the same basic skeleton, organs, nervous systems, hormones, and behaviors.

(B) We assume that we are the world's standard, that all things should be compared to us. Such an assumption makes us overlook a lot.

(C) Just as different models of automobiles each have an engine, drive train, four wheels, doors, and seats, we differ mainly in terms of our outside contours and a few internal tweaks. But like naive car buyers, most people see only animals' varied exteriors.

* contour: 윤곽, 외형 ** tweak: 조정, 개조

① (A) − (C) − (B)   ② (B) − (A) − (C)   ③ (B) − (C) − (A)
④ (C) − (A) − (B)   ⑤ (C) − (B) − (A)

주어진 글 다음에 이어질 글의 순서로 가장 적절한 것을 고르시오.

> It can be difficult to decide the place of fine art, such as oil paintings, watercolours, sketches or sculptures, in an archival institution.

(A) The best archival decisions about art do not focus on territoriality (this object belongs in my institution even though I do not have the resources to care for it) or on questions of monetary value or prestige (this object raises the cultural standing of my institution). The best decisions focus on what evidential value exists and what is best for the item.

(B) But art can also carry aesthetic value, which elevates the job of evaluation into another realm. Aesthetic value and the notion of artistic beauty are important considerations, but they are not what motivates archival preservation in the first instance.

(C) Art can serve as documentary evidence, especially when the items were produced before photography became common. Sketches of soldiers on a battlefield, paintings of English country villages or portraits of Dutch townspeople can provide the only visual evidence of a long-ago place, person or time.

* archival: 기록(보관소)의 ** prestige: 명성, 위신 *** realm: 영역

① (A) − (C) − (B)   ② (B) − (A) − (C)   ③ (B) − (C) − (A)
④ (C) − (A) − (B)   ⑤ (C) − (B) − (A)

13 23학년도 6월 평가원 37번   [정답과 해설 166page]

주어진 글 다음에 이어질 글의 순서로 가장 적절한 것을 고르시오.

> In economics, there is a principle known as the *sunk cost fallacy*. The idea is that when you are invested and have ownership in something, you overvalue that thing.

(A) Sometimes, the smartest thing a person can do is quit. Although this is true, it has also become a tired and played-out argument. Sunk cost doesn't always have to be a bad thing.

(B) This leads people to continue on paths or pursuits that should clearly be abandoned. For example, people often remain in terrible relationships simply because they've invested a great deal of themselves into them. Or someone may continue pouring money into a business that is clearly a bad idea in the market.

(C) Actually, you can leverage this human tendency to your benefit. Like someone invests a great deal of money in a personal trainer to ensure they follow through on their commitment, you, too, can invest a great deal up front to ensure you stay on the path you want to be on.

         * leverage: 이용하다

① (A) − (C) − (B)   ② (B) − (A) − (C)   ③ (B) − (C) − (A)
④ (C) − (A) − (B)   ⑤ (C) − (B) − (A)

14 25학년도 9월 평가원 36번   [정답과 해설 169page]

주어진 글 다음에 이어질 글의 순서로 가장 적절한 것을 고르시오.

> If learning were simply a matter of accumulating lists of facts, then it shouldn't make any difference if we are presented with information that is just a little bit beyond what we already know or totally new information.

(A) If we are trying to understand something totally new, however, we need to make larger adjustments to the units of the patterns we already have, which requires changing the strengths of large numbers of connections in our brain, and this is a difficult, tiring process.

(B) The adjustments are clearly smallest when the new information is only slightly new — when it is compatible with what we already know, so that the old patterns need only a little bit of adjustment to accommodate the new knowledge.

(C) Each fact would simply be stored separately. According to connectionist theory, however, our knowledge is organized into patterns of activity, and each time we learn something new we have to modify the old patterns so as to keep the old material while adding the new information.

         * compatible: 양립하는

① (A) − (C) − (B)   ② (B) − (A) − (C)   ③ (B) − (C) − (A)
④ (C) − (A) − (B)   ⑤ (C) − (B) − (A)

주어진 글 다음에 이어질 글의 순서로 가장 적절한 것을 고르시오.

> Plants show finely tuned adaptive responses when nutrients are limiting. Gardeners may recognize yellow leaves as a sign of poor nutrition and the need for fertilizer.

(A) In contrast, plants with a history of nutrient abundance are risk averse and save energy. At all developmental stages, plants respond to environmental changes or unevenness so as to be able to use their energy for growth, survival, and reproduction, while limiting damage and nonproductive uses of their valuable energy.

(B) Research in this area has shown that plants are constantly aware of their position in the environment, in terms of both space and time. Plants that have experienced variable nutrient availability in the past tend to exhibit risk-taking behaviors, such as spending energy on root lengthening instead of leaf production.

(C) But if a plant does not have a caretaker to provide supplemental minerals, it can proliferate or lengthen its roots and develop root hairs to allow foraging in more distant soil patches. Plants can also use their memory to respond to histories of temporal or spatial variation in nutrient or resource availability.

* nutrient: 영양소 ** fertilizer: 비료 *** forage: 구하러 다니다

① (A) - (C) - (B) ② (B) - (A) - (C) ③ (B) - (C) - (A)
④ (C) - (A) - (B) ⑤ (C) - (B) - (A)

주어진 글 다음에 이어질 글의 순서로 가장 적절한 것을 고르시오.

> Recently, a number of commercial ventures have been launched that offer social robots as personal home assistants, perhaps eventually to rival existing smart-home assistants.

(A) They might be motorized and can track the user around the room, giving the impression of being aware of the people in the environment. Although personal robotic assistants provide services similar to those of smart-home assistants, their social presence offers an opportunity that is unique to social robots.

(B) Personal robotic assistants are devices that have no physical manipulation or locomotion capabilities. Instead, they have a distinct social presence and have visual features suggestive of their ability to interact socially, such as eyes, ears, or a mouth.

(C) For instance, in addition to playing music, a social personal assistant robot would express its engagement with the music so that users would feel like they are listening to the music together with the robot. These robots can be used as surveillance devices, act as communicative intermediates, engage in richer games, tell stories, or be used to provide encouragement or incentives.

* locomotion: 이동 ** surveillance: 감시

① (A) - (C) - (B) ② (B) - (A) - (C) ③ (B) - (C) - (A)
④ (C) - (A) - (B) ⑤ (C) - (B) - (A)

주어진 글 다음에 이어질 글의 순서로 가장 적절한 것을 고르시오.

> Experts have identified a large number of measures that promote energy efficiency. Unfortunately many of them are not cost effective. This is a fundamental requirement for energy efficiency investment from an economic perspective.

(A) And this has direct repercussions at the individual level: households can reduce the cost of electricity and gas bills, and improve their health and comfort, while companies can increase their competitiveness and their productivity. Finally, the market for energy efficiency could contribute to the economy through job and firms creation.

(B) There are significant externalities to take into account and there are also macroeconomic effects. For instance, at the aggregate level, improving the level of national energy efficiency has positive effects on macroeconomic issues such as energy dependence, climate change, health, national competitiveness and reducing fuel poverty.

(C) However, the calculation of such cost effectiveness is not easy: it is not simply a case of looking at private costs and comparing them to the reductions achieved.

* repercussion: 반향, 영향 ** aggregate: 집합의

① (A) - (C) - (B)　　② (B) - (A) - (C)　　③ (B) - (C) - (A)
④ (C) - (A) - (B)　　⑤ (C) - (B) - (A)

주어진 글 다음에 이어질 글의 순서로 가장 적절한 것을 고르시오.

> Negotiation can be defined as an attempt to explore and reconcile conflicting positions in order to reach an acceptable outcome.

(A) Areas of difference can and do frequently remain, and will perhaps be the subject of future negotiations, or indeed remain irreconcilable. In those instances in which the parties have highly antagonistic or polarised relations, the process is likely to be dominated by the exposition, very often in public, of the areas of conflict.

(B) In these and sometimes other forms of negotiation, negotiation serves functions other than reconciling conflicting interests. These will include delay, publicity, diverting attention or seeking intelligence about the other party and its negotiating position.

(C) Whatever the nature of the outcome, which may actually favour one party more than another, the purpose of negotiation is the identification of areas of common interest and conflict. In this sense, depending on the intentions of the parties, the areas of common interest may be clarified, refined and given negotiated form and substance.

* reconcile: 화해시키다 ** antagonistic: 적대적인 *** exposition: 설명

① (A) - (C) - (B)　　② (B) - (A) - (C)　　③ (B) - (C) - (A)
④ (C) - (A) - (B)　　⑤ (C) - (B) - (A)

주어진 글 다음에 이어질 글의 순서로 가장 적절한 것을 고르시오.

> A firm is deciding whether to invest in shipbuilding. If it can produce at sufficiently large scale, it knows the venture will be profitable.

(A) There is a "good" outcome, in which both types of investments are made, and both the shipyard and the steelmakers end up profitable and happy. Equilibrium is reached. Then there is a "bad" outcome, in which neither type of investment is made. This second outcome also is an equilibrium because the decisions not to invest reinforce each other.

(B) Assume that shipyards are the only potential customers of steel. Steel producers figure they'll make money if there's a shipyard to buy their steel, but not otherwise. Now we have two possible outcomes — what economists call "multiple equilibria."

(C) But one key input is low-cost steel, and it must be produced nearby. The company's decision boils down to this: if there is a steel factory close by, invest in shipbuilding; otherwise, don't invest. Now consider the thinking of potential steel investors in the region.

* equilibrium: 균형

① (A) − (C) − (B)　　② (B) − (A) − (C)　　③ (B) − (C) − (A)
④ (C) − (A) − (B)　　⑤ (C) − (B) − (A)

주어진 글 다음에 이어질 글의 순서로 가장 적절한 것을 고르시오.

> The fruit ripening process brings about the softening of cell walls, sweetening and the production of chemicals that give colour and flavour. The process is induced by the production of a plant hormone called ethylene.

(A) If ripening could be slowed down by interfering with ethylene production or with the processes that respond to ethylene, fruit could be left on the plant until it was ripe and full of flavour but would still be in good condition when it arrived at the supermarket shelf.

(B) In some countries they are then sprayed with ethylene before sale to the consumer to induce ripening. However, fruit picked before it is ripe has less flavour than fruit picked ripe from the plant. Biotechnologists therefore saw an opportunity in delaying the ripening and softening process in fruit.

(C) The problem for growers and retailers is that ripening is followed sometimes quite rapidly by deterioration and decay and the product becomes worthless. Tomatoes and other fruits are, therefore, usually picked and transported when they are unripe.

* deterioration: (품질의) 저하

① (A) − (C) − (B)　　② (B) − (A) − (C)　　③ (B) − (C) − (A)
④ (C) − (A) − (B)　　⑤ (C) − (B) − (A)

주어진 글 다음에 이어질 글의 순서로 가장 적절한 것을 고르시오.

> Green products involve, in many cases, higher ingredient costs than those of mainstream products.

(A) They'd rather put money and time into known, profitable, high-volume products that serve populous customer segments than into risky, less-profitable, low-volume products that may serve current noncustomers. Given that choice, these companies may choose to leave the green segment of the market to small niche competitors.

(B) Even if the green product succeeds, it may cannibalize the company's higher-profit mainstream offerings. Given such downsides, companies serving mainstream consumers with successful mainstream products face what seems like an obvious investment decision.

(C) Furthermore, the restrictive ingredient lists and design criteria that are typical of such products may make green products inferior to mainstream products on core performance dimensions (e.g., less effective cleansers). In turn, the higher costs and lower performance of some products attract only a small portion of the customer base, leading to lower economies of scale in procurement, manufacturing, and distribution.

* segment: 조각 ** cannibalize: 잡아먹다 *** procurement: 조달

① (A) - (C) - (B)　　　② (B) - (A) - (C)　　　③ (B) - (C) - (A)
④ (C) - (A) - (B)　　　⑤ (C) - (B) - (A)

주어진 글 다음에 이어질 글의 순서로 가장 적절한 것을 고르시오.

> Watch the birds in your backyard. If one bird startles and flies off, others will follow, not waiting around to assess whether the threat is real. They have been infected by emotional contagion.

(A) Marc wondered whether the birds in line were more fearful because they didn't know what their flockmates were doing. Emotional contagion would have been impossible for individual grosbeaks in the linear array except with their nearest neighbors.

(B) In a long-term research project that Marc did with some of his students on patterns of antipredatory scanning by western evening grosbeaks, they found that birds in a circle showed more coordination in scanning than did birds who were feeding in a line.

(C) The birds in a line, who could only see their nearest neighbor, not only were less coordinated when scanning, but also were more nervous, changing their body and head positions significantly more than grosbeaks in a circle, where it was possible for each grosbeak to see every other grosbeak.

* grosbeak: 콩새류(類) ** array: 정렬

① (A) - (C) - (B)　　　② (B) - (A) - (C)　　　③ (B) - (C) - (A)
④ (C) - (A) - (B)　　　⑤ (C) - (B) - (A)

23 23학년도 수능 37번

[정답과 해설 196page]

주어진 글 다음에 이어질 글의 순서로 가장 적절한 것을 고르시오.

> The most commonly known form of results-based pricing is a practice called *contingency pricing*, used by lawyers.

(A) Therefore, only an outcome in the client's favor is compensated. From the client's point of view, the pricing makes sense in part because most clients in these cases are unfamiliar with and possibly intimidated by law firms. Their biggest fears are high fees for a case that may take years to settle.

(B) By using contingency pricing, clients are ensured that they pay no fees until they receive a settlement. In these and other instances of contingency pricing, the economic value of the service is hard to determine before the service, and providers develop a price that allows them to share the risks and rewards of delivering value to the buyer.

(C) Contingency pricing is the major way that personal injury and certain consumer cases are billed. In this approach, lawyers do not receive fees or payment until the case is settled, when they are paid a percentage of the money that the client receives.

* intimidate: 위협하다

① (A) - (C) - (B) ② (B) - (A) - (C) ③ (B) - (C) - (A)
④ (C) - (A) - (B) ⑤ (C) - (B) - (A)

24 22학년도 6월 평가원 36번

[정답과 해설 199page]

주어진 글 다음에 이어질 글의 순서로 가장 적절한 것을 고르시오.

> Spatial reference points are larger than themselves. This isn't really a paradox: landmarks are themselves, but they also define neighborhoods around themselves.

(A) In a paradigm that has been repeated on many campuses, researchers first collect a list of campus landmarks from students. Then they ask another group of students to estimate the distances between pairs of locations, some to landmarks, some to ordinary buildings on campus.

(B) This asymmetry of distance estimates violates the most elementary principles of Euclidean distance, that the distance from A to B must be the same as the distance from B to A. Judgments of distance, then, are not necessarily coherent.

(C) The remarkable finding is that distances from an ordinary location to a landmark are judged shorter than distances from a landmark to an ordinary location. So, people would judge the distance from Pierre's house to the Eiffel Tower to be shorter than the distance from the Eiffel Tower to Pierre's house. Like black holes, landmarks seem to pull ordinary locations toward themselves, but ordinary places do not.

* asymmetry: 비대칭

① (A) - (C) - (B) ② (B) - (A) - (C) ③ (B) - (C) - (A)
④ (C) - (A) - (B) ⑤ (C) - (B) - (A)

주어진 글 다음에 이어질 글의 순서로 가장 적절한 것을 고르시오.

> There are a number of human resource management practices that are necessary to support organizational learning.

(A) Their role should be to assist, consult, and advise teams on how best to approach learning. They must be able to develop new mechanisms for cross-training peers — team members — and new systems for capturing and sharing information. To do this, human resource development professionals must be able to think systematically and understand how to promote learning within groups and across the organization.

(B) For example, performance evaluation and reward systems that reinforce long-term performance and the development and sharing of new skills and knowledge are particularly important. In addition, the human resource development function may be dramatically changed to keep the emphasis on continuous learning.

(C) In a learning organization, every employee must take the responsibility for acquiring and transferring knowledge. Formal training programs, developed in advance and delivered according to a preset schedule, are insufficient to address shifting training needs and encourage timely information sharing. Rather, human resource development professionals must become learning facilitators.

① (A) － (C) － (B)　　　　② (B) － (A) － (C)　　　　③ (B) － (C) － (A)
④ (C) － (A) － (B)　　　　⑤ (C) － (B) － (A)

주어진 글 다음에 이어질 글의 순서로 가장 적절한 것을 고르시오.

> Wildfire is a natural phenomenon in many Australian environments. The intentional setting of fire to manage the landscape was practised by Aboriginal people for millennia.

(A) However, the pattern of burning that stockmen introduced was unlike previous regimes. When conditions allowed, they would set fire to the landscape as they moved their animals out for the winter. This functioned to clear woody vegetation and also stimulated new plant growth in the following spring.

(B) Although grasses were the first kinds of plants to recolonize the burnt areas they were soon succeeded by further woody plants and shrubs. About the only strategy to prevent such regrowth was further burning — essentially using fire to control the consequences of using fire.

(C) The young shoots were a ready food source for their animals when they returned. However, the practice also tended to reinforce the scrubby growth it was intended to control.

* regime: 양식　** scrubby: 관목이 우거진

① (A) － (C) － (B)　　　　② (B) － (A) － (C)　　　　③ (B) － (C) － (A)
④ (C) － (A) － (B)　　　　⑤ (C) － (B) － (A)

▌접속사 점검하기.

1. 역접 표현/ 접속사 정리

But, However		(Al/Even) though	
Still		Despite	
Yet		In spite of	
Conversely		Even so	
In contrast		Nevertheless	
On the contrary		Nonetheless	
On the other hand		Regardless	
While		Even if	
Even if it is true		Rather/Instead	

2. 예시 표현/ 접속사 정리

For example		Consider	
For instance		Given	
Suppose		To name a few	

3. 인과관계 표현/ 접속사 정리

Because		As	
Because of		Since	
Therefore		Thus	
So		As a result	
In turn		As a consequence	
Contribute to		Cause	
Lead to		Result from	
In the end		Eventually	

4. 재진술 표현/ 접속사 정리

In other words		That is to say	
In brief		To sum up	
Namely		That is	
In essence		In short	
Indeed		Put more generally	

5. 나열 표현/ 접속사 정리

In this way		Further	
Likewise		Moreover	
Similarly		Alternatively	

5-2 문장삽입은 단절과 근거를 찾아야 한다.

먼저, 다음 기출 문제를 풀어봅시다.

17학년도 6월 평가원 39번

> That is why people experience jet lag when traveling across time zones.

In humans, body clocks are responsible for daily changes in blood pressure, body temperature, hormones, hunger, and thirst, as well as our sleep-wake cycles. (①) These biological rhythms, which we experience as internal time, are probably older than sleep, developed over the course of millions of years of evolution. (②) They facilitate physiological and behavioral changes on a roughly twenty-four-hour cycle no matter what is happening outside, whether a cold front moves in or clouds block the light of the sun. (③) Their internal clocks continue to run in accordance with the place they left behind, not the one to which they have come, and it can take some time to realign the two. (④) The most remarkable thing is that our internal body clocks can be readjusted by environmental cues. (⑤) We may get jet lag for a few days when we ask our body clocks to adapt to a vastly different schedule of day and night cycles on the other side of the Earth, but they can do it.

* facilitate: 쉽게 하다 ** realign: 재조정하다

③번을 고르셨나요? ⑤번을 고르셨나요? 다른 걸 고르셨다면 정말 special한 20%에 들어가셨습니다.
⑤번을 고른 학생들은 아직 문장삽입이라는 유형을 이해하지 못한 학생입니다.
'jet lag'라는 생소한 단어가 ⑤번 이후 처음 제시되었기 때문에 고르셨을 겁니다.
③번을 '지시사 단절' 혹은 'their'이 가리키는 대상이 없어 논리적 오류 발생으로 판단한 학생은 문장삽입 유형을 잘 이해하고 있습니다.

그렇다면 왜 ⑤번이 안되고 ③번이 정답이 될까요?

그 이유는 문장삽입의 첫 번째 정답의 근거가 단절이기 때문입니다. 평가원은 중복 정답없이 한 개의 정답을 출제해야 합니다. 즉, 어떠한 학생들, 강사들도 인정할 수 밖에 없는 정답을 만들어야 합니다.

그저 소재가 중복된 것이 정답의 근거라면

'jet lag', '시차'의 의미로 인해서

(④) The most remarkable thing is that our internal body clocks can be readjusted by environmental cues.

④번 뒷 문장 'our internal body clocks'도 시차와 관련된 의미이므로 ④번도 정답이 가능합니다.

④번은 아니라고 생각하시나요? 왜 그런가요? 객관적인 근거인가요?

평가원은 누군가에게는 자연스럽고 누군가에게는 자연스럽지 않은 것을 정답의 근거로 제시하지 않습니다. 중복 정답의 가능성이 크기 때문입니다. 객관적인 논리적 결함 (단절)을 지문에서 출제하여 주어진 문장을 통해 결함을 해소할 수 있도록 합니다. 물론 논리적 연결 (주어진 문장과 지문 사이 연결)도 신경을 써야 합니다. 정답을 찾을 때는 단절을 중심으로 찾되, '논리적 연결성'은 시험장에서 정답은 검토하는 수단으로 사용해야 합니다.

이를 정리하면

Ⅰ. 주어진 문장을 해석하여 앞 뒷 내용을 생각한다.
Ⅱ. 지문에서 단절을 찾는다.
Ⅲ. 주어진 문장을 단절이 있는 곳에 넣어 논리적 연결을 확인한다.

평가원이 출제하는 단절의 종류는

1. 지시사 단절 2. 접속사 단절 3. 내용 단절 3가지입니다.

한 가지씩 확인해봅시다.

지시사 단절

지시사 단절이란 한 문장에 존재하는 지시사가 지칭하는 대상이 앞 문장에서 존재하지 않는 경우를 이야기합니다. 우리가 순서 유형에서 배운 것과 동일합니다.

다음 문제를 풀어봅시다.

This dynamic can be illustrated with the example of parents who place equal value on convenience and concern for the environment.

Our total set of values and their relative importance to us constitute our value system. (①) The way that we behave in a given situation is often influenced by how important one value is to us relative to others. (②) For instance, deciding whether to spend Saturday afternoon relaxing with your family or exercising will be determined by the relative importance that you place on family versus health. (③) You feel value conflict when you do something that is consistent with one value but inconsistent with another equally important value. (④) They may experience value conflict if they buy disposable diapers for their babies. (⑤) Consumers facing such decisions consider not only the product's immediate consumption outcomes but also the product's general effect on society, including how the manufacturer behaves (e.g., toward the environment).

* diaper: 기저귀

This dynamic can be illustrated with the example of parents who place equal value on convenience and concern for the environment.

Our total set of values and their relative importance to us constitute our value system. (①) The way that we behave in a given situation is often influenced by how important one value is to us relative to others. (②) For instance, deciding whether to spend Saturday afternoon relaxing with your family or exercising will be determined by the relative importance that you place on family versus health. (③) You feel value conflict when you do something that is consistent with one value but inconsistent with another equally important value. (④) **They** may experience value conflict if they buy disposable diapers for their babies. (⑤) Consumers facing such decisions consider not only the product's immediate consumption outcomes but also the product's general effect on society, including how the manufacturer behaves (e.g., toward the environment).

* diaper: 기저귀

Ⅰ. 주어진 문장에서 환경에 대한 편리함과 걱정에 동일한 가치를 둔 부모의 예시를 통해 그 역동적인 것을 설명할 수 있다고 합니다.

Ⅱ. ④번 뒷 문장의 'They'는 가치 충돌을 경험할지도 모르는 사람입니다. 하지만 ④번 앞 문장에서는 복수 명사가 존재하지 않습니다. 그러므로 ④번 뒷 문장 'They'가 지칭하는 대상이 ④번 앞 문장에서 존재하지 않습니다.

Ⅲ. 주어진 문장에시 'parents'가 복수 명사이고 아이의 기저귀를 구매할지 말지 가치 충돌을 경험하는 사람이므로 ④번이 정답이 됩니다.

이렇듯 지시사가 지칭하는 대상이 존재하지 않을 경우 단절을 근거로 성납을 찾을 수 있습니다. 그러므로 문장삽입 문제를 푸실 때 지시사를 인식하며 이 지시사가 지칭하는 대상을 잘 찾으셔야 합니다.

🅷 해석

우리의 일련의 전체 가치와 우리에게 있어 그것(가치)들의 상대적 중요성으로 우리의 가치 체계는 구성된다. 우리가 어떤 주어진 상황에서 행동하는 방식은 하나의 가치가 다른 것들에 비해 우리에게 얼마나 중요한가에 의해 자주 영향을 받는다. 예를 들어 토요일 오후를 가족과 함께 편안하게 쉬면서 보낼 것인지 아니면 운동을 하면서 보낼 것인지 정하는 것은 가족 대 건강에 대해 여러분이 부가하는 상대적 중요성에 의해 결정될 것이다. 여러분은 하나의 가치와는 일치하지만, 똑같이 중요한 또 다른 하나의 가치와는 일치하지 않는 어떤 것을 할 때 '가치 갈등'을 느낀다. 이러한 역학은 편의성과 환경에 대한 우려에 똑같은 가치를 두는 부모들의 예에서도 분명히 볼 수 있다. 그들이 자신의 아기를 위해 일회용 기저귀를 산다면 그들은 가치 갈등을 경험할 수도 있다. 그러한 결정에 직면한 소비자는 그 제품의 직접적인 소비 결과뿐만 아니라, 그 제조업체가 (예를 들면 환경에 대하여) 어떻게 행동하는지를 포함하여, 그 제품이 사회에 미치는 전반적인 영향도 또한 고려한다.

접속사 단절

접속사 단절이란 접속사에 의해서 논리적 연결이 되어야 하지만 되지 않는 경우를 이야기합니다.
우리가 순서에서 배운 것처럼 'A but A'의 전개 혹은 'B moreover A'와 같은 전개는 논리적 결함이 생기므로
단절이 발생합니다.

다음 문제를 풀어봅시다.

17학년도 9월 평가원 38번

> Even so, research confirms the finding that nonverbal cues are more credible than verbal cues, especially when verbal and nonverbal cues conflict.

Researchers have reported various nonverbal features of sarcasm. (①) Most disagree as to whether nonverbal cues are essential to the perception of sarcasm or the emotion that prompts it. (②) Also, nonverbal cues are better indicators of speaker intent. (③) As the nature of sarcasm implies a contradiction between intent and message, nonverbal cues may "leak" and reveal the speaker's true mood as they do in deception. (④) Ostensibly, sarcasm is the opposite of deception in that a sarcastic speaker typically intends the receiver to recognize the sarcastic intent; whereas, in deception the speaker typically intends that the receiver not recognize the deceptive intent. (⑤) Thus, when communicators are attempting to determine if a speaker is sarcastic, they compare the verbal and nonverbal message and if the two are in opposition, communicators may conclude that the speaker is being sarcastic.

* sarcasm: 비꼼 ** ostensibly: 표면상

> Even so, research confirms the finding that nonverbal cues are more credible than verbal cues, especially when verbal and nonverbal cues conflict.

Researchers have reported various nonverbal features of sarcasm. (①) Most disagree as to whether nonverbal cues are essential to the perception of sarcasm or the emotion that prompts it. (②) **Also,** nonverbal cues are better indicators of speaker intent. (③) As the nature of sarcasm implies a contradiction between intent and message, nonverbal cues may "leak" and reveal the speaker's true mood as they do in deception. (④) Ostensibly, sarcasm is the opposite of deception in that a sarcastic speaker typically intends the receiver to recognize the sarcastic intent; whereas, in deception the speaker typically intends that the receiver not recognize the deceptive intent. (⑤) Thus, when communicators are attempting to determine if a speaker is sarcastic, they compare the verbal and nonverbal message and if the two are in opposition, communicators may conclude that the speaker is being sarcastic.

* sarcasm: 비꼼 ** ostensibly: 표면상

Ⅰ. 그럼에도 불구하고, 연구는 특히 언어적 신호와 비언어적 신호가 충돌할 때, 비언어적 신호가 언어적 신호보다 더 믿을만 하다는 결과를 확인했다고 합니다. 주어진 문장 앞에는 이와 반대되는 내용이 제시되어야 합니다.

Ⅱ. ②번 앞 문장에서 비언어적 신호가 비꼼의 인지나 감정을 촉진시키는 것에 필수적이라는 것에 관해서 대부분이 반대한다고 합니다. 즉 비언어적 신호가 중요하다는 것에 대부분이 반대한다고 합니다. ②번 뒷 문장에서 'Also'를 제시하며 비언어적 신호가 말하는 사람이 가지는 의도의 더 좋은 지표라고 합니다. ②번 앞 문장은 비언어적 신호가 의도를 알려주지 않는다는 내용을 제시하지만 ②번 뒷 문장은 비언어적 신호가 의도를 알 수 있다는 내용을 제시하므로 ②번 문장의 'Also'로 나열될 수 없습니다. 그러므로 ②번에서 단절이 발생합니다.

Ⅲ. ②번 앞 문장에서 비언어적 신호가 중요하다는 것을 반대한다는 (−) 내용이 제시되었고 주어진 문장이 ②번 뒷 문장과 같이 비언어적 신호의 장점을 제시하므로 정답은 ②번이 됩니다.

§ 해석

연구자들은 빈정거림의 다양한 비언어적 특성들을 보고했다. 대부분의 연구자들은 비언어적 신호가 빈정거림 또는 그것을 촉발하는 감정을 인지하는 데 필수적인 것인지에 대해 의견이 다르다. 그렇다 하더라도 연구는 특히 언어적 신호와 비언어적 신호가 상충할 때에는 비언어적 신호가 언어적 신호보다 더 신빙성이 있다는 연구 결과를 확증해 준다. 또한, 비언어적 신호가 화자의 의도를 더 잘 보여 준다. 빈정거림의 본질이 의도와 메시지 사이의 모순을 암시하므로, 속임수를 쓸 때 그러는 것처럼 비언어적 신호가 '새어 나와' 말하는 사람의 진정한 기분 상태를 드러낼지도 모른다. 일반적으로 빈정대는 말을 하는 사람은 받아들이는 사람이 그 빈정대는 의도를 알아차리기를 바라지만, 반면에 속임수를 쓸 때는 일반적으로 화자가 듣는 사람이 그 속이려는 의도를 알아차리지 못했으면 하고 바란다는 점에서 표면상으로 빈정거림은 속임과 반대되는 것이다. 따라서 의사 전달자들은 어떤 화자가 빈정대는 것인지 판단하려고 할 때, 언어적 메시지와 비언어적 메시지를 비교하며 두 개가 서로 반대이면 그 화자가 빈정대고 있다는 결론을 내릴 수 있다.

내용 단절

내용 단절이란 접속사 없이 연결될 수 없는 내용들이 연결된 경우를 이야기합니다. 예를 들어 '(-) 내용과 (+)
내용이 역접의 표현 없이 제시된 경우' 혹은 'A라는 소재에 대한 내용. B라는 소재에 대한 내용으로
제시되었는데 나열의 표현이 제시되지 않은 경우'가 있습니다.

다음 문제를 풀어봅시다.

16학년도 수능 38번

> Even so, it is not the money per se that is valuable, but the fact that it can potentially yield more
> positive experiences.

  Money — beyond the bare minimum necessary for food and shelter — is nothing more than a means
to an end. Yet so often we confuse means with ends, and sacrifice happiness (end) for money (means).
It is easy to do this when material wealth is elevated to the position of the ultimate end, as it so often
is in our society. (①) This is not to say that the accumulation and production of material wealth
is in itself wrong. (②) Material prosperity can help individuals, as well as society, attain higher levels
of happiness. (③) Financial security can liberate us from work we do not find meaningful and from
having to worry about the next paycheck. (④) Moreover, the desire to make money can challenge
and inspire us. (⑤) Material wealth in and of itself does not necessarily generate meaning or lead
to emotional wealth.

* per se: 그 자체로

Even so, it is not the money per se that is valuable, but the fact that it can potentially yield more positive experiences.

Money — beyond the bare minimum necessary for food and shelter — is nothing more than a means to an end. Yet so often we confuse means with ends, and sacrifice happiness (end) for money (means). It is easy to do this when material wealth is elevated to the position of the ultimate end, as it so often is in our society. (①) This is not to say that the accumulation and production of material wealth is in itself wrong. (②) Material prosperity can help individuals, as well as society, attain higher levels of happiness. (③) Financial security can liberate us from work we do not find meaningful and from having to worry about the next paycheck. (④) Moreover, the desire to make money can challenge and inspire us. (⑤) Material wealth in and of itself does not necessarily generate meaning or lead to emotional wealth.

* per se: 그 자체로

Ⅰ. 주어진 문장에서 그럼에도 불구하고, 돈 그 자체로 중요한 것이 아니라 그것이 잠재적으로 더 많은 긍정적인 경험을 생산한다는 것이라고 합니다. 주어진 문장 앞에서는 돈의 장점이 제시되어야 함을 알 수 있습니다.

Ⅱ. ⑤번 앞 문장에서는 돈을 만들려는 욕구가 도전적이고 우리에게 영감을 준다고 합니다. 하지만 ⑤번 뒷 문장에서는 물질적인 부 그 자체로 반드시 의미를 발생시키거나 감정적인 부를 야기하지 않는다고 합니다. ⑤번 앞 문장에서는 돈이 (+)로 제시되고 ⑤번 뒷 문장에서는 (-)로 제시되었지만 역접의 표현이 존재하지 않으므로 ⑤번에서 단절이 발생합니다.

Ⅲ. 주어진 문장에서 'Even so'가 역접의 표현이고, ⑤번 뒷 문장에서 제시된 논 그 사체로 귀중한 것은 아니라는 내용을 보여주고 있으므로 정답은 ⑤번이 됩니다.

δ 해석

음식과 거처에 필요한 기본적인 최소한의 범위를 벗어나는 돈은 목적에 대한 수단에 불과하다. 하지만 아주 흔히 우리는 수단을 목적과 혼동하여 돈(수단)을 위해서 행복(목적)을 희생한다. 우리 사회에서 아주 흔히 그렇듯이, 물질적 부유함이 궁극적인 목적의 위치로 높여질 때에 이렇게 하기 쉽다. 이것은 물질적 부의 축적과 생산이 그것 자체로서 잘못된 것이라고 말하는 것이 아니다. 물질적 풍요는 사회뿐만 아니라 개인이 더 높은 수준의 행복을 얻을 수 있도록 도와줄 수 있다. 재정적 안정은 우리가 의미 있다고 생각하지 않는 일로부터 그리고 다음 번 월급에 대해서 걱정해야 하는 것으로부터 우리를 해방시켜 줄 수 있다. 더욱이, 돈을 벌고자 하는 욕구는 우리에게 도전 정신을 심어 주고 영감을 줄 수 있다. 그렇다고 하더라도, 가치가 있는 것은 돈 '그 자체로서'가 아니라 그것이 잠재적으로 더 긍정적인 경험을 만들어 낼 수 있다는 사실이다. 물질적 부유함이 본질적으로 그리고 그 자체로서 의미를 만들어 내거나 감정적인 풍요로움을 반드시 가져오는 것은 아니다.

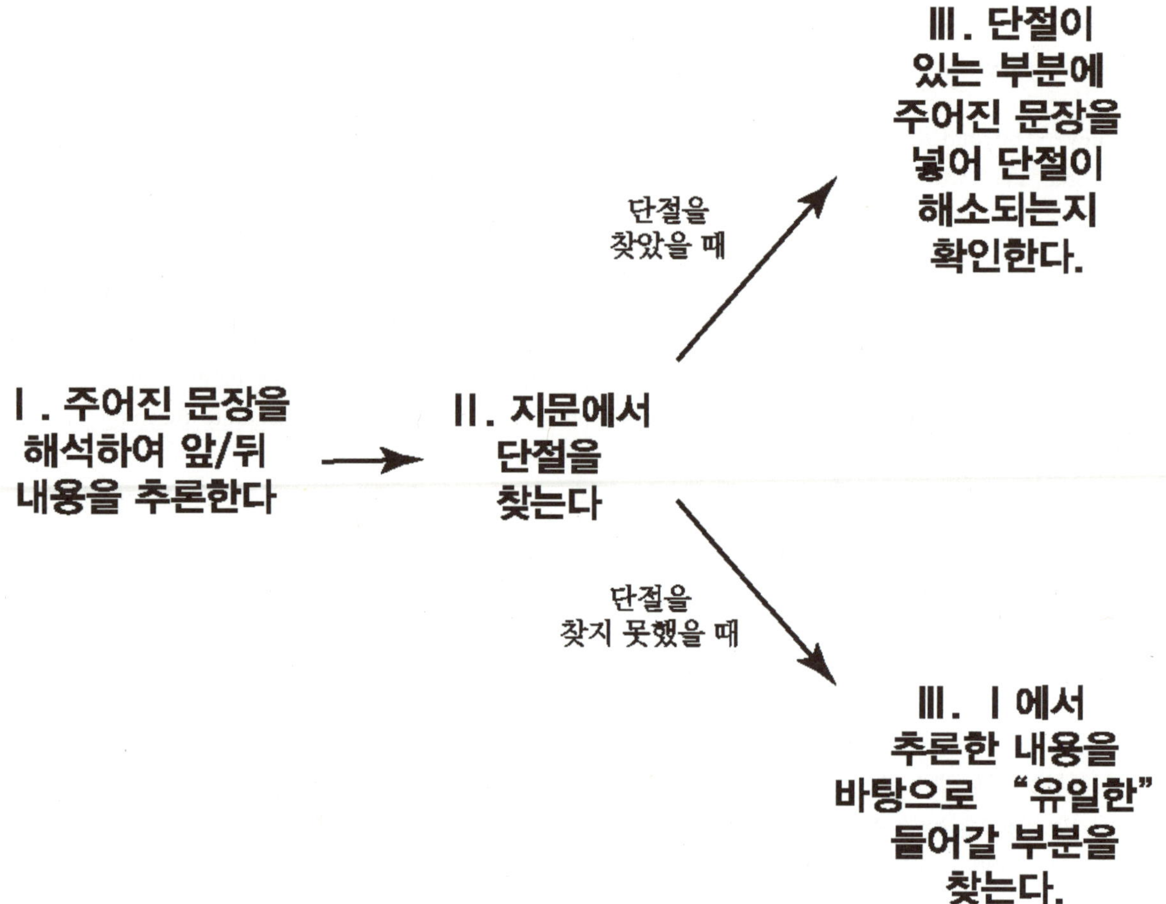

체화를 통해 더 연습해 봅시다.

체화

다음 지문에서 단절이 발생한 부분을 찾고
1. 지시사 단절 2. 접속사 단절 3. 내용 단절 중 어느 것인지 파악해봅시다.

01

17학년도 수능 38번

What is the best order for a report, paper or other technical document? Of course, it must be logical; but that means simply that the paper must have connection and sequence, and a variety of orders is possible under this heading. Too many writers interpret the term logical to mean chronological, and it has become habitual to begin reports and papers with careful reviews of previous work. (①) Usually, this is tactically weak. (②) Therefore, to rehearse to them the findings of previous work is simply to bore them with unnecessary reminders. (③) The interesting thing for them is the new information — the new findings and conclusions. (④) So it is usually best to start with those pieces of information. (⑤) To give a long chronological account of work or procedures is normally appropriate only when the essential point of the paper is the chronological sequence.

* chronological: 연대순의

1. 지시사 단절
2. 접속사 단절
3. 내용 단절

02

15학년도 9월 평가원 38번

Studies do show that motorists are more likely to yield to pedestrians in marked crosswalks than at unmarked crosswalks. But as some researchers found, that does not necessarily make things safer. (①) When they compared the way pedestrians crossed at both kinds of crosswalks on roads with considerable traffic volumes, they found that people at unmarked crosswalks tended to look both ways more often, waited more often for gaps in traffic, and crossed the road more quickly. (②) Researchers suspect that both drivers and pedestrians are more aware that drivers should yield to pedestrians in marked crosswalks. (③) Not knowing traffic safety laws, it turns out, is actually a good thing for pedestrians. (④) Because they do not know whether cars are supposed to stop, they act more cautiously. (⑤) Marked crosswalks, by contrast, may give pedestrians an unrealistic picture of their own safety.

1. 지시사 단절
2. 접속사 단절
3. 내용 단절

03

People make extensive use of searching images. One unexpected context is sorting. Suppose you have a bag of small hardware — screws, nails, and so on — and you decide to organize them into little jars. You dump the stuff out on a table and begin separating the items into coherent groups. (①) It is possible to do this by randomly picking up individual objects, one by one, identifying each one, and then moving it to the appropriate jar. (②) But what most people do is very different. (③) They put them in the jar and then go back and do the same for a different kind of item. (④) So the sorting sequence is nonrandom, producing runs of items of a single type. (⑤) It is a faster, more efficient technique, and much of the increased efficiency is due to the use of searching images.

1. 지시사 단절
2. 접속사 단절
3. 내용 단절

04

In mature markets, breakthroughs that lead to a major change in competitive positions and to the growth of the market are rare. (①) Because of this, competition becomes a zero sum game in which one organization can only win at the expense of others. (②) However, where the degree of competition is particularly intense a zero sum game can quickly become a negative sum game, in that everyone in the market is faced with additional costs. (③) As an example of this, when one of the major high street banks in Britain tried to gain a competitive advantage by opening on Saturday mornings, it attracted a number of new customers who found the traditional Monday-Friday bank opening hours to be a constraint. (④) However, faced with a loss of customers, the competition responded by opening on Saturdays as well. (⑤) In essence, this proved to be a negative sum game.

1. 지시사 단절
2. 접속사 단절
3. 내용 단절

체화 해설

01

What is the best order for a report, paper or other technical document? Of course, it must be logical; but that means simply that the paper must have connection and sequence, and a variety of orders is possible under this heading. Too many writers interpret the term logical to mean chronological, and it has become habitual to begin reports and papers with careful reviews of previous work. (①) Usually, this is tactically weak. (②) Therefore, to rehearse to **them** the findings of previous work is simply to bore them with unnecessary reminders. (③) The interesting thing for them is the new information — the new findings and conclusions. (④) So it is usually best to start with those pieces of information. (⑤) To give a long chronological account of work or procedures is normally appropriate only when the essential point of the paper is the chronological sequence.

* chronological: 연대순의

1. 지시사 단절 2. 접속사 단절 3. 내용 단절

⎔ 해설

②번 뒷 문장에서 그러므로, 'them'에게 이전 작업의 연구 결과를 다시 들려주는 것은 불필요하게 상기시키는 것으로 그들을 지루하게 한다고 합니다. ②번 앞 내용에서 이전 작업의 연구 결과를 들었을 때 지루할 'them'이 제시되지 않았습니다. 1. 지시사 단절입니다.

02

Studies do show that motorists are more likely to yield to pedestrians in marked crosswalks than at unmarked crosswalks. But as some researchers found, that does not necessarily make things safer. (①) When they compared the way pedestrians crossed at both kinds of crosswalks on roads with considerable traffic volumes, they found that people at unmarked crosswalks tended to look both ways more often, waited more often for gaps in traffic, and crossed the road more quickly. (②) Researchers suspect that **both drivers and pedestrians are more aware that drivers should yield to pedestrians in marked crosswalks. (③) Not knowing traffic safety laws, it turns out, is actually a good thing for pedestrians.** (④) Because they do not know whether cars are supposed to stop, they act more cautiously. (⑤) Marked crosswalks, by contrast, may give pedestrians an unrealistic picture of their own safety.

1. 지시사 단절 2. 접속사 단절 **3. 내용 단절**

⎔ 해설

③번 앞 문장에서 표시가 있는 건널목에서 운전자가 반드시 보행자에게 양보를 해야한다는 것을 운전자와 보행자 둘 다 잘 인지하고 있다고 합니다. 하지만 ③번 뒷 문장에서 교통 안전 규칙을 모르는 것이 보행자들에게 좋은 일이라고 합니다. 이는 서로 상반되는 내용이 역접의 표현 없이 제시되었으므로 3. 내용 단절입니다.

03

People make extensive use of searching images. One unexpected context is sorting. Suppose you have a bag of small hardware — screws, nails, and so on — and you decide to organize them into little jars. You dump the stuff out on a table and begin separating the items into coherent groups. (①) It is possible to do this by randomly picking up individual objects, one by one, identifying each one, and then moving it to the appropriate jar. (②) But what most people do is very different. (③) They put **them** in the jar and then go back and do the same for a different kind of item. (④) So the sorting sequence is nonrandom, producing runs of items of a single type. (⑤) It is a faster, more efficient technique, and much of the increased efficiency is due to the use of searching images.

1. 지시사 단절 2. 접속사 단절 3. 내용 단절

8 해설

③번 뒷 문장에서 그들은 'them'을 항아리 속에 넣고 다시 돌아가 다른 종류의 물품에 대하여 똑같은 것을 한다고 합니다. ③번 앞 내용에서 'They'인 '사람들'이 항아리 속에 넣어야할 대상이 존재하지 않으므로 'them'이 지칭하는 대상이 없습니다. 1. 지시사 단절입니다.

04

In mature markets, breakthroughs that lead to a major change in competitive positions and to the growth of the market are rare. (①) Because of this, competition becomes a zero sum game in which one organization can only win at the expense of others. (②) However, where the degree of competition is particularly intense a zero sum game can quickly become a negative sum game, in that everyone in the market is faced with additional costs. (③) As an example of this, when one of the major high street banks in Britain tried to gain a competitive advantage by opening on Saturday mornings, it attracted a number of new customers who found the traditional Monday-Friday bank opening hours to be a constraint. (④) However, faced with a loss of customers, the competition responded by opening on Saturdays as well. (⑤) **In essence**, this proved to be a negative sum game.

1. 지시사 단절 **2. 접속사 단절** 3. 내용 단절

8 해설

⑤번 뒷 문장에서 'In essence'를 통해 앞 문장을 그것은 네거티브 게임으로 판명났다는 내용으로 재진술합니다. 하지만 ⑤번 앞 문장에서 고객의 감소에 직면하자, 경쟁 상대도 토요일에 문을 열며 대응했다고 합니다. 토요일에 문을 여는 것 자체가 네거티브 게임으로 재진술될 수 없으므로 2. 접속사 단절에 해당합니다.

 만약 시험장에서 단절을 못 찾았거나, 단절이 존재하지 않으면 어떻게 해야 하나요?

 상대평가에서 절대평가로 전환된 이후 가끔씩 단절이 없는 문제가 출제되고 있습니다. 단절을 찾지 못하거나 지문에서 단절이 존재하지 않는 경우 결국, 주어진 문장의 내용과 근거를 통해 정답을 찾아야 합니다. 우리가 배운 Ⅰ단계에서 주어진 문장을 통해서 주어진 문장의 앞과 뒷 내용을 추론하는 사고 과정과 Ⅲ단계에서 주어진 문장을 해당 번호에 삽입했을 때 논리적 결함의 존재 여부를 판단하는 과정은 단절이 존재하지 않을 때도 해야 하는 사고 과정입니다. 또한 문장 삽입 문제를 처음 접했을 때 단절의 유무를 판단할 수 없으므로 Ⅱ번 과정을 통해서 단절이 존재하는 지 존재하지 않는지 반드시 찾아야 합니다. 즉 이 책에서 제시하는 문장 삽입 풀이 방법은 단절이 존재할 때와 존재하지 않을 때를 모두 고려한 방식이므로 모든 문제에 적용할 수 있기 때문에 모든 문제에서 Ⅰ, Ⅱ, Ⅲ단계를 진행하시면 됩니다. 심화에서 단절이 존재하지 않을 때 사고과정을 연습하고 중. 최. 평.에서 단절이 존재하지 않는 경우를 같이 풀어보며 단절이 존재하지 않을 때, 풀이 방식을 적용하는 것을 이해해 봅시다.

심화 (1) 단절이 찾지 못하거나 없을 때

시험때 단절을 찾지 못했거나 문제 자체에서 단절이 존재하지 않을 때도, 즉 단절이 없을 때 우리가 배운 Ⅰ, Ⅱ, Ⅲ단계를 잘 지키면 정답을 찾을 수 있습니다. 단절이 없을 경우 Ⅰ단계에서 찾은 주어진 문장의 단서와 Ⅲ단계 최종 확인 단계를 통해서 답을 찾으면 됩니다. 연습해 봅시다.

01

> Such norms are without doubt controls on deviant behavior, but for most people the less formal sanctions, the spontaneous displays of approval or disapproval, prove more effective.

In our society, for example, there are courts of law and means of judging criminals which are so complex that only specialists can understand them. Some sociologists attach great importance to such highly formalized sanctions and have even defined the organized group as one in which the social structure is protected and reinforced through formal sanctions. (①) Those who are about to violate some rule are often stopped short by the show of displeasure on the part of others. (②) Ridicule and gossip are especially effective. (③) In some cases deviant parties may be excluded informally, even when they continue to retain membership in the group. (④) Among the most effective of the informal sanctions is the deprivation of mutual services, the refusal of others to honor the claims of the violator's role. (⑤) Since roles consist of reciprocating claims and obligations, they cannot be maintained without the cooperation of others in complementary roles.

* deviant: 일탈적인 ** sanction: 제재 *** reciprocate: ~을 서로 주고받다

02

> Complete families thought about emigrating, only to find out that the Depression was a worldwide phenomenon and that relatives who had stayed behind in the old world were suffering as much as they were.

From today's perspective, it is difficult to imagine the depth of the Great Depression, and the desperation and deprivation it created among people from all walks of life and social conditions. (①) Complete industries disappeared, the ranks of the unemployed swelled to unthinkable levels, families lost their life savings and had no one to turn to. (②) Homes and farms were repossessed by the thousands. (③) Soup kitchens could not serve enough meals to those going hungry, banks collapsed in rapid succession, and children stopped going to school. (④) Not only that: uncles and cousins who had gone to faraway places, such as Argentina or Australia, were in even worse conditions. (⑤) There were no jobs, no relief, and nowhere to go.

* repossess: 압류하다

03

> The reason for the reversal was that women applied in greater numbers to departments with lower acceptance rates than to the departments to which men predominantly applied.

Quite often, a party seeking to show statistical significance combines data from different sources to create larger numbers, and hence greater significance for a given disparity. Conversely, a party seeking to avoid finding significance disaggregates data insofar as possible. (①) In a discrimination suit brought by female faculty members of a medical school, plaintiffs aggregated faculty data over several years, while the school based its statistics on separate departments and separate years. (②) The argument for disaggregation is that pooled data may be quite misleading. (③) A well-known study showed that at the University of California at Berkeley female applicants for graduate admissions were accepted at a lower rate than male applicants. (④) When the figures were broken down by department, however, it appeared that in most departments the women's acceptance rate was higher than the men's. (⑤) The departments were therefore variables that confounded the association between sex and admission.

* disaggregate: 구성요소로 분해하다
** plaintiff: (민사 소송의) 원고

04

> Guided imagery instructions were given to the participants to help them generate images for the false event (e.g., "Visualize what it might have been like and the memory will probably come back to you").

In a study, 77 undergraduate students were interviewed. (①) During these interviews, they were presented with various events (e.g., falling on their head, getting a painful wound, or being sent to a hospital emergency room). (②) They were told that, according to their parents, these events had occurred in their childhood. (③) The interviewer gave further details about the events supposedly given by the parents. (④) Unknown to the interviewees, the events were invented by the researchers and had never happened to the participants according to their parents. (⑤) Results indicated that 26% of students "recovered" a complete memory for the false event, and another 30% recalled aspects of the false experience.

> Such norms are without doubt controls on deviant behavior, but for most people the less formal sanctions, the spontaneous displays of approval or disapproval, prove more effective.

In our society, **for example**, there are courts of law and means of judging criminals which are so complex that only specialists can understand them. Some sociologists attach great importance to such highly formalized sanctions and have even defined the organized group as one in which the social structure is protected and reinforced through formal sanctions. (①) Those who are about to violate some rule are often stopped short by the show of displeasure on the part of others. (②) Ridicule and gossip are especially effective. (③) In some cases deviant parties may be excluded informally, even when they continue to retain membership in the group. (④) Among the most effective of the informal sanctions is the deprivation of mutual services, the refusal of others to honor the claims of the violator's role. (⑤) **Since** roles consist of reciprocating claims and obligations, they cannot be maintained without the cooperation of others in complementary roles.

* deviant: 일탈적인 ** sanction: 제재

*** reciprocate: ~을 서로 주고받다

§ 해석 ｜ 정답 : ① ｜

예를 들어, 우리 사회에는 매우 복잡해서 전문가만이 이해할 수 있는 사법 재판소와 범죄자들을 심판하는 수단이 있다. 일부 사회학자들은 그러한 고도의 공식화된 제재에 굉장한 중요성을 부여하고 심지어 조직화된 집단을 공식적인 제재를 통해 사회 구조가 보호되고 강화되는 집단으로 규정하기까지 했다. 그러한 규범은 의심의 여지 없이 일탈 행위를 제어하는 것이지만, 대부분의 사람들에게는 덜 공식적인 제재, 즉 승인이나 못마땅함의 자연스러운 표현이 더 효과적이라는 것이 드러난다. 어떤 규칙을 막 위반하려 하는 사람들은 흔히 다른 사람들 쪽에서의 불쾌감의 표시에 의해 (하려던 것을) 급히 멈추게 된다. 조롱과 험담은 특히 효과적이다. 경우에 따라서 일탈자들은 심지어 그들이 그 집단에서 구성원의 자격을 계속 유지하고 있을 때 조차도 비공식적으로 배척당할지도 모른다. 상호 서비스의 박탈, 즉 위반자의 역할 권리 주장을 존중하는 것을 다른 이들이 거부하는 것은 비공식적인 제재 중에서 가장 효과적인 것에 속한다. 역할은 권리 주장과 의무를 서로 주고 받는 것으로 구성되기 때문에, 그것들은 보완적인 역할을 하는 다른 이들의 협조 없이는 유지될 수 없다.

§ 해설

Ⅰ. 주어진 문장의 'Such norms'를 통해 앞에서는 규범이 제시되어야 하며 주어진 문장의 내용이 덜 공식적인 제재인 승인이나 못마땅함의 자연스러운 표현에 더 효과적으로 일탈 행위를 제어하게 된다고 하므로 주어진 문장의 뒤에서는 덜 공식적인 제재에 대해서 언급되어야 합니다.

Ⅱ. ①번에서는 앞 문장을 뒷 문장이 구체화하고 있으며, ②번에서는 앞 문장에 대한 예시가 뒷 문장에서 제시되고 있습니다. ③번 뒷 문장에서는 덜 공식적인 제재의 다른 측면을 보여주며 ④번 뒷 문장에서는 ③번 뒷 문장에 대한 예시를 보여주고 있습니다. ⑤번 뒷 문장은 ④번 뒷 문장을 일반화하므로 단절을 발견하기 어렵습니다.

Ⅲ. 단절이 보이지 않으므로 주어진 문장의 단서를 통해서 정답을 추론해야 합니다. ①번 앞 문장에서는 일부 사회학자들이 공식화된 제재에 중요성을 부여했다고 합니다. ①번 뒷 문장에서는 규칙을 위반하려는 사람들은 다른 사람들의 불쾌감에 표시에 의해 일탈 행위를 중단한다고 합니다. 즉 ①번 앞 문장에서는 공식적인 제재인 'Such norms'에 대해서 언급하고 있고 ①번 뒷 문장에서는 덜 공식적인 제재중 하나인 못마땅함의 자연스러운 표현이 더 효과적인 상황을 제시하므로 정답은 ①번이 됩니다.

Complete families thought about emigrating, only to find out that the Depression was a worldwide phenomenon and that relatives who had stayed behind in the old world were suffering as much as they were.

From today's perspective, it is difficult to imagine the depth of the Great Depression, and the desperation and deprivation it created among people from all walks of life and social conditions. (①) Complete industries disappeared, the ranks of the unemployed swelled to unthinkable levels, families lost their life savings and had no one to turn to. (②) Homes and farms were repossessed by the thousands. (③) Soup kitchens could not serve enough meals to those going hungry, banks collapsed in rapid succession, and children stopped going to school. (④) Not only that: uncles and cousins who had gone to faraway places, such as Argentina or Australia, were in even worse conditions. (⑤) There were no jobs, no relief, and nowhere to go.

* repossess: 압류하다

⬛

⠿ 해석 ㅣ정답 : ④ㅣ

오늘날의 관점에서 대공황의 깊이와 그것이 온갖 계층과 사회적 여건의 사람들 사이에서 일으켰던 절망과 박탈을 상상하는 것은 어렵다. 완전한 산업들이 사라졌고 실업자군은 생각할 수 없는 수준으로 팽창했으며, 가족들은 평생 저축한 돈을 잃었고 의지할 사람이 아무도 없었다. 주택과 농장은 수천씩 압류되었다. 무료 급식소들은 배고픈 사람들에게 충분한 음식을 제공할 수 없었고, 은행들은 빠르게 잇달아 파산했으며, 아이들은 등교를 중지했다. <u>가족 전체가 이민 가는 것에 대해 생각했지만, 결국 대공황이 전 세계적 현상이고 구세계에 남아있던 친척들이 자신들이 그런 만큼 매우 고통받고 있다는 것을 알게 될 뿐이었다.</u> 그것만이 아니었는데, 아르헨티나나 호주와 같은 먼 곳에 갔던 삼촌들과 사촌들은 훨씬 더 열악한 여건에 처해있었다. 일자리도 없고 구호도 없고 갈 곳도 없었다.

⠿ 해설

Ⅰ. 주어진 문장에서 전체 가족이 이민가는 것을 고려했지만 대공황은 전 세계적인 현상이였으며 구세계에서 사는 친척들이 역시 고통받고 있다는 것과 관련된 내용이 뒤에서 제시되어야 합니다.

Ⅱ. ①번 앞 문장에서 대공황의 깊이와 대공황이 많은 사람들에게 절망과 박탈을 일으켰다는 것을 상상하는 것은 어렵다고 합니다. ①번 뒷 문장에서부터 ④번 뒷 문장까지 이에 대한 예시가 나열되며 ⑤번 뒷 문장은 ④번 뒷 문장의 예시를 구체화한다고 볼 수 있습니다. 그러므로 단절이 보이지 않습니다.

Ⅲ. 주어진 문장에서 대공황이 전 세계적인 상황임과 친척들 역시 힘든 상황임을 제시합니다. ④번 뒷 문장에서 아르헨티나나 호주와 같은 먼 곳에 갔던 삼촌들과 사촌들은 훨씬 더 열악한 여건에 처해있다고 하므로 주어진 문장에서 대공황의 전 세계적인 상황과 친척들이 열악하다는 내용을 구체화합니다. 또한 ④번 뒷 문장과 주어진 문장은 ④번 뒷 문장의 'Not only that'으로 나열되므로 정답은 ④번이 됩니다.

* 'Not only that'이 나열의 표현인 것을 파악하고 ④번에서 나열 단절을 느꼈다면 영어적 이해도가 높은 학생입니다. 나열 단절을 파악한 경우 쉽게 정답을 고를 수 있는 문제입니다.

03

The reason for **the reversal** was that women applied in greater numbers to departments with lower acceptance rates than to the departments to which men predominantly applied.

Quite often, a party seeking to show statistical significance combines data from different sources to create larger numbers, and hence greater significance for a given disparity. **Conversely**, a party seeking to avoid finding significance disaggregates data insofar as possible. (①) In a discrimination suit brought by female faculty members of a medical school, plaintiffs aggregated faculty data over several years, **while** the school based its statistics on separate departments and separate years. (②) The argument for disaggregation is that pooled data may be quite misleading. (③) **A well-known study showed** that at the University of California at Berkeley female applicants for graduate admissions were accepted at a lower rate than male applicants. (④) When the figures were broken down by department, **however**, it appeared that in most departments the women's acceptance rate was higher than the men's. (⑤) The departments were **therefore** variables that confounded the association between sex and admission.

* disaggregate: 구성요소로 분해하다
** plaintiff: (민사 소송의) 원고

상당히 자주, 통계적 유의성을 보여주고자 하는 당사자는 상이한 출처들의 자료를 결합하여 더 큰 숫자를 만들고, 따라서 주어진 격차에 더 큰 유의성을 부여한다. 정반대로, 유의성을 발견하지 않으려고 하는 당사자는 가능한 한 자료를 구성요소로 분해한다. 한 의과 대학의 여 교직원들이 제기한 차별 소송에서 원고들은 몇 년 동안 교직원 자료를 모았고, 반면 학교는 별도의 학과와 별개 년의 통계를 근거로 삼았다. 구성요소로의 분해를 옹호하는 주장은 모아진 자료가 상당히 오도할 수 있다는 것이다. 잘 알려진 한 연구는 캘리포니아 대학 버클리 캠퍼스에서 대학원 입학을 위한 여성 지원자들이 남성 지원자들보다 더 낮은 비율로 받아들여졌다는 것을 보여주었다. 그러나 학과별로 수치를 세분화했을 때 대부분의 학과에서 여성의 합격률이 남성의 합격률보다 더 높은 것으로 나타났다. <u>반전의 이유는 여성들은 남성들이 주로 지원한 학과보다 합격률의 더 낮은 학과에 더 많이 지원했기 때문이었다.</u> 그러므로 학과가 성별과 입학 사이 연광성의 틀렸음을 입증하는 변수였다.

📩 해설

Ⅰ. 주어진 문장의 'the reversal'가 지칭하는 대상이 주어진 문장 앞에 존재해야 하며 여성들은 남성들이 주로 지원한 학과보다 합격률이 더 낮은 학과에 더 많이 지원한 것과 관련된 내용이 주어진 문장 뒤에서 제시되어야 합니다.

Ⅱ. ①번 앞 문장은 유의성을 발견하지 않으려고 하는 당사자는 자료를 세분화한다고 합니다. ①번 뒷 문장에서 통계적 유의성을 증명하려는 여 교직원들은 총체적인 자료를 제시하고 통계적 유의성을 발견하지 않으려고 하는 세분화한다고 하므로 ①번 뒷 문장은 ①번 앞 문장의 예시가 됩니다. ②번 뒷 문장에서 세분화를 주장하는 쪽에서 총체적인 자료가 오해를 불러일으킨다고 하며 앞 문장을 구체화합니다. ③번 뒷 문장에서는 대학원 입힉에 여성 지원지들이 남성 지원자들보다 더 낮은 비율로 받아들여졌다고 하며 ②번 뒷 문장의 예시를 제시합니다. ④번 뒷 문장에서 하지만 학과별로 수치를 세분화했을 때 여성의 합격률이 남성의 합격률보다 더 높은 것으로 니디난다고 히며 ③번 뒷 문장을 전환합니다. 이러한 ④번 뒷 문장의 내용은 ⑤번 뒷 문장에서는 성별과 입학 사이의 연관성이 없다는 부분에 대한 근거에 해당하므로 단절이 보이지 않습니다.

Ⅲ. 주어진 문장 앞에서는 'the reversal'이 존재해야 합니다 ③번 뒷 문장에서는 총체적으로 봤을 때 여성이 남성보다 합격률이 낮다고 제시하고 ④번 뒷 문장에서는 세분화하여 봤을 때 여성의 합격률이 남성의 합격률보다 높다는 내용의 전환이 발생합니다. 주어진 문장의 'the reversal'은 ③번 뒷 문장과 ④번 뒷 문장에서의 전환을 지칭하므로 정답은 ⑤번이 됩니다.

04

> Guided imagery instructions were given to the participants to help them generate images for the false event (e.g., "Visualize what it might have been like and the memory will probably come back to you").

In a study, 77 undergraduate students were interviewed. (①) During these interviews, they were presented with various events (e.g., falling on their head, getting a painful wound, or being sent to a hospital emergency room). (②) They were told that, according to their parents, these events had occurred in their childhood. (③) The interviewer gave further details about the events supposedly given by the parents. (④) Unknown to the interviewees, the events were invented by the researchers and had never happened to the participants according to their parents. (⑤) **Results** indicated that 26% of students "recovered" a complete memory for the false event, and another 30% recalled aspects of the false experience.

§ 해석 | 정답 : ⑤ |

한 연구에서 77명의 학부생들이 면접을 보았다. 이 면접 동안에 (예를 들어 머리가 땅에 닿으면서 넘어지거나, 고통스러운 상처를 입거나, 병원 응급실로 후송되는 것과 같은) 다양한 사건이 그들에게 제시되었다. 그들의 부모에 따르면 이러한 사건들이 그들의 어린 시절에 일어났었다고 그들은 들었다. 면접관은 아마도 부모가 주었을 사건의 추가적인 세부 사항을 주었다. 면접받는 사람들은 몰랐지만 이 사건들은 연구원들이 꾸며낸 것이고, 참가자들의 부모에 따르면 참가자들에게 결코 발생한 적이 없다는 것이었다. <u>참가자들이 거짓 사건에 대한 이미지를 생성하는 것을 돕기 위해 유도된 심상에 대한 설명 (예를 들어, "그것이 어땠을 것 같은지를 마음속에 그려보면, 아마도 그 기억이 당신에게 떠오를 것입니다.")이 주어졌다.</u> 26 퍼센트의 학생들이 거짓 사건에 대한 완전한 기억을 '회복했고' 또 다른 30 퍼센트의 학생들이 거짓된 경험의 이모저모를 회상했다는 결과가 나왔다.

---

§ 해설

Ⅰ. 주어진 문장의 'the false event'가 지칭하는 것이 주어진 문장 앞에서 제시되어야 하며 주어진 문장 뒤에서는 참가자들이 거짓 사건에 대한 이미지를 생성화는 것과 관련된 내용이 제시되어야 합니다.

Ⅱ. ①번 앞 문장에서 면접이 제시되며 ①번 뒷 문장에서 ①번 앞 문장에서 제시한 면접의 과정이 제시되기 시작합니다. ②번 뒷 문장에서 제시받은 사건들이 어린 시절 그들에게 발생한 사건들이었다고 하며 ①번 뒷 문장의 내용을 부연 설명합니다. ③번 뒷 문장에서는 면접관들이 사건에 대한 세부 사항을 주었다고 하며 면접 과정 중 변화를 제시하고 ④번 뒷 문장에서 그 사건은 면접관들에 의해서 만들어진 것이며 부모에 따르면 참가자들에게 발생하지 않은 사건이라고 하며 ③번 뒷 문장에서 제시한 세부 사항을 구체화합니다. ⑤번 뒷 문장에서 26 퍼센트의 학생들은 거짓 사건에 대한 기억을 완전히 회복히고 30 퍼센트의 학생들은 회상했다는 면접의 결과를 제시하므로 단절이 보이지 않습니다.

Ⅲ. 단절이 보이지 않으므로 주어진 문장을 통해서 정답을 찾아야 합니다. ⑤번 앞 문장에서 면접관들이 참가자들에게 준 세부 사항은 면접관들이 꾸며낸 것이라고 제시하였고 이는 주어진 문장의 'the false event'에 해당하고 ④번 뒷 문장과 주어진 문장의 결과로 ⑤번 뒷 문장이 제시되기 때문에 정답은 ⑤번이 됩니다.

| 심화 (2) 나열 단절 찾기

많은 수험생들이 가장 단절을 느끼기 어려워하는 유형이 나열 단절입니다.
나열 단절은 A. Similarly, A'이 아닌 A. Similarly, not A 혹은 A. Similarly B와 같이 반대 내용이 나열되거나
앞 문장과 다른 내용으로 나열되는 경우를 지칭합니다. 비기출 문제를 풀어보며 나열 단절을 파악하는 연습을
해봅시다.

01

> Also, we must create and maintain a noncommercial public media system as well as independent alternative media that exist outside the control of transnational corporations and advertisers.

A well-functioning democracy requires a media system that provides diverse sources of information and encourages civic participation. (①) The government once considered the airwaves such an integral part of our democracy that politicians decided the public should own and control them. (②) It is time for the public to reclaim the responsibility of producing quality media from the corporate conglomerates. (③) The first step is to break up the concentration of media power. (④) Let's give control to a greater number of smaller companies that could legitimately compete with a broader range of information. (⑤) The rise of independent political blogs, and that of alternative podcasts, radio networks and television channels are all examples of citizens rising up to take back control of our media.

* airwaves: 방송 전파 ** conglomerate: 대기업

02

> They rarely believe they can handle such illnesses themselves because they have no sense of being in control over the workings of their heart.

Severe depression is not something people failure, kidney disease, or gallstones. (①) When patients with congestive heart failure develop difficulty breathing, they are usually grateful for treatment that relieves their distress. (②) We also do not sense our brains at work, but we feel in control of our minds. (③) This sense of being in control of our minds allows those with depression to believe they can pull themselves out of the severe depression. (④) In my experience, once older adults understand that depression is a disease of the brain, and not something they have control over, they become more open to considering treatment. (⑤) It's not that they can't handle their problems any longer; rather, their brain has let them down. I often say to my patients, "It's not you; it's your brain."

* congestive heart failure: 울혈성 심부전 ** gallstone: 담석

03

In 2000 she could access the Internet from her home computer at 2:00 a.m. if necessary and find an answer within minutes.

In the 1990s the Internet became the newest entrant in the baby advice field. Major manufacturers of baby equipment as well as the neighbor down the street set up Web sites to help parents care for their babies. (①) Chat rooms brought mothers from all around the country together online to discuss, question, and support each other. (②) The Internet meant that the speed of information available to mothers had compressed from weeks and months in the early 1900s to near instantaneous by 2000. (③) In the 1910s a mother with a baby care question that was unanswerable in her immediate surroundings could write to the Children's Bureau and wait for a reply. (④) Depending on her location and the post office this entire process might take several weeks. (⑤) Hospitals and pediatricians also embraced the Internet and Web sites written by and directed by them were set up across the country.

* entrant: 신입 회원
** The (United States) Children's Bureau: 미국 아동국
(1912년에 아이와 엄마의 건강을 증진하기 위해 창설된 미국의 기관)
*** pediatrician: 소아과 의사

04

Culinary professionals and food scientists are increasingly cutting this waste by taking the constituents of animal products (fats, proteins, nutrients, water) directly from plants and assembling them into the architecture of meat.

The ace in the hole for the inevitability of the end of animal farming is the incredible inefficiency of making meat, dairy, and eggs from animals. Farmed animals consume calories and nutrients from plants, and they use that energy to do a lot more than produce meat, dairy, and eggs. (①) They have all the normal bodily functions like breathing, movement, and growing by-products like hoofs, organs, and hair. (②) These processes mean fanned animals have a caloric conversion ratio of 10:1 or more. (③) For every ten calories of food we feed them, we get only about one calorie of meat in return. (④) And for every ten grams of plant-based protein, we get at most two grams of animal-based protein. (⑤) They can also make cultured meat like the Memphis Meats meatball, real animal flesh made by using cell cultures to grow meat in the same process that happens inside an animal's body, so it's molecularly identical to conventional meat.

* ace in the hole: 비장의 무기 ** culinary: 요리의

심화 (2) 나열 단절 찾기 해설

01

> Also, we **must** create and maintain a noncommercial public media system as well as independent alternative media that exist outside the control of transnational corporations and advertisers.

A well-functioning democracy requires a media system that provides diverse sources of information and encourages civic participation. (①) The government once considered the airwaves such an integral part of our democracy that politicians decided the public **should** own and control them. (②) It is time for the public to reclaim the responsibility of producing quality media from the corporate conglomerates. (③) The first step is to break up the concentration of media power. (④) Let's give control to a greater number of smaller companies that could legitimately compete with a broader range of information. (⑤) The rise of independent political blogs, and that of alternative podcasts, radio networks and television channels are all examples of citizens rising up to take back control of our media.

* airwaves: 방송 전파 ** conglomerate: 대기업

ⓗ 해석 [정답 : ⑤]

잘 작동하는 민주주의는 다양한 정보원을 제공하고 시민참여를 장려하는 미디어 시스템을 필요로 한다. 정부는 한때 방송 전파를 우리 민주주의의 매우 필수적인 부분으로 간주하여 정치인들은 일반 국민이 그것을 소유하고 지배해야 한다고 결정했다. 이제는 일반 국민이 대기업으로부터 양질의 미디어를 생산할 책임을 되찾을 때다. 첫 번째 단계는 미디어 권력의 집중을 깨는 것이다. 더 폭넓은 범위의 정보를 가지고 합법적으로 경쟁할 수 있는 더 많은 수의 소규모 회사에게 통제권을 주자. 또한 우리는 초국가적인 기업과 광고주의 통제 밖에 존재하는 독립적인 대안 미디어뿐만 아니라 비상업적인 공공 미디어 시스템도 만들어내고 유지해야 한다. 독립적인 정치 블로그의 출현과 대안적인 팟캐스트, 라디오 방송망, 텔레비전 채널의 출현은 모두 우리의 미디어 지배권을 되찾기 위해 시민들이 들고 일어나는 사례들이다.

ⓗ 해설

Ⅰ. 주어진 문장에서 연결사 'Also'를 통해서 독립적인 대안 미디어와 비상업적인 공공 미디어 시스템을 만들어내고 유지해야 하는 것과 비슷한 내용이 앞 문장에 등장해야 합니다.

Ⅱ. ⑤번 앞 문장에서 소규모 회사에게 통제권을 줘야 한다고 합니다. 그런데 ⑤번 뒷 문장에서는 독립적인 정치 블로그의 출현과 대안적인 팟캐스트 등 독립적인 대안 미디어와 비상업적인 공공 미디어 시스템에 대한 예시를 나열하고 있는 것은 소규모 회사에게 통제권을 주는 것이라 볼 수 없습니다. 그렇기 때문에 ⑤번에서 단절이 발생합니다.

Ⅲ. ⑤번 뒷 문장이 주어진 문장에서 언급된 독립적인 대안 미디어와 비상업적 공공 미디어 시스템에 대한 예시이므로 정답은 ⑤번이 됩니다.

02

> They rarely believe they can handle such illnesses themselves because they have no sense of being in control over the workings of their heart.

Severe depression is not something people failure, kidney disease, or gallstones. (①) When patients with congestive heart failure develop difficulty breathing, they are usually grateful for treatment that relieves their distress. (②) We also do not sense our brains at work, **but** we feel in control of our minds. (③) This sense of being in control of our minds allows those with depression to believe they can pull themselves out of the severe depression. (④) In my experience, once older adults understand that depression is a disease of the brain, and not something they have control over, they **become** more open to considering treatment. (⑤) It's not that they can't handle their problems any longer; **rather**, their brain has let them down. I often say to my patients, "It's not you; it's your brain."

* congestive heart failure: 울혈성 심부전 ** gallstone: 담석

⊗ 해석 [정답 : ②]

울혈성 심부전, 신장병, 또는 담석에서 사람들이 스스로 벗어날 수 없는 것처럼, 심한 우울증도 사람들이 스스로 벗어날 수 있는 것이 아니다. 울혈성 심부전을 앓는 환자들은 숨 쉬는데 어려움을 겪을 때, 자신의 고통을 덜어주는 치료에 대해서 대개 감사한다. 그들은 자신의 심장 작동을 통제하고 있다는 인식이 없기에 그런 질병을 스스로 다스릴 수 있다고 믿는 경우는 거의 없다. 우리는 우리 뇌가 작동하는 것도 인식하지 못하지만, 우리가 정신을 통제하고 있다고 느낀다. 정신을 통제하고 있다는 이러한 느낌은 우울증이 있는 사람들이 심각한 우울증에서 스스로 빗어날 수 있다고 믿게 한다. 내 경험에서, 나이 든 성인이 우울증은 뇌의 질병이고 자신이 통제할 수 있는 것이 아니라는 것을 일단 이해하면, 치료법을 고려하는 것에 더 개방적이 된다. 그들이 자신의 문제를 더는 다룰 수 없다는 것이 아니라, 오히려 그들의 뇌가 그들을 저버린 것이다. 나는 환자들에게 "문제는 여러분이 아니라, 여러분의 뇌입니다."라고 자주 말한다.

⊗ 해설

Ⅰ. 주어진 문장에서 'They'와 'such illnesses'가 지칭하는 것을 찾을 필요가 있습니다. 또한 주어진 문장의 내용인 자신의 신체 부위를 통제한다는 인식이 없는 것이나, 질병을 스스로 다스릴 수 없다는 것과 관련된 내용의 글이 앞 뒤에 제시될 수 있음을 기억하고 지문을 읽어야 합니다.

Ⅱ. ②번 앞 문장에서 울혈성 심부전을 가지고 있는 환자들은 그들의 치료에 대해서 감사해한다고 했습니다. 그런데 ②번 뒷 문장에서는 우리가 뇌가 작동하는 것도 인식하지 못하지만, 정신을 통제하고 있다고 느낀다고 했는데, 환자들이 치료에 대해서 감사해하는 것과 우리가 정신을 통제하는 것이라는 서로 관련이 없는 내용이 'also'로 연결되었으므로 내용적 단절이 발생합니다.

Ⅲ. 주어진 문장의 그들의 심장 박동을 통제하고 있다는 인식이 없다는 내용은 ②번 뒷 문장의 뇌가 작동하는 것을 인식하지 못한다는 내용으로 이어지고 있습니다. 또한 주어진 문장의 'They'와 'such illnesses'는 각각 ②번 앞 문장의 'patients'와 'congestive heart failure'를 지칭하고 있습니다. 그러므로 정답은 ②번이 되어야 합니다.

03

In 2000 she could access the Internet from her home computer at 2:00 a.m. if necessary and find an answer within minutes.

In the 1990s the Internet became the newest entrant in the baby advice field. Major manufacturers of baby equipment as well as the neighbor down the street set up Web sites to help parents care for their babies. (①) Chat rooms brought mothers from all around the country together online to discuss, question, and support each other. (②) The Internet meant that the speed of information available to mothers had compressed from weeks and months in the early 1900s to near instantaneous by 2000. (③) In the 1910s a mother with a baby care question that was unanswerable in her immediate surroundings could write to the Children's Bureau and wait for a reply. (④) Depending on her location and the post office this entire process might take several weeks. (⑤) Hospitals and pediatricians also embraced the Internet and Web sites written by and directed by them were set up across the country.

* entrant: 신입 회원
** The (United States) Children's Bureau: 미국 아동국
(1912년에 아이와 엄마의 건강을 증진하기 위해 창설된 미국의 기관)
*** pediatrician: 소아과 의사

⑧ 해석 [정답 : ⑤]

1900년대에 인터넷은 육아 조언 분야에 가장 최근의 신입 회원이 되었다. 도로를 따라 이웃에 사는 사람뿐만 아니라 주요 유아용품 제조업체들이 부모들이 아이를 돌보는 데 도움을 주기 위해 웹사이트를 만들었다. 채팅방은 서로 논의하고, 질문하고, 응원하기 위해 전국의 엄마들을 온라인으로 모았다. 인터넷은 엄마들이 이용할 수 있는 정보의 속도가 1900년대 초의 몇 주와 몇 달에서 2000년에는 거의 즉시로 압축되었다는 것을 의미했다. 1910년대에는 자신의 가까운 이웃에서 답을 얻을 수 없는 육아 관련 질문이 있는 엄마가 아동국에 편지를 쓰고 답장을 기다릴 수 있었다. 엄마의 위치와 우체국에 따라 이러한 전 과정이 몇 주가 걸릴 수도 있었다. <u>2000년에는 필요하다면 새벽 2시에 가정의 컴퓨터에서 인터넷에 접속하여 몇 분안에 해답을 찾을 수 있었다.</u> 병원과 소아과 의사들도 인터넷을 받아들였고 그들에 의해 만들어지고 관리를 받는 웹사이트들이 전국에서 개설되었다.

⑧ 해설

Ⅰ. 주어진 문장의 'In 2000'이나 '2:00 a.m.'을 통해 지문의 시간적인 흐름을 파악하며 글을 읽어야 할 필요가 있습니다.

Ⅱ. ⑤번 앞 문장에서는 'In 1910'에 관한 내용이 등장합니다. 편지를 쓰고 답장을 기다리는 데 위치에 따라 몇 주가 걸릴 수도 있었다는 내용이 그러합니다. 그런데 ⑤번 뒤 문장에서는 병원과 소아과 의사들이 인터넷을 받아들였고, 웹사이트들이 전국에서 개설되었다는 내용입니다. 이것은 'In 2000'에 관한 내용이므로 'also'로 연결될 수 없기 때문에 단절이 발생합니다.

Ⅲ. 그러므로 2000년의 이야기가 언급되는 주어진 문장은 ⑤번에 들어가야 합니다. ⑤번 뒤 문장에서 의사들도 인터넷을 받아들였다는 내용을 통해 주어진 문장의 'In 2000'의 인터넷에 관한 내용이 전개되었음을 알 수 있습니다.

04

> Culinary professionals and food scientists are increasingly cutting this waste by taking the constituents of animal products (fats, proteins, nutrients, water) directly from plants and assembling them into the architecture of meat.

The ace in the hole for the inevitability of the end of animal farming is the incredible inefficiency of making meat, dairy, and eggs from animals. Farmed animals consume calories and nutrients from plants, and they use that energy to do a lot more than produce meat, dairy, and eggs. (①) They have all the normal bodily functions like breathing, movement, and growing by-products like hoofs, organs, and hair. (②) These processes mean fanned animals have a caloric conversion ratio of 10:1 or more. (③) For every ten calories of food we feed them, we get only about one calorie of meat in return. (④) And for every ten grams of plant-based protein, we get at most two grams of animal-based protein. (⑤) They can also make cultured meat like the Memphis Meats meatball, real animal flesh made by using cell cultures to grow meat in the same process that happens inside an animal's body, **so** it's molecularly identical to conventional meat.

* ace in the hole: 비장의 무기 ** culinary: 요리의

---

⑧ 해석 | 정답 : ⑤ |

축산의 종말이 불가피함을 보여주는 비장의 무기는 동물로 고기, 유제품, 달걀을 생산하는 것의 믿을 수 없는 비효율이다. 가축들은 식물로부터 칼로리와 영양소를 섭취하여, 그 에너지를 이용해서 고기, 유제품, 그리고 달걀을 생산하는 것보다 훨씬 더 많은 것을 한다. 그것들은 호흡, 동작, 그리고 발굽, 장기와 털과 같은 부산물을 기르는 것과 같은 모든 정상적인 신체 기능을 한다. 이 과정들은 가축들이 10:1이나 그 이상의 칼로리 환산 비율을 갖는 것을 의미한다. 그들에게 먹이는 매 10칼로리의 먹이에 대해서, 겨우 1칼로리 정도의 고기를 대가로 얻는다. 그리고 식물성 단백질 매 10g에 대해서, 많이 봐야 동물성 단백질 2g을 얻는다. <u>요리 전문가들과 식품 과학자들은 동물 제품의 성분(지방, 단백질, 영양소, 수분)을 식물에서 직접 추출하여 그것들을 고기의 구조로 조립함으로써 이러한 낭비를 점점 더 줄이고 있다.</u> 그들은 또한 Memphis Meats의 미트볼과 같은 배양된 고기를 만들 수 있는데, 이것은 세포 배양을 이용하여 동물의 몸 안에서 일어나는 것과 똑같은 과정으로 고기가 자라게 함으로써 만들어지는 진짜 동물의 살이어서, 그것은 종래의 고기와 분자적으로 동일하다.

⑧ 해설

Ⅰ. 주어진 문장의 'this waste'를 통해 앞 문장에는 줄이고 있는 낭비에 대한 설명이 등장해야 합니다. 또한 뒷 문장에는 동물 제품의 성분을 식물에서 직접적으로 추출하는 것에 대한 구체적 예시가 언급될 수 있음을 염두에 두고 지문을 읽을 필요가 있습니다.

Ⅱ. ⑤번 앞 문장에서는 식물성 단백질 10g에 대해서 동물성 단백질 2g을 얻는다고 했습니다. 그런데 ⑤번 뒷 문장에서는 세포 배양을 이용하여 분자적으로 동일한 고기를 만들 수 있다고 했습니다. 식물성 단백질과 동물성 단백질을 비교하는 것과 다른 고기를 만들어내는 것은 비슷한 내용이라고 볼 수 없기 때문에 'also'로 이어질 수 없습니다.

Ⅲ. ⑤번 앞 문장에서 식물성 단백질과 동물성 단백질의 교환은 주어진 문장의 'this waste'에 해당합니다. 또한 ⑤번 뒷 문장에서 주어진 문장의 낭비를 해결하는 구체적 방안이 제시되고 있습니다. 그러므로 정답은 ⑤번이 됩니다.

01 25학년도 9월 평가원 38번

글의 흐름으로 보아, 주어진 문장이 들어가기에 가장 적절한 곳을 고르시오.

> If not, the robot might endlessly chase itself rather than the blocks.

People involved in the conception and engineering of robots designed to perceive and act know how fundamental is the ability to discriminate oneself from other entities in the environment. Without such an ability, no goal-oriented action would be possible. (①) Imagine that you have to build a robot able to search for blocks scattered in a room in order to pile them. (②) Even this simple task would require that your machine be able to discriminate between stimulation that originates from its own machinery and stimulation that originates from the blocks in the environment. (③) Suppose that you equip your robot with an artificial eye and an artificial arm to detect, grab, and pile the blocks. (④) To be successful, your machine will have to have some built-in system enabling it to discriminate between the detection of a block and the detection of its own arm. (⑤) Your robot would engage in circular, self-centered acts that would drive it away from the target or external goal.

* entity: 실재물(物)

02 25학년도 수능 39번

글의 흐름으로 보아, 주어진 문장이 들어가기에 가장 적절한 곳을 고르시오.

> In reality, objects do not conform to a linear lifecycle model; instead, they undergo breakdowns, await repairs, are stored away, or find themselves relegated to the basement, only to be rediscovered and repurposed later.

By their very nature, the concepts of maintenance and repair are predominantly examined from a process-oriented perspective. (①) The focus in related scholarly discourse often revolves around the lifespan or lifecycle of objects and technologies. (②) In this context, maintenance and repair are considered practices that have the potential to prolong the existence of objects, ensuring their sustained utilization over an extended period. (③) Krebs and Weber critically engage with anthropomorphic metaphors that imply a biography of things, appropriately highlighting that conventional understanding of the lifecycle of a technology, from its acquisition to its disposal from the household, provides an incomplete definition. (④) Additionally, objects may enter recycling or second-hand cycles, leading to a dynamic afterlife marked by diverse applications. (⑤) As such, the life of an object exhibits a far more complicated and adaptive path than a simplistic linear progression.

* relegate: 추방하다 ** anthropomorphic: 의인화된

03 24학년도 6월 평가원 38번

글의 흐름으로 보아, 주어진 문장이 들어가기에 가장 적절한 곳을 고르시오.

> Instead, much like the young child learning how to play 'nicely', the apprentice scientist gains his or her understanding of the moral values inherent in the role by absorption from their colleagues — socialization.

As particular practices are repeated over time and become more widely shared, the values that they embody are reinforced and reproduced and we speak of them as becoming 'institutionalized'. (①) In some cases, this institutionalization has a formal face to it, with rules and protocols written down,and specialized roles created to ensure that procedures are followed correctly. (②) The main institutions of state — parliament, courts, police and so on — along with certain of the professions, exhibit this formal character. (③) Other social institutions, perhaps the majority, are not like this; science is an example. (④) Although scientists are trained in the substantive content of their discipline, they are not formally instructed in 'how to be a good scientist'. (⑤) We think that these values, along with the values that inform manyof the professions, are under threat, just as the value of the professions themselves is under threat.

* apprentice: 도제, 견습 ** inherent: 내재된

04 24학년도 9월 평가원 38번

글의 흐름으로 보아, 주어진 문장이 들어가기에 가장 적절한 곳을 고르시오.

> Because the manipulation of digitally converted sounds meant the reprogramming of binary information, editing operations could be performed with millisecond precision.

The shift from analog to digital technology significantly influenced how music was produced. First and foremost, the digitization of sounds — that is, their conversion into numbers — enabled music makers to undo what was done. (①) One could, in other words, twist and bend sounds toward something new without sacrificing the original version. (②) This "undo" ability made mistakes considerably less momentous, sparking the creative process and encouraging a generally more experimental mindset. (③) In addition, digitally converted sounds could be manipulated simply by programming digital messages rather than using physical tools, simplifying the editing process significantly. (④) For example, while editing once involved razor blades to physically cut and splice audiotapes, it now involved the cursor and mouse-click of the computer-based sequencer program, which was obviously less time consuming. (⑤) This microlevel access at once made it easier to conceal any traces of manipulations (such as joining tracks in silent spots) and introduced new possibilities for manipulating sounds in audible and experimental ways.

* binary: 2진법의 ** splice: 합쳐 있다

중. 최. 평. 해설

01 25학년도 9월 평가원 38번 (정답률 56%)

글의 흐름으로 보아, 주어진 문장이 들어가기에 가장 적절한 곳을 고르시오.

> If not, the robot might endlessly chase itself rather than the blocks.

People involved in the conception and engineering of robots designed to perceive and act know how fundamental is the ability to discriminate oneself from other entities in the environment. Without such an ability, no goal-oriented action would be possible. (①) Imagine that you **have to** build a robot able to search for blocks scattered in a room in order to pile them. (②) Even this simple task would require that your machine be able to discriminate between stimulation that originates from its own machinery and stimulation that originates from the blocks in the environment. (③) Suppose that you equip your robot with an artificial eye and an artificial arm to detect, grab, and pile the blocks. (④) To be successful, your machine will **have to** have some built-in system enabling it to discriminate between the detection of a block and the detection of its own arm. (⑤) Your robot would engage in circular, self-centered acts that would drive it away from the target or external goal.

* entity: 실재물(物)

해설 [정답 : ⑤]

Ⅰ. 주어진 문장에서 그렇지 않으면 로봇이 블록보다는 자기 자신을 끝없이 쫓아갈 수도 있다고 합니다. 앞 내용이 되지 않으면 자기 자신을 끊임없이 쫓아간다고 하므로, 앞에는 자기 자신을 끝없이 쫓아가지 않는 방법이 제시되어야 하며, 뒤에는 자기 자신을 끝없이 쫓아가는 내용이 제시되어야 합니다.

Ⅱ. ⑤번 앞 문장에서는 성공하기 위해서, 너의 기계는 그것이 블록 감지와 자신의 팔 감지를 구별할 수 있게 해주는 어떠한 내장된 시스템을 가지고 있어야만 한다고 합니다. ⑤번 뒷 문장에서는 너의 로봇은 로봇을 목표물이나 외부 목표에서 멀어지게 하는 순환적이고 자기 중심적인 행동을 하게 된다고 합니다. ⑤번 앞 문장은 목표를 달성하기 위한 내용이 제시되고 ⑤번 뒷 문장에서는 목표에서 멀어지는 내용이 제시되므로 역접의 내용 없이 두 문장이 연결될 수 없습니다. 즉 내용 단절이 발생합니다.

Ⅲ. ⑤번에서 발생한 내용 단절은 주어진 문장의 역접의 내용인 'If not'을 통해 해소가 되며, ⑤번 앞 문장은 자기 자신을 끝없이 쫓아가지 않기 위한 블록 감지와 로봇 자신의 팔을 감지하는 것을 구별하는 내용이 제시되고 ⑤번 뒷 문장은 스스로 돌게 되어 목표에서 멀어지게 되는 내용이 제시되므로 정답은 ⑤번이 됩니다.

주. If not, the robot / might endlessly chase / itself (rather than the blocks).

구▶ 그렇지 않으면 로봇이 블록보다는 자기 자신을 끝없이 쫓아갈 수도 있다고 합니다.

독▶ 앞에 제시된 내용이 아니면 로봇이 블록을 쫓아 가는 것이 아닌 스스로를 쫓아간다고 합니다.

Ⅰ. People (involved in the conception and engineering of robots (designed to perceive and act)) /
know / how fundamental / is / the ability (to discriminate / oneself from other entities in the
environment).

* entity: 실재물(物)

구▶ 'discriminate A from B'는 'A를 B로부터 구별하다'를 의미합니다.

- 인지하고 행동하도록 설계된 로봇의 개념과 엔지니어링에 참여한 사람들은 환경에서 자신을 (= 로봇 자신을) 주위의 다른 실재물로부터 구별하는 능력이 얼마나 근본적인지 (= 중요한지) 알고 있다고 합니다.

독▶ 인지하고 행동하는 로봇을 개발하는 사람들은 로봇이 그 스스로를 다른 것들과 구별하는 것이 매우 중요하다고 합니다.

Ⅱ. (Without such an ability), no goal-oriented action / would be / possible.

구▶ 그러한 능력이 (= 다른 것들과 자신을 구별하는 능력이) 없으면, 목표 지향적인 행동이 불가능하다고 합니다.

독▶ 다른 것과 자신을 구별하지 못하면 목표 지향적인 행동이 불가능하다고 합니다.

Ⅲ. Imagine / that you / **have to** build / a robot (able to search for blocks (scattered in a room)) (in
order to pile them).

구▶ 너가 블록을 쌓기 위해 빙에 흩어져 있는 블록을 찾을 수 있는 로봇을 만들어야만 한다고 상상해 보라고 합니다.

독▶ 'have to'가 제시되었으므로 중심 문장
- 블록을 쌓기 위해서 블록을 찾을 수 있는 로봇을 만든다고 상상해보라고 합니다.

Ⅳ. Even this simple task / would require / that your machine / be able to discriminate (between
stimulation (that originates from / its own machinery) and stimulation (that originates from / the
blocks) (in the environment).

구▶ 'between A and B'는 'A와 B 사이'를 의미합니다.

- 이 간단한 작업은 너의 기계가 환경에서 기계로부터 유래된 자극과 블록으로부터 유래된 자극을 구별할 수 있어야 한다는 것을 요구한다고 합니다.

독▶ Ⅰ번 문장에서 제시된 다른 실재물과 로봇 자신을 구별해야 한다는 내용을 블록을 찾는 로봇을 예시로 하여 블록을 찾는 로봇은 스스로부터의 자극과 블록으로부터의 자극을 구별해야만 한다고 합니다.

Ⅴ. Suppose / that you / equip / your robot (with an artificial eye and an artificial arm) (to detect, grab, and pile the blocks).

구▶ 너가 로봇에 블록을 감지하고 잡고 쌓도록 하기 위해서 인공적인 눈과 팔을 설치했다고 가정해보라고 합니다.

독▶ 블록을 감지하고 잡고 쌓을 수 있는 인공적인 눈과 팔을 로봇에 설치했다고 가정하라고 합니다.

Ⅵ. To be successful, your machine / will **have to** have / some built-in system (enabling / it / to discriminate (between the detection of a block and the detection of its own arm)).

구▶ 'enable A to-V'는 'A가 V하는 것을 가능하게 하다'를 뜻합니다.
  - 'between A and B'는 'A와 B 사이'를 의미합니다.
  - 성공하기 위해서, 너의 기계는 (= 로봇은) 그것이 (= 로봇이) 블록 감지와 자신의 팔 감지를 구별할 수 있게 해주는 어떠한 내장된 시스템을 가지고 있어야만 한다고 합니다.

독▶ 'have to'가 제시되었으므로 중심 문장
  - 블록을 쌓는다는 목표에 성공하기 위해서는 블록의 감지와 로봇 자신의 팔 감지를 구별할 수 있어야만 한다고 합니다.

Ⅶ. Your robot / would engage in / circular, self-centered acts (that would drive / it away from the target or external goal).

구▶ 너의 로봇은 로봇을 목표물이나 외부 목표에서 멀어지게 하는 순환적이고 자기 중심적인 행동을 하게 된다고 합니다.

독▶ 로봇이 목표와 멀어지는 순환적이고 자기 중심적인 행동, 즉 블록을 쌓지 않고 스스로 빙빙 도는 행동을 하게 된다고 합니다.

글의 흐름으로 보아, 주어진 문장이 들어가기에 가장 적절한 곳을 고르시오.

> In reality, objects do not conform to a linear lifecycle model; **instead**, they undergo breakdowns, await repairs, are stored away, or find themselves relegated to the basement, only to be rediscovered and repurposed later.

By their very nature, the concepts of maintenance and repair are predominantly examined from a process-oriented perspective. (①) The focus in related scholarly discourse often revolves around the lifespan or lifecycle of objects and technologies. (②) In this context, maintenance and repair are considered practices that have the potential to prolong the existence of objects, ensuring their sustained utilization over an extended period. (③) Krebs and Weber critically engage with anthropomorphic metaphors that imply a biography of things, appropriately highlighting that conventional understanding of the lifecycle of a technology, from its acquisition to its disposal from the household, provides an incomplete definition. (④) **Additionally**, objects may enter recycling or second-hand cycles, **leading to** a dynamic afterlife marked by diverse applications. (⑤) As such, the life of an object exhibits a far more complicated and adaptive path than a simplistic linear progression.

* relegate: 추방하다 ** anthropomorphic: 의인화된

해설 [정답 : ④]

Ⅰ. 주어진 문장에서 실제로, 물건은 선형의 수명 모델에 순응하시 않는다고 합니다. 대신에 그들은 고장을 겪거나, 수리를 기다리거나, 저장되거나, 그들 스스로 지하로 추방되었다는 발견했다가, 결국 나중에 다시 발견되고 목적이 바뀌기도 한다고 합니다. 주어진 문장 뒷 부분에서는 물건이 고상이나 수리 혹은 목적이 바뀌는 것에 대해서 제시되어야 합니다.

Ⅱ. ④번 앞 문장에서는 기술의 수명 주기에 대한 관례적인 이해가 불완전한 정의를 제공한다고 합니다. ④번 뒷 문장에서는 추가적으로, 물건은 재활용 또는 중고품 순환 과정으로 들어갈 수 있어서, 다양한 용도의 역동적인 생후를 야기한다고 합니다. ④번 앞 문장에 기술의 수명 주기에 대한 불완전한 정의가 'Additionally'로 나열이 되기 위해서는 기술의 수명 주기에 대한 오해나 불완전한 정의에 대한 내용이 제시되어야 합니다. 하지만 ④번 뒷 문장에서는 물건이 재활용 또는 중고품 순환 과정을 통해 다양한 용도로 사용될 수 있다는 내용으로 접속사 단절 즉, 심화 (2)에서 배웠던 나열 단절에 해당합니다.

Ⅲ. ④번 뒷 문장에서 물건의 목적이 바뀌는 재활용 또는 중고품 순환 과정이 제시되었고, 주어진 문장의 내용은 ④번 뒷 문장과 나열될 수 있으므로 정답은 ④번이 됩니다.

주. In reality, objects / do not conform to / a linear lifecycle model; **instead**, they / undergo / breakdowns, await repairs, are stored away, or find / themselves / relegated to the basement, (only to be rediscovered and repurposed later).

* relegate: 추방하다

구 'only to-V'는 '결국 V하다'를 의미합니다.

- 실제로, 물건은 선형의 수명 모델에 순응하지 않는다. 대신에 그들은 (= 물체들은) 고장을 겪거나, 수리를 기다리거나, 저장되거나, 그들 스스로 지하로 추방되었다는 발견했다가, 결국 나중에 다시 발견되고 목적이 바뀌기도 한다고 합니다.

독 'instead'가 제시되었으므로 중심 문장

- 물체들은 선형의 수명 모델이라는 것이 적용되지 않고 고장을 겪거나 수리를 기다리는 등 다른 모델을 적용해야 한다고 합니다.

* re (다시) + purpose (목적을 가지다) = repurpose - 목적을 재설정하다, 목적이 바뀌다.

Ⅰ. By their very nature, the concepts (of maintenance and repair) / are predominantly examined (from a process-oriented perspective).

구 바로 그 본질에 의해서, 유지와 수리의 개념은 과정 지향적인 관점으로부터 주로 조사된다고 합니다. (= 검토된다고 합니다.)

독 유지와 수리는 과정 지향적인 관점을 적용받는다고 합니다.

Ⅱ. The focus (in related scholarly discourse) / often revolves around / the lifespan or lifecycle (of objects and technologies).

구 관련된 학문적인 담론의 초점은 물건과 기술의 수명 또는 생애 주기를 중심으로 이루어진다고 합니다.

독 초점은 물건과 기술의 수명 또는 생애 주기에 있다고 합니다.

Ⅲ. In this context, maintenance and repair / are considered / practices (that have / the potential to prolong the existence of objects, ensuring their sustained utilization over an extended period).

구 'consider + O + O.C'는 'O를 O.C라고 여기다'를 의미합니다.

- 이러한 상황에서, 유지와 수리는 물건의 존재를 지속하여 장기간 동안 지속적인 활용을 보장할 수 있는 잠재력을 가진 행위로 여겨진다고 합니다.

독 물건과 기술의 수명 또는 생애 주기에 집중하는 관점에서 유지와 수리는 물건의 활용을 보장할 수 있는 행위라고 합니다.

Ⅳ. Krebs and Weber / critically engage with / anthropomorphic metaphors (that imply / a biography of things), (appropriately highlighting that conventional understanding of the lifecycle of a technology, (from its acquisition to its disposal from the household), provides / an incomplete definition).

** anthropomorphic: 의인화된

구▶ 'from A to B'는 'A부터 B까지'를 의미합니다.

- Krebs와 Weber는 물건의 일대기를 암시하는 의인화된 은유를 비판적으로 참여하여 (= 사용하여) 기술의 수명 주기에 대한 관례적인 이해가, 기술의 획득으로부터 가정에서의 기술의 처분까지 불완전한 정의를 제공한다는 점을 적절히 강조한다고 합니다.

독▶ Krebs와 Weber는 기술의 수명 주기에 대한 일반적인 이해들이 기술에 대한 불완전한 정의를 제공한다고 합니다.

Ⅴ. **Additionally**, objects / may enter / recycling or second-hand cycles, (**leading to** a dynamic afterlife marked by diverse applications).

구▶ 추가적으로, 물건은 재활용 또는 중고품 순환 과정으로 들어갈 수 있어서, 다양한 용도의 역동적인 생후를 야기한다고 합니다.

독▶ 'Additionally'와 'lead to'가 제시되었으므로 중심 문장
- 물건은 재활용 또는 중고품 순환 과정을 통해 다양한 용도로 사용됨으로써 기술의 생명 주기가 길다고 합니다.

* second (두 번째로) + hand (손) = second-hand - 두 번째로 손을 댄 즉, 중고

Ⅵ. As such, the life of an object / exhibits / a far more complicated and adaptive path (than a simplistic linear progression).

구▶ 그와 같이, 물건의 생애는 단순한 선형 진행보다 더욱 복잡하고 적응적인 경로를 보인다고 합니다.

독▶ 물건의 인생은 단순한 진행보다는 더욱 복잡한 경로를 보인다고 합니다.

글의 흐름으로 보아, 주어진 문장이 들어가기에 가장 적절한 곳을 고르시오.

> **Instead**, much like the young child learning how to play 'nicely', the apprentice scientist gains his or her understanding of the moral values inherent in the role by absorption from their colleagues — socialization.

  As particular practices are repeated over time and become more widely shared, the values that they embody are reinforced and reproduced and we speak of them as becoming 'institutionalized'. (①) In some cases, this institutionalization has a formal face to it, with rules and protocols written down, and specialized roles created to ensure that procedures are followed correctly. (②) The main institutions of state — parliament, courts, police and so on — along with certain of the professions, exhibit this formal character. (③) Other social institutions, perhaps the majority, are not like this; science is an example. (④) Although scientists are trained in the substantive content of their discipline, they are not formally instructed in 'how to be a good scientist'. (⑤) We think that these values, along with the values that inform many of the professions, are under threat, just as the value of the professions themselves is under threat.

* apprentice: 도제, 견습   ** inherent: 내재된

해설 [정답 : ⑤]

Ⅰ. 주어진 문장에서는 대신, 마치 착하게 노는 법을 배우는 어린아이처럼 견습 과학자는 동료들로부터 흡수, 즉 사회화를 통해 그 역할에 내재한 도덕적 가치에 대한 이해를 얻는다고 합니다. 주어진 문장에 접속사 'Instead'가 있으므로, 주어진 문장 앞에는 과학자들이 도덕적 가치를 교육받지 않는 것과 같은 대조되는 내용이 들어갈 가능성이 높습니다.

Ⅱ. 지문에서 과학이라는 주제는 ③번 뒷 문장에서 예시로 처음 언급됩니다. ④번 뒷 문장에서는 'they are not formally instructed in 'how to be a good scientist'' 과학자들은 학문의 내용에 대해서는 훈련받지만, 좋은 과학자가 되는 방법에 대해서는 교육받지 않는다고 합니다. ⑤번 뒷 문장에서는 우리는 이러한 가치가 위협받고 있다고 생각하는데, 이 가치에 대한 설명은 ④번 뒷 문장에서 찾아볼 수 없으므로 단절이 발생합니다.

Ⅲ. 주어진 문장에서는 대신에 과학자들은 사회화를 통해 도덕적 가치에 대한 이해를 얻는다고 했습니다. 이것은 ④번 뒷 문장에서 과학자들이 '좋은 과학자가 되는 방법'에 대한 내용으로 이어지며, ⑤번 뒷 문장에서 가치들에 대한 설명이 되므로 주어진 문장은 ⑤번에 들어가야 합니다.

주. **Instead**, much like the young child learning / how to play 'nicely', the apprentice scientist / gains / his or her understanding of the moral values inherent (in the role) by absorption from their colleagues — socialization.

* apprentice: 도제, 견습   ** inherent: 내재된

구▶ 대신, 마치 '착하게' 노는 법을 배우는 어린아이처럼 견습 과학자는 동료들로부터의 흡수, — 사회화를 통해 그 역할에 내재한 도덕적 가치에 대한 이해를 얻는다고 합니다.

독▶ 'instead'가 제시되므로 중심 문장
　- 앞 문장의 경우, 견습 과학자가 학습하지 못하는 내용과 같은 대조되는 내용이 언급되어야 합니다.

Ⅰ. As particular practices / are repeated / over time / and become more widely shared, the values / that / they / embody / are reinforced / and reproduced / and we / speak of them as becoming 'institutionalized'.

구▶ 특정 관행이 오랜 기간 반복되고 더 널리 공유됨에 따라, 그 관행이 구현하는 가치는 강화되고 재생산되며 우리는 그것들이 '제도화'된다고 말한다고 합니다.

독▶ 제도화의 정의에 관해서 설명하는 문장입니다.

Ⅱ. In some cases, this institutionalization / has / a formal face to it, with rules and protocols written down, and specialized roles created to ensure / that / procedures / are followed correctly.

구▶ 어떤 경우에는 이러한 제도화는 공시적인 면모를 갖추기두 하는데, 규칙과 프로토콜이 문서화되고 절차가 올바르게 지켜지도록 확실히 하고자 전문화된 역할이 만들어진다고 합니다.

독▶ Ⅰ번 분상의 제도화에 대한 보충 설명 문장입니디.

Ⅲ. The main institutions (of state — parliament, courts, police and so on — along with certain of the professions), / exhibit this formal character.

구▶ 의회, 법원, 경찰 등 — 국가의 주요 기관이 일부 전문직과 더불어 이러한 공식적인 성격을 보여 준다고 합니다.

독▶ 제도화의 성질을 가진 기관들의 예시가 언급되고 있습니다.

Ⅳ. Other social institutions, perhaps the majority, / are not like this; science / is / an example.

구▶ 다른 사회 기관들, 아마도 대다수는 이와 같지 않을 것인데 과학이 그 예라고 합니다.

독▶ Ⅲ번 문장의 내용이 전환되며, 공식적 성격이 없는 예시로 과학을 언급하고 있습니다.

Ⅴ. Although scientists / are trained in the substantive content (of their discipline), they / are not formally instructed (in 'how to be a good scientist').

> 구▶ '의문사 to-V'는 '의문사를 V하는지'를 의미합니다.
> - 과학자들은 자기 학문의 실질적인 내용에 대해서는 훈련받겠지만, '어떻게 좋은 과학자가 되는지'에 대해서는 공식적으로 교육받지 않는다고 합니다.

> 독▶ 과학자들이 과학자의 도덕성에 관해서 교육받지 않는 것은 과학의 비공식적인 성격의 예시가 되는 문장입니다.

Ⅵ. We / think / that / these values, (along with the values / that / inform / many of the professions), / are under threat, just as the value (of the professions themselves) / is under threat.

> 구▶ 우리는 이러한 가치가 그 전문직에 관한 많은 것을 알려주는 가치와 더불어, 그 전문직 자체의 가치가 위협받고 있는 것과 꼭 마찬가지로 위협받고 있다고 생각한다고 합니다.

04 24학년도 9월 모의평가 38번 (정답률 24%)

글의 흐름으로 보아, 주어진 문장이 들어가기에 가장 적절한 곳을 고르시오.

> **Because** the manipulation of digitally converted sounds meant the reprogramming of binary information, editing operations could be performed **with millisecond precision**.

The shift from analog to digital technology significantly influenced how music was produced. First and foremost, the digitization of sounds — that is, their conversion into numbers — enabled music makers to **undo** what was done. (①) One could, in other words, twist and bend sounds toward something new without sacrificing the original version. (②) This "undo" ability made mistakes considerably less momentous, sparking the creative process and encouraging a generally more experimental mindset. (③) **In addition**, digitally converted sounds could be manipulated simply by programming digital messages rather than using physical tools, **simplifying the editing process significantly.** (④) **For example**, while editing once involved razor blades to physically cut and splice audiotapes, it now involved the cursor and mouse-click of the computer-based sequencer program, which was obviously less time consuming. (⑤) This microlevel access at once made it easier to conceal any traces of manipulations (such as joining tracks in silent spots) and introduced new possibilities for manipulating sounds in audible and experimental ways.

* binary: 2진법의 ** splice: 합쳐 잇다

해설 [정답 : ⑤]

Ⅰ. 주어진 문장에서는 디지털로 변환된 소리의 조작은 2신법의 정보를 재프로그래밍하는 것을 의미했으므로, 편집 작업은 1,000분의 1초의 정밀도로 수행될 수 있었다고 합니다.

Ⅱ. Ⅰ번 문장에서는 아날로그에서 디지털 기술로의 전환이 음악이 어떻게 제작되는지에 큰 영향을 미쳤다고 했고, 'enabled music makers to undo what was done', 즉, 음악 제작자로 하여금 행해졌던 일을 취소할 수 있게, 즉, 원상태로 돌릴 수 있도록 했다고 합니다. Ⅱ번 문장에서 원래 버전을 희생하지 않고 새로운 것을 향해 소리를 비틀고 굽힐 수 있다는 내용이 'undo'를 설명합니다. Ⅲ번 문장에서 Ⅱ번 문장의 'undo' 개념을 'This "undo" ability'로 지칭하고 있습니다. Ⅳ번 문장에서는 'in addition'이라는 표현이 나오는데, 이는 다른 범주를 이야기하기에 Ⅲ번 문장과 연결할 수 있다는 확신을 가지기 힘듭니다. 따라서, 완전한 단절이 발생하는 지점을 찾아야 합니다.

Ⅲ. 그렇다면 주어진 문장과 비교하여 내용을 확인해봅시다. 먼저 주어진 문장에서는 'editing operations could be performed with millisecond precision.', 편집 작업은 1,000분의 1초의 정밀도로 수행될 수 있었다고 했습니다. 주어진 문장이 없으면 ⑤번 뒤의 Ⅵ번 문장에서 'This microlevel access'이 지칭하는 대상이 없어 단절이 일어나기 때문에 주어진 문장은 ⑤번에 위치해야 합니다.

주. (Because the manipulation (of digitally converted sounds) / meant / the reprogramming (of binary information), editing operations / could be / performed (with millisecond precision).

* binary: 2진법의

구 디지털로 변환된 소리의 조작이 이진법 정보의 재프로그래밍을 의미하기 때문에, 편집 작업을 1000분의 1초의 정밀도로 수행할 수 있다고 합니다.

독 '1000분의 1초'라는 구체적 수치가 나왔기 때문에 아주 미세한 단위를 나타내는 표현을 주목해야 합니다.

Ⅰ. The shift (from analog to digital technology) significantly / influenced / (how music / was / produced). First and foremost, the digitization of sounds — that is, their conversion into numbers — enabled / music makers / to undo (what / was / done).

구 아날로그에서 디지털 기술로의 전환은 음악이 어떻게 제작되는지에 큰 영향을 미쳤다고 합니다. 무엇보다도, 소리의 디지털화 즉, '그것을 숫자로 변환하는 것'은 음악 제작자들에게 한 일을 취소할 수 있게 했다고 합니다.

독 '무엇보다도'의 표현으로 알 수 있듯이 여기서 핵심은 '한 일을 취소하다' 입니다.

Ⅱ. One / could, (**in other words**), twist and bend / sounds (toward something new) (without sacrificing / the original version).

구 다시 말해, 원래 버전을 희생하지 않고 새로운 것을 향해 소리를 비틀고 굽힐 수 있다고 합니다.

독 '한 일을 취소하다'라는 표현이 '원래 버전을 희생하지 않고'라는 표현으로 다시 등장했습니다.

Ⅲ. This "undo" ability / made / mistakes / considerably less momentous, (sparking the creative process and encouraging a generally more experimental mindset).

구 이 "취소" 기능은 실수를 훨씬 덜 중요하게 만들어 창의적 과정을 자극하고 일반적으로 더 실험적인 마음가짐을 장려했다고 합니다.

독 이 "취소" 기능이라고 지칭하며 '취소 기능은 원래 버전을 희생하지 않고'라는 표현을 나타냅니다.

Ⅳ. (In addition), digitally converted sounds / could be / manipulated (simply by programming digital messages rather than using physical tools), (simplifying / the editing process significantly).

구 또한, 디지털로 변환된 소리는 물리적 도구를 사용하는 대신 디지털 메시지를 프로그래밍하여 조작할 수 있어 편집과정을 크게 단순화시켰다고 합니다.

Ⅴ. **For example**, (while editing / once involved / razor blades (to physically cut and splice audiotapes)), it / now involved / the cursor and mouse-click (of the computer-based sequencer program), (which / was / obviously less time consuming).

** splice: 합쳐 잇다

구▶ 예를 들면, 편집은 한때 오디오 테이프를 물리적으로 자르고 이어붙이기 위해 면도날을 사용했지만, 이제는 컴퓨터 기반 시퀀서 프로그램의 커서와 마우스 클릭을 사용하게 되었는데, 이는 분명히 시간을 덜 소비했다고 합니다.

독▶ Ⅳ문장의 '물리적 도구를 사용하는 대신 디지털 메시지를 프로그래밍하여 조작'을 자세하게 설명합니다.

Ⅵ. This microlevel access / at once / made / it / easier / (to conceal any traces of manipulations) (such as joining tracks in silent spots) and introduced / new possibilities / (for manipulating / sounds (in audible and experimental ways)).

구▶ 이 초 미세한 수준의 접근은 어떠한 조작의 흔적(예: 조용한 곳에서 트랙을 합치는 것과 같은)을 숨기기 더 쉽게 만들었으며, 소리를 들을 수 있고 실험적인 방법으로 조작하는 새로운 가능성을 도입했다고 합니다.

독▶ '1000분의 1초'라는 구체적 수치를 지칭하는 '이 초 미세한 수준의 접근'이 등장했으므로 주어진 문장은 Ⅵ문장 앞에 위치해야 합니다.

┃절. 모. 평. (절대평가 모든 평가원 기출)

01 25학년도 9월 평가원 39번 [정답과 해설 208page]

글의 흐름으로 보아, 주어진 문장이 들어가기에 가장 적절한 곳을 고르시오.

> Unfortunately, at the scales, accuracy, and precision most useful to protected area management, the future not only promises to be unprecedented, but it also promises to be unpredictable.

To decide whether and how to intervene in ecosystems, protected area managers normally need a reasonably clear idea of what future ecosystems would be like if they did not intervene. (①) Management practices usually involve defining a more desirable future condition and implementing management actions designed to push or guide ecosystems toward that condition. (②) Managers need confidence in the likely outcomes of their interventions. (③) This traditional and inherently logical approach requires a high degree of predictive ability, and predictions must be developed at appropriate spatial and temporal scales, often localized and near-term. (④) To illustrate this, consider the uncertainties involved in predicting climatic changes, how ecosystems are likely to respond to climatic changes, and the likely efficacy of actions that might be taken to counter adverse effects of climatic changes. (⑤) Comparable uncertainties surround the nature and magnitude of future changes in other ecosystem stressors.

* adverse: 해로운 ** magnitude: 크기

02 21학년도 수능 39번 [정답과 해설 211page]

글의 흐름으로 보아, 주어진 문장이 들어가기에 가장 적절한 곳을 고르시오.

> Note that copyright covers the expression of an idea and not the idea itself.

Designers draw on their experience of design when approaching a new project. This includes the use of previous designs that they know work — both designs that they have created themselves and those that others have created. (①) Others' creations often spark inspiration that also leads to new ideas and innovation. (②) This is wellknown and understood. (③) However, the expression of an idea is protected by copyright, and people who infringe on that copyright can be taken to court and prosecuted. (④) This means, for example, that while there are numerous smartphones all with similar functionality, this does not represent an infringement of copyright as the idea has been expressed in different ways and it is the expression that has been copyrighted. (⑤) Copyright is free and is automatically invested in the author, for instance, the writer of a book or a programmer who develops a program, unless they sign the copyright over to someone else.

* infringe: 침해하다 ** prosecute: 기소하다

글의 흐름으로 보아, 주어진 문장이 들어가기에 가장 적절한 곳을 고르시오.

> Rather, it evolved naturally as certain devices were found in practice to be both workable and useful.

Film has no grammar. (①) There are, however, some vaguely defined rules of usage in cinematic language, and the syntax of film — its systematic arrangement — orders these rules and indicates relationships among them. (②) As with written and spoken languages, it is important to remember that the syntax of film is a result of its usage, not a determinant of it. (③) There is nothing preordained about film syntax. (④) Like the syntax of written and spoken language, the syntax of film is an organic development, descriptive rather than prescriptive, and it has changed considerably over the years. (⑤) "Hollywood Grammar" may sound laughable now, but during the thirties, forties, and early fifties it was an accurate model of the way Hollywood films were constructed.

* preordained: 미리 정해진

글의 흐름으로 보아, 주어진 문장이 들어가기에 가장 적절한 곳을 고르시오.

> It may be easier to reach an agreement when settlement terms don't have to be implemented until months in the future.

Negotiators should try to find ways to slice a large issue into smaller pieces, known as using *salami tactics*. (①) Issues that can be expressed in quantitative, measurable units are easy to slice. (②) For example, compensation demands can be divided into cents-per-hour increments or lease rates can be quoted as dollars per square foot. (③) When working to fractionate issues of principle or precedent, parties may use the time horizon (when the principle goes into effect or how long it will last) as a way to fractionate the issue. (④) Another approach is to vary the number of ways that the principle may be applied. (⑤) For example, a company may devise a family emergency leave plan that allows employees the opportunity to be away from the company for a period of no longer than three hours, and no more than once a month, for illness in the employee's immediate family.

* increment: 증가 ** fractionate: 세분하다

글의 흐름으로 보아, 주어진 문장이 들어가기에 가장 적절한 곳을 고르시오.

> At the next step in the argument, however, the analogy breaks down.

Misprints in a book or in any written message usually have a negative impact on the content, sometimes (literally) fatally. (①) The displacement of a comma, for instance, may be a matter of life and death. (②) Similarly most mutations have harmful consequences for the organism in which they occur, meaning that they reduce its reproductive fitness. (③) Occasionally, however, a mutation may occur that increases the fitness of the organism, just as an accidental failure to reproduce the text of the first edition might provide more accurate or updated information. (④) A favorable mutation is going to be more heavily represented in the next generation, since the organism in which it occurred will have more offspring and mutations are transmitted to the offspring. (⑤) By contrast, there is no mechanism by which a book that accidentally corrects the mistakes of the first edition will tend to sell better.

* analogy: 유사 ** mutation: 돌연변이

글의 흐름으로 보아, 주어진 문장이 들어가기에 가장 적절한 곳을 고르시오.

> A problem, however, is that supervisors often work in locations apart from their employees and therefore are not able to observe their subordinates' performance.

In most organizations, the employee's immediate supervisor evaluates the employee's performance. (①) This is because the supervisor is responsible for the employee's performance, providing supervision, handing out assignments, and developing the employee. (②) Should supervisors rate employees on performance dimensions they cannot observe? (③) To eliminate this dilemma, more and more organizations are implementing assessments referred to as 360-degree evaluations. (④) Employees are rated not only by their supervisors but by coworkers, clients or citizens, professionals in other agencies with whom they work, and subordinates. (⑤) The reason for this approach is that often coworkers and clients or citizens have a greater opportunity to observe an employee's performance and are in a better position to evaluate many performance dimensions.

* subordinate: 부하 직원

글의 흐름으로 보아, 주어진 문장이 들어가기에 가장 적절한 곳을 고르시오.

> There's a reason for that: traditionally, park designers attempted to create such a feeling by planting tall trees at park boundaries, building stone walls, and constructing other means of partition.

Parks take the shape demanded by the cultural concerns of their time. Once parks are in place, they are no inert stage — their purposes and meanings are made and remade by planners and by park users. Moments of park creation are particularly telling, however, for they reveal and actualize ideas about nature and its relationship to urban society. (①) Indeed, what distinguishes a park from the broader category of public space is the representation of nature that parks are meant to embody. (②) Public spaces include parks, concrete plazas, sidewalks, even indoor atriums. (③) Parks typically have trees, grass, and other plants as their central features. (④) When entering a city park, people often imagine a sharp separation from streets, cars, and buildings. (⑤) What's behind this idea is not only landscape architects' desire to design aesthetically suggestive park spaces, but a much longer history of Western thought that envisions cities and nature as antithetical spaces and oppositional forces.

* aesthetically: 미적으로 ** antithetical: 대조적인

글의 흐름으로 보아, 주어진 문장이 들어가기에 가장 적절한 곳을 고르시오.

> Continuous emissions measurement can be costly, particularly where there are many separate sources of emissions, and for many pollution problems this may be a major disincentive to direct taxation of emissions.

Environmental taxes based directly on measured emissions can, in principle, be very precisely targeted to the policy's environmental objectives. (①) If a firm pollutes more, it pays additional tax directly in proportion to the rise in emissions. (②) The polluter thus has an incentive to reduce emissions in any manner that is less costly per unit of abatement than the tax on each unit of residual emissions. (③) The great attraction of basing the tax directly on measured emissions is that the actions the polluter can take to reduce tax liability are actions that also reduce emissions. (④) Nevertheless, the technologies available for monitoring the concentrations and flows of particular substances in waste discharges have been developing rapidly. (⑤) In the future, it may be possible to think of taxing measured emissions in a wider range of applications.

* abatement: 감소 ** liability: 부담액

글의 흐름으로 보아, 주어진 문장이 들어가기에 가장 적절한 곳을 고르시오.

> Also, it has become difficult for companies to develop new pesticides, even those that can have major beneficial effects and few negative effects.

　Simply maintaining yields at current levels often requires new cultivars and management methods, since pests and diseases continue to evolve, and aspects of the chemical, physical, and social environment can change over several decades. (①) In the 1960s, many people considered pesticides to be mainly beneficial to mankind. (②) Developing new, broadly effective, and persistent pesticides often was considered to be the best way to control pests on crop plants. (③) Since that time, it has become apparent that broadly effective pesticides can have harmful effects on beneficial insects, which can negate their effects in controlling pests, and that persistent pesticides can damage non-target organisms in the ecosystem, such as birds and people. (④) Very high costs are involved in following all of the procedures needed to gain government approval for new pesticides. (⑤) Consequently, more consideration is being given to other ways to manage pests, such as incorporating greater resistance to pests into cultivars by breeding and using other biological control methods.

* pesticide: 살충제 ** cultivar: 품종 *** breed: 개량하다

글의 흐름으로 보아, 주어진 문장이 들어가기에 가장 적절한 곳을 고르시오.

> Without any special legal protection for trade secrets, however, the secretive inventor risks that an employee or contractor will disclose the proprietary information.

　Trade secret law aims to promote innovation, although it accomplishes this objective in a very different manner than patent protection. (①) Notwithstanding the advantages of obtaining a patent, many innovators prefer to protect their innovation through secrecy. (②) They may believe that the cost and delay of seeking a patent are too great or that secrecy better protects their investment and increases their profit. (③) They might also believe that the invention can best be utilized over a longer period of time than a patent would allow. (④) Once the idea is released, it will be "free as the air" under the background norms of a free market economy. (⑤) Such a predicament would lead any inventor seeking to rely upon secrecy to spend an inordinate amount of resources building high and impassable fences around their research facilities and greatly limiting the number of people with access to the proprietary information.

* patent: 특허 ** predicament: 곤경

11 22학년도 수능 39번

글의 흐름으로 보아, 주어진 문장이 들어가기에 가장 적절한 곳을 고르시오.

> As long as the irrealism of the silent black and white film predominated, one could not take filmic fantasies for representations of reality.

Cinema is valuable not for its ability to make visible the hidden outlines of our reality, but for its ability to reveal what reality itself veils — the dimension of fantasy. (①) This is why, to a person, the first great theorists of film decried the introduction of sound and other technical innovations (such as color) that pushed film in the direction of realism. (②) Since cinema was an entirely fantasmatic art, these innovations were completely unnecessary. (③) And what's worse, they could do nothing but turn filmmakers and audiences away from the fantasmatic dimension of cinema, potentially transforming film into a mere delivery device for representations of reality. (④) But sound and color threatened to create just such an illusion, thereby destroying the very essence of film art. (⑤) As Rudolf Arnheim puts it, "The creative power of the artist can only come into play where reality and the medium of representation do not coincide."

* decry: 공공연히 비난하다 ** fantasmatic: 환상의

12 22학년도 9월 평가원 38번

글의 흐름으로 보아, 주어진 문장이 들어가기에 가장 적절한 곳을 고르시오.

> It was not until relatively recent times that scientists came to understand the relationships between the structural elements of materials and their properties.

The earliest humans had access to only a very limited number of materials, those that occur naturally: stone, wood, clay, skins, and so on. (①) With time, they discovered techniques for producing materials that had properties superior to those of the natural ones; these new materials included pottery and various metals. (②) Furthermore, it was discovered that the properties of a material could be altered by heat treatments and by the addition of other substances. (③) At this point, materials utilization was totally a selection process that involved deciding from a given, rather limited set of materials, the one best suited for an application based on its characteristics. (④) This knowledge, acquired over approximately the past 100 years, has empowered them to fashion, to a large degree, the characteristics of materials. (⑤) Thus, tens of thousands of different materials have evolved with rather specialized characteristics that meet the needs of our modern and complex society, including metals, plastics, glasses, and fibers.

글의 흐름으로 보아, 주어진 문장이 들어가기에 가장 적절한 곳을 고르시오.

> Yes, some contests are seen as world class, such as identification of the Higgs particle or the development of high temperature superconductors.

Science is sometimes described as a winner-take-all contest, meaning that there are no rewards for being second or third. This is an extreme view of the nature of scientific contests. (①) Even those who describe scientific contests in such a way note that it is a somewhat inaccurate description, given that replication and verification have social value and are common in science. (②) It is also inaccurate to the extent that it suggests that only a handful of contests exist. (③) But many other contests have multiple parts, and the number of such contests may be increasing. (④) By way of example, for many years it was thought that there would be "one" cure for cancer, but it is now realized that cancer takes multiple forms and that multiple approaches are needed to provide a cure. (⑤) There won't be one winner — there will be many.

* replication: 반복 ** verification: 입증

글의 흐름으로 보아, 주어진 문장이 들어가기에 가장 적절한 곳을 고르시오.

> I have still not exactly pinpointed Maddy's character since wickedness takes many forms.

Imagine I tell you that Maddy is bad. Perhaps you infer from my intonation, or the context in which we are talking, that I mean morally bad. Additionally, you will probably infer that I am disapproving of Maddy, or saying that I think you should disapprove of her, or similar, given typical linguistic conventions and assuming I am sincere. (①) However, you might not get a more detailed sense of the particular sorts of way in which Maddy is bad, her typical character traits, and the like, since people can be bad in many ways. (②) In contrast, if I say that Maddy is wicked, then you get more of a sense of her typical actions and attitudes to others. (③) The word 'wicked' is more specific than 'bad'. (④) But there is more detail nevertheless, perhaps a stronger connotation of the sort of person Maddy is. (⑤) In addition, and again assuming typical linguistic conventions, you should also get a sense that I am disapproving of Maddy, or saying that you should disapprove of her, or similar, assuming that we are still discussing her moral character.

* connotation: 함축

15 21학년도 9월 평가원 38번

글의 흐름으로 보아, 주어진 문장이 들어가기에 가장 적절한 곳을 고르시오.

> As long as you do not run out of copies before completing this process, you will know that you have a sufficient number to go around.

We sometimes solve number problems almost without realizing it. (①) For example, suppose you are conducting a meeting and you want to ensure that everyone there has a copy of the agenda. (②) You can deal with this by labelling each copy of the handout in turn with the initials of each of those present. (③) You have then solved this problem without resorting to arithmetic and without explicit counting. (④) There are numbers at work for us here all the same and they allow precise comparison of one collection with another, even though the members that make up the collections could have entirely different characters, as is the case here, where one set is a collection of people, while the other consists of pieces of paper. (⑤) What numbers allow us to do is to compare the relative size of one set with another.

* arithmetic: 산수

16 24학년도 9월 평가원 39번

글의 흐름으로 보아, 주어진 문장이 들어가기에 가장 적절한 곳을 고르시오.

> In the case of specialists such as art critics, a deeper familiarity with materials and techniques is often useful in reaching an informed judgement about a work.

Acknowledging the making of artworks does not require a detailed, technical knowledge of, say, how painters mix different kinds of paint, or how an image editing tool works. (①) All that is required is a general sense of a significant difference between working with paints and working with an imaging application. (②) This sense might involve a basic familiarity with paints and paintbrushes as well as a basic familiarity with how we use computers, perhaps including how we use consumer imaging apps. (③) This is because every kind of artistic material or tool comes with its own challenges and affordances for artistic creation. (④) Critics are often interested in the ways artists exploit different kinds of materials and tools for particular artistic effect. (⑤) They are also interested in the success of an artist's attempt — embodied in the artwork itself — to push the limits of what can be achieved with certain materials and tools.

* affordance: 행위유발성 ** exploit: 활용하다

글의 흐름으로 보아, 주어진 문장이 들어가기에 가장 적절한 곳을 고르시오.

> When the team painted fireflies' light organs dark, a new set of bats took twice as long to learn to avoid them.

Fireflies don't just light up their behinds to attract mates, they also glow to tell bats not to eat them. This twist in the tale of the trait that gives fireflies their name was discovered by Jesse Barber and his colleagues. The glow's warning role benefits both fireflies and bats, because these insects taste disgusting to the mammals. (①) When swallowed, chemicals released by fireflies cause bats to throw them back up. (②) The team placed eight bats in a dark room with three or four fireflies plus three times as many tasty insects, including beetles and moths, for four days. (③) During the first night, all the bats captured at least one firefly. (④) But by the fourth night, most bats had learned to avoid fireflies and catch all the other prey instead. (⑤) It had long been thought that firefly bioluminescence mainly acted as a mating signal, but the new finding explains why firefly larvae also glow despite being immature for mating.

* bioluminescence: 생물 발광 (發光)
** larvae: larva(애벌레)의 복수형

글의 흐름으로 보아, 주어진 문장이 들어가기에 가장 적절한 곳을 고르시오.

> As a result, they are fit and grow better, but they aren't particularly long-lived.

When trees grow together, nutrients and water can be optimally divided among them all so that each tree can grow into the best tree it can be. If you "help" individual trees by getting rid of their supposed competition, the remaining trees are bereft. They send messages out to their neighbors unsuccessfully, because nothing remains but stumps. Every tree now grows on its own, giving rise to great differences in productivity. (①) Some individuals photosynthesize like mad until sugar positively bubbles along their trunk. (②) This is because a tree can be only as strong as the forest that surrounds it. (③) And there are now a lot of losers in the forest. (④) Weaker members, who would once have been supported by the stronger ones, suddenly fall behind. (⑤) Whether the reason for their decline is their location and lack of nutrients, a passing sickness, or genetic makeup, they now fall prey to insects and fungi.

* bereft: 잃은 ** stump: 그루터기
*** photosynthesize: 광합성하다

글의 흐름으로 보아, 주어진 문장이 들어가기에 가장 적절한 곳을 고르시오.

> On top of the hurdles introduced in accessing his or her money, if a suspected fraud is detected, the account holder has to deal with the phone call asking if he or she made the suspicious transactions.

 Each new wave of technology is intended to enhance user convenience, as well as improve security, but sometimes these do not necessarily go hand-in-hand. For example, the transition from magnetic stripe to embedded chip slightly slowed down transactions, sometimes frustrating customers in a hurry. (①) Make a service too burdensome, and the potential customer will go elsewhere. (②) This obstacle applies at several levels. (③) Passwords, double-key identification, and biometrics such as fingerprint-, iris-, and voice recognition are all ways of keeping the account details hidden from potential fraudsters, of keeping your data dark. (④) But they all inevitably add a burden to the use of the account. (⑤) This is all useful at some level — indeed, it can be reassuring knowing that your bank is keeping alert to protect you — but it becomes tiresome if too many such calls are received.

* fraud: 사기

글의 흐름으로 보아, 주어진 문장이 들어가기에 가장 적절한 곳을 고르시오.

> This is particularly true since one aspect of sleep is decreased responsiveness to the environment.

 The role that sleep plays in evolution is still under study. (①) One possibility is that it is an advantageous adaptive state of decreased metabolism for an animal when there are no more pressing activities. (②) This seems true for deeper states of inactivity such as hibernation during the winter when there are few food supplies, and a high metabolic cost to maintaining adequate temperature. (③) It may be true in daily situations as well, for instance for a prey species to avoid predators after dark. (④) On the other hand, the apparent universality of sleep, and the observation that mammals such as cetaceans have developed such highly complex mechanisms to preserve sleep on at least one side of the brain at a time, suggests that sleep additionally provides some vital service(s) for the organism. (⑤) If sleep is universal even when this potential price must be paid, the implication may be that it has important functions that cannot be obtained just by quiet, wakeful resting.

* metabolism: 신진대사 ** mammal: 포유동물

글의 흐름으로 보아, 주어진 문장이 들어가기에 가장 적절한 곳을 고르시오.

> This makes sense from the perspective of information reliability.

The dynamics of collective detection have an interesting feature. Which cue(s) do individuals use as evidence of predator attack? In some cases, when an individual detects a predator, its best response is to seek shelter. (①) Departure from the group may signal danger to nonvigilant animals and cause what appears to be a coordinated flushing of prey from the area. (②) Studies on dark-eyed juncos (a type of bird) support the view that nonvigilant animals attend to departures of individual group mates but that the departure of multiple individuals causes a greater escape response in the nonvigilant individuals. (③) If one group member departs, it might have done so for a number of reasons that have little to do with predation threat. (④) If nonvigilant animals escaped each time a single member left the group, they would frequently respond when there was no predator (a false alarm). (⑤) On the other hand, when several individuals depart the group at the same time, a true threat is much more likely to be present.

* predator: 포식자 ** vigilant: 경계하는 *** flushing: 날아오름

글의 흐름으로 보아, 주어진 문장이 들어가기에 가장 적절한 곳을 고르시오.

> In particular, they define a group as two or more people who interact with, and exert mutual influences on, each other.

In everyday life, we tend to see any collection of people as a group. (①) However, social psychologists use this term more precisely. (②) It is this sense of mutual interaction or inter-dependence for a common purpose which distinguishes the members of a group from a mere aggregation of individuals. (③) For example, as Kenneth Hodge observed, a collection of people who happen to go for a swim after work on the same day each week does not, strictly speaking, constitute a group because these swimmers do not interact with each other in a structured manner. (④) By contrast, a squad of young competitive swimmers who train every morning before going to school is a group because they not only share a common objective (training for competition) but also interact with each other in formal ways (e.g., by warming up together beforehand). (⑤) It is this sense of people coming together to achieve a common objective that defines a "team".

* exert: 발휘하다 ** aggregation: 집합

글의 흐름으로 보아, 주어진 문장이 들어가기에 가장 적절한 곳을 고르시오.

> Compounding the difficulty, now more than ever, is what ergonomists call information overload, where a leader is overrun with inputs—via e-mails, meetings, and phone calls—that only distract and confuse her thinking.

 Clarity is often a difficult thing for a leader to obtain. Concerns of the present tend to seem larger than potentially greater concerns that lie farther away. (①) Some decisions by their nature present great complexity, whose many variables must come together a certain way for the leader to succeed. (②) Alternatively, the leader's information might be only fragmentary, which might cause her to fill in the gaps with assumptions—sometimes without recognizing them as such. (③) And the merits of a leader's most important decisions, by their nature, typically are not clear-cut. (④) Instead those decisions involve a process of assigning weights to competing interests, and then determining, based upon some criterion, which one predominates. (⑤) The result is one of judgment, of shades of gray; like saying that Beethoven is a better composer than Brahms.

* ergonomist: 인간 공학자 ** fragmentary: 단편적인

글의 흐름으로 보아, 주어진 문장이 들어가기에 가장 적절한 곳을 고르시오.

> Retraining current employees for new positions within the company will also greatly reduce their fear of being laid off.

 Introduction of robots into factories, while employment of human workers is being reduced, creates worry and fear. (①) It is the responsibility of management to prevent or, at least, to ease these fears. (②) For example, robots could be introduced only in new plants rather than replacing humans in existing assembly lines. (③) Workers should be included in the planning for new factories or the introduction of robots into existing plants, so they can participate in the process. (④) It may be that robots are needed to reduce manufacturing costs so that the company remains competitive, but planning for such cost reductions should be done jointly by labor and management. (⑤) Since robots are particularly good at highly repetitive simple motions, the replaced human workers should be moved to positions where judgment and decisions beyond the abilities of robots are required.

글의 흐름으로 보아, 주어진 문장이 들어가기에 가장 적절한 곳을 고르시오.

> Personal stories connect with larger narratives to generate new identities.

The growing complexity of the social dynamics determining food choices makes the job of marketers and advertisers increasingly more difficult. (①) In the past, mass production allowed for accessibility and affordability of products, as well as their wide distribution, and was accepted as a sign of progress. (②) Nowadays it is increasingly replaced by the fragmentation of consumers among smaller and smaller segments that are supposed to reflect personal preferences. (③) Everybody feels different and special and expects products serving his or her inclinations. (④) In reality, these supposedly individual preferences end up overlapping with emerging, temporary, always changing, almost tribal formations solidifying around cultural sensibilities, social identifications, political sensibilities, and dietary and health concerns. (⑤) These consumer communities go beyond national boundaries, feeding on global and widely shared repositories of ideas, images, and practices.

* fragmentation: 파편화 ** repository: 저장소

글의 흐름으로 보아, 주어진 문장이 들어가기에 가장 적절한 곳을 고르시오.

> This active involvement provides a basis for depth of aesthetic processing and reflection on the meaning of the work.

There are interesting trade-offs in the relative importance of subject matter (i.e., figure) and style (i.e., background). (①) In highly representational paintings, plays, or stories, the focus is on subject matter that resembles everyday life and the role of background style is to facilitate the construction of mental models. (②) Feelings of pleasure and uncertainty carry the viewer along to the conclusion of the piece. (③) In highly expressionist works, novel stylistic devices work in an inharmonious manner against the subject matter thereby creating a disquieting atmosphere. (④) Thus, when the work is less "readable" (or easily interpreted), its departure from conventional forms reminds the viewer or reader that an "aesthetic attitude" is needed to appreciate the whole episode. (⑤) An ability to switch between the "pragmatic attitude" of everyday life and an "aesthetic attitude" is fundamental to a balanced life.

* aesthetic: 미학의 ** pragmatic: 실용주의의

Chapter

06

문법

6-1 형식

형식이란?

모든 문법책을 펴면 가장 먼저 나오는 단원, 바로 형식입니다. 형식하면 무엇이 떠오르나요?
1형식부터 5형식까지의 형식의 구조, 혹은 내신 문제에 지겹도록 나오는 지각동사, 수여동사, 사역동사 등이 있을 겁니다.

형식에 대해 알아보기 전에 앞서서 이것부터 생각해 봅시다.

영어에서 형식이란 무엇일까요?

형식이란 영어의 문장들을 구분하는 기준입니다.
즉, 여러분이 아무 문장을 하나 만들 때, 책에서 영어로 된 문장을 하나 볼 때, 이것을 '동사'에 따라 구분하는 것이 바로 형식입니다.

형식의 구조

1형식 : 주어(S) + 동사(V)
2형식 : 주어(S) + 동사(V) + 보어(C)
3형식 : 주어(S) + 동사(V) + 목적어(O)
4형식 : 주어(S) + 동사(V) + 간접목적어(I.O) + 직접목적어(D.O)
5형식 : 주어(S) + 동사(V) + 목적어(O) + 목적격보어(O.C)

영어의 모든 문장을 그 종류에 따라 5가지로 구분해서 문장을 파악하기 좀 더 쉽게 하기 위해 배우는 것이 바로 형식이며, 여러분이 형식을 알아둬야 하는 이유입니다.

An interesting aspect of human psychology is that we tend to like things more and find them more <u>appealing</u> if everything about those things is not obvious the first time we experience them.

다음 문장은 어법상 옳은 문장일까요?

정답은 ○입니다.

find가 5형식 동사로 사용됐으므로,
aspect(주어) + find(동사) + them(목적어) + appealing(목적격보어)
순으로 이어지고 있으며,
목적격 보어 자리에는 형용사가 들어갈 수 있으므로 형용사의 역할을 할 수 있는 현재분사 appealing이 들어가야 합니다.

이 한 문장에만 형식, 품사, 형용사, 분사를 모두 섞은 문제 풀이가 필요합니다. 이렇게 형식은 형식 자체 다른 문법과 연계되어 나오기 때문에 모든 문법과 함께 학습하는 것이 필요합니다.

• 주요 2형식 동사 : be, keep, seem, become, stay, get 지각동사 look, taste, feel, smell 등
• 주요 5형식 동사 : call, name, consider, find, 사역동사 make, let, have 등

가장 흔한 문제 출제 방식은 2, 5형식의 보어를 이용한 형용사/부사 구분 문제나, 분사 문세로 나오는 것입니다. 각 단원에서 다시 한번 설명하겠습니다.

6-2 수 일치

▌쉽디 쉬운 단원?

명사가 단수, 복수인지에 따라 동사를 변화시키는 것

수 일치를 학생들이 많이 틀리는 이유는 결코 단원이 어려워서가 아닙니다. 평가원이 쳐두는 낚시에 걸리는 학생들이 많기 때문입니다.

> He (go / goes) to school everyday.

이 문제를 틀리는 학생은 없습니다.
주어가 He라는 것을, 동사가 go라는 것을 아주 명확하게 알 수 있기 때문이죠.

하지만 영어의 모든 문장이 주어, 동사만으로 간단하게 끝나는 경우는 없으며, 수식어구, 전치사구, 준동사구, 관계사절 등등의 다양한 잡다한 표현들이 추가되면서 문장이 길어지고 명사들이 난무하면 여러분은 헷갈리기 시작합니다.

> The pyramid, the result of the efforts of many workers, (is / are) still standing there today.

평가원의 흔한 낚시 중 하나입니다. the pyramid, result, efforts, workers, 등 많은 명사들이 나오지만 동사의 주어는 The pyramid이므로 동사는 is가 됩니다. 동사 바로 앞의 workers를 주어로 착각하는 학생들은 평가원의 덫에 빠진 것입니다.

단순히 주어에 수에 따른 동사만을 물어보는 것 외에도, 대명사를 it / them으로 구분하여 수를 파악해야 하는 문법 문제도 존재합니다. 핵심은, '동작의 주체를 명확하게 파악하는 것'이며, 이를 위해서는 정확한 해석이 필요합니다. 문법은 문법 지식만으로 풀기보다는 정밀한 해석을 통해 주어와 동사를 제대로 파악하려는 노력이 필요합니다.

▌체화

- Malinowski, the classic anthropological fieldworker, describes the early stages of fieldwork as ' strange, sometimes unpleasant, sometimes intensely interesting adventure which soon (adopts / adopt) quite a natural course.'

- It refers to those who (claims / claim) to be proficient at countless tasks, but cannot perform a single one of them well.

- By comparison, evaluation of performances such as diving, gymnastics, and figure skating is more subjective — although elaborate scoring rules help make (it / them) more objective.

- There is a deep cavern on the island, containing the bones and arms of the Indians, who, it is supposed, (was / were) buried there.

- both major breakthroughs, like understanding the genetic structure of life, and smaller (one / ones), such as advances in mathematics or basic chemistry.

- Malinowski, the classic anthropological fieldworker, describes the early stages of fieldwork as 'strange, sometimes unpleasant, sometimes intensely interesting adventure which soon (**adopts** / adopt) quite a natural course.'

→ 관계대명사 which의 선행사가 adventure이므로 동사로는 adopts가 와야 합니다.

- It refers to those who (claims / **claim**) to be proficient at countless tasks, but cannot perform a single one of them well.

→ 관계대명사 who의 선행사가 복수인 those이므로, 복수동사인 claim이 쓰여야 합니다.

- By comparison, evaluation of performances such as diving, gymnastics, and figure skating is more subjective — although elaborate scoring rules help make (**it** / them) more objective.

→ 대명사가 evaluation을 대신하므로 단수인 it이 쓰여야 합니다.

- There is a deep cavern on the island, containing the bones and arms of the Indians, who, it is supposed, (was / **were**) buried there.

→ 관계대명사 who의 선행사가 the Indians이므로 복수형 동사인 were이 쓰여야 합니다.

- both major breakthroughs, like understanding the genetic structure of life, and smaller (one / **ones**), such as advances in mathematics or basic chemistry.

→ 앞의 breakthroughs를 대신하는 대명사가 쓰여야하므로 복수형 부정대명사 ones가 쓰여야 합니다.

6-3 병렬 구조

▌수 일치의 동사 버전?

수 일치가 주어와 연결되는 동사를 파악하는 것이 중요하다면,
병렬 구조는 동사와 연결되는 동사를 파악하는 것이 핵심입니다.

다음 문제를 풀어봅시다.

20학년도 6월 평가원

For example, we might hear a song on the radio for the first time that catches our interest and (decide / decides) we like it.

문장을 해석하면 다음과 같습니다.

예를 들어,
우리는 라디오에서 우리의 관심을 끄는 노래를 처음 듣고, 그 노래가 마음에 든다고 결정할 수 있다.

결정하는 게 누구죠? 바로 '우리'입니다. 우리가 노래를 듣고, 결정하는 것입니다.
즉, decide는 hear과 연결되므로, 답은 decide가 됩니다.

병렬 구조는 수 일치와 같은 방식으로 문제를 풀 수 있습니다.
정확한 해석. 여러분이 지문을 정확하게 해석해야 하는 이유는 단순히 지문의 빈칸, 주제들을 파악하기 위해서뿐만이 것이 아니라는 것을 기억할 필요가 있습니다.

체화

- The purser accepted the responsibility for the valuables and (remarking / remarked), "It's all right. I'l be very glad to take care of them for you.

- We try to support the present with the future and (think / thinking) of arranging things we cannot control, for a time we have no certainty of reaching.

- The ears of a rabbit are longer than (that / those) of a cat.

• The purser accepted the responsibility for the valuables and (remarking / **remarked**), "It's all right. I'l be very glad to take care of them for you.

→ 동사 accepted와 병렬 구조를 이루어야 하므로 remarked가 쓰여야 합니다.

• We try to support the present with the future and (**think** / thinking) of arranging things we cannot control, for a time we have no certainty of reaching.

→ 동사 try와 병렬구조를 이루면서 주어인 We에 연결되는 think가 쓰여야 합니다.

• The ears of a rabbit are longer than (that / **those**) of a cat.

→ 토끼의 귀와 고양이의 귀를 병렬로 비교하고 있으므로 대명사는 ears가 됩니다. 복수 대명사를 지칭하는 those가 쓰여야 합니다.

memo

대(代)동사란?

대동사는 대신해서 쓰이는 동사를 의미합니다.

대신해서 쓰이는 명사가 대명사라면, 대신해서 쓰이는 동사가 대동사입니다.

대동사에는 do, be, have가 있으며, 각 동사들의 활용은 다음과 같습니다.

- do/does : 일반 동사를 대신함
- be동사 : be동사를 대신함
- have/has : 현재 완료를 대신함

어떤 식으로 문제에 나오는지, 바로 예시 문제로 들어가 봅시다.

16학년도 9월 평가원 (고2)

It not only cleans clothes, but it <u>is</u> so with far less water, detergent, and energy than washing by hand requires.

cleans라는 동사가 일반 동사로 쓰였으므로,
but 뒤의 앞에 나온 동사를 대신하여 is가 아닌 does가 들어가야 합니다.

대동사가 쓰였다는 것만 파악한다면 문제의 난이도가 급락하지만,
이것을 파악하지 못한다면 어? 수 일치 문제인가? 라고 생각하고 그대로 틀려버리는 문법이 바로 대동사입니다.
모든 문법은 주어와 동사를 잡는 것부터 시작하는 것이 기본이라는 것을 기억합시다.

6-5 재귀대명사

주어=목적어

형식 단원에서 한 번 설명했지만, 재귀대명사는 동작의 주체인 주어와, 대상인 목적어가 같을 때, 사용하는
대명사입니다.

- He called the name of the students
  → He(주어) + called(동사) + the name(목적어) → He≠the name

- He called himself a patriot
  → He(주어) + called(동사) + himself(목적어) + patriot(목적격보어) → He=himself

재귀대명사의 형태
- 단수 : myself, yourself, herself, himself, itself, oneself
- 복수 : ourselves, yourselves, themselves

재귀대명사를 이용한 문법문제는 다음과 같은 경우가 있습니다.

18학년도 6월 평가원

He is quick to inform friends and relatives as soon as their infant holds her head up, reaches for
objects, sits by (himself / herself), and walks alone.

목적어의 동작은 sits가 됩니다.
그렇다면 주어와 목적어는 어차피 같으므로,
앉는 사람이 He라면 답은 himself가, infant라면 herself가 답이 되겠죠. 문장에서는 infant가 holds, reaches,
sits, walks라는 행위를 하는 것이 병렬로 연결되어 있으므로 sits의 주어는 infant가 되며, 답은 herself가 됩니다.

재귀대명사 역시 기존에 설명한 해석으로 푸는 문제들과 크게 다르지 않습니다.
정확한 해석을 통해 주어와 동사를 정확하게 파악하나면 꽤나 수월하게 풀 수 있는 단원입니다.

주어 ↔ 동사

도치란 주어와 동사의 위치가 바뀌는 것이 도치입니다. 문법책을 펴면 도치는 일반적으로 마지막에 위치하는 경우가 많습니다. 덕분에 역설적으로 도치를 제대로 알고 있는 학생이 굉장히 드뭅니다.

먼저 도치를 왜 할까요?

국어의 예를 봅시다.

나랑 지금 장난 하냐?
라는 문장을
장난 지금 나랑 하냐?
로 바꾸어 봅시다.

문법적으로 잘못된 문장이긴 하지만, '장난'이라는 단어로 문장이 시작되기 때문에 글을 읽으면서 상대적으로 '장난'이라는 목적어에 집중하게 됩니다.

이렇듯 도치를 하는 이유는 앞으로 튀어나오는 구를 강조하기 위해서입니다.

영어에서 도치는 주로 4가지 상황에서 일어납니다.
1. 부정 표현을 문장 맨 앞에서 강조할 때
2. 부사(구)나 보어를 강조할 때
3. so, neither, nor을 사용할 때
4 가정법 문장에서 if가 생략될 때

이중 수능 문법에는 주로 2번이 많이 사용되는데, 그 과정을 한 번 보겠습니다.
You can play only after dinner.

이 문장에서 부사구 only after lunch를 강조하기 위해 문장 맨 앞으로 보낸 다음

Only after dinner you can play.

그 다음 주어와 동사의 위치를 바꿉니다.

Only after dinner can you play.

이것이 도치의 기본적인 과정입니다.

동사와 주어에 무엇인지에 따라 도치의 형태가 바뀝니다.

만약 be동사가 사용된다면, be동사와 주어를 도치합니다.

ex) he is → is he

만약 조동사가 사용된다면, 조동사와 주어만을 도치합니다.

ex) he can read → can he read

만약 동사가 일반동사만 사용된 경우, 대동사 do를 사용하여 도치합니다.

ex) they say → do they say
    he said → did he say

모든 문제가 객관식인 수능에서 도치를 어떻게 하는 지를 물어보지는 않을 테고, 도치는 어떻게 문법 문제로 출제될까요?

주로 수 일치와 연관되어 출제됩니다.

20학년도 9월 평가원

Only when the information is repeated can its possessor <u>turn</u> the fact that he knows something into something socially valuable like social recognition, prestige, and notoriety.

* prestige: 명성 ** notoriety: 악명

이 문장의 turn은 문법적으로 맞을까요?

Only when the information is repeated라는 부사구가 강조되기 위해 문장 맨 앞으로 나오면서 도치가 되었습니다.
원래의 주어와 동사는 its possessor과 can turn이었는데, 이것이 도치되었으므로 turn은 문법적으로 옳습니다.

도치를 전혀 모르는 학생이라면, its possessor만 보고
응? 주어 단수인데? turns!
이렇게 풀기 때문에 문제가 되는 겁니다.

도치 구문의 핵심은 먼저 도치 구문이라는 것을 알아내는 것.
그리고 강조된 부사구가 어디까지인지를 찾은 다음, 도치된 주어와 동사를 제대로 파악하는 것

이 과정들이 연습이 되어야 합니다.
간간히 복병으로 튀어나와 정답률을 깎아먹는 주범이니 많은 문장들을 보며 익숙해지는 과정이 필요합니다.

memo

수동태란?

수동태에 대해 나름 열심히 공부한 학생들이라면 수동태가 뭐야? 라는 질문에 '주어가 동작을 받는 대상입니다' 라고 답을 할 것입니다.
그렇다면 수동태에 대해 알아보기 이전에 수동태라는 것이 왜 존재하는지부터 알아봅시다.

다음 두 문장을 봅시다.

    A. David broke the window.
    B. The window was broken by David.

A 문장은 능동태, B 문장은 수동태 문장입니다.
두 문장 모두 말하는 객관적인 내용은 같습니다. David가 창문을 깼다는 것이죠.
하지만 실제로 두 문장은 상당히 다릅니다.
A 문장은 주어가 David이므로 문장에서 중요한 건 바로 창문을 깬 사람인 David입니다.
반면 B 문장에서 강조하는 것은 바로 깨진 것인 The window입니다. David가 깬 것이 화장실 거울이 아니라, 접시가 아니라, 바로 유리창이라는 것입니다.

이렇게 수동태는 동작의 대상을 강조하기 위해 사용됩니다. 능동태는 동작의 주체를 강조하는 것이므로 여기서 차이를 알 수 있습니다.
그러므로 동작의 대상이 문장에 나와야 되기 때문에 수동태를 사용하기 위해선 목적어가 반드시 필요합니다.

수동태가 수능 문법에서는 바로 이 대상과 주체를 혼동하도록 출제가 됩니다.

The suitcase that I had lost after work (found / was founded) at the office.

명사는 3개(The suitcase, I, work)가 등장하지만 여기서 that I had lost after work는 The suitcase를 수식하기 위한 관계사절입니다. The suitcase는 스스로가 찾을 수 없기 때문에 능동태로 사용될 수 없으며, The suitcase가 회사에서 발견되었다는 수동태로 사용되었으므로 was founded가 답이 됩니다.

주어와 동사와의 관계를 잘 파악합시다. 주어가 동작을 하는 '주체'가 되면 능동태, 주어가 동작을 받는 '대상'이 되면 수동태입니다.

* 능동태를 수동태로 바꾸면 목적어가 주어가 되기 때문에 수동태 문장에 목적어가 존재한다면 문법적으로 잘못된 문장이라고 판단하는 경우가 있습니다.
대부분의 경우가 다음과 같은 판단이 적절하나 예외가 있습니다.
4형식에서는 동사가 'I.O', 'D.O'라는 두 개의 목적어를 가집니다.
그러므로 수동태로 바뀌더라도 두 개의 목적어 중 한 개만 주어로 바뀔 뿐 남은 한 개의 목적어는 동사 뒤에 위치하게 됩니다. 그러므로 수동태로 바뀌어도 문장에 목적어가 존재할 수 있음을 알아두셔야 합니다.

• He gave me a present

  → I was given a present by him. (수동태지만, present라는 목적어가 존재)
  → A present was given (to) me by him (수동태지만, me라는 목적어가 존재)

- People are rarely (bitten / biting) by a mosquito in winter

- A polygraph can (detect / be detected) people who confuse the investigation with the facts hidden.

- Jack is believed to have (been crossed / crossed) the frontier last night.

- But then, by an unfortunate accident, as the mannered man raised a slippery slice of tofu to his lips, he (placed / was placed) the tiniest bit of excess pressure on his chopsticks, propelling his tofu through the air and onto his neighbor' lap.

- Regardless of the type of information (disclosed / disclosing), clients must be certain.

• People are rarely (**bitten** / biting) by a mosquito in winter

→ 주어 People이 물린다는 뜻의 동사 bite의 대상이므로 수동태 **bitten**

• A polygraph can (**detect** / be detected) people who confuse the investigation with the facts hidden.

→ 주어 Polygraph가 목적어 people을 직접 탐지해내므로 능동태 **detect**

• Jack is believed to have (been crossed / **crossed**) the frontier last night.

→ 주어 Jack이 직접 목적어 frontier를 건너므로 능동태 **crossed**

• But then, by an unfortunate accident, as the mannered man raised a slippery slice of tofu to his lips, he (**placed** / was placed) the tiniest bit of excess pressure on his chopsticks, propelling his tofu through the air and onto his neighbor' lap.

→ he가 주어이고 뒤에 목적어로 **the tiniest bit of excess pressure**가 왔으므로 능동형인 **placed**가 와야 합니다.

• Regardless of the type of information (**disclosed** / disclosing), clients must be certain.

→ 명사 **type of information**이 공개되었으므로 수동태 **disclosed**

6-8 to 부정사

to 부정사와 명사적 용법

to 부정사의 부정사는 무슨 뜻일까요?

흔하게 생각하는 부정문의 부정이 아닌, 不(아닐 부) 定(정할 정) 자를 써서, 정해지지 않았다는 뜻입니다.

후에 배울 분사는 형용사로만, 동명사는 명사로만 쓰임이 정해져 있는 것과는 다르게, to 부정사는 얼핏 봤을 때, 이것이 어떤 품사로 쓰일지 알 수가 없기 때문에 to 부정사라고 부르는 것이며, 그 용법에 따라 3가지 경우로 나뉘게 됩니다.

1. 명사적 용법

to 부정사가 명사처럼 사용되는 경우입니다. 명사의 역할을 그대로 하기 때문에 다른 명사와 같이 문장의 주어, 목적어, 보어가 될 수 있습니다.

---

to 부정사의 명사적 용법

주　　　어 : <u>To learn</u> English is difficult. (영어를 <u>배우는 것</u>은 어렵다)

목　적　어 : She wants <u>to change</u> the book. (그녀는 책을 <u>바꾸는 것</u>을 원한다)

주격보어 : My plan is <u>to finish</u> the homework before dinner. (내 계획은 저녁 전까지 숙제를 <u>끝내는 것</u>이다)

목적격보어 : I requested them <u>to work</u> harder. (나는 그들에게 열심히 <u>일하는 것</u>을 요청했다)

잘 이해가 가지 않는다면 형식 단원을 복습해봅시다. 5가지 형식 중에서 명사는 주어, 목적어, 보어의 역할을 할 수 있으며, 그 자리에 명사의 역할을 할 수 있는 to 부정사가 들어간 것입니다.

▌to 부정사의 형용사적 용법과 부사적 용법

형용사적 용법은 두 가지입니다. 각각의 경우를 봅시다.

16학년도 수능 36번

명사 수식 : He needs some books <u>to read.</u> (그는 <u>읽을</u> 책이 필요하다)
보　　어 : We are about <u>to finish</u> the test. (우리는 시험을 <u>끝낼 예정</u>이다)

형용사의 역할 그대로, 명사를 수식해 ~할 N으로 해석될 수 있고

2형식 동사 뒤에서 주어를 보충하는 보어의 역할을 할 수 있습니다.

부사의 역할은 네 가지입니다.

---
to 부정사의 부사적 용법

동사　수식 : I studied hard <u>to pass</u> the test. (나는 시험을 <u>통과하기 위해</u> 열심히 공부했다)
형용사 수식 : This textbook is easy <u>to read</u>. (이 책은 <u>읽기</u> 쉽다)
부사　수식 : The ball is too fast <u>to catch.</u> (그 공은 너무 빨라서 <u>잡을</u> 수 없었다)
문장　수식 : <u>To be honest</u>, I love you. (<u>솔직히 말하면</u>, 너를 사랑해)

이렇듯 to 부정사의 용법은 원래 명사, 형용사, 부사가 하는 역할에 to 부정사가 들어간 것입니다.
각각 모든 용법을 달달달 외우려고 하기보다는 to 부정사가 들어간 문장을 봤을 때,
아 이건 명사적/형용사적/부사적 용법이구나. 라는 것을 구분할 줄 알고,
그 자리에 to 부정사가 들어가는 것이 옳은지를 중심으로 연습하는 것이 좋습니다.

* to 부정사의 용법을 바로 파악하는 가장 좋은 방법 중 하나는 문장의 동사를 파악하는 것입니다.
　우리가 "구"에서 봤듯이 많은 동사들은 정해진 형태로 형식을 가지고 오게 됩니다.
　예를 들어 타동사에 해당하는 'want'의 경우 타동사이기 때문에 동사 뒤에 목적어가 와야 합니다.
　만약 to부정사가 'want'의 뒤에 오고 문장이 끝났다면, 'want' 뒤에 위치하는 'to 부정사'는 명사적 용법에
　해당하여 목적어로 사용됩니다

동 / 명사

to 부정사를 배울 때처럼 한자를 통해 접근해봅시다.

動(움직일 동) 名(이름 명) 詞(말 사)

동사+명사 이것이 동명사의 정의입니다. 원래는 동사인데, 끝에 -ing를 붙여 문장 속에서 명사 역할을 할 수 있게 만든 것입니다. 동사와 명사라는 두 집합 사이의 교집합이라고 볼 수 있으며, 동사와 명사의 성질을 모두 가지고 있는 것이 특징입니다.

• 명사 : 명사의 역할을 하므로 문장에서 주어, 목적어, 보어의 역할을 한다.
• 동사 : 목적어나 보어를 동반해서 쓸 수 있고, 부사의 수식을 받을 수 있다.

동명사는 '~하는 것, ~하기'라고 해석되며, 명사, 형용사, 부사로 전부 쓰이는 to 부정사와 다르게 동명사는 명사의 역할만을 합니다.

• 주　어 : Watching movies is my hobby. (영화를 보는 것은 내 취미다)
• 목적어 : I enjoy playing a guitar. (나는 기타 치는 것을 즐긴다)
• 보　어 : My hobby is reading a book. (내 취미는 책을 읽는 것이다)

memo

역할이 나뉘는 동사의 변형 구조

to 부정사가 명사, 형용사, 부사의 세 가지 품사, 동명사가 명사의 역할을 한다면 분사는 형용사의 역할을 합니다.

분사에서 기억해 두셔야 하는 것은 세가지입니다.

1. 현재분사와 과거분사

현재분사는 동사 뒤에 -ing를 붙이고, 능동, 진행의 의미를 나타내며, '~하는, ~하고 있는'이라고 해석합니다.
과거분사는 동사의 p.p.형이며, 수동, 완료의 의미를 나타냅니다. '~된, ~해진'이라고 해석합니다.

> **현재분사와 과거분사**
>
> 현재분사 : Look at the <u>sleeping</u> baby. (자고 있는 아기를 봐)
> 과거분사 : Do not touch the <u>closed</u> window. (닫힌 창문을 만지지 마세요)

2. 감정을 나타내는 분사

동사들 중에는 기쁨, 슬픔, 지루함, 흥분과 같은 다양한 감정들을 나타내는 동사들이 있습니다. 이러한 동사들이
분사 형태로 바뀔 때에 그 의미가 서로 달라지는 것을 알아야 합니다.

shock, '충격을 주다'라는 뜻의 동사입니다.

- shocking : 현재분사이며, '충격적인(충격을 주는)'이라는 뜻
- shocked : 과거분사이며, '충격을 받은'이라는 뜻

그렇다면 '충격적인'과 '충격을 받은'은 어떻게 다를까요?
두 예문을 통해 알아봅시다.

> **감정을 나타내는 분사**
>
> shocking news : 충격적인 소식
> shocked audience : 충격을 받은 관중들

현재분사인 shocking은 능동의 의미임으로 수식 대상인 news가 직접적으로 충격이라는 감정을 주는 것이고,
과거분사인 shocked는 수동의 의미이므로 수식 대상인 audience가 충격이라는 감정을 받은 것이 됩니다.

분사의 역할

분사는 형용사의 역할을 하므로 명사를 수식하고, 보어의 역할을 합니다.

분사의 역할

명사 수식 : I installed a <u>blocking</u> program. (나는 <u>차단하는</u> 프로그램을 설치했다)
보　　어 : He looks <u>confused</u>. (그는 <u>혼란스러워</u> 보인다)

* 동명사와 현재분사는 뭐가 다른가요?
  동명사와 현재분사는 모두 똑같이 생겼습니다. 하지만 현재분사는 '~하는'이라는 뜻을 가지는 형용사이고, 동명사는 '~하는 것'이라는 뜻의 명사입니다.
  단어 자체만 보고서는 그것이 동명사인지 현재분사인지를 알 수 없으며 문장 안에서 어떻게 쓰였는지를 보고 구분을 해야 합니다.

- 동 명 사 : <u>Running</u> is basic exercise. (<u>달리기</u>는 기본적인 운동이다)
- 현재분사 : The <u>running</u> marathoner looks exhausted. (<u>달리는</u> 마라토너는 지쳐 보인다)

- Examine your thoughts, and you will find them wholly (to occupy / occupied) with the past or the future.
  to occupy

- On January 10, 1992, a ship (traveled / traveling) through rough seas lost 12 cargo containers, one of which held 28,800 floating bath toys.

- Tory Higgins and his colleagues had university students read a personality description of someone and then (summarize / summarized) it for someone else who was believed either to like or to dislike this person.

- He goes on to describe his daily routine of strolling through the village (observed / observing) the intimate details of family life, and as he tells it, such observations seem possible and accessible.

- We've done everything we can (contain / to contain) costs without compromising quality.

▌체화 해설

- Examine your thoughts, and you will find them wholly (to occupy / **occupied**) with the past or the future.

  → **'find+목적어+목적보어'의 구문으로 목적어인 them이 occupy의 대상이므로 수동의 의미를 지니는 과거분사 occupied가 쓰여야 합니다.**

- On January 10, 1992, a ship (traveled / **traveling**) through rough seas lost 12 cargo containers, one of which held 28,800 floating bath toys.

  → **거친 바다를 항해하던 배 한 척이라는 뜻으로, 능동의 의미로 a ship을 수식하는 traveling이 쓰여야 합니다.**

- Tory Higgins and his colleagues had university students read a personality description of someone and then (**summarize** / summarized) it for someone else who was believed either to like or to dislike this person.

  → **read와 함께 사역동사 had의 목적격보어 역할을 할 수 있는 원형부정사 summarize가 쓰여야 합니다.**

- He goes on to describe his daily routine of strolling through the village (observed / **observing**) the intimate details of family life, and as he tells it, such observations seem possible and accessible.

  → **뒤에 the intimate details of family life라는 목적어가 있으므로 과거분사인 observed가 아니라 현재분사인 observing이 쓰여야 합니다.**

- We've done everything we can (contain / **to contain**) costs without compromising quality.

  → **We can은 everything을 수식하는 관계대명사절이고, 문장 전체를 수식하는 to 부정사가 필요하므로 to contain이 쓰여야 합니다.**

너무나도 어려운 그 단원

지겹도록 배우지만 지겹도록 까먹는 그 단원, 관계대명사입니다.

항상 문법을 배우기 전에 내가 배우는 게 무엇인지를 봐야 합니다.

관계대명사란 무엇일까요?

어렵게 생각할 것 없이 이 단어를 쪼개보면 관계+대명사가 됩니다.

관계대명사라는 것은 관계사+대명사이며, 두 문장을 연결하는 접속사의 역할과,
문장에서 반복되는 단어를 대신하는 대명사의 역할 수행합니다.

예시로 먼저 이해해 봅시다.

    A. I have a brother.
    B. He lives in Seattle.

두 문장에 공통되는 부분인 brother가 있으므로 관계대명사를 사용하여 하나의 문장으로 만들 수 있습니다.

I have a brother [he lives in Seattle.]
여기서 의미가 좀 더 명확한 brother를 남기고, he를 삭제합니다. 그 경우 남겨진 a brother는 선행사가 됩니다.

I have a brother [lives in Seattle.]
여기서 반복되는 부분인 brother를 대신하는 명사와, 두 문장을 연결하는 접속사의 역할을 수행하는 관계대명사를 넣습니다.

I have a brother [who lives in Seattle.]
다시 설명하면 이 문장의 관계대명사 who는 선행사인 brother를 대신하는 대명사와,
두 문장을 연결하는 관계사의 역할을 동시에 하고 있는 것입니다.

선생님들이 말하는 관계대명사 뒤의 부분이 불완전한 문장인 이유도 바로 여기에 있습니다. 이 대명사의 역할을 하는 관계대명사가 빠지면, 관계대명사절은 주어, 목적어 등 하나가 반드시 빠져 버린 상태이기 때문에 불완전한 문장이 될 수밖에 없는 것입니다.

▌관계대명사의 격

관계대명사에는 주격, 목적격, 소유격이 있습니다.

어렵게 생각하지 마세요. <u>관계대명사</u>가 <u>관계대명사절</u> 안에서 어떤 역할을 하는지에 따라 구분됩니다.

> **관계대명사의 격**
>
> 주격 : 관계대명사가 관계대명사절에서 주어 역할을 하면 주격
> 목적격 : 관계대명사가 관계대명사절에서 목적어 역할을 하면 목적격
> 소유격 : 관계대명사가 관계대명사절에서 소유격 역할을 하면 소유격

예시로 이해해 봅시다.

He is a new student [who transferred from another school].

이 문장에서 관계대명사절만을 봅시다. 동사 transferred의 주체가 없습니다. 즉, who가 관계대명사절 안에서 주어 역할을 하므로 who는 주격 관계대명사입니다.

그럼 이 문장을 다시 두 개의 문장으로 쪼개 볼까요?

- <u>He</u> is <u>a new student</u>.
- <u>He</u> transferred from another school.

who가 두 번째 문장에서 He를 대신하여 쓰인 것입니다.
He는 두 번째 문장에서 주어 역할을 하며, 이것이 주격 관계대명사가 되는 것입니다.

- I visited my uncle [whom I hadn't seen for years].

관계대명사절에서 동사 hadn't seen 뒤의 목적어가 없습니다.
그러므로 whom은 관계대명사절에서 목적어 역할을 하므로 목적격 관계대명사가 됩니다.

이 문장 역시 쪼개 봅시다.

- I visited <u>my uncle</u>.
- I hadn't seen <u>him</u> for years.

whom은 두 번째 문장에서 목적어 him을 대신하여 쓰였습니다.
whom이 목적격 관계대명사가 되는 이유입니다.

• I met a man [whose restaurant is famous].

whose는 뒤에 나온 명사 restaurant가 선행사인 a man의 소유임을 나타냅니다.

역시 쪼개 봅시다.

• I met a man.
• His restaurant is famous.

식당의 남자의 것이므로 남자에게 소속된 것이며,
그 소유를 의미하는 His가 관계대명사 whose로 바뀐 것입니다.

▌주로 쓰이는 관계대명사

1. who

who는 바로 앞의 격을 이용하여 설명했기 때문에 패스하겠습니다.
who는 선행사가 사람인 경우에 쓰며, 주격은 who, 목적격은 whom, 소유격은 whose입니다.

2. which

관계대명사 which는 who와는 반대로 선행사가 사람이 아닌 경우에 사용합니다.
주격은 which, 목적격 역시 which, 소유격은 whose(=of which)입니다.
예를 통해 이해해 봅시다.

• 주격 The bus [which goes to the museum] has just left.
  ← The bus has just left. + The bus(주어) goes to the museum.

• 목적격 She wore a dress [which she bought in France].
  ← She wore a dress + She bought it(목적어) in France.

• 소유격 She finally finished the work [whose deadline is almost over].
  ← She finally finished the work + Its(소유격) deadline is almost over.

3. that

관계대명사로 쓰이는 that은 선행사가 사람이든 아니든 상관없이 쓸 수 있습니다.
쉽게 말해서 위에 예문들에 쓰인 who, whom, which를 that으로 모두 바꿔 써도 되는 것이죠.

하지만

1. that은 소유격이 없습니다.

2. 계속적 용법으로는 사용할 수 없습니다. ex) ~, that (X)

3. 전치사+관계대명사로 사용할 수 없습니다. ex) of that, from that (X)

that은 굉장히 보편적으로 사용되는 관계사이기 때문에, 사용하는 경우보다는 사용할 수 없는 경우를 기억해 두시는 게 좋습니다.

4. what

관계대명사 what은 선행사를 포함하는 관계대명사입니다.

He showed me <u>the jacket</u> [<u>that</u> he bought]. 그는 자기가 산 재킷을 내게 보여주었다
→ He showed me <u>what</u> he bought. 그는 자기가 산 것을 나에게 보여주었다.

선행사 the jacket과 that을 모두 합쳐서 what으로 쓰인 경우입니다.

관계대명사 what의 특징으로는

1. that과 마찬가지로 소유격이 없습니다.

2. what 앞에 선행사가 오지 않습니다.

3. what 뒤에는 불완전한 문장이 옵니다.

4. '~한 것'이라고 해석됩니다.

관계부사

관계부사는 관계사+부사가 되니, 접속사의 역할과 부사의 역할을 동시에 수행하는 것이라 볼 수 있습니다.

바로 예시로 들어가 봅시다.

• I like the house.
• Paul lives in the house.

이 두 문장을 합치면 다음과 같습니다.

• I like the house [Paul lives in the house].

의미가 겹치는 부사 in the house를 생략합니다.

• I like the house [Paul lives].

생략한 부사의 의미를 포함하는 관계사를 넣습니다.

• I like the house [where Paul lives].

이렇게 where는 두 문장을 연결하는 접속사의 역할과, in the house라는 부사의 역할을 동시에 하고 있습니다.

이렇게 관계대명사절에서 생략되는 것은 문장의 구성 요소가 아닌 부사이므로, 관계부사 뒤에 오는 문장은 완전한 문장이 되는 것입니다.

when

관계부사 when은 선행사가 시간과 관련된 말일 때 사용합니다.

• I still remember the day [when she came to my office].
  ← I still remember the day. + She came to my office <u>on the day(부사)</u>.

where

관계부사 where은 선행사가 장소와 관련된 말일 때 사용합니다.

• The meeting was held in the office [where he first met his wife].
  ← The meeting was held in the office. + He first met his wife <u>at the office(부사)</u>.

관계부사 why는 선행사가 이유와 관련된 말일 때 사용합니다.

• I don't know the reason [why she's mad at me].
  ← I don't know the reason. + She's mad at me for some reason(부사).

관계부사 how는 선행사가 방법과 관련된 말일 때 사용합니다.

하지만, how는 다른 관계부사와 다르게 how 스스로 선행사의 역할까지 할 수 있기 때문에 선행사 the way와 같이 쓸 수 없으며, how만을 쓰거나 the way만을 사용해야 합니다.

• We will change [how we take care of a problem].
  ← We will change the way. + we take care of a problem in a way(부사).

모든 관계부사는 that, 그리고 전치사 + which로 바꿔쓸 수 있습니다.

❙ 복합관계사

먼저 복합관계대명사는 관계대명사+ever 형태의 관계사를 말하며, 기본적으로 앞 관계대명사에 ever(언제나, 항상)의 의미를 추가하여 해석합니다. 관계대명사절은 선행사를 뒤에서 꾸며주는 형용사절이지만, 복합관계사절은 선행사를 포함하는 명사절이나 부사절이 됩니다.

who(m)ever 명사절 anyone who ~하는 누구든지
whoever fails the test has to take the retest. 누구든지 시험을 떨어진 사람은 재시험을 봐야 한다.
He wants to know whoever did this. 그는 누구든 이걸 한 사람을 알고 싶다.
who(m)ever 부사절 no matter who 누가 ~하더라도
whoever you ask, you will not be able to solve the problem. 누구에게 묻는다 해도, 너는 그 문제를 풀 수 없을 거다.

whichever 명사절 anything that ~하는 어느 것이든지
you are free to choose whichever one you want. 너는 원하는 어떤 것이든지 고를 수 있다.
whichever 부사절 no matter which 어느 것이 ~하더라도
I don't care about it, whichever you choose. 네가 어느 것을 선택하더라도, 나는 신경 쓰지 않는다.

whatever 명사절 anything that ~하는 무엇이든지
You can do whatever you want. 너는 네가 원하는 것이 무엇이든지 할 수 있다.
whatever 부사절 no matter what 무엇을 ~하더라도
Whatever it is, please tell me. 그것이 무엇이든지 간에, 나에게 말해줘.

복합관계대명사도 기본적으로 관계대명사이므로 ① 뒤에는 불완전한 절이 이어지지만, ② 선행사를 포함하며, ③ 관계대명사 that은 복합관계대명사절을 만들 수 없습니다.

그 다음은 복합관계부사입니다. 관계대명사가 관계부사로 바뀌었으니, 기본적으로 관계부사+ever의 구조를 취하며, 시간/장소/방법의 부사절과 양보의 부사절로 나뉩니다.

whenever 시간의 부사절 at any time when ~할 때는 언제나
whenever I try to discuss my financial problem, they don't want to hear it. 내 재정적인 문제를 상의하려고 할 때마다 그들은 듣고 싶어 하지 않는다.
whenever 양보의 부사절 no matter when 언제 ~하더라도
You can begin whenever you're ready. 네가 준비되었을 때 언제라도 시작할 수 있다

wherever 장소의 부사절 at any place where ~하는 곳은 어디든
You can take the exam wherever you want. 당신이 원하는 어떤 곳에서도 시험을 치를 수 있습니다.
wherever 양보의 부사절 no matter where 어디에서 ~하더라도
Wherever they go, I'll follow them. 그들이 어디를 가든, 나는 그들을 따라갈 것이다.

however 방법의 부사절 in any way ~하는 어떤 식으로든
however 양보의 부사절 no matter how 아무리 ~하더라도
However hard I study, I think I'm going to fail the test. 내가 얼마나 열심히 공부해도, 나는 시험에 떨어질 것 같다.

복합관계부사의 경우에는 ① 뒤에는 완전한 절이 이어지며, ② 선행사를 포함하고, ③ 관계부사 why는 복합관계부사절을 만들 수 없습니다.

관계사의 구분

who / whom

관계대명사의 격을 묻습니다. 주격 관계대명사 who 뒤의 불완전 절에는 주어가 없고, 목적격 관계대명사 whom의 뒤에는 목적어가 없습니다.

who, which, what / where, when, how, why

관계대명사와 관계부사를 구분해야 합니다. 관계대명사 뒤에는 불완전한 절이, 관계부사 뒤에는 완전한 절이 옵니다.

who / which

선행사에 따라 구분합니다. 선행사가 사람이면 who, 사물이면 which가 옵니다.

who, which / what

역시 선행사를 봐야 합니다. who, which는 선행사가 존재하며, what은 선행사를 포함한 관계대명사이므로 선행사가 없습니다.

when / where

선행사가 시간이면 when, 장소면 where가 됩니다.

who / whoever

who가 관계대명사로 쓰였다면 선행사가 있고, whoever는 선행사가 없지만, who가 의문사로도 쓰일 수 있으므로 선행사의 유무로 파악하는 것을 추천하진 않습니다. 정확한 문장 해석을 통해 각각의 단어의 의미를 정확하게 파악해야 합니다. 다른 관계사와 복합관계사의 경우도 마찬가지입니다.

that / what

관계대명사 that과 what이라면 that은 선행사가 있고, 뒷 절이 불완전하지만, what은 선행사가 없으며, 뒷 절이 불완전합니다.
명사절 접속사인 that과 what이라면 모두 선행사가 없지만 that 뒤는 완전한 절, what 뒤는 불완전한 절이 옵니다. 그러므로 뒤 절의 완전/불완전 여부에 따라 풀면 됩니다.

that / which

that은 which와 바꿔 쓸 수 있으므로, that이 쓸 수 없는 경우를 기억해야 합니다. 계속적 용법 (콤마), 전치사 뒤에는 that이 나올 수 없습니다.

which / in which

which 뒷 절은 불완전, in which 뒤는 완전한 절이 옵니다.

▌체화

- After seven months, the first toys made landfall on beaches near Sitka, Alaska, 3,540 kilometers from (what / where) they were lost.

- He judged by the sound (which / that) the fall was a mere slip and could not have hurt Meredith.

- Nevertheless, they begin to believe (what / that) they are saying.

- Sir Arthur Conan Doyle, the creator of Sherlock Holmes, had a great sense of delicacy (where / which) other persons' feelings were concerned.

- Everyone looked at (what / how) the man held his chopsticks, so that they could imitate him.

- I recently saw a news interview with an acquaintance (who / whom) I was certain was going to lie about a few particularly sensitive issues, and lie she did.

- We can read the news of the day, or the latest on business, entertainment or (however / whatever) news on the websites of the New York Times, the Guardian or almost any other major newspaper in the world.

- To oversimplify, basic ideas bubble out of universities and laboratories (in which / which) a group of researchers work together.

▎체화 해설

- After seven months, the first toys made landfall on beaches near Sitka, Alaska, 3,540 kilometers from (what / **where**) they were lost.

  → 뒷 절이 완전하고, ~한 장소라고 해석되므로 관계부사 where이 쓰여야 합니다.

- He judged by the sound (which / **that**) the fall was a mere slip and could not have hurt Meredith.

  → 관계대명사 뒷 절이 완전한 문장이므로 that이 쓰여야 합니다.

- Nevertheless, they begin to believe (**what** / that) they are saying.

  → believe와 are saying의 목적어 역할을 동시에 하는 선행사를 포함한 관계대명사인 what이 쓰여야 합니다.

- Sir Arthur Conan Doyle, the creator of Sherlock Holmes, had a great sense of delicacy (**where** / which) other persons' feelings were concerned.

  → 뒷 절이 완전하므로 관계부사 where이 쓰여야 합니다.

- Everyone looked at (what / **how**) the man held his chopsticks, so that they could imitate him.

  → 뒷 절이 완전하므로 관계부사 how가 쓰여야 합니다.

- I recently saw a news interview with an acquaintance (**who** / whom) I was certain was going to lie about a few particularly sensitive issues, and lie she did.

  → 관계대명사절 안에서 'I was certain'이 삽입절로 쓰여 주격 관계대명사가 필요하므로 who가 와야 합니다.

• We can read the news of the day, or the latest on business, entertainment or (however / **whatever)** news on the websites of the New York Times, the Guardian or almost any other major newspaper in the world.

→ 해석상 '어떤 뉴스든지'라는 의미이므로 **whatever**가 적절합니다.

• To oversimplify, basic ideas bubble out of universities and laboratories (**in which** / which) a group of researchers work together.

→ **which**의 선행사는 **universities and laboratories**이고 관계대명사 뒷 절이 완전한 문장이며, '대학과 실험실에서'의 의미를 전달하므로 전치사 **in**과 결합되어야 합니다.

동사와 동사의 변형

모든 문장은 주어와 동사를 가집니다. 접속사는 성분과 성분, 절과 절을 연결하므로 접속사가 늘어난다면 동사는 그에 비례하여 늘어나게 됩니다. 문법 문제의 밑줄 친 부분이 동사인지, 혹은 동사처럼 생긴 다른 용법인지를 잘 봐야 합니다. 동사처럼 생긴 다른 무언가로는 주로 바로 앞에 배웠던 to 부정사, 동명사, 분사가 되는데, 이 세 가지는 모두 동사를 변형하여 만들기 때문에 동사처럼 보이지만 동사의 역할은 할 수 없습니다.

그러므로 문법 문제의 문장에서 동사에 밑줄이 쳐져 있을 때, 이것이 '동사'인지, '동사의 모습을 한 다른 것'인지를 잘 봐야 합니다.

> **2011학년도 수능 변형**
>
> But people who are daring in taking a wholehearted stand for truth often <u>achieving</u> results that surpass their expectations.

문장에서 주어는 people이 확실합니다. 그렇다면 people의 동사는 뭐가 될까요? are daring은 관계대명사 who에 이어지는 동사, surpass 역시 관계대명사 that의 동사이므로 주어 persons의 동사가 아닙니다.

> **2011학년도 수능 변형**
>
> But persons (who are daring in taking a wholehearted stand) (for truth) often <u>achieving</u> results (that surpass their expectations).

수식어구와 관계사절을 제외한 문장은 다음과 같습니다. achieving은 be동사가 없이 단독으로는 동사의 역할을 할 수 없으니 문장의 동사는 존재하지 않는다는 모순에 빠져 버립니다. 그러므로 동사는 achieving이 되어야 하므로 동사의 역할을 할 수 없는 achieving을 achieve와 같은 일반동사로 바꿔야 하는 것입니다.

분사, 동명사, to 부정사의 내용의 연장선상에 있는 단원이라고 볼 수 있습니다.
각각의 단원들이

• 너, 현재분사와 과거분사 구분 가능하니?
• 너, 분사와 to 부정사 구분 가능하니?
• 너, 동명사와 to 부정사 구분 가능하니?

에 대해 질문하고 있다면,

이번 단원은

- 너, 이 자리에 들어가야 하는 게 동사인지 분사인지 구분 가능하니?
- 너, 이 자리에 들어가야 하는 게 동사인지 동명사인지 구분 가능하니?
- 너, 이 자리에 들어가야 하는 게 동사인지 to 부정사인지 구분 가능하니?

에 대해 물어보고 있습니다.
문법 문제 풀이의 시작은 주어와 동사를 찾는 것입니다.
동사를 찾는 습관, 그리고 동사의 변형 과정인 부정사, 동명사, 분사를 잘 구분하고 서로 혼동하지 않도록
합시다.

▌체화

- But persons who are daring in taking a wholehearted stand for truth often (achieving / achieve) results that surpass their expectations.

- However, if you are eating burgers and ice-cream to feel comforted, relaxed and happy, (trying / try) to replace them with broccoli and carrot juice is like dealing with a leaky bathroom tap by repainting the kitchen.

- It is true that the questions (dealt / dealing) with very personal issues, but I have found that in general, no matter how touchy the question, if a person is telling the truth his or her manner will not change significantly or abruptly.

▌체화 해설

- But persons who are daring in taking a wholehearted stand for truth often (achieving / **achieve**) results that surpass their expectations.

  → 주어인 **persons**에 연결되는 동사가 없으므로 **achieve**가 들어가야 합니다.

- However, if you are eating burgers and ice-cream to feel comforted, relaxed and happy, (**trying** / try) to replace them with broccoli and carrot juice is like dealing with a leaky bathroom tap by repainting the kitchen.

  → 문장은 주절의 주어가 없기 때문에 명사 역할을 할 수 있는 **trying**이나 **to try**가 들어가야 하며, 이 주어는 동사 **is**와 연결됩니다.

- It is true that the questions (**dealt** / dealing) with very personal issues, but I have found that in general, no matter how touchy the question, if a person is telling the truth his or her manner will not change significantly or abruptly.

  → **that**절 안에서 **the questions**를 주어로 하는 동사가 와야 하므로 **deal**의 과거형인 **dealt**가 와야 합니다.

6-13 형용사와 부사

용법의 차이

모든 문장은 주어와 동사를 가집니다. 접속사는 성분과 성분, 절과 절을 연결하므로 접속사가 늘어난다면 동사는 그에 비례해서 늘어납니다. 형용사는 명사를 수식하고, 부사는 동사, 형용사, 부사, 문장을 수식합니다. 초등학교 때부터 배우는 내용이니 이 두 품사를 모르는 수험생은 아마 없을 겁니다.

하지만 형용사는 한 가지 용법이 더 있습니다. 바로 보어의 역할을 한다는 것입니다.

• I am kind / kindly

를 틀리는 학생은 없습니다.

• He looked sad / sadly

sadly는 동사를 수식하니까 looked를 수식한다고 보는 수험생은 없을 거라고 믿습니다.
look은 2형식 동사인 지각동사이므로 보어를 필요로 하는데, 보어의 역할을 할 수 있는 단어는 sad밖에 없으므로 당연히 형용사 sad가 와야 합니다. Chapter 6-1에서 2형식, 5형식 동사만을 적어둔 이유는 바로 2, 5형식 문장이 보어를 필요로 하기 때문입니다. 2, 5형식 동사와 뒤에 주격/목적격 보어 자리에 부사를 집어넣고 수식여부를 헷갈리게 하는 방식입니다.

하지만 영어에 절대라는 것은 없습니다. 다음 문장을 봅시다.

2016학년도 수능

In both cases the focus is <u>exclusively</u> on the object, with no attention paid to the possibility that some force outside the object might be relevant.

분명히 문장에는 2형식 동사 is가 쓰였는데, 부사 exclusively는 어법상 틀리지 않았습니다. 그 이유는 exclusively가 수식하는 것이 주어 focus가 아니라, 부사절인 전치사구 on the object이기 때문입니다. 결국 해석을 통해 수식하는 것을 잘 파악합시다. 주격보어, 목적격 보어를 쓰인 형용사도 결국 각각 주어, 목적어를 수식해주는 것이니 형용사의 용법이 바뀌는 것이 아닙니다.

체화

- But it soon became (evident / evidently) that their knowledge was limited and of no practical value.

- (So / Such) imprudent are we that we wander about in times that are not ours and do not think of the one that belongs to us.

- This sounds (obvious / obviously), but countless efforts at habit change ignore its implications.

- Sometimes the variation is as (subtle / subtly) as a pause.

- As a source of plot, character, and dialogue, the novel seemed more (suitable / suitably)

• But it soon became (**evident** / evidently) that their knowledge was limited and of no practical value.

 → **become**의 보어 역할을 할 수 있는 형용사 **evident**가 들어가야 합니다.

• (**So** / Such) imprudent are we that we wander about in times that are not ours and do not think of the one that belongs to us.

 → 형용사 **imprudent** 앞에 올 수 있는 것은 부사인 **so**이며, **such**는 'such+관사+형용사+명사'의 어순으로 사용돼야 합니다.

• This sounds (**obvious** / obviously), but countless efforts at habit change ignore its implications.

 → 불완전자동사 **sounds**의 보어 역할을 할 수 있는 형용사 **obvious**가 와야 합니다.

• Sometimes the variation is as (**subtle** / subtly) as a pause.

 → 2형식 동사 **is**의 보어 역할을 할 수 있는 형용사 **subtle**이 와야 합니다.

• As a source of plot, character, and dialogue, the novel seemed more (**suitable** / suitably)

 → 동사 **seemed**의 보어 역할을 할 수 있는 형용사 **suitable**이 와야 합니다.

연습문제

01

[정답과 해설 286page]

다음 글의 밑줄 친 부분 중 어법상 틀린 것은?

 Speculations about the meaning and purpose of prehistoric art ① <u>rely</u> heavily on analogies drawn with modern-day hunter-gatherer societies. Such primitive societies, ② <u>as</u> Steven Mithen emphasizes in The Prehistory of the Modern Mind, tend to view man and beast, animal and plant, organic and inorganic spheres, as participants in an integrated, animated totality. The dual expressions of this tendency are anthropomorphism (the practice of regarding animals as humans) and totemism (the practice of regarding humans as animals), both of ③ <u>which</u> spread through the visual art and the mythology of primitive cultures. Thus the natural world is conceptualized in terms of human social relations. When considered in this light, the visual preoccupation of early humans with the nonhuman creatures ④ <u>inhabited</u> their world becomes profoundly meaningful. Among hunter-gatherers, animals are not only good to eat, they are also good to think about, as Claude Lévi-Strauss has observed. In the practice of totemism, he has suggested, an unlettered humanity "broods upon ⑤ <u>itself</u> and its place in nature."

* speculation: 고찰 ** analogy: 유사점 *** brood: 곰곰이 생각하다

02

[정답과 해설 286page]

다음 글의 밑줄 친 부분 중 어법상 틀린 것은?

 Psychologists who study giving behavior ① <u>have</u> noticed that some people give substantial amounts to one or two charities, while others give small amounts to many charities. Those who donate to one or two charities seek evidence about what the charity is doing and ② <u>what</u> it is really having a positive impact. If the evidence indicates that the charity is really helping others, they make a substantial donation. Those who give small amounts to many charities are not so interested in whether what they are ③ <u>doing</u> helps others — psychologists call them warm glow givers. Knowing that they are giving makes ④ <u>them</u> feel good, regardless of the impact of their donation. In many cases the donation is so small — $10 or less — that if they stopped ⑤ <u>to think</u>, they would realize that the cost of processing the donation is likely to exceed any benefit it brings to the charity.

다음 글의 밑줄 친 부분 중 어법상 틀린 것은?

Not all organisms are able to find sufficient food to survive, so starvation is a kind of disvalue often found in nature. It also is part of the process of selection ① <u>by which</u> biological evolution functions. Starvation helps filter out those less fit to survive, those less resourceful in finding food for ② <u>themselves</u> and their young. In some circumstances, it may pave the way for genetic variants ③ <u>to take</u> hold in the population of a species and eventually allow the emergence of a new species in place of the old one. Thus starvation is a disvalue that can help make ④ <u>possible</u> the good of greater diversity. Starvation can be of practical or instrumental value, even as it is an intrinsic disvalue. ⑤ <u>What</u> some organisms must starve in nature is deeply regrettable and sad. The statement remains implacably true, even though starvation also may sometimes subserve ends that are good.

다음 글의 밑줄 친 부분 중 어법상 틀린 것은?

An interesting aspect of human psychology is that we tend to like things more and find them more ① <u>appealing</u> if everything about those things is not obvious the first time we experience them. This is certainly true in music. For example, we might hear a song on the radio for the first time that catches our interest and ② <u>decide</u> we like it. Then the next time we hear it, we hear a lyric we didn't catch the first time, or we might notice ③ <u>what</u> the piano or drums are doing in the background. A special harmony ④ <u>emerges</u> that we missed before. We hear more and more and understand more and more with each listening. Sometimes, the longer ⑤ <u>that</u> takes for a work of art to reveal all of its subtleties to us, the more fond of that thing — whether it's music, art, dance, or architecture — we become.

* subtleties: 중요한 세부 요소[사항]들

다음 글의 밑줄 친 부분 중 어법상 **틀린** 것은?

Most historians of science point to the need for a reliable calendar to regulate agricultural activity as the motivation for learning about what we now call astronomy, the study of stars and planets. Early astronomy provided information about when to plant crops and gave humans ① <u>their</u> first formal method of recording the passage of time. Stonehenge, the 4,000-year-old ring of stones in southern Britain, ② <u>is</u> perhaps the best-known monument to the discovery of regularity and predictability in the world we inhabit. The great markers of Stonehenge point to the spots on the horizon ③ <u>where</u> the sun rises at the solstices and equinoxes — the dates we still use to mark the beginnings of the seasons. The stones may even have ④ <u>been used</u> to predict eclipses. The existence of Stonehenge, built by people without writing, bears silent testimony both to the regularity of nature and to the ability of the human mind to see behind immediate appearances and ⑤ <u>discovers</u> deeper meanings in events.

* monument: 기념비 ** eclipse: (해·달의) 식(蝕) *** brood: 증언

다음 글의 밑줄 친 부분 중 어법상 **틀린** 것은?

Though most bees fill their days visiting flowers and collecting pollen, some bees take advantage of the hard work of others. These thieving bees sneak into the nest of an ① <u>unsuspecting</u> "normal" bee (known as the host), lay an egg near the pollen mass being gathered by the host bee for her own offspring, and then sneak back out. When the egg of the thief hatches, it kills the host' offspring and then eats the pollen meant for ② <u>its</u> victim. Sometimes called brood parasites, these bees are also referred to as cuckoo bees, because they are similar to cuckoo birds, which lay an egg in the nest of another bird and ③ <u>leaves</u> it for that bird to raise. They are more ④ <u>technically</u> called cleptoparasites. Clepto means "thief" in Greek, and the term cleptoparasite refers specifically to an organism ⑤ <u>that</u> lives off another by stealing its food. In this case the cleptoparasite feeds on the host' hard-earned pollen stores.

* brood parasite: (알을 대신 기르도록 하는) 탁란 동물

다음 글의 밑줄 친 부분 중 어법상 **틀린** 것은?

  People from more individualistic cultural contexts tend to be motivated to maintain self-focused agency or control ① <u>as</u> these serve as the basis of one's self-worth. With this form of agency comes the belief that individual successes ② <u>depending</u> primarily on one's own abilities and actions, and thus, whether by influencing the environment or trying to accept one's circumstances, the use of control ultimately centers on the individual. The independent self may be more ③ <u>driven</u> to cope by appealing to a sense of agency or control. However, people from more interdependent cultural contexts tend to be less focused on issues of individual success and agency and more motivated towards group goals and harmony. Research has shown ④ <u>that</u> East Asians prefer to receive, but not seek, more social support rather than seek personal control in certain cases. Therefore, people ⑤ <u>who</u> hold a more interdependent self-construal may prefer to cope in a way that promotes harmony in relationships.

* self-construal: 자기구성

다음 글의 밑줄 친 부분 중 어법상 **틀린** 것은?

  The lack of real, direct experience in and with nature has caused many children to regard the natural world as mere abstraction, that fantastic, beautifully filmed place ① <u>filled</u> with endangered rainforests and polar bears in peril. This overstated, often fictionalized version of nature is no more real — and yet no less real — to them than the everyday nature right outside their doors, ② <u>waits</u> to be discovered in a child' way, at a child' pace. Consider the University of Cambridge study which found that a group of eight-year-old children was able to identify ③ <u>substantially</u> more characters from animations than common wildlife species. One wonders whether our children' inherent capacity to recognize, classify, and order information about their environment — abilities once essential to our very survival — is slowly devolving to facilitate life in ④ <u>their</u> increasingly virtualized world. It' all part of ⑤ <u>what</u> Robert Pyle first called "he extinction of experience."

* peril: 위험 ** devolve: 퇴화하다

다음 글의 밑줄 친 부분 중 어법상 **틀린** 것은?

　Competitive activities can be more than just performance showcases ① <u>which</u> the best is recognized and the rest are overlooked. The provision of timely, constructive feedback to participants on performance ② <u>is</u> an asset that some competitions and contests offer. In a sense, all competitions give feedback. For many, this is restricted to information about whether the participant is an award- or prizewinner. The provision of that type of feedback can be interpreted as shifting the emphasis to demonstrating superior performance but not ③ <u>necessarily</u> excellence. The best competitions promote excellence, not just winning or "beating" others. The emphasis on superiority is what we typically see as ④ <u>fostering</u> a detrimental effect of competition. Performance feedback requires that the program go beyond the "win, place, or show" level of feedback. Information about performance can be very helpful, not only to the participant who does not win or place but also to those who ⑤ <u>do</u>.

* foster: 조장하다 ** detrimental: 유해한

다음 글의 밑줄 친 부분 중 어법상 **틀린** 것은?

　To begin with a psychological reason, the knowledge of another's personal affairs can tempt the possessor of this information ① <u>to repeat</u> it as gossip because as unrevealed information it remains socially inactive. Only when the information is repeated can its possessor ② <u>turn</u> the fact that he knows something into something socially valuable like social recognition, prestige, and notoriety. As long as he keeps his information to ③ <u>himself</u>, he may feel superior to those who do not know it. But knowing and not telling does not give him that feeling of "superiority that, so to say, latently contained in the secret, fully ④ <u>actualizing</u> itself only at the moment of disclosure." This is the main motive for gossiping about well-known figures and superiors. The gossip producer assumes that some of the "fame" of the subject of gossip, as ⑤ <u>whose</u> "friend" he presents himself, will rub off on him.

* prestige: 명성 ** notoriety: 악명
*** latently: 잠재적으로

11 19학년도 6월 평가원

다음 글의 밑줄 친 부분 중 어법상 틀린 것은?

Humans are so averse to feeling that they're being cheated ① that they often respond in ways that seemingly make little sense. Behavioral economists — the economists who actually study ② what people do as opposed to the kind who simply assume the human mind works like a calculator — have shown again and again that people reject unfair offers even if ③ it costs them money to do so. The typical experiment uses a task called the ultimatum game. It's pretty straightforward. One person in a pair is given some money — say $10. She then has the opportunity to offer some amount of it to her partner. The partner only has two options. He can take what's offered or ④ refused to take anything. There's no room for negotiation; that's why it's called the ultimatum game. What typically happens? Many people offer an equal split to the partner, ⑤ leaving both individuals happy and willing to trust each other in the future.

* averse to: ~을 싫어하는 ** ultimatum: 최후통첩

12 19학년도 수능

다음 글의 밑줄 친 부분 중 어법상 틀린 것은?

"Monumental" is a word that comes very close to ① expressing the basic characteristic of Egyptian art. Never before and never since has the quality of monumentality been achieved as fully as it ② did in Egypt. The reason for this is not the external size and massiveness of their works, although the Egyptians admittedly achieved some amazing things in this respect. Many modern structures exceed ③ those of Egypt in terms of purely physical size. But massiveness has nothing to do with monumentality. An Egyptian sculpture no bigger than a person's hand is more monumental than that gigantic pile of stones ④ that constitutes the war memorial in Leipzig, for instance. Monumentality is not a matter of external weight, but of "inner weight". This inner weight is the quality which Egyptian art possesses to such a degree that everything in its seems to be made of primeval stone, like a mountain range, even if it is only a few inches across or ⑤ carved in wood.

* gigantic: 거대한 ** primeval: 원시 시대의

13 20학년도 3월 교육청

다음 글의 밑줄 친 부분 중 어법상 <u>틀린</u> 것은?

When children are young, much of the work is demonstrating to them that they ① <u>do</u> have control. One wise friend of ours who was a parent educator for twenty years ② <u>advises</u> giving calendars to preschoolage children and writing down all the important events in their life, in part because it helps children understand the passage of time better, and how their days will unfold. We can't overstate the importance of the calendar tool in helping kids feel in control of their day. Have them ③ <u>cross</u> off days of the week as you come to them. Spend time going over the schedule for the day, giving them choice in that schedule wherever ④ <u>possible</u>. This communication expresses respect —they see that they are not just a tagalong to your day and your plans, and they understand what is going to happen, when, and why. As they get older, children will then start to write in important things for themselves, ⑤ <u>it</u> further helps them develop their sense of control.

14 20학년도 7월 교육청

다음 글의 밑줄 친 부분 중 어법상 <u>틀린</u> 것은?

Metacognition simply means "thinking about thinking," and it is one of the main distinctions between the human brain and that of other species. Our ability to stand high on a ladder above our normal thinking processes and ① <u>evaluate</u> why we are thinking as we are thinking is an evolutionary marvel. We have this ability ② <u>because</u> the most recently developed part of the human brain —the prefrontal cortex — enables self-reflective, abstract thought. We can think about ourselves as if we are not part of ③ <u>ourselves</u>. Research on primate behavior indicates that even our closest cousins, the chimpanzees, ④ <u>lacking</u> this ability (although they possess some self-reflective abilities, like being able to identify themselves in a mirror instead of thinking the reflection is another chimp). The ability is a double-edged sword, because while it allows us to evaluate why we are thinking ⑤ <u>what</u> we are thinking, it also puts us in touch with difficult existential questions that can easily become obsessions.

15 20학년도 10월 교육청

[정답과 해설 289page]

다음 글의 밑줄 친 부분 중 어법상 틀린 것은?

Mathematical practices and discourses should be situated within cultural contexts, student interests, and reallife situations ① <u>where</u> all students develop positive identities as mathematics learners. Instruction in mathematics skills in isolation and devoid of student understandings and identities renders them ② <u>helpless</u> to benefit from explicit instruction. Thus, we agree that explicit instruction benefits students but propose that incorporating culturally relevant pedagogy and consideration of nonacademic factors that ③ <u>promoting</u> learning and mastery must enhance explicit instruction in mathematics instruction. Furthermore, teachers play a critical role in developing environments ④ <u>that</u> encourage student identities, agency, and independence through discourses and practices in the classroom. Students who are actively engaged in a contextualized learning process are in control of the learning process and are able to make connections with past learning experiences ⑤ <u>to foster</u> deeper and more meaningful learning.

* render: (어떤 상태가 되게) 만들다 ** pedagogy: 교수법

16 20학년도 4월 교육청

[정답과 해설 290page]

다음 글의 밑줄 친 부분 중 어법상 틀린 것은?

Mental representation is the mental imagery of things that are not actually present to the senses. In general, mental representations can help us learn. Some of the best evidence for this ① <u>comes</u> from the field of musical performance. Several researchers have examined ② <u>what</u> differentiates the best musicians from lesser ones, and one of the major differences lies in the quality of the mental representations the best ones create. When ③ <u>practicing</u> a new piece, advanced musicians have a very detailed mental representation of the music they use to guide their practice and, ultimately, their performance of a piece. In particular, they use their mental representations to provide their own feedback so that they know how ④ <u>closely</u> they are to getting the piece right and what they need to do differently to improve. The beginners and intermediate students may have crude representations of the music ⑤ <u>that</u> allow them to tell, for instance, when they hit a wrong note, but they must rely on feedback from their teachers to identify the more subtle mistakes and weaknesses.

* crude: 투박한

17 19학년도 4월 교육청

다음 글의 밑줄 친 부분 중 어법상 <u>틀린</u> 것은?

The present moment feels special. It is real. However much you may remember the past or anticipate the future, you live in the present. Of course, the moment ① <u>during which</u> you read that sentence is no longer happening. This one is. In other words, it feels as though time flows, in the sense that the present is constantly updating ② <u>itself</u>. We have a deep intuition that the future is open until it becomes present and ③ <u>that</u> the past is fixed. As time flows, this structure of fixed past, immediate present and open future gets carried forward in time. Yet as ④ <u>naturally</u> as this way of thinking is, you will not find it reflected in science. The equations of physics do not tell us which events are occurring right now — they are like a map without the "you are here" symbol. The present moment does not exist in them, and therefore neither ⑤ <u>does</u> the flow of time.

18 19학년도 10월 교육청

다음 글의 밑줄 친 부분 중 어법상 <u>틀린</u> 것은?

The modern adult human brain weighs only 1/50 of the total body weight but uses up to 1/5 of the total energy needs. The brain's running costs are about eight to ten times as high, per unit mass, as ① <u>those</u> of the body's muscles. And around 3/4 of that energy is expended on neurons, the ② <u>specialized</u> brain cells that communicate in vast networks to generate our thoughts and behaviours. An individual neuron ③ <u>sends</u> a signal in the brain uses as much energy as a leg muscle cell running a marathon. Of course, we use more energy overall when we are running, but we are not always on the move, whereas our brains never switch off. Even though the brain is metabolically greedy, it still outclasses any desktop computer both in terms of the calculations it can perform and the efficiency ④ <u>at which</u> it does this. We may have built computers that can beat our top Grand Master chess players, but we are still far away from designing one that is capable of recognizing and picking up one of the chess pieces as ⑤ <u>easily</u> as a typical three-year-old child can.

다음 글의 밑줄 친 부분 중 어법상 **틀린** 것은?

The idea that hypnosis can put the brain into a special state, ① <u>in which</u> the powers of memory are dramatically greater than normal, reflects a belief in a form of easily unlocked potential. But it is false. People under hypnosis generate more "memories" than they ② <u>do</u> in a normal state, but these recollections are as likely to be false as true. Hypnosis leads them to come up with more information, but not necessarily more accurate information. In fact, it might actually be people's beliefs in the power of hypnosis that ③ <u>leads</u> them to recall more things: If people believe that they should have better memory under hypnosis, they will try harder to retrieve more memories when hypnotized. Unfortunately, there's no way to know ④ <u>whether</u> the memories hypnotized people retrieve are true or not — unless of course we know exactly what the person should be able to remember. But if we ⑤ <u>knew</u> that, then we'd have no need to use hypnosis in the first place!

* hypnosis: 최면

다음 글의 밑줄 친 부분 중 어법상 **틀린** 것은?

Baylor University researchers investigated ① <u>whether</u> different types of writing could ease people into sleep. To find out, they had 57 young adults spend five minutes before bed ② <u>writing</u> either a to-do list for the days ahead or a list of tasks they'd finished over the past few days. The results confirm that not all pre-sleep writing is created equally. Those who made to-do lists before bed ③ <u>were</u> able to fall asleep nine minutes faster than those who wrote about past events. The quality of the lists mattered, too; the more tasks and the more ④ <u>specific</u> the to-do lists were, the faster the writers fell asleep. The study authors figure that writing down future tasks ⑤ <u>unloading</u> the thoughts so you can stop turning them over in your mind. You're telling your brain that the task will get done — just not right now.

21 18학년도 4월 교육청

다음 글의 밑줄 친 부분 중 어법상 <u>틀린</u> 것은?

According to Pierre Pica, understanding quantities approximately in terms of estimating ratios is a universal human intuition. In fact, humans who do not have numbers have no choice but ① <u>to see</u> the world in this way. By contrast, understanding quantities in terms of exact numbers is not a universal intuition; it is a product of culture. The precedence of approximations and ratios over exact numbers, Pica suggests, ② <u>is</u> due to the fact that ratios are much more important for survival in the wild than the ability to count. ③ <u>Faced</u> with a group of spear-wielding adversaries, we needed to know instantly whether there were more of them than us. When we saw two trees we needed to know instantly ④ <u>that</u> had more fruit hanging from it. In neither case was it ⑤ <u>necessary</u> to enumerate every enemy or every fruit individually. The crucial thing was to be able to make quick estimates of the relative amounts.

* enumerate: 일일이 세다

22 18학년도 7월 교육청

다음 글의 밑줄 친 부분 중 어법상 <u>틀린</u> 것은?

When it comes to medical treatment, patients see choice as both a blessing and a burden. And the burden falls primarily on women, who are ① <u>typically</u> the guardians not only of their own health, but that of their husbands and children. "It is an overwhelming task for women, and consumers in general, ② <u>to be</u> able to sort through the information they find and make decisions," says Amy Allina, program director of the National Women's Health Network. And what makes it overwhelming is not only that the decision is ours, but that the number of sources of information ③ <u>which</u> we are to make the decisions has exploded. It's not just a matter of listening to your doctor lay out the options and ④ <u>making</u> a choice. We now have encyclopedic lay-people's guides to health, "better health" magazines, and the Internet. So now the prospect of medical decisions ⑤ <u>has</u> become everyone's worst nightmare of a term paper assignment, with stakes infinitely higher than a grade in a course.

* lay-people: 비전문가

23 18학년도 10월 교육청 [정답과 해설 291page]

다음 글의 밑줄 친 부분 중 어법상 틀린 것은?

The Internet allows information to flow more ① <u>freely</u> than ever before. We can communicate and share ideas in unprecedented ways. These developments are revolutionizing our self-expression and enhancing our freedom. But there's a problem. We're heading toward a world ② <u>where</u> an extensive trail of information fragments about us will be forever preserved on the Internet, displayed instantly in a search result. We will be forced to live with a detailed record ③ <u>beginning</u> with childhood that will stay with us for life wherever we go, searchable and accessible from anywhere in the world. This data can often be of dubious reliability; it can be false; or it can be true but deeply ④ <u>humiliated</u>. It may be increasingly difficult to have a fresh start or a second chance. We might find ⑤ <u>it</u> harder to engage in self-exploration if every false step and foolish act is preserved forever in a permanent record.

* dubious: 의심스러운

24 18학년도 3월 교육청 [정답과 해설 292page]

다음 글의 (A), (B), (C)에 들어갈 말로 알맞은 것을 고르시오.

The old maxim "I'll sleep when I'm dead" is unfortunate. (A) [Adopt / Adopting] this mind-set, and you will be dead sooner and the quality of that life will be worse. The elastic band of sleep deprivation can stretch only so far before it snaps. Sadly, human beings are in fact the only species that will deliberately deprive (B) [them / themselves] of sleep without legitimate gain. Every component of wellness, and countless seams of societal fabric, are being eroded by our costly state of sleep neglect: human and financial alike. So much so that the World Health Organization (WHO) has now declared a sleep loss epidemic throughout industrialized nations. It is no coincidence that countries (C) [where / which] sleep time has declined most dramatically over the past century, such as the US, the UK, Japan, and South Korea, and several in Western Europe, are also those suffering the greatest increase in rates of physical diseases and mental disorders.

	(A)	(B)	(C)
①	Adopt	them	where
②	Adopt	themselves	where
③	Adopt	themselves	which
④	Adopting	themselves	which
⑤	Adopting	them	which

다음 글의 밑줄 친 부분 중 어법상 <u>틀린</u> 것은?

The most dramatic and significant contacts between civilizations were ① <u>when</u> people from one civilization conquered and eliminated the people of another. These contacts normally were not only violent but brief, and ② <u>they</u> occurred only occasionally. Beginning in the seventh century A.D., relatively ③ <u>sustained</u> and at times intense intercivilizational contacts did develop between Islam and the West and Islam and India. Most commercial, cultural, and military interactions, however, were within civilizations. While India and China, for instance, were on occasion invaded and subjected by other peoples (Moguls, Mongols), both civilizations ④ <u>having</u> extensive times of "warring states" within their own civilization as well. Similarly, the Greeks fought each other and traded with each other far more often than they ⑤ <u>did</u> with Persians or other non-Greeks.

다음 글의 밑줄 친 부분 중 어법상 <u>틀린</u> 것은?

People seeking legal advice should be assured, when discussing their rights or obligations with a lawyer, ① <u>which</u> the latter will not disclose to third parties the information provided. Only if this duty of confidentiality is respected ② <u>will people</u> feel free to consult lawyers and provide the information required for the lawyer to prepare the client's defense. Regardless of the type of information ③ <u>disclosed</u>, clients must be certain that it will not be used against them in a court of law, by the authorities or by any other party. It is generally considered to be a condition of the good functioning of the legal system and, thus, in the general interest. Legal professional privilege is ④ <u>much</u> more than an ordinary rule of evidence, limited in its application to the facts of a particular case. It is a fundamental condition on which the administration of justice as a whole ⑤ <u>rests</u>.

* confidentiality: 비밀 유지

27 17학년도 4월 교육청

다음 글의 밑줄 친 부분 중 어법상 틀린 것은?

In early modern Europe, transport by water was usually much cheaper than transport by land. An Italian printer calculated in 1550 ① <u>that</u> to send a load of books from Rome to Lyons would cost 18 scudi by land compared with 4 by sea. Letters were normally carried overland, but a system of transporting letters and newspapers, as well as people, by canal boat ② <u>developed</u> in the Dutch Republic in the seventeenth century. The average speed of the boats was a little over four miles an hour, ③ <u>slow</u> compared to a rider on horseback. On the other hand, the service was regular, frequent and cheap, and allowed communication not only between Amsterdam and the smaller towns, but also between one small town and another, thus ④ <u>equalizing</u> accessibility to information. It was only in 1837, with the invention of the electric telegraph, that the traditional link between transport and the communication of messages ⑤ <u>were</u> broken.

* scudi: 이탈리아의 옛 은화 단위(scudo)의 복수형

28 17학년도 3월 교육청

다음 글의 밑줄 친 부분 중 어법상 틀린 것은?

One of the simplest and most effective ways to build empathy in children ① <u>is</u> to let them play more on their own. Unsupervised kids are not reluctant to tell one another how they feel. In addition, children at play often take on other roles, pretending to be Principal Walsh or Josh's mom, happily forcing ② <u>themselves</u> to imagine how someone else thinks and feels. Unfortunately, free play is becoming rare. Boston College research professor Peter Gray has documented a continuous and ③ <u>ultimately</u> dramatic decline in children's opportunities to play and explore in their own chosen ways over the past fifty years in the United States and other developed countries. The effects have been especially ④ <u>damaged</u>, he argues, to empathy. He concludes that a decline of empathy and a rise in narcissism are exactly ⑤ <u>what</u> we would expect to see in children who have little opportunity to play socially.

* empathy: 공감, 감정 이입

29 22학년도 수능

다음 글의 밑줄 친 부분 중 어법상 틀린 것은?

Like whole individuals, cells have a life span. During thcir life cycle (cell cycle), cell size, shape, and metabolic activities can change dramatically. A cell is "born" as a twin when its mother cell divides, ① <u>producing</u> two daughter cells. Each daughter cell is smaller than the mother cell, and except for unusual cases, each grows until it becomes as large as the mother cell ② <u>was</u>. During this time, the cell absorbs water, sugars, amino acids, and other nutrients and assembles them into new, living protoplasm. After the cell has grown to the proper size, its metabolism shifts as it either prepares to divide or matures and ③ <u>differentiates</u> into a specialized cell. Both growth and development require a complex and dynamic set of interactions involving all cell parts. ④ <u>What</u> cell metabolism and structure should be complex would not be surprising, but actually, they are rather simple and logical. Even the most complex cell has only a small number of parts, each ⑤ <u>responsible</u> for a distinct, well-defined aspect of cell life.

* metabolic: 물질대사의 ** protoplasm: 원형질

30 21학년도 10월 교육청

다음 글의 밑줄 친 부분 중 어법상 틀린 것은?

According to its dictionary definition, an anthem is both a song of loyalty, often to a country, and a piece of 'sacred music', definitions that are both applicable in sporting contexts. This genre is dominated, although not exclusively, by football and has produced a number of examples ① <u>where</u> popular songs become synonymous with the club and are enthusiastically adopted by the fans. More than this they are often spontaneous expressions of loyalty and identity and, according to Desmond Morris, have 'reached the level of something ② <u>approached</u> a local art form'. A strong element of the appeal of such sports songs ③ <u>is</u> that they feature 'memorable and easily sung choruses in which fans can participate'. This is a vital part of the team's performance ④ <u>as</u> it makes the fans' presence more tangible. This form of popular culture can be said ⑤ <u>to display</u> pleasure and emotional excess in contrast to the dominant culture which tends to maintain 'respectable aesthetic distance and control'.

* synonymous: 밀접한 연관을 갖는 ** tangible: 확실한

31 22학년도 9월 평가원

다음 글의 밑줄 친 부분 중 어법상 <u>틀린</u> 것은?

Accepting whatever others are communicating only pays off if their interests correspond to ours —think cells in a body, bees in a beehive. As far as communication between humans is concerned, such commonality of interests ① <u>is</u> rarely achieved; even a pregnant mother has reasons to mistrust the chemical signals sent by her fetus. Fortunately, there are ways of making communication work even in the most adversarial of relationships. A prey can convince a predator not to chase ② <u>it</u>. But for such communication to occur, there must be strong guarantees ③ <u>which</u> those who receive the signal will be better off believing it. The messages have to be kept, on the whole, ④ <u>honest</u>. In the case of humans, honesty is maintained by a set of cognitive mechanisms that evaluate ⑤ <u>communicated</u> information. These mechanisms allow us to accept most beneficial messages —to be open while— rejecting most harmful messages —to be vigilant.

* fetus: 태아 ** adversarial: 반대자의 *** vigilant: 경계하는

32 21학년도 7월 교육청

다음 글의 밑줄 친 부분 중 어법상 <u>틀린</u> 것은?

The idea that people ① <u>selectively</u> expose themselves to news content has been around for a long time, but it is even more important today with the fragmentation of audiences and the proliferation of choices. Selective exposure is a psychological concept that says people seek out information that conforms to their existing belief systems and ② <u>avoid</u> information that challenges those beliefs. In the past when there were few sources of news, people could either expose themselves to mainstream newswhere they would likely see beliefs ③ <u>expressed</u> counter to their own -or they could avoid news altogether. Now with so many types of news constantly available to a full range of niche audiences, people can easily find a source of news ④ <u>that</u> consistently confirms their own personal set of beliefs. This leads to the possibility of creating many different small groups of people with each strongly ⑤ <u>believes</u> they are correct and everyone else is wrong about how the world works.

* fragmentation: 분열 ** proliferation: 급증 *** niche: 틈새

다음 글의 밑줄 친 부분 중 어법상 틀린 것은?

The world's first complex writing form, Sumerian cuneiform, followed an evolutionary path, moving around 3500 BCE from pictographic to ideographic representations, from the depiction of objects to ① that of abstract notions. Sumerian cuneiform was a linear writing system, its symbols usually ② set in columns, read from top to bottom and from left to right. This regimentation was a form of abstraction: the world is not a linear place, and objects do not organize ③ themselves horizontally or vertically in real life. Early rock paintings, thought to have been created for ritual purposes, were possibly shaped and organized ④ to follow the walls of the cave, or the desires of the painters, who may have organized them symbolically, or artistically, or even randomly. Yet after cuneiform, virtually every form of script that has emerged has been set out in rows with a clear beginning and endpoint. So ⑤ uniformly is this expectation, indeed, that the odd exception is noteworthy, and generally established for a specific purpose.

* cuneiform: 쐐기 문자 ** regimentation: 조직화

다음 글의 밑줄 친 부분 중 어법상 틀린 것은?

Recognizing ethical issues is the most important step in understanding business ethics. An ethical issue is an identifiable problem, situation, or opportunity that requires a person to choose from among several actions that may ① be evaluated as right or wrong, ethical or unethical. ② Learn how to choose from alternatives and make a decision requires not only good personal values, but also knowledge competence in the business area of concern. Employees also need to know when to rely on their organizations' policies and codes of ethics or ③ have discussions with co-workers or managers on appropriate conduct. Ethical decision making is not always easy because there are always gray areas ④ that create dilemmas, no matter how decisions are made. For instance, should an employee report on a co-worker engaging in time theft? Should a salesperson leave out facts about a product's poor safety record in his presentation to a customer? Such questions require the decision maker to evaluate the ethics of his or her choice and decide ⑤ whether to ask for guidance.

35 23학년도 6월 평가원

다음 글의 밑줄 친 부분 중 어법상 <u>틀린</u> 것은?

Ecosystems differ in composition and extent. They can be defined as ranging from the communities and interactions of organisms in your mouth or ① <u>those</u> in the canopy of a rain forest to all those in Earth's oceans. The processes ② <u>governing</u> them differ in complexity and speed. There are systems that turn over in minutes, and there are others ③ <u>which</u> rhythmic time extends to hundreds of years. Some ecosystems are extensive ('biomes', such as the African savanna); some cover regions (river basins); many involve clusters of villages (micro-watersheds); others are confined to the level of a single village (the village pond). In each example there is an element of indivisibility. Divide an ecosystem into parts by creating barriers, and the sum of the productivity of the parts will typically be found to be lower than the productivity of the whole, other things ④ <u>being</u> equal. The mobility of biological populations is a reason. Safe passages, for example, enable migratory species ⑤ <u>to survive.</u>

* canopy: 덮개 ** basin: 유역

36 23학년도 수능

[정답과 해설 295page]

다음 글의 밑줄 친 부분 중 어법상 <u>틀린</u> 것은?

Trends constantly suggest new opportunities for individuals to restage themselves, representing occasions for change. To understand how trends can ultimately give individuals power and freedom, one must first discuss fashion's importance as a basis for change. The most common explanation offered by my informants as to why fashion is so appealing is ① <u>that</u> it constitutes a kind of theatrical costumery. Clothes are part of how people present ② <u>them</u> to the world, and fashion locates them in the present, relative to what is happening in society and to fashion's own history. As a form of expression, fashion contains a host of ambiguities, enabling individuals to recreate the meanings ③ <u>associated</u> with specific pieces of clothing. Fashion is among the simplest and cheapest methods of self-expression: clothes can be ④ <u>inexpensively</u> purchased while making it easy to convey notions of wealth, intellectual stature, relaxation or environmental consciousness, even if none of these is true. Fashion can also strengthen agency in various ways, ⑤ <u>opening</u> up space for action.

* stature: 능력

기출의 파급효과

영어 영역

영어(하)

해설

orbi books

빠른 정답

Chapter 4-1
절. 모. 평.

문항번호	정 답	문항번호	정 답	문항번호	정 답	문항번호	정 답	문항번호	정 답
1	④	2	④	3	③	4	③	5	③
6	③	7	④	8	③	9	④	10	④
11	③	12	③	13	④				

Chapter 4-2
절. 모. 평.

문항번호	정 답	문항번호	정 답	문항번호	정 답	문항번호	정 답	문항번호	정 답
1	③	2	④	3	⑤	4	⑤	5	④
6	③	7	⑤	8	④	9	④	10	④
11	④	12	④	13	⑤				

Chapter 4-3
절. 모. 평.

문항번호	정 답	문항번호	정 답	문항번호	정 답	문항번호	정 답	문항번호	정 답
1	②	2	⑤	3	②	4	③	5	③
6	④	7	③	8	②	9	①	10	④
11	③	12	③	13	①	14	③	15	②
16	⑤	17	③	18	⑤	19	①	20	④
21	④	22	③	23	②	24	⑤	25	①
26	⑤	27	③	28	②				

Chapter 5-1

절. 모. 평.

문항번호	정 답	문항번호	정 답	문항번호	정 답	문항번호	정 답	문항번호	정 답
1	②	2	②	3	⑤	4	⑤	5	④
6	④	7	②	8	③	9	④	10	⑤
11	②	12	⑤	13	②	14	⑤	15	⑤
16	②	17	⑤	18	④	19	⑤	20	⑤
21	⑤	22	③	23	④	24	①	25	③
26	①								

Chapter 5-2

절. 모. 평.

문항번호	정 답	문항번호	정 답	문항번호	정 답	문항번호	정 답	문항번호	정 답
1	④	2	④	3	④	4	④	5	④
6	②	7	⑤	8	④	9	④	10	④
11	④	12	④	13	③	14	④	15	③
16	③	17	⑤	18	②	19	⑤	20	⑤
21	③	22	②	23	②	24	⑤	25	⑤
26	⑤								

Chapter 6

연습문제

문항번호	정 답	문항번호	정 답	문항번호	정 답	문항번호	정 답	문항번호	정 답
1	④	2	②	3	⑤	4	⑤	5	⑤
6	③	7	②	8	②	9	①	10	④
11	④	12	②	13	⑤	14	④	15	③
16	④	17	④	18	③	19	③	20	⑤
21	④	22	③	23	④	24	②	25	④
26	①	27	⑤	28	④	29	④	30	②
31	③	32	⑤	33	⑤	34	②	35	③
36	②								

Chapter
04
전개상 흐름 파악

01 25학년도 6월 평가원 35번　　　　　　　　　(정답률 83%)

다음 글에서 전체 흐름과 관계 <u>없는</u> 문장은?

> Avian song learning occurs in two stages: first, songs **must** be memorized and, second, they **must** be practiced. In some species these two events overlap, **but** in others memorization can occur before practice by several months, providing an impressive example of long-term memory storage. ① The young bird's initial efforts to reproduce the memorized song are usually not successful. ② These early songs may have uneven pitch, irregular tempo, and notes that are out of order or poorly reproduced. ③ **However**, sound graphs of songs recorded over several weeks or months reveal that during this practice period the bird fine-tunes his efforts until he produces an accurate copy of the memorized template. ④ An important idea to emerge from the study of birdsong is that song learning is shaped by preferences and limitations. ⑤ This process requires hearing oneself sing; birds are unable to reproduce memorized songs if they are deafened after memorization **but** before the practice period.
>
> * avian: 조류의

해설 [정답 : ④]

지문은 조류의 노래 학습이 이루어지는 과정을 설명하고 있습니다.

④번 문장에서는 'important idea to emerge from the study of birdsong is that song learning is shaped by preferences and limitations' 새소리 연구를 통해 드러나는 아이디어는 노래 학습이 선호하는 것과 한계점에 의해 형성된다고 했습니다.

그런데 ③번 문장에서 'during this practice period the bird fine-tunes his efforts until he produces an accurate copy' 연습 기간 동안 새가 암기된 복사본을 정확하게 모방할 때까지 미세 조정의 노력을 기울인다는 것, ⑤번 문장에서 'process requires hearing oneself sing' 이 과정에서 새들은 자신이 노래하는 것을 들어야 한다고 하는 내용은 모두 조류의 노래 학습 과정의 일부분과 관련된 내용이 이어지고 있는데, 새소리 연구와 관련된 ④번 문장의 내용은 조류의 학습 과정과는 관련이 없습니다. 그러므로 정답은 ④번이 됩니다.

Ⅰ. Avian song learning / occurs / in two stages: first, songs / **must** be memorized / and, second, they / **must** be practiced.

* avian: 조류의

구 ▶ 조류의 노래 학습은 두 단계로 이루어지는데, 첫째로는, 노래를 암기해야 하고 둘째로는, 노래를 연습해야 한다고 합니다.

독 ▶ 'must'가 제시되었으므로 중심 문장
- 조류의 노래 학습 과정을 언급하고 있습니다.

Ⅱ. In some species / these two events / overlap, **but** in others / memorization / can occur / before practice / by several months, providing / an impressive example (of long-term memory storage.)

구▶ 일부 종에서는 이 두 가지 일이 겹치기도 하지만, 다른 종에서는 연습 전 몇 달 동안 암기가 이루어질 수 있는데, 이는 장기 기억 저장의 인상적인 예를 제공한다고 합니다.

독▶ 'but'이 제시되었으므로 중심 문장
  - 두 과정이 겹치는 경우와 암기-연습 순으로 이어지는 경우가 나열되고 있습니다.

①. The young bird's initial efforts / to reproduce / the memorized song / are usually not / successful.

구▶ 어린 새가 암기한 노래를 재현하려는 초기의 노력은 대체로 성공적이지 못하다고 합니다.

독▶ 암기한 노래를 제대로 재현하지 못하는 새의 사례가 언급됩니다.

* initiate (시작하다) + -ial (형용사형 접사) = initial – 처음의, 초기의

②. These early songs / may have / uneven pitch, irregular tempo, and notes (that / are / out of order / or poorly reproduced).

구▶ 이러한 초기의 노래에는 고르지 않은 음정과 불규칙한 박자, 그리고 순서가 맞지 않거나 제대로 재현되지 않은 음이 있을 수도 있다고 합니다.

독▶ 초기의 노래가 음정, 박자, 순서가 제대로 맞지 않는 것은 ①번 문장의 사례가 됩니다.

③. **However**, sound graphs (of songs recorded / over several weeks or months) / reveal / that (during this practice period) the bird / fine-tunes / his efforts / until / he / produces / an accurate copy (of the memorized template.)

구▶ 하지만 몇 주 또는 몇 달에 걸쳐 녹음된 노래의 음향 그래프를 보면, 이 연습 기간 동안 새가 암기된 본보기를 정확하게 모방할 때까지 미세 조정의 노력을 기울인다는 것을 알 수 있다고 합니다.

독▶ 'However'가 제시되었으므로 앞 뒷 문장이 중심 문장
  - ②번 문장에서 언급된 새들이 암기한 노래의 불완전함을 조정하기 위해 노력하는 내용이 언급됩니다.

* template – 템플릿, 견본

④. An important idea (to emerge (from the study of birdsong)) / is / that song learning / is shaped (by preferences and limitations.)

구▶ 새소리 연구를 통해 드러날 수 있는 중요한 아이디어는 노래 학습은 선호하는 것과 한계점에 의해 형성된다는 것이라고 합니다.

독▶ 노래의 학습은 선호와 한계에 의해 형성된다고 했는데, Ⅰ번 문장에서는 노래와 학습이 암기와 연습을 통해 일어난다고 했으므로 다른 내용이 언급된다고 볼 수 있습니다.

⑤. This process / requires / hearing oneself sing; birds / are unable to reproduce / memorized songs /
if they / are deafened / after memorization / **but** before the practice period.

구 이 과정에서는 자신이 노래하는 것을 들어야 하는데, 만약 새들이 암기한 후이지만 연습 기간 전에
귀가 먹으면 암기된 노래를 재현할 수 없다고 합니다.

독 'but'이 제시되었으므로 중심 문장
- 'This process'는 ③번 문장의 암기된 노래를 모방하기 위해 미세 조정하는 것을 말하며, 이 과정 중
자신이 노래하는 것을 듣는 것이 재현에 있어서 중요하다고 말하고 있습니다.

다음 글에서 전체 흐름과 관계 <u>없는</u> 문장은?

　Kinship ties continue to be important today. In modern societies such as the United States people frequently have family get-togethers, they telephone their relatives regularly, and they provide their kin with a wide variety of services. ① Eugene Litwak has referred to this pattern of behaviour as the 'modified extended family'. ② It is an extended family structure **because** multigenerational ties are maintained, **but** it is modified **because** it does not usually rest on co-residence between the generations and most extended families do not act as corporate groups. ③ **Although** modified extended family members often live close by, the modified extended family does not require geographical proximity and ties are maintained even when kin are separated by considerable distances. ④ The oldest member of the family makes the decisions on important issues, no matter how far away family members live from each other. ⑤ **In contrast to** the traditional extended family where kin always live in close proximity, the members of modified extended families may freely move away from kin to seek opportunities for occupational advancement.

* kin: 친족 ** proximity: 근접

해설 [정답 : ④]

④번 문장 전까지는 수정된 확대 가족은 가족 구성원들이 멀리 떨어져 있더라도 유대 관계를 유지한다는 내용이며 ⑤번 문장 역시 이러한 수정된 확대 가족의 특징으로 인해서 수정된 확대 가족의 구성원들이 멀리 떨어져 이주할 수 있다고 합니다. 하지만 ④번 문장에서는 가족 구성원들이 멀리 떨어져 있더라도 최고 연장자가 중요한 사안에 대해서 결정한다는 내용이므로 가족 구성원들이 멀리 떨어져 있다는 같은 소재이지만 다른 내용이 전개되고 있으므로 정답은 ④번이 됩니다.

Ⅰ. Kinship ties / continue to be / important today.

* kin: 친족

구▶ 친족 유대 관계는 오늘날 계속 중요하다고 합니다.

Ⅱ. In modern societies (such as the United States people / frequently have / family get-togethers), they / telephone / their relatives regularly, and they / provide / their kin (with a wide variety (of services)).

구▶ 'provide A with B'는 'A에게 B를 제공하다'를 의미합니다.
- 자주 가족 모임을 가지는 미국과 같은 현대 사회에서, 그들은 (= 친족들은) 그들의 친척들에게 정기적으로 전화하고, 그들의 친족들에게 매우 다양한 서비스를 제공한다고 합니다.

① . Eugene Litwak / has referred to / this pattern of behaviour (as the 'modified extended family').

> **구** 'refer to A as B'는 'A를 B라고 언급하다'를 의미합니다.
>   - 'Eugene Litwak'은 그러한 패턴의 행동을 (= 친족들에게 정기적으로 전화하고 다양한 서비스를 제공하는 것을) '수정된 확대 가족'이라고 언급한다고 합니다.

② . It / is / an extended family structure / **because** multigenerational ties / are maintained, / **but** it is modified / **because** it / does not usually rest on / co-residence (between the generations) / and most extended families / do not act as / corporate groups.

> **구** 'rest on A'는 'A에 의존하다'를 의미합니다.
>   - 그것은 (= 수정된 확대 가족은) 다세대의 유대 관계가 유지되기 때문에 확대된 가족 구조이지만, 그것은 (= 수정된 확대 가족은) 보통 세대 간 공동 거주에 기초를 두지 않고 대부분의 확대된 가족이 공동 집단으로서 기능하지 않기 때문에 수정된다고 합니다.

> **독** 'because'가 제시되었으므로 중심 문장
>   - '수정된 확대 가족이란' 다양한 세대의 유대 관계가 유지되어 있기도 하지만, 옛날과 같은 공동 거주에는 기초를 두지 않기 때문에 수정되었다고 합니다.

③ . **Although** modified extended family members often / live close by, / the modified extended family / does not require / geographical proximity / and ties / are maintained / even when kin / are separated (by considerable distances).

** proximity: 근접

> **구** 비록 수정 확대 가족의 구성원들이 보통 가까이 살지 않지만, 수정 확대 가족은 지리적 근접이 필요하지 않으며, 유대 관계는 친척이 상당히 멀리 떨어져 있더라도 유지된다고 합니다.

> **독** 'Although'가 제시되었으므로 중심 문장
>   - ②번 문장을 재진술하고 있으며, 지리적 근접이 필요하지 않고 멀리 떨어져 있더라도 유대 관계를 유지하는 것은 ②번 문장에서 수정된 확대 가족이 공동 거주에 의존하지 않는 것과 대응됩니다.

④ . The oldest member of the family / makes / the decisions (on important issues), no matter how far away family members / live / from each other.

> **구** 'no matter how S + V'는 '얼마나 S가 V하더라도'를 의미합니다.
>   - 가장 나이든 가족의 구성원이 얼마나 가족 구성원들이 멀리 떨어져 살지라도, 중요한 문제에 관해서 결정한다고 합니다.

> **독** ③번 문장까지는 가족 구성원들이 멀리 떨어져 있더라도 가족 간에 유대 관계를 유지한다는 내용이지만, ④번 문장에서는 가족 구성원들이 멀리 떨어져 있더라도 연장자가 중대한 사항에 대해서 결정은 한다는 내용이므로, 같은 소재이지만 다른 내용이 전개되고 있습니다. 즉, ④번 문장 전 내용은 수정된 확대 가족 자체를 설명하고 있지만 ④번 문장에서는 그 가족의 의사결정 방식에 대해서 제시하므로 같은 소재이지만 다른 내용이 전개되고 있습니다.

⑤. **<u>In contrast to</u>** the traditional extended family (where kin always live in close proximity), /

the members of modified extended families / may freely move / away from kin (to seek /

opportunities for occupational advancement).

구▸ 친족들이 가까운 근접성에서 살았던 전통의 확대 가족과는 다르게, 수정된 확대 가족의 구성원들은
자유롭게 멀리 이주해가서 직업상 발전을 위한 기회를 추구할 수 있다고 합니다.

독▸ 'In contrast to'가 제시되었으므로 중심 문장
 - 과거와는 달리 수정된 확대 가족은 멀리 이주할 수 있다고 합니다.

다음 글에서 전체 흐름과 관계 <u>없는</u> 문장은?

Interestingly, experts do not suffer as much as beginners when performing complex tasks or combining multiple tasks. **Because** experts have extensive practice within a limited domain, the key component skills in their domain tend to be highly practiced and more automated. ① Each of these highly practiced skills then demands relatively few cognitive resources, effectively lowering the total cognitive load that experts experience. ② **Thus**, experts can perform complex tasks and combine multiple tasks relatively easily. ③ Furthermore, beginners are excellent at processing the tasks when the tasks are divided and isolated. ④ This is **not because** they necessarily have more cognitive resources than beginners; rather, **because of** the high level of fluency they have achieved in performing key skills, they can do more with what they have. ⑤ Beginners, **on the other hand**, have not achieved the same degree of fluency and automaticity in each of the component skills, and thus they struggle to combine skills that experts combine with relative ease and efficiency.

해설 [정답 : ③]

글의 핵심 주제는 전문가는 영역 내에서 연습을 통해 기술이 고도로 숙련되고 자동화되어 있어서, 초보자보다 복잡하거나, 많은 과제를 수월하게 해결한다는 것입니다. ③번 문장은 초보자들의 특징, 그중에서도 장점을 언급하고 있는데, ②번 문장에서는 전문가들의 장점을 언급하고 있으므로, 같은 내용을 나열하는 접속사 'Furthermore'로 연결될 수 없습니다. 또한 ④번 문장에서 'high level of fluency they have achieved', 높은 수준의 능숙함을 가지고 있는 것 역시 전문가들의 특징이므로, ③번 문장은 더더욱 지문의 흐름과 관계가 없습니다.

Ⅰ. Interestingly, experts / do not suffer / as much as beginners / when / performing complex tasks / or combining multiple tasks.

> 구▶ 흥미롭게도, 전문가들은 복잡한 과제를 수행하거나 많은 과제를 결합할 때 초보자만큼 어려움을 겪지 않는다고 합니다.

> 독▶ 전문가의 입장에서 전문가와 초보자를 비교하고 있는 문장입니다.

Ⅱ. **Because** experts / have / extensive practice (within a limited domain), the key component skills (in their domain) / tend to be highly practiced / and more automated.

> 구▶ 전문가는 제한된 영역 내에서 광범위한 연습을 하므로, 그들의 영역에서의 핵심 구성 기술은 고도로 숙련되고 더 자동화되어 있는 경향이 있다고 합니다.

> 독▶ 'because'가 언급되고 있으므로 중심 문장
> - 전문가의 특징이 Ⅰ번 문장에 이어 나열되고 있습니다.

①. Each (of these highly practiced skills) / then demands / relatively few cognitive resources, effectively lowering / the total cognitive load / that / experts / experience.

> **구** 그래서 고도로 숙련된 이러한 각각의 기술은 비교적 적은 인지 자원이 필요하여, 전문가가 경험하는 총 인지 부하를 효과적으로 낮춘다고 합니다.

> **독** II번 문장의 숙련된 기술이 전문가들의 총 인지 부하를 낮춘다는 내용으로 이어지고 있습니다.

②. **Thus**, experts / can perform / complex tasks / and combine / multiple tasks relatively easily.

> **구** 따라서 전문가는 비교적 쉽게 복잡한 과제를 수행하고 많은 과제를 결합할 수 있다고 합니다.

> **독** 'thus'가 언급되므로 중심 문장
> - II번, ①번 문장에서 언급된 전문가의 특징을 요약해서 제시하고 있습니다.

③. Furthermore, beginners / are / excellent (at processing the tasks) / when / the tasks / are divided and isolated.

> **구** 게다가, 초보자는 과제가 분할되고 분리될 때 그것을 처리하는 데 탁월하다고 합니다.

> **독** 초보자들의 장점에 관한 내용이 언급되고 있습니다.

④. This / is / **not because** / they / necessarily have / more cognitive resources than beginners; rather, **because of** the high level of fluency / they / have achieved in performing key skills, they / can do / more with (what / they / have).

> **구** 이것은 그들이 반드시 초보자보다 더 많은 인지적 자원을 가지고 있기 때문인 것은 아니며, 오히려 핵심 기술을 수행하면서 달성한 높은 수준의 능숙함 때문에 그들은 자신들이 가지고 있는 것으로 더 많은 것을 할 수 있다고 합니다.

> **독** 'because'로 원인을 나열하므로 중심 문장
> - 전문가가 초보자보다 우위에 있는 원인을 제시하고 있습니다.

⑤. Beginners, **on the other hand**, / have not achieved / the same degree (of fluency and automaticity) in each of the component skills, and **thus** they / struggle to combine skills / that / experts / combine with relative ease and efficiency.

> **구** 반면에, 초보자는 각각의 구성 기술에서 동일한 수준의 능숙함과 자동성을 달성하지 못했으며, 따라서 그들은 전문가가 비교적 쉽고 효율적으로 결합하는 기술을 결합하려고 애쓴다고 합니다.

> **독** 'on the other hand'로 내용이 전환되므로 중심 문장
> - 전문가와는 다른 초보자의 특징을 대조하여 언급하고 있습니다.

다음 글에서 전체 흐름과 관계 <u>없는</u> 문장은?

> The animal in a conflict between attacking a rival and fleeing may initially not have sufficient information to enable it to make a decision straight away. ① If the rival is likely to win the fight, then the optimal decision would be to give up immediately and not risk getting injured. ② **But** if the rival is weak and easily defeatable, then there could be considerable benefit in going ahead and obtaining the territory, females, food or whatever is at stake. ③ Animals under normal circumstances maintain a very constant body weight and they eat and drink enough for their needs at regular intervals. ④ By taking a little extra time to collect information about the opponent, the animal is more likely to reach a decision that maximizes its chances of winning than if it takes a decision without such information. ⑤ Many signals are now seen as having this information gathering or 'assessment' function, directly **contributing to** the mechanism of the decision-making process by supplying vital information about the likely outcomes of the various options.

해설 [정답 : ③]

나머지 문장들에서는 동물들이 적과 싸울지 도망갈지 갈등하는 상황에서 정보를 얻는 과정에 대한 내용이 제시됩니다. 하지만 ③번 문장에서는 동물이란 같은 소재에서 체중을 유지하고 규칙적인 간격으로 먹고 마신다는 무관한 내용이 제시되었습니다. 그러므로 정답은 ③번이 됩니다.

Ⅰ. The animal (in a conflict between attacking a rival and fleeing) / may initially not have / sufficient information (to enable / it / to make / a decision straight away.

> 구 ▶ 'between A and B'는 'A와 B사이'를 의미합니다.
> - 'enable A to-V'는 'A가 V하는 것을 가능하게 하다'를 뜻합니다.
> - 적을 공격하는 것과 도망가는 것 사이의 갈등에서 동물은 처음에 곧바로 그것이 (= 동물이) 결정을 내리는 것을 가능하게 할 충분한 정보가 없을 수도 있다고 합니다.

① If the rival / is likely to win / the fight, then the optimal decision / would be to give up immediately and not risk getting injured.

> 구 ▶ 만약 그 적이 싸움에서 이길 가능성이 높다면, 최선의 선택은 즉시 포기하는 것이고 다칠 위험을 감수하지 않는 것이라고 합니다.
> 독 ▶ 동물이 적과 싸울지 도망갈지 갈등하는 상황에서 적이 강하다면 도망가는 것을 선택한다고 합니다.

② <u>**But**</u> if the rival / is / weak and easily defeatable, then there could be / considerable benefit (in going ahead and obtaining the territory, females, food or whatever is at stake).

> 구▶ 'in V-ing'는 'V함에 있어서'를 의미합니다.
> - 'whatever'은 '무엇이든지 간에'로 해석하시면 됩니다.
> - 그러나 만약 그 적이 약하고 쉽게 패배시킬 수 있다면, 싸우고 영역, 암컷, 음식, 또는 성패가 달려있는 무엇이든지 간에 얻음으로써 상당한 이익이 있을 수도 있다고 합니다.

> 독▶ 'But'이 제시되었으므로 중심 문장
> - 동물이 적과 싸울지 도망갈지 갈등하는 상황에서 적이 강할 때와는 달리 약할 때는 싸우는 것이 좋다고 합니다.

 * at stake - 성패가 달려 있는

③ Animals (under normal circumstances) / maintain / a very constant body weight and they / eat and drink (enough for their needs at regular intervals).

> 구▶ 일반적인 상황에서 동물들은 일관적인 체중을 유지하며 그들은 (= 동물들은) 규칙적인 간격으로 그들의 (= 동물들의) 필요를 충분히 해결할 수 있도록 먹고 마신다고 합니다.

> 독▶ 나머지 선지들에서는 동물들이 적과 싸울지 도망갈지 갈등하는 상황에서 정보를 얻는 과정에 대한 내용이 제시됩니다. 하지만 ③번 선지에서는 동물이란 같은 소재에서 체중을 유지하고 규칙적인 간격으로 먹고 마시는 무관한 내용이 제시되었습니다.

④ By taking / a little extra time (to collect / information) (about the opponent), the animal /is more likely to reach / a decision (that maximizes / its chances of winning than if it / takes / a decision (without such information)).

> 구▶ 'By V-ing'는 'V함으로써'를 의미합니다.
> - 상대방에 대한 정보를 모으는 약간의 추가 시간을 가짐으로써, 동물은 그러한 정보없이 (= 상대방에 대한 정보없이) 결정을 내릴 때보다 이길 수 있는 가능성을 최대화하는 결정에 접근할 가능성이 높아진다고 합니다.

> 독▶ 상대방에 대한 정보를 모음으로써 가장 이득이 되는 결정을 할 가능성을 높인다고 합니다.

⑤ Many signals / are now seen as having / this information gathering or 'assessment' function, (directly <u>**contributing to**</u> / the mechanism of the decision-making process (by supplying / vital information (about the likely outcomes of the various options))).

> 구▶ 'see A as B'는 'A를 B로써 간주하다'를 뜻합니다. 이 문장에서 수동태로 사용되었으므로 'A be seen as B'가 되어 'A가 B로써 간주되다'로 해석하시면 됩니다.
> - 'By V-ing'는 'V함으로써'를 의미합니다.
> - 많은 신호들은 오늘날 정보 수집 혹은 평가 기능을 가지는 것으로 간주되어, 다양한 선택들의 가능한 결과들에 대한 중요한 정보를 제공함으로써 직접적으로 결정 수립 과정에 기여한다고 합니다.

> 독▶ 'contributing to'가 제시되었으므로 중심 문장
> - 많은 신호들을 통해 상대방에 대한 정보를 얻고 평가하여 이를 통해 적과 싸울지 도망갈지 결정한다고 합니다.

다음 글에서 전체 흐름과 관계 <u>없는</u> 문장은?

Actors, singers, politicians and countless others recognise the power of the human voice as a means of communication beyond the simple decoding of the words that are used. Learning to control your voice and use it for different purposes is, **therefore**, one of the most important skills to develop as an early career teacher. ① The more confidently you give instructions, the higher the chance of a positive class response. ② There are times when being able to project your voice loudly will be very useful when working in school, and knowing that you can cut through a noisy classroom, dinner hall or playground is a great skill to have. ③ **In order to** address serious noise issues in school, students, parents and teachers **should** search for a solution together. ④ **However**, I would always advise that you use your loudest voice incredibly sparingly and avoid shouting as much as possible. ⑤ A quiet, authoritative and measured tone has so much more impact than slightly panicked shouting.

해설 [정답 : ③]

③번 문장에서는 목소리를 통해서 학급을 통제하는 ①번, ②번과는 달리, 학교 내 소음 문제에 대해서 제시하고 있습니다. 또한 ④번 문장에서는 큰 목소리를 적게 사용하는 것을 추천한다고 합니다. 이는 학교에서 선생님 목소리의 중요성과 효과를 의미하는데, ③번 문장은 학교 내 소음 문제와 해결책을 제시하고 있습니다. 즉, 같은 소재에서 다른 내용을 제시하고 있습니다. 또한 ③번 문장의 학교 내 소음 문제에 대해서 해결책이 필요하다는 맥락을 중심으로 보았을 때 ③번 문장과 같은 맥락의 내용으로 ③번 문장과 ④번 문장은 'However'을 통해서 전환될 수 없습니다. 그러므로 정답은 ③번입니다.

Ⅰ. Actors, singers, politicians and countless others / recognise / the power of the human voice (as a means of communication) (beyond the simple decoding of the words (that are used)).

> 구▶ 배우, 가수, 정치가, 그리고 무수한 다른 사람들은 사용된 단어의 단순한 해독을 넘어서는 의사소통 수단으로써 사람 목소리가 가지는 힘에 대해 인식하고 있다고 합니다.

> 독▶ 사람의 목소리가 가지는 힘을 많은 사람들이 인식하고 있다고 합니다.

Ⅱ. Learning to control your voice and use it (for different purposes) / is, **therefore**, / one of the most important skills (to develop as an early career teacher).

> 구▶ 따라서, 다양한 목적을 위해 너의 목소리를 통제하고 사용하는 것을 배우는 것은 경력 초기의 교사로서 발전하기 위한 중요한 기술 중 하나라고 합니다.

> 독▶ 'therefore'이 제시되었으므로 중심 문장
> - 교사로서 목소리를 통제하고 사용하는 것을 배우는 것이 매우 중요하다고 합니다.

①. The more confidently you / give / instructions, the higher the chance of a positive class response.

> **구** 'The + 비교급 S + V, The + 비교급 S' + V' '은 '더욱 S가 V할수록, S'이 V'하다'로 해석하시면
> 됩니다.
> - 너가 더 자신감있게 지시를 하면 할수록 긍정적인 학급의 반응이 나올 확률이 높다고 합니다.

> **독** II번 문장에서 제시된 목소리를 통제하고 사용하는 것에 대한 예시가 제시되고 있습니다.

②. There are times (when being able to project your voice / loudly will be / very useful) (when working in school, and knowing / that you / can cut (through a noisy classroom, dinner hall or playground) / is / a great skill to have.)

> **구** 목소리를 크게 내보내는 것은 매우 유용할 때가 있는데, 너가 학교에서 일하거나 너가 시끄러운 교실,
> 식당이나 운동장에서 자를 수 있다는 것을 (= 목소리로 통제할 수 있다는 것을) 아는 것은 가지고
> 있어야 할 훌륭한 기술이라고 합니다.

> **독** 큰 목소리를 낼 수 있는 것은 시끄러운 상황에서도 통제할 수 있도록 하는 중요한 기술이라고 합니다.
> ①번 문장에 이어서 목소리를 통제하고 사용하는 것에 대한 예시가 제시되었습니다.

③. (**In order to** address serious noise issues in school), students, parents and teachers / **should** search for / a solution together.

> **구** 학교 내에서 심각한 소음 문제를 다루기 위해서, 학생, 학부모, 선생님들은 함께 해결책을 찾아야만
> 한다고 합니다.

> **독** 'In order to'와 'should'가 제시되었으므로 중심 문장
> - 목소리를 통해서 학급을 통제하는 ①번, ②번과는 달리, 학교 내 소음 문제에 대해서 제시하고
> 있습니다.

④. **However**, I / would always advise / that you / use / your loudest voice incredibly sparingly and avoid / shouting (as much as possible).

> **구** 그러나, 나는 너가 큰 목소리를 놀라울 정도로 적게 사용하고 가능한 소리치는 것을 피하는 것을 항상
> 조언한다고 합니다.

> **독** 'However'가 제시되었으므로 앞 뒷 문장 중심 문장
> - 큰 목소리를 통해서 상황을 통제할 수 있지만 가능한 적게 이러한 방식을 사용하는 것을 추천한다고
> 합니다.

* sparingly - 적게, 드물게

⑤. A quiet, authoritative and measured tone / has so much more impact (than slightly panicked shouting).

> **구** 조용하고, 권위있는 조절된 목소리가 약간의 당황한 고함보다 더 효과적이라고 합니다.

> **독** 큰 목소리를 통해서 상황을 통제할 수 있지만 큰 목소리보다 조용하고 권위적인 목소리가 더 효과적이라고
> 합니다.

다음 글에서 전체 흐름과 관계 <u>없는</u> 문장은?

> In a highly commercialized setting such as the United States, it is not surprising that many landscapes are seen as commodities. **In other words**, they are valued **because of** their market potential. Residents develop an identity in part based on how the landscape can generate income for the community. ① This process involves more than the conversion of the natural elements into commodities. ② The landscape itself, including the people and their sense of self, takes on the form of a commodity. ③ Landscape protection in the US traditionally focuses on protecting areas of wilderness, typically in mountainous regions. ④ Over time, the landscape identity can evolve into a sort of "logo" that can be used to sell the stories of the landscape. ⑤ **Thus**, California's "Wine Country," Florida's "Sun Coast," or South Dakota's "Badlands" shape how both outsiders and residents perceive a place, and these labels build a set of expectations associated with the culture of those who live there.

해설 [정답 : ③]

②번과 ④번 문장에서는 모두 경관의 상품화를 다루고 있지만, ③번 문장에서는 경관의 상품화와 관련된 내용이 아닌 경관의 보호와 관련된 내용이 등장하므로 ③번 문장은 경관의 보호라는 같은 소재로 다른 내용을 다루고 있습니다. 그러므로 정답은 ③번이 되어야 합니다.

Ⅰ. In a highly commercialized setting (such as the United States), it / is not / surprising / that many landscapes / are seen as / commodities).

> 구▶ 'it be동사 + 형용사 + that절'은 가주어/진주어 의심
> - 'it'이 지칭하는 대상이 없으므로 가주어/진주어
> - 'A be seen as B'는 'A가 B로써 여겨지다'를 의미합니다.
> - 미국과 같이 고도로 상업화된 환경에서 많은 경관들이 상품으로 여겨지는 것은 놀라운 일이 아니라고 합니다.

Ⅱ. **In other words**, they / are valued (**because of** their market potential).

> 구▶ 다시 말해, 시장 잠재력이 경관을 가치 있게 한다고 합니다.
> 독▶ 'In other words'가 제시되었으니 재진술의 표현, 'because of'도 제시되었으니 중심 문장입니다.

Ⅲ. Residents / develop / an identity (in part) (based on how the landscape / can generate / income (for the community)).

> 구▶ 주민들이 경관이 어떻게 소득을 창출하는가에 부분적으로 기초하여 정체성을 발전시킨다고 합니다.

①. This process / involves / more than the conversion of the natural elements (into commodities).

> **구** 이러한 과정에는 자연의 요소를 상품으로 전환하는 것 이상의 것이 포함된다고 합니다.

> **독** Ⅲ번 문장의 주민들이 경관이 어떻게 소득을 창출하는가에 기초하여 정체성을 발전시킨다는 내용이 'This process'로 언급되고, 이 과정에는 자연의 요소를 상품으로 전환하는 것 이상의 것이 포함된다고 합니다.

②. The landscape itself, (including the people and their sense of self), takes on / the form (of a commodity).

> **구** 사람들과 그 자아의식을 포함하여 경관 자체가 상품의 형태를 띠게 된다고 합니다.

③. Landscape protection (in the US traditionally) / focuses on / protecting areas (of wilderness, typically in mountainous regions).

> **구** 미국에서 경관 보호는 일반적으로 산악 지대의 황무지를 보호하는 데 초점을 두고 있다고 합니다.

> **독** 경관을 보호하는 새로운 내용이 처음 등장합니다.

④. Over time, the landscape identity / can evolve / into a sort of "logo" (that can be used to sell / the stories of the landscape).

> **구** 시간이 흐르면서 경관 정체성은 경관에 대한 이야기를 판매하기 위해 사용되는 "로고"로 발전할 수 있다고 합니다.

> **독** ③번 문장에서는 경관의 보호와 관련된 내용이 아닌 다시 경관의 상품화와 관련된 내용이 등장하므로 단절이 발생합니다. ③번 문장은 경관이라는 같은 소재로 경관의 보호라는 다른 말을 다루고 있습니다. 그러므로 정답은 ③번이 되어야 합니다.

⑤. **Thus**, California's "Wine Country," Florida's "Sun Coast," or South Dakota's "Badlands" / shape / how both outsiders and residents / perceive / a place, and these labels / build / a set (of expectations) (associated with the culture of those (who live there)).

> **구** 그래서, California의 "Wine Country", Florida의 "Sun Coast", 또는 South Dakota의 "Badlands"는 외지인과 거주자가 모두 장소를 인식하는 방식을 형성하며, 이런 호칭들은 그곳에 사는 사람들의 문화와 관련된 기대치를 형성한다고 합니다.

> **독** 예시로 언급된 California's "Wine Country," Florida's "Sun Coast," or South Dakota's "Badlands"는 ④번 문장의 'logo'의 예시로 언급되고 있음을 알 수 있습니다.

07 23학년도 9월 평가원 35번 (정답률 76%)

다음 글에서 전체 흐름과 관계 <u>없는</u> 문장은?

Because plants tend to recover from disasters more quickly than animals, they are essential to the revitalization of damaged environments. Why do plants have this preferential ability to recover from disaster? It is largely **because**, unlike animals, they can generate new organs and tissues throughout their life cycle. ① This ability is **due to** the activity of plant meristems — regions of undifferentiated tissue in roots and shoots that can, in response to specific cues, differentiate into new tissues and organs. ② If meristems are not damaged during disasters, plants can recover and ultimately transform the destroyed or barren environment. ③ You can see this phenomenon on a smaller scale when a tree struck by lightning forms new branches that grow from the old scar. ④ In the form of forests and grasslands, plants regulate the cycling of water and adjust the chemical composition of the atmosphere. ⑤ In addition to regeneration or resprouting of plants, disturbed areas can also recover through reseeding.

* revitalization: 소생

해설 [정답 : ④]

지문에서 반복되는 핵심 주제는 식물의 재생력입니다. Ⅲ번 문장에서 식물이 재해로부터 회복할 수 있는 이유는 식물이 'generate new organs and tissues', 새로운 장기와 조직을 생성할 수 있기 때문이라고 했고, 이 식물의 재생 능력은 선지 문장에 걸쳐 언급되고 있습니다. 그런데 ④번 문장에서는 식물은 물의 순환을 조절하고, 대기의 화학적 구성을 조정한다고 했는데, 이것은 식물의 재생에서 벗어난 내용의 지문이므로 전체 흐름과 관계가 없는 문장입니다. 그러므로 정답은 ④번이 됩니다.

Ⅰ. **Because** / plants / tend / to recover (from disasters more quickly / than animals), they / are / essential (to the revitalization (of damaged environments)).

* revitalization: 소생

- [구] 식물은 동물보다 더 빨리 재해로부터 회복하는 경향이 있기 때문에 손상된 환경의 소생에 필수적이라고 합니다.

- [독] 'Because'가 제시되었으므로 중심 문장
  - 동물과 대비되는 식물의 재생 특성이 언급됩니다.

Ⅱ. Why / do / plants / have / this preferential ability / to recover (from disaster)?

- [구] 왜 식물에게는 재해로부터 회복할 수 있는 이런 특별한 능력이 있을까?

Ⅲ. It / is / largely **because**, unlike animals, they / can generate / new organs and tissues (throughout their life cycle).

- [구] 그것은 대체로 식물이 동물과 달리 생애 주기 내내 새로운 장기와 조직을 생성할 수 있기 때문이다.

- [독] 'because'가 제시되었으므로 중심 문장

①. This ability / is / **due to** the activity (of plant meristems) ― regions / of undifferentiated tissue / in roots and shoots / that can, in response to specific cues, differentiate / into new tissues and organs.

> **구** 이러한 능력은 식물의 분열 조직, 즉 특정 신호에 반응하여 새로운 세포 조직과 기관으로 분화할 수 있는, 뿌리와 싹에 있는 미분화 세포 조직 부위의 활동 때문이라고 합니다.

> **독** 'due to'가 제시되었으므로 중심 문장
> - 'meristems'의 뜻을 모르더라도, 'differentiate into new tissues', 새로운 조직으로 분화한다는 내용을 통해 식물의 재생 능력에 대한 설명이 이어지고 있음을 알 수 있습니다.

②. If / meristems / are not damaged (during disasters), plants / can recover and ultimately transform / the destroyed or barren environment.

> **구** 재해 시에 분열 조직이 손상되지 않으면, 식물은 회복해서 파괴되거나 척박한 환경을 궁극적으로 변화시킬 수 있다고 합니다.

> **독** 식물의 'meristems'와 재생 능력이 환경을 변화시킬 수 있다는 것은 1번 문장에 대한 설명이 됩니다.

③. You / can see / this phenomenon (on a smaller scale) (when / a tree / struck / by lightning forms / new branches / that / grow (from the old scar)).

> **구** 번개 맞은 나무가 오래된 상처에서 자라나는 새로운 가지를 형성할 때 더 작은 규모로 이러한 현상을 볼 수 있다고 합니다.

> **독** 식물인 나무가 재생하는 것에 대한 예시 문장입니다.

④. (In the form / of forests and grasslands), plants / regulate / the cycling (of water) and adjust / the chemical composition (of the atmosphere).

> **구** 숲과 초원의 형태로, 식물은 물의 순환을 조절하고 대기의 화학적 구성을 조정한다고 합니다.

> **독** 식물이 물의 순환, 대기의 화학적 구성을 조정한다는 내용은 앞에서 언급된 재생 능력과는 관련이 없는 내용입니다.

⑤. In addition to regeneration or resprouting (of plants), disturbed areas / can also recover / through reseeding.

> **구** 식물의 재생이나 재발아 외에도, 교란된 지역은 재파종을 통해서도 회복할 수 있다고 합니다.

> **독** 'regeneration or resprouting of plants', 식물의 재생이나 재발아를 통해 식물의 재생과 관련된 내용이 이어져야 함을 추론할 수 있습니다.

08 21학년도 수능 35번　　　　　　　　　　　　　　　　　　　(정답률 75%)

다음 글에서 전체 흐름과 관계 <u>없는</u> 문장은?

> Workers are united by laughing at shared events, even ones that may initially spark anger or conflict. Humor reframes potentially divisive events into merely "laughable" ones which are put in perspective as subservient to unifying values held by organization members. Repeatedly recounting humorous incidents reinforces unity based on key organizational values. ① One team told repeated stories about a dumpster fire, something that does not seem funny on its face, **but** the reactions of workers motivated to preserve safety sparked laughter **as** the stories were shared multiple times by multiple parties in the workplace. ② Shared events that cause laughter can indicate a sense of belonging since "you **had to** be there" to see the humor in them, and non-members were not and do not. ③ Since humor can easily capture people's attention, commercials tend to contain humorous elements, such as funny faces and gestures. ④ Instances of humor serve to enact bonds among organization members. ⑤ Understanding the humor may even be required as an informal badge of membership in the organization.
>
> * subservient: 도움이 되는

해설 [정답 : ③]

이 지문에서 유머가 조직 구성원들 간의 단합을 증가시킨다는 내용이 재진술됩니다. 하지만 ③번에서는 유머가 사람들의 집중을 이끌어 상업에 사용된다는 내용이므로 유머라는 같은 소재이지만 다른 내용이 전개되는 무관한 문장입니다.

Ⅰ. Workers / are united (by laughing at shared events), even ones / that may initially spark / anger or conflict.

　🔲구 'by V-ing'는 'V함으로써'를 의미합니다.
　　- 직원들은 공유된 사건, 심지어 처음에는 분노나 갈등을 발생시킬 수 있는 사건에 대해서도 웃음으로써 단합된다고 합니다.

Ⅱ. Humor / reframes / potentially divisive events (into merely "laughable" ones) (which are put in perspective as subservient / to unifying values (held by organization members)).

　　　　　　　　　　　　　　　　　　　　　　　　　　　* subservient: 도움이 되는

　🔲구 유머는 조직 구성원들에 의해 간직되는 통합 가치에 도움이 된다는 관점에서 그저 '재미있는 사건'으로 잠재적으로 분리될 수 있는 사건 (분열될 수 있는 사건)을 재구성한다고 합니다.

　🔲독 Ⅰ번 문장의 민감한 사건이더라도 웃음으로써 단합된다는 내용을 재진술하고 있습니다.

　* re- (다시) + frame (틀에 넣다, 구성하다) = reframe - 재구성하다

Ⅲ. Repeatedly recounting humorous incidents / reinforces / unity (based on key organizational values).

> **구** 재미있는 사건을 반복하는 것은 중요한 조직의 가치에 기반을 두어 통합성을 강화시킨다고 합니다.

> **독** 유머가 단합을 강화시킨다는 앞 내용을 재진술하고 있습니다.

① One team / told / repeated stories (about a dumpster fire), something (that does not seem / funny (on its face)), **but** the reactions of workers (motivated to preserve safety) / sparked / laughter (as the stories / were shared multiple times by multiple parties in the workplace).

> **구** 어떤 팀에서 쓰레기 수납장 화제에 관한 이야기를 되풀이 하는데, 그것은 표면적으로는 재미있어 보이지 않지만, 이야기가 직장에서 다른 모음에 의해 여러 번 공유되었기 때문에 안전을 보호하기 위해 동료의 반응이 웃음을 발생시킨다고 합니다.

> **독** ‘but’이 제시되었고 ‘as’가 ‘때문에’로 해석되므로 중심 문장!
> - 반복되는 이야기가 어떻게 통합성을 강화하는지 제시하고 있습니다.

② Shared events (that cause / laughter) / can indicate / a sense of belonging / **since** “you / had to be there” to see / the humor in them, / and non-members / were not and do not.

> **구** 웃음을 야기한 공유된 사건이 소속감을 나타내는데, 유머를 이해하기 위해서는 “너는 거기에 있어야만 하다”고, 구성원이 아닌 사람들은 그럴 수 없기 때문이라고 합니다.

> **독** ‘cause’, ‘since’, ‘had to’가 제시되었으므로 중심 문장!

③ Since humor / can easily capture / people’s attention, / commercials / tend to contain / humorous elements, (such as funny faces and gestures).

> **구** 유머가 쉽게 사람들의 주의를 집중시킬 수 있기 때문에, 상업은 재밌는 얼굴이나 몸짓과 같은 재미있는 요소를 포함시키는 경향이 있다고 합니다.

④ Instances (of humor) / serve to enact / bonds (among organization members).

> **구** ‘serve to-V’는 ‘V하는 역할을 하다’를 의미합니다.
> - 유머의 사례는 조직 구성원들 간의 유대감을 만드는 역할을 한다고 합니다.

> **독** 유머가 조직 구성원들의 단합을 강화시킨다는 내용을 재진술하고 있습니다.

⑤ Understanding the humor / may even be required (as an informal badge of membership in the organization).

> **구** 유머를 이해하는 것은 조직 구성원임을 나타내는 비공식적 신분증으로 요구될 수 있다고 합니다.

> **독** 유머를 이해하기 위해서는 조직에 소속되어야 하고 유머는 단합을 증가시킨다는 내용이 재진술되고 있습니다.

다음 글에서 전체 흐름과 관계 없는 문장은?

> Since their introduction, information systems have substantially changed the way business is conducted. ① This is particularly true for business in the shape and form of cooperation between firms that involves an integration of value chains across multiple units. ② The resulting networks do not only cover the business units of a single firm **but** typically also include multiple units from different firms. ③ **As a consequence**, firms do not only need to consider their internal organization **in order to** ensure sustainable business performance; they also **need to** take into account the entire ecosystem of units surrounding them. ④ Many major companies are fundamentally changing their business models by focusing on profitable units and cutting off less profitable ones. ⑤ **In order to** allow these different units to cooperate successfully, the existence of a common platform is crucial.

해설 [정답 : ④]

이 지문에서는 정보 체계가 도입됨에 따라서 회사들이 사업을 수행할 때, 서로의 부분들이 연결된다고 합니다. 하지만 ④번 문장에서는 회사들이 수익성이 높은 부분에 집중하고 수익성이 낮은 부분은 잘라낸다고 하므로 회사라는 같은 소재를 사용하지만 다른 내용을 제시하고 있습니다. 그러므로 정답은 ④번이 됩니다.

Ⅰ. (Since their introduction), information systems / have substantially changed / the way / business / is conducted.

> **구** 정보 체계의 도입 이래로, 정보 체계는 사업이 수행되는 방식을 상당히 변화시켜 왔다고 합니다.

① This / is particularly / true (for business (in the shape and form of cooperation (between firms))) (that involves / an integration of value chains (across multiple units)).

> **구** 그것은 (= 정보 체계가 사업이 수행되는 방식을 변화시킨 것은) 특히 다수의 부분에 걸쳐 가치 사슬의 통합을 수반하는 기업들 간의 협력 형태와 유형의 사업에서 사실이라고 합니다.

> **독** 정보 체계가 특히 기업들 간의 협력 형태와 유형을 상당히 변화시켰다고 합니다.

② The resulting networks / do not only cover / the business units of a single firm **but** typically also include / multiple units (from different firms).

> 구 'not only A but also B'는 'A뿐만 아니라 B'를 의미합니다.
> - 결과적인 네트워크들은 하나의 기업 사업 부분을 포함할 뿐만 아니라 전형적으로 다양한 회사로부터 다양한 부분을 포함한다고 합니다.

> 독 'but'이 제시되었으므로 중심 문장
> - ①번 문장을 재진술하여, 정보 체계로 인한 결과가 하나의 회사를 연결하는 것뿐만 아니라 다양한 회사들을 연결하였다고 합니다.

③ **As a consequence**, firms / do not only **need to** consider / their internal organization (**in order to** ensure / sustainable business performance); (but을 대신하여 사용됨) they / also **need to** take into account / the entire ecosystem of units surrounding them.

> 구 'not only A but also B'는 'A뿐만 아니라 B'를 의미합니다. 이 문장에서는 'but'을 대신하여 ';'을 사용하였습니다.
> - 결과적으로 회사들은 안정적인 사업 수행을 보장하기 위해서 그들의 내부 조직을 고려할 필요가 있을 뿐만 아니라, 그들은 (= 회사들은) 또한 그들을 둘러싼 부분의 전체적인 환경도 고려할 필요가 있다고 합니다.

> 독 'As a consequence'와 'need to', 'in order to'가 제시되었으므로 중심 문장
> - ①번, ②번 문장과 같은 맥락으로 정보 체계로 인해서 회사들은 내부 조직뿐만 아니라 그들을 둘러싼 전체적인 상황을 고려할 필요가 있다고 합니다.

④ Many major companies / are fundamentally changing / their business models (by focusing on / profitable units and cutting off / less profitable ones).

> 구 'by V-ing'는 'V함으로써'를 의미합니다.
> - 많은 주요 기업들은 수익성이 있는 부분에는 집중하고 수익성이 낮은 부분을 잘라 냄으로써 그들의 사업 모델을 근본적으로 변경한다고 합니다.

⑤ **In order to** allow / these different units / to cooperate successfully, / the existence (of a common platform) / is / crucial.

> 구 'allow + O + to-V'는 'O가 V하는 것을 허락하다'를 의미합니다.
> - 그들의 다양한 부분들이 성공적으로 협동하는 것을 허락하기 위해서, 공통 플랫폼의 존재가 중요하다고 합니다.

> 독 'In order to-V'가 인과 관계를 제시하므로 중심 문장
> - ①, ②, ③번 문장에서 제시된 회사들이 서로 연결된 상황에서 성공적으로 협동하기 위해서는 공통의 플랫폼이 중요하다고 합니다.

다음 글에서 전체 흐름과 관계 <u>없는</u> 문장은?

The best dealers offer a much broader service than merely having their goods on display and 'selling from stock'. Once they know the needs of a particular collector they can actively seek specific items to fill gaps in the collection. ① **Because** it is their business, to which they devote themselves full-time, they will inevitably have a much wider network than any non-professional collector can ever develop. ② As a matter of course they can enquire about the availability of pieces from dealers in other cities and, most crucially in some categories, from overseas. ③ They will be routinely informed of news of all auctions and important private sales, and **should** be well-enough connected to hear occasionally of items which are not yet quite on sale **but** might be available for a certain price. ④ The main advantage of buying from a dealer is getting personalised service on your purchases. ⑤ **In turn**, they can circulate their own contacts with 'want-lists' of desired items or subjects, multiplying their client collectors' chances of expanding their collections.

해설 [정답 : ④]

④번 문장은 판매업자로부터 구매하는 것의 주요 이점은 구매품에 대해 개인화된 서비스를 받는 것이라고 합니다. ①번 ~ ③번 문장들은 최고의 판매업자들이 그들의 네트워크, 조직망을 통해서 정보를 얻는 것에 대한 내용이지만 ④번 문장은 판매업자로부터 물건을 구매하는 것의 이점에 대해서 제시하므로, 같은 소재 다른 내용에 해당합니다.

Ⅰ. The best dealers / offer / a much broader service than merely having their goods (on display and 'selling from stock').

> 구▸ 최고의 판매업자는 단순히 상품을 전시하고 '재고로 있는 것을 판매하는 것'보다 훨씬 더 폭넓은 서비스를 제공한다고 합니다.

> 독▸ 제일 많이 판매하는 사람은 단순히 상품을 전시하고 판매하는 것보다 더 많은 서비스를 제공한다고 합니다.

Ⅱ. Once they / know / the needs of a particular collector they / can actively seek / specific items (to fill gaps in the collection).

> 구▸ 그들이 (= 판매업자들이) 특정 수집가의 필요를 알게 될 때, 그들은 (= 판매업자들은) 소장품들의 빈틈을 채우기 위해서 특정한 물품을 활동적으로 찾을 수 있다고 합니다.

> 독▸ 판매업자들이 특정 수집가의 필요를 알게되면 판매업자들은 수집가의 필요를 충족하기 위해 특정 물품을 적극적으로 찾는다고 합니다.

①. **<u>Because</u>** it / is / their business, (to which they / devote / themselves full-time), they / will inevitably have / a much wider network than any non-professional collector / can ever develop.

- **구** 그것은 (= 수집가들을 위해 특정한 물품을 찾는 것은) 그들의 (= 판매자들의) 전업이기 때문에, 그들은 어떠한 비전문 수집가가 구축할 수 있는 것보다도 훨씬 더 넓은 조직망을 필연적으로 갖게 된다고 합니다.

- **독** 'Because'가 제시되었으므로 중심 문장
  - 물품을 찾는 것은 판매업자들의 전업이므로 넓은 조직망을 가지게 된다고 합니다.

②. (As a matter of course) they / can enquire about the availability of pieces (from dealers in other cities and, most crucially in some categories, from overseas).

- **구** 당연하게도 그들은 (= 판매업자들은) 다른 도시의 판매업자들에게, 그리고 가장 중요하게 일부 범주에서는 해외의 판매업자들에게도 작품의 구매 가능 여부를 문의할 수 있다고 합니다.

- **독** ①번 문장에서 제시된 판매업자들의 넓은 조직망을 구체화하여 제시하고 있습니다.

③. They / will be routinely informed of / news of all auctions and important private sales, and **should** be well-enough connected to hear / occasionally of items (which are not yet quite on sale **but** might be available for / a certain price).

- **구** 그들은 (= 판매업자들은) 모든 경매와 중요한 개인 판매 소식에 대해서 정기적으로 정보를 받을 것이고, 아직 판매되지 않았지만 특정한 가격에 구매할 수 있을 물품에 대해 가끔 소식을 들을 수 있도록 충분하게 연결되었을 것이라고 합니다.

- **독** 'should'와 'but'이 제시되었으므로 중심 문장
  - 판매업자들은 ①번 문장에서 제시된 넓은 조직망을 통해서 모든 경매와 개인 판매소식 등에 대한 정보를 알 수 있다고 합니다.

④. The main advantage (of buying from a dealer) / is getting / personalised service (on your purchases).

- **구** 판매업자로부터 구매하는 것의 주요 이점은 구매품에 대해 개인화된 서비스를 받는 것이라고 합니다.

- **독** ①번 ~ ③번 문장들은 최고의 판매업자들이 그들의 네트워크, 조직망을 통해서 정보를 얻는 것에 대한 내용이지만 ④번 문장은 판매업자로부터 물건을 구매하는 것의 이점에 대해서 제시하므로, 같은 소재 다른 내용에 해당합니다.

⑤. **<u>In turn</u>**, they / can circulate / their own contacts (with 'want-lists' of desired items or subjects), (multiplying their client collectors' chances of expanding their collections).

[구] 결국에, 그들은 (= 판매업자들은) 원하는 물품이나 대상의 '필요 리스트'를 자신들이 연락하는 사람들에게 배포하여, 자신들의 고객인 수집가들의 소장품 확장 기회를 증대시킬 수 있다고 합니다.

[독] 'In turn'이 제시되었으므로 중심 문장
  - 최고의 판매업자들은 '필요 리스트'를 만들어 조직망을 통해 전달함으로써 자신의 고객들에게 상품을 팔 수 있게 된다고 합니다.

다음 글에서 전체 흐름과 관계 <u>없는</u> 문장은?

A variety of theoretical perspectives provide insight into immigration. Economics, which assumes that actors engage in utility maximization, represents one framework. ① From this perspective, it is assumed that individuals are rational actors, i.e., that they make migration decisions based on their assessment of the costs as well as benefits of remaining in a given area versus the costs and benefits of leaving. ② Benefits may include **but** are not limited to short-term and long-term monetary gains, safety, and greater freedom of cultural expression. ③ People with greater financial benefits tend to use their money to show off their social status by purchasing luxurious items. ④ Individual costs include **but** are not limited to the expense of travel, uncertainty of living in a foreign land, difficulty of adapting to a different language, uncertainty about a different culture, and the great concern about living in a new land. ⑤ Psychic costs associated with separation from family, friends, and the fear of the unknown also should be taken into account in cost-benefit assessments.

* psychic: 심적인

해설 [**정답 : ③**]

지문의 주된 내용은 이민을 여부를 결정하는 비용과 관련된 것입니다. 경제학적 관점에서 이주를 결정하는 것은 떠나는 것과 남는 것의 비용과 편익을 비교하고 평가함으로써 내려진다는 내용의 글에서 금전적 혜택이 큰 사람들은 사치품을 구매하여 자신의 사회적 지위를 과시한다는 ③번 문장의 내용은 지문의 흐름과 관계가 없습니다. 그러므로 정답은 주제와 관련 없는 다른 소재를 말하고 있는 문장인 ③번이 됩니다.

Ⅰ. A variety of theoretical perspectives / provide / insight (into immigration).

　　구▶ 다양한 이론적 관점은 이주에 대한 통찰을 제공한다고 합니다.

Ⅱ. Economics, (which assumes / that actors / engage in / utility maximization), / represents / one framework.

　　구▶ 행위자들이 효용 극대화에 참여 한다고 상정하는 경제학은 하나의 틀을 제시한다고 합니다.

　　독▶ Ⅰ번 문장의 이론적 관점에 대한 것으로 경제학을 설명하고 있습니다.

①. From this perspective, it is assumed / that individuals / are / rational actors, i.e., / that they / make / migration decisions (based on their assessment / of the costs as well as benefits / of remaining in a given area / versus the costs and benefits of leaving.

　　구▶ 이런 관점에서는 개인은 합리적인 행위자라고, 즉 그들은 특정한 지역을 떠나는 것의 비용 및 편익과 대비하여 남는 것의 비용과 편익 모두에 대한 자신의 평가에 근거하여 이주 결정을 내린다고 추정된다고 합니다.

　　독▶ 비용 및 편익과 대비하여 이주 결정을 내리는 것은 Ⅱ번 문장의 경제학적 관점으로 통찰하는 것과 연결됩니다.

②. Benefits may include / **but** are not limited to / short-term and long-term monetary gains, safety, and greater freedom (of cultural expression).

- 구▶ 편익은 단기적 및 장기적인 금전적 이득, 안전, 문화적 표현의 더 큰 자유를 포함할 수도 있지만 이에 국한되지는 않는다고 합니다.
- 독▶ 'but'이 언급되므로 중심 문장
  - ①번 문장에서 언급된 편익과 관련된 보충 설명 문장입니다.

③. People (with greater financial benefits) tend to use / their money (to show off / their social status) (by purchasing luxurious items).

- 구▶ 더 큰 금전적 혜택이 있는 사람들은 사치품을 구입함으로써 자신의 사회적 지위를 과시하기 위해 돈을 쓰는 경향이 있다고 합니다.
- 독▶ 사회적 지위 과시를 위해 사치품을 소비하는 사람들에 대한 새로운 주제가 나옵니다.

④. Individual costs / include **but** are not limited to / the expense of travel, uncertainty (of living in a foreign land), difficulty (of adapting to a different language), uncertainty (about a different culture), and the great concern (about living in a new land).

- 구▶ 개인적 비용은 이동 비용, 타지에서 사는 것의 불확실성, 다른 언어에 적응하는 것의 어려움, 다른 문화에 대한 불확실성, 새로운 지역에서 사는 것에 대한 큰 염려를 포함하지만 이에 국한되지는 않는다고 합니다.
- 독▶ 'but'이 언급되므로 중심 문장
  - 다시 경제학적으로 이민을 고려하는 내용의 문장입니다.
* at the expense of - ~를 희생하면서

⑤. Psychic costs (associated with separation / from family, friends, and the fear (of the unknown)) / also should be taken into account / in cost-benefit assessments.

* psychic: 심적인

- 구▶ 'take into account'는 '~를 고려하다'를 의미합니다.
  - 가족, 친구와의 이별과 미지의 것에 대한 두려움과 관련된 심리적 비용 또한 비용-편익 평가에서 고려되어야 한다고 합니다.

12 24학년도 9월 평가원 35번 (정답률 68%)

다음 글에서 전체 흐름과 관계 <u>없는</u> 문장은?

Although organizations are offering telecommuting programs in greater numbers than ever before, acceptance and use of these programs are still limited by a number of factors. ① These factors include manager reliance on face-to-face management practices, lack of telecommuting training within an organization, misperceptions of and discomfort with flexible workplace programs, and a lack of information about the effects of telecommuting on an organization's bottom line. ② **Despite** these limitations, at the beginning of the 21st century, a new "anytime, anywhere" work culture is emerging. ③ Care **must** be taken to select employees whose personal and working characteristics are best suited for telecommuting. ④ Continuing advances in information technology, the expansion of a global workforce, and increased desire to balance work and family are only three of the many factors that will gradually reduce the current barriers to telecommuting as a dominant workforce development. ⑤ With implications for organizational cost savings, especially with regard to lower facility costs, increased employee flexibility, and productivity, telecommuting is increasingly of interest to many organizations.

* telecommute: (컴퓨터로) 집에서 근무하다

해설 [정답 : ③]

1번 문장에서 키워드를 잡아보면, '원격 근무 프로그램'이 됩니다. 여러 요인들에 의해 제한되고 있는 상황입니다. ①번 문장에서는 여러 요인들에 대한 설명이 나오고 있고, ②번 문장에서는 'Despite'가 나왔기 때문에 여러 요인에도 불구하고, '원격 근무 프로그램'이 활성화되어야 한다고 판단합니다. 그후 이에 대한 구체적인 설명으로 여러 요인에도 불구하고 '왜 원격 근무 프로그램이 활성화 되는가?'에 대한 내용이 이어져야 논리적으로 일치하게 되는데, ③번 문장의 내용인 '원격 근무에 가장 적합한 개인적 및 업무적 특성을 가진 직원을 선택하는 데 주의를 기울여야 한다'라는 내용으로 흐름에 맞지 않습니다. ④번 문장에서 원격 근무가 활성화되고 있는 원인이 나오므로 '왜 원격 근무 프로그램이 활성화되는가?'에 대한 보강설명으로 논리적으로 글이 이어집니다. 그러므로 전체 흐름과 무관한 문장은 ③번 문장이 됩니다.

---

1. (**Although** organizations / are / offering / telecommuting programs (in greater numbers than ever before), acceptance and use of these programs / are / still limited (by a number of factors).

* telecommute: (컴퓨터로) 집에서 근무하다

구▶ 조직들이 이전보다 더 많은 수의 원격 근무 프로그램을 제공하고 있지만, 이러한 프로그램의 수용과 사용은 여전히 여러 요인에 의해 제한되고 있다고 합니다.

①. These factors / include / manager reliance (on face-to-face management practices), lack of telecommuting training (within an organization), misperceptions of and discomfort (with flexible workplace programs), and a lack of information (about the effects of telecommuting) (on an organization's bottom line).

구▶ 이러한 요인에는 대면 관리 방식에 대한 관리자의 의존, 조직 내에서의 원격 근무 교육 부족, 유연한 근무 장소 프로그램에 대한 잘못된 인식과 불편함, 그리고 원격 근무가 조직의 수익에 미치는 영향에 대한 정보 부족이 포함된다고 합니다.

②. (**Despite** these limitations), (at the beginning of the 21st century), a new "anytime, anywhere" work culture / is / emerging.

구▶ 이러한 제한들에도 불구하고, 21세기 초에는 새로운 "언제 어디서나"의 근무 문화가 등장하고 있다고 합니다.

③. Care / **must** be / taken (to select / employees) (whose personal and working characteristics are best suited (for telecommuting)).

구▶ 원격 근무에 가장 적합한 개인적 및 업무적 특성을 가진 직원을 선발하는 데 주의를 기울여야 한다고 합니다.

독▶ 전체 흐름과 무관한 문장입니다.

④. (Continuing / advances (in information technology)), the expansion of a global workforce, and increased desire to balance work and family / are / only three of the many factors (that / will gradually reduce / the current barriers (to telecommuting as a dominant workforce development)).

구▶ 정보 기술의 지속적인 발전, 글로벌 인력의 확장, 그리고 일과 가정의 균형을 맞추려는 증가하는 욕구는 현재 원격 근무를 주요한 인력 발전 방식으로 만드는 데 있어서의 장벽을 점차 줄여나갈 많은 요인들 중 단지 세 가지에 불과하다고 합니다.

⑤. (With implications for organizational cost savings), (especially with regard to lower facility costs, increased employee flexibility, and productivity), telecommuting / is increasingly / of interest (to many organizations).

구▶ 특히 시설 비용 절감과 관련된 조직의 비용 절감, 증가된 직원의 유연성, 그리고 생산성 측면에서의 영향을 고려할 때, 원격 근무는 더 많은 조직의 관심사가 되고 있다고 합니다.

13 21학년도 6월 평가원 35번 (정답률 55%)

다음 글에서 전체 흐름과 관계 <u>없는</u> 문장은?

One of the most widespread, and sadly mistaken, environmental myths is that living "close to nature" out in the country or in a leafy suburb is the best "green" lifestyle. Cities, **on the other hand**, are often blamed as a major cause of ecological destruction—artificial, crowded places that suck up precious resources. **Yet**, when you look at the facts, nothing could be farther from the truth. ① The pattern of life in the country and most suburbs involves long hours in the automobile each week, burning fuel and pumping out exhaust to get to work, buy groceries, and take kids to school and activities. ② City dwellers, **on the other hand**, have the option of walking or taking transit to work, shops, and school. ③ The larger yards and houses found outside cities also create an environmental cost in terms of energy use, water use, and land use. ④ This illustrates the tendency that most city dwellers get tired of urban lives and decide to settle in the countryside. ⑤ It's clear that the future of the Earth depends on more people gathering together in compact communities.

* compact: 밀집한

해설 [**정답 : ④**]

이 지문에서 시골 혹은 교외가 친환경적이라는 통념과는 달리 시골에서 자동차를 더 많이 이용해 더 많은 배기가스를 배출하고 환경적 비용이 발생한다고 합니다. 즉 시골에서 거주하는 것을 (-)로 제시합니다. 하지만 ④번 문장에서는 도시 거주자가 도시 생활에 지치고 시골에 정착하는 경향을 제시하는 시골에 대한 (+)를 제시하기 때문에 반대 문장으로 무관한 문장입니다.

Ⅰ. One of the most widespread, and sadly mistaken, environmental myths / is that living ("close to nature" out in the country or in a leafy suburb) is / the best "green" lifestyle.

> 구▶ 가장 널리 퍼져있고 아쉽게도 잘못된, 환경에 대한 통념은 시골이나 잎이 우거진 교외에서 '자연과 가까이' 사는 것이 최고의 '친환경적인' 생활 방식이라는 것이라고 합니다.

* leaf (잎) + -y (형용사형 접사) = leafy - 잎스러운 ⇒ 잎이 우거진

Ⅱ. Cities, **on the other hand**, / are often blamed (as a major cause of ecological destruction—artificial), (crowded places that suck up / precious resources).

> 구▶ 'blame A as B'는 'A를 B로 비난하다'를 의미합니다.
> - 반면에, 도시들은 귀중한 자원들을 빨아먹는 인공적이고 혼잡한 장소인 자연 생태 파괴의 주요 원인으로 비난받는다고 합니다.

> 독▶ 'on the other hand'를 통해서 역접이 이루어지므로 앞 뒷 문장 중심 문장!
> - 시골, 교외와 도시를 비교하고 있습니다.

Ⅲ. <u>Yet</u>, when you / look at / the facts, / nothing / could be (farther from the truth).

> 구▶ 'nothing could be farther from the truth'는 'nothing could be farther from the truth than it' 에서 'than it'이 생략된 구조입니다.
> - 직역하면 '그것보다 진실에서 더 멀어지는 것은 없다' ⇒ '그것은 사실이 아니다'가 됩니다.
> - 그러나, 네가 사실을 볼 때, 사실이 아니라고 합니다.

> 독▶ 'Yet'이 제시되었으므로 중심 문장!

① The pattern of life (in the country and most suburbs) / involves long hours (in the automobile) each week, (burning fuel and pumping out exhaust) (to get to work, buy groceries, and (get, buy와 take를 연결) take kids to school and activities).

> 구▶ 시골과 대부분의 교외의 생활양식은 출근하고, 식료품을 사고, 아이들을 학교와 활동에 데리고 가기 위해 연료를 소모하고 배기가스를 배출하며 매주 자동차 안에서 오랜 시간 동안 있는 것을 포함한다고 합니다.

* exhaust - 고갈시키다, 배기가스

② City dwellers, <u>on the other hand</u>, / have / the option (of walking or taking transit) (to work, shops, and school).

> 구▶ 반면에 도시 거주자들은 일터, 상점, 학교로 걸어가거나 대중교통을 선택할 수 있다고 합니다.

> 독▶ 'on the other hand'가 제시되었으므로 앞 뒷 문장 중심 문장!
> - 통념과는 달리 시골 생활은 자동차를 이용하며 많은 배기가스를 배출하지만 도시 생활은 걸어다니거나 대중교통을 이용할 수 있다고 합니다.

③ The larger yards and houses (found outside cities) / also create / an environmental cost (in terms of energy use, water use, and land use).

> 구▶ 'in terms of A'는 'A에 관해서'를 의미합니다.
> - 도시 밖에 설립된 큰 마당과 집은 또한 에너지 사용, 물 사용, 토지 사용에 관해서 환경적인 비용을 만든다고 합니다.

> 독▶ 시골 혹은 교외에서 생활의 다른 단점을 제시하고 있습니다.

④ This / illustrates / the tendency (that most city dwellers / get tired of / urban lives / and decide to settle in the countryside).

> 구▶ 그것은 도시 거주자들이 도시 생활에 지치고 시골에 정착하는 것을 결정하는 경향을 설명한다고 합니다.

⑤ It 's clear / that the future (of the Earth) depends on / more people / gathering together in compact
communities.

* compact: 밀집한

구▶ 'It be동사 + 형용사 + that'은 가주어/진주어 의심!
- 'It'이 지칭하는 대상이 없으므로 가주어/진주어
- 지구의 미래가 더 많은 사람들이 밀집한 공동체 속에 모이는 것에 의존하는 것은 분명하다고 합니다.

독▶ 'compact communities'는 'city'를 지칭합니다.

01 21학년도 6월 평가원 30번　　　　　　　　　　(정답률 64%)

다음 글의 밑줄 친 부분 중, 문맥상 낱말의 쓰임이 적절하지 <u>않은</u> 것은?

Chunking is vital for cognition of music. If we **had to** encode it in our brains note by note, we'd ① <u>struggle</u> to make sense of anything more complex than the simplest children's songs. Of course, most accomplished musicians can play compositions containing many thousands of notes entirely from ② <u>memory</u>, without a note out of place. **But** this seemingly awesome accomplishment of recall is made ③ <u>improbable</u> by remembering the musical process, not the individual notes as such. If you ask a pianist to start a Mozart sonata from bar forty-one, she'll probably **have to** ④ <u>mentally</u> replay the music from the start until reaching that bar — the score is not simply laid out in her mind, to be read from any random point. It's rather like describing how you drive to work: you don't simply recite the names of roads as an abstract list, **but have to** construct your route by mentally retracing it. When musicians make a mistake during rehearsal, they wind back to the ⑤ <u>start</u> of a musical phrase ('let's take it from the second verse') before restarting.

* chunking: 덩어리로 나누기 ** bar: (악보의) 마디

해설 [정답 : ③]

Ⅳ번 문장에서 그렇지만 겉보기에는 굉장한 것 같은 이러한 기억의 성취는 보통 말하는 그런 개별적인 음을 기억하는 것이 아니라 음악적인 과정을 기억함으로써 '일어날 것 같지 않게 되는' 것이라고 합니다. 이러한 기억의 성취는 Ⅲ번 문장의 기억으로 연주하는 음악가들을 말합니다. Ⅲ번 문장에서 음악가들이 기억으로 연주하는 것은 이러한 기억의 성취가 발생한 것이라고 봐야 하기 때문에 ③ 'improbable'을 'possible'과 같은 단어로 바꾸어야 합니다.

Ⅰ. Chunking / is / vital / for cognition of music.

* chunking: 덩어리로 나누기

구▶ 덩어리로 나누는 것은 음악의 인식에서 아주 중요하다고 합니다.

Ⅱ. If we / **had to** encode / it in our brains note by note, / we'd ① <u>struggle</u> to make sense of / anything (more complex than the simplest children's songs).

구▶ 만일 우리가 그것을 하나씩 뇌에서 부호화해야 한다면 우리는 더 복잡한 것은 어느 것이나 이해하기 위해 '몸부림치게'될 것이라고 합니다.

독▶ 'have to'가 제시되었으므로 중심 문장

Ⅲ. Of course, most accomplished musicians / can play / compositions (containing / many thousands of notes) (entirely from ② memory, without a note out of place).

구▶ 물론, 기량이 뛰어난 음악가들은 한 음도 틀리지 않고 수천 개의 음을 포함하는 작품을 완전히 '기억'으로 연주할 수 있다고 합니다.

Ⅳ. **But** this seemingly awesome accomplishment of recall / is made ③ improbable (by remembering / the musical process, not the individual notes as such).

구▶ 'by V-ing'는 'V함으로써'를 의미합니다.
- 그렇지만 겉보기에는 굉장한 것 같은 이러한 기억의 성취는 보통 말하는 그런 개별적인 음을 기억하는 것이 아니라 음악적인 과정을 기억함으로써 '일어날 것 같지 않게 되는'것이라고 합니다.

독▶ 'But'이 제시되었으므로 앞 뒷 문장 중심 문장
- 이러한 기억의 성취는 Ⅲ번 문장의 기억으로 연주하는 음악가들을 말합니다. Ⅲ번 문장에서 음악가들이 기억으로 연주하는 것은 이러한 기억의 성취가 발생한 것이라고 봐야 하기 때문에 ③ 'improbable'을 'possible'과 같은 단어로 바꾸어야 합니다.

Ⅴ. If you / ask / a pianist / to start a Mozart sonata from bar forty-one, / she'll probably **have to** ④ mentally replay / the music from the start (until reaching that bar) — the score / is not simply laid out (in her mind), (to be read from any random point).

** bar: (악보의) 마디

구▶ 'ask + I.O + D.O'는 'I.O에게 D.O를 질문하다/요청하다'를 의미합니다.
- 개별적인 음을 기억하는 것이 아닌 것에 대한 예시로 만일 피아니스트에게 모차르트 소나타를 41번 마디로부터 시작해 달라고 요청하면, 그녀는 — 악보가 어떠한 임의의 시점에서도 읽힐 수 있게 그녀의 머릿속에 들어있지 않아서 아마도 그 음악을 처음부터 '머릿속으로' 재생해서 그 마디까지 와야 할 것이라고 합니다.

독▶ 'have to'가 제시되었으므로 중심 문장
- 이는 음을 개별적으로 기억하는 것이 아닌 것이라고 볼 수 있습니다.

Ⅵ. It's rather like describing / how you / drive to work: you / don't simply recite / the names of roads as an abstract list, **but have to construct** / your route by mentally retracing it.

구▶ 'not A but B'는 'A가 아니라 B'를 의미합니다.
- 그것은 우리가 운전해서 직장에 가는 방법을 설명하는 것과 같다고 합니다. 또한 우리는 추상적인 목록으로 길의 이름을 열거하는 것이 아니고 마음속에서 그것을 되짚어감으로써 여러분의 경로를 구성해야 한다고 합니다.

독▶ 'but'과 'have to'가 제시되었으므로 중심 문장

Ⅶ. When musicians / make / a mistake (during rehearsal), they / wind back / to the ⑤ <u>start</u> of a
musical phrase ('let's take it from the second verse') before restarting.

구 음악가들이 리허설 중에 실수한다면, 그들은 다시 시작하기 전에 한 악구의 '시작'으로 (되)돌아간다고
합니다.

독 이것은 Ⅵ번 문장의 마음속에서 그것을 되짚어가는 것이므로 다시 처음으로 돌아간다고 볼 수
있습니다.

다음 글의 밑줄 친 부분 중, 문맥상 낱말의 쓰임이 적절하지 <u>않은</u> 것은?

Sport can **trigger** an emotional response in its consumers of the kind rarely brought forth by other products. Imagine bank customers buying memorabilia to show loyalty to their bank, or consumers ① <u>identifying</u> so strongly with their car insurance company that they get a tattoo with its logo. We know that some sport followers are so ② <u>passionate</u> about players, teams and the sport itself that their interest borders on obsession. This addiction provides the emotional glue that binds fans to teams, and maintains loyalty even in the face of on-field ③ <u>failure</u>. **While** most managers can only dream of having customers that are as passionate about their products as sport fans, the emotion **triggered** by sport can also have a negative impact. Sport's emotional intensity can mean that organisations have strong attachments to the past through nostalgia and club tradition. **As a result**, they may ④ <u>increase</u> efficiency, productivity and the need to respond quickly to changing market conditions. **For example**, a proposal to change club colours in order to project a more attractive image may be ⑤ <u>defeated</u> **because** it breaks a link with tradition.

* memorabilia: 기념품 ** obsession: 집착

해설 [**정답 : ④**]

Ⅴ번 문장에서 스포츠팬의 팀에 대한 높은 충성심이 부정적 영향을 끼칠 수 있다고 합니다. 그러므로 Ⅵ번, Ⅶ번 문장에서는 스포츠팬의 높은 충성심으로 인한 단점이 제시되어야 하지만 Ⅶ번 문장의 'increase'는 장점을 제시하고 있으므로 'increase'가 'decrease'나 'ignore'와 같은 말로 바뀌어야 합니다. 또한 Ⅷ번 문장의 더 매력적인 이미지를 위한 것은 Ⅶ번 문장의 변화하는 시장 조건에 반응하는 것과 대응됩니다. 하지만 이러한 대응은 전통에 의해서 실패한다고 하므로 ④번이 정답인 것을 확인 할 수 있습니다.

Ⅰ. Sport / can **trigger** / an emotional response (in its consumers of the kind (rarely brought forth by other products)).

> 구▶ 스포츠는 소비자에게 다른 상품에서는 야기하지 못하는 종류의 감정적 반응을 불러일으킬 수 있다고 합니다.

> 독▶ 'trigger'이 제시되었으므로 중심 문장
> - 스포츠 ⇒ 소비자의 감정적 반응이라고 합니다.

* bring forth - 야기하다, 불러일으키다

Ⅱ. Imagine / bank customers (buying memorabilia) (to show / loyalty to their bank), / or consumers ① <u>identifying</u> (so strongly) with their car insurance company that they / get / a tattoo (with its logo).

* memorabilia: 기념품

> 구▸ 'identify with A'는 'A와 동일시하다'를 의미합니다.
> - 은행 고객이 그들 은행에 대한 충성심을 보여주기 위해 기념품을 구입하거나, 고객이 그들 자동차 보험 회사에 대해서 매우 강한 동일시를 하여 그들이 회사 로고를 문신한다고 상상해 보라고 합니다.

> 독▸ 스포츠가 아닌 다른 제품에서 소비자가 감정적 반응을 보이는 것을 상상해보라고 합니다.

Ⅲ. We / know / that some sport followers / are / so ② <u>passionate</u> (about players, teams and the sport itself) / that their interest / borders on / obsession.

** obsession: 집착

> 구▸ 'so + 형용사 + that + S + V'는 '너무 형용사하여 S가 V하다'를 의미합니다.
> - 우리는 몇몇 스포츠팬들이 선수, 팀, 그리고 그 스포츠 자체에 매우 열정적 이여서 그들의 관심이 집착과 가깝다는 것을 알고 있다고 합니다.

> 독▸ Ⅱ번 문장에서 제시된 다른 제품에서 소비자들이 감정적 반응을 보여주는 것과는 반대로 스포츠에서 소비자가 감정적으로 반응하는 것은 이미 알고 있는 사실이라고 합니다.

* border (경계, V. 경계에 접하다) + on (붙어 있는 이미지)
= border on - 경계에 붙어있는 ⇒ ~와 가깝다.

Ⅳ. This addiction / provides / the emotional glue (that binds / fans / to teams), / and maintains / loyalty (even in the face of on-field ③ <u>failure</u>).

> 구▸ 'bind A to B'는 'A와 B를 묶다'를 의미합니다.
> - 그러한 중독은 (= 스포츠에 팬들이 감정적으로 반응하는 것은) 팬과 팀을 묶는 감정적인 끈끈함을 제공하고 경기장에서 일어나는 실패에도 불구하고 충성심을 유지한다고 합니다.

> 독▸ 스포츠 팬이 스포츠에 감정적인 반응을 보여주는 것은 팀이 경기에서 실패하더라도 충성심을 유지하고 팀과 팬 사이의 유대 관계를 형성한다고 합니다.

Ⅴ. <u>**While**</u> most managers / can only dream (of having / customers (that are as passionate about their products as sport fans)), / the emotion (<u>**triggered**</u> by sport) / can also have / a negative impact.

> 구▸ 대부분의 경영자들은 스포츠팬만큼 그들 제품에 열정적인 고객을 가지는 것을 꿈꾸는 반면에, 스포츠로부터 야기되는 감정은 부정적인 영향을 미칠 수 있다고 합니다.

> 독▸ 'While'이 제시되었으니 중심 문장
> - 대부분의 경영자들은 소비자들이 스포츠팬만큼 충성심을 보여주기 원할 정도로 스포츠팬의 충성심이 이득이 되는 것으로 보이지만 부정적인 측면 또한 존재한다고 합니다.

Ⅵ. Sport's emotional intensity / can mean / that organisations / have / strong attachments (to the past) (through nostalgia and club tradition).

> 구▶ 스포츠의 감정적 강도는 (= 팬과 팀사이의 감정적으로 강한 유대는) 조직이 향수와 클럽 전통을 통해 과거에 대한 강한 애착이 있다는 것을 의미한다고 합니다.

> 독▶ 예를 들어, 무패 우승 시절을 (= 박지성이 맨유 이적하기 전 시절을) 그리워하는 아스날 팬이나, 마지막 우승인 92년을 그리워하는 롯데 팬이 있습니다.

Ⅶ. **As a result**, they / may ④ increase / efficiency, productivity and the need (to respond quickly to changing market conditions).

> 구▶ 결과적으로, 그들은 효율성, 생산성, 그리고 빠르게 변화하는 시장 조건에 반응할 필요성을 증가시킬 수 있다고 (⇒ 감소시킬 수 있다 혹은 무시할 수 있다고) 합니다.

> 독▶ 'As a result'를 통해서 결과를 제시하므로 중심 문장
> - Ⅴ번 문장에서 스포츠팬의 팀에 대한 높은 충성심이 부정적 영향을 끼칠 수 있다고 합니다. 그러므로 Ⅵ번, Ⅶ번 문장에서는 스포츠팬의 높은 충성심으로 인한 단점이 제시되어야 하지만 Ⅶ번 문장의 'increase'는 장점을 제시하고 있으므로 'increase'가 'decrease'나 'ignore'와 같은 말로 바뀌어야 합니다.

Ⅷ. **For example**, a proposal (to change club colours) (in order to project / a more attractive image) may be ⑤ **defeated** **because** it / breaks / a link with tradition.

> 구▶ 예를 들어, 더 매력적인 이미지를 투영하기 위해서 클럽 색깔을 바꾸자는 제안은 그것이 (= 클럽 색깔을 바꾸는 것이) 전통과의 관계를 끊기 때문에 실패할 것이라고 합니다.

> 독▶ 'For example'과 'because'가 제시되었으므로 중심 문장
> - 더 매력적인 이미지를 위한 것은 Ⅶ번 문장의 변화하는 시장 조건에 반응하는 것과 대응됩니다. 하지만 이러한 대응은 전통에 의해서 실패한다고 하므로 ④번이 정답인 것을 확인할 수 있습니다.

다음 글의 밑줄 친 부분 중, 문맥상 낱말의 쓰임이 적절하지 <u>않은</u> 것은?

How the bandwagon effect occurs is demonstrated by the history of measurements of the speed of light. <u>**Because**</u> this speed is the basis of the theory of relativity, it's one of the most frequently and carefully measured ① <u>quantities</u> in science. As far as we know, the speed hasn't changed over time. <u>**However**</u>, from 1870 to 1900, all the <u>**experiments found**</u> speeds that were too high. Then, from 1900 to 1950, the ② <u>opposite</u> happened—all <u>**the experiments found**</u> speeds that were too low! This kind of error, where results are always on one side of the real value, is called "bias." It probably happened <u>**because**</u> over time, experimenters subconsciously adjusted their results to ③ <u>match</u> what they expected to find. If a result fit what they expected, they kept it. If a result didn't fit, they threw it out. They weren't being intentionally dishonest, just ④ <u>influenced</u> by the conventional wisdom. The pattern only changed when someone ⑤ <u>lacked</u> the courage to report what was actually measured instead of what was expected.

* bandwagon effect: 편승 효과

해설 [정답 : ⑤]

지문이 이해하기 어렵지 않습니다. 실험자들이 통념에 영향을 받아 기대된 것과 결과가 일치하면 유지하고 일치하지 않는다면 그 결과를 버리는 방향으로 연구를 했기 때문에 편승 효과와 편향이 발생한다고 합니다. 예상한 것 대신에 실제로 측정된 것을 발표할 용기가 있을 때만 패턴이 바뀌므로 정답은 ⑤번이 됩니다.

Ⅰ. How the bandwagon effect / occurs / is demonstrated (by the history of measurements of the speed of light).

* bandwagon effect: 편승 효과

> 구 편승 효과가 어떻게 발생하는 지는 빛의 속도 측정의 역사로 입증된다고 합니다.

Ⅱ. **Because** this speed / is / the basis of the theory of relativity, / it's / one of the most frequently and carefully measured ① quantities (in science).

> 구 왜냐하면 이 속도는 상대성 이론의 기초이기 때문에, 과학에서 가장 빈번하고 면밀하게 측정되는 물리량 중 하나라고 합니다.

> 독 'Because'가 제시되었으므로 중심 문장!
> - 빛의 속도가 상대성 이론의 기초 ⇒ 가장 면밀하게 측정되는 물리량이라고 이해하시면 됩니다.

Ⅲ. As far as we / know, / the speed / hasn't changed over time.

> 구 'as far as'는 '~하는 한'을 의미합니다.
> - 우리가 아는 한, 그 속도는 시간이 지나도 변화하지 않는다고 합니다.

Ⅳ. **However**, from 1870 to 1900, all the experiments / **found** / speeds (that were / too high).

> 구▶ 'from A to B'는 'A부터 B까지'를 의미합니다.
> - 하지만 1870년부터 1900년까지 모든 실험은 너무 빠른 속도를 발견했다고 합니다.

> 독▶ 'However'가 제시되므로 앞 뒷 문장 중심 문장!
> - 실험도 제시되었습니다!

Ⅴ. Then, (from 1900 to 1950), the ② opposite happened—all **the experiments / found** / speeds (that were too low)!

> 구▶ 그 후, 1900년부터 1950년까지 그 반대현상이 일어나, 모든 실험이 너무 느린 속도를 발견했다고 합니다.

> 독▶ 실험이 제시되었으니 중심 문장!

Ⅵ. This kind (of error), (where results / are always on one side of the real value), is called / "bias."

> 구▶ 결과가 항상 실제 값의 한 쪽에 있는 이런 종류의 오류를 "편향"이라 부른다고 합니다.

Ⅶ. It / probably happened / **because** (over time), experimenters subconsciously / adjusted / their results (to ③ match / what they / expected to find).

> 구▶ 그것은 시간이 지나면서 실험자들이 자신들이 발견할 것이라 기대한 것과 일치하도록 잠재의식적으로 결과를 조정했기 때문에 발생했다고 합니다.

> 독▶ 'because'를 통해서 인과관계를 제시하므로 중심 문장!
> - 기대한 결과와 일치하도록 결과 조정 ⇒ 편향 발생

Ⅷ. If a result / fit / what they / expected, they / kept / it. If a result / didn't fit, / they / threw / it / out.

> 구▶ 만약 결과가 예상한 것과 일치하다면, 그들은 그것을 유지한다. 만약 결과가 일치하지 않는다면, 그들은 그것을 버렸다고 합니다.

Ⅸ. They / weren't being intentionally / dishonest, just ④ influenced (by the conventional wisdom).

> 구▶ 그들이 의도적으로 부정직한 게 아니라, 단지 통념에 영향을 받았을 뿐이라고 합니다.

Ⅹ. The pattern / only changed / when someone / ⑤ lacked / the courage (to report / what was actually measured (instead of what was expected)).

> 구▶ 그 패턴은 누군가가 예상된 것 대신에 실제로 측정된 것을 보고할 용기가 부족했을 때, 바뀌었다고 합니다.

> 독▶ 용기가 부족할 때가 아닌 용기가 있을 때 통념에 영향을 받아 실제 결과를 왜곡하는 패턴이 바뀌는 것이므로 'lack'이 아니라 'had'가 와야 합니다.

다음 글의 밑줄 친 부분 중, 문맥상 낱말의 쓰임이 적절하지 <u>않은</u> 것은?

Although the wonders of modern technology have provided people with opportunities beyond the wildest dreams of our ancestors, the good, as usual, is weakened by a downside. One of those downsides is that anyone who so chooses can pick up the virtual megaphone that is the Internet and put in their two cents on any of an infinite number of topics, regardless of their ① <u>qualifications</u>. After all, on the Internet, there are no regulations ② <u>preventing</u> <u>a kindergarten teacher (A)</u> from <u>offering medical advice (B)</u> or <u>a physician (A)</u> from <u>suggesting ways to safely make structural changes to your home (B)</u>. **As a result**, <u>misinformation (A)</u> gets disseminated as information, and it is not always easy to ③ <u>differentiate</u> the two. This can be particularly frustrating for <u>scientists (B)</u>, who spend their lives <u>learning how to understand the intricacies of the world (B)</u> around them, only to have their work summarily ④ <u>challenged</u> by <u>people whose experience with the topic can be measured in minutes (A)</u>. This frustration is then ⑤ <u>diminished</u> by the fact that, to the general public, both the <u>scientist (B)</u> and the <u>challenger (A)</u> are awarded equal credibility.

* put in one's two cents: 의견을 말하다 ** disseminate: 퍼뜨리다

*** intricacy: 복잡성

해설 [정답 : ⑤]

만약 지문이 이해가 되지 않았다면 Chapter 2-2에서 배운 A / B 치환을 사용하셔도 됩니다. 비전문가와 전문가를 각각 A, B로 치환하여 정리해본다면 글을 이해하기 조금 더 수월합니다. Ⅱ번 문장에서는 인터넷상에서 자격에 상관없이 의견을 말할 수 있다고 했고, Ⅳ번 문장에서는 이 상황에서 비전문가들의 잘못된 정보가 퍼지게 된다고 했습니다. 이것은 지문의 virtual megaphone, 가상의 확성기라는 비유적인 표현이며, 이 상황 속에서 전문가와 비전문가의 정보가 같은 신뢰성을 부여받는 것이 전문가의 좌절감을 줄어들게 한다고 볼 수 없으므로 정답은 ⑤번이 되며, 'diminished'를 'amplified'와 같은 단어로 바꿔야 합니다.

Ⅰ. **Although** the wonders (of modern technology) / have provided / people (with opportunities / beyond the wildest dreams / of our ancestors), the good, as usual, is weakened (by a downside).

> 구 'provide A with B'는 'A에게 B를 제공하다'를 의미합니다.
> - 현대 기술의 경이로움이 사람들에게 우리 조상들은 꿈에도 생각해 본 적이 없을 만큼의 기회를 제공했지만, 늘 그렇듯이 좋은 점은 부정적인 면에 의해 약화된다고 합니다.

> 독 'Although'가 제시되었으므로 중심 문장
> - 현대 기술의 단점에 관한 내용이 언급될 것임을 알 수 있습니다.

Ⅱ. One (of those downsides) is / that / anyone (who so chooses) / can pick up / the virtual megaphone (that / is / the Internet) / and put in their two cents / on any (of an infinite number of topics), regardless of their ① qualifications.

* put in one's two cents: 의견을 말하다

구▶ 그 부정적인 면 중 하나는 그렇게 하기로 선택한 사람은 누구나 자신의 자격에 상관없이 인터넷이라는 가상의 확성기를 집어 들고 무한히 많은 주제 중 어느 것에 대해서라도 의견을 말할 수 있다는 것이라고 합니다.

독▶ 현대 기술의 단점은 자격에 상관없이 모두가 자신의 의견을 제공할 수 있다는 것이라고 합니다.
  - 'virtual megaphone', 가상의 확성기는 현대 기술이라는 눈에 보이지 않는 기술을 통해 의견을 타인에게 전달하는 것을 비유적으로 표현한 것입니다.

Ⅲ. After all, on the Internet, there / are / no regulations / ② preventing / a kindergarten teacher (A) / from offering medical advice (B) or a physician (A) / from suggesting ways / to safely make / structural changes / to your home (B).

구▶ 결국, 인터넷에는 유치원 선생님이 의학적인 조언을 제공하거나 의사가 여러분의 집에 안전하게 구조적인 변화를 줄 수 있는 방법을 제안하는 것을 막는 규정이 없다고 합니다.

독▶ 예시 문장입니다. 주제로 치환하면 다음과 같습니다.
  - 유치원 선생님, 의사 = 자격 없는 개인
  - 의학적인 조언, 집 구조 변화 방법 제안 = 의견 제시
  - 자격이 없고 지식이 부족한 개인이 제시하는 잘못된 의견이 인터넷이라는 기술을 통해 확대된다는 것입니다.

Ⅳ. **As a result**, misinformation (A) / gets disseminated / as information, and it / is / not always easy / to ③ differentiate the two.

** disseminate: 퍼뜨리다

구▶ 'It + be 동사 + 보어 + to 부정사'는 가주어/진주어입니다.
  - 결과적으로, 잘못된 정보가 정보로 퍼지게 되고, 그 둘을 구별하는 것이 항상 쉽지만은 않다고 합니다.

독▶ 'As a result'가 제시되었으므로 중심 문장
  - Ⅲ번 문장에서 개인들이 제공하는 의견이 잘못됐다는 것을 의미하며, 이것을 올바른 정보와 구별하는 것이 어렵다고 합니다.

Ⅴ. This / can be / particularly frustrating / for <u>scientists (B)</u>, who / spend / their lives / <u>learning how / to understand / the intricacies / of the world (B)</u> / around them, only / to have / their work / summarily ④ <u>challenged</u> (by <u>people whose</u> / experience (with the topic) / <u>can be measured in minutes (A)</u>).

*** intricacy: 복잡성

구▶ 이것은 과학자에게 특히 좌절감을 줄 수 있는데, 그들은 자기 주변 세상의 복잡성을 이해하는 방법을 배우느라 일생을 보내지만 결국 그들의 연구는 그 주제에 대한 경험이 분 단위로 측정될 수 있는 사람들에게 즉석으로 도전을 받게 된다고 합니다.

독▶ Ⅲ번 문장과 비교를 해야 하는 문장입니다.
- 과학자 = 전문가 ↔ 비전문가 = 유치원 선생님, 의사
- 이러한 정보를 구별하는 것이 어려우므로, 전문가인 과학자가 제공하는 의견은 비전문가들의 잘못된 의견과 구별하기 어렵다는 것입니다.

Ⅵ. This frustration / is then ⑤ <u>diminished</u> (by the fact / that, to the general public, both <u>the scientist (B)</u> and the <u>challenger (A)</u> / are awarded / equal credibility).

구▶ 그러면 일반 대중들의 눈에는 과학자와 도전자 둘 다 동등한 신뢰성을 부여받는다는 사실에 의해 이 좌절감은 줄어든다고 합니다.

독▶ 전문가인 과학자와 비전문가인 도전자의 의견들이 동등한 신뢰를 부여받을 수 없지만, 현대 기술 때문에 이것이 현실화가 되며, 이 경우, 과학자가 느끼는 좌절감을 증가할 것임을 알 수 있습니다.

다음 글의 밑줄 친 부분 중, 문맥상 낱말의 쓰임이 적절하지 않은 것은?

Why is the value of place so important? From a historical perspective, until the 1700s textile production was a hand process using the fibers available within a ① <u>particular</u> geographic region, for example, cotton, wool, silk, and flax. Trade among regions ② <u>increased</u> the availability of these fibers and associated textiles made from the fibers. The First Industrial Revolution and subsequent technological advancements in manufactured fibers ③ <u>added</u> to the fact that fibers and textiles were no longer "place-bound." Fashion companies created and consumers could acquire textiles and products made from textiles with little or no connection to where, how, or by whom the products were made. This ④ <u>countered</u> a disconnect between consumers and the products they use on a daily basis, a loss of understanding and appreciation in the skills and resources necessary to create these products, and an associated disregard for the human and natural resources necessary for the products' creation. **Therefore**, renewing a value on place ⑤ <u>reconnects</u> the company and the consumer with the people, geography, and culture of a particular location.

* textile: 직물

해설 [정답 : ④]

Ⅰ번 문장에서는 'the value of place'를 주제어로 주었고 그것을 아주 중요하다고 했습니다. 이를 설명하기 위해 Ⅱ번 문장에서 1700년대 직물 생산과 특정 지리적 지역 내에서 사용 가능한 섬유와의 연관성을 보여주며, 장소의 가치에 대해 설명하고 있습니다. Ⅳ번 문장 뒤부터 제1차 산업 혁명의 결과로 더 이상 직물이 장소에 국한되지 않는 점을 예로 들며, 장소의 가치가 중요해지지 않는 역접의 논리가 등장합니다. 그러므로 Ⅳ번 문장을 기준으로 논리적으로 대조를 이루고 있습니다. 그러므로 Ⅳ번 문장에서 단절을 막는 것이 아닌 단절을 유발한다는 내용이 나와야 하므로 'countered'를 'resulted in 또는 caused'로 바꾸어야 합니다.

Ⅰ. Why is / the value of place / so important?

구▶ "장소의 가치는 왜 매우 중요한가요?"라고 합니다.

독▶ 주제어는 'the value of place'입니다.

Ⅱ. From a historical perspective, until the 1700s textile production / was / a hand process (using the fibers available) (within a ① <u>particular</u> geographic region, for example, cotton, wool, silk, and flax).

* textile: 직물

구▶ 역사적 관점에서 보면, 1700년대까지 직물 생산은 특정 지리적 지역 내에서 사용 가능한 섬유, 예를 들면, 면, 양모, 실크, 아마를 사용한 수작업 과정이었다고 합니다.

독▶ Ⅰ번 문장에서 나온 'the value of place'를 설명합니다.

Ⅲ. Trade among regions / ② increased / the availability of these fibers and associated textiles (made from the fibers).

구▶ 지역 간의 무역은 이러한 섬유와 그 섬유로 만든 직물의 이용성을 증가시켰다고 합니다.

독▶ 조금씩 'the value of place'의 중요도가 낮아지는 것을 설명합니다. '역접의 논리'의 빌드업입니다.

Ⅳ. The First Industrial Revolution and subsequent technological advancements (in manufactured fibers) (③ added to the fact that fibers and textiles) were no longer "place-bound."

구▶ 제1차 산업 혁명과 그 이후의 제조 섬유에 대한 기술적 발전은 섬유와 직물이 더 이상 "장소에 구속되지 않는다는" 사실을 더해주었다고 합니다.

독▶ 제1차 산업혁명 이후로'로 이어지는 내용은 'the value of place'의 중요성이 낮아진 것을 의미합니다. 그러므로 '역접의 논리'로 판단합니다.

Ⅴ. Fashion companies / created and consumers / could acquire / textiles and products (made from textiles) (with little or no connection) (to where, how, or by whom the products / were / made).

구▶ 패션 회사들은 제품이 어디에서, 어떻게, 누구에 의해 만들어졌는지와의 연결이 거의 없거나 전혀 없는 직물과 직물로 만든 제품을 만들고 소비자들은 그것을 획득할 수 있었다고 합니다.

독▶ 'the value of place'의 중요성이 낮아진 것을 패션 회사들의 제품을 예시로 들어 설명하고 있습니다.

Ⅵ. This / ④ countered / a disconnect (between consumers and the products) (they use (on a daily basis)), a loss of understanding and appreciation (in the skills and resources) (necessary to create these products), and an associated disregard (for the human and natural resources) (necessary for the products' creation).

구▶ 이것은 소비자와 그들이 매일 사용하는 제품 간의 단절을 막았으며 이러한 제품을 만드는 데 필요한 기술과 자원에 대한 이해와 감사의 손실, 그리고 제품의 창조에 필요한 인간과 자연 자원에 대한 무시를 막아준 것이기도 했다고 합니다.

독▶ Ⅱ번 문장에서 설명한 '장소의 중요성의 하락'의 결과로 제품과 소비자와의 단절을 설명합니다. 소비자와 상품의 단절을 막은 것이 아니라 유발한 것이 글의 흐름과 일치하기 때문에 'countered'를 'resulted in 또는 caused'로 바꾸어야 합니다.

Ⅶ. Therefore, renewing a value on place / ⑤ reconnects / the company and the consumer (with the people, geography, and culture of a particular location).

구▶ 따라서, 장소에 대한 가치를 재확인하는 것은 회사와 소비자를 특정 위치의 사람들, 지리, 문화와 다시 연결한다고 합니다.

독▶ Ⅳ번 문장에서 설명한 대로 제품과 소비자는 단절되어 있는데, 만약 장소에 대한 가치를 다시 새롭게 하면 전에 단절되어 있던 요소들이 다시 연결될 것이라는 내용으로 글을 마무리합니다.

다음 글의 밑줄 친 부분 중, 문맥상 낱말의 쓰임이 적절하지 <u>않은</u> 것은?

It has been suggested that "organic" methods, defined as those in which only natural products can be used as inputs, would be less damaging to the biosphere. Large-scale adoption of "organic" farming methods, **however**, would ① <u>reduce</u> yields and increase production costs for many major crops. Inorganic nitrogen supplies are ② <u>essential</u> for maintaining moderate to high levels of productivity for many of the non-leguminous crop species, **because** organic supplies of nitrogenous materials often are either limited or more expensive than inorganic nitrogen fertilizers. In addition, there are ③ <u>benefits</u> to the extensive use of either manure or legumes as "green manure" crops. In many cases, weed control can be very difficult or require much hand labor if chemicals cannot be used, and ④ <u>fewer</u> people are willing to do this work as societies become wealthier. Some methods used in "organic" farming, **however**, such as the sensible use of crop rotations and specific combinations of cropping and livestock enterprises, can make important ⑤ <u>contributions</u> to the sustainability of rural ecosystems.

* nitrogen fertilizer: 질소 비료 ** manure: 거름

*** legume: 콩과(科) 식물

해설 [정답 : ③]

'In addition'은 나열의 표현입니다. 나열은 긍정적인 내용들을 연결해주거나 부정적인 내용들을 연결해주는 역힐을 하지 긍정적인 내용과 부정적인 내용을 연결해주지 못합니다. (긍정적인 내용과 부정적인 내용을 연결해주는 것은 역접의 접속사가 합니다) 그러므로, II번 문장, III번 문장에서 친환경적인 유기농에 대해서 유기농 경작은 생산량을 낮추고 생신 비용을 높인다는 부정적인 내용이 제시되었는데, IV번 문장에서 나열을 통해 친환경적인 거름에 대해서 긍정적인 내용을 제시하는 것은 단절이 발생하게 됩니다. 그러므로 benefits을 disadvantage 혹은 constraints로 바꾸어야 합니다.

I. It / has been suggested / that "organic" methods, (defined as those (in which only natural products / can be used (as inputs))), / would be less damaging to / the biosphere.

구 ▶ 'It + be suggested + that + S + V'는 가주어/진주어로 기억하시면 됩니다.
- 'defined as A'는 'A로써 정의되다'로 해석하시면 됩니다.
- 'be used as B'는 'B로써 사용되다'를 의미합니다.
- 'be damaging to D'는 'D에 피해를 끼치다'를 뜻합니다.
- 천연 제품들이 생산으로써 사용된 것으로 정의되는 '유기농' 방식은 생물권에 적은 피해를 끼치는 것으로 제시되어 왔다고 합니다.

* bio (생물의) + sphere (영역) = biosphere - 생물권

Ⅱ. Large-scale adoption (of "organic" farming methods), **however**, / would ① <u>reduce</u> / yields and increase / production costs (for many major crops).

구▶ 그러나 "유기농" 경작 방식의 대규모 채택은 많은 주요 작물들의 생산량을 감소시키고 생산비를 증가시키게 된다.

독▶ 'however'가 제시되었으므로 앞 뒷 문장 중심 문장입니다.
- "유기농" 생산 방식이 자연 환경에 적은 영향을 끼칠 것으로 보였지만 실제로는 주요 작물의 생산량을 감소시키고 생산 비용을 증가시킨다고 합니다.

* yield - n. 생산량

Ⅲ. Inorganic nitrogen supplies / are / ② <u>essential</u> / for maintaining moderate (to high levels of productivity) (for many of the non-leguminous crop species), **because** organic supplies of nitrogenous materials / often are / either limited or more expensive / than inorganic nitrogen fertilizers.

* nitrogen fertilizer: 질소 비료 *** legume: 콩과(科) 식물

구▶ 'either A or B'는 'A혹은 B'를 의미합니다.
- 유기농이 아닌 질소 공급은 많은 비콩과 식물 종의 생산성을 높은 수준으로 유지하기 위해서 필수적인데, 왜냐하면 질소 물질의 유기농 공급은 종종 유기농이 아닌 질소 비료보다 제한되거나 비싸기 때문이라고 합니다.

독▶ 'because'가 제시되었으므로 중심 문장입니다.
- 유기농이 아닌 질소 비료가 유기농 질소 물질보다 제한되지 않고 싸기 때문에 비콩과 식물종의 생산량을 유지하기 위해서는 필수적이라고 합니다.

Ⅳ. In addition, there / are / ③ <u>benefits</u> (to the extensive use of either manure or legumes as "green manure" crops).

** manure: 거름 *** legume: 콩과(科) 식물

구▶ 'either A or B'는 'A혹은 B'를 의미합니다.
- 게다가, "친환경적인 거름"으로써, 거름 혹은 작물의 광범위한 사용은 이익이 (⇒ 단점이) 있다고 합니다.

독▶ 'In addition'은 나열의 표현입니다. 나열은 긍정적인 내용들을 연결해 주거나 부정적인 내용들을 연결해 주는 역할을 하지 긍정적인 내용과 부정적인 내용을 연결해 주지 못합니다. (긍정적인 내용과 부정적인 내용을 연결해주는 것은 역접의 접속사가 합니다) 그러므로, Ⅲ번 문장에서 친환경적인 유기농에 대한 부정적인 내용이 제시되었는데, Ⅳ번 문장에서 나열을 통해 친환경적인 거름에 대해서 긍정적인 내용을 제시하는 것은 단절이 발생하게 됩니다. 그러므로 이익을 단점으로 바꾸어야 합니다.

Ⅴ. (In many cases), weed control / can be / very difficult or require / much hand labor / if chemicals / cannot be used, and ④ <u>fewer</u> people / are willing to do / this work (as societies / become / wealthier).

구▶ 많은 경우, 화학 물질을 사용할 수 없다면, 잡초를 통제하는 것은 매우 어렵고, 많은 노동력을 요구하는데, 사회가 부유할수록, 그러한 일들을 (= 잡초를 통제하는 일들을) 기꺼이 하는 사람들은 거의 없다고 합니다.

독▶ 화학 물질을 사용하지 않는다면, 많은 노동력을 투자해야 잡초를 통제할 수 있지만, 사회가 발전할수록 이러한 일을 하길 원하는 사람은 없다고 합니다.

* weed - 잡초

Ⅵ. Some methods (used in "organic" farming), **however**, (such as the sensible use of crop rotations and specific combinations of cropping and livestock enterprises), / can make / important ⑤ <u>contributions</u> (to the sustainability of rural ecosystems).

구▶ 하지만, 돌려 짓기의 합리적 사용과 경작과 가축 경영의 특징적인 조합과 같은 "유기농" 경작에서 사용되는 방법들은 농촌 생태계의 지속 가능성에 중요한 기여를 할 수 있다고 합니다.

독▶ 'however'가 제시되었으므로 앞 뒷 문장 중심 문장
　- Ⅴ번 문장까지의 내용인 유기농 경작의 한계점을 전환하여 유기농 경작이 생태계에는 중요한 기여를 한다고 합니다.

* crop (작물) + rotation (순환) = crop rotation - 작물 순환 = 돌려 짓기
** sustain (유지하다) + ability (가능성) = sustainability - 지속가능성

다음 글의 밑줄 친 부분 중, 문맥상 낱말의 쓰임이 적절하지 <u>않은</u> 것은?

Everywhere we turn we hear about almighty "cyberspace"! The hype promises that we will leave our boring lives, put on goggles and body suits, and enter some metallic, three-dimensional, multimedia otherworld. When the Industrial Revolution arrived with its great innovation, the motor, we didn't leave our world to go to some ① <u>remote</u> motorspace! **On the contrary**, we brought the motors into our lives, as automobiles, refrigerators, drill presses, and pencil sharpeners. This ② <u>absorption</u> has been so complete that we refer to all these tools with names that declare their usage, not their "motorness." These innovations **led to** a major socioeconomic movement precisely **because** they entered and ③ <u>affected</u> profoundly our everyday lives. People have not changed fundamentally in thousands of years. Technology changes constantly. It's the one that **must** ④ <u>adapt</u> to us. That's exactly what will happen with information technology and its devices under human-centric computing. The longer we continue to believe that computers will take us to a magical new world, the longer we will ⑤ <u>maintain</u> their natural fusion with our lives, the hallmark of every major movement that aspires to be called a socioeconomic revolution.

* hype: 과대광고 ** hallmark: 특징

해설 [정답 : ⑤]

Ⅶ번 문장부터 Ⅹ번 문장까지 사람은 변화하지 않지만 기술은 변화하기 때문에 적응하는 과정이 있다고 합니다. Ⅺ번 문장에서 컴퓨터가 새로운 세계로 우리를 데려간다는 것은 Ⅷ번 문장의 기술이 지속적으로 변화하는 것을 재진술 한 것입니다. 즉, 기술은 변화하지만 사람은 변화하지 않는다고 합니다. 또한 우리와 컴퓨터의 자연스러운 융합은 우리가 변화한 기술에 적응하는 것으로 기술이 오랫동안 지속적으로 변화할수록 우리는 지속적으로 적응하는 과정을 거쳐야만 하기 때문에 ⑤번 'maintain'을 'delay'로 바꾸어야 합니다.

Ⅰ. Everywhere (we / turn) we / hear (about almighty "cyberspace")!

> **구** 우리가 돌아다니는 어디에서나 우리는 강력한 "가상 공간"에 대해 듣는다고 합니다.

Ⅱ. The hype / promises / that we / will leave / our boring lives, put on / goggles and body suits, and enter / some metallic, three-dimensional, multimedia otherworld.

* hype: 과대광고

> **구** 'A, B, and C' 병렬 구조입니다.
> - 그 과대광고는 (= 우리가 어디에서나 강력한 "가상 공간"에 대해 듣는다는 말은) 우리가 지루한 삶을 떠나 고글과 바디 수트를 착용하고, 어떤 금속성의, 3차원의 멀티미디어인 다른 공간으로 접속한다는 것을 약속한다고 합니다.

Ⅲ. When the Industrial Revolution / arrived (with its great innovation, the motor), we / didn't leave / our world (to go to some ① <u>remote</u> motorspace)!

구 위대한 혁신인 모터와 함께 산업 혁명이 도착했을 때, 우리는 어떤 먼 모터 공간으로 가기 위해서 우리의 세계를 떠날 수 없었다고 합니다.

독 산업 혁명이 도래했을 때 우리는 가상 공간으로 갈 수 없었다고 합니다.

Ⅳ. **On the contrary**, we / brought / the motors (into our lives, as automobiles, refrigerators, drill presses, and pencil sharpeners).

구 반대로, 우리는 모터를 자동차, 냉장고, 드릴 프레스, 연필깎이로써 우리의 삶으로 가져왔다고 합니다.

독 'On the contrary'를 통해서 전환하므로 중심 문장
  - 우리가 산업 혁명을 통해 모터를 이용하게 되며, 비록 가상 공간으로 갈 수는 없었지만 모터들을 삶 안으로 가져오며 다양한 가전제품을 사용할 수 있었다고 합니다.

Ⅴ. This ② <u>absorption</u> / has been / so complete that we / refer to / all these tools (with names that declare / their usage, not their "motorness.")

구 'so A that'은 '너무 A해서 ~하다'로 해석하시면 됩니다.
  - 그러한 흡수는 (= 가전제품들을 삶으로 가져온 것은) 너무 완전해서 우리는 그것들의 (= 가전제품들의) 모터성이 아니라 그들의 사용에 대해서 언급하는 이름들로 모든 그러한 도구들을 언급하게 되었다고 합니다.

독 우리는 우리의 삶 속으로 들어온 가전제품에 모터성이 아닌 사용을 밝히는 이름으로 이름 붙였다고 합니다.

Ⅵ. These innovations / **led to** / a major socioeconomic movement precisely **because** they / entered and ③ <u>affected</u> profoundly / our everyday lives.

구 그러한 혁신들은 (= 가전제품들은) 정확하게 주요한 사회경제적 움직임을 야기하는 데, 그들이 우리의 일상생활에 들어왔고 영향을 끼쳤기 때문이라고 합니다.

독 'lead to'와 'because'가 제시되었으므로 중심 문장
  - 우리의 삶 속에 들어온 가전제품들은 우리의 일상생활에 많은 영향을 끼쳤다고 합니다.

Ⅶ. People / have not changed fundamentally (in thousands of years).

구 수천년동안 사람들은 근본적으로 변화하지 않았다고 합니다.

Ⅷ. Technology / changes constantly.

구 기술은 지속적으로 변화해왔다고 합니다.

Ⅸ. It's the one (that **must** ④ <u>adapt</u> to / us).

> 구▶ 그것이 우리가 반드시 적응해야 하는 것이라고 합니다.

> 독▶ 'must'가 제시되었으므로 중심 문장
> - 사람은 변화하지 않았지만 기술은 변화하였기 때문에 사람들이 기술에 적응해야 한다고 합니다.

Ⅹ. That's exactly / what will happen (with information technology and its devices under human-centric computing).

> 구▶ 그것이 (= 사람들이 기술에 적응하는 것이) 정보 기술과 그 장치들이 인간 중심의 컴퓨터 사용 아래에 일어날 일이라고 합니다.

> 독▶ 우리가 컴퓨터를 사용하게 되면서 정보 기술들과 그 장치들에 적응해야 한다고 합니다.

Ⅺ. The longer we / continue to believe / that computers / will take / us (to a magical new world), the longer we / will ⑤ <u>maintain</u> / their natural fusion (with our lives), the hallmark of every major movement (that aspires to be called / a socioeconomic revolution).

** hallmark: 특징

> 구▶ 'The 비교급 S + V, The 비교급 S' + V''는 '더욱 S가 V하는 것을 비교급 할수록, S'이 V'하는 것이 비교급된다'라고 해석하시면 됩니다.
> - 우리가 컴퓨터가 우리를 마법같은 새로운 세계로 (= 가상 세계로) 데려간다는 것을 오랫동안 믿으면 믿을수록, 우리는 컴퓨터와 우리 삶의 자연스러운 융합이 더 오래 유지될 (⇒ 지연될) 것인데, 이는 사회경제적 혁명이라고 불리는 것을 열망하는 모든 주요한 운동의 특징이라고 합니다.

> 독▶ Ⅷ번 문장부터 Ⅹ번 문장까지 사람은 변화하지 않지만 기술은 변화하기 때문에 적응하는 과정이 있다고 합니다. 즉 Ⅺ번 문장에서 컴퓨터가 새로운 세계로 우리를 데려갈수록 우리는 그러한 세계에 적응해야 하기 때문에 우리의 삶과 컴퓨터 사이의 자연스러운 융합인 적응은 유지가 아닌 지연될 것입니다.

다음 글의 밑줄 친 부분 중, 문맥상 낱말의 쓰임이 적절하지 <u>않은</u> 것은?

Internalization depends on supports for autonomy. Contexts that use controlling strategies such as salient rewards and punishments or evaluative, selfesteem-hooking pressures are ① <u>least</u> likely to lead people to value activities as their own. This is not to say that controls don't ② <u>work</u> to produce behavior — decades of operant psychology prove that they can. It is rather that the more salient the external control over a person's behavior, the more the person is likely to be merely externally regulated or introjected in his or her actions. **Consequently**, the person does not ③ <u>develop</u> a value or investment in the behaviors, but instead remains dependent on external controls. **Thus**, parents who reward, force, or cajole their child to do homework are more likely to have a child who does so only when rewarded, cajoled, or forced. The salience of external controls ④ <u>drives</u> the acquisition of self-responsibility. Alternatively, parents who supply reasons, show an emotional understanding of difficulties overcoming problems, and use a ⑤ <u>minimum</u> of external incentives are more likely to cultivate a sense of willingness and value for work in their child.

* autonomy: 자율성 ** salient: 두드러진 *** introject: 투입하다

해설 [정답 : ④]

ㅣ번 문장에서는 'Internalization depends on supports for autonomy' 내면화는 자율성에 대한 지지에 의존한다고 했는데, 이는 자율성에 내면하가 중요한 역할을 한다는 것을 보여줍니다.

지문에서는 이어 내면화와 반대되는 외부화는 자율성에 대한 부정적인 영향을 준다는 내용을 이어서 설명합니다.

Ⅳ번 문장의 'the more salient the external control ~, the more the person is likely to be merely externally regulated' 사람의 통제에 대한 외부 통제가 두드러질수록, 사람은 자신의 행동에서 외부적으로 규제될 가능성이 높다고 한 것을 통해 알 수 있습니다.

그런데 Ⅶ번 문장에서는 'the salience of external controls drives the acquisition of self-responsibility' 외적 통제가 두드러지면 자기 책임감의 습득이 촉진된다고 했는데, 이는 틀린 내용이며, 오히려 두드러진 외적 통제로 인해 자기 책임감의 습득이 제대로 이뤄지지 않는다는 내용이 들어가야 합니다.

그러므로 정답은 ④번이며, drives을 undermines와 같은 단어로 바꿔야 합니다.

ㅣ. Internalization / depends on / supports (for autonomy).

* autonomy: 자율성

구▶ 내면화는 자율성에 대한 지지에 의존한다고 합니다.

독▶ 내면화의 특징이 언급됩니다.

Ⅱ. Contexts (that / use / controlling strategies / such as salient rewards and punishments or evaluative, selfesteem-hooking pressures) are ① <u>least</u> likely to lead / people / to value activities as their own).

** salient: 두드러진

구▶ 'lead A to-V'는 'A가 V하도록 이끌다'를 의미합니다.
- 'value A as B'는 'A를 B로써 가치있게 여기다'를 뜻합니다.
- 두드러진 보상과 처벌 또는 평가하는, 자존감을 건드리는 압박과 같은 통제 전략을 사용하는 상황에서는 사람들이 활동을 자신의 것으로 가치 있게 여기게 될 가능성이 거의 없다고 합니다.

독▶ 활동을 자신의 것으로 여기지 않는 것은 Ⅰ번 문장의 자율성이 없는 것을 의미하며, 그 원인으로 보상이나 처벌, 평가, 압박과 같은 통제 전략이 제시됩니다.

Ⅲ. This / is / not to say / that controls / don't ② <u>work</u> / to produce behavior — decades (of operant psychology) / prove / that / they / can.

구▶ 이것은 통제가 행동을 유발하는데 효과가 없다는 말은 아닌데 수십 년에 걸친 조작적 심리학은 통제가 행동을 유발할 수 있다는 것을 증명한다고 합니다.

독▶ Ⅱ번 문장에서 자율성을 상실시키는 통제 전략이 행동을 어느 정도 유발할 수 있다는 순기능으로 언급하고 있습니다.

Ⅳ. It / is / rather that / the more salient / the external control (over a person's behavior), the more the person / is likely to be merely externally regulated or introjected (in his or her actions).

*** introject: 투입하다

구▶ 'the more A, the more B'는 'A하면 할수록 B하다'를 의미합니다.
- 그 말은 오히려 사람의 행동에 대한 외부 통제가 더 두드러질수록, 그 사람은 자신의 행동에서 외부적으로만 규제되거나 투입될 가능성이 더 높다는 것이라고 합니다.

독▶ 행동에서 외부적으로 규제되거나 투입되는 것 역시 Ⅰ번 문장의 자율성이 없어지는 것이며, 이것은 외부 통제 때문이므로 Ⅱ번 문장의 내용으로 돌아온 것을 알 수 있습니다.

Ⅴ. <u>**Consequently**</u>, the person / does not ③ <u>develop</u> / a value or investment in the behaviors, but instead / remains / dependent (on external controls.)

구▶ 결과적으로 그 사람은 행동에 대한 가치나 투자를 발전시키지 않고, 대신에 외부 통제에 의존하는 상태로 남는다고 합니다.

독▶ 'Consequently'가 제시되었으므로 중심 문장
- 통제 전략으로 인해 자율성이 없어지는 것에 대한 부정적인 결과가 언급됩니다.

Ⅵ. **<u>Thus</u>**, parents (who reward, force, or cajole / their child to do homework) are more likely to have

/ a child (who / does so only when rewarded, cajoled, or forced).

> 따라서 자녀에게 숙제를 하도록 보상을 주거나, 강요하거나, 회유하는 부모는 보상받거나, 회유당하거나, 강요받을 때만 그렇게 하는 자녀를 가질 가능성이 높다고 합니다.

> 'Thus'가 제시되었으므로 중심 문장
> - 보상, 강요, 회유하는 것은 모두 통제 전략의 예시이며, 이로 인해 그렇게 강요받을 때만 숙제를 하는 자녀들은 Ⅴ번 문장의 외부 통제에 의존하는 사람들의 사례가 됩니다.

* cajole – 꼬드기다, 회유하다

Ⅶ. The salience (of external controls) / ④ <u>drives</u> / the acquisition (of self-responsibility.)

> 외적 통제가 두드러지면 자기 책임감의 습득이 촉진된다고 합니다.

Ⅷ. Alternatively, parents (who / supply / reasons, / show / an emotional understanding of difficulties / overcoming problems, and use / a ⑤ <u>minimum</u> of external incentives) / are more likely to cultivate

/ a sense of willingness and value for work (in their child.)

> 그 대신에 이유를 제시하고, 문제를 극복하는 어려움에 대해 정서적 이해를 보여주고, 최소한의 외적 인센티브를 사용하는 부모는 자녀에게 과업에 대한 자발적 의지와 가치에 대한 식별력을 길러줄 가능성이 더 높다고 합니다.

> 반대되는 사례가 언급되고 있는 문장입니다. 외적 인센티브를 줄이고 정서적 이해를 보여주는 부모는 외적 통제를 사용하지 않는 사례에 해당하며, 그로 인해 자녀의 과업에 대한 자발적 의지와 식별력을 길러주는 것은 자녀들이 자율성을 가질 수 있도록 이어지는 긍정적인 사례에 해당합니다.

다음 글의 밑줄 친 부분 중, 문맥상 낱말의 쓰임이 적절하지 <u>않은</u> 것은?

In recent years urban transport professionals globally have largely acquiesced to the view that automobile demand in cities needs to be managed rather than accommodated. Rising incomes inevitably **lead to** increases in motorization. Even without the imperative of climate change, the physical constraints of densely inhabited cities and the corresponding demands of accessibility, mobility, safety, air pollution, and urban livability all ① <u>limit</u> the option of expanding road networks purely to accommodate this rising demand. **As a result**, as cities develop and their residents become more prosperous, ② <u>persuading</u> people to choose not to use cars becomes an increasingly key focus of city managers and planners. Improving the quality of ③ <u>alternative</u> options, such as walking, cycling, and public transport, is a central element of this strategy. **However**, the most direct approach to ④ <u>accommodating</u> automobile demand is making motorized travel more expensive or restricting it with administrative rules. The contribution of motorized travel to climate change ⑤ <u>reinforces</u> this imperative.

* acquiesce: 따르다 ** imperative: 불가피한 것

*** constraint: 압박

해설 [정답 : ④]

지문에서 자동차 수요를 관리하는 것과 수용하는 것은 반대되는 개념으로 제시되었습니다. Ⅴ번 문장까지는 자동차 수요를 수용할 수 없는 이유와 자동차 수요를 조절하는 방법에 대해서 제시되었습니다. 하지만 Ⅵ번 문장에서는 자동차 수요를 수용하는 방식에 대해서 제시되었고 또한, 자동차 여행을 비싸게 만들거나 제한하는 것은 자동차 수요 그 자체를 제한하는 것이지 자동차 수요를 도로망 확장을 통해 수용하는 것이 아니므로 'accommodating'을 'managing'으로 바꾸어야 합니다.

Ⅰ. (In recent years) urban transport professionals / globally have largely acquiesced to / the view (that automobile demand (in cities) / needs to be managed (rather than accommodated)).

* acquiesce: 따르다

[구] 최근 몇 년 동안 도시 교통 전문가들은 전 세계적으로 도시에서 자동차 수요가 수용되어야 하기보다는 조절되어야 한다는 관점을 대체로 따르고 있다고 합니다.

[독] 도시 교통 전문가들은 자동차 수요에 맞춰 도로를 늘리거나 차선을 넓히는 것 (= 수용)이 아닌 자동차 수요 자체를 조절해야 한다는 관점을 따르고 있다고 합니다.

Ⅱ. Rising incomes / inevitably **lead to** increases (in motorization).

[구] 'motor'는 '모터, 전동기 혹은 자동차'를 의미합니다. 접미사 'zation'은 '~화'하다를 의미합니다. 그러므로 'motorization'은 '자동차화'를 의미합니다.
- 증가된 소득은 불가피하게 자동차화의 증가를 야기한다고 합니다.

[독] 'lead to'가 제시되었으므로 중심 문장
- 소득이 증가함에 따라 자동차 수요가 증가하였다고 합니다.

Ⅲ. (Even without the imperative of climate change), the physical constraints of densely inhabited cities and the corresponding demands (of accessibility, mobility, safety, air pollution, and urban livability) all / ① limit / the option of expanding road networks purely (to accommodate / this rising demand).

** imperative: 불가피한 것 *** constraint: 압박

[구] 불가피한 기후 변화없이, 인구 밀도가 높은 도시의 물리적인 압박과 접근성, 이동성, 안전성, 대기 오염 그리고 도시 거주 적합성에 상응하는 수요들은 모두 증가하는 수요에 상응하기 위해 도로망을 확장하는 선택권을 제한한다고 합니다.

[독] Ⅰ번 문장에서 증가하는 자동차의 수요를 도로망을 확장하는 것으로 수용할 수 없는 이유가 Ⅲ번 문장에서 제시되고 있습니다.

Ⅳ. **As a result**, as cities / develop and their residents / become / more prosperous, ② persuading / people / to choose not to use cars / becomes / an increasingly key focus of city managers and planners.

[구] 'persuade A to-V'는 'A가 to-V하도록 설득하다'를 의미합니다.
  - 결과적으로, 도시들이 발전하고 그들의 (= 도시들의) 거주민들이 더 풍요로워졌기 때문에, 사람들이 자동차를 사용하지 않는 것을 선택하도록 설득하는 것이 도시 관리자와 계획자들의 가장 중요한 사항이 되었다고 합니다.

[독] 'As a result'가 제시되었으므로 중심 문장
  - Ⅲ번 문장에서 제시되었듯이 증가하는 자동차의 수요를 순전히 도로망을 확장하는 것으로 수용할 수 없기 때문에 사람들이 자동차를 이용하지 않도록 설득하는 것이 중요해졌다고 합니다. 사람들이 자동차를 이용하지 않도록 도시 관리자와 계획자들이 설득하는 것은 Ⅰ번 문장에서 자동차 수요를 조절해야 한다는 내용의 재진술입니다.

Ⅴ. Improving the quality of ③ alternative options, (such as walking, cycling, and public transport), / is / a central element of this strategy.

[구] 걷기, 자전거 타기, 대중교통과 같은 대안적인 선택들의 질을 상승시키는 것이 그러한 전략의 (= 자동차의 수요를 조절하는 전략의) 핵심 요소라고 합니다.

[독] Ⅳ번 문장에서 제시된 사람들이 자동차를 사용하지 않도록 설득하는 것의 핵심 요소가 걷기, 자전거 타기, 대중교통과 같은 대안적인 선택들의 질을 상승시키는 것이라고 합니다.

Ⅵ. **<u>However</u>**, the most direct approach (to ④ <u>accommodating</u> automobile demand) / is making / motorized travel / more expensive or restricting / it (with administrative rules).

구▶ 'make + O + O.C'는 'O를 O.C로 만들다'를 의미합니다.
- 그러나, 자동차 수요를 수용하는 가장 직접적인 관점은 자동차 여행을 좀 더 비싸게 만들거나 행정 규정으로 그것을 (= 자동차 여행을) 제한하는 것이라고 합니다.

독▶ 'However'가 제시되었으므로 앞 뒷 문장 중심 문장
- 지문에서 자동차 수요를 관리하는 것과 수용하는 것은 반대되는 개념으로 제시되었습니다. Ⅴ번 문장까지는 자동차 수요를 수용할 수 없는 이유와 자동차 수요를 조절하는 방법에 대해서 제시되었습니다. 하지만 Ⅵ번 문장에서는 자동차 수요를 수용하는 방식에 대해서 제시되었고 또한, 자동차 여행을 비싸게 만들거나 제한하는 것은 자동차 수요 그 자체를 제한하는 것이지 자동차 수요를 도로망 확장을 통해 수용하는 것이 아니므로 'accommodating'을 'managing'으로 바꾸어야 합니다.

Ⅶ. The contribution (of motorized travel) to climate change / ⑤ <u>reinforces</u> / this imperative.

구▶ 자동차 여행의 기후 변화에 대한 기여는 이러한 불가피한 것을 (= 자동차 수요를 제한하는 것을) 강화한다고 합니다.

독▶ 자동차의 수요를 조절해야 하는 또 다른 이유로 기후 변화를 제시하고 있습니다.

다음 글의 밑줄 친 부분 중, 문맥상 낱말의 쓰임이 적절하지 <u>않은</u> 것은?

If I say to you, 'Don't think of a white bear', you will find it difficult not to think of a white bear. In this way, 'thought suppression can actually increase the thoughts one wishes to suppress instead of calming them'. One common **example** of this is that people on a diet who try not to think about food often begin to think much ① <u>more</u> about food. This process is **therefore** also known as the rebound effect. The ② <u>ironic</u> effect seems to be caused by the interplay of two related cognitive processes. This dual-process system involves, first, an intentional operating process, which consciously attempts to locate thoughts ③ <u>unrelated</u> to the suppressed ones. Second, and simultaneously, an unconscious monitoring process tests whether the operating system is functioning effectively. If the monitoring system encounters thoughts inconsistent with the intended ones, it prompts the intentional operating process to ensure that these are replaced by ④ <u>inappropriate</u> thoughts. **However**, it is argued, the intentional operating system can fail **due to** increased cognitive load **caused** by fatigue, stress and emotional factors, and so the monitoring process filters the inappropriate thoughts into consciousness, making them highly ⑤ <u>accessible</u>.

해설 [정답 : ④]

지문을 완전히 이해하기에는 어렵지만 정답은 원래 문장의 반댓말이라는 것을 생각했다면 쉽게 답이 보이는 문제라고 생각합니다. 'inappropriate'가 제시되었을 때 생각해야 하는 것은 반대말인 'appropriate'여야 합니다. 의도된 것과 일치하지 않는 생각을 마주쳤다면 (생각하지 않으려고 하는 생각과 마주쳤다면), 적절한 생각 (무관한 생각)으로 대체해야 한다고 지문에서 제시됩니다. 그러므로 정답은 ④번이 됩니다.

Ⅰ. If I say to you, / 'Don't think of a white bear', you / will find / it / difficult / not to think of a white bear.

> **구** 'find + it + 형용사 + to-V'는 가목적어/진목적어 의심
> - 'it'이 지칭하는 대상이 없으므로 가목적어/진목적어
> - 만약 내가 너에게 '백곰에 대해서 생각하지 말라'고 한다면, 너는 백곰에 대해서 생각하지 않는 것이 어렵다는 것을 알게 될 것이라고 합니다.

Ⅱ. (In this way), 'thought suppression / can actually increase / the thoughts (one / wishes to suppress instead of calming them').

> **구** 이러한 방식으로, '사고의 억제는 억압하고 싶은 생각을 가라앉히는 대신, 그것을 사실은 증가시킬 수 있다'고 합니다.

Ⅲ. One common **example** (of this) / is that people (on a diet) (who try / not to think about food) often begin to think / much ① <u>more</u> about food.

> 구▶ 이것에 대한 흔한 예시는 다이어트를 하고 있어서 음식에 대해 생각하지 않으려고 노력하는 사람들이 흔히 음식에 대해 훨씬 더 많이 생각하기 시작한다는 것이라고 합니다.

> 독▶ 'example'이 제시되었으니 앞 문장 중심 문장!

Ⅳ. This process / is **therefore** also known (as the rebound effect).

> 구▶ 따라서 그 과정은 반등 효과로 알려져 있다고 합니다.

> 독▶ 'therefore'이 제시되었으므로 중심 문장!
> - 반등 효과 = 생각하지 않으려고 하지만 실제로는 더 생각이 증가함

Ⅴ. The ② <u>ironic</u> effect / seems to be **caused** (by the interplay of two related cognitive processes).

> 구▶ 그 역설적인 영향은 두 가지 인지 과정의 상호작용에 의해 야기되는 것 같다고 합니다.

> 독▶ 'cause'가 제시되었으니 중심 문장!
> - 두 가지 인지 과정의 상호작용 ⇒ 반등 효과

Ⅵ. This dual-process system / involves, first, / an intentional operating process, (which consciously attempts to locate / thoughts (③ <u>unrelated</u> to the suppressed ones)).

> 구▶ 우선 이 이중 체계는 의도적인 운영 과정을 포함하는데, 이는 의식적으로 억제된 생각과 무관한 생각을 찾아내려고 시도한다고 합니다.

Ⅶ. Second, (and simultaneously), an unconscious monitoring process / tests / whether the operating system / is functioning effectively.

> 구▶ 'whether'은 '~인지 아닌지'를 의미합니다.
> - 두 번째로, 동시에, 무의식적인 감시 과정은 운영 체계가 효과적으로 작동하는지 아닌지 검사한다고 합니다.

Ⅷ. If the monitoring system / encounters / thoughts (inconsistent with the intended ones), it / prompts / the intentional operating process (to ensure / that these / are replaced by ④ <u>inappropriate</u> thoughts).

> 구▶ 만약 감시 체계가 의도된 생각과 일치하지 않는 생각을 마주친다면, 그것은 의도적인 운영 과정을 그것들을 부적절한 생각으로 대체하는 것을 보증하기 위해서 자극시킨다고 합니다.

> 독▶ 의도된 생각과 일치하지 않는 생각을 마주치면 생각하지 않으려고 노력하는 생각과 관련 없는 적절한 생각으로 바꿔야 합니다. 그러므로 'inappropriate' ⇒ 'appropriate'로 바꿔야 합니다.

Ⅸ. **However**, it is argued, the intentional operating system / can fail (**due to** increased cognitive load) (**caused** by fatigue, stress and emotional factors), / and so the monitoring process / filters / the inappropriate thoughts (into consciousness), (making / them / highly ⑤ accessible).

구▶ 'filter A into B'는 'A를 걸러서 B 안으로 투입시키다'를 의미합니다.
- 하지만, 주장되는 것은 의도적인 운영체계는 피로, 스트레스, 감정적 요인들에 의해 생긴 인지 부하의 증가 때문에 멈출 수 있고, 그래서 감시 과정이 부적절한 생각을 걸러서 의식으로 스며들게 해, 그것의 접근성을 높게 만든다는 것이라고 합니다.

독▶ 'However'로 인해서 앞 뒷 문장 중심 문장, 'due to'와 'caused'도 제시했습니다.
- 인지 부화 증가 ⇒ 의도적인 작동 체계 (생각하지 않으려고 노력하는 것) 멈춤 ⇒ 감시 과정이 부적절한 생각을 의식으로 스며들게 함 ⇒ 생각 접근성 상승으로 이해하시면 됩니다.

(A), (B), (C)의 각 네모 안에서 문맥에 맞는 낱말로 가장 적절한 것은?

To the extent that an agent relies on the prior knowledge of its designer rather than on its own percepts, we say that the agent lacks autonomy. A rational agent **should** be autonomous — it **should** learn what it can to (A) [**compensate** / prepare] for partial or incorrect prior knowledge. **For example**, a vacuum-cleaning agent that learns to foresee where and when additional dirt will appear will do better than one that does not. As a practical matter, one seldom requires complete autonomy from the start: when the agent has had little or no experience, it would **have to** act (B) [purposefully / **randomly**] unless the designer gave some assistance. **So**, just as evolution provides animals with enough built-in reflexes to survive long enough to learn for themselves, it would be reasonable to provide an artificial intelligent agent with some initial knowledge as well as an ability to learn. After sufficient experience of its environment, the behavior of a rational agent can become effectively (C) [**independent** / protective] of its prior knowledge. **Hence**, the incorporation of learning allows one to design a single rational agent that will succeed in a vast variety of environments.

해설 [정답 : ④]

(A) : 부정확한 사전 지식을 (A)할 수 있도록 학습해야 한다고 했습니다. (A) 뒤의 Ⅲ번 문장에서는 예시로 'learns to foresee where and when additional dirt will appear', 다른 먼지가 어디에서, 언제 나타날지 예측하도록 학습하는 진공 청소기의 에이전트가 언급되는데, 이는 사전 지식을 보완하는 것이므로 (A)에는 compensate, '보완하다'가 들어가야 합니다.

(B) : (B) 문장에서는 'one seldom requires complete autonomy from the start', 처음부터 완전한 자율성이 필요하지 않다고 했습니다. (B)의 에이전트가 경험이 없을 때, 설계자가 지원을 제공하지 않으면, 에이전트의 자율성이 존재하지 않는 것이므로 무작위로 행동한다고 봐야 합니다. 그러므로 (B)에는 randomly, '임의로'가 들어가야 합니다.

(C) : (C)는 (B)와 반대되는 내용입니다. (C) 문장에서는 'After sufficient experience of its environment', 환경을 충분히 경험한 에이전트는 자율성을 얻게 될 것이므로, (C)에는 independent, '독립적인'이 들어가야 합니다.

Ⅰ. To the extent (that an agent / relies on / the prior knowledge (of its designer) rather than (on its own percepts)), we / say / that / the agent / lacks / autonomy.

> **구** 에이전트가 자신이 지각한 내용보다 설계자의 사전 지식에 의존하는 경우, 우리는 그 에이전트가 자율성이 부족하다고 말한다고 합니다.

> **독** 에이전트의 자율성은, 설계자의 사전 지식의 의존 여부에 달려 있음을 알 수 있습니다.

* 에이전트는 '대리인'을 의미하기도 하는데, 특정 목적에 대해 사용자를 대신하여 작업을 수행하는 자율 프로세스를 의미하는 IT용어로 사용되었습니다. 분명히 지엽적인 내용이긴 하지만, '사용자를 대신해 활동하는 것'이라는 것은 이해하고 지문에 접근해야 합니다.

Ⅱ. A rational agent / **should** be / autonomous — it / **should** learn / what / it / can / to

(A) [**compensate** / prepare] for partial or incorrect prior knowledge.

> **구** 합리적인 에이전트는 자율적이어야 하는데, 불완전하거나 부정확한 사전 지식을 보완하기 위해 무엇을 준비해야 하는지 학습해야 한다고 합니다.

> **독** 'should'가 언급되었으므로 중심 문장
> - 합리적인 에이전트의 조건으로 자율성과 지식을 보완하는 능력에 대해서 언급하고 있습니다.

Ⅲ. **For example**, a vacuum-cleaning agent (that / learns / to foresee / where and when / additional dirt / will appear) will do / better than one / that / does not.

> **구** 예를 들어, 또 다른 먼지가 어디에서 그리고 언제 나타날지 예측하는 방법을 학습하는 진공 청소 에이전트는 그렇게 하지 않는 것보다 더 잘할 것이라고 합니다.

> **독** 'for example'이 제시되었으므로 앞 문장이 중심 문장
> - Ⅱ번 문장의 예시 문장입니다. 먼지에 대해서 예측하는 방법을 학습하는 에이전트는 Ⅱ번 문장의 사전 지식을 보완하는 것의 예시가 됩니다.

Ⅳ. As a practical matter, one / seldom requires / complete autonomy (from the start): when / the agent / has had / little or no experience, it / would **have to** act (B) [purposefully / **randomly**] unless / the designer / gave / some assistance.

> **구** 현실적으로는 처음부터 완전한 자율성이 거의 필요하지 않은데, 에이전트가 경험이 거의 없거나 전혀 없을 때, 설계자가 약간의 지원을 제공하지 않는다면, 그것은 임의로 작동해야 할 것이라고 합니다.

> **독** 'have to'가 제시되었으므로 중심 문장
> - 처음부터 자율성이 필요하지 않다고 했으므로, 설계자의 지원이 없으면 자율성 없이 임의로 작동할 것임을 추론할 수 있습니다.

Ⅴ. **So**, just as evolution / provides / animals (with enough built-in reflexes (to survive long enough (to learn for themselves))), it / would be / reasonable / to provide / an artificial intelligent agent (with some initial knowledge as well as an ability to learn).

> 구 'it + be동사 + 형용사 + to-V'는 가주어/진주어 의심
> - 'it'이 지칭하는 대상이 없으므로 가주어/진주어
> - 따라서 진화가 동물이 스스로 학습할 수 있을 만큼 충분히 오래 생존할 수 있도록 필요한 만큼의 타고난 반사 신경을 제공하는 것처럼, 인공 지능 에이전트에게 학습할 수 있는 능력뿐만 아니라 약간의 초기 지식을 제공하는 것이 합리적일 것이라고 합니다.

> 독 'so'가 제시되었으므로 중심 문장
> - Ⅱ번 문장의 내용을 동물의 예시를 들어 재진술하고 있습니다.

Ⅵ. After sufficient experience (of its environment), the behavior (of a rational agent) / can become / effectively (C) [**independent** / protective] of its prior knowledge.

> 구 환경을 충분히 경험한 후, 합리적인 에이전트의 행동은 사전 지식으로부터 사실상 독립할 수 있다고 합니다.

> 독 Ⅱ번 문장에서 합리적인 에이전트는 자율적이라고 했으므로 설계자의 지식으로부터 독립한 에이전트가 합리적임을 알 수 있습니다.

Ⅶ. **Hence**, the incorporation (of learning) / allows / one / to design / a single rational agent / that / will succeed (in a vast variety of environments).

> 구 'allow A to-V' - A가 V하는 것을 허락하다
> - 따라서 학습의 통합은 아주 다양한 환경에서 성공할 하나의 합리적 에이전트를 설계할 수 있게 한다고 합니다.

> 독 'hence'가 제시되었으므로 중심 문장

다음 글의 밑줄 친 부분 중, 문맥상 낱말의 쓰임이 적절하지 <u>않은</u> 것은?

  In economic systems what takes place in one sector has impacts on another; demand for a good or service in one sector is derived from another. **For instance**, a consumer buying a good in a store will likely **trigger** the replacement of this product, which will generate ① <u>demands</u> for activities such as manufacturing, resource extraction and, of course, transport. What is different about transport is that it cannot exist alone and a movement cannot be ② <u>stored</u>. An unsold product can remain on the shelf of a store until bought (often with discount incentives), **but** an unsold seat on a flight or unused cargo capacity in the same flight remains unsold and cannot be brought back as additional capacity ③ <u>later</u>. In this case an opportunity has been ④ <u>seized</u>, **since** the amount of transport being offered has exceeded the demand for it. The derived demand of transportation is often very difficult to reconcile with an equivalent supply, and actually transport companies would prefer to have some additional capacity to accommodate ⑤ <u>unforeseen</u> demand (often at much higher prices).

* reconcile: 조화시키다

해설 [**정답 : ④**]

③번 문장에서는 항공편의 미판매 좌석이나 미사용 화물 용량은 차후 추가 용량으로 돌아오지 않는다고 했는데, ④번 문장에서는 제공받는 운송량이 수요를 초과했기 때문에 기회가 포착되었다고 했습니다. 추가 용량으로 돌아오지 않는 것은 기회가 점유되는 것이라 볼 수 없습니다. 초과된 운송량이 차후 추가되지 않으므로 기회가 오히려 사라진다고 봐야 하며, 'seized'를 'lost'와 같은 단어로 바꿔야 합니다.

Ⅰ. In economic systems / what takes place / in one sector / has impacts on another; demand / for a good or service / in one sector / is derived from another.

  구▶ 경제 시스템에서는 한 부문에서 일어나는 일이 다른 부문에 영향을 미치며, 한 부문에서의 재화나 서비스에 대한 수요는 다른 부문에서 파생된다고 합니다.

Ⅱ. **For instance**, a consumer / buying a good / in a store / will likely **trigger** / the replacement / of this product, which will generate / ① <u>demands</u> for activities / such as manufacturing, resource extraction and, of course, transport.

  구▶ 예를 들어, 상점에서 상품을 구매하는 소비자는 아마 이 상품의 보충을 촉발할 것이고, 이것은 제조, 자원 추출, 그리고 물론 운송과 같은 활동에 대한 수요를 창출할 것이라고 합니다.

  독▶ 'For instance'를 통해서 예시를 제시하므로 앞 문장 중심 문장, 'trigger'을 통해서 인과관계를 제시하므로 중심 문장입니다.
   - Ⅰ번 문장의 한 부문의 일(= 상품을 구매하는 소비자)이 다른 부문에 영향(상품의 보충, 수요 창출)을 미치는 경제 시스템에 관한 예시 문장입니다.
   - 소비자가 상품을 구매했으니, 그에 대한 수요를 창출한다고 볼 수 있습니다.

III. What is different / about transport / is that it / cannot exist alone / and a movement / cannot be ② <u>stored</u>.

> 구▶ 운송이 (상품과) 다른 점은 그것이 혼자서는 존재할 수 없고 이동은 저장될 수 없다는 것이라고 합니다.

> 독▶ II번 문장의 상품을 구매하는 것과 운송을 비교하고 있습니다.

IV. An unsold product / can remain / on the shelf of a store / until bought (often with discount incentives), **but** an unsold seat / on a flight or unused cargo capacity / in the same flight / remains unsold / and cannot be brought back / as additional capacity ③ <u>later</u>.

> 구▶ 'bring'은 '가져오다', back은 '다시 돌아오는 이미지'입니다. 그러므로 'bring back'은 '다시 되돌리다'를 의미하게 됩니다.
> - 팔리지 않은 상품은 (흔히 할인 인센티브로) 구매될 때까지 매장 진열대에 남아 있을 수 있지만, 항공편의 팔리지 않은 좌석이나 동일 항공편의 미사용 화물 적재 용량은 팔리지 않은 상태로 남게 되며 이후에 추가 용량으로 되돌릴 수 없다고 합니다.

> 독▶ 'but'이 제시되었으므로 중심 문장
> - 팔리지 않은 상품은 상품, 항공편의 팔리지 않는 좌석은 운송에 관한 예시입니다. 팔리지 않는 좌석이 이후에 추가적으로 수용될 수 없으므로 III번 문장의 이동이 저장될 수 없다는 것에 대한 근거가 됩니다.

V. In this case / an opportunity / has been ④ <u>seized</u>, **since** / the amount of transport (being offered) / has exceeded / the demand for it.

> 구▶ 이 경우, 제공되는 운송량이 그것에 대한 수요를 초과하였기 때문에 기회가 포착되었다고 합니다.

> 독▶ 'since'가 'because'와 같은 뜻으로 사용되었으므로 중심 문장
> - 제공되는 운송량이 그것의 수요를 초과했다는 것은 팔리지 않는 것을 말합니다. 그러므로 여기서 'opportunity'는 IV번 문장에서 제시된 팔리지 않은 좌석이나 미사용 화물 적재 용량을 추가 용량으로 되돌리는 것을 의미하게 됩니다. 즉, 팔리지 않는 운송량이 기회가 포착되었다고 볼 수 없으므로 'seized'를 'lost'와 같은 단어로 바꿔야 합니다.

VI. The derived demand (of transportation) / is often very difficult (to reconcile with / an equivalent supply), and actually transport companies / would prefer to have / some additional capacity / to accommodate ⑤ <u>unforeseen</u> demand (often at much higher prices).

* reconcile: 조화시키다

> 구▶ 파생된 운송 수요는 흔히 (그에) 상응하는 공급과 조화를 이루기가 매우 어려워서, 실제로 운송 회사들은 (흔히 훨씬 더 높은 가격으로) 예측하지 못한 수요를 수용할 수 있는 얼마간의 추가 용량을 갖는 것을 선호할 것이라고 합니다.

> 독▶ 운송의 수요와 공급이 조화를 이룬다는 것은 제공되는 운송량이 수요와 일치하는 것을 의미하며, 이것이 매우 어렵기 때문에, 회사가 추가적인 용량을 갖는 것은 예측하지 못한 수요를 수용하기 위해서라고 볼 수 있습니다.

13 25학년도 9월 평가원 30번 (정답률 33%)

다음 글의 밑줄 친 부분 중, 문맥상 낱말의 쓰임이 적절하지 <u>않은</u> 것은?

We all like to think of ourselves as rational actors, careful and considered in our thinking, capable of sound and reliable judgments. We might believe that we generally consider different points of view and make ① <u>informed</u> decisions. We are, **in fact**, "predictably irrational," as psychologist Dan Ariely titled his book on the topic. All of us engage in automatic, reflexive thinking, typically taking the ② <u>easier</u> path and conserving mental effort. **Although** we each may have the subjective impression that we are careful thinkers, we often make snap judgments or no real judgments at all. In addition, numerous biases inhibit or override reflective, deliberative thought; intuitive theories can also interfere with ③ <u>acceptance</u> of accurate scientific explanations. Understanding more about how our minds work and how biases may operate can make us each ④ <u>less</u> subject to fallacious reasoning, more rational, and more aware of the problems in others' thinking. Learning to understand the built-in ⑤ <u>rationality</u> of our mental processes can also help us improve our ability to inform others more effectively.

* intuitive: 직관적인 ** fallacious: 오류가 있는

해설 [**정답** : ⑤]

Ⅵ번, Ⅶ번 문장에서 우리는 우리 마음에 내재된 편견과 직관 등을 이해하고 인식해야 더 합리적인 판단이 가능하다고 합니다. Ⅷ번 문장에서는 이를 재진술하여 마음에 내재된 편견과 직관을 이해하는 것이 우리가 다른 사람들에게 더 효과적으로 정보를 전달하는 능력을 키울 수 있다는 내용이 제시됩니다. 즉 Ⅷ번 문장에서 우리의 정신 과정에는 합리성이 아닌 편견과 직관과 같은 비합리성 혹은 한계가 내재되어 있으며, 이를 이해해야 한다는 것이므로 정답은 ⑤번이 됩니다.

* ④번을 41%의 학생들이 골랐습니다. ④번이 있는 Ⅶ번 문장은 Ⅵ번 문장에 이어 우리 마음에 있는 편견이나 직관을 이해하고 인식하는 것이 우리에게 좋은 영향을 끼칠 것이라는 내용이 제시될 것입니다. ④번에서 우리가 오류가 있는 추론에 덜 종속되게 된다. 즉, 우리가 오류가 있는 추론에 덜 빠지게 된다는 것은 오류를 범하지 않게 된다는 내용이므로 편견이나 직관을 이해하는 것이 긍정적인 영향을 끼친다고 합니다. 그러므로 ④번은 적절한 어휘입니다.

Ⅰ. We / all like to think of / ourselves as rational actors, (careful and considered in our thinking, capable of sound and reliable judgments).

구 ▶ 'think of A as B'는 'A를 B라고 간주하다'를 의미합니다.

- 우리는 모두 자신을 신중하고 사려 깊이 생각하며 타당하고 신뢰할 수 있는 판단을 내릴 수 있는 합리적인 행위자라고 간주하고 싶어한다고 합니다.

독 ▶ 우리는 스스로를 생각이 깊고 믿을 수 있는 합리적인 사람이라고 생각하고 싶어한다고 합니다.

Ⅱ. We / might believe that we / generally consider / different points of view and make / ① <u>informed</u> decisions.

> **구** 우리가 일반적으로 다양한 관점을 고려하고 정보에 입각한 결정을 만든다고 믿을 지도 모른다고 합니다.

> **독** 우리는 우리가 일반적으로 다양한 관점을 생각하고 근거를 통한 결정을 하는 것을 믿는다고 합니다.

Ⅲ. We / are, **in fact**, "predictably irrational," (as psychologist Dan Ariely / titled / his book on the topic).

> **구** 사실, 우리는 심리학자 Dan Ariely가 이 주제에 관한 자신의 책에 붙인 제목처럼 "예측할 수 있게 비합리적"이라고 합니다.

> **독** 'in fact'가 제시되었으므로 중심 문장
> - 우리는 예측할 수 있는 비합리적인 속성을 가지고 있다고 합니다.

Ⅳ. All of us / engage in / automatic, reflexive thinking, (typically taking the ② <u>easier</u> path and conserving mental effort).

> **구** 우리 모두는 자동적이고 반사적인 생각에 참여하며, 전형적으로 더 쉬운 길을 택하고 정신적 노력을 보존한다고 합니다.

> **독** 모든 사람들은 자동적이고 반사적으로 더 쉬운 길을 선택하고 정신적 노력을 안하는 길을 택한다고 합니다.

Ⅴ. **Although** we each / may have / the subjective impression (that we / are / careful thinkers), we / often make / snap judgments or no real judgments (at all).

> **구** 우리는 각자 자신이 신중하게 생각한다는 주관적 인상을 가질 수도 있지만, 우리는 순간적인 판단을 내리거나 실제 판단을 전혀 하지 않는 경우가 흔하다고 합니다.

> **독** 'Although'가 제시되었으므로 중심 문장
> - 우리는 우리 스스로가 생각하는 사람이라고 인식하지만, 실제로 우리는 성급한 판단을 내리거나 남의 판단을 따라가고 실제로는 판단을 하지 않는 경우가 있다고 합니다.

Ⅵ. In addition, numerous biases / inhibit or override / reflective, deliberative thought; intuitive theories / can also interfere with / ③ <u>acceptance</u> of accurate scientific explanations.

* intuitive: 직관적인

> **구** 게다가, 수많은 편견이 성찰적이고 신중한 사고를 억제하거나 무시하는데, 직관적인 이론도 정확한 과학적 설명의 수용을 간섭할 수도 있다고 합니다.

> **독** 우리가 가지고 있는 편견들이 우리의 성찰적이고 신중한 사고를 방해하며, 우리의 직관적인 이론 역시, 과학적인 설명을 수용함에 있어서 이를 방해할 수도 있다고 합니다.

VII. Understanding more about how our minds / work and how biases / may operate / can make / us / each ④ <u>less</u> subject to fallacious reasoning, more rational, and more aware of the problems (in others' thinking).

** fallacious: 오류가 있는

구 ▶ 'make + O + O.C'는 'O가 O.C하도록 만들다'를 의미합니다.

- 우리의 마음이 어떻게 작용하고 편견이 어떻게 작용할 수 있는지 더 많이 이해하는 것은 우리 각자가 오류가 있는 추론에 덜 종속되게 하고, 더 합리적이고 다른 사람의 사고의 문제점을 더 잘 인식하도록 만든다고 합니다.

독 ▶ Ⅵ번 문장에서 제시된 우리의 편견이나 직관이 어떻게 작용하는지를 이해해야, 우리가 오류를 덜 범하고 더 합리적으로 생각하며, 문제점을 더 잘 인식할 수 있다고 합니다.

VIII. Learning to understand the built-in ⑤ <u>rationality</u> of our mental processes / can also help / us / improve / our ability (to inform others more effectively).

구 ▶ 'help + O + O.C'는 'O가 O.C하도록 돕다'를 의미합니다.

- 우리의 정신 과정에 내재된 합리성을 (⇒ 비합리성을) 이해하는 것을 배우는 것은 우리가 다른 사람들에게 더 효과적으로 정보를 전달하는 능력을 향상하는 데 도움이 될 수 있다고 합니다.

독 ▶ Ⅵ번, Ⅶ번 문장에서 우리는 우리 마음에 내재된 편견과 직관 등을 이해하고 인식해야 더 합리적인 판단이 가능하다고 합니다. Ⅷ번 문장에서는 이를 재진술하여 마음에 내재된 편견과 직관을 이해하는 것이 우리가 다른 사람들에게 더 효과적으로 정보를 전달하는 능력을 키울 수 있다는 내용이 제시됩니다. 즉 Ⅷ번 문장에서 우리의 정신 과성에는 합리성이 아닌 편건과 직관과 같은 비힙리성 혹은 한계가 내재되어 있으며, 이를 이해해야 한다는 것이므로 정답은 ⑤번이 됩니다.

[01~02] 다음 글을 읽고, 물음에 답하시오.

Imagine grabbing a piece of paper between your thumb and index finger. Maybe you already are, as you turn this page. We use this type of forceful, pad-to-pad precision gripping without thinking about it, and literally in a snap. **Yet** it was a breakthrough in human evolution. Other primates exhibit some kinds of precision grips in the handling and use of objects, **but** not with the kind of (a) <u>efficient</u> opposition that our hand anatomy allows. In a single hand, humans can easily hold and manipulate objects, even small and delicate ones, **while** adjusting our fingers to their shape and reorienting them with (b) <u>displacements</u> of our fingertip pads. Our relatively long, powerful thumb and other anatomical attributes, including our flat nails (which nearly all primates possess), make this (c) <u>possible</u>. Just picture trying — and failing — to dog-ear this page with pointy, curved claws.

With a unique combination of traits, the human hand shaped our history. No question, stone tools couldn't have become a keystone of human technology and subsistence (d) <u>without</u> hands that could do the job, along with a nervous system that could regulate and coordinate the necessary signals. Anybody who's ever attempted to make a spear tip or arrowhead from a rock knows that it (e) <u>excludes</u> strong grips, constant rotation and repositioning, and forceful, careful strikes with another hard object. And even with a fair amount of know-how, it can be a bloody business.

* primate: 영장류 ** anatomy: 해부학 *** subsistence: 생계

01 25학년도 수능 41번   (정답률 67%)

윗글의 제목으로 가장 적절한 것은?

해설 [정답 : ②]

인간이 다른 영장류나 동물들에 비해 발달된 손에 의해서 발전하는 것에 대한 내용으로 도배가 되어있는 지문입니다. Ⅳ번 문장에서 효율적인 손을 가지는 것이 인류 발전의 돌파구라고 하였으며, Ⅸ번 문장에서는 인류의 손이 인류의 역사를 만들었다고 합니다. 주제를 파악하기 쉬운 지문입니다.

①번 선지 : 인간과 다른 영장류 사이의 해부학적 거리
- 영장류와는 달리 인간은 상대적으로 긴 엄지 손가락을 가지고 있다고 했습니다. 하지만 지문의 내용은 영장류와 달리 발달된 손에 의한 인류의 발전이라는 내용이므로 ①번 선지는 주제의 일부만 포함하고 있습니다. 즉, 포괄하지 않은 선지에 해당합니다.
②번 선지 : 인간의 손: 진화 경로의 결정적 도약
- 정답입니다.
③번 선지 : 우리의 손 : 예상하지 못한 진화의 결과
- 14%의 수험생들이 고른 선지입니다. 우리의 손이 발달된 것을 예상하였는지, 예상하지 못했는지에 관한 내용이 지문에 없습니다. 또한 지문에서 손이 진화의 돌파구가 되었다며, 진화와 손에 관한 내용이 제시되었지만 진화된 지문의 손에 의한 인류의 역사와 발전에 대해서는 선지에서 제시되지 않았습니다. 즉 포괄하지 않은 선지에 해당합니다.
④번 선지 : 인류의 그립 : 인류 생존의 딜레마
- 딜레마가 없습니다.
⑤번 선지 : 도구의 일상적 사용에 숨겨진 힘
- 무관한 선지입니다.

밑줄 친 (a) ~ (e) 중에서 문맥상 낱말의 쓰임이 적절하지 <u>않은</u> 것은?

해설 [정답 : ⑤]

Ⅴ번과 Ⅵ번 문장을 통해서 우리는 다른 영장류들과 달리 상대적으로 길고 강한 엄지를 통해서 효율적인 그립이 가능하다는 것을 알 수 있습니다. 이는 Ⅹ번 문장에서 손이 없으면 석기를 사용할 수 없다는 내용으로 이어집니다. Ⅺ번 문장에서는 Ⅴ, Ⅵ번 문장의 효율적인 그립을 구체화하여 강한 그립, 지속적인 회전과, 재배치, 그리고 다른 단단한 물체로의 강하고 조심스러운 충돌이라고 제시하므로 이는 석기를 사용하기 위해 필요한 것입니다. 그러므로 (e)의 'excludes'를 'requires', '요구하다'로 바꾸어야 합니다. 그래서 정답은 ⑤번이 됩니다.

Ⅰ. Imagine grabbing / a piece of paper (between your thumb and index finger).

> 구 'between A and B'는 'A와 B 사이'를 의미합니다.
> - 너의 엄지 손가락과 집게 손가락 사이에 한 장의 종이를 쥐는 것을 상상해보라고 합니다.

> 독 종이를 손가락으로 잡는 것을 상상해 보라고 합니다.

Ⅱ. Maybe you / already are, as you / turn / this page.

> 구 아마도 너는 이 페이지를 넘기면서 하고 있을지도 모른다고 합니다.

> 독 페이지를 넘기면서 이미 손가락으로 종이를 잡고 있을지도 모른다고 합니다.

Ⅲ. We / use / this type of forceful, pad-to-pad precision gripping (without thinking about it, and literally in a snap).

> 구 우리는 이러한 유형의 힘을 쓰는 손가락 끝 살이 맞닿는 정밀하게 쥐는 법을 그것에 대한 (= 쥐는 법에 대한) 생각 없이 글자 그대로 순식간에 사용한다고 합니다.

> 독 종이를 손가락으로 잡는 것은 어떠한 생각 없이 순식간에 이루어 진다고 합니다.

Ⅳ. Yet it / was / a breakthrough in human evolution.

> 구 그러나 그것은 (= 손가락으로 종이를 잡는 것은) 인류의 발전에서 돌파구였다고 합니다.

> 독 'Yet'이 제시되었으므로 앞 뒷 문장 중심 문장
> - 이러한 손가락으로 잡는 것이 인류 발전의 킥이었다고 합니다.

Ⅴ. Other primates / exhibit / some kinds of precision grips (in the handling and use of objects), **but** not with the kind of (a) <u>efficient</u> opposition (that our hand anatomy / allows).

* primate: 영장류 ** anatomy: 해부학

구▶ 다른 영장류들은 물건을 다루고 사용함에 있어서 몇 가지 종류의 정확한 그립을 보여주지만 우리 손의 해부학이 허락하는 효율적인 맞대음이 (= 손가락끼리의 맞대음이) 아니라고 합니다.

독▶ 'but'이 제시되었으므로 중심 문장
- 침팬지나 원숭이 등 다른 영장류들도 그립을 할 수는 있지만 인류만큼 효율적인 그립은 하지 못한다고 합니다.

Ⅵ. (In a single hand), humans / can easily hold and manipulate / objects, (even small and delicate ones), **while** adjusting / our fingers / to their shape and reorienting them (with (b) <u>displacements</u> of our fingertip pads).

구▶ 'adjust A to B'는 'A를 B에 맞춰 조정하다'를 의미합니다.
- 한손으로, 인류는 심지어 작고 섬세하다 하더라도 물건을 쉽게 잡고 조작할 수 있으며, 우리의 손가락을 그들의 (= 물건들의) 모양에 맞춰 조정하고 우리의 손가락 살 부분의 이동으로 그것들의 (= 물건들의) 방향을 바꿀 수도 있다고 합니다.

독▶ 'while'이 제시되었으므로 중심 문장
- 인류는 손쉽게 물건들을 한손으로 잡고 조작할 수 있으며, 우리의 손가락을 물건의 모양에 맞춰 조절하거나 손가락을 이용하여 물건들의 방향도 바꿀 수 있다고 합니다. 이는 Ⅴ번 문장에서 제시된 인류가 할 수 있는 효율적인 그립에 대한 구체적인 진술에 해당합니다.

* re (다시) + orient (방향) = reorient – 다시 방향을 설정하다, 방향을 바꾸다.

* dis (흩어지는) + place (장소, 두다) = displace – 옮기다.

Ⅶ. Our relatively long, powerful thumb and other anatomical attributes, (including our flat nails (which nearly all primates possess)), make / this / (c) <u>possible</u>.

* primate: 영장류 ** anatomy: 해부학

구▶ 'make + O + O.C'는 'O가 O.C하도록 만들다'를 의미합니다.
- 우리의 상대적으로 길고 강력한 엄지 손가락과 (거의 모든 영장류가 소유한) 우리의 평평한 손톱을 포함한 다른 해부학적 속성들이 그것을 (= 효율적인 그립을) 가능하게 만든다고 합니다.

독▶ 대부분의 영장류들이 가지고 있는 우리의 평평한 손톱을 포함한 해부학적 특징들과 다른 영장류들에 비해 길고 강력한 엄지들이 인류가 효율적인 그립을 할 수 있도록 만든다고 합니다.

Ⅷ. Just picture trying — and failing — to dog-ear / this page (with pointy, curved claws).

구▶ 'dog-ear'이 'to-V'로 동사로 사용되었습니다. '개의 귀'를 동사로 생각하면 '개의 귀처럼 만들다'로 생각할 수 있고, 문장 안에서 '이 페이지를 개의 귀처럼 만들다'를 생각하면 개의 귀가 접히듯이 '모서리를 접다.'의 뜻이 됩니다. 시험장에서는 추론이 불가능하고 넘어가야 하는 단어가 아닐까 싶습니다.
- 끝이 뾰족하고 굽은 발톱으로 이 페이지의 모서리를 접으려다가 실패하는 모습을 생각해보라고 합니다.

독▶ 영장류가 가지는 평평한 손톱이 아닌 뾰족하고 굽은 발톱으로는 페이지의 모서리를 접을 수 없다는 내용을 제시합니다.

Ⅸ. (With a unique combination of traits), the human hand / shaped / our history.

구▶ 고유한 특성의 조합으로, 인류의 손은 인류의 역사를 만들었다고 합니다.

독▶ 모든 영장류가 가지고 있는 평평한 손톱과 인류만이 가지고 있는 길고 강한 엄지를 통해서 인류의 역사가 만들어졌다고 합니다.

Ⅹ. No question, stone tools / couldn't have become / a keystone of human technology and subsistence (d) <u>without</u> hands (that could do / the job), (along with a nervous system (that could regulate and coordinate / the necessary signals)).

*** subsistence: 생계

구▶ 의심할 여지 없이, 필요한 신호를 조절하고 조정할 수 있는 신경계와 함께, 그 일을 할 수 있는 손이 없었다면 돌 도구는 (= 석기는) 인간의 기술과 생계의 핵심이 될 수 없었다고 합니다.

독▶ 손을 조절할 수 있는 신경계와 함께 일을 할 수 있게 해주는 손이 없었다면, 석기가 인류의 기술과 생계의 핵심이 될 수 없었다고 합니다. 즉, 손이 있어서 인류가 석기를 사용할 수 있었다고 합니다.

Ⅺ. Anybody (who's ever attempted to make / a spear tip or arrowhead from a rock) / knows / that it / (e) <u>excludes</u> / strong grips, constant rotation and repositioning, and forceful, careful strikes (with another hard object).

구▶ 돌로 창이나 화살촉을 만들려고 시도하는 누구라도 그것이 (= 돌로 만든 창이나 화살촉이) 강한 그립, 지속적인 회전과, 재배치, 그리고 다른 단단한 물체로의 강하고 조심스러운 충돌을 배제하는 것을 (⇒ 요구한다는 것을) 안다고 합니다.

독▶ 돌로 만든 창이나 화살촉, 즉, 석기들을 위해서는 강한 그립이나 지속적인 회전 등의 효율적인 그립과 정교한 손이 있어야 한다고 합니다.

Ⅻ. And even with a fair amount of know-how, it / can be / a bloody business.

구▶ 그리고 상당한 정도의 요령을 가지고서도, 이것은 피가 흐르는 사업이 될 수 있다고 합니다.

독▶ 돌로 만든 창이나 화살촉에 대해서 잘 다룬다고 하더라도, 석기를 다루는 작업이 어렵다고 합니다. 즉, 효율적인 손을 가지고 있는 인간도 어려운데, 효율적인 손을 가지지 못하는 영장류나 손이 발달하지 않은 다른 동물들은 석기를 다룰 수 없다는 것을 의미합니다.

Classifying things together into groups is something we do all the time, and it isn't hard to see why. Imagine trying to shop in a supermarket where the food was arranged in random order on the shelves: tomato soup next to the white bread in one aisle, chicken soup in the back next to the 60-watt light bulbs, one brand of cream cheese in front and another in aisle 8 near the cookies. The task of finding what you want would be (a) <u>time-consuming</u> and extremely difficult, if not impossible. In the case of a supermarket, someone **had to** (b) <u>design</u> the system of classification. But there is also a ready-made system of classification embodied in our language. The word "dog," **for example**, groups together a certain class of animals and distinguishes them from other animals. Such a grouping may seem too (c) <u>abstract</u> to be called a classification, **but** this is only **because** you have already mastered the word. As a child learning to speak, you **had to** work hard to (d) <u>learn</u> the system of classification your parents were trying to teach you. Before you got the hang of it, you probably made mistakes, like calling the cat a dog. If you hadn't learned to speak, the whole world would seem like the (e) <u>unorganized</u> supermarket; you would be in the position of an infant, for whom every object is new and unfamiliar. In learning the principles of classification, **therefore**, we'll be learning about the structure that lies at the core of our language.

03 22학년도 수능 41번   (정답률 65%)

윗글의 제목으로 가장 적절한 것은?

해설 [정답 : ②]

①번 선지 : 영업과 언어 학습 전략의 유사성
 - 언어 학습에 대한 의의를 제시하고 있지 언어 학습 전략에 대해서는 언급되지 않았습니다.

②번 선지 : 분류: 언어의 본질적 특성
 - XI번 문장에서 분류가 언어의 중심에 있는 구조라고 했고, 언어에서 분류의 체계가 중요하다고 했으므로 정답 선지입니다.

③번 선지 : 범주화를 통한 언어학적 문제의 탐색
 - 범주화가 분류와 같은 말이지만 지문에서는 언어학적 문제에 대해서 제시되지 않았습니다. 언급되지 않은 선지입니다.

④번 선지 : 이미 존재하는 분류 시스템이 정말 더 나은가?
 - 분류 체계를 비교하지 않았습니다. 언급되지 않은 선지입니다.

⑤번 선지 : 언어 교육에서 분류 활용의 딜레마
 - 딜레마가 제시되기 위해서는 장점과 단점 모두 제시되어야 합니다. 하지만 언어 교육의 단점이 제시되지 않았습니다.

밑줄 친 (a) ~ (e) 중에서 문맥상 낱말의 쓰임이 적절하지 <u>않은</u> 것은?

해설 [정답 : ③]

Ⅴ번 문장에서 우리 언어에도 이미 만들어진 분류 체계가 있다고 합니다. Ⅵ번 문장에서는 이에 대한 예시로 '강아지'라는 단어를 제시하며 단어를 통해서 다른 동물들과 구별할 수 있다고 합니다. 즉, 단어로 그룹을 구성함으로써 다른 동물들과 구별할 수 있다고 합니다. 그러므로 Ⅶ번 문장에서는 단어에 숙달했기 때문에, 너무 추상적이여서 그룹짓는 것을 분류라고 부를 수 없다는 것이 아닌 너무 당연해서 분류라고 부를 수 없는 것이 됩니다. 그래서 'abstract'를 'obvious'로 바꾸어야 합니다.

Ⅰ. Classifying / things together (into groups) / is / something (we / do / all the time), and it / isn't / hard / to see why.

> 구 ▶ 'classify A into B'는 'A를 B로 분류하다'를 의미합니다.
> - 'It + be동사 + 형용사 + to-V'는 가주어/진주어입니다.
> - 사물들을 함께 그룹으로 분류하는 것은 우리가 항상 하는 것이고, 그 이유를 보는 것을 어렵지 않다고 합니다.

Ⅱ. Imagine / trying to shop (in a supermarket) (where the food / was arranged (in random order) (on the shelves): tomato soup **(A)** (next to the white bread in one aisle), chicken soup **(B)** (in the back next to the 60-watt light bulbs), one brand of cream cheese **(C)** (in front) and another **(D)** (in aisle 8 near the cookies).

> 구 ▶ 'A, B, C, and D' 병렬구조로 제시되었습니다.
> - 음식이 무작위 순서로 선반에 배치되어있는 슈퍼마켓에서 쇼핑을 하려고 한다고 생각해 봐라, 토마토 수프는 흰 빵 옆에 있고, 치킨 수프는 뒤 쪽에 있는 60와트 전구 옆에 있고, 한 크림치즈 브랜드는 앞 쪽에, 또 다른 하나는 쿠키 근처의 8번 통로에 있다고 합니다.

> 독 ▶ 음식들이 그룹으로 분류되어 있지 않은 슈퍼마켓을 예시로 들고 있습니다.

Ⅲ. The task of finding (what you / want) / would be / (a) <u>time-consuming</u> and extremely difficult, if not impossible.

> 구 ▶ 네가 원하는 것을 찾는 업무는 불가능하지 않더라도 시간이 많이 걸리고 극도로 어려울 것이라고 합니다.

> 독 ▶ 그룹으로 분류되지 않은 슈퍼마켓에서 원하는 것을 찾는 것은 시간이 오래 걸리고 어렵다고 합니다.

Ⅳ. (In the case of a supermarket), someone / **had to** (b) design / the system of classification.

> 구▶ 슈퍼마켓의 경우에서, 누군가는 반드시 분류의 체계를 설계해야만 한다고 합니다.

> 독▶ 'had to'가 제시되었으니 중심 문장
> - 분류가 되지 않으면, 시간이 오래걸리고 어렵기 때문에, 분류의 체계가 설계되어야만 한다고 합니다.

Ⅴ. **But** there / is also / a ready-made system of classification (embodied in our language).

> 구▶ 그러나, 또한 우리의 언어에 구체화되어 있는 이미 만들어진 분류의 체계가 있다고 합니다.

> 독▶ 'But'이 제시되었으니 앞 뒷 문장 중심 문장
> - 언어에서도 분류의 체계가 있다고 합니다.

Ⅵ. The word "dog," **for example**, / groups together / a certain class of animals and distinguishes / them / from other animals.

> 구▶ 'distinguish + A + from B'는 'A를 B로부터 분류하다'를 의미합니다.
> - "강아지"라는 단어는 특정한 부류의 동물들을 같이 그룹짓고 다른 동물로부터 그들을 (= 강아지로 그룹지어진 동물들을) 분류한다고 합니다.

> 독▶ 'for example'이 제시되었으니 앞 문장 중심 문장
> - 언어에 있는 분류의 체계에 대한 예시로 강아지를 제시하고 있습니다.

Ⅶ. Such a grouping / may seem (too (c) abstract) to be called / a classification, **but** this / is only **because** you / have already mastered / the word.

> 구▶ 'too + 형용사 + to-V'는 '너무 형용사해서 V하기 힘들다'로 해석하시면 됩니다.
> - 'call + O + O.C'는 'O를 O.C라고 부르다'를 의미합니다. 이 문장에서는 수동태로 제시되어 'be called + O.C' 형태로 제시되었습니다.
> - 그러한 분류는 너무 추상적이여서 (⇒ 구체적이여서) 분류라고 부르기 힘든 것처럼 보이지만, 그것은 오직 네가 이미 단어에 숙달했기 때문이라고 합니다.

> 독▶ 'but, because'가 제시되었으니 중심 문장

Ⅷ. As a child learning (to speak), you / **had to work** / hard (to (d) learn / the system of classification (your parents / were trying to teach / you).

> 구▶ 'teach + I.O + D.O'는 'I.O에게 D.O를 가르치다'를 의미합니다. 이 문장에서는 관계 대명사가 생략된 형태로 원래 문장은 'teach you classification'이라고 생각하시면 됩니다.
> - 아이들이 말하는 것을 배우는 것처럼, 너는 너의 부모가 너에게 가르치려고 노력한 분류의 체계를 배우기 위해서 노력을 해야만 했다고 합니다.

> 독▶ 'had to'가 제시되었으니 중심 문장
> - 언어의 분류 체계를 배우기 위해서 우리는 많은 노력을 했다고 합니다.

Ⅸ. Before you / got / the hang of it, you / probably made / mistakes, like calling / the cat / a dog.

> 구▶ 'call + O + O.C'는 'O를 O.C라고 부르다'로 해석하시면 됩니다.
> - 너가 그것을 이해하기 전에, 너는 아마도 고양이를 강아지라고 부르는 것과 같은 실수를 했을 것이라고 합니다.

> * get the hang of A - A를 이해하다.

Ⅹ. If you / hadn't learned to speak, / the whole world / would seem like / the (e) unorganized supermarket; you / would be (in the position of an infant), for whom every object / is / new and unfamiliar.

> 구▶ 너가 배우지 않았다면, 전체 세계는 조직되지 않은 (= 분류되지 않은) 슈퍼마켓처럼 보였을 것이고, 너는 아이의 위치에서 모든 사물들이 새롭고 친숙하지 않았을 것이라고 합니다.

> 독▶ 언어의 분류 체계를 배우지 않았다면, 세계를 어린아이처럼 새롭고 친숙하지 않게 인식했을 것이라고 합니다.

Ⅺ. (In learning / the principles of classification), **therefore**, we'll be learning / (about the structure) (that lies (at the core of our language)).

> 구▶ 'In + V-ing'는 'V함에 있어서'를 의미합니다.
> - 그러므로 분류의 원리를 배움에 있어서, 우리는 우리 언어의 중심에 놓여있는 구조에 대해서 배우고 있는 것이라고 합니다.

> 독▶ 'therefore'이 제시되었으므로 중심 문장
> - 언어의 분류 체계를 배우지 않으면 세계를 낯설게 바라보기 때문에, 분류의 원리를 배우는 것이 우리 언어의 중심에 놓여있는 구조를 배우는 것이라고 합니다.

[05~06] 다음 글을 읽고, 물음에 답하시오.

Our irresistible tendency to see things in human terms—that we are often mistaken in attributing complex human motives and processing abilities to other species— does not mean that an animal's behavior is not, **in fact**, complex. **Rather**, it means that the complexity of the animal's behavior is not purely a (a) <u>product</u> of its internal complexity. Herbert Simon's "parable of the ant" makes this point very clearly. Imagine an ant walking along a beach, and (b) <u>visualize</u> tracking the trajectory of the ant as it moves. The trajectory would show a lot of twists and turns, and would be very irregular and complicated. One could then suppose that the ant had equally complicated (c) <u>internal</u> navigational abilities, and work out what these were likely to be by analyzing the trajectory to infer the rules and mechanisms that could produce such a complex navigational path. The complexity of the trajectory, **however**, "is really a complexity in the surface of the beach, not a complexity in the ant." **In reality**, the ant may be using a set of very (d) <u>complex</u> rules: it is the interaction of these rules with the environment that actually produces the complex trajectory, not the ant alone. **Put more generally**, the parable of the ant illustrates that there is no necessary correlation between the complexity of an (e) <u>observed</u> behavior and the complexity of the mechanism that produces it.

* parable: 우화 ** trajectory: 이동 경로

05 21학년도 수능 41번 (정답률 58%)

윗글의 제목으로 가장 적절한 것은?

해설 [정답 : ③]

인간의 관점에서 보면 동물의 행동이 복잡성을 띠고 동물의 내적이 복잡하다고 생각되지만 실제로는 그것이 아니라, 복잡한 환경과 상호작용하는 동물의 단순한 규칙이 동물의 행동을 복잡한 것처럼 보이게 만든다는 내용으로 재진술된 지문입니다.

①번 선지 : 환경의 복잡성에 이르는 신비의 문을 열라!
- 지문에서 동물의 행동이 복잡한 것에 대해서 제시하지 환경의 복잡성에 대해서 제시하지 않으므로 포괄하지 않는 선지에 해당합니다.
②번 선지 : 인간과 동물의 평화로운 공존 - 무관한 선지입니다.
③번 선지 : 무엇이 동물 행동의 복잡성을 만드는가?
- 동물 행동의 복잡성은 동물이 복잡한 것이 아니라 동물과 환경간의 상호작용으로 인해서 만들어진다고 하므로 정답 선지입니다.
④번 선지 : 동물의 딜레마: 인간 세계에서 자신의 길을 찾아가기
- 동물의 복잡성의 원인에 대한 내용이 동물의 딜레마로 보일 수 있으나 인간 세계에서 동물이 자신의 길을 찾아가는 내용은 무관합니다.
⑤번 선지 : 인간 행동 복잡성에 미치는 환경의 영향
- 환경 ⇒ 동물에 미치는 영향 ⇒ 인간이 동물 행동의 복잡성을 확인함이 지문의 내용이지 환경 ⇒ 인간 행동의 복잡성이 아니므로 오답 선지입니다.

밑줄 친 (a) ~ (e) 중에서 문맥상 낱말의 쓰임이 적절하지 <u>않은</u> 것은?

해설 [정답 : ④]

(d)가 포함된 문장 앞 문장에서 이동 경로의 복잡성 (동물 행동의 복잡성)은 해변 지면 (환경)의 복잡성이지 개미 (동물) 자체의 복잡성이 아니라고 합니다. (d)가 포함된 문장은 'In reality'를 통해서 이 문장을 재진술하므로 개미가 이용하는 규칙은 'complex', '복잡한'것이 아닌 반댓말인 'simple', '단순한'것이여야 함을 알 수 있습니다.

Ⅰ. Our irresistible tendency (to see / things in human terms) — (that we / are often mistaken / in attributing complex human motives and processing abilities (to other species)) — / does not mean / that an animal's behavior / is / not, **in fact**, complex.

> 구 'in V-ing'는 'V함에 있어서'를 의미합니다.
> - 'attribute A to B'는 'A를 B의 탓으로 돌리다'를 뜻합니다.
> - 인간의 관점에서 사물을 보는 우리의 저항할 수 없는 경향, 즉 우리가 복잡한 인간의 동기와 처리하는 능력을 다른 종들에게 탓함에 있어서 (=원인을 찾는데 있어서) 실수하는 것은 실제로 동물의 행동이 복잡하지 않다는 것을 의미하지 않는다고 합니다.

> 독 'in fact'가 제시되었으므로 중심 문장
> - 복잡한 인간의 동기와 처리하는 능력을 다른 종들에게 탓하는 것 (= 인간의 행동이 복잡한 것)이 동물의 행동은 복잡하지 않다는 것을 의미하는 것이 아니라고 합니나.

Ⅱ. **Rather**, it / means / that the complexity of the animal's behavior / is not purely / a (a) <u>product</u> (of its internal complexity).

> 구 오히려, 그것은 동물 행동의 복잡성이 순전히 동물의 내적 복잡성의 산물이 아니라는 의미라고 합니다.

> 독 'Rather'이 제시되었으므로 중심 문장
> - 동물의 행동이 복잡하지 않다는 것을 의미하는 것이 아닌 동물 행동의 복잡성이 내적 복잡성의 산물이 아니라는 것을 의미한다고 합니다.

Ⅲ. Herbert Simon's "parable of the ant" / makes / this point very clearly.

* parable: 우화

> 구 Herber Simon의 "개미 우화"는 이 관점을 매우 분명하게 만든다고 합니다.

Ⅳ. Imagine / an ant (walking along a beach), and (b) <u>visualize</u> / tracking the trajectory of the ant (as it moves).

** trajectory: 이동 경로

> 구 개미 한 마리가 해변을 따라 걷는 것을 상상하고, 그 개미가 이동함에 따라 그 이동 경로를 추적하는 것을 시각화 해보라고 합니다.

* visual (시각의) + -ize (~화 하다) = visualize - 시각화하다

Ⅴ. The trajectory / would show / a lot of twists and turns, and would be / very irregular and complicated.

　　[구] 그 이동 경로는 많은 뒤틀림과 전환을 보여주고 매우 불규칙적이며 복잡할 것이라고 합니다.

Ⅵ. One / could then suppose / that the ant / had equally complicated / (c) internal navigational abilities, and (suppose와 work out을 연결) work out / what these / were likely to be (by analyzing the trajectory) (to infer / the rules and mechanisms (that could produce / such a complex navigational path)).

　　[구] 'by V-ing'는 'V함으로써'를 의미합니다.
　　　- 그러면 누군가는 그 개미가 동등하게 복잡한 내적 항해 능력을 가지고 있다고 가정하고, 그런 복잡한 항해 경로를 만들어 낼 수 있는 규칙과 체계를 추론하기 위해서 그 이동 경로를 분석함으로써 이것이 무엇일 수 있는지를 알 수 있을 것이라고 합니다.

Ⅶ. The complexity of the trajectory, **however**, "is really / a complexity (in the surface of the beach), not a complexity in the ant."

　　[구] 하지만, 이동 경로의 복잡성은 "실제로 해변 지면에서의 복잡성이지 개미 안에서의 복잡성이 아니다"라고 합니다.

　　[독] 'however'가 제시되었으므로 앞 뒷 문장 중심 문장
　　　- 개미가 복잡한 항해 경로를 만들어 낼 수 있는 복잡한 능력이 있을 것이라고 가정하지만, 실제로는 해변이 복잡한 것이지 개미가 (개미의 내적) 복잡한 것이 아니라고 합니다.

Ⅷ. **In reality**, the ant / may be using / a set of very (d) complex rules: it / is / the interaction (of these rules) (with the environment) (that actually produces / the complex trajectory), not the ant alone.

　　[구] 사실, 그 개미는 일련의 매우 복잡한 규칙을 사용하는 데, 그것은 개미 혼자서가 아닌 복잡한 이동경로를 만들어 내는 환경과의 상호작용에 대한 규칙이라고 합니다.

　　[독] 'In reality'는 '실제로'를 뜻하며 'In fact'와 같은 의미이므로 재진술을 하는 중심 문장
　　　- 실제로, 복잡한 이동 경로를 만드는 환경과의 상호 작용의 규칙인 복잡한 (⇒ 단순한) 규칙을 사용한다고 합니다.

Ⅸ. **Put more generally**, the parable of the ant / illustrates / that there / is / no necessary correlation (between the complexity of an (e) observed behavior and the complexity of the mechanism that produces it).

　　[구] '(co)relation between A and B'는 'A와 B의 (상관) 관계'를 의미합니다.
　　　- 더 일반적으로, 개미 우화는 관찰된 행동의 복잡성과 복잡한 행동을 만들어 내는 체계의 복잡성 사이의 필연적인 상관관계가 없음을 설명한다고 합니다.

　　[독] 'Put more generally'는 '더 일반적으로 말하면'을 의미하므로 재진술의 표현 중심 문장
　　　- 즉, 행동의 복잡성과 그것을 만들어내는 체계의 복잡성 (개미의 내적 복잡성)간의 필연적인 상관관계는 없다고 합니다.

The right to privacy may extend only to the point where it does not restrict someone else's right to freedom of expression or right to information. The scope of the right to privacy is (a) <u>similarly</u> restricted by the general interest in preventing crime or in promoting public health. **However**, when we move away from the property-based notion of a right (where the right to privacy would protect, **for example**, images and personality), to modern notions of private and family life, we find it (b) <u>easier</u> to establish the limits of the right. This is, of course, the strength of the notion of privacy, in that it can adapt to meet changing expectations and technological advances.

In sum, *what* is privacy today? The concept includes a claim that we should be unobserved, and that certain information and images about us **should** not be (c) <u>circulated</u> without our permission. *Why* did these privacy claims arise? They arose **because** powerful people took offence at such observation. Furthermore, privacy incorporated the need to protect the family, home, and correspondence from arbitrary (d) <u>interference</u> and, in addition, there has been a determination to protect honour and reputation. *How* is privacy protected? Historically, privacy was protected by restricting circulation of the damaging material. **But** if the concept of privacy first became interesting legally as a response to reproductions of images through photography and newspapers, more recent technological advances, such as data storage, digital images, and the Internet, (e) <u>pose</u> new threats to privacy. The right to privacy is now being reinterpreted to meet those challenges.

* arbitrary: 임의의

07 22학년도 6월 평가원 41번 　　　　　　　　　　　　　　　　(정답률 70%)

윗글의 제목으로 가장 적절한 것은?

해설 [정답 : ③]

첫 번째 문단에서 사생활의 범위를 설정하는 것은 어렵다고 하며, 두 번째 문단에서는 전통적으로 설정된 사생활의 개념이 현대로 오면서 다양한 요구가 생기고 새로운 기술로 인한 위협으로 인해서 변화한다고 합니다. 두 문단을 연결하면 사생활은 변화하고 있다는 문맥을 알 수 있습니다. 단문 주제 같은 경우 모든 문단을 포괄해야 합니다.

①번 선지 : 사생활 보호 기술들의 부작용
　　- 사생활 보호 기술들에 대한 내용이 제시되지 않았으므로 무관한 선지입니다.
②번 선지 : 사생활 주장에 대한 법적 영역과 충돌들
　　- 사생활의 범위를 설정하는 것은 어렵다는 내용이 첫 번째 문단에서 제시되었으나 법적으로 어떻게 어렵고 이로 인한 갈등이 발생하는 지에 대한 내용은 제시되지 않았습니다. 언급되지 않은 선지에 해당합니다.
③번 선지 : 사생활에 대한 권리: 발전하는 개념들과 실행들
　　- 사생활에 대한 개념이 현대에 맞게 변화하고 있다고 하므로 정답 선지에 해당합니다.
④번 선지 : 느슨한 사생활 규제로부터 누가 진짜로 이득을 얻는가?
　　- 질문 선지는 질문에 대한 답이 지문에서 제시되어야 합니다. 하지만 사생활에 이득을 얻는 사람에 대한 내용이 제시되어있지 않습니다. 또한 사생활 규제가 느슨하다는 내용도 제시되지 않았으므로 무관한 선지입니다.
⑤번 선지 : 적은 것이 많은 것이다: 사생활에 대한 국가의 개입을 줄여라! - 무관한 선지입니다.

밑줄 친 (a) ~ (e) 중에서 문맥상 낱말의 쓰임이 적절하지 <u>않은</u> 것은?

해설 [**정답 :** ②]

Ⅰ번, Ⅱ번 문장에서 사생활의 권리가 제한된다고 합니다. Ⅲ번 문장에서 사생활의 권리가 쉽다는 내용이 전개될 경우 Ⅰ번, Ⅱ번 문장과 같은 내용이 제시되기 때문에 'However'을 통해서 Ⅰ번, Ⅱ번과 역접을 이룰 수 없습니다. 그러므로 'easier'이 아닌 'harder'과 같은 내용이 제시되어야 합니다.

Ⅰ. The right (to privacy) / may extend only to / the point (where it / does not restrict /

someone else's right to freedom of expression or right to information).

> **구▶** 사생활에 대한 권리는 다른 사람의 표현의 자유에 대한 권리나 정보에 대한 권리를 제한하지 않는 정도까지만 확대될 수 있다고 합니다.

Ⅱ. The scope (of the right to privacy) / is (a) <u>similarly</u> restricted (by the general interest (in

preventing crime or in promoting public health)).

> **구▶** 'in V-ing'는 'V함에 있어서'를 의미합니다.
> - 사생활에 대한 권리의 범위는 범죄를 예방하거나 공공의 건강을 증진함에 있어서 일반적인 이익에 의해서 제한된다고 합니다.

> **독▶** Ⅰ번 문장에서 제시된 사생활에 대한 권리가 제한되는 것을 구체적으로 보여주고 있습니다.

Ⅲ. **However**, when we / move away / from the property-based notion (of a right) (where the right to

privacy / would protect, **for example**, images and personality), / to modern notions (of private and

family life), we / find / it / (b) <u>easier</u> / to establish the limits of the right.

> **구▶** 'from A to B'는 'A부터 B까지'를 의미합니다.
> - 'find (5형식 동사) + it + 형용사 + to-V'는 가목적어/진목적어입니다.
> - 하지만, 우리가 속성에 기반을 둔 권리 개념에서 (예를 들어, 사생활에 대한 권리가 이미지와 인격을 보호할 개념) 사생활과 가족의 생활이라는 현대적 개념으로 옮겨갈 때, 우리는 그 권리의 한계를 (= 사생활 권리의 한계를) 설정하기 쉽다는 것을 (⇒ 어렵다는 것을) 알게 된다고 합니다.

> **독▶** 'However', 'for example'이 제시되었으므로 중심 문장
> - 사생활 권리의 개념이 현대적 개념으로 옮겨갈 때, 한계를 설정하는 것이 어렵다고 합니다.
> - Ⅰ번, Ⅱ번 문장에서 사생활의 권리가 제한된다고 합니다. Ⅲ번 문장에서 사생활의 권리가 쉽다는 내용이 전개될 경우 Ⅰ번, Ⅱ번 문장과 같은 내용이 제시되기 때문에 'However'을 통해서 Ⅰ번, Ⅱ번과 역접을 이룰 수 없습니다. 그러므로 'easier'이 아닌 'harder'과 같은 내용이 제시되어야 합니다.

Ⅳ. This / is, (of course), / the strength of the notion of privacy, / in that it / can adapt to meet / changing expectations and technological advances.

> 구 ▶ 'in that S V'는 'S가 V라는 점에서'를 의미합니다.
> - 물론, 이것은 (= 사생활 권리의 한계가 어렵다는 것은) 변화하는 기대와 기술 진보에 충족하기 위해 적응할 수 있다는 점에서 사생활 개념의 장점이라고 합니다.

> * 'Of course'는 '물론'을 뜻하므로 반론에 대하여 설명합니다. 문법적인 요소로 양보절이지만 'Of course'가 제시되면 정보를 나열한다고만 생각하시면 됩니다.

Ⅴ. In sum, *what* is privacy today? The concept / includes / a claim (that we / **should be unobserved)**, / and that certain information and images (about us) / **should** not be (c) circulated (without our permission).

> 구 ▶ 요컨대, 오늘날 사생활은 무엇인가? 그 개념은 (= 사생활은) 우리는 관찰되지 않아야 한다는 것과 우리에 대한 특정한 정보가 우리의 허락 없이는 순환되지 않아야만 한다는 (= 유포되지 않는다는) 주장을 포함한다고 합니다.

> 독 ▶ 'should'가 제시되었으므로 중심 문장
> - 사생활이란 우리의 허락 없이는 우리를 관찰할 수 없고 우리의 정보를 남에게 알릴 수 없다는 것을 의미한다고 합니다.

Ⅵ. *Why* did these privacy claims / arise? They / arose / **because** powerful people / took / offence (at such observation).

> 구 ▶ 왜 이러한 시생활이 발생했을까? 그들은 (= 사생활에 대한 개념은) 강력한 사람들이 그러한 관찰에서 공격적이었기 (= 불쾌했기) 때문이라고 합니다.

> 독 ▶ 'because'가 제시되었으므로 중심 문장
> - 사람들이 관찰될 때 불쾌함을 느끼기 때문에 사생활이라는 개념이 등장했다고 합니다.

Ⅶ. Furthermore, privacy / incorporated / the need (to protect / the family, home, and correspondence) (from arbitrary (d) interference) and, in addition, there has been / a determination (to protect / honour and reputation).

* arbitrary: 임의의

> 구 ▶ 'protect A from B'는 'A를 B로부터 지키다'를 의미합니다.
> - 게다가, 사생활은 가족, 가정, 그리고 상응을 임의의 간섭으로부터 지킬 필요를 구현하였고, 추가적으로, 명예와 평판을 보호하려는 결심이 있었다고 합니다.

> 독 ▶ 사생활은 가족, 가정을 임의의 간섭으로부터 지키고 명예와 평판을 지키려는 필요에 의해서 발생했다고 합니다.

*   determination - 결심
**   honour - 명예
*** reputation - 평판

Ⅷ. *How* is privacy protected? Historically, privacy / was protected (by restricting / circulation (of the damaging material)).

> 구▶ 'by V-ing'는 'V함으로써'를 의미합니다.
> - 사생활은 어떻게 보호될까? 역사적으로 사생활은 피해를 주는 물질의 순환을 제한함으로써
>   보호되었다고 합니다.

Ⅸ. **But** if the concept of privacy / first became / interesting legally (as a response to reproductions of images) (through photography and newspapers), / more recent technological advances, (such as data storage, digital images, and the Internet), / (e) pose / new threats (to privacy).

> 구▶ 그러나, 만약 사생활의 개념이 첫 번째로 사진과 신문을 통한 이미지 재생산에 대한 대응으로 법적으로
>   흥미를 끌었다면, 자료 저장, 디지털 이미지, 그리고 인터넷과 같은 더욱 최근의 기술적 진보들이
>   사생활에 대한 새로운 위험을 제기한다고 합니다.

> 독▶ 'But'이 제시되므로 앞 뒷 문장 중심 문장
> - 만약 사생활의 개념이 이미지 재생산을 제한하는 것이라면 새로운 기술이 사생활에 대한 위협이
>   되었을 것이라고 합니다.

Ⅹ. The right (to privacy) / is now being reinterpreted (to meet / those challenges).

> 구▶ 지금 사생활의 권리는 그러한 어려움을 (= 새로운 기술로 인한 새로운 위험을) 충족하기 위해서
>   (= 대처하기 위해서) 새롭게 해석되고 있다고 합니다.

> 독▶ 새로운 기술로 인해서 사생활의 개념이 변화할 필요가 있다고 합니다.

In many mountain regions, rights of access to water are associated with the possession of land—until recently in the Andes, **for example**, land and water rights were (a) <u>combined</u> so water rights were transferred with the land. However, through state land reforms and the development of additional sources of supply, water rights have become separated from land, and may be sold at auction. This **therefore** (b) <u>favours</u> those who can pay, rather than ensuring access to all in the community. The situation arises, **therefore**, where individuals may hold land with no water. In Peru, the government grants water to communities separately from land, and it is up to the community to allocate it. Likewise in Yemen, the traditional allocation was one measure (tasah) of water to one hundred 'libnah' of land. This applied only to traditional irrigation supplies—from runoff, wells, etc., where a supply was (c) <u>guaranteed</u>. Water derived from the capture of flash floods is not subject to Islamic law as this constitutes an uncertain source, and is **therefore** free for those able to collect and use it. **However**, this traditional allocation per unit of land has been bypassed, partly by the development of new supplies, **but** also by the (d) <u>decrease</u> in cultivation of a crop of substantial economic importance. This crop is harvested throughout the year and **thus** requires more than its fair share of water. The economic status of the crop (e) <u>ensures</u> that water rights can be bought or bribed away from subsistence crops.

* irrigation: 관개(灌漑) ** bribe: 매수하다 *** subsistence crop: 생계용 작물

09 21학년도 6월 평가원 41번   (정답률 56%)

윗글의 제목으로 가장 적절한 것은?

해설 [정답 : ①]

토지에 따른 분배를 적용하지 않는 물 권리에 관한 지문입니다. 많은 지역에서 물을 이용할 권리와 토지의 소유가 연관되어 있는데, 새로운 공급의 개발을 통한 물의 증가나, 경제적으로 중요한 작물 재배의 증가와 같은 경우에는 이러한 분배가 적용되지 않는다는 내용의 지문입니다.

①번 선지 : 더는 토지에 얽매이지 않는 물 권리
  - 정답 선지입니다. 토지와 물에 대한 권리가 서로 관련이 없는 상황들을 설명하며 물 권리를 주장할 수 있는 내용을 다루고 있습니다.

②번 선지 : 물 권리 매매 전략
  - 마지막 문장에서 언급된 물 권리를 사거나 매수하는 내용은 경제적 작물의 재배 증가로 인해 토지와 분리되어 매매되는 것입니다. 토지와 관련된 선지가 아니므로 지문을 포괄하지 않은 선지로 볼 수 있습니다.

③번 선지 : 물 저장 방법: 산 대(對) 사막 - 물을 저장하는 내용은 지문에서 찾아볼 수 없습니다.

④번 선지 : 산악 지역에 안정적이지 않은 물 공급
  - 새로운 물 공급이 개발될 때 토지를 이용하지 않고도 물 권리가 주장된다는 내용의 지문입니다. 안정적이지 못한 물 공급과 관련된 내용은 지문에서 찾아볼 수 없습니다.

⑤번 선지 : 끝없는 논쟁: 우리는 어떤 작물을 재배해야 하는가
  - 어떤 작물을 재배해야하는가에 대한 지문이 아니며, 경제적으로 중요한 작물을 재배할 때 물 권리가 토지와 관계없이 거래될 수 있다는 것입니다.

10 21학년도 6월 평가원 42번 (정답률 63%)

밑줄 친 (a) ~ (e) 중에서 문맥상 낱말의 쓰임이 적절하지 <u>않은</u> 것은?

해설 [정답 : ④]

Ⅹ번 문장에서는 이러한 중요한 작물은 일 년 내내 수확되고, 적정한 양의 물을 필요로 한다고 했습니다. 이러한 작물은 Ⅸ번 문장의 경제적으로 중요한 작물을 말하는데, 이것이 일 년 내내 수확된다는 것으로 보아 작물의 재배 감소로 볼 수 없습니다. 'decrease'는 'increase'와 같은 단어로 바꿔야 합니다.

Ⅰ. (In many mountain regions), rights of access (to water) / are associated with / the possession (of land) — (until recently in the Andes), **for example**, land and water rights / were (a) <u>combined</u> so water rights / were transferred (with the land).

> 구▶ 많은 산악 지역에서, 물을 이용할 권리는 토지의 소유와 연관되어 있다고 합니다 — 예를 들어 최근까지 안데스 산맥은 토지와 물 권리가 '통합되어' 이전 되었다고 합니다.

> 독▶ 'for example'이 제시되었으므로 중심 문장
> - 물과 토지가 연관되어 있기 때문에 이 권리가 통합되었다고 봐야 합니다.

Ⅱ. **However**, (through state land reforms and the development of additional sources of supply), water rights / have become separated (from land), and may be sold / at auction.

> 구▶ 그러나 주 토지 개혁과 추가 공급원을 통해, 물 권리가 토지와 분리되어 경매에 붙여질 수 있었다고 합니다.

> 독▶ 'However'가 제시되었으므로 앞 뒷 문장 중심 문장
> - 새로운 내용이 등장하고 있습니다.

Ⅲ. This / **therefore** (b) <u>favours</u> / those (who can pay), (rather than ensuring / access (to all) (in the community)).

> 구▶ 그러므로 이것(물과 토지가 분리되어 경매되는 것)은 지역사회의 모든 사람에게 이용할 권리를 보장하기보다는 비용을 지불할 수 있는 사람에게 '유리하다'고 합니다.

> 독▶ 'therefore'로 결과가 제시되므로 중심 문장

Ⅳ. The situation / arises, **therefore**, where individuals / may hold / land (with no water).

> 구▶ 따라서 개인들이 물이 없는 땅을 보유하는 상황이 생긴다고 합니다.

> 독▶ 'therefore'로 결과가 제시되므로 중심 문장

Ⅴ. In Peru, / the government / grants / water (to communities separately from land), / and it / is /
up to the community / to allocate it.

> 구▶ 'it be동사 + 형용사 + to-V'는 가주어/진주어 의심
> - 'it'이 지칭하는 대상이 없으므로 가주어/진주어
> - 페루에서는 정부가 토지와는 별도로 토지와는 별개로 지역사람들에게 물을 주고, 그 물을 분배하는
>   것은 공동체의 몫이라고 합니다.

> 독▶ 물 권리가 토지와 분리된 예시가 등장하고 있습니다.

Ⅵ. Likewise in Yemen, the traditional allocation / was / one measure (*tasah*) of water (to one hundred
'*libnah*' of land).

> 구▶ 예멘에서도, 전통적인 분배는 100 'libnah'의 토지에 1 'tasha'의 물로 분배되었다고 합니다.

> 독▶ 이를 통해 물의 비용을 지불할 수 있는 사람이 더 유리하다고 볼 수 있습니다.

Ⅶ. This / applied only to / traditional irrigation supplies — (from runoff, wells, etc.), (where a supply
/ was (c) <u>guaranteed</u>.)

* irrigation: 관개(灌漑)

> 구▶ 이것은 — 공급이 '보장된' 유수, 우물 등의 전통적인 관개 공급에만 적용되었다고 합니다.

Ⅷ. Water (derived from the capture of flash floods) / is not subject to / Islamic law (as this /
constitutes / an uncertain source, and is / <u>**therefore**</u> free (for those) (able to collect and use / it).

> 구▶ 갑작스런 홍수로 인해 생긴 물은 불확실한 수원으로 여겨졌기 때문에 이슬람 율법에 영향을 받지
>   않았고, 그래서 물을 모아 사용할 수 있는 사람에게는 무료였다고 합니다.

> 독▶ 'therefore'이 제시되었으므로 중심 문장
> - Ⅵ번 문장의 비용을 지불하고 물을 받는 것과는 빈대되는 내용이 등장하고 있습니다.

Ⅸ. <u>**However**</u>, this traditional allocation (per unit of land) / has been bypassed, (partly
by the development of new supplies), <u>**but**</u> also by the (d) <u>decrease</u> (in cultivation of a crop of
substantial economic importance).

> 구▶ 'not only A but also B'는 'A뿐만 아니라 B'를 의미합니다.
> - 그러나 토지에 따른 이런 전통적인 분배는 새로운 공급의 전개뿐만이 아니라 경제적으로 중요한 작물의
>   재배 '감소'로도 회피되었다고 합니다.

> 독▶ 'However'와 'but'이 제시되므로 중심 문장
> - 새로운 공급의 전개로 인해 토지에 의한 분배가 회피되었다는 것은 Ⅷ번 문장에서 홍수로 인한
>   물은 토지 단위로 분배하지 않고 무료로 사용할 수 있었다는 뜻입니다.

Ⅹ. This crop / is harvested (throughout the year) / and **thus** requires / more than its fair share of

water.

구▶ 이러한 작물은 일 년 내내 수확되고, 적정한 양의 물을 필요로 한다고 합니다.

독▶ 'thus'가 제시되었으므로 중심 문장
- 이러한 작물은 Ⅸ번 문장의 경제적으로 중요한 작물을 말하는데, 이것이 일 년 내내 수확된다는 것으로
보아 작물의 재배 감소로 볼 수 없습니다. 'decrease'는 'increase'와 같은 단어로 바꿔야 합니다.

Ⅺ. The economic status of the crop / (e) <u>ensures</u> / that water rights / can be bought or bribed (away

from subsistence crops).

** bribe: 매수하다 *** subsistence crop: 생계용 작물

구▶ 이 작물의 경제적 지위는 생계형 작물로부터 물 권리를 사거나 매수할 수 있도록 '보장한다'고 합니다.

독▶ Ⅸ번 문장에서 중요 작물의 재배 증가로 인해 토지에 의한 분배가 회피되었다고 했기 때문에 토지의
개입 없이 물 권리의 거래를 보장한다고 봐야 합니다.

Climate change experts and environmental humanists alike agree that the climate crisis is, at its core, a crisis of the imagination and much of the popular imagination is shaped by fiction. In his 2016 book *The Great Derangement*, anthropologist and novelist Amitav Ghosh takes on this relationship between imagination and environmental management, arguing that humans have failed to respond to climate change at least in part because fiction (a) <u>fails</u> to believably represent it. Ghosh explains that climate change is largely absent from contemporary fiction **because** the cyclones, floods, and other catastrophes it brings to mind simply seem too "improbable" to belong in stories about everyday life. **But** climate change does not only reveal itself as a series of (b) <u>extraordinary</u> events. In fact, as environmentalists and ecocritics from Rachel Carson to Rob Nixon have pointed out, environmental change can be "imperceptible"; it proceeds (c) <u>rapidly</u>, only occasionally producing "explosive and spectacular" events. Most climate change impacts cannot be observed day-to-day, **but** they become (d) <u>visible</u> when we are confronted with their accumulated impacts.

Climate change evades our imagination **because** it poses significant representational challenges. It cannot be observed in "human time," which is why documentary filmmaker Jeff Orlowski, who tracks climate change effects on glaciers and coral reefs, uses "before and after" photographs taken several months apart in the same place to (e) <u>highlight</u> changes that occurred gradually.

* anthropologist: 인류학자 ** catastrophe: 큰 재해 *** evade: 피하다

11 23학년도 9월 평가원 41번 (정답률 61%)

윗글의 제목으로 가장 적절한 것은?

해설 [정답 : ③]

기후 위기는 근본적으로 상상력의 위기이며, 기후 변화는 실제로 오랜 시간 점진적으로 일어나는데, 소설과 같은 대중적 상상력이 그것을 인간이 인식하지 못하도록 막는다는 내용의 지문입니다. 그러므로 글의 제목으로 가장 적절한 선지는 ③번이 됩니다.

①번 선지 : 현재의 기후 문제에 대한 다양한 태도
  - 일관적인 주장을 하는 글이지 다양한 태도가 나열된다고 볼 수 없습니다.
②번 선지 : 느리지만 중요하다: 생태 운동의 역사
  - 생태 운동과 관련된 지문이 아닙니다.
③번 선지 : 기후 변화를 표현하는 데 있어서 상상력의 침묵
  - 정답 선지입니다.
④번 선지 : 뚜렷한 위협: 지역에서 퍼져 나가는 기후 재앙들
  - 기후 재앙은 지문에서 언급되지만, 기후 재앙은 일상생활과 동떨어져 우리가 상상하기를 어렵게 하는 것이므로 뚜렷한 위협이라고 볼 수 없습니다.
⑤번 선지 : 환경주의와 생태 비평의 흥망성쇠
  - 생태 비평은 지문에서 언급되지 않습니다.

밑줄 친 (a) ~ (e) 중에서 문맥상 낱말의 쓰임이 적절하지 <u>않은</u> 것은?

해설 [정답 : ③]

(c) 문장에서는 환경 변화는 감지할 수 없을 수 있는데, 그것은 '빠르게' 진행되며, 단지 때때로 폭발적이고 극적인 사건들을 만들어 낼 뿐이라고 합니다. 그런데 빠르게 진행되는 환경 변화는 (c) 문장의 'imperceptible', 감지할 수 없는, (d) 문장의 'cannot be observed day-to-day', 매일 관찰될 수 없다고 하는 내용으로 미루어 보아 기후 변화가 '빠르게' 진행된다고 볼 수 없으며, (c)의 'rapidly'는 'gradually'와 같은 단어로 바꿔야 합니다.

I . Climate change experts and environmental humanists / alike agree / that / the climate crisis / is, at its core, / a crisis (of the imagination) and much of the popular imagination / is shaped (by fiction).

> 구▶ 기후 변화 전문가들과 환경 인문주의자들은 기후 위기가 근원적으로 상상력의 위기이며 대중적 상상력의 많은 부분이 소설에 의해 형성된다는 데 똑같이 동의한다고 합니다.

> 독▶ 기후 위기는 소설에 의해 만들어진 대중들의 상상력의 위기와 같다고 합니다.

II . In his 2016 book *The Great Derangement,* anthropologist and novelist Amitav Ghosh / takes on / this relationship (between imagination / and environmental management), arguing / that / humans / have failed / to respond (to climate change) (at least in part) because / fiction / (a) <u>fails</u> / to believably represent / it.

* anthropologist: 인류학자

> 구▶ 인류학자이자 소설가인 Amitav Ghosh는 자신의 2016년도 책 'The Great Derangement'에서 상상과 환경 관리 사이의 이러한 관계를 다루면서, 인간이 기후 변화에 대응하는 데 실패한 것은 최소한 부분적으로는 소설이 그것을 믿을 수 있게 표현하지 못하기 때문이라고 주장한다고 합니다.

> 독▶ 소설이 대중들이 기후 위기를 믿을 수 있도록 표현하지 못한다는 것은, 대중들의 상상력을 성하도록 소설이 쓰이고 있지 못하다는 것을 의미합니다.

III . Ghosh / explains / that / climate change / is / largely absent (from contemporary fiction) **because** / the cyclones, floods, and other catastrophes (it / brings / to mind) simply seem / too "improbable" (to belong / in stories / about everyday life).

** catastrophe: 큰 재해

> 구▶ Ghosh는 기후 변화는 그것이 상기시키는 사이클론, 홍수, 그리고 다른 큰 재해들이 그야말로 일상생활에 관한 이야기에 속하기에는 너무 '있을 것 같지 않은' 것처럼 보이기 때문에 현대 소설에 대체로 존재하지 않는다고 설명한다고 합니다.

> 독▶ 'because'가 제시되었으므로 중심 문장
> - 대중들이 재해들을 있을 것 같지 않은 일들로 여기는 것 역시 소설이 기후 위기와 관련하여 대중들의 상상력을 형성하지 못했다는 것을 의미합니다.

Ⅳ. **But** climate change / does not only reveal / itself (as a series / of (b) extraordinary events).

> 구▶ 그러나 기후 변화는 일련의 놀라운 사건들로만 자신을 드러내는 것은 아니라고 합니다.

> 독▶ 'But'이 제시되었으므로 앞 뒷 문장 중심 문장
> - 'extraordinary event', 놀라운 사건들은 Ⅲ번 문장에서 제시된 사이클론, 홍수와 같은 재해들을 지칭하며, 이것들만으로 기후 변화가 존재하는 것은 아니라고 하는 내용으로 전환됩니다.

Ⅴ. In fact, as environmentalists and ecocritics (from Rachel Carson to Rob Nixon) have pointed out, environmental change / can be / "imperceptible"; it / proceeds (c) rapidly, only occasionally / producing "explosive and spectacular" events.

> 구▶ 사실, Rachel Carson에서 Rob Nixon에 이르는 환경론자들과 생태 비평가들이 지적했듯이, 환경 변화는 '감지할 수 없을' 수 있는데, 즉 그것은 빠르게 진행되며, 단지 이따금 '폭발적이고 극적인' 사건들을 만들어 낼 뿐이라고 합니다.

> 독▶ 눈에 띄는 재해들과 대비되게 감지할 수 없는 환경 변화에 관한 내용이며, 이것은 가끔 폭발적인 사건을 만들어낼 뿐, 대부분 느리고 완만하게 진행되어야 한다는 것을 알 수 있습니다.

Ⅵ. Most climate change impacts / cannot be observed day-to-day, **but** / they / become / (d) visible / when / we / are confronted with / their accumulated impacts.

> 구▶ 대부분의 기후 변화의 영향은 매일 관찰될 수는 없지만, 우리가 그것들의 축적된 영향에 직면할 때 그것들은 가시화된디고 합니다.

> 독▶ 'but'이 제시되었으므로 중심 문장
> - 관찰될 수 없는 기후 변화 역시 Ⅴ번 문장의 감지할 수 있는 기후 변화와 같은 내용임을 알 수 있습니다.

Ⅶ. Climate change / evades / our imagination / **because** / it / poses / significant representational challenges.

*** evade: 피하다

> 구▶ 기후 변화는 그것이 중요한 표현상의 문제를 제기하기 때문에 우리의 상상에서 벗어난다고 합니다.

> 독▶ 'because'가 제시되었으므로 중심 문장
> - 왜 대중이 기후 변화를 믿을 수 없는 지에 대한 설명이 되는 문장입니다. 기후 변화는 허리케인과 같이 가끔 일어나는 폭발적인 사건과, 눈에 보이지 않는 점진적인 사건들로 구성되는데, 눈에 보이지 않는 사건들은 대중들이 인식할 수 없고, 소설에서 묘사하는 재해들은 비현실적으로 묘사되므로 결과적으로 대중들은 기후 변화에 대한 상상력을 형성하기가 어렵기 때문입니다.

Ⅷ. It / cannot be observed / in "human time," which / is / why documentary filmmaker Jeff Orlowski, who / tracks / climate change effects (on glaciers and coral reefs), uses / "before and after" photographs / taken several months apart (in the same place) / to (e) <u>highlight</u> / changes / that / occurred gradually.

구▶ 그것은 '인간의 시간' 동안에는 관찰될 수 없는데, 그것이 빙하와 산호초에 미치는 기후 변화의 영향을 추적하는 다큐멘터리 영화 제작자 Jeff Orlowski가 점진적으로 일어난 변화를 강조하기 위해 수개월 간격으로 같은 장소에서 찍은 '전과 후' 사진을 이용하는 이유라고 합니다.

독▶ Jeff Orlowski가 점진적 변화를 보여주기 위한 사진을 이용하는 것은 대중들이 인식할 수 없는 눈에 보이지 않는 기후 변화의 모습을 대중들에게 이해시키기 위해서라는 것을 알 수 있습니다.

Once an event is noticed, an onlooker **must** decide if it is truly an emergency. Emergencies are not always clearly (a) <u>labeled</u> as such; "smoke" pouring into a waiting room may be **caused** by fire, or it may merely indicate a leak in a steam pipe. Screams in the street may signal an attack or a family quarrel. A man lying in a doorway may be having a coronary — or he may simply be sleeping off a drunk.

A person trying to interpret a situation often looks at those around him to see how he **should** react. If everyone else is calm and indifferent, he will tend to remain so; if everyone else is reacting strongly, he is likely to become alert. This tendency is not merely blind conformity; ordinarily we **derive** much valuable information about new situations from how others around us behave. It's a (b) <u>rare</u> traveler who, in picking a roadside restaurant, chooses to stop at one where no other cars appear in the parking lot.

But occasionally the reactions of others provide (c) <u>accurate</u> information. The studied nonchalance of patients in a dentist's waiting room is a poor indication of their inner anxiety. It is considered embarrassing to "lose your cool" in public. In a potentially acute situation, then, everyone present will appear more (d) <u>unconcerned</u> than he is in fact. A crowd can **thus** force (e) <u>inaction</u> on its members by implying, through its passivity, that an event is not an emergency. Any individual in such a crowd fears that he may appear a fool if he behaves as though it were.

* coronary: 관상동맥증 ** nonchalance: 무관심, 냉담

13 23학년도 6월 평가원 41번 (정답률 63%)

윗글의 제목으로 가장 적절한 것은?

해설 [정답 : ①]

첫 번째 문단에서는 우리가 응급 상황인지 아닌지에 대해 판단함에 있어서 어려움이 많다는 내용을 제시하고 있고 두 번째 문단에서는 어려운 응급 상황인지 아닌지를 판단하기 위해 다른 사람들의 반응을 통해서 정보를 얻어 우리가 응급 상황인시 아닌지를 판단할 수 있다고 합니다. 이는 세 번째 문단에서 전환되어 군중에게 바보처럼 보이지 않기 위해서 우리가 군중이 목격한 사건에 대해 무관심한 것처럼 우리도 무관심하게 강요받게 된다는 내용이므로 우리가 응급 상황인지 아닌지 판단하는 상황에서 군중의 영향을 제시하고 있습니다.

①번 선지 : 우리는 독립적으로 판단하는가? 군중의 영향 - 정답 선지입니다.

②번 선지 : 승리 전략: 다른 사람에 의해 바보 취급을 당하지 않기 위해서는 어떻게 해야 하는가

    - 마지막 문장에서 우리는 군중에게 바보처럼 보이지 않기 때문에 군중과 같이 무관심을 보인다고 합니다. 하지만 이 내용은 But이 제시된 IX번 문장 이후의 내용으로 ②번 선지는 포괄하지 않는 선지에 해당합니다.

③번 선지 : 응급 상황이 우리의 사고방식에 영향을 끼치는가?

    - 응급 상황이 우리의 사고방식에 영향을 끼치는 "비상 상황 ⇒ 우리의 반응"이 아닌 다른 사람들을 통해서 우리의 응급 상황인지 아닌지에 대한 판단을 제시하는 "다른 사람의 반응 ⇒ 우리의 반응"에 대한 내용입니다. 언급되지 않은 선지에 해당합니다.

④번 선지 : 이웃과 조화를 향해 발걸음을 내딛기 - 무관한 선지입니다.

⑤번 선지 : 응급 상황에서 다른 사람을 돕는 방법

    - 응급 상황이란 같은 소재이지만 응급 상황인지 아닌지 판단하는데에 있어 군중의 영향을 제시하는 지문과는 달리 응급 상황에서 다른 사람을 돕는 방법에 대해 언급하고 있으므로 언급되지 않은 선지에 해당합니다.

밑줄 친 (a) ~ (e) 중에서 문맥상 낱말의 쓰임이 적절하지 <u>않은</u> 것은?

해설 [**정답 : ③**]

Ⅷ번 문장까지 우리는 다른 사람들의 반응을 통해서 행동한다는 내용이 제시되었습니다. 만약 이러한 경향이 정확한 정보를 얻는 것이라면 'But'을 통해서 전환될 수 없습니다. 또한 Ⅹ번 문장 이후 군중의 무관심 속에서 그 사건이 응급 상황이든 아니든 반응하지 않는 것을 강요받는 내용이 제시되므로 (C)가 적절하지 않은 어휘임을 알 수 있습니다. 'accurate'를 'inaccurate'로 바꾸어야 합니다.

Ⅰ. Once an event / is noticed, an onlooker / **must** decide / if it / is truly / an emergency.

> 구 ▶ 'if'가 목적절을 이끌 경우 '~인지 아닌지'로 해석하시면 됩니다.
> - 어떤 사건이 목격될 때, 목격자는 반드시 그것이 (= 목격한 사건이) 진정한 응급 상황인지 아닌지 결정해야만 한다고 합니다.

> 독 ▶ 'must'가 제시되었으므로 중심 문장.
> - 어떠한 사건을 목격했을 목격자는 그 사건이 응급 상황인지 판단해야 한다고 합니다.

Ⅱ. Emergencies / are not always clearly (a) <u>labeled</u> (as such); "smoke" (pouring into / a waiting room) / may be **caused** (by fire), or it / may merely indicate / a leak (in a steam pipe).

> 구 ▶ 'label A as B'는 'A를 B로 생각하다'를 의미합니다. 이 문장에서는 수동태로 사용되어 'A be labeled as B'의 구조로 제시되었습니다.
> - 응급 상황들은 항상 분명하게 대기실에 쏟아진 "연기"는 화재에 의해 발생할 수도 있고 단순히 증기 파이프의 누출로 나타날 수도 있는 것처럼 생각되지 않는다고 합니다.

> 독 ▶ 'cause'가 제시되었으므로 중심 문장.
> - 연기가 항상 화재에 의해서만 발생하지는 않는 것처럼 목격한 사건이 응급 상황인지를 판단하는 것은 어렵다고 합니다.

Ⅲ. Screams (in the street) / may signal / an attack or a family quarrel.

> 구 ▶ 거리에서의 비명은 공격에 대한 신호일 수 있고 가족간 다툼의 신호일 수도 있다고 합니다.

Ⅳ. A man (lying in a doorway) / may be having / a coronary — or he / may simply be sleeping off / a drunk.

* coronary: 관상동맥증

구 'door'은 '문'을 의미하고 'way'는 '길'을 의미합니다. 'doorway'는 문 앞에 있는 길이니 '출입구'로 이해하시면 됩니다.
- 출입구에 누워있는 남자는 관상동맥증일 수도 있고 혹은 술에 취해 잠을 자는 중일 수도 있다고 합니다.

독 Ⅱ번 문장에서 제시된 응급 상황인지 판단하기 어려운 상황을 Ⅲ번 문장과 Ⅳ번 문장에서 제시하고 있습니다.

Ⅴ. A person (trying to interpret a situation) / often looks (at those around him) (to see / how he / **should** react).

구 상황을 해석하는 것을 시도하는 사람들은 어떻게 그가 (= 상황을 해석하는 사람이) 반응해야만 할지를 판단하기 위해서 그의 주변을 본다고 합니다.

독 'should'가 제시되었으므로 중심 문장
- 상황을 판단하기 위해서 주변을 본다고 합니다.

Ⅵ. If everyone else / is / calm and indifferent, he / will tend to remain so; if everyone else / is reacting strongly, he / is likely to become / alert.

구 만약 모든 사람들이 평온하고 무관심하다면 그는 (= 상황을 판단하는 사람은) 그러한 상태를 (= 평온하고 무관심한 상태를) 유지하는 경향이 있고, 만약 모든 사람들이 강하게 반응한나면, 그는 기민할 (= 다른 사람들처럼 강하게 반응할) 확률이 높다고 합니다.

독 주변 사람들의 반응 정도에 따라 상황에 대한 반응을 결정하는 것을 제시하고 있습니다.

Ⅶ. This tendency / is not merely / blind conformity; ordinarily we / **derive** / much valuable information (about new situations) (from how others (around us) behave).

구 그러한 경향은 (= 주변 사람들의 반응 정도에 따라 상황에 대한 반응을 결정하는 경향은) 단순히 맹목적인 순응이 아니라 보통 우리는 우리 주변 사람들이 어떻게 행동하는 지를 통해서 새로운 상황에 대한 많은 귀중한 정보들을 이끌어 낸다고 합니다.

독 'derive'를 통해서 인과 관계를 제시하므로 중심 문장
- 우리는 우리 주변 사람들의 행동을 통해서 새로운 상황에 대한 정보를 얻는다고 합니다.

VIII. It's / a (b) <u>rare</u> traveler who, (in picking a roadside restaurant), / chooses to stop (at one) (where no other cars / appear (in the parking lot)).

> 구 'It + be 동사 + 사람 명사 + who'는 가주어/진주어입니다.
> - 'in V-ing'는 'V함에 있어서'를 의미합니다.
> - 길가의 식당을 선택함에 있어서 주차장에 어떠한 차량도 보이지 않는 식당에서 멈추고 그 식당을 선택하는 사람들은 거의 없다고 합니다.

> 독 다른 사람들의 행동을 통해서 새로운 상황에 대한 정보를 얻는 것의 예시에 해당합니다.

IX. <u>**But**</u> occasionally the reactions of others / provide / (c) <u>accurate</u> information.

> 구 그러나 때때로 다른 사람들의 반응은 정확한 (⇒ 부정확한) 정보를 제공한다고 합니다.

> 독 'But'이 제시되었으므로 앞 뒷 문장 중심 문장
> - VIII번 문장까지 우리는 다른 사람들의 반응을 통해서 행동한다는 내용이 제시되었습니다. 만약 이러한 경향이 정확한 정보를 얻는 것이라면 'But'을 통해서 전환될 수 없으므로 (C)가 잘못 사용된 어휘임을 알 수 있습니다.

X. The studied nonchalance of patients (in a dentist's waiting room) / is / a poor indication of their inner anxiety.

** nonchalance: 무관심, 냉담

> 구 치과 대기실에서 연구된 환자의 무관심은 그들의 (= 환자들의) 내적 불안을 잘 나타내지 않는다고 합니다.

XI. It / is considered / embarrassing (to "lose your cool") (in public).

> 구 'consider + O + O.C'로 5형식으로 사용될 경우 'O를 O.C라고 생각하다'라는 뜻을 가집니다. 이 문장에서 수동태 형태로 사용되어 'O be considered O.C'로 제시되었습니다.
> - 그것은 (= 환자들의 무관심은) 사람들 앞에서 '냉정을 잃는 것'에 대한 부끄러움으로 생각된다고 합니다.

> 독 다른 사람들이 냉담해 보이는 것은 다른 사람들 앞에서 냉정을 잃는 것에 대한 부끄러움이지 실제로 냉담한 것은 아니라고 합니다.

XII. (In a potentially acute situation), then, everyone present / will appear / more (d) <u>unconcerned</u> than he is in fact.

> 구 잠재적으로 급한 상황에서, 다른 사람들의 존재는 그들의 (= 다른 사람들의) 실제보다 더 무관심한 것처럼 보일 수 있다고 합니다.

> 독 다른 사람들의 존재로 인해서 사람들이 본인이 느끼는 것보다 더 무관심하게 행동할 수도 있다고 합니다.

XIII. A crowd / can **thus** force / (e) <u>inaction</u> (on its members) (by implying, (through its passivity), that an event / is not / an emergency).

> 구 ‘force A on B’는 ‘A를 B에 강요하다’를 의미합니다.
> - ‘by V-ing’는 ‘V함으로써’를 뜻합니다.
> - 따라서 군중은 그것의 (= 군중의) 사람들에게 수동성을 통해 사건이 비상 상황이 아님을 암시함으로써 행동하지 않는 것을 강요할 수 있다고 합니다.

> 독 ‘thus’가 제시되었으므로 중심 문장
> - 군중의 실제와는 달리 무관심을 보임으로써 다른 사람들에게 무관심을 보일 것을 강요할 수 있다고 합니다.

XIV. Any individual (in such a crowd) / fears / that he / may appear / a fool if he / behaves / as though it were.

> 구 ‘as though’는 ‘마치 ~인 것처럼’을 의미합니다. 이 문장은 ‘it were emergency’에서 ‘emergency’가 생략되었습니다.
> - 그러한 군중에서 (= 무관심을 보이는 군중에서) 어떠한 개인도 만약 그가 마치 응급 상황인 것처럼 행동한다면 바보처럼 보이는 것을 두려워한다고 합니다.

> 독 군중이 무관심을 보이는 상황에서 응급 상황인 것처럼 강하게 반응할 경우 바보처럼 보이는 것을 걱정하여 군중들과 같이 무관심을 보이게 된다고 합니다.

One way to avoid contributing to overhyping a story would be to say nothing. **However**, that is not a realistic option for scientists who feel a strong sense of responsibility to inform the public and policymakers and/or to offer suggestions. Speaking with members of the media has (a) <u>advantages</u> in getting a message out and perhaps receiving favorable recognition, **but** it runs the risk of misinterpretations, the need for repeated clarifications, and entanglement in never-ending controversy. **Hence**, the decision of whether to speak with the media tends to be highly individualized. Decades ago, it was (b) <u>unusual</u> for Earth scientists to have results that were of interest to the media, and consequently few media contacts were expected or encouraged. In the 1970s, the few scientists who spoke frequently with the media were often (c) <u>criticized</u> by their fellow scientists for having done so. The situation now is quite different, as many scientists feel a responsibility to speak out **because of** the importance of global warming and related issues, and many reporters share these feelings. In addition, many scientists are finding that they (d) <u>enjoy</u> the media attention and the public recognition that comes with it. At the same time, other scientists continue to resist speaking with reporters, thereby preserving more time for their science and (e) <u>running</u> the risk of being misquoted and the other unpleasantries associated with media coverage.

* overhype: 과대광고하다 ** entanglement: 얽힘

15 24학년도 수능 41번 (정답률 59%)

윗글의 제목으로 가장 적절한 것은?

해설 [**정답** : ②]

과학자와 언론 간의 대화의 장단점을 정리하여 서술하는 지문입니다. 장점으로는 메시지를 알려지게 하고, 인정을 받을 수 있다는 점이 있으며, 단점으로는 오해를 일으키고 반복적인 해명과 논란에 얽힐 수 있다는 점이 있습니다. 다음으로 지문에서는 언론 접촉에 대해서 과학자가 인식하는 점도 점차 긍정적으로 바뀌었다고 언급하며, 이 양날의 검인 언론 대화의 내용을 모두 포함한 선지가 정답이 됩니다.

①번 선지 : 과학자와 언론 간의 골치 아픈 관계
   - 골치 아픈 관계라는 선지는 과학자와 언론 간의 접촉의 순기능을 포함하고 있지 않으므로 오답 선지입니다.
②번 선지 : 과학자의 선택: 언론과 접할 것인가, 말 것인가?
   - 과학자와 언론 간의 접촉의 장단점을 포함하고 있는 정답 선지입니다.
③번 선지 : 과학자여! 언론에 말할 때 조심하세요
   - 과학자와 언론 간의 대화를 부정적으로만 보고 있는 선지이므로 오답입니다.
④번 선지 : 과학적 진실과 언론의 주목에 대한 딜레마
   - 과학자와 언론 간의 대화라는 핵심 주제에서 벗어나 있는 선지입니다.
⑤번 선지 : 누가 기후 문제에 책임이 있나, 과학자인가, 언론인가?
   - 기후 문제의 책임을 알아내는 지문이라고 볼 수 없습니다.

16 24학년도 수능 42번 (정답률 58%)

밑줄 친 (a) ~ (e) 중에서 문맥상 낱말의 쓰임이 적절하지 <u>않은</u> 것은?

해설 [**정답 : ⑤**]

지문에서는 언론과의 접촉의 단점으로 오해를 일으키고 반복적인 해명과 논란에 얽힐 수 있다는 점을 언급하고 있습니다. 그런데 (e) 문장에서는 'scientists continue to resist speaking with reporters, thereby preserving more time for their science and running the risk of being misquoted' 과학자들은 기자들과의 대화를 계속 물리치며, 그렇게 함으로써 자신의 과학을 위해 더 많은 시간을 지키고, 잘못 인용되는 위험과 언론 보도와 관련된 다른 불쾌한 상황을 감수한다고 했습니다. 언론과 대화를 하지 않는 과학자들에게는 이러한 위험 자체가 발생하지 않으므로 과학자들이 언론과 불편한 상황을 감수한다고 볼 수 없습니다. 그러므로 'running'을 'avoiding'과 같은 단어로 바꿔야 합니다.

Ⅰ. One way (to avoid contributing to overhyping a story) / would be / to say nothing.

* overhype: 과대광고하다

> **구▶** 이야기를 과대광고하는 것에 대한 기여를 피하는 한 가지 방법은 아무 말도 하지 않는 것이라고 합니다.

> **독▶** 이야기를 과장하는 것을 피하기 위해서는 말을 아예 하지 말라고 합니다.

Ⅱ. **However**, that / is not / a realistic option for scientists / who / feel / a strong sense of responsibility to inform the public and policymakers and/or to offer suggestions.

> **구▶** 그러나 그것은 대중과 정책 입안자에게 정보를 전하고/전하거나 제안을 제공해야 한다는 강한 책임감을 느끼는 과학자들에게는 현실적인 선택안이 아니라고 합니다.

> **독▶** 'however'가 제시되었으므로 중심 문장
> - Ⅰ번 문장에서 언급된 해결책은 과학자들이 선택할 수 없다고 합니다.

Ⅲ. Speaking (with members of the media) / has / (a) <u>advantages</u> in getting a message out and perhaps receiving favorable recognition, **but** / it / runs / the risk of misinterpretations, the need for repeated clarifications, and entanglement in never-ending controversy.

** entanglement: 얽힘

> **구▶** 언론 구성원들과의 대화는 메시지를 알려지게 하고 아마 호의적인 인정을 받을 수 있다는 장점이 있지만, 오해를 일으키고 반복적인 해명이 필요하며 끝없는 논란에 얽힐 위험을 감수한다고 합니다.

> **독▶** 'but'이 제시되었으므로 중심 문장
> - 과학자들과 언론인들과의 대화의 장점으로는 메시지를 알리고 인정을 받을 수 있다는 것이 있고, 반대로 단점으로는 오해를 유발하여 해명과 논란에 시달릴 수 있다는 것을 말하고 있습니다.

Ⅳ. **Hence**, the decision (of whether to speak with the media) / tends to be highly individualized.

> 구▶ 따라서 언론과 대화할지 여부는 아주 개인적으로 결정되는 경향이 있다고 합니다.

> 독▶ 'hence'로 결과를 제시하므로 중심 문장
> - Ⅲ번 문장의 단점을 회피하기 위해 보인, 언론과의 대화에 대한 과학자들의 태도가 달랐다는 것을 언급합니다.

Ⅴ. Decades ago, it / was / (b) <u>unusual</u> for Earth scientists / to have / results / that / were of interest to the media, and consequently few media contacts / were expected or encouraged.

> 구▶ 'for N to-V'에서 'to-V'앞에 있는 'N'은 의미상 주어
> - 수십 년 전에 지구과학자들이 언론의 흥미를 끄는 연구 결과를 발표하는 것은 드문 일이었고, 따라서 언론과의 접촉을 기대하거나 권장하는 것은 거의 없었다고 합니다.

> 독▶ 과거에는 언론과 접촉을 하는 과학자들이 거의 없었다고 합니다.

Ⅵ. In the 1970s, the few scientists (who / spoke frequently (with the media)) / were often (c) <u>criticized</u> by their fellow scientists for having done so.

> 구▶ 1970년대에는, 언론과 자주 대화하는 소수의 과학자들은 흔히 그렇게 한 것에 대해 동료 과학자들로부터 비난을 받았다고 합니다.

> 독▶ Ⅴ번 문장의 예시이자 결과로 언론과 접촉을 한 과학자들은 비난을 받게 되었다고 합니다.

Ⅶ. The situation now / is / quite different, as many scientists / feel / a responsibility to speak out **because of** the importance of global warming and related issues, and many reporters / share / these feelings.

> 구▶ 지금은 상황이 아주 다른데, 많은 과학자가 지구 온난화와 관련 문제의 중요성 때문에 공개적으로 말해야 한다는 책임감을 느끼고 있으며 많은 기자도 이런 감정들을 공유하고 있기 때문이라고 합니다.

> 독▶ 'because of'가 제시되었으므로 중심 문장
> - 현대 과학자들은 과거와는 다르게 언론과 접촉을 많이 하고 있으며, 그 원인으로는 과학자들과 기자들이 느끼는 책임감 때문이라고 합니다.

Ⅷ. In addition, many scientists / are finding / that / they / (d) <u>enjoy</u> / the media attention and the public recognition / that / comes with it.

> 구▶ 게다가, 많은 과학자는 자신이 언론의 주목과 그에 따른 대중의 인정을 즐기고 있다는 사실을 알아 가고 있다고 합니다.

> 독▶ 과학자들이 언론과 대화를 하는 또 다른 이유로 과학자들이 언론의 주목과 그로 인한 대중의 인정을 좋아하고 있기 때문이라는 점이 언급됩니다.

Ⅸ. At the same time, other scientists / continue to resist speaking with reporters, thereby preserving more time (for their science) and (e) <u>running</u> the risk (of being misquoted) and the other unpleasantries / associated with media coverage.

구 동시에, 다른 과학자들은 기자들과의 대화를 계속 물리치며, 그렇게 함으로써 자신의 과학을 위해 더 많은 시간을 지켜 내고, 잘못 인용되는 위험과 언론 보도와 관련된 다른 불쾌한 상황을 감수한다고 합니다.

독 Ⅷ번 문장의 과학자들과는 대조적으로 기자들과 대화를 하지 않는 과학자들도 여전히 존재한다는 것을 보여주고 있습니다.

[17~18] 다음 글을 읽고, 물음에 답하시오.

If we understand critical thinking as: 'the identification and evaluation of evidence to guide decision-making', then ethical thinking is about identifying ethical issues and evaluating these issues from different perspectives to guide how to respond. This form of ethics is distinct from higher levels of conceptual ethics or theory. The nature of an ethical issue or problem from this perspective is that there is no clear right or wrong response. It is **therefore** (a) <u>essential</u> that students learn to think through ethical issues rather than follow a prescribed set of ethical codes or rules. There is a **need to** (b) <u>encourage</u> recognition that, **although** being ethical is defined as acting 'in accordance with the principles of conduct that are considered correct', these principles vary both between and within individuals. What a person (c) <u>values</u> relates to their social, religious, or civic beliefs influenced by their formal and informal learning experiences. Individual perspectives may also be context (d) <u>dependent</u>, meaning that under different circumstances, at a different choices. **Therefore**, in order to analyse ethical issues and think ethically it is necessary to understand the personal factors that influence your own 'code of behaviour' and how these may (e) <u>coincide</u>, alongside recognizing and accepting that the factors that drive other people's codes and decision making may be different.

17 25학년도 6월 평가원 41번 (정답률 63%)

윗글의 제목으로 가장 적절한 것은?

해설 [정답 : ③]

개인의 올바른 윤리적 사고를 위한 조건을 설명하고 있는 지문입니다. 필자의 직접적인 주장은 'principles vary both between and within individuals' 윤리적 행동의 원칙의 기준이 개인마다 다르다는 것을 이해해야 한다는 V번 문장에서 언급되고 있으며, 다음 VI번 문장부터 원칙 기준이 다양한 원인으로 'relates to their social, religious, or civic beliefs influenced by their formal and informal learning experiences' 사회, 종교, 시민 의식 등의 구체적 사례들을 언급하며 주제를 확대하여 설명하고 있습니다.

①번 선지 : 비판적 추론: 윤리적 의사결정으로 가는 길
　　－ 윤리적 의사결정으로 비판적 추론을 언급하는 지문이 아닙니다.

②번 선지 : 윤리가 행동 규범에 미치는 광범위한 영향
　　－ 윤리가 행동 규범에 미치는 영향이 아니라, 행동 규범이 윤리적 의사결정에 영향을 미치는 지문입니다.

③번 선지 : 윤리적 사고: 개인의 마음을 거니는 여정
　　－ 윤리적 사고, 그 조건으로 개인마다 다른 윤리적 원칙을 언급하는 지문이므로 정답 선지입니다.

④번 선지 : 타인의 눈에 비친 윤리 이론 탐구
　　－ 윤리 이론 탐구가 아닌 윤리 행동의 원칙을 설명하고 있으며, 타인의 눈으로 보는 것이 아닌 자신의 원리를 사용하는 것이므로 정답이 될 수 없습니다.

⑤번 선지 : 윤리적 선택이 항상 우선인가?
　　－ 윤리적 선택을 우선시한다는 내용의 지문이라 보기 어렵습니다.

밑줄 친 (a) ~ (e) 중에서 문맥상 낱말의 쓰임이 적절하지 <u>않은</u> 것은?

해설 [**정답 : ⑤**]

Ⅴ번 문장에서 'principles vary both between and within individuals' 윤리적 행동의 원칙의 기준이 개인마다 다르다는 것을 이해해야 한다고 했습니다. 다음 개인마다 영향을 받는 선택 기준을 나열하는 문장에 이어서, Ⅷ번 문장에서는 'it is necessary to understand the personal factors that influence your own 'code of behaviour' and how these may coincide' 윤리적으로 사고하기 위해서 자신의 행동 규범에 영향을 미치는 개인적 요인과 이 요인들이 어떻게 일치할 수 있는지를 이해해야 한다고 했습니다. 분명히 지문에서는 이 요인들이 개인마다 다르다고 했고, 이어서 'factors that drive other people's codes and decision making may be different' 다른 사람에게 영향을 미치는 요소들도 다르다고 하는 내용이 언급되는 것 역시 행동 규범에 미치는 요소들이 다양하다는 것과 같은 내용이 되므로 'coincide'를 'vary'와 같은 단어로 바꿔야 합니다.

Ⅰ. If we / understand / critical thinking / as: 'the identification and evaluation (of evidence) (to guide decision-making)', then ethical thinking / is / about identifying ethical issues and evaluating these issues (from different perspectives) (to guide / how to respond).

구▶ 우리가 비판적 사고를 '의사결정을 안내하기 위한 증거의 검증 및 평가'로 이해한다면, 윤리적 사고는 윤리적 사인을 식별하고 이러한 사안을 다양한 관점에서 평가하여 어떻게 대응할지를 안내하는 것이라고 합니다.

독▶ 윤리적 사고에 관한 정의가 언급되고 있습니다.

Ⅱ. This form (of ethics) / is / distinct (from higher levels of conceptual ethics or theory).

구▶ 이러한 형태의 윤리는 더 높은 수준의 개념적 윤리나 이론과는 구별된다고 합니다.

Ⅲ. The nature (of an ethical issue or problem) (from this perspective) / is that there / is / no clear right or wrong response.

구▶ 이러한 관점에서 윤리적 사안이나 문제의 본질은 명백하게 옳거나 그른 대응이 없다는 것이라고 합니다.

독▶ 다시 Ⅰ번 문장으로 돌아와서 윤리적 문제의 본질로서 명확한 대응책은 존재하지 않는다고 말하고 있습니다.

Ⅳ. It / is / **therefore** / (a) underline{essential} / that / students / learn / to think through ethical issues rather than
/ follow / a prescribed set (of ethical codes or rules.)

구▶ 따라서 학생들은 규정된 일련의 윤리 규범이나 규칙을 따르는 것보다는 윤리적 문제를 충분히
생각하는 법을 배우는 것이 필수적이라고 합니다.

독▶ 'therefore'이 제시되었으므로 중심 문장
- Ⅲ번 문장에 이어, 윤리적 문제에 관한 정해진 대응책이 없으므로 윤리적 규범을 따르는 것은 의미가
없고, 문제에 관해서 생각하는 것이 중요하다고 말하고 있습니다.

* prescribe - ① 규정하다 ② 처방하다

Ⅴ. There / is / a **need to** (b) underline{encourage} / recognition that, (although being ethical / is defined / as
acting 'in accordance with / the principles of conduct (that are considered / correct')),
these principles / vary both between and within individuals.

구▶ 비록 윤리적인 행동이 '옳다고 여겨지는 행동 원칙에 따라' 행동하는 것으로 정의된다고 하더라도,
이러한 원칙은 개인 간 그리고 개인 내에서도 다를 수 있다는 인식을 장려할 필요가 있다고 합니다.

독▶ 'need to'가 제시되었으므로 중심 문장
- 윤리적 행동에 원칙이 없다는 것은, 사람마다 그 원칙에 대한 인식이 다르다고 말하고 있는 내용입니다.

* in accordance with - ~에 따라서

Ⅵ. What a person (c) underline{values} / relates / to their social, religious, or civic beliefs (influenced by their
formal and informal learning experiences).

구▶ 개인이 가치 있게 여기는 것은 그들의 공식적이고 또 비공식적인 학습 경험에 의해 영향받은 사회적,
종교적, 혹은 시민으로서의 신념과 관련이 있다고 합니다.

독▶ 개인이 가치를 인식하는 데에 영향을 주는 것들이 언급되고 있습니다.

Ⅶ. Individual perspectives / may also be / context (d) dependent, meaning / that / under different
circumstances, / at a different choices.

구▶ 개인의 관점은 또한 상황에 따라 달라질 수도 있는데, 이는 다른 환경에서, 다른 시간에, 그들이 다른
감정을 느끼고 있을 때, 동일한 개인이 다른 선택을 할 수도 있음을 의미한다고 합니다.

독▶ 개인의 관점이 상황에 따라 달라지는 것은 Ⅴ번 문장의 개인 내에서도 다를 수 있다는 인식을
의미합니다.

Ⅷ. **Therefore**, in order to analyse / ethical issues / and think ethically / it / is / necessary / to understand / the personal factors (that influence / your own 'code of behaviour') and how these / may (e) <u>coincide</u>, alongside recognizing and accepting / that the factors (that drive / other people's codes and decision making) / may be / different.

[구] 따라서 윤리적 사안을 분석하고 윤리적으로 사고하기 위해서는 자신의 '행동 규범'에 영향을 미치는 개인적 요인들과 이것들이 어떻게 일치할 수 (⇒ 다양할 수) 있는지 이해하며, 그와 동시에 다른 사람들의 행동 규범과 의사결정에 영향을 미치는 요소들이 다를 수 있다는 점을 인식하고 받아들이는 것이 필요하다고 합니다.

[독] 'Therefore'이 제시되었으므로 중심 문장
- 지문의 주제를 직접적으로 언급하는 문장입니다. 윤리적 사고를 위해서는 자신의 규범에 영향을 주는 요소들, 다른 사람들의 행동 규범에 영향을 주는 요소들이 모두 다르다는 것을 인지하고 있어야 한다는 것입니다.

There is evidence that even very simple algorithms can outperform expert judgement on simple prediction problems. **For example**, algorithms have proved more (a) <u>accurate</u> than humans in predicting whether a prisoner released on parole will go on to commit another crime, or in predicting whether a potential candidate will perform well in a job in future. In over 100 studies across many different domains, half of all cases show simple formulas make (b) <u>better</u> significant predictions than human experts, and the remainder (except a very small handful), show a tie between the two. When there are a lot of different factors involved and a situation is very uncertain, simple formulas can win out by focusing on the most important factors and being consistent, **while** human judgement is too easily influenced by particularly salient and perhaps (c) <u>irrelevant</u> considerations. A similar idea is supported by further evidence that 'checklists' can improve the quality of expert decisions in a range of domains by ensuring that important steps or considerations aren't missed when people are feeling (d) <u>relaxed</u>. **For example**, treating patients in intensive care can require hundreds of small actions per day, and one small error could cost a life. Using checklists to ensure that no crucial steps are missed has proved to be remarkably (e) <u>effective</u> in a range of medical contexts, from preventing live infections to reducing pneumonia.

* parole: 가석방 ** salient: 두드러진 *** pneumonia: 폐렴

19 23학년도 수능 41번
(정답률 54%)

윗글의 제목으로 가장 적절한 것은?

해설 [정답 : ①]

알고리즘을 사용하는 것이 전문가의 예측을 능가한다는 내용이 재진술되어 있습니다. 또한 요인들이 많거나 불안정한 상황에서 사람의 판단은 관련이 없을지도 모르는 고려 사항에 의해 영향을 받을 수도 있지만 알고리즘들은 중요한 요인에 집중하고 일관성을 유지하여 효과적이라고 합니다. 알고리즘들을 이용할 수 있는 체크리스트들을 전문가들이 사용할 때 전문가들이 중요한 단계나 고려 사항을 놓치지 않음으로써 결정의 질을 높일 수 있다고 하므로 이 글의 주제는 체크리스트와 같은 알고리즘을 사용하는 것이 결정의 질을 높인다가 됩니다.

①번 선지 : 의사 결정을 할 때의 단순한 공식의 힘 - 정답 선지입니다.
②번 선지 : 항상 우선순위를 결정하라: 빅데이터 관리 요령 - 무관한 선지입니다.
③번 선지 : 알고리즘의 실수: 단순함의 신화
　　- 알고리즘에 대한 소재가 동일하지만 지문에서는 알고리즘을 사용함으로써 얻게 되는 장점에 대해서 제시되었습니다. ③번 선지는 알고리즘의 단점에 대해서 제시하고 있으므로 언급되지 않은 선지입니다.
④번 선지 : 준비하라! 만일의 경우를 대비해 체크리스트를 만들어라
　　- 21%의 수험생이 고른 오답 선지입니다. 이 지문에서 체크리스트가 중요하게 제시되었지만 체크리스트는 알고리즘에 대한 예시입니다. 그러므로 포괄적이지 않은 선지에 해당합니다.
⑤번 선지 : 인간의 판단이 알고리즘을 이기는 방법
　　- ⑤번 선지는 인간의 판단이 알고리즘보다 우수하다고 합니다. 즉, 선지는 '사람의 판단 > 알고리즘'이라고 합니다. 하지만 지문에서 사람의 판단은 불안정한 상황에서 관련이 없을 수 있는 고려 사항들에 영향을 받거나 중요한 단계나 고려 사항을 놓칠 수 있으므로 알고리즘이 더 우수하다고 합니다. '알고리즘 > 사람의 판단'이므로 방향 바꾸기 선지에 해당합니다.

밑줄 친 (a) ~ (e) 중에서 문맥상 낱말의 쓰임이 적절하지 <u>않은</u> 것은?

해설 [정답 : ④]

불안정한 상황의 예시에 해당하는 강력한 치료가 필요한 환자들에게는 많은 행동들이 필요하며 작은 실수 하나로도 생명을 잃을 수도 있다고 합니다. Ⅵ번 문장은 Ⅴ번 문장에 대한 예시로 강력한 치료가 필요한 환자들을 치료하는 것은 작은 실수로도 생명을 빼앗을 수도 있으므로, 사람들이 편안함을 느낄 때에 대한 예시로 적절하지 않습니다. 그러므로 'relax'를 'uncertain' 혹은, Ⅳ번 문장에서 제시된 요소들, 즉, 행동들이 많은 상황으로 'overload'로 바꿔야 합니다.

Ⅰ. There is / evidence (that even very simple algorithms / can outperform / expert judgement (on simple prediction problems)).

> **구** 'out'은 '~을 나가는 이미지'로 생각하시면 됩니다. 'outperform' '~을 나가는 이미지' + '수행하다'이므로 '~을 능가하다'로 이해하시면 됩니다.
>   - 심지어 매우 단순한 알고리즘들도 간단한 예측 문제들에 대한 전문가의 판단을 능가하는 증거가 있다고 합니다.

> **독** 간단한 알고리즘들이라도 전문가의 판단보다 좋을 수 있다고 합니다.

Ⅱ. **For example**, algorithms / have proved / more (a) <u>accurate</u> than humans (in predicting / whether a prisoner released on parole / will go on / to commit another crime), or (in predicting / whether a potential candidate / will perform well (in a job in future)).

* parole: 가석방

> **구** 'in V-ing'는 'V함에 있어서'를 의미합니다.
>   - 'whether'이 목적절로 제시된 경우 '~인지 아닌지'로 해석하시면 됩니다.
>   - 예를 들어, 알고리즘들은 가석방으로 판단된 죄수가 다른 범죄를 저지를지 아닐지에 대한 예측을 함에 있어서, 또한 잠재적인 후보자가 미래에 그의 역할을 잘 수행할지 아닐지에 대한 예측을 함에 있어서 사람보다 더 정확하다는 것이 증명되어졌다고 합니다.

> **독** 'For example'이 제시되었으므로 앞 문장 중심 문장
>   - 알고리즘들이 사람보다 더 정확한 예측을 했던 사례들을 제시하고 있습니다.

Ⅲ. (In over 100 studies across many different domains), half of all cases / show / simple formulas /
make / (b) <u>better</u> significant predictions than human experts, and the remainder / (except a very
small handful), show / a tie (between the two).

구▶ 다양한 영역의 100개가 넘는 연구에서, 모든 경우 중 절반의 간단한 공식들이 (= 알고리즘들이)
　　 전문가들보다 더 좋고 중요한 예측들을 만드는 것을 보여줬으며, 나머지 절반에서 (= 매우 작은 경우를
　　 제외하고) 두 개가 (= 전문가와 알고리즘이) 비겼다고 합니다.

독▶ Ⅱ번 문장에 이어서 알고리즘이 전문가들보다 좋은 판단을 한 예시를 제시하고 있습니다.

Ⅳ. When there are / a lot of different factors involved and a situation / is / very uncertain, simple
formulas / can win out (by focusing on / the most important factors and being consistent), **while**
human judgement / is too easily influenced (by particularly salient and perhaps (c) <u>irrelevant</u>
considerations).

** salient: 두드러진

구▶ ‘by V-ing’는 ‘V함으로써’를 의미합니다.
　　 - 관련된 다양한 요인들이 있고 상황이 매우 부정확할 때 (= 불안할 때), 간단한 공식들은 매우 중요한
　　　 요인들에 집중함으로써, 일관성을 가짐으로써 승리할 수 있는 반면, (= 효과적인 반면) 사람의 판단은
　　　 특정하게 두드러지거나 아마도 관련이 없는 고려 사항들에 너무 쉽게 영향을 받는다고 합니다.

독▶ ‘while’이 제시되었으므로 중심 문장
　　 - 알고리즘들은 상황이 요인들이 너무 많고 상황이 불안정해도 중요한 요인들에만 집중하여 효과적인
　　　 반면 사람의 판단, 즉, 전문가의 판단은 관련이 없는 사항에도 영향을 받는다고 합니다.

Ⅴ. A similar idea / is supported (by further evidence) (that ‘checklists’ / can improve / the quality of
expert decisions (in a range of domains) (by ensuring / that important steps or considerations /
aren't missed (when people / are feeling (d) <u>relaxed</u>)).

구▶ ‘by V-ing’는 ‘V함으로써’를 의미합니다.
　　 - 비슷한 생각이 ‘체크리스트’가 사람들이 편안함을 (⇒ 불안감을) 느낄 때 중요한 단계나 고려 사항들을
　　　 놓치지 않는 것을 보증함으로써 한 영역의 전문가의 결정에 대한 질을 개선시킬 수 있다는 증거로 인해
　　　 지지된다고 합니다.

독▶ ‘checklist’가 있으면 불안한 상황에서도 전문가들의 판단이 더욱 좋아진다고 합니다. 이는 ‘checklist’가
　　 전문가의 판단에 도움이 되었다는 것이고 ‘checklist’가 없다면 전문가의 판단에서 중요한 단계나 고려 사항이
　　 누락될 수 있다는 내용입니다. 그러므로 불안한 상황에서 사람의 판단이 흔들릴 수 있다는 Ⅳ번 문장의
　　 내용을 재진술하였습니다.

Ⅵ. **<u>For example</u>**, treating patients (in intensive care) / can require / hundreds of small actions per day, and one small error / could cost / a life.

구▶ 예를 들어, 강력한 케어로 (= 중환자실에 있는 환자처럼 집중 치료로) 환자들을 치료하는 것은 하루에 수백 개의 작은 행동들이 요구될 수 있으며, 하나의 작은 실수가 생명을 빼앗아 갈 수도 있다고 합니다.

독▶ 'For example'이 제시되었으므로 앞 문장 중심 무장
- 불안정한 상황의 예시에 해당하는 강력한 치료가 필요한 환자들에게는 많은 행동들이 필요하며 작은 실수 하나로도 생명을 잃을 수도 있다고 합니다. Ⅵ번 문장은 Ⅴ번 문장에 대한 예시로 강력한 치료가 필요한 환자들을 치료하는 것은 작은 실수로도 생명을 빼앗을 수도 있으므로, 사람들이 편안함을 느낄 때에 대한 예시로 적절하지 않습니다. 그러므로 'relax'를 'uncertain' 혹은, Ⅳ번 문장에서 제시된 요소들, 즉, 행동들이 많은 상황으로 'overload'로 바꿔야 합니다.

Ⅶ. Using checklists (to ensure / that no crucial steps / are missed) / has proved to be remarkably (e)<u>effective</u> (in a range of medical contexts), (from preventing live infections to reducing pneumonia).

*** pneumonia: 폐렴

구▶ 'from A to B'는 'A부터 B까지'로 해석하시면 됩니다.
- 중요한 단계를 놓치지 않는 것을 보증하기 위해서 체크리스트들을 사용하는 것은 감염을 막는 것에서부터 폐렴을 줄이는 것까지 의학적 상황에서 매우 효과적인 것으로 증명되어졌다고 합니다.

독▶ 전문가들이 중요한 단계를 놓치지 않기 위해서 체크리스트를 사용하는 것은 매우 효과적이라고 합니다.

To the extent that sufficient context has been provided, the reader can come to a well-crafted text with no expert knowledge and come away with a good approximation of what has been intended by the author. The text has **become** a public document and the reader can read it with a (a) <u>minimum</u> of effort and struggle; his experience comes close to what Freud has described as the deployment of "evenly-hovering attention." He puts himself in the author's hands (some have had this experience with great novelists such as Dickens or Tolstoy) and he (b) <u>follows</u> where the author leads. The real world has vanished and the fictive world has taken its place. **Now consider the other extreme**. When we come to a badly crafted text in which context and content are not happily joined, we **must** struggle to understand, and our sense of what the author intended probably bears (c) <u>close</u> correspondence to his original intention. An out-of-date translation will give us this experience; as we read, we **must** bring the language up to date, and understanding comes only at the price of a fairly intense struggle with the text. Badly presented content with no frame of reference can provide (d) <u>the same</u> experience; we see the words **but** have no sense of how they are to be taken. The author who fails to provide the context has (e) <u>mistakenly</u> assumed that his picture of the world is shared by all his readers and fails to realize that supplying the right frame of reference is a critical part of the task of writing.

* deployment: (전략적) 배치
** evenly-hovering attention: 고르게 주의를 기울이는 것

21 21학년도 9월 평가원 41번 (정답률 55%)

윗글의 제목으로 가장 적절한 것은?

해설 [정답 : ④]

지문에서 충분한 문맥이 제공될 때와 충분한 문맥이 제공되지 않는 경우로 나누어 충분한 문맥의 중요성을 강조하고 있습니다. 충분한 문맥이 제공될 때는 독자가 적은 노력으로 작가가 의도한 것을 이해할 수 있다고 합니다. 반면 충분한 문맥이 제공되지 않는 경우 많은 노력을 해야하고 작가가 의도한 것과 무관하게 이해하게 된다고 합니다.

①번 선지 : 현실과 상상의 세계 사이에 벽 세우기
 - 충분한 문맥이 제공될 때 현실 세계가 사라지고 상상의 세계가 발생하지만 충분한 문맥이 제공될 때의 효과에 불과하므로 포괄하지 않는 선지입니다.
②번 선지 : 창의적 글 읽기: 작가의 의도를 넘어서는 것 - 무관한 선지입니다.
③번 선지 : 효과적인 글쓰기를 위한 독자 경험의 유용성
 - 글쓰기라는 동일한 소재를 제시하고 있지만 독자의 경험이 글쓰기와 관련되어 있다는 내용으로 무관한 선지입니다.
④번 선지 : 글쓰기에서의 문맥: 텍스트 이해를 위한 등대
 - 독자가 텍스트를 이해하기 위해서는 충분한 문맥을 제공해야 한다고 하므로 정답 선지입니다.
⑤번 선지 : 자기 자신의 말에 갇히다: 작가들의 좁은 견해 - 무관한 선지입니다.

22 21학년도 9월 평가원 42번 (정답률 48%)

밑줄 친 (a) ~ (e) 중에서 문맥상 낱말의 쓰임이 적절하지 <u>않은</u> 것은?

해설 [정답 : ③]

지문에서 문맥이 충분히 제공될 때와는 달리 문맥이 충분히 제공되지 않을 때는 많은 노력을 해야 하고 단어들을 어떻게 받아들여야 할지 이해하지 못한다고 하므로 (c)를 포함하는 문장에서 작가가 의도한 것에 대한 우리의 이해는 작가의 본래 의도와 'close', '밀접한' 것이 아닌 'little', '무관'해야 하므로 정답은 ③번이 됩니다.

Ⅰ. To the extent (that sufficient context / has been provided), / the reader / can come to / a well-crafted text (with no expert knowledge)) and come away with / a good approximation (of what has been intended by the author)).

> **구** 'come (오다) + to (어디를 향하는 이미지) = come to - 다가가다'가 된 반면
> 'come (오다) + away (붙어있다가 멀어지는 이미지) = come away - 떠나다'가 됩니다.
> - 충분한 맥락이 제공된 경우, 독자는 전문적 지식 없이도 잘 만들어진 텍스트에 다가가고 작가가 의도한 것과 아주 근접한 것을 가지고 떠날 수 있다고 합니다.

Ⅱ. The text / has become / a public document and the reader / can read / it (with a (a) <u>minimum</u> of effort and struggle); his experience / comes close to / what Freud / has described (as the deployment of "evenly-hovering attention.")

* deployment: (전략적) 배치 ** evenly-hovering attention: 고르게 주의를 기울이는 것

> **구** 'describe A as B'는 'A를 B라고 묘사하다'를 의미합니다.
> - 그 텍스트는 공적 문서가 되어가며, 독자는 그것을 '최소한의' 노력과 분투로 읽을 수 있게 된다고 합니다. 그의 경험은 Freud가 "고르게 주의를 기울이는 것"의 배치라고 묘사한 것과 가까워진다고 합니다.

> **독** 결과의 'become'이 제시되었으므로 중심 문장
> - 독자들이 쉽게 접근하는 텍스트는 공적 문서가 되며, 적은 노력과 분투로 읽을 수 있다고 합니다.

Ⅲ. He / puts / himself (in the author's hands) (some / have had / this experience (with great novelists such as Dickens or Tolstoy)) and he / (b) <u>follows</u> / where the author / leads.

> **구** 그는 작가의 손에 자신 스스로를 두고 (어떤 사람들이 Dickens나 Tolstoy와 같은 위대한 소설가와 이런 경험을 가졌던 것과 같이) 그는 작가가 이끄는 곳을 '따라간다고' 합니다.

Ⅳ. The real world / has vanished and the fictive world / has taken / its place.

> **구** 실제 세계는 사라지고 상상의 세계가 그 자리를 채운다고 합니다.

*   vanish - 사라지다, 죽다
** fictive - 상상의

Ⅴ. **Now consider the other extreme**.

> 구▸ 이제 반대의 경우를 생각해 봅시다.

> 독▸ 반대의 경우를 생각해보자는 것은 전환의 표현으로 앞 뒷 문장이 중심 문장입니다.

Ⅵ. When we / come to / a badly crafted text (in which context and content / are not happily joined), / we / **must** struggle to understand, / and our sense (of what the author intended) probably bears /

(c) <u>close</u> correspondence (to his original intention).

> 구▸ 'bear'가 동사로 쓰일 경우 '지니다, 견디다'를 의미합니다.
> - 우리가 문맥과 내용이 적절하게 결합하지 않는, 제대로 만들어지지 않은 텍스트의 경우, 우리는 이해하려고 노력해야만 하고, 작가가 의도한 것에 대한 우리의 인지는 아마도 그의 본래 의도와는 '밀접한' 관련성을 가질 것이라고 합니다.

> 독▸ 'must'가 제시되었고 전환의 표현 뒷 문장이므로 중심 문장
> - 제대로 만들어진 텍스트와 달리 제대로 만들어지지 않은 텍스트는 이해하려고 노력해야만 하고 작가가 의도한 것에 대한 우리의 이해는 작가의 본래 의도와는 무관한 관련성을 지닌다고 합니다. 지문에서 문맥이 충분히 제공되지 않을 때는 많은 노력을 해야하고 단어들을 어떻게 받아들여야 할지 이해하지 못한다고 하므로 (c)를 포함하는 문장에서 작가가 의도한 것에 대한 우리의 이해는 작가의 본래 의도와 'close', '밀접한'것이 아닌 'little', '무관'해야 하므로 정답은 ③번이 됩니다.

Ⅶ. An out-of-date translation / will give / us / this experience; (as we read), we / must bring / the language (up to date), and understanding / comes only (at the price of a fairly intense struggle (with the text)).

> 구▸ 'give + I.O + D.O'는 'I.O에게 D.O를 주다'를 의미합니다.
> - 'at the price of A'는 'A의 대가로'를 뜻합니다.
> - 구식의 번역은 우리에게 이런 경험을 주는데, 우리가 읽을 때, 우리는 최신의 언어를 가져와야만 하며, 이해는 텍스트와 꽤 강력한 분투의 대가로 다가온다고 합니다.

> 독▸ 'must'가 제시되었으므로 중심 문장
> - 제대로 만들어지지 않은 텍스트와 마찬가지로, 구식의 번역은 우리가 이해하기 위해서는 많은 노력을 해야만 한다고 합니다.

Ⅷ. Badly presented content (with no frame of reference) / can provide / (d) <u>the same</u> experience; we / see / the words **but** have / no sense (of how they are to be taken).

> 구▸ 참조의 틀이 없는 잘못 제시된 내용은 '같은' 경험을 제공하는데, 우리는 단어들을 보지만 어떻게 그것들을 받아들여야 하는지 이해하지 못한다고 합니다.

> 독▸ 'but'이 제시되므로 중심 문장
> - Ⅵ번, Ⅶ번 문장과 마찬가지로 참고할 내용 없이 잘못 제시된 내용도 우리가 이해하지 못한다고 합니다.

IX. The author (who fails to provide / the context) / has (e) <u>mistakenly</u> assumed / that his picture (of the world) / is shared (by all his readers) / and fails to realize / that supplying the right frame (of reference) / is / a critical part of the task of writing.

구▶ 문맥을 제공하지 못한 작가는 세상에 대한 자신의 그림을 모든 독자가 공유한다고 '잘못' 가정하고, 적절한 참조의 틀을 제공하는 것이 글을 쓰는 일의 중대한 부분임을 깨닫지 못한다고 합니다.

[23~24] 다음 글을 읽고, 물음에 답하시오.

In studies examining the effectiveness of vitamin C, researchers typically divide the subjects into two groups. One group (the experimental group) receives a vitamin C supplement, and the other (the control group) does not. Researchers observe both groups to determine whether one group has fewer or shorter colds than the other. The following discussion describes some of the pitfalls inherent in an experiment of this kind and ways to (a) <u>avoid</u> them. In sorting subjects into two groups, researchers **must** ensure that each person has an (b) <u>equal</u> chance of being assigned to either the experimental group or the control group. This is accomplished by randomization; **that is**, the subjects are chosen randomly from the same population by flipping a coin or some other method involving chance. Randomization helps to ensure that results reflect the treatment and not factors that might influence the grouping of subjects. Importantly, the two groups of people **must** be similar and **must** have the same track record with respect to colds to (c) <u>rule out</u> the possibility that observed differences in the rate, severity, or duration of colds might have occurred anyway. If, **for example**, the control group would normally catch twice as many colds as the experimental group, then the findings prove (d) <u>nothing</u>. In experiments involving a nutrient, the diets of both groups **must** also be (e) <u>different</u>, especially with respect to the nutrient being studied. If those in the experimental group were receiving less vitamin C from their usual diet, then any effects of the supplement may not be apparent.

* pitfall: 함정

23 22학년도 9월 평가원 41번   (정답률 51%)

윗글의 제목으로 가장 적절한 것은?

해설 [정답 : ②]

실험을 할 때 집단을 구분하는 올바른 방법에 관한 지문입니다. 비타민 C가 감기에 끼치는 영향을 파악하기 위한 실험을 예로 든 지문에서는, 실험에 내재한 함정들을 피하려면, 즉 실험 대상자의 분류가 결과에 영향을 미치지 않도록 하려면, 집단을 추출할 때 임의로 배정해야 하며, 두 집단 모두 감기와 관련한 동일한 기록을 가지고 있도록 설정해야 한다는 것입니다. 그렇게 하지 않는다면, 실험의 결과는 아무것도 입증하지 못하게 됩니다.

①번 선지 : 완벽한 계획과 불완전한 결과: 연구의 슬픈 현실
   - 완벽한 계획이라도 불완전한 결과로 이어질 수 있다는 내용의 지문이 아닙니다. 오히려 실험 계획에 대한 통제가 완벽하지 않으면 결과가 아무것도 입증할 수 없다는 내용에 가깝습니다.

②번 선지 : 상관없는 요인이 결과에 영향을 미치지 않도록 해라!
   - 정답 선지입니다. 실험 집단 분류의 임의성, 감기에 관련된 동일한 기록, 동일한 식단 등은 모두 상관없는 요인이 결과에 영향을 미치지 않도록 하기 위한 예시로서 언급되었습니다.

③번 선지 : 실험 연구에 참여하는 인간 실험 대상자들을 보호해라!
   - 실험 참가자들의 인권과 관련된 내용이 아닙니다.

④번 선지 : 어떤 영양분이 감기를 더 잘 막을 수 있을까?
   - 감기와 비타민 C의 실험은 변인을 올바르게 통제해야 하는 것에 대한 예시일 뿐이지, 글의 제목이 될 수 없습니다.

⑤번 선지 : 영양에 대한 심층 분석: 인간의 건강을 위한 핵심 요소
   - ④번과 같은 이유로 답이 될 수 없습니다.

밑줄 친 (a) ~ (e) 중에서 문맥상 낱말의 쓰임이 적절하지 <u>않은</u> 것은?

해설 [**정답 : ⑤**]

글에서는 연구 결과에 외부 요인이 영향을 미치지 않도록 실험 집단과 통제 집단을 통제해야 한다고 했습니다. 그래서 그에 대한 예로 Ⅷ번 문장에서 감기와 관련하여 두 집단의 사람들이 비슷하고 동일한 기록을 가지고 있어야 한다는 예시가 언급되고 있습니다. 그러므로 (e) 문장에서도 영양분을 포함하는 실험에서 두 집단의 식단은 당연히 같아야 하므로 (e) 'different'를 비슷하다는 뜻의 'similar'과 같은 단어로 바꿔야 합니다.

Ⅰ. In studies / examining the effectiveness of vitamin C, researchers typically divide / the subjects / into two groups.

> 구▸ 'divide A into B'는 'A를 B로 나누다'를 의미합니다.
> - 비타민 C의 효과를 조사하는 연구에서, 연구원들은 일반적으로 실험 대상자들을 두 집단으로 나눈다.

> 독▸ 비타민 C의 효과를 조사하는 실험 과정이 등장하고 있습니다.

Ⅱ. One group (the experimental group) receives a vitamin C supplement, and the other (the control group) does not.

> 구▸ 한 집단(실험 집단)은 비타민 C 보충제를 받고 「다른 집단(통제 집단)은 비타민 C 보충제를 받지 않는다.

> 독▸ 두 집단의 차이점이 언급됩니다.

> * supplement - 보충물

Ⅲ. Researchers / observe / both groups / to determine / whether one group / has / fewer or shorter colds than the other.

> 구▸ 'whether A or B'는 'A인지 B인지'를 의미합니다.
> - 연구원들은 한 집단이 다른 집단보다 감기에 더 적게 또는 더 짧게 걸리는지를 알아내기 위해 두 집단 모두를 관찰한다.

Ⅳ. The following discussion / describes / some of the pitfalls / inherent (in an experiment of this kind / and ways to (a) <u>avoid</u> them).

> * pitfall: 함정

> 구▸ 이어지는 논의는 이러한 종류의 실험에 내재한 함정 중 일부와 이를 피하는 방법을 설명한다.

> 독▸ 비타민 C에 관한 실험에서 실험에 내재된 함정으로 글의 내용이 전환됩니다.

Ⅴ. In sorting subjects into two groups, researchers / **must** ensure / that each person / has an (b) <u>equal</u> chance / (of being assigned to / either the experimental group or the control group).

> 구 'assign A to B'는 'A를 B에 할당하다'를 의미합니다.
> - 'either A or B'는 'A와 B 중 하나'를 의미합니다.
> - 실험 대상자를 두 집단으로 분류할 때, 연구원들은 반드시 각 개인이 실험 집단 또는 통제 집단 둘 중 한 곳에 배정될 확률이 동일하도록 해야 한다.

> 독 'must'가 언급되므로 중심 문장
> - Ⅳ번 문장의 함정들을 피하는 방법에 대한 예시 문장입니다.

Ⅵ. This is accomplished by randomization; **that is**, the subjects / are chosen randomly (from the same population) by flipping a coin / or some other method involving chance.

> 구 'by V-ing'는 'V함으로써'를 의미합니다.
> - 이는 임의 추출에 의해 달성되는데 즉 실험 대상자는 동전 던지기나 우연이 포함된 어떤 다른 방법에 의해 동일 모집단에서 임의로 선정된다.

> 독 'that is'가 언급되므로 중심 문장
> - Ⅴ번 문장에서 이어지는 내용입니다. 동전 던지기와 같은 확률이 동일한 방법을 통해 실험 집단들을 분류해야 한다는 것입니다.

Ⅶ. Randomization / helps / to ensure / that results / reflect / the treatment and not factors / that might influence / the grouping of subjects.

> 구 임의 추출은 반드시 결과에 처리가 반영되도록, 실험 대상자의 분류에 영향을 줄지도 모르는 요인은 반영되지 않도록 하는 데 도움이 된다.

> 독 임의 추출을 해야 하는 이유는 실험 대상자의 분류에 영향을 주는 요인을 배제해야 하기 때문임을 알 수 있습니다.

Ⅷ. Importantly, the two groups (of people) / **must** be / similar / and **must** have / the same track record / with respect to colds to (c) <u>rule out</u> the possibility / that observed / differences (in the rate, severity), or duration of colds / might have occurred anyway.

> 구 중요한 것은, 감기의 비율, 심각성, 또는 지속 기간에서 관찰된 차이가 어떤 식으로든 일어났을지도 모른다는 가능성을 배제하기 위해 감기와 관련하여 두 집단의 사람들이 비슷하고 동일한 기록을 가지고 있어야 한다는 것이다.

> 독 'must'가 언급되므로 중심 문장
> - 실험 관찰에 영향을 줄 수 있는 가능성을 배제하기 위해 두 집단은 최대한 동일한 상태를 유지해야 한다는 것임을 알 수 있습니다.

IX. If, <u>**for example**</u>, the control group / would normally catch / twice as many colds / as the experimental group, then the findings prove (d) <u>nothing</u>.

> 구 예를 들어, 만약 통제 집단이 보통 실험 집단보다 감기에 무려 두 배나 많이 걸리는 경우, 연구 결과는 아무것도 입증하지 못한다.

> 독 'for example'이 제시되었으므로 앞 문장 중심 문장
> - 두 집단이 감기에 걸리는 비율에서 차이가 발생한다는 것은 Ⅷ번 문장에 감기와 관련하여 두 집단이 비슷한 기록을 가지고 있지 않기 때문에, 실험의 결과가 의미가 없고 비타민 C 보충제의 효과를 분명하게 알 수 없게 됩니다. 즉 Ⅳ번 문장에서 언급된 실험의 함정에 빠진 예시라고 볼 수 있습니다.

X. In experiments involving a nutrient, the diets (of both groups) / <u>**must**</u> also be / (e) <u>different</u>, especially (with respect to the nutrient being studied).

> 구 'with respect to A'는 'A에 대한 관점에서'를 의미합니다.
> - 영양분을 포함하는 실험에서, 두 집단의 식단 또한 달라야(→ 비슷해야) 하며, 연구 중인 영양분에 관련해서 특히 그래야 한다.

> 독 'must'가 언급되므로 중심 문장
> - 두 집단의 사람들이 서로 비슷한 기록을 가지고 있도록 해야 한다고 했으므로 실험이 외부 요인에 영향을 받지 않으려면 두 집단의 식단은 서로 비슷해야 하며, 'different'를 'similar'과 같은 단어로 바꿔야 합니다.

XI. If those / in the experimental group / were receiving less vitamin C / from their usual diet, then any effects / of the supplement / may not be apparent.

> 구 만약 실험 집단에 속한 사람들이 평소 식단에서 비타민 C를 적게 섭취하고 있었다면, 보충제의 어떤 효과도 분명하지 않을 수 있다.

> 독 두 집단이 섭취한 비타민 C의 양이 다르므로 역시 실험의 결과가 의미가 없게 되는 경우입니다.

[25~26] 다음 글을 읽고, 물음에 답하시오.

One reason we think we forget most of what we learned in school is that we underestimate what we actually remember. Other times, we know we remember something, **but** we don't recognize that we learned it in school. Knowing where and when you learned something is usually called context information, and context is handled by (a) <u>different</u> memory processes than memory for the content. **Thus**, it's quite possible to retain content without remembering the context.

For example, if someone mentions a movie and you think to yourself that you heard it was terrible **but** can't remember (b) <u>where</u> you heard that, you're recalling the content, **but** you've lost the context. Context information is frequently (c) <u>easier</u> to forget than content, and it's the source of a variety of memory illusions. **For instance**, people are (d) <u>unconvinced</u> by a persuasive argument if it's written by someone who is not very credible (e.g., someone with a clear financial interest in the topic). **But** in time, readers' attitudes, on average, change in the direction of the persuasive argument. Why? **Because** readers are likely to remember the content of the argument **but** forget the source — someone who is not credible. If remembering the source of knowledge is difficult, you can see how it would be (e) <u>challenging</u> to conclude you don't remember much from school.

* illusion: 착각

25 24학년도 9월 평가원 41번

(정답률 52%)

윗글의 제목으로 가장 적절한 것은?

해설 [정답 : ①]

기억을 제대로 하지 못하는 원인인 맥락 정보의 부재를 설명하는 지문입니다. 맥락 정보의 특징, 그 상실로 인해 발생하는 기억 오류와 같은 지문의 내용을 포함한 선지가 답이 될 가능성이 높습니다.

①번 선지 : 학교에서 배운 것이 없는가?: 기억이 어떻게 당신을 속이는가
- 학교에서 배운 것이 없다 – 기억 오류, 기억이 어떻게 당신을 속이는가 - 그 원인인 맥락 정보의 부재를 모두 포괄하는 정답 선지입니다.

②번 선지 : 우리가 선택적으로 잊어버리는 이유: 내용의 신뢰성
- 선택적으로 잊어버리는 것은 기억 오류의 예시로 볼 수 있지만, 그 원인은 내용의 신뢰성이 아니기 때문에 오답 선지입니다.

③번 선지 : 내용과 맥락 사이의 끊임없는 싸움
- 내용 정보와 맥락 정보 중 맥락 정보의 특징과 관련된 내용이므로 오답입니다.

④번 선지 : 학생들이 학교에서 더 많이 그리고 더 잘 배울 수 있는 방법
- 학생들의 학습에 관한 지문이 아닙니다.

⑤번 선지 : 기억 형성을 위해 여러분의 초점을 누구에서 무엇으로 전환하라
- 역시 기억 문제에 대한 원인을 잘못 언급한 선지이므로 오답입니다.

밑줄 친 (a) ~ (e) 중에서 문맥상 낱말의 쓰임이 적절하지 <u>않은</u> 것은?

해설 [정답 : ⑤]

Ⅰ번 문장에서 'we forget most of what we learned in school', 우리가 학교에서 배운 것 대부분을 잊어버린다고 했습니다. 그렇다면 지문에서 이 원인에 대한 내용을 정리하면 다음과 같습니다. Ⅴ번 문장에서 'but can't remember where you heard that, you're recalling the content, but you've lost the context', 어디에서 들었는지 기억할 수 없다면, 내용은 기억하지만 맥락은 잃어버린 것이다. Ⅵ번 문장에서 'it's the source of a variety of memory illusions' 맥락 정보는 다양한 기억 착각의 근원이다. 그런데 (e) 문장에서는 'If remembering the source of knowledge is difficult, you can see how it would be challenging to conclude you don't remember much from school.' 지식의 출처를 기억하는 게 어렵다면, 네가 학교에서 배운 것을 기억하지 못한다고 결론 내리기가 어렵다고 했습니다. 지식의 출처를 기억하지 못하는 것은 맥락 정보를 잃어버린 경우인데, 이 경우 배운 것을 제대로 기억하지 못한다고 결론을 내리기가 어렵다고 볼 수 없습니다. 오히려 결론을 내리기가 쉽다고 봐야 하며, 'challenging'은 쉽다는 뜻의 'easy'와 같은 단어로 바꿔야 합니다.

Ⅰ. One reason (which (we think) <u>we / forget / most (of what we learned in school))</u> / is / (that we / underestimate (what we / actually remember).

> **구** 우리가 학교에서 배운 대부분의 것들을 잊어버렸다고 생각하는 한 가지 이유는 우리가 실제로 기억하는 깃을 과소평가하기 때문이라고 합니다.

> **독** 이 글의 중심 키워드는 '학교에서 배운 것' 그리고 속성은 '대부분 잊어버렸다고 생각하는 것' 그리고 그 원인은 '학교에서 배운 것을 과소평가하는 것'입니다.

Ⅱ. Other times, we / know / that we / remember / something, <u>**but**</u> we / don't recognize / that we / learned / it (in school).

> **구** 다른 때에는 우리가 무언가를 기억한다는 것을 알지만, 그것을 학교에서 배웠다는 것을 인식하지 못한다고 합니다.

> **독** 학교에서 배운 것을 과소평가하기에 일어나는 일입니다.

Ⅲ. Knowing (where and when you / learned / something) / is usually / called context information, and context / is / handled (by (a) <u>different</u> memory processes than memory for the content).

> **구** 어디서 그리고 언제 무언가를 배웠는지 알고 있는 것을 보통 맥락 정보라고 부르며, 맥락은 내용에 대한 기억과는 다른 기억 과정에 의해 처리된다고 합니다.

> **독** 왜 학교에서 배운 것을 기억하지 못하고 과소평가하는지에 대한 분석의 요소로 '맥락 정보'를 소개하고 있습니다.

Ⅳ. **Thus**, it's quite possible (to retain content (without remembering the context)).

구▶ 따라서 맥락을 기억하지 않고 내용만 유지하는 것이 가능하다고 합니다.

독▶ 맥락 즉, 학교에서 배웠다는 것을 기억하지 못하고 지식만을 기억하고 있습니다.

Ⅴ. **For example**, (if someone / mentions / a movie and you / think (to yourself) (that you / heard (that it / was / terrible)) **but** can't remember ((b) <u>where</u> you / heard / that)), you're / recalling the content, **but** you've / lost / the context.

구▶ 예를 들어, 누군가가 영화에 대해 언급하고, 그것이 끔찍하다고 들었지만 어디서 들었는지 기억할 수 없다면, 당신은 내용을 회상하고 있지만, 당신은 맥락을 잃어버린 것이라고 합니다.

독▶ 'For example'이 있으니 앞 문장 중심문장, 또한 'but'이 제시되었으니 중심문장

Ⅵ. Context information / is / frequently (c) <u>easier</u> (to forget than content), and it's the source (of a variety of memory illusions).

* illusion: 착각

구▶ 맥락 정보는 종종 내용보다 잊기 쉽고, 다양한 기억에 대한 착각의 원인이라고 합니다.

독▶ 왜 학교에서 배운 지식을 과소평가하는지에 대한 추가 설명입니다.

Ⅶ. **For instance**, people / are / (d) <u>unconvinced</u> (by a persuasive argument) (if it's written (by someone (who / is not very / credible)) (e.g., someone with a clear financial interest in the topic).

구▶ 예를 들어, 사람들은 그것이 그다지 신뢰할 만한 사람에 의해 쓰여지지 않았다면 설득력 있는 논쟁에 납득되지 않는다고 합니다. (예: 주제에 대한 명확한 금전적 이해관계를 가진 사람).

독▶ 맥락 정보에 대한 다른 범주의 지식을 설명하고 있습니다. 즉, 범주가 학교에서 신뢰하지 못할 만한 사람으로 이동했습니다.

Ⅷ. **But** in time, readers' attitudes, on average, / change (in the direction of the persuasive argument).

구▶ 그러나 시간이 지나면, 독자들의 태도는 평균적으로 설득적인 논쟁의 방향으로 변한다고 합니다.

독▶ 맥락 정보의 특성으로 인한 결과입니다.

Ⅸ. Why? **Because** readers / are likely to / remember / the content (of the argument) but forget / the source — someone (who / is not / credible).

구▶ 왜냐하면 독자들은 논쟁의 내용을 기억할 가능성이 있지만, 신뢰할 수 없는 사람이라는 출처를 잊어버릴 가능성이 높기 때문이라고 합니다.

X. (If remembering the source of knowledge / is / difficult), you / can see / (how it / would be / (e) challenging) (to conclude (that you / don't remember / much (from school))).

구 지식의 출처를 기억하는 것이 어렵다면, 학교에서 배운 것 중 많은 것을 기억하지 못한다고 결론 내리는 것이 어려울 것이라고 합니다.

독 이 글 전체가 맥락은 잊어버리고 지식만을 기억하기에 생기는 학교지식에 대한 과소평가에 대한 글이기 때문에 학교에서 배운 것 중 많은 것을 기억하지 못한다고 결론을 내리는 것이 쉬울 것이라고 판단을 내려야 합니다.

Many negotiators assume that all negotiations involve a fixed pie. Negotiators often approach integrative negotiation opportunities as zero-sum situations or win-lose exchanges. Those who believe in the mythical fixed pie assume that parties' interests stand in opposition, with no possibility for integrative settlements and mutually beneficial trade-offs, **so** they (a) <u>suppress</u> efforts to search for them. In a hiring negotiation, a job applicant who assumes that salary is the only issue may insist on $75,000 when the employer is offering $70,000. Only when the two parties discuss the possibilities further do they discover that moving expenses and starting date can also be negotiated, which may (b) <u>block</u> resolution of the salary issue. The tendency to see negotiation in fixed-pie terms (c) <u>varies</u> depending on how people view the nature of a given conflict situation. This was shown in a clever experiment by Harinck, de Dreu, and Van Vianen involving a simulated negotiation between prosecutors and defense lawyers over jail sentences. Some participants were told to view their goals in terms of personal gain (e.g., arranging a particular jail sentence will help your career), others were told to view their goals in terms of effectiveness (a particular sentence is most likely to prevent recidivism), and still others were told to focus on values (a particular jail sentence is fair and just). Negotiators focusing on personal gain were most likely to come under the influence of fixed-pie beliefs and approach the situation (d) <u>competitively</u>. Negotiators focusing on values were least likely to see the problem in fixed-pie terms and more inclined to approach the situation cooperatively. Stressful conditions such as time constraints contribute to this common misperception, which in turn may **lead to** (e) <u>less</u> integrative agreements.

* prosecutor: 검사 ** recidivism: 상습적 범행

27 24학년도 6월 평가원 41번 (정답률 57%)

윗글의 제목으로 가장 적절한 것은?

해설 [정답 : ③]

협상가들은 협상을 고정된 파이의 관점에서 접근하는데, 이에 대한 단점들을 언급하는 지문입니다. Ⅲ번 문장의 'no possibility for integrative settlements and mutually beneficial trade-offs' 절충안을 찾으려는 노력을 억제한다는 내용과, Ⅸ번 문장의 'approach the situation competitively' 고정된 파이의 영향을 받아 상황에 경쟁적으로 접근하는데, 이것은 ⅩⅠ번 문장의 'less integrative agreements' 오해와 합의 도출 실패로 이어질 수 있다는 내용으로 이어집니다. 이는 모두 고정된 파이의 관점에서 협상에 접근하는 것에 대한 부정적인 사례에 해당합니다.

①번 선지 : 고정된 파이: 제로섬 게임에서 성공의 열쇠

　　- 고정된 파이의 장점은 지문에서 찾아볼 수 없습니다.

②번 선지 : 고정된 파이는 네게 가장 큰 급여를 받는 방법을 알려준다.

　　- 급여만을 바라보고 협상하는 고정된 파이는 오히려 문제 해결을 어렵게 하므로 정답이 될 수 없습니다.

③번 선지 : 협상가들이여, 고정된 파이라는 미신에서 깨어나라!

　　- 정답 선지입니다. 고정된 파이라는 글의 주제를 부정적으로 인식하고 있습니다.

④번 선지 : 더 공정한 징역형을 원하는가? 고정된 파이를 고수하라.

　　- 반대 선지입니다.

⑤번 선지 : 어떤 대안이 고정된 파이 효과를 극대화하는가?

　　- 고정된 파이 효과를 극대화하는 대안은 지문에서 찾아볼 수 없습니다.

밑줄 친 (a) ~ (e) 중에서 문맥상 낱말의 쓰임이 적절하지 <u>않은</u> 것은?

해설 [정답 : ②]

Ⅲ번 문장에서는 'no possibility for integrative settlements and mutually beneficial trade-offs, so they suppress efforts', 허구의 고정된 파이를 믿는 사람들은 당사자들이 절충안의 가능성이 없는 반대 입장에 있다고 가정하기 때문에 이를 찾으려는 노력을 억누른다고 했습니다. Ⅴ번 문장에서는 'moving expenses and starting date can also be negotiated', 급여 협상 과정에서 이사 비용과 시작 날짜를 협상하는 예시가 언급되고 있는데, 이것은 고정된 파이를 늘리는 것이 아닌 협상 과정에서 통합적인 합의와 상호 이익이 될 수 있는 협상 전개의 내용이므로 오히려 문제를 해결할 수 있다고 봐야 합니다. 그러므로 (b)의 'block'을 'facilitate'와 같은 단어로 바꿔야 합니다.

Ⅰ. Many negotiators / assume / that / all negotiations / involve / a fixed pie.

> 구▶ 많은 협상가는 모든 협상이 고정된 파이를 수반한다고 가정한다고 합니다.

> 독▶ 지문에서 파이는, 음식이 아닌 몫이나 이익을 의미한다고 생각해야 합니다.

Ⅱ. Negotiators / often approach / integrative negotiation opportunities / as zero-sum situations or win-lose exchanges.

> 구▶ 'approach A as B'는 'A를 B로 접근하다'를 의미합니다.
> - 협상가들은 자주 통합 협상 기회를 제로섬 상황이나 승패 교환으로 접근한다고 합니다.

> 독▶ 제로섬(누가 얻는 만큼 반드시 누가 잃는 상황)=승패 교환

Ⅲ. Those (who / believe in the mythical fixed pie) / assume (that / parties' interests / stand in opposition), with no possibility for integrative settlements and mutually beneficial trade-offs, **so** they / (a) <u>suppress</u> efforts to search for them.

> 구▶ 허구의 고정된 이익을 믿는 사람들은 당사자들의 이해관계가 통합적인 합의와 상호 이익이 되는 절충안의 가능성이 없는 반대 입장에 있다고 가정하기 때문에 이를 찾으려는 노력을 억누른다고 합니다.

> 독▶ 'so'가 언급되므로 중심 문장
> - Ⅱ번 문장에서처럼 협상을 제로섬 게임(손해가 반드시 발생)으로 접근할 경우, 발생하는 결과에 대한 문장입니다. 이 경우, 상호 이득이 협상에서 절대로 발생할 수 없기 때문에, 절충안(상호 이득이 되는 상황)을 찾으려고 하지 않는다는 것을 의미합니다.

Ⅳ. In a hiring negotiation, a job applicant / who / assumes (that / salary / is / the only issue) may insist on $75,000 / when / the employer / is offering $70,000.

> **[구]** 고용 협상에서 급여가 유일한 문제라고 생각하는 구직자는 고용주가 7만 달러를 제시할 때 7만 5천 달러를 요구할 수 있다고 합니다.

> **[독]** 급여가 유일한 문제라고 생각하는 것은 협상의 파이를 급여로 고정시키는 것에 대한 예시가 되는 문장입니다. 그 결과 Ⅲ번 문장에서처럼 절충안이 잘 발생하지 않게 된다고 추론할 수 있습니다.

Ⅴ. (Only when the two parties / discuss the possibilities further) do / they / discover / that / moving expenses and starting date / can also be negotiated, which / may (b) <u>block</u> / resolution (of the salary issue.)

> **[구]** 부사절 'Only when the two parties discuss the possibilities further'가 앞으로 오면서 의문문 어순 도치가 되었습니다.
> - 두 당사자가 가능성에 대해 더 자세히 논의할 때만 이사 비용과 시작 날짜 또한 협상할 수 있다는 사실을 발견하게 되는데, 이는 급여 문제의 해결을 방해할 수 있을 것이라고 합니다.

> **[독]** 이 경우, Ⅳ번 문장에서의 협상의 몫이 이사 비용과 날짜로 확대되게 되며, 이것은 협상의 파이가 고정되지 않고 늘어나는 결과로 이어지므로 문제 해결을 촉진한다고 봐야 합니다.

Ⅵ. The tendency (to see negotiation in fixed-pie terms) / (c) <u>varies</u> depending on how / people / view / the nature of a given conflict situation.

> **[구]** 협상을 고정된 파이 관점에서 보는 경향은 사람들이 주어진 갈등 상황의 본질을 어떻게 보느냐에 따라 달라진다고 합니다.

> **[독]** 새로운 주장으로 글의 주제가 확대됩니다.

Ⅶ. This / was shown in a clever experiment (by Harinck, de Dreu, and Van Vianen) involving a simulated negotiation (between prosecutors and defense lawyers over jail sentences).

* prosecutor: 검사

> **[구]** 이는 Harinck, de Dreu와 Van Vianen의, 징역형에 대한 검사와 피고측 변호인 간의 모의 협상을 포함하는 기발한 실험에서 밝혀졌다고 합니다.

> **[독]** Ⅵ번 문장의 내용을 증명하는 실험이 처음으로 언급됩니다.

VIII. Some participants / were told to view their goals / in terms of personal gain (e.g., arranging a particular jail sentence will help your career), others / were told to view their goals / in terms of effectiveness (a particular sentence is most likely to prevent recidivism), and still others / were told to focus on values (a particular jail sentence is fair and just).

** recidivism: 상습적 범행

구▶ 어떤 참가자들은 개인적 이득의 관점에서 그들의 목표를 보라는 말(예를 들어, 특정 징역형을 정하는 것이 당신의 경력에 도움이 될 것이다)을 들었고, 다른 참가자들은 그들의 목표를 효과성의 관점에서 보라는 말(특정 형은 상습적 범행을 방지할 가능성이 가장 크다)을 들었으며, 그리고 또 다른 참가자들은 가치에 초점을 맞추라는 말(특정 징역형은 공정하고 정당하다)을 들었다고 합니다.

독▶ 실험에서 참가자들은 세 가지 관점으로 협상 목표를 설정하게 됩니다.
ⅰ. 개인적 이득의 관점(개인적 경력에 도움이 된다)
ⅱ. 효과성의 관점(차후 범행을 방지하는 효과가 있다)
ⅲ. 가치의 관점(공정과 정당성의 가치를 중시한다)

IX. Negotiators (focusing on personal gain) / were most likely to come under the influence of fixed-pie beliefs / and approach the situation (d) competitively.

구▶ 개인적 이득에 초점을 맞춘 협상가들은 고정된 파이에 대한 믿음의 영향을 받아 상황에 경쟁적으로 접근할 가능성이 가장 컸다고 합니다.

독▶ ⅰ번 관점의 경우에는 협상 상황을 경쟁적으로 접근하게 되며, 고정된 파이에 대한 믿음이 좋지 않다는 것을 보여 주는 문장입니다.

X. Negotiators (focusing on values) were least likely to see the problem in fixed-pie terms and more inclined to approach the situation cooperatively.

구▶ 가치에 초점을 맞춘 협상가들은 문제를 고정된 파이 관점에서 볼 가능성이 가장 낮았고 상황에 협력적으로 접근하려는 경향이 더 컸다고 합니다.

독▶ ⅲ번 관점에 집중할 경우, 협력적으로 접근한다고 합니다. 이를 요약하면,
ⅰ. 개인적 이득의 관점: 경쟁적 접근↑, 협력적 접근↓
ⅱ. 효과성의 관점: 경쟁적 접근−, 협력적 접근−
ⅲ. 가치의 관점: 경쟁적 접근↓, 협력적 접근↑
고정된 파이 관점이 높을수록 협상에 경쟁적으로 임하며, 반대로 낮을수록 협력적으로 접근해 합의에 이를 가능성이 더 높다고 볼 수 있습니다.

XI. Stressful conditions (such as time constraints) contribute to this common misperception, which in turn may **lead to** (e) less integrative agreements.

구▶ 시간 제약과 같은 스트레스가 많은 조건은 이러한 흔한 오해의 원인이 되며, 이는 결국 덜 통합적인 합의로 이어질 수 있다고 합니다.

독▶ 'lead to'로 결과가 언급되므로 중심 문장
- 좋은 협상 결과로 이어지지 않는 원인으로 스트레스가 많은 조건을 설명하고 있습니다.

memo

Chapter
05

간접 쓰기

01 22학년도 수능 36번   (정답률 72%)

주어진 글 다음에 이어질 글의 순서로 가장 적절한 것을 고르시오.

> ① According to the market response model, it is increasing prices that drive providers to search for new sources, innovators to substitute, consumers to conserve, and alternatives to emerge.

(A)

① Many examples of **such "green taxes"** exist.

② Facing landfill costs, labor expenses, and related costs in the provision of garbage disposal, **for example**, some cities have required households to dispose of all waste in special trash bags, purchased by consumers themselves, and often costing a dollar or more each.

(B)

① Taxing certain goods or services, and so increasing prices, **should result in** either decreased use of these resources or creative innovation of new sources or options.

② The money raised through **the tax** can be used directly by the government either to supply services or to search for alternatives.

(C)

① **The results** have been greatly increased recycling and more careful attention by consumers to packaging and waste.

② By internalizing the costs of trash to consumers, there has been an observed decrease in the flow of garbage from households.

해설 [정답 : ②]

주어진 지문에서 시장 반응 모형에서는 가격이 인상하면 공급자가 새로운 자원을 찾는 등 다양한 활동을 한다고 합니다.

(A)의 ①번 문장부터 그러한 '환경세'에 대한 예시가 시작됩니다. (A)의 ②번 문장에서 매립 비용등을 충당하기 위해서 몇몇 도시들은 가정에서 나오는 폐기물을 소비자가 구입한 쓰레기 봉투에 담게 했다고 합니다. 이는 (C)의 ①번 문장으로 이어져, 소비자에 의해서 재활용이 증가했다고 합니다. 이는 (A)의 ②번 문장에 대한 결과이므로 (A) 다음에는 (C)가 와야 합니다.

(A) - (C)가 결정되었기 때문에 우리는 '환경세'에 대한 예시가 (B)에 대한 예시인지 주어진 지문에 대한 예시인지 파악해야 합니다. 주어진 지문에서는 세금에 대한 내용이 존재하지 않습니다. 반면, (B)의 ①번 문장에서 가격이 인상되면 가격이 인상된 자원들의 사용은 감소할 것이고, 새로운 자원이 새롭게 생길 것이라고 합니다. 또한 (B)의 ②번 문장에서는 세금을 통해 조성된 돈은 대안을 모색하는 데 사용하는 등 세금을 사용하는 방식에 대해서 서술되어 있습니다. 즉, (A)의 ①번 문장 such "green taxes"는 (B)의 ②번 문장 'the tax'를 지칭하므로 정답은 (B)-(A)-(C)가 됩니다.

주 ①. According to the market response model, / it is / increasing prices / that drive / providers / to search for new sources, / innovators / to substitute, / consumers / to conserve, / and alternatives / to emerge.

구▶ 'It is + N + that + 불완전한 문장'은 'It that 강조 구문'입니다.
- 'drive + O + to-V'는 'O가 V하도록 이끌다'를 의미합니다.
- 시장 반응 모델에 따르면, 증가하는 가격은 공급자들이 새로운 자원을 찾도록 하고, 혁신가가 대체하도록 하고, 소비자가 보존하도록 (= 아껴 쓰도록) 하며, 그리고 대안이 생기도록 이끈다고 합니다.

(A) ①. Many examples of such "green taxes" / exist.

구▶ 그러한 "환경세"에는 많은 예시들이 존재한다고 합니다.

(A) ②. Facing / landfill costs, labor expenses, and related costs (in the provision of garbage disposal), for example, some cities / have required / households / to dispose of / all waste (in special trash bags), (purchased by consumers themselves, and often costing / a dollar or more each).

구▶ 'require + O + to-V'는 'O가 V하는 것을 요구하다'를 의미합니다.
- 예를 들어, 쓰레기 매립 비용, 인건비, 쓰레기 처리의 공급에 관련된 비용들에 직면한 몇몇 도시들은 가정이 모든 폐기물을 소비자가 직접 구입한, 흔히 1달러 또는 그 이상의 비용이 발생하는 특별한 쓰레기 봉투안에서 처리하도록 요구해왔다고 합니다.

독▶ 'for example'이 제시되었으므로 앞 문장 중심 문장
- 환경세에 대한 예시로 쓰레기 봉투가 제시되고 있습니다.

(B) ①. Taxing certain goods or services, (and so increasing prices), should result in / either decreased use (of these resources) / or creative innovation (of new sources or options).

구▶ 'either A or B'는 'A혹은 B'를 의미합니다.
- 특정한 물건과 서비스에 과세하여 가격이 인상되는 것은 반드시 자원의 사용이 감소되거나 혹은 새로운 자원과 옵션에 대한 창조적인 혁신이 야기된다고 합니다.

독▶ 'so'와 'result in'을 통해서 인과 관계를 제시하므로 중심 문장
- 과세로 인해서 가격이 상승하면 과세된 자원의 사용이 감소하고 새로운 자원에 대한 창의적인 혁신이 발생한다고 합니다.

(B) ②. The money (raised through the tax) / can be used / directly (by the government) (either to supply services or to search for alternatives).

구▶ 'either A or B'는 'A 혹은 B'를 의미합니다.
- 세금에 의해 증가된 돈은 정부에 의해서 직접적으로 서비스를 제공하거나 대안을 찾기 위해서 사용될 수 있다고 합니다.

(C) ①. **The results** / have been greatly increased / recycling and more careful attention (by consumers to packaging and waste).

구▸ 그 결과로, 재활용이 크게 증가하였고 소비자가 포장과 폐기물에 더욱 세밀하게 주의를 기울였다고 합니다.

독▸ 'The results'를 통해서 결과를 제시하므로 중심 문장

(C) ②. By internalizing / the costs of trash to consumers, / there / has been / an observed decrease (in the flow of garbage from households).

구▸ 'by V-ing'는 'V함으로써'를 의미합니다.
- 소비자에게 쓰레기의 비용을 내면화함으로써, 가정에서 나오는 쓰레기의 흐름이 감소되었다고 합니다.

주어진 글 다음에 이어질 글의 순서로 가장 적절한 것을 고르시오.

> ① The objective of battle, to "throw" the enemy and to make him defenseless, may temporarily blind commanders and even strategists to the larger purpose of war.
> ② War is never an isolated act, nor is it ever only one decision.

(A)

① To be political, a political entity or a representative of a political entity, whatever its constitutional form, **has to** have an intention, a will.

② That intention **has to** be clearly expressed.

(B)

① In the real world, war's larger purpose is always a political purpose.

② It transcends the use of force.

③ This insight was famously captured by Clausewitz's most famous phrase, "War is a mere continuation of politics by other means."

(C)

① **And** one side's will **has to** be transmitted to the enemy at some point during the confrontation it does not **have to** be publicly communicated.

② A violent act and its larger political intention **must** also be attributed to one side at some point during the confrontation.

③ History does not know of acts of war without eventual attribution.

* entity: 실체 ** transcend: 초월하다

해설 [**정답** : ②]

주어진 지문에서 전쟁은 고립된 행동이 아니며 하나의 결정이 아니라고 합니다. (B)의 ①번 문장에서 전쟁의 목적이 정치적 목적이라는 것을 처음 제시합니다. (A)의 ①번 문장과 (C)의 ①번, ②번 문장 모두 정치적 목적을 제시하므로 (B)가 주어진 지문 뒤에 와야합니다.

(A)의 ①번, ②번 문장에서 정치적이기 위해서는 정치적 실체가 의도를 가지고 있어야만 하며 그 의도가 분명해야만 한다고 합니다. 이는 전쟁이 정치적 목적을 달성하기 위한 조건에 해당합니다. 이는 (C)의 ①번 문장의 'And'로 이어져 (C)의 ①번에서 마주하는 동안 한쪽의 의지가 적에게 전달되어야 한다는 내용으로 제시됩니다. 'And'를 통해서 나열이 되므로 (C)와 (B)는 연결될 수 없으며, (A)가 (C) 앞에 와야합니다. 또한 (C)의 ②번 문장에서 'also'를 통해서 전쟁이 정치적 목적을 달성하기 위한 조건으로 적을 탓하는 내용이 제시되는 것을 통해서도 알 수 있습니다. 그러므로 정답은 (B)-(A)-(C)가 됩니다.

주 ①. The objective of battle, (to "throw" / the enemy and to make / him / defenseless), /

may temporarily blind / commanders and even strategists (to the larger purpose of war).

> 구 ▶ ' "throw" the enemy', '적을 던지다' = '적을 무찌르다'는 의미가 됩니다.
> - 'make + O + O.C'는 'O를 O.C하게 만들다'를 뜻합니다.
> - 'blind'는 '보지 못하는'인데 동사로 사용하였으므로 '보지 못하게 하다'를 나타냅니다.
> - 전투의 목표, 적군을 무찌르고 그들을 방어하지 못하게 만드는 것은, 일시적으로 지휘관과
>   전략가까지도 전쟁의 더 큰 목적을 보지 못하게 할 수도 있다고 합니다.

> * objective - 목적

주 ②. War / is never / an isolated act, / nor is / it / ever only one decision.

> 구 ▶ 'nor'이라는 부정어가 문장 앞에 왔으므로 의문문 어순으로 도치됩니다.
> - 전쟁은 결코 고립된 행위가 아니며, 또한 단 하나의 결정도 아니라고 합니다.

(A) ①. To be political, / a political entity or a representative of a political entity, (whatever its

constitutional form), / **has to** have / an intention, a will.

> * entity: 실체

> 구 ▶ 'whatever'은 '무엇이든지 간에'를 뜻합니다.
> - 'will'이 명사로 쓰이면 '의지'라는 의미를 가집니다.
> - 정치적으로 되려면, 정치적 실제 혹은 정치적 실체의 대표자는, 구성의 형태가 무엇이든지 간에,
>   의도, 즉 의지가 있어야만 한다고 합니다.

> 독 ▶ 'have to'가 제시되었으므로 중심 문장!
> - 정치적이기 위해서는 정치적 실체가 의도를 가져야만 한다고 합니다.

(A) ②. That intention / **has to** be clearly expressed.

> 구 ▶ 그러한 의도는 분명하게 표현되어야만 한다고 합니다.

> 독 ▶ 'have to'가 제시되었으므로 중심 문장!
> - 그러한 정치적 의도는 분명하게 표현되어야 한다고 합니다.

(B) ①. (In the real world), war's larger purpose / is always / a political purpose.

> 구 ▶ 실제 세계에서 전쟁의 큰 목적은 항상 정치적 목적이라고 합니다.

(B) ②. It / transcends / the use of force.

> ** transcend: 초월하다

> 구 ▶ 그것은 힘의 사용을 초월한다고 합니다.

(B) ③. This insight / was famously captured (by Clausewitz's most famous phrase, "War / is / a mere continuation of politics (by other means).")

구▶ 'means'는 '수단, 방법'을 나타냅니다. (≠ mean 의미, 비열한)
- 이 통찰은 Clausewitz의 가장 유명한 말인 "전쟁은 다른 수단으로 단지 정치를 계속하는 것에 불과하다"라는 말에 의해 유명하게 포착되었다고 합니다.

독▶ 전쟁은 다른 수단으로 정치를 계속하는 것에 불과하다는 말에 포착되었다는 것은 상황이 이 말을 따른다는 의미이므로 전쟁이 정치를 계속하는 것이라고 합니다.
- 그러므로 (B) ①번 문장을 재진술 합니다.

(C) ①. **And** one side's will / **has to** be transmitted to / the enemy (at some point) (during the confrontation) (it / does not **have to** be publicly communicated).

구▶ 그리고, 한쪽의 의지는 대치하는 동안 어느 시점에 적에게 전달되어야만 한다. (그것이 공개적으로 전달될 필요는 없다)고 합니다.

독▶ 'have to'가 제시되었으므로 중심 문장!
- 한쪽의 의지가 적에게 전달되어야만 한다고 합니다.

(C) ②. A violent act and its larger political intention / **must** also be attributed to / one side (at some point) (during the confrontation).

구▶ 'attribute A to B'는 'A를 B에 탓으로 돌리다'를 의미합니다.
- 폭력적인 행위와 더 큰 정치적 의도 또한 대치하는 동안 어느 시점에 한쪽의 탓이 되어야만 한다고 합니다.

독▶ 전쟁의 목적이 정치적으로 되기 위한 조건을 설명하고 있습니다.

(C) ③. History / does not know of / acts of war (without eventual attribution).

구▶ 역사는 궁극적인 남탓 없이는 전쟁 행위에 대해 알지 못한다고 합니다.

독▶ 전쟁은 남탓이 있어야 한다고 하며 (C) ②번 문장을 재진술합니다.

주어진 글 다음에 이어질 글의 순서로 가장 적절한 것을 고르시오.

> ① In spite of the likeness between the fictional and real world, the fictional world deviates from the real one in one important respect.

(A)

① The author has selected the content according to his own worldview and his own conception of relevance, in an attempt to be neutral and objective or convey a subjective view on the world.

② Whatever the motives, the author's subjective conception of the world stands between the reader and the original, untouched world on which the story is based.

(B)

① **Because of** the inner qualities with which the individual is endowed through heritage and environment, the mind functions as a filter; every outside impression that passes through it is filtered and interpreted.

② **However**, the world the reader encounters in literature is already processed and filtered by another consciousness.

(C)

① The existing world faced by the individual is in principle an infinite chaos of events and details before it is organized by a human mind.

② This chaos only gets processed and modified when perceived by a human mind.

* deviate: 벗어나다 ** endow: 부여하다 *** heritage: 유산

해설 [정답 : ⑤]

주어진 문장에서 허구 세계와 실제 세계는 유사하지만 허구 세계가 중요한 부분에서 실제 세계로부터 벗어난다고 합니다.

(A)의 ①번 문장에서는 작가는 중립적이고 객관적이며 세계에 대한 주관적인 관점을 전달하려는 시도에서 그들 고유의 관점에 따라서 내용을 선택한다고 합니다. 이는 (A)의 ②번 문장에서 재진술됩니다. 이러한 작가에 대한 내용은 (B)의 ②번 문장에서 문학에서 독자가 접하는 세계는 다른 의식들에 의해서 처리되고 여과되었다는 내용에서 처음 제시되므로 (A)는 (B) 다음에 와야 합니다.

(C)의 ①번 문장에서는 개인이 직면한 존재하는 세계는 인간의 마음이 세계를 조직하기 전까지는 사건과 세부 사항의 혼돈 상황이라고 합니다. 이는 (C)의 ②번 문장에서 인간의 마음이 혼란한 세계를 인식할 때 혼란이 처리되고 수정된다고 합니다. 이는 (B)의 ①번 문장에서 마음이 필터로써 기능한다는 내용과 이어지므로 (B)는 (C) 다음에 와야 합니다. 그러므로 정답은 (C)-(B)-(A)가 됩니다.

* 심화 (2) 전환 대응 훈련에서 연습한 것을 그대로 적용할 수 있습니다. 실제로 전환을 잘 파악한 저의 과외생은 이 문제를 30초컷 할 수 있었다고 합니다.

주 ①. (In spite of the likeness between the fictional and real world), the fictional world / deviates (from the real one) (in one important respect).

* deviate: 벗어나다

구 'between A and B'은 'A와 B 사이'를 의미합니다.
- 허구와 실제 세계 사이의 유사성에도 불구하고, 허구 세계는 한 가지 중요한 측면에서 실제 세계로부터 벗어난다고 합니다.

* likeness - 유사성

(A) ①. The author / has selected / the content (according to his own worldview and his own conception of relevance), (in an attempt to be / neutral and objective / or convey / a subjective view on the world).

구 'in an attempt to-V'는 'V하려는 시도에서'로 해석하시면 됩니다.
- 저자는 중립적이고 객관적이며 혹은 세계에 대한 주관적인 견해를 전달하는 시도에서, 그의 고유한 세계 관점과 적절성에 대한 고유의 개념에 따라서 내용을 선택해 왔다고 합니다.
독 즉, 저자는 글을 통해서 본인의 관점을 독자에게 전달해 왔다고 합니다.

(A) ②. Whatever the motives, / the author's subjective conception (of the world) / stands / between the reader and the original, untouched world (on which the story / is based).

구 'Whatever'은 '무엇이든지 간에'로 해석하시면 됩니다.
- 'between A and B'은 'A와 B 사이'를 의미합니다.
- 동기가 무엇이든지 간에, 저자들의 세계에 대한 주관적인 개념은 독자와 이야기의 기반이 되는 근본적인 손대지 않은 세계 사이에 존재한다고 합니다.
독 저자들이 생각하는 세계는 독자에게 전달해야 하지만 주관적이기 때문에 독자와 원래의 손대지 않은 세계 (= 저자들의 세계) 사이에 존재한다고 합니다.

(B) ①. **Because of** the inner qualities (with which the individual / is endowed (through heritage and environment)), the mind / functions as / a filter; every outside impression (that passes through / it) is filtered and interpreted.

** endow: 부여하다 *** heritage: 유산

구 'functions as N'은 'N으로써 기능하다'로 해석하시면 됩니다.
- 개인이 유산과 환경을 통해서 부여받은 내적 특성 때문에, 마음은 필터로써 기능하는데, 그것은 그것을 (= 필터를) 통과하는 모든 외부 인상들을 여과하고 해석한다고 합니다.
독 'Because of'가 제시되었으므로 중심 문장

(B) ②. **However**, the world (the reader / encounters in literature) / is already processed and filtered (by another consciousness).

- 구 ▶ 하지만, 독자들이 문학에서 마주하는 세계는 이미 다른 의식들에 의해서 가공되어 있고 여과되어 있다고 합니다.

- 독 ▶ 'However'가 제시되었으므로 앞 뒷 문장 중심 문장
  - (B) ①번 문장에서 마음이 외부 인상들을 (= 세계에 대해서) 여과하고 해석한다고 했지만, 문학에서는 이미 여과되고 가공되어 있다고 합니다.

(C) ①. The existing world (faced by the individual) / is / (in principle) an infinite chaos (of events and details) (before it / is organized (by a human mind)).

- 구 ▶ 개인이 마주한 존재하는 세계는 원칙적으로 인간의 마음에 의해서 조직되기 전에 사건과 세부 사항들의 무한한 혼돈 상태라고 합니다.

- 독 ▶ 인간의 마음에 의해서 세계가 조직되지 않을 때는 혼돈의 상태라고 합니다.

(C) ②. This chaos / only gets processed and modified / when perceived by a human mind.

- 구 ▶ 'get + p.p'는 'be + p.p'와 동일한 수동태입니다.
  - 그러한 혼란들은 인간의 마음에 의해서 인식될 때 처리되고 변경된다고 합니다.

- 독 ▶ 인간의 마음에 의해 혼란한 세계가 인식될 때 혼란이 끝난다고 합니다.

주어진 글 다음에 이어질 글의 순서로 가장 적절한 것을 고르시오.

① When two natural bodies of water stand at different levels, building a canal between them presents a <u>complicated engineering problem</u>.

(A)

① <u>Then the upper gates open</u> and the ship passes through.

② For downstream passage, the process works the opposite way.

③ The ship enters the lock from the upper level, and water is pumped from the lock until the ship is in line with the lower level.

(B)

① When a vessel is going upstream, <u>the upper gates stay closed</u> as the ship enters the lock at the lower water level.

② The downstream gates are then closed and more water is pumped into the basin.

③ The rising water lifts the vessel to the level of the upper body of water.

(C)

① <u>To make up for the difference in level</u>, engineers build one or more water "steps," called locks, that carry ships or boats up or down between the two levels.

② A lock is an artificial water basin.

③ It has a long rectangular shape with concrete walls and <u>a pair of gates</u> at each end.

* rectangular: 직사각형의

해설 [정답 : ⑤]

주어진 문장에서는 두 곳의 자연 수역이 서로 다른 수위에 있을 때, 그것들 사이에 운하를 건설하는 것은 복잡한 공학적 문제를 만들어낸다고 합니다.

(C)의 ①번 문장에서 'To make up for the difference in level', 수위의 차이를 보전하기 위해서 공학자들은 물 "계단"을 만든다고 했습니다. 이것은 주어진 문장의 공학적 문제를 해결하기 위한 방법을 시행하는 것이므로 주어진 문장 뒤에는 (C)가 와야 합니다.

(C)의 ②③번 문장에서 로크의 양쪽 끝에는 문이 있다고 하며 문이 처음으로 언급되고, (A), (B) 모두 위쪽, 아래쪽 문이 언급됩니다. 그러므로 (A)와 (B)의 순서를 파악해봅시다. (A)의 ①번 문장에서 그러고 나면 위쪽 문이 열린다고 했고, (B)의 ①번 문장에서는 위쪽 문이 닫혀 있다고 합니다.

(A)의 ①번 문장에서 접속사 'Then'이 다음에 일어나는 상황을 나타내므로, (B)의 문이 닫힌 상태를 유지하다가, (B) ③번 문장에서 상승하는 물이 선박을 위쪽 문 높이 수준까지 끌어올린 과정의 다음에 문이 열린다는 내용으로 연결돼야 합니다. 그러므로 (A)는 (B) 뒤에 와야 하며, 정답은 (C)-(B)-(A)가 됩니다.

주 ①. When / two natural bodies of water / stand / at different levels, building / a canal (between them) / presents / a complicated engineering problem.

구▶ 두 곳의 자연 수역이 서로 다른 수위에 있을 때, 그것들 사이에 운하를 건설하는 것은 복잡한 공학적 문제를 만들어 낸다고 합니다.

독▶ 서로 다른 수위의 수역, 운하 건설, 공학적 문제라는 주제 단어들의 특성을 지문을 통해 파악해야 할 필요가 있습니다.

(A) ①. Then the upper gates / open and the ship / passes through.

구▶ 그러고 나면 위쪽 문이 열리고 배가 통과한다고 합니다.

독▶ 운하에서 하류 통행에서 배가 통과하는 과정으로 전환됩니다. 그러므로 (A)의 앞에는 상류 통행에 대한 설명이 언급되어야 함을 알 수 있습니다.

(A) ②. For downstream passage, the process / works / the opposite way.

구▶ 하류 통행의 경우, 그 과정은 정반대로 작동한다고 합니다.

(A) ③. The ship / enters / the lock (from the upper level), and water / is pumped / from the lock (until the ship / is / in line (with the lower level)).

구▶ 배가 위쪽 수위의 로크로 들어오고, 배가 더 낮은 수위와 일치할 때까지 물이 로크로부터 양수된다고 합니다.

독▶ 하류 통행에 대한 설명 문장입니다.

(B) ①. When a vessel / is going / upstream, <u>the upper gates / stay / closed</u> (as the ship / enters / the lock (at the lower water level)).

구▶ 선박이 상류로 올라가고 있을 때는, 배가 더 낮은 수위에 있는 잠금장치에 들어서는 동안 위쪽 문은 닫혀 있다고 합니다.

독▶ 상류 통행 과정이 처음으로 언급되는 문장입니다.

(B) ②. The downstream gates / are then closed / and more water / is pumped / into the basin.

구▶ 그리고 나서 하류의 문이 닫히고 더 많은 물이 웅덩이 안으로 양수된다고 합니다.

(B) ③. The rising water / lifts / the vessel (to the level (of the upper body (of water))).

구▶ 상승하는 물이 선박을 위쪽의 물 높이 수준까지 끌어올린다고 합니다.

독▶ 상류 통행 과정에 대한 설명 문장입니다.

(C) ①. To make up for the difference in level, engineers / build / one or more water "steps," called

locks, that / carry / ships or boats (up or down) (between the two levels).

구▶ 수위의 차이를 보전하기 위해 공학자들은 두 수위 사이에서 배나 보트를 위아래로 운반하는, 로크라고 부르는 하나 이상의 물 '계단'을 만든다고 합니다.

독▶ 로크라는 개념이 처음으로 언급되므로 로크와 관련된 내용에서는 처음으로 언급되어야 하는 문장임을 알 수 있습니다.

(C) ②. A lock / is / an artificial water basin.

구▶ 로크는 인공적인 물웅덩이라고 합니다.

(C) ③. It / has / a long rectangular shape (with concrete walls) and a pair of gates (at each end).

* rectangular: 직사각형의

구▶ 그것은 콘크리트 벽과 양 끝에 한 쌍의 문이 있는 긴 직사각형 모양을 하고 있다고 합니다.

독▶ 로크에 대한 설명 문장입니다.

주어진 글 다음에 이어질 글의 순서로 가장 적절한 것을 고르시오.

> ① **Studies** of people struggling with major health problems show that the majority of respondents report they derived benefits from their adversity.
>
> ② Stressful events sometimes force people to develop new skills, reevaluate priorities, learn new insights, and acquire new strengths.

(A)

① High levels of adversity predicted poor mental health, as expected, but people who had faced intermediate levels of adversity were healthier than those who experienced little adversity, suggesting that moderate amounts of stress can foster resilience.

② **A follow-up study** found a similar link between the amount of lifetime adversity and subjects' responses to laboratory stressors.

(B)

① Intermediate levels of adversity were predictive of the greatest resilience.

② **Thus**, **having to** deal with a moderate amount of stress may build resilience in the face of future stress.

(C)

① **In other words**, the adaptation process initiated by stress can lead to personal changes for the better.

② **One study** that measured participants' exposure to thirty-seven major negative events found a curvilinear relationship between lifetime adversity and mental health.

* resilience: 회복력

해설 [정답 : ④]

주어진 지문에서 자신이 겪은 역경에서 이익을 얻었고, 스트레스를 주는 사건은 이득이 된다고 합니다. (C)의 ②번 문장에서 'One study'를 통해 역경과 정신 건강 사이의 관계를 발견했다고 합니다. 이러한 역경과 정신 건강 사이의 관계는 (A)의 ①번 문장에서 제시되므로 (C) 뒤에는 (A)가 와야 합니다.

(A)의 ①번 문장에서 적당한 양의 스트레스가 회복력을 촉진하고 ②번 문장에서 후속 연구에서 피실험자들이 겪은 역경의 양과 피실험자들이 실험 중 주어진 스트레스 요인에 반응하는 것 사이에서 비슷한 관계를 발견했다고 합니다. (B)의 ①번 문장에서 적절한 역경은 회복력을 예측할 수 있다고 (A)의 ②번 문장을 재진술합니다. 그러므로 (A) 뒤에는 (B)가 와야 합니다. 또한 (C)의 ①번 문장의 'In other words'를 통해서 주어진 지문의 ②번 문장이 재진술되므로 정답은 (C)-(A)-(B)가 됩니다.

주 ①. **Studies** of people (struggling with major health problems) / show / that the majority (of

respondents) / report / they derived benefits (from their adversity).

구▶ 중대한 건강 문제에 노력하는 (=해결하려는) 사람들에 대한 연구는 대다수의 응답자들이 자신이 겪은
역경으로부터 이익을 얻었다고 보고한다는 것을 보여준다고 합니다.

독▶ 'Study', '연구'가 제시되었으므로 중심 문장!
- 중대한 건강 문제를 해결하려는 사람들이 역경으로부터 이익을 얻었다고 생각한다고 합니다.

*   struggle with - 노력하다
** adversity - 역경

주 ②. Stressful events / sometimes force / people / to develop new skills, reevaluate priorities, learn

new insights, and (develop, reevaluate, learn 그리고 acquire을 연결) acquire new strengths.

구▶ 'force A to-V'는 'A가 V하는 것을 강요하다'를 의미합니다.
- 스트레스를 주는 사건은 때때로 사람들이 새로운 기술을 개발하고, 우선순위를 재평가하고, 새로운
통찰을 배우고, 새로운 강점을 얻게 강요한다고 (=만든다고) 합니다.

(A) ①. High levels (of adversity) / predicted / poor mental health, as expected, / **but** people (who

had faced / intermediate levels of adversity) / were / healthier than those (who experienced /

little adversity), suggesting / that moderate amounts of stress / can foster / resilience.

* resilience: 회복력

구▶ 높은 수준의 역경은 예상대로 나쁜 전신 건강을 예측했지만, 적절한 수준의 역경에 직면한 사람들은
역경을 거의 경험하지 않았던 사람들보다 더 건강했는데, 이것은 적당한 양의 스트레스가 회복력을
촉진할 수 있음을 제시한다고 합니다.

독▶ 'but'이 제시되었으므로 중심 문장!
- 높은 수준의 역경은 좋지 못한 건강이 예상되지만 적절한 역경은 사람들 더 건강하게 한다고
합니다.

(A) ②. **A follow-up study** / found / a similar link (between the amount of lifetime adversity and

subjects' responses to laboratory stressors.).

구▶ 'between A and B'는 'A와 B 사이'를 의미합니다.
- 이후 연구는 삶에서 역경의 양과 피실험자들이 실험 중 주어진 스트레스 요인에 반응하는 것 사이의
유사한 관계를 발견했다고 합니다.

독▶ 후속 연구가 제시되었으므로 중심 문장!
- 일생동안 역경의 양과 피실험자의 스트레스 요인에 대한 반응에 관계가 있다고 합니다.

(B) ①. Intermediate levels of adversity / were / predictive of the greatest resilience.

> 구 적절한 수준의 역경이 가장 큰 회복력을 예측했다고 합니다.

* predict (예측하다) + -ive (형용사형 접사) = predictive - 예측하는

(B) ②. **Thus**, **having to** deal with / a moderate amount of stress / may build / resilience (in the face of future stress).

> 구 그러므로, 적당한 양의 스트레스를 다뤄야만 하는 것은 미래에 직면한 스트레스에서 회복력을 만들 수 있다고 합니다.

> 독 'Thus'가 제시되었으므로 중심 문장!
> - 적당한 스트레스 ⇒ 미래 스트레스에 대한 회복력을 기름으로 이해하시면 됩니다.

(C) ①. **In other words**, the adaptation process (initiated by stress) can **lead to** / personal changes for the better.

> 구 다시 말해, 스트레스에 의해 시작된 적응 과정은 더 나은 쪽으로 개인적 변화를 가져올 수 있다고 합니다.

> 독 'In other words'와 'lead to'가 제시되었으므로 중심 문장!
> - 스트레스 ⇒ 적응 과정 ⇒ 더 나은 개인적 변화로 이해하시면 됩니다.

(C) ②. **One study** (that measured / participants' exposure (to thirty-seven major negative events)) / found / a curvilinear relationship (between lifetime adversity and mental health).

> 구 참가자들의 서른일곱 가지 주요 부정적인 사건 경험을 측정한 연구는 생애에서 겪은 역경과 정신 건강 사이의 곡선 관계를 발견했다고 합니다.

> 독 연구가 제시되었으므로 중심 문장!
> - 생애 역경과 정신 건강 사이의 관계를 발견했다고 합니다.

* curvilinear - 곡선의

주어진 글 다음에 이어질 글의 순서로 가장 적절한 것을 고르시오.

---

① The growing complexity of computer software has direct implications for our global safety and security, particularly as the physical objects upon which we depend — things like **cars**, **airplanes**, bridges, tunnels, and implantable medical devices — transform themselves into **computer code**.

(A)

① As all this code grows in size and complexity, so too do the number of errors and software bugs.

② According to a study by Carnegie Mellon University, commercial software typically has twenty to thirty bugs for every thousand lines of code — 50 million lines of code means 1 million to 1.5 million **potential errors to be exploited**.

(B)

① **This** is the basis for all malware attacks that take advantage of these computer bugs to get the code to do something it was not originally intended to do.

② As computer code grows more elaborate, software bugs flourish and security suffers, with increasing consequences for society at large.

(C)

① Physical things are increasingly becoming **information technologie**s.

② **Cars** are "computers we ride in," and **airplanes** are nothing more than "flying Solaris boxes attached to bucketfuls of industrial control systems."

* exploit: 활용하다

해설 [정답 : ④]

주어진 문장에서 컴퓨터 소프트웨어 복잡성의 증가는 전 세계의 안전과 보안에 직접적인 영향을 주는데, 자동차, 비행기 등과 같은 우리가 의존하는 물리적 대상들이 컴퓨터 코드로 변해간다고 합니다. (C)의 ②번 문장에서 'Cars are "computers we ride in"', 자동차는 우리가 타는 컴퓨터이고, 'airplanes are "flying Solaris boxes"', 비행기는 비행 솔라리스 박스라고 언급하는 것은 주어진 문장에서 자동차와 비행기들이 컴퓨터 코드로 변하는 예시에 대한 구체적인 설명이 되므로 (C)는 주어진 문장 뒤에 와야 합니다.

(A)의 ①번 문장에서는 'all this code grows in size and complexity', 모든 코드가 크기와 복잡성이 증가한다고 했고, 이것은 (C)의 물리적 대상이 코드로 변해가는 내용에서 이어질 수 있습니다.
(B)의 ①번 문장에서는 'this is the basis for all malware attacks', 이것이 악성 소프트웨어 공격의 기반이라고 했습니다. 이것 역시 (C)의 내용이 소프트웨어 공격의 원인으로 작용하는 새로운 내용으로 이어질 수 있으므로 (A)와 (B) 모두 (C) 뒤에 올 수 있습니다.

그러므로 (A)와 (B) 사이의 순서를 파악해야 합니다. (A)의 ②번 문장에서는 'potential errors to be exploited', 수많은 잠재적 오류가 악용될 수 있다고 합니다. 이것은 (B)의 ①번 문장의 'This'를 지칭하며, 소프트웨어 공격의 기반이 된다는 내용으로 이어져야 하므로 (B)는 (A) 뒤에 와야 합니다. 그러므로 정답은 (C)-(A)-(B)가 됩니다.

주 ①. The growing complexity (of computer software) / has / direct implications (for our global safety and security), particularly as the physical objects / upon which / we / depend — things like cars, airplanes, bridges, tunnels, and implantable medical devices — transform / themselves / into computer code.

> 구 ▶ transform A into B - A를 B로 바꾸다
> - 컴퓨터 소프트웨어 복잡성의 증가는 전 세계의 안전과 보안에 직접적인 영향을 주는데, 우리가 의존하는 물리적 대상, — 자동차, 비행기, 교량, 터널, 이식형 의료 기기와 같은 것들이 — 컴퓨터 코드로 변해감에 따라 특히 그렇다고 합니다.

> 독 ▶ 물리적인 대상들이 오늘날 컴퓨터 코드로 변해감에 따라 컴퓨터 소프트웨어의 복잡성이 증가하면서 안전과 보안에 영향을 준다고 합니다.

(A) ①. As all this code / grows / in size and complexity, so too / do / the number of errors and software bugs.

> 구 ▶ 부사구 'so too'가 앞으로 도치되면서 주어가 동사와 도치되었습니다.
> - 이 모든 코드가 크기와 복잡성이 증가함에 따라, 오류와 소프트웨어 버그 수 또한 증가한다고 합니다.

> 독 ▶ 코드의 성질에 따라 오류와 버그의 수 역시 비례하여 증가한다는 것을 알 수 있습니다.

(A) ②. According to a study (by Carnegie Mellon University), commercial software / typically has / twenty to thirty bugs (for every thousand lines of code) — 50 million lines of code / means / 1 million to 1.5 million potential errors / to be exploited.

* exploit: 활용하다

> 구 ▶ Carnegie Mellon 대학교의 연구에 따르면, 상용 소프트웨어에는 보통 코드 1,000줄당 20~30개의 버그가 있어서, — 5천만 줄의 코드는 1백만~150만 개의 잠재적 오류가 악의적으로 이용될 수 있다는 것을 의미한다고 합니다.

> 독 ▶ 소프트웨어 속에 존재하는 버그의 비율, 그리고 그 버그들이 악의적으로 사용될 수 있다는 사실에 관한 예시 문장입니다.

(B) ①. This / is / the basis for all malware attacks / that / take advantage of / these computer bugs / to get the code / to do something / it / was not originally intended to do.

> 구 ▶ 'take advantage of A' - A를 이용하다
> - 이것이 코드가 원래 하도록 의도되지 않았던 것을 하기 위해 이 컴퓨터 버그를 이용하는 모든 악성 소프트웨어 공격의 근간이라고 합니다.

> 독 ▶ (A)-②번 문장에서 언급된 수많은 잠재적인 버그들이 악성 소프트웨어 공격의 뿌리가 된다는 것을 알 수 있습니다.

(B) ②. As computer code / grows / more elaborate, software bugs / flourish / and security / suffers, with increasing consequences for society at large.

구▶ 컴퓨터 코드가 더 정교해짐에 따라, 소프트웨어 버그는 창궐하고 보안은 악화되어, 사회 전반에 미치는 영향이 커진다고 합니다.

독▶ 컴퓨터 소프트웨어의 복잡성이 주어진 문장에서 언급된 안전과 보안에 부정적인 영향을 주고 있음을 확인할 수 있습니다.

(C) ①. Physical things / are increasingly becoming / information technologies.

구▶ 물리적 사물은 점점 더 정보 기술이 되어가고 있다고 합니다.

독▶ 주어진 문장에서 이어지는 내용으로, 물리적 사물들이 컴퓨터 코드로 변해간다는 주어진 문장의 내용이 정보 기술이 되어간다는 내용으로 이어지고 있습니다.

(C) ②. Cars / are / "computers / we / ride in," and airplanes / are / nothing more than "flying Solaris boxes / attached to bucketfuls of industrial control systems."

구▶ 자동차는 '우리가 타는 컴퓨터'이고, 비행기는 '수많은 산업 제어 시스템에 부착된 비행 솔라리스 박스'에 불과하다고 합니다.

독▶ (C)-①의 예시 문장으로, 자동차(물리적 사물)가 '타는 컴퓨터(정보 기술)'인 것, 비행기(물리적 사물)가 '제어 시스템에 부착된 비행 솔라리스 박스(정보 기술)'인 것임을 통해 알 수 있습니다.

주어진 글 다음에 이어질 글의 순서로 가장 적절한 것을 고르시오.

> ① A fascinating species of water flea exhibits a kind of flexibility that evolutionary biologists call adaptive plasticity.

(A)

① That's a clever trick, **because** producing spines and a helmet is costly, in terms of energy, and conserving energy is essential for an organism's ability to survive and reproduce.

② The water flea only expends the energy **needed to** produce spines and a helmet when it **needs to**.

(B)

① If the baby water flea is developing into an adult in water that includes the chemical signatures of creatures that prey on water fleas, it develops a helmet and spines to defend itself against predators.

② If the water around it doesn't include the chemical signatures of predators, the water flea doesn't develop these protective devices.

(C)

① **So** it may well be that this plasticity is an adaptation: a trait that came to exist in a species **because** it contributed to reproductive fitness.

② There are many cases, across many species, of adaptive plasticity.

③ Plasticity is conducive to fitness if there is sufficient variation in the environment.

* spine: 가시돌기 ** conducive: 도움되는

해설 [정답 : ②]

주어진 지문에서 물벼룩의 매력적인 종들은 진화 생물학자들이 적응적 가변성이라고 부르는 유연성을 보여준다고 합니다. (A)의 ①번 문장에서 그것은 가시돌기와 헬멧을 만드는 것이 에너지적 관점에서 비싸고 에너지를 보존하는 것이 생존과 번식에 필수적이기 때문에 영리한 방식이라고 합니다. (B)의 ①번 문장에서는 어린 물벼룩이 포식자에 노출된 환경에서 자랐을 때는 헬멧과 가시돌기를 발달시키지만 ②번 문장에서 포식자에 노출되지 않은 환경에서는 헬멧과 가시돌기를 발달시키지 않는다고 하므로 이는 (A)의 ①번 문장에서 제시한 가시돌기와 헬멧을 만드는 것에 대한 서술이며, (A)의 ①번 문장 'That'이 지칭하는 내용인 것을 알 수 있습니다. 그러므로 (A)는 (B) 뒤에 와야 합니다.

(B) - (A)가 확실하므로 (C) - (B) - (A)와 (B) - (A) - (C) 중 안되는 것을 찾으면 됩니다. (C)의 ①번 문장에서 그러한 가변성은 적응이고 생식 적합성에 기여한다고 합니다. 그러한 가변성이 주어진 문장의 'adaptive plasticity'를 지칭한다면 주어진 지문 뒤에 (C)가 와야 합니다. 그러나 (C)의 ②번, ③번 문장에서 다양한 종들에 대해서 제시하지만 (B) - (A)는 물벼룩, 하나의 종만 제시하므로 (C)는 (B) - (A) 앞에 올 수 없습니다. 즉, (C)는 (B) - (A) 뒤에 와야 합니다.

또한 (B) - (A)에서 서술된 물벼룩의 가변성에 대한 내용이 (C)의 'this plasticity'로 지칭되며, 주어진 지문과 (B)에서 제시된 물벼룩에 대한 내용이 연결되므로 정답은 (B)-(A)-(C)가 됩니다.

주 ①. A fascinating species of water flea / exhibits / a kind of flexibility (that evolutionary biologists / call / adaptive plasticity).

구▶ 'call A B'는 'A를 B라고 부르다'를 의미합니다.
- 'plastic'은 '플라스틱'을 뜻하지만 '딱딱한 플라스틱'뿐만 아니라 '비닐'과 같은 '가변적인 소재'도 지칭합니다. 'plastic bag'이 우리가 흔히 얘기하는 '비닐봉지'를 뜻합니다. 그러므로 'plasticity'는 '변화기 쉬움', '가변성'으로 이해하시면 됩니다.
- 물벼룩의 매력적인 종들은 진화 생물학자들이 적응적 가변성이라고 부르는 유연성을 보여준다고 합니다.

(A) ①. That's / a clever trick, **because** producing spines and a helmet / is costly, (in terms of energy), and conserving energy / is / essential for an organism's ability (to survive and reproduce).

* spine: 가시돌기

구▶ 그것은 영리한 방법인데, 가시돌기나 헬멧을 만드는 것은 에너지의 관점에서 비용이 비싸고, 에너지를 보존하는 것은 생존하고 번식하는 생물체의 능력에서 필수적이기 때문이라고 합니다.

독▶ 'because'가 제시되었으므로 중심 문장
- 가시돌기나 헬멧을 (= 머리 보호 장치를) 만드는 것은 비싸고 생물체에게 필수적이기 때문에 '그것'이 매우 영리한 방법이라고 합니다.

(A) ②. The water flea / only expends / the energy (**needed to** produce spines and a helmet) (when it **needs to**).

구▶ 물벼룩은 오직 필요할 때만 가시돌기와 헬멧을 만드는 데 필요한 에너지를 소비한다고 합니다.

독▶ 'need to'가 제시되었으므로 중심 문장
- 물벼룩은 필요한 상황에서만 가시돌기와 헬멧을 만든다고 합니다.

(B) ①. If the baby water flea / is developing (into an adult in water) (that includes / the chemical signatures of creatures (that prey on / water fleas)), it / develops / a helmet and spines (to defend itself against predators).

구▶ 'defend A against B'는 'B에 대항하여 A를 보호하다'를 의미합니다.
- 만약 물벼룩의 어린 개체가 물벼룩을 잡아먹는 생물체의 화학적 신호를 포함한 물에서 성체로 성장한다면, 그것은 (= 물벼룩은) 포식자에 대항하여 스스로를 보호하기 위해서 헬멧과 가시돌기를 발달시킨다고 합니다.

독▶ 포식자가 있는 환경에서 자란 물벼룩은 스스로를 보호하기 위해 헬멧과 가시돌기를 발달시킨다고 합니다.

(B) ②. If the water (around it) doesn't include / the chemical signatures of predators, the water flea / doesn't develop / these protective devices.

구▶ 만약 그것 주위의 (= 물벼룩 주위의) 물에서 포식자의 화학적 신호가 포함되어 있지 않다면, 그 물벼룩은 그러한 방어 장치들을 (= 헬멧과 가시돌기들을) 발달시키지 않을 것이라고 합니다.

독▶ 포식자가 없다면 물벼룩은 헬멧과 가시돌기들을 발달시키지 않는다고 합니다.

(C) ①. **So** it / may well be / that this plasticity / is / an adaptation: a trait (that came to exist (in a species)) **because** it / contributed to / reproductive fitness.

구▶ 그래서 그러한 가변성은 적응이고, 그 특성은 생물 종에 존재하는데, 왜냐하면 그것은 (= 가변성은) 생식 적합성에 기여하기 때문이라고 합니다.

독▶ 'So'와 'because'가 제시되었으므로 중심 문장
- 그러한 가변성은 생식 적합성에 기여하므로 적응의 결과라고 합니다.

(C) ②. There are / many cases, (across many species), of adaptive plasticity.

구▶ 다양한 종들을 포함하여 적응적 가변성의 많은 경우가 있다고 합니다.

(C) ③. Plasticity / is conducive to / fitness if there is / sufficient variation (in the environment).

** conducive: 도움되는

구▶ 만약 환경에서 충분한 차이가 있다면 가변성은 적합성에 도움이 된다고 합니다.

독▶ 환경에서 충분한 차이가 있다면 가변성은 도움이 된다고 합니다.

08 23학년도 9월 평가원 37번 (정답률 54%)

주어진 글 다음에 이어질 글의 순서로 가장 적절한 것을 고르시오.

> ① Culture operates in ways we can consciously consider and discuss but also in ways of which we are far less cognizant.

(A)
① In some cases, **however**, we are far less aware of why we believe a certain claim to be true, or how we are to explain why certain social realities exist.
② Ideas about the social world become part of our worldview without our necessarily being aware of the source of the particular idea or that we even hold the idea at all.

(B)
① When we have to offer an account of our actions, we consciously understand which excuses might prove acceptable, given the particular circumstances we find ourselves in.
② In such situations, we use cultural ideas as we would use a particular tool.

(C)
① We select the cultural notion as we would select a screwdriver: certain jobs call for a Phillips head while others require an Allen wrench.
② Whichever idea we insert into the conversation to justify our actions, the point is that our motives are discursively available to us. They are not hidden.

* cognizant: 인식하는 ** discursively: 만연하게

해설 [**정답 : ③**]

연결사, 예시, 반복 등 순서 문제에서 나오는 단서들을 모두 활용하여 풀 수 있는 정석적인 문제입니다. 먼저 주어진 문장에서 문화는 우리가 의시적으로 고려하고 논의할 수 있는 방식뿐만 아니라, 우리가 훨씬 덜 인식하는 방향으로도 작동한다고 합니다.

(B)의 ①번 문장에서는 'we consciously understand', 우리는 우리가 처한 상황에 어떤 변명이 용인될지 의식적으로 이해한다고 했습니다. 이것은 주어진 문장의 consciously consider, 의식적으로 고려하는 것에 대한 내용이 반복되고 있으므로 주어진 문장 뒤에는 (B)가 와야 합니다.

(B)의 ②번 문장에서는 'a particular tool', 우리는 특정한 도구를 사용하는 것처럼 문화적 관념을 사용한다고 했습니다. (C)의 ①번 문장에서는 우리가 스크류드라이버를 사용하는 것처럼 문화적 개념을 사용한다고 했는데, 이것은 (B)의 특정한 도구를 사용하는 것에 대한 구체적인 예시가 되므로 (C)는 (B) 뒤에 와야 합니다.

(C)의 ②번 문장에서는 우리의 동기가 우리에게 만연하게 이용가능하며, 숨겨져 있지 않다고 했습니다. (A)의 ①번 문장에서는 우리는 어떤 경우에는 우리가 어떤 주장을 사실이라고 믿는지에 대해 훨씬 덜 알려져 있다고 했습니다. 이것은 (C)의 ②번 문장의 동기를 이용할 수 있다는 것과 반대되는 내용이 되며, 연결사 'however'를 통해 전환되므로 (A)는 (C) 뒤에 와야 합니다. 그러므로 정답은 (B)-(C)-(A)가 됩니다.

주 ①. Culture / operates (in ways) we / can consciously consider / and discuss **but** also (in ways / of which / we / are / far less cognizant).

* cognizant: 인식하는

구▶ 문화는 우리가 의식적으로 고려하고 논의할 수 있는 방식뿐만 아니라 우리가 훨씬 덜 인식하는 방식으로도 작동한다고 합니다.

독▶ 'but'이 제시되었으므로 중심 문장
- 문화를 의식적, 무의식적으로 인식하는 방식에 대한 문장입니다.

(A) ①. In some cases, **however**, we / are / far less aware (of why / we / believe a certain claim / to be true, or how / we / are / to explain why / certain social realities / exist).

구▶ 하지만 우리는 어떤 경우에는 우리가 왜 어떤 주장을 사실이라고 믿는지 또는 어떤 사회적 현실이 존재하는 이유를 어떻게 우리가 설명할 것인지에 대해 훨씬 덜 알고 있다고 합니다.

독▶ 'however'가 제시되었으므로 중심 문장
- 이유를 설명해야 하는 것에 대해 덜 알고 있다는 것은 주어진 문장의 문화가 우리가 덜 인식하는 방향으로 작동하는 것에 대한 예시 문장이 됩니다.

(A) ②. Ideas (about the social world) / become / part (of our worldview) (without our necessarily being / aware / of the source / of the particular idea / or that / we / even hold / the idea / at all).

구▶ 사회적 세계에 대한 관념은 우리가 특정한 관념의 출처에 대해서 혹은 심지어 우리가 그 관념을 갖고 있다는 것조차 반드시 알고 있지 않은 상태에서도 우리 세계관의 일부가 된다고 합니다.

독▶ (A)-①의 반복 문장입니다.

(B) ①. When / we / have to offer / an account (of our actions), we / consciously understand / which excuses / might prove / acceptable, given the particular circumstances (we / find / ourselves in).

구▶ 우리의 행동에 관해 설명을 제시해야 할 때, 우리는 우리가 처한 특정한 상황 하에 어떤 변명이 용인되는 것으로 판명될 수도 있는지를 의식적으로 이해한다고 합니다.

독▶ 어떤 변명이 받아들여질지를 의식적으로 이해하는 것은 주어진 문장의 의식적으로 논의하는 방식에 대한 예시가 되는 문장입니다.

(B) ②. In such situations, we / use / cultural ideas (as we / would use / a particular tool).

구▶ 그런 상황에서 우리는 특정 도구를 사용하는 것처럼 문화적 관념을 사용한다고 합니다.

독▶ 문화적 관념을 도구처럼 사용하는 것 역시 우리가 문화를 의식적으로 논의하는 방식으로 작동하는 것에 대한 설명이 되는 문장입니다.

(C) ①. We / select / the cultural notion (as / we / would select / a screwdriver): certain jobs / call (for a Phillips head) while others / require / an Allen wrench.

구▶ 우리는 스크류드라이버를 선택하는 것처럼 문화적 개념을 선택한다고 합니다. 어떤 일은 십자 드라이버 헤드를 필요로 하지만 다른 일은 육각 랜치를 필요로 한다고 합니다.

독▶ 십자 드라이버와 랜치를 상황에 따라 다르게 사용해야 하는 스크류드라이버의 예시는 선택적으로 문화적 개념을 고르는 것에 대한 예시로 언급되었습니다.

(C) ②. Whichever idea (we / insert / into the conversation / to justify our actions), the point / is / that / our motives / are / discursively available / to us. They / are not hidden.

** discursively: 만연하게

구▶ 우리의 행동을 정당화하기 위해 대화에 어떤 생각을 넣든, 요점은 우리의 동기가 우리에게 만연하게 이용 가능하다는 것이라고 하며, 그것들은 숨겨져 있지 않다고 합니다.

독▶ 우리가 스스로 동기를 사용할 수 있다는 것은 도구를 고르듯이 문화적 개념을 사용하는 것에 대한 예시 문장입니다.

주어진 글 다음에 이어질 글의 순서로 가장 적절한 것을 고르시오.

① The intuitive ability to classify and generalize is undoubtedly a useful feature of life and research, **but** it carries a high cost, such as in our tendency to stereotype generalizations about people and situations.

(A)

① Intuitively and quickly, we mentally sort things into groups based on what we perceive the differences between them to be, and that is the basis for stereotyping.

② Only afterwards do we examine (or not examine) more evidence of how things are differentiated, and the degree and significance of the variations.

(B)

① Our brain performs these tasks efficiently and automatically, usually without our awareness.

② The real danger of stereotypes is not their inaccuracy, but their lack of flexibility and their tendency to be preserved, even when we have enough time to stop and consider.

(C)

① For most people, the word stereotype arouses negative connotations: it implies a negative bias.

② **But**, **in fact**, stereotypes do not differ in principle from all other generalizations; generalizations about groups of people are not necessarily always negative.

* intuitive: 직관적인　** connotation: 함축

해설 [정답 : ④]

주어진 문장에서는 'The intuitive ability to classify and generalize is undoubtedly a useful feature … but it carries a high cost' 분류하고 일반화하려는 직관적인 능력은 유용한 특징이지만, 그것은 일반화를 고정 관념화하는 경향에 있어서 대가를 수반한다고 합니다. 수능 영어에서 대가 즉, 'a high cost'는 부정적인 의미를 지닙니다. 그러므로 주어진 문장에 연결되는 문장은 일반화하려는 직관적인 능력에 대한 부정적인 의미를 조금 더 구체화하는 문장인 (C)가 와야 합니다. (C)-① 에 나오는 'For most people, the word stereotype arouses negative connotations'이 바로 그 문장입니다.

(C)-②번 문장에서는 But이 나오기 때문에 대조의 논리를 나타내는 이분법 문장이고 바로 앞의 일반화하는 직관적 능력의 부정적인 측면을 뒤집는 'stereotypes do not differ … generalizations; generalizations about groups of people are not necessarily always negative'이라는 문장이 나오며 고정관념은 일반화와 다르지 않으며, 그것이 부정적인 것도 아니라고 합니다. 다음 (B)-①번 문장을 (C)-②번 문장으로 연결하려면 (B)-①번 문장의 'these tasks'가 문장에 존재하지 않으므로 (A)-①번 문장과 연결해야 함을 알 수 있습니다.

(A)-②번 문장에서는 'Only afterwards do we examine more evidence', 그 후에야 우리는 더 많은 증거를 조사한다고 했습니다. 이것은 고정관념과 일반화의 과정이 마무리된 경우인데, (B)-①번 문장에서는 'Our brain performs these tasks efficiently and automatically, usually without our awareness.', 우리의 뇌는 인식하지 못하는 사이에 이러한 일을 효율적이고 자동적으로 수행한다고 했습니다. 이것은 (A)에서 언급된 일반화의 과정을 'these tasks'로 지칭하고 있으므로 (B)는 (A) 뒤에 와야 합니다. 그러므로 정답은 (C)-(A)-(B)가 됩니다.

주 ①. The intuitive ability (to classify and generalize) / is / undoubtedly / a useful feature (of life and research), **but** it / carries / a high cost, (such as in our tendency) to stereotype generalizations about people and situations).

* intuitive: 직관적인

구▶ 분류하고 일반화하는 직관적 능력은 의심할 여지 없이 생활과 연구의 유용한 특징이다, 그러나 그것은 사람들과 상황에 대한 일반화를 하려는 고정관념과 같은 경향성이라는 높은 비용을 수반한다고 합니다.

독▶ 분류하고 일반화하는 직관적 능력의 문제점을 부각하여 주어진 문장을 시작하고 있습니다.

(A) ①. (Intuitively and quickly), we / mentally / sort / things (into groups) (based on (what we / perceive / the differences (between them) to be)), and that / is / the basis (for stereotyping).

구▶ 직관적이고 빠르게 우리는 그들 사이의 차이점을 인식하는 것을 기반으로 물건들을 정신적으로 그룹으로 분류하며, 그것이 고정관념의 기초라고 합니다.

독▶ 물건들을 정신적 그룹으로 분류하는 것을 고정관념의 기초라고 설명합니다. 이 문장만으로는 고정관념의 긍정적인 측면을 설명한다고 보기는 어렵습니다.

(A) ②. (Only afterwards) do we / examine (or not examine) / more evidence (of how things / are / differentiated, and the degree and significance of the variations).

구▶ 그 후에야 우리는 물건들이 어떻게 구별되는지, 변화의 정도와 중요성에 대한 더 많은 증거를 조사하거나 (또는 조사하지 않게) 된다고 합니다.

독▶ 이 문장까지 보았을 때 물건들을 정신적으로 분류해 고정관념을 사용하는 것은 우리가 물건들은 구별하고 변화의 성노에 대해서 조사하는 행위를 할 수 있게 하는 원동력 정도로 이해할 수 있습니다. (C)문장에서 우리가 목표로 하였던 정보인 긍정적 측면이라고 확언하기는 힘듭니다.

(B) ①. Our brain / performs / these tasks (efficiently and automatically, usually without our awareness).

구▶ 우리의 뇌는 이러한 작업을 효율적이고 자동적으로 수행하며, 대개 우리가 인식하지 못하는 상태에서 그렇게 한다고 합니다.

독▶ 이 문장에서 나오는 '이러한 작업들'이라는 표현으로 물건들을 구별하고 변화의 정도에 조사하는 행위를 지칭해서 순서의 힌트를 찾을 수 있습니다.

(B) ②. The real danger of stereotypes / is / not their inaccuracy, but their lack of flexibility and their tendency (to be preserved), even (when we / have / enough time (to stop and consider)).

구▶ 고정관념의 진짜 위험은 그들의 부정확성이 아니라, 그들의 유연성 부족과 우리가 멈추고 고려할 충분한 시간이 있을 때에도 보존되려는 경향이라고 합니다.

독▶ 이 마지막 문장이 고정관념의 진짜 부정적인 측면이기 때문에 (A)보다 (B)의 문장이 후 순위에 와야 한다는 단서를 제공합니다.

(C) ①. (For most people), the word $\overset{s}{\text{stereotype}}$ / $\overset{v}{\text{arouses}}$ / negative $\overset{o}{\text{connotations}}$: it $\overset{s}{}$ / $\overset{v}{\text{implies}}$ / a negative $\overset{o}{\text{bias}}$.

** connotation: 함축

> **구** 대부분의 사람들에게 고정관념이라는 단어는 부정적인 함축을 불러일으킨다고 합니다. 그것은 부정적 편견을 의미한다고 합니다.

> **독** 이렇게 고정관념이 부정적 편견이라는 부정적인 함축을 불러일으킨다는 내용은 고정관념이 수반하는 높은 비용이라는 주어진 문장의 내용을 구체적으로 설명하고 있습니다.

(C) ②. **But**, **in fact**, $\overset{s}{\text{stereotypes}}$ / $\overset{v}{\text{do not differ}}$ (in principle from all other generalizations); generalizations about groups of $\overset{s}{\text{people}}$ / $\overset{v}{\text{are not necessarily always}}$ / $\overset{c}{\text{negative}}$.

> **구** 그러나 사실, 고정관념은 원칙적으로 다른 모든 일반화와 다르지 않다고 합니다; 사람들의 그룹에 대한 일반화는 반드시 항상 부정적이라는 것은 아니라고 합니다.

> **독** 고정관념이 수반하는 높은 비용에 대해서 설명한 후에 '그러나'의 논리 기능어로 논리를 역접시켜 고정관념에 반드시 부정적인 측면만 있는 것이 아니라 긍정적인 측면도 있다는 내용으로 전환하고 있습니다. 그러므로 (C)문장 뒤에는 어떠한 긍정적인 측면이 있는지 설명하는 문장을 기대할 수 있습니다.

주어진 글 다음에 이어질 글의 순서로 가장 적절한 것을 고르시오.

> ① The fossil record provides evidence of evolution.
> ② The story the fossils tell is one of change.
> ③ Creatures existed in the past that are no longer with us.
> ④ Sequential changes are found in many fossils showing the change of certain features over time from a common ancestor, as in the case of the horse.

(A)

① If multicelled organisms were **indeed** found to have evolved before single-celled organisms, then the theory of evolution would be rejected.

② A good scientific theory always allows for the possibility of rejection.

③ The fact that we have not found such a case in countless examinations of the fossil record strengthens the case for evolutionary theory.

(B)

① The fossil record supports this prediction — multicelled organisms are found in layers of earth millions of years after the first appearance of single-celled organisms.

② **Note** that the possibility always remains that the opposite could be found.

(C)

① Apart from demonstrating that evolution did occur, the fossil record also provides tests of the predictions made from evolutionary theory.

② **For example**, the theory predicts that single-celled organisms evolved before multicelled organisms.

해설 [**정답 : ⑤**]

주어진 지문에서 화석 기록은 진화의 증거를 보여준다고 합니다. (A), (B), (C)의 첫 문장들을 보면 (A)의 ①번 문장에서 다세포 생물들이 단세보 생물보다 먼저 진화된 것이 발견되었을 때 그 이론이 거절된다고 합니다. (B)의 ①번 문장에서는 화석 기록은 그러한 예측을 지지한다고 합니다. (C)의 ①번 문장에서는 진화가 일어났음을 입증하는 것 외에도 진화 이론으로부터 만들어진 예측을 시험할 수 있다고 합니다. 주어진 지문에서 '그 이론'에 대해서 제시되지 않았으므로 (A)는 주어진 지문 뒤에 올 수 없고 '그 예측'도 제시되지 않았으므로 (B)도 올 수 없습니다. 그러므로 주어진 지문 뒤에는 (C)가 와야 합니다.

(B)의 '그 예측'은 단세포 생물들이 처음 출현하고 수백만 년 후에 다세포 생물들이 발견되었다는 것으로 (C)의 ②번 문장에서 제시된 단세포 생물들이 다세포 생물들 이전에 진화한 예측을 지칭합니다. 그러므로 (C) 다음에 (B)가 와야 합니다.

(A)의 ①번 문장에서 다세포 생물들이 단세포 생물보다 먼저 진화된 것이 발견되었을 때 그 이론이 거절된다는 것은 (B)의 ②번 문장에서 반대가 발견될 가능성이 항상 존재한다는 내용을 구체화한 것으로 다세포 생물이 단세포 생물들이 처음 출현하고 수백만 년 후에 발견되는 것과 반대되는, 다세포 생물들이 단세포 생물이 출현하기 전에 발견되는 것에 대한 설명이 나와있습니다. 또한 (A)의 '그 이론'은 (B)에서 제시된 '다세포 생물들이 단세포 생물이 출현하고 수백만 년 후에 발견되었다'는 것으로 (B) 다음에 (A)가 와야 합니다. 그러므로 정답은 (C)-(B)-(A)가 됩니다.

주 ①. The fossil record / provides / evidence of evolution.

구 화석 기록은 진화의 증거를 제공한다고 합니다.

주 ②. The story (the fossils / tell) / is / one of change.

구 화석이 말하는 이야기는 변화 중 하나라고 합니다.

주 ③. Creatures / existed (in the past) (that are no longer with us).

구 관계대명사가 긴 경우 수식하는 명사 뒤가 아닌 문장의 끝에 존재할 수 있습니다. 이 문장의 경우 관계대명사 'that'은 'Creatures'를 수식합니다.
- 더 이상 우리와 함께하지 않는 생물체들이 과거에 존재했다고 합니다.

주 ④. Sequential changes / are found (in many fossils) (showing / the change of certain features (over time from a common ancestor, as in the case of the horse)).

구 말의 경우에서처럼, 시간이 지남에 따라 공통의 조상으로부터 특정한 특징의 변화를 보여주는 많은 화석들에서 일련의 변화가 발견된다고 합니다.

독 시간이 지남에 따라 특정한 특징이 변화한다는 것은 주 ①번 문장에서 제시된 진화에 대한 재진술입니다. 즉, 많은 화석들에서 진화에 해당하는 일련의 변화가 보인다고 합니다.

(A) ①. If multicelled organisms / were **indeed** found to have evolved (before single-celled organisms), then the theory of evolution / would be rejected.

구 만약 다세포 생물이 단세포 생물보다 먼저 진화한 것으로 발견된다면, 그 진화 이론은 거부될 것이라고 합니다.

독 'indeed'는 재진술의 표현이자 강조의 표현입니다. 그러므로 중심 문장입니다.

(A) ②. A good scientific theory / always allows for / the possibility of rejection.

구 좋은 과학 이론은 항상 거절의 가능성을 허락한다고 합니다.

(A) ③. The fact (that we / have not found / such a case (in countless examinations of the fossil record)) / strengthens / the case (for evolutionary theory).

구 우리가 화석 기록에 대한 수 많은 조사에서 그러한 경우를 (= 다세포 생물이 단세포 생물보다 먼저 진화한 경우를) 발견하지 못해왔다는 사실은 진화 이론의 근거를 강화한다고 합니다.

(B) ①. The fossil record / supports / this prediction — multicelled organisms / are found (in layers of earth millions of years after the first appearance of single-celled organisms).

　구▶ 그 화석 기록은 그러한 예측을 지지하는데, 다세포 생물들은 단세포 생물들이 처음 출현하고 수백만 년 후의 지구 지층에서 발견되었다고 합니다.

(B) ②. **Note** that the possibility / always remains that the opposite / could be found.

　구▶ 동격절이 긴 경우 수식하는 명사 뒤가 아닌 문장의 끝에 존재할 수 있습니다. 이 문장의 경우 동격 'that'은 'the possibility'를 수식합니다.
　- 그 반대가 발견될 가능성이 항상 남아 있다는 것에 주목하라고 합니다.

　독▶ 명령문이 사용되었으므로 중심 문장
　- 다세포 생물들은 단세포 생물이 처음 출현하고 수백만 년 후 지구 지층에서 발견되었지만 다세포 생물들이 단세포 생물이 처음 출현하기 전에 발견될 가능성이 남아있다는 것에 주목하라고 합니다.

(C) ①. Apart from demonstrating / that evolution / did occur, the fossil record / also provides / tests of the predictions (made from evolutionary theory).

　구▶ 진화가 일어났다는 것을 증명하는 것 외에도, 화석 기록은 진화 이론으로부터 만들어진 예측의 검증을 제공한다고 합니다.

　독▶ 화석 기록은 진화를 나타낼 뿐만 아니라 진화 이론의 예측을 검증할 수 있다고 합니다.

(C) ②. **For example**, the theory / predicts / that single-celled organisms / evolved (before multicelled organisms).

　구▶ 예를 들어, 그 이론은 (= 진화 이론은) 단세포 생물이 다세포 생물 이전에 진화했다고 예측한다고 합니다.

　독▶ 'For example'이 제시되었으므로 앞 문장 중심 문장

주어진 글 다음에 이어질 글의 순서로 가장 적절한 것을 고르시오.

> ① In the fifth century B.C.E., the Greek philosopher Protagoras pronounced, "Man is the measure of all things."
>
> ② **In other words**, we feel entitled to ask the world, "What good are you?"

(A)

① Abilities said to "make us human" ― empathy, communication, grief, toolmaking, and so on ― all exist to varying degrees among other minds sharing the world with us.

② Animals with backbones (fishes, amphibians, reptiles, birds, and mammals) all share the same basic skeleton, organs, nervous systems, hormones, and behaviors.

(B)

① We assume that we are the world's standard, that all things **should** be compared to us.

② Such an assumption makes us overlook a lot.

(C)

① Just as different models of automobiles each have an engine, drive train, four wheels, doors, and seats, we differ mainly in terms of our outside contours and a few internal tweaks.

② **But** like naive car buyers, most people see only animals' varied exteriors.

* contour: 윤곽, 외형 ** tweak: 조정, 개조

해설 [정답 : ②]

주어진 지문에서 인간은 만물의 척도이며, 우리는 세계를 향해 "너는 무엇을 잘하는가?"라고 질문할 자격이 있다고 합니다. 즉 인간이 세계의 중심이라고 합니다. (B)의 ①번 문장에서 우리는 우리가 세상의 기준이라고 생각한다고 합니다. 이는 주어진 지문의 내용을 재진술하는 것이므로 주어진 지문 뒤에 (B)가 와야 합니다.

(B)의 ②번 문장에서 이러한 가정은 많은 것들을 간과하게 만든다고 합니다. (A)의 ①번 문장에서 인간이 특별하다고 생각하는 감정 등이 다른 것들과 공유한다는 것과 (C)의 ①번 문장에서 자동차처럼 많은 것을 공유하고 주로 외형과 몇 가지 내부적인 조정만 다르다는 것 모두 간과하는 것을 제시한다고 볼 수 있습니다. 그러므로 우리는 (A) - (C)와 (C) - (A) 중 논리적 결함이 생기는 것을 찾아야 합니다. (C) - (A)의 경우 (C)의 ②번 문장은 대부분의 사람들은 오직 사람과는 다른 동물들의 외형만 본다고 합니다. 하지만 (A)의 ①번 문장은 인간이 특별하다고 생각하는 것들이 다른 것과 공유한다는 내용이므로 (C)의 ②번 문장과 (A)의 ①번 문장은 역접의 표현 없이 연결될 수 없습니다. (A) - (C)는 (A)의 ①번, ②번 문장에서 (B)의 ②번 문장에서 제시된 사람들이 간과하는 것을 구체화하여 인간과 다른 것의 공통점을 제시하고 (C)의 ①번, ②번 문장을 통해서 (A)의 내용을 비유적으로 표현하는 것으로 볼 수 있으므로 정답은 (B)-(A)-(C)가 됩니다.

주 ①. (In the fifth century B.C.E.)., the Greek philosopher Protagoras / pronounced, / "Man / is / the measure of all things."

구▶ 기원전 5세기에, 그리스 철학자 Protagoras는 "인간은 만물의 척도이다"라고 선언했다고 합니다.

주 ②. **In other words**, we / feel entitled to ask / the world, / "What good are you?"

구▶ 'feel'도 2형식으로 사용될 수 있으므로 'feel p.p'는 'be p.p'와 동일하다고 보시면 됩니다.
  - 'be entitle to-V'는 'V할 자격을 부여받다'를 의미합니다.
  - 다시 말해서, 우리는 세상에 "너는 무엇을 잘하는가?"라고 질문할 자격이 있다 느낀다고 합니다.

독▶ 'In other words'를 통해서 재진술하므로 중심 문장!
  - 우리는 세상에게 무슨 쓸모가 있냐고 질문할 자격이 있다고 합니다.

(A) ①. Abilities (said to "make / us / human") — (empathy, communication, grief, toolmaking, and so on) — all / exist to / varying degrees (among other minds sharing the world with us).

구▶ 'make + O + O.C'는 'O를 O.C하게 만들다'를 의미합니다.
  - '우리를 인간답게 만들어 준다고' 이야기되는 능력들, 즉 공감, 의사소통, 슬픔, 도구 만들기 등, 모두 우리와 세상을 공유하는 다른 마음을 지닌 존재에서 다양한 정도로 존재한다고 합니다.

(A) ②. Animals (with backbones) (fishes, amphibians, reptiles, birds, and mammals) all / share / the same basic skeleton, organs, nervous systems, hormones, and behaviors.

구▶ 척추동물 (어류, 양서류, 파충류, 조류, 포유류) 모두 기본 골격, 기관, 장기, 신경 체계, 그리고 행동들을 공유한다고 합니다.

독▶ (A)의 ①번 문장과 ②번 문장을 통해서 인간이 다른 동물들과 다르다고 생각하는 마음 역시 다른 동물들도 가지고 있고 생물학적인 것도 공유하고 있다고 제시하고 있습니다.

(B) ①. We / assume / that we / are / the world's standard, that all things / **should** be compared (to us).

구▶ 우리는 우리가 세계의 기준이고, 모든 것들은 우리와 비교되어야만 한다고 가정한다고 합니다.

독▶ 'should'가 제시되었으므로 중심 문장!

(B) ②. Such an assumption / makes / us / overlook a lot.

구▶ 'make + O + O.C'는 'O를 O.C하게 만들다'를 의미합니다.
  - 그러한 가정은 우리를 더 많은 것을 간과하도록 만든다고 합니다.

(C) ①. (Just as different models of automobiles each / have / an engine, drive train, four wheels, doors,

and seats), we / differ mainly (in terms of our outside contours and a few internal tweaks).

* contour: 윤곽, 외형 ** tweak: 조정, 개조

구 'Just as'는 '마치 ~인 것처럼'을 의미합니다.
- 'in terms of'는 '~에 관해서'를 뜻합니다.
- 마치 다양한 자동차 모델들이 각각 엔진, 동력 전달 체계, 네 개의 바퀴와 문, 그리고 좌석을 가지고 있는 것처럼, 우리는 주로 외부 윤곽과 몇 가지 내부적인 조정에 관해 다르다고 합니다.

(C) ②. **But** like naive car buyers, / most people / see / only animals' varied exteriors.

구 그러나 순진한 자동차 구매자들처럼, 대부분의 사람들은 오직 동물들의 다양한 외형만 본다고 합니다.

독 'But'이 제시되었으므로 중심 문장!
- 우리는 다양한 자동차들이 똑같은 구성을 하고 있는 것처럼 외형과 몇 가지 조정만 다르고 나머지는 비슷하지만, 사람들은 다른 외형만을 바라본다고 합니다.

주어진 글 다음에 이어질 글의 순서로 가장 적절한 것을 고르시오.

> ① It can be difficult to decide the place of fine art, such as oil paintings, watercolours, sketches or sculptures, in an archival institution.

(A)

① The best archival decisions about art do not focus on territoriality (this object belongs in my institution **even though** I do not have the resources to care for it) or on questions of monetary value or prestige (this object raises the cultural standing of my institution).

② The best decisions focus on what evidential value exists and what is best for the item.

(B)

① **But** art can **also** carry aesthetic value, which elevates the job of evaluation into another realm.

② Aesthetic value and the notion of artistic beauty are important considerations, **but** they are not what motivates archival preservation in the first instance.

(C)

① Art can serve as documentary evidence, especially when the items were produced before photography became common.

② Sketches of soldiers on a battlefield, paintings of English country villages or portraits of Dutch townspeople can provide the only visual evidence of a long-ago place, person or time.

* archival: 기록(보관소)의 ** prestige: 명성, 위신 *** realm: 영역

해설 [**정답 : ⑤**]

주어진 지문에서 미술의 위치를 기록 보관 기관에서 정하는 것은 어려울 수 있다고 합니다.

(C)의 ①번 문장에서 예술은 사진이 보편화 되기 전에 증거의 역할을 했다고 하며 ②번 문장에서는 이를 구체화하여 제시합니다. 이는 (B)에서 예술이 미적 가치를 지닐 수 있다는 내용과 'But'으로 소재가 전환되어 'also'로 나열될 수 있으므로 (C) 다음에는 (B)가 와야 합니다.

(B)의 ②번 문장에서 미적 가치와 예술적 아름다움의 개념은 기록 보존의 동기를 부여하는 것은 아니라고 합니다. (A)의 ①번 문장에서 최선의 기록 보관 결정은 영토권과 금전적 가치나 위신의 문제에 초점을 두지 않는다고 하며, (B)의 ②번 문장에서 제시한 기록 보존의 동기가 아닌 것을 나열합니다. 그러므로 (B) 뒤에는 (A)가 와야 합니다. 그래서 정답은 (C)-(B)-(A)가 됩니다.

* 주어진 지문이 기록 보관이 어렵다는 것을 제시하므로 같은 소재인 기록 보관에 대해서 제시하는 (A)가 주어진 지문 뒤에 올 수 있습니다. 그럼에도 (A) - (C) - (B)가 정답이 될 수 없는 이유는 (A)와 (C)가 연결될 수 없기 때문입니다. (A)는 예술이 증거적 가치가 있다는 것을 전제로 예술이 어떠한 증거 가치가 있고 무엇이 최선인지에 초점을 맞춘다고 합니다. 하지만 (C)에서 예술이 증거의 역할을 할 수 있다는 것을 처음 제기하므로 (A) 뒤에 (C)가 오는 것은 논리적 결함이 생깁니다. 그러므로 (A)-(C)-(B)는 정답이 될 수 없습니다.

주 ①. It / can be difficult / to decide / the place of fine art, (such as oil paintings, watercolours, sketches or sculptures), (in an archival institution).

* archival: 기록(보관소)의

구▶ 'It be동사 + 형용사 + to-V'는 가주어/진주어 의심
- 'It'이 지칭하는 대상이 없으므로 가주어/진주어
- 유화, 수채화, 스케치 혹은 조각과 미세한 미술의 위치를 기록 보관 기관에서 정하는 것은 어려울 수 있다고 합니다.

(A) ①. The best archival decisions (about art) / do not focus on / territoriality (this object / belongs (in my institution) / **even though** I / do not have / the resources (to care for it)) or / on questions of monetary value or prestige (this object / raises / the cultural standing of my institution).

** prestige: 명성, 위신

구▶ 미술에 관한 가장 최선의 기록 보관 결정은 영토권 (비록 이 물건은 내가 그것을 돌볼 자원이 없더라도 내 기관에 속해 있다)나 금전적 가치나 위신의 문제 (이 물건은 내 기관의 문화적 지위를 높인다)에 초점을 두지 않는다고 합니다.

독▶ 'even though'가 제시되었으므로 중심 문장!
- 최선의 기록 보관 결정은 돌볼 자원이 없지만 기관에 속해있는 거나 기관의 문화적 지위에 초점을 맞추지 않는다고 합니다.

(A) ②. The best decisions / focus on / what evidential value / exists and what is / best (for the item).

구▶ 최선의 결정은 어떤 증거적 가치가 존재하고 품목에 무엇이 최선인지에 초점을 맞춘다고 합니다.

(B) ①. **But** art / can **also** carry / aesthetic value, which elevates / the job of evaluation (into another realm).

*** realm: 영역

구▶ 'elevate A into B'는 'A를 B로 상승시키다'를 의미합니다.
- 그러나, 미술은 또한 미적 가치를 가질 수 있는데, 이는 평가의 일을 다른 영역으로 상승시킨다고 합니다.

독▶ 'But'이 제시되었으므로 중심 문장!

(B) ②. Aesthetic value and the notion (of artistic beauty) / are / important considerations, **but** they /
are not / what motivates / archival preservation (in the first instance).

구▶ 미학적 가치와 예술적 아름다움의 개념은 중요한 고려사항이지만, 그들은 기록 보존의 동기를
우선적으로 부여하는 것은 아니라고 합니다.

독▶ 'but'이 제시되었으므로 중심 문장!
- 미학적 가치와 예술적 아름다움에 대한 개념은 중요하지만 우선적으로 기록 보관의 동기가 되는
것은 아니라고 합니다.

(C) ①. Art / can serve as / documentary evidence, / especially when the items / were produced (before
photography / became / common).

구▶ 'serve as A'는 'A의 역할을 하다'를 의미합니다.
- 예술은 문서적인 기록의 역할을 하는데, 특히 그 물품이 사진이 흔해지기 전에 만들어졌을 때
그러하다고 합니다.

(C) ②. Sketches (of soldiers on a battlefield), paintings (of English country villages) or portraits (of
Dutch townspeople) / can provide / the only visual evidence (of a long-ago place, person or
time).

구▶ 전쟁터에 있는 군인들의 스케치, 영국 시골 마을의 그림 또는 네덜란드 시민들의 초상화는 옛날의
상소, 사람 또는 시절에 대한 유일한 시각적 증거를 제공할 수 있다고 합니다.

독▶ (C)의 ①번 문장에서 제시된 예술의 증거로 역할 하는 것을 구체화하여 재진술하고 있습니다.

13 23학년도 6월 평가원 37번 (정답률 45%)

주어진 글 다음에 이어질 글의 순서로 가장 적절한 것을 고르시오.

> ① In economics, there is a principle known as the *sunk cost fallacy*.
> ② The idea is that when you are invested and have ownership in something, <u>you overvalue that thing</u>.

(A)

① Sometimes, the smartest thing a person can do is quit.

② **Although** this is true, it has also become a tired and played-out argument.

③ Sunk cost doesn't always **have to** be a bad thing.

(B)

① This **leads** people **to** continue on paths or pursuits that **should** clearly be abandoned.

② **For example**, people often remain in terrible relationships simply **because** they've invested a great deal of themselves into them.

③ Or someone may continue pouring money into a business that is clearly a bad idea in the market.

(C)

① Actually, you can leverage this human tendency to your benefit.

② Like someone invests a great deal of money in a personal trainer to ensure they follow through on their commitment, you, too, can invest a great deal up front to ensure you stay on the path you want to be on.

* leverage: 이용하다

해설 [정답 : ②]

주어진 지문에서 매몰 비용 오류에 대해서 제시되고 있습니다. 매몰 비용 오류란 사람들이 본인들이 투자했거나 가지고 있는 것에 대해 과대 평가를 하고 있다고 합니다. (A), (B), (C)의 ①번 문장 모두 매몰 비용에 대해서 제시하고 있기 때문에 주어진 지문 뒤에 올 수 있습니다. 그러므로, (A), (B), (C) 사이의 관계를 파악해야 합니다.

(A)의 ①번 문장에서는 사람들이 할 수 있는 것 중 가장 똑똑한 것은 그만 두는 것이라며 매몰 비용을 버리는 것에 대한 내용이 제시되었지만 (A)의 ③번 문장에서 매몰 비용이 항상 좋지 않은 것은 아니라며 전환하고 있습니다. 즉, (A)는 매몰 비용에 대한 단점에서 장점으로 전환하는 부분에 해당하므로 (B)와 (C)가 매몰 비용에 대한 단점이 제시되는지 장점이 제시되는지에 따라 순서를 확정지을 수 있습니다.

(B)의 ①번 문장에서 '그것'은 사람들을 버려야만 하는 길과 추구를 계속하게 한다고 합니다. 이는 매몰 비용의 단점에 해당하고 (B)의 ③번 문장에서도 매몰 비용의 단점이 제시되고 있으므로 (B)는 (A) 앞에 제시되어야 합니다. (B)의 '그것'은 주어진 지문의 사람들이 자신이 투자하고 가지고 있는 것에 과대 평가하는 것을 지칭합니다.

(C)의 ①번 문장에서 너는 '그러한 인간의 경향'을 너의 이익으로 이용할 수 있다고 합니다. '그러한 인간의 경향'은 매몰 비용을 지칭하며 매몰 비용에 대한 장점이 제시되고 있으므로 (C)는 (A) 뒤에 제시되어야 합니다. 그러므로 정답은 (B)-(A)-(C)가 됩니다.

주 ①. In economics, there / is / a principle (known as the sunk cost fallacy).

구▶ 경제학에서, 매몰 비용 오류로 알려진 원리가 있다고 합니다.

주 ②. The idea / is that when you / are invested and have / ownership (in something), you / overvalue / that thing.

구▶ 그 관점은 (= 매몰 비용 오류는) 너가 투자를 했거나 무언가에 대한 소유권이 있을 때, 너가 그것에 대해 과대평가하는 것이라고 합니다.

(A) ①. Sometimes, the smartest thing (a person / can do) is / quit.

구▶ 때때로, 사람이 할 수 있는 가장 똑똑한 것은 관두는 것이라고 합니다.

(A) ②. **Although** this / is / true, it / has also become / a tired and played-out argument.

구▶ 비록 그것이 (= 때때로 사람이 할 수 있는 가장 똑똑한 것은 관두는 것이) 사실일지라도, 그것은 또한 지루하고 효력이 떨어진 주장일 수 있다고 합니다.

독▶ 'Although'가 제시되었으므로 중심 문장

* played-out - 효력이 떨어진

(A) ③. Sunk cost / doesn't always **have to** be / a bad thing.

구▶ 매몰 비용이 항상 안좋은 것은 아니라고 합니다.

독▶ 'have to'가 제시되었으므로 중심 문장
  - 매몰 비용의 단점에서 장점으로 전환되는 것을 파악할 수 있습니다.

(B) ①. This / **leads** people **to continue** (on paths or pursuits (that **should** clearly be abandoned)).

구▶ 'lead A to-V'는 'A가 V하도록 야기하다'를 의미합니다.
  - 그것은 사람들이 분명하게 버려야만 하는 길과 추구를 계속하도록 야기한다고 합니다.

독▶ 'lead to'와 'should'가 제시되었으므로 중심 문장

(B) ②. **For example**, people / often remain (in terrible relationships simply) **because** they've invested / a great deal of themselves (into them).

구▶ 예를 들어, 사람들은 종종 단순히 안 좋은 관계들에 남아 있는데, 그들이 (= 사람들이) 자신의 많은 것을 그것에 (= 그 관계에) 투자했기 때문이라고 합니다.

독▶ 'For example'이 제시되었으므로 앞 문장 중심 문장, 'because'가 제시되었으므로 중심 문장입니다.
  - 사람들은 버려야 하는 길이나 추구를 자신들이 많이 투자했다는 이유로 유지한다고 합니다.

(B) ③. Or someone / may continue / pouring money into a business (that is clearly / a bad idea in the market).

> **구** 'pour A into B'는 'A를 B에 쏟아 붓다'를 의미합니다.
> - 혹은 누군가는 시장에서 분명하게 나쁜 아이디어인 사업에 돈을 쏟아 붓는 것을 지속할 수도 있다고 합니다.

> **독** 매몰 비용을 버리지 않음으로써 생기는 문제점에 대해서 제시되고 있습니다.

(C) ①. Actually, you / can leverage / this human tendency (to your benefit).

* leverage: 이용하다

> **구** 실제로, 너는 그러한 인간의 경향을 너의 이익을 위해 이용할 수 있다고 합니다.

(C) ②. Like someone / invests / a great deal of money (in a personal trainer) (to ensure / they / follow through (on their commitment)), you, too, / can invest / a great deal up front (to ensure / you / stay (on the path (you / want to be on))).

> **구** 누군가 많은 양의 돈을 개인 트레이너에게 투자하여, 그들이 (= 개인 트레이너들이) 그들 스스로의 약속에 따르는 것을 보증하는 것처럼 너 역시 너가 있고 싶은 경로에 확실히 있기 위해 먼저 많은 것을 투자할 수 있다고 합니다.

> **독** (C) ①번 문장에서 제시된 그러한 인간의 경향을 너의 이익을 위해 이용되는 구체적인 내용이 제시되고 있습니다.

주어진 글 다음에 이어질 글의 순서로 가장 적절한 것을 고르시오.

> ① If learning were simply a matter of accumulating lists of facts, then it **shouldn't** make any difference if we are presented with information that is just a little bit beyond what we already know or totally new information.

(A)

① If we are trying to understand something totally new, **however**, we **need to** make larger adjustments to the units of the patterns we already have, which requires changing the strengths of large numbers of connections in our brain, and this is a difficult, tiring process.

(B)

① The adjustments are clearly smallest when the new information is only slightly new — when it is compatible with what we already know, **so that** the old patterns need only a little bit of adjustment to accommodate the new knowledge.

(C)

① Each fact would simply be stored separately.

② According to connectionist theory, **however**, our knowledge is organized into patterns of activity, and each time we learn something new we **have to** modify the old patterns **so as to** keep the old material while adding the new information.

* compatible: 양립하는

해설 [정답 : ⑤]

주어진 지문에서는 학습이 간단하게 사실의 목록을 축적하는 문제라면, 우리가 이미 알고 있는 것을 조금 넘어서는 정보가 제공되거나 완전히 새로운 정보가 제공되더라도 아무런 차이가 없을 것이라고 합니다. 즉, 새로운 정보를 단순히 저장할 때를 제시합니다.

(C)-①번 문장에서 약간만 새로운 정보와 완전히 새로운 정보를 지칭하는 'Each fact'를 통해서 주어진 지문 다음에 (C)가 와야함을 쉽게 알 수 있습니다. 정답은 (C)-(A)-(B) 혹은 (C)-(B)-(A)가 되어야 합니다. (A)-(B)인지 (B)-(A)인지만 판단하면 됩니다.

(A)-①번 문장은 완전히 새로운 것을 이해할 때는 우리는 수많은 연결 강도의 변경을 요구하며, 어렵고 피곤한 과정이라고 합니다. 주어진 지문에서 조금 새로운 것과 완전히 새로운 것의 차이를 제시했으므로, (A)-①번 문장의 'however'을 통해 (A) 앞에는 조금 새로운 정보에 대한 내용이 나와야 함을 알 수 있습니다. 조금 새로운 정보에 대한 내용은 (B)-①번 문장에서 제시하고 있으므로 (C)-(B)-(A)가 되어야 합니다.

혹은 (C)-②번 문장에서 연결 이론에 따르면 우리는 새로운 정보를 추가하면서 과거의 지식을 지키기 위해 과거의 패턴들을 수정해야만 한다고 합니다. (A)-①번 문장에서는 하지만, 완전히 새로운 정보일 경우 더 큰 조정이 필요하다고 합니다. (C)-②번 문장에서는 새로운 것을 배울 때 기존의 것에 수정이 필요하다고 하고 (A)-①번 문장에서도 완전히 새로운 정보는 더 큰 조정이 필요하다고 합니다. 즉, (C)-②번 문장과 (A)-①번 문장은 'however'를 통해서 연결될 수 없으므로 정답은 (C)-(B)-(A)가 되어야 합니다.

주 ①. If learning / were simply / a matter of accumulating lists of facts, then it / **shouldn't** make / any difference if we / are presented with / information (that is just / a little bit beyond (what we / already know)) or totally new information.

구▶ 학습이 간단하게 사실의 목록을 축적하는 문제라면, 우리가 이미 알고 있는 것을 조금 넘어서는 정보가 제공되거나 완전히 새로운 정보가 제공되더라도 아무런 차이가 없을 것이라고 합니다.

독▶ 'should'가 제시되었으므로 중심 문장
- 학습이 단순히 사실을 배우는 것뿐이라면, 우리는 이미 알고 있는 것보다 조금 새로운 정보와 완전히 새로운 정보를 받게 됨에 있어서 간단하게 배우기만 하면 되므로 차이가 없을 것이라고 합니다.

(A) ①. If we / are trying to understand / something totally new, **however**, we / **need to** make / larger adjustments (to the units of the patterns we / already have), which requires / changing the strengths of large numbers of connections (in our brain), and this / is / a difficult, tiring process.

구▶ 그러나 완전히 새로운 것을 이해하려고 한다면, 우리는 이미 가지고 있는 패턴의 단위를 더 크게 조정해야만 하는데, 이는, 우리의 뇌에 있는 수많은 연결 강도의 변경을 요구하며, 이것은 (= 뇌에 있는 수많은 연결 강도의 변경을 요구하는 것은) 어렵고 피곤한 과정이라고 합니다.

독▶ 'however'과 'need to'가 제시되었으므로 중심 문장
- 완전히 새로운 것을 이해할 때는 우리는 수많은 연결 강도의 변경을 요구하며, 어렵고 피곤한 과정이라고 합니다. 주어진 지문에서 조금 새로운 것과 완전히 새로운 것의 차이를 제시했으므로, (A)-①번 문장의 'however'을 통해 (A) 앞에는 조금 새로운 정보에 대한 내용이 나와야 함을 알 수 있습니다.

(B) ①. The adjustments / are clearly / smallest when the new information / is / only slightly new ― when it / is / compatible (with what we / already know), **so that** the old patterns / need / only a little bit of adjustment (to accommodate the new knowledge).

* compatible: 양립하는

구▶ 'so that'은 '~하기 위해서'를 의미합니다.
- 새로운 정보가 약간만 새로울 때, 즉 그것이 (= 정보가) 우리가 이미 알고 있는 것과 양립할 수 있어서 (= 크게 충돌하는 지점이 없어서 서로 공존할 수 있어서) 새로운 지식을 (= 약간만 새로운 지식을) 수용하기 위해 기존 패턴을 약간만 조정하면 될 때 조정은 가장 작다고 합니다.

독▶ 'so that'이 제시되었으므로 중심 문장
- 새로운 정보가 기존 정보와 충돌하는 지점이 적어서 공존할 수 있을 때 조정이 가장 작다고 합니다.

(C) ①. Each fact / would simply be stored separately.

구▶ 각각의 사실은 단순하게 개별적으로 저장될 것이라고 합니다.

독▶ 각각의 사실이 따로 따로 저장될 뿐이라고 합니다.

(C) ②. (According to connectionist theory), **however**, our knowledge / is organized (into patterns of activity), and each time (we / learn / something new) / we / **have to** modify / the old patterns **so as to** keep the old material (while adding the new information).

구▶ 그러나 연결주의 이론에 따르면, 우리의 지식은 활동 패턴으로 조직되어, 우리가 새로운 것을 배우는 각각의 순간에 우리는 새로운 정보를 추가하면서 과거의 물질을 (= 지식들을) 지키기 위해 과거의 패턴들을 수정해야만 한다고 합니다.

독▶ 'however'가 제시되었으므로 앞 뒷 문장 중심문장, 'have to'와 'so as to'가 제시되었으므로 중심 문장

- 연결 주의 이론에 따르면 우리가 새로운 것을 배울 때마다 과거의 지식을 지키면서 새로운 지식을 추가하기 위해 과거의 패턴들을 수정해야만 한다고 합니다.

주어진 글 다음에 이어질 글의 순서로 가장 적절한 것을 고르시오.

> ① Plants show finely tuned adaptive responses when nutrients are limiting.
> ② **Gardeners** may recognize yellow leaves as a sign of poor nutrition and the need for fertilizer.

(A)
① **In contrast**, plants with a history of nutrient abundance are <u>risk averse</u> and save energy.
② At all developmental stages, plants respond to environmental changes or unevenness so as to be able to use their energy for growth, survival, and reproduction, while limiting damage and nonproductive uses of their valuable energy.

(B)
① Research in this area has shown that plants are constantly aware of their position in the environment, in terms of <u>both space and time</u>.
② Plants that have experienced variable nutrient availability in the past tend to exhibit **risk-taking behaviors**, such as spending energy on root lengthening instead of leaf production.

(C)
① **But** if a plant does not have **a caretaker** to provide supplemental minerals, it can proliferate or lengthen its roots and develop root hairs to allow foraging in more distant soil patches.
② Plants can also use their memory to respond to <u>histories of temporal or spatial variation</u> in nutrient or resource availability.

* nutrient: 영양소 ** fertilizer: 비료 *** forage: 구하러 다니다

해설 [정답 : ⑤]

주어진 지문에서는 'Plants show finely tuned adaptive responses when nutrients are limiting. Gardeners may recognize yellow leaves as a sign of poor nutrition and the need for fertilizer', 식물은 영양분이 제한적일 때, 미세하게 조정된 적응 반응을 보이고, 정원사는 노란 잎을 영양 부족과 비료가 필요하다는 신호로 인식할 수도 있다고 합니다. (C)-①번 문장에서는 'But if a plant does not have a caretaker to provide supplemental minerals', 식물에 미네랄을 보충해 줄 관리자가 없을 경우를 언급하는데, 이것은 주어진 문장의 정원사라는 관리자가 존재하는 상황에서 존재하지 않는 상황으로 전환된 내용이므로 (C)는 주어진 문장 뒤에 와야 합니다.

(C)-②번 문장에서는 'Plants can also use their memory to respond to histories of temporal or spatial variation', 식물은 시간적 혹은 공간적 변화의 역사에 대응하기 위해 자신의 기억을 사용한다고 했습니다. (B)-①번 문장에서는 'in terms of both space and time', 식물은 공간과 시간 모두의 측면에서 환경에서 자신의 위치를 인식한다고 했는데, 이것은 (C)의 시공간적 변화에 대응하는 식물의 반응에 대한 재진술이므로 (B)는 (C) 뒤에 와야 합니다.

(B)의 ②번 문장에서는 'tend to exhibit risk-taking behaviors', 과거에 다양한 영양소 가용성을 경험한 식물은 위험을 감수하는 행동을 보이는 경향이 있다고 했습니다. (A)의 ①번 문장에서는 'plants with a history of nutrient abundance are risk averse and save energy', 반면 영양분이 풍부했던 이력을 가진 식물은 위험을 회피하고 에너지를 절약한다고 했는데, 이 내용은 (B)의 내용을 'In contrast'로 역접시켜 설명하고 있습니다. 그러므로 (A)는 (B) 뒤에 와야 하며, 정답은 (C)-(B)-(A)가 됩니다.

주 ①. Plants / show / finely tuned adaptive responses (when nutrients / are / limiting).

구▶ 식물은 영양소가 부족할 때 세밀하게 조정되는 적응 반응을 보인다고 합니다.

독▶ 주어진 문장의 핵심 내용은 식물의 영양소가 부족할 때의 대응 전략인 조정 반응입니다.

주 ②. Gardeners / may recognize / yellow leaves (as a sign of poor nutrition and the need for fertilizer).

구▶ 정원사들은 노란색 잎을 영양 부족의 징후로 인식하며, 이는 비료가 필요함을 나타낸다고 합니다.

독▶ 대응 전략인 조정 반응의 예를 노란색 잎으로 설명하고 있습니다. 이 조정 반응을 통해 정원사들이 식물의 영양 상태를 알 수 있다고 합니다.

(A) ①. In contrast, plants (with a history of nutrient abundance) / are / risk averse and save / energy.

구▶ 반면에, 영양물질이 풍부한 과거를 가진 식물들은 위험을 피하고 에너지를 절약한다고 합니다.

독▶ 영양물질에 대한 가용성이 변동적이지 않으면 위험을 회피한다고 합니다. '반면에'라는 표현으로 논지의 역접을 나타내고 (B)문장 마지막에 나왔던 '위험을 감수한다'와 정반대의 표현이 되므로 (A)문장은 (B)문장의 뒤에 위치하게 됩니다.

(A) ②. (At all developmental stages), plants / respond (to environmental changes or unevenness) (so as to be able to use their energy) (for growth, survival, and reproduction), (while limiting / damage and nonproductive uses (of their valuable energy)).

구▶ 모든 발달 단계에서, 식물은 성장, 생존, 그리고 번식을 위해 에너지를 사용할 수 있도록 환경 변화나 불균형에 반응하며, 소중한 에너지의 손상과 비생산적인 사용을 제한한다고 합니다.

(B) ①. Research (in this area) has shown (that plants / are / constantly aware (of their position in the environment, in terms of both space and time)).

구▶ 이 분야의 연구는 식물이 공간과 시간 측면에서 자신의 환경 내 위치를 항상 인식하고 있다는 것을 보여준다고 합니다.

독▶ (C)에서 우리가 보았던 시간적, 공간적 변수에 대한 반응이라는 기억이 이 문장에서 "시간과 공간의 관점으로"라는 표현으로 다시 등장해 순서에 대한 단서를 제공합니다.

(B) ②. Plants (that / have experienced / variable nutrient availability in the past) tend to exhibit risk-taking behaviors, (such as spending energy on root lengthening instead of leaf production).

구▶ 과거에 영양소의 변동적인 공급을 경험한 식물들은 위험을 감수하는 행동을 보이는 경향이 있는데, 이는 잎 생산 대신 뿌리를 길게 하는 데 에너지를 소비하는 것과 같은 행동을 포함합니다.

독▶ 영양소의 가용성이 변동적이면 식물은 위험을 감수합니다.

(C) ①. **But** (if a plant / does not / have / **a caretaker** (to provide / supplemental minerals)), it / can proliferate or lengthen / its roots and develop / root hairs (to allow / foraging in more distant soil patches).

구▶ 그러나 식물이 보충 미네랄을 제공해줄 관리자가 없다면, 더 멀리 있는 토양 조각에서 포식을 허용하기 위해 뿌리를 번식시키거나 길게 하고 뿌리털을 발달시킬 수 있다고 합니다.

독▶ 이 문장에서는 역접의 표현인 '그러나'를 사용하여 정원사가 없는 상황에서의 식물의 대응 전략을 설명하고 있습니다. 이 문장에서 '관리자'라는 표현이 주어진 문장의 '정원사'를 지칭하는 표현입니다. 현재 평가원에서 단순 대명사가 아닌 다른 표현으로 이전 문장의 표현을 지칭하는 경우가 많습니다.

(C) ②. Plants / can also / use / their memory (to respond (to histories of temporal or spatial variation in nutrient or resource availability)).

구▶ 식물은 또한 영양소나 자원의 시간적 또는 공간적 변동의 역사에 반응하기 위해 그들의 기억을 사용할 수 있다고 합니다.

독▶ 이 문장에서 사용한 '또한'이라는 표현을 주목해야 합니다. 여기서 '또한'은 위의 문장에서 알 수 있었던 식물의 대응 전략인 뿌리를 번식하거나 뿌리털을 길게 하는 전략과 다른 대응 전략인 식물의 '기억'을 예비하는 표현입니다.

주어진 글 다음에 이어질 글의 순서로 가장 적절한 것을 고르시오.

> ① Recently, a number of commercial ventures have been launched that offer social robots as personal home assistants, perhaps eventually to rival existing smart-home assistants.

(A)

① They might be motorized and can track the user around the room, giving the impression of being aware of the people in the environment.

② **Although** personal robotic assistants provide services similar to those of smart-home assistants, their **social presence** offers an opportunity that is unique to social robots.

(B)

① Personal robotic assistants are devices that have no physical manipulation or locomotion capabilities.

② **Instead**, they have a distinct social presence and have **visual features** suggestive of their ability to interact socially, such as eyes, ears, or a mouth.

(C)

① **For instance**, in addition to playing music, a social personal assistant robot would express its engagement with the music so that users would feel like they are listening to the music together with the robot.

② These robots can be used as surveillance devices, act as communicative intermediates, engage in richer games, tell stories, or be used to provide encouragement or incentives.

* locomotion: 이동 ** surveillance: 감시

해설 [**정답 : ②**]

주어진 문장에서는 많은 벤처 기업들이 시작한 소셜 로봇을 개인용 가정 도우미로 사용하는 것은 스마트홈 도우미와 경쟁하게 될 것이라고 합니다.

(B)-①에서는 로봇 도우미는 신체 조작이나 이동 능력이 없다고 했고, (B)-②에서는 로봇들은 사회적 존재감이 있고, 사회적 상호작용이 가능한 시각적 특징이 있다고 합니다. 즉 (B)는 사회적 로봇 도우미의 장점과 단점을 언급하고 있으므로, 소셜 로봇의 등장을 언급한 주어진 문장 뒤에 연결되는 것이 적절합니다.

(A)-①에서 그것들은 동력화될 수 있으며, 실내에서 사용자들을 추적할 수 있는데, 그것이 환경 내의 사람들은 감지한다는 느낌을 준다고 합니다. (A)-②에서도 역시 사회적 존재감이 로봇에게만 특유한 기회를 제공한다고 했으므로 (A)-①은 소셜 로봇과 관련된 지문인데, 이것은 (B)-①의 'have no physical manipulation or locomotion capabilities', 소셜 로봇이 이동 능력이 없다는 것과 반대되는 내용이 됩니다.

B-②를 다시 보면, 소셜 로봇의 시각적 특징을 가지고 있다고 했습니다. 그러므로 (A)-①의 'They'는 (B)-②의 'visual features'를 지칭합니다. 즉 내용은
(B)-①: 로봇은 이동 능력이 없다.
(B)-②: 대신에 로봇은 시각적 특징이 있다.
(A)-①: 그것들은 동력화될 수 있다.는 내용으로 이어지고 있습니다.

(C)-①에서는 예를 들어 소셜 도우미 로봇은 음악을 재생할 뿐만 아니라 사용자가 로봇과 함께 음악을 듣는 것처럼 느끼도록 음악과의 교감을 표현한다고 했습니다. 이것은 (A)-②의 로봇의 사회적 존재감이 소셜 로봇에게만 특유한 기회를 제공하는 것에 대한 예시가 되므로 (C)는 (A) 뒤에 와야 합니다.

* (C)가 (A), (B) 중 무엇의 예시인지를 파악하는 것이 핵심입니다. 로봇이 사용자와 함께 음악을 듣는 것처럼 느끼게 하는 것은 (A)의 예시이지, 로봇의 시각적 특징을 언급하는 (B)의 예시가 될 수 없습니다. 그래서 (C)는 (A)의 뒤에 와야 합니다.

주 ①. Recently, a number of commercial ventures / have been launched / that offer / social robots (as personal home assistants, / perhaps eventually to rival / existing smart-home assistants).

구 최근에, 소셜 로봇을 개인용 가정 도우미로 제공하는 많은 상업적인 벤처 기업들이 진출해 왔는데, 아마도 결국 기존의 스마트홈 도우미와 경쟁하게 될 것이라고 합니다.

독 가정 도우미로 사용하는 소셜 로봇이 기존의 스마트홈 도우미와 경쟁한다고 합니다.

(A) ①. They / might be motorized / and can track / the user (around the room), giving the impression / of being aware of the people (in the environment).

구 그것들은 동력화될 수 있으며 실내에서 사용자를 추적할 수 있는데, 환경 내의 사람들을 감지한다는 인상을 준다고 합니다.

독 이것들이 움직이며 사용자를 추적하고 감지할 수 있다고 합니다.

(A) ②. **Although** personal robotic assistants / provide / services (similar to those of smart-home assistants), their social presence / offers / an opportunity / that is unique to social robots.

구 개인용 로봇 도우미는 스마트홈 도우미와 비슷한 서비스를 제공하긴 하지만, 그들의 사회적 존재감은 소셜 로봇에게만 특유한 기회를 제공한다고 합니다.

독 'Although'가 제시되었으므로 중심 문장
- 사회적 존재감은 소셜 로봇에게만 존재하는 특수한 기능이라고 합니다.

(B) ①. Personal robotic assistants / are / devices / that have / no physical manipulation or locomotion capabilities.

* locomotion: 이동

구 개인용 로봇 도우미는 신체 조작이나 이동 능력이 없는 장치라고 합니다.

독 로봇의 단점에 가까운 특징이 언급됩니다.

(B) ②. **<u>Instead</u>**, they / have / a distinct social presence / and have visual features / suggestive of their ability (to interact socially, such as eyes, ears, or a mouth).

구▶ 대신에, 그것들에게는 뚜렷한 사회적 존재감이 있고 눈, 귀 또는 입과 같은 사회적 상호작용을 할 수 있는 능력을 암시하는 시각적 특징들을 가지고 있다고 합니다.

독▶ 'Instead'가 제시되었으므로 앞 뒷 문장 중심 문장
- (B) ①번 문장과 다르게, 소셜 로봇의 장점에 가까운 특징으로 사회적 존재감이 있는 것과 사회적 상호작용이 가능한 시각적 특징이 등장합니다.

(C) ①. **<u>For instance</u>**, (in addition to playing music), a social personal assistant robot would express / its engagement with the music / so that users / would feel like / they are listening to / the music together with the robot.

구▶ 예를 들어, 소셜 개인용 도우미 로봇은 음악을 재생할 뿐만 아니라 사용자가 로봇과 함께 그 음악을 듣는 것처럼 느끼도록 음악과의 교감을 표현한다고 합니다.

독▶ 사용자가 로봇과 함께 음악을 듣는 것처럼 느끼게 하는 것은 Ⅴ번 문장의 사회적 존재감에 대한 예시가 됩니다.

(C) ②. These robots / can be used / as surveillance devices, act as communicative intermediates, engage in richer games, tell stories, or be used to provide / encouragement or incentives.

** surveillance: 감시

구▶ 이들 로봇은 보안 감시 장치로 사용될 수 있거나, 통신 매개체의 역할을 하거나, 더 다채로운 게임에 참여하거나, 이야기를 들려주거나, 격려나 동기를 제공하는 데 사용될 수 있다고 합니다.

독▶ 역시 소셜 로봇에서만 가능한 기능의 사례들이 언급되고 있습니다.

주어진 글 다음에 이어질 글의 순서로 가장 적절한 것을 고르시오.

① Experts have identified a large number of measures that promote energy efficiency.
② Unfortunately many of them are not cost effective.
③ This is a fundamental requirement for energy efficiency investment from an economic perspective.

(A)

① **And** this has direct repercussions at the individual level: households can reduce the cost of electricity and gas bills, and improve their health and comfort, while companies can increase their competitiveness and their productivity.
② Finally, the market for energy efficiency could **contribute to** the economy through job and firms creation.

(B)

① There are significant externalities to take into account and there are also macroeconomic effects.
② **For instance**, at the aggregate level, improving the level of national energy efficiency has positive effects on macroeconomic issues such as energy dependence, climate change, health, national competitiveness and reducing fuel poverty.

(C)

① **However**, the calculation of **such cost effectiveness** is not easy: it is not simply a case of looking at private costs and comparing them to the reductions achieved.

* repercussion: 반향, 영향 ** aggregate: 집합의

해설 [정답 : ⑤]

주어진 지문에서 전문가들은 에너지 효율을 증가시키는 다수의 대책을 확인했고 그 중 많은 것이 비용 효율적이지 않았다고 합니다. 그리고 주어진 지문 ③번 문장에서 비용 효율은 에너지 효율을 위한 투자에 필요조건이라고 합니다. (C)의 ①번 문장에서 'However'가 제시되었고 'such cost effectiveness'가 지칭하는 대상이 (C) 앞에 존재해야 합니다. 주어진 지문에서 'cost effective'가 제시되었고, 비용 효율은 에너지 효율 투자의 근본적인 필요조건이라는 ③번 문장과 비용 효율성의 계산이 쉽지 않다는 (C)의 ①번 문장이 역접을 이루므로 주어진 지문 다음에 (C)가 와야 합니다.

(A)의 ①번 문장에서 'And'로 인해 (A)의 앞에는 개인적 차원에 영향을 끼치는 것과 나열될 수 있는 것이 와야 하지만 (C)의 계산이 어렵다는 내용과는 나열될 수 없으므로 (C) 뒤에 올 수 없습니다.
반면에 (B)의 ①번 문장에서는 비용 효율을 계산하기 쉽지 않은 이유로 상당한 외부효과와 거시 경제적 효과를 제시하므로 (B)가 (C) 다음에 와야 합니다.

(B)의 ②번 문장에서 예시를 통해 집합적인 수준에서의 영향을 제시하고 이를 (A)의 ①번 문장에서 'And'를 통해 개인적 수준으로 나열하므로 정답은 (C)-(B)-(A)가 됩니다.

주 ①. Experts / have identified / a large number of measures (that promote / energy efficiency).

구 전문가들은 에너지 효율을 증가시키는 다수의 대책을 확인해왔다고 합니다.

주 ②. Unfortunately many of them / are not / cost effective.

구 불행하게도, 그것들 중 많은 것이 비용 효율적이지 않았다고 합니다.

주 ③. This / is / a fundamental requirement (for energy efficiency investment) (from an economic

perspective).

구 'This'는 'cost effective'를 지칭합니다.
- 그것은 경제적 관점에서 에너지 효율을 위한 투자에 근본적인 필요조건이라고 합니다.

(A) ①. **And** this / has / direct repercussions (at the individual level): households / can reduce / the cost

(of electricity and gas bills), and improve / their health and comfort, **while** companies /

can increase / their competitiveness and their productivity.

* repercussion: 반향, 영향

구 그리고 그것은 개인적 차원에서 직접적인 영향을 미치는데, 가정은 전기 비용과 가스 요금을 줄이고 그들의 건강과 편안함을 증가시킬 수 있는 반면에, 회사는 자체 경쟁력과 생산력을 증가시킬 수 있다고 합니다.

독 'while'이 '반면에'로 사용되었으므로 중심 문장!

(A) ②. Finally, the market (for energy efficiency) / could contribute to / the economy (through job and

firms creation).

구 마침내, 에너지 효율 시장은 일자리와 기업 창출을 통해서 경제에 기여할 수 있다고 합니다.

독 'contribute to'가 제시되었으니 중심 문장!
- 일자리와 기업 창출 ⇒ 에너지 효율 시장의 경제 기여로 이해하시면 됩니다.

(B) ①. There are / significant externalities (to take into account) and there are also /

macroeconomic effects.

구 'take into account'는 '고려하다'를 의미합니다.
- 고려해야 할 상당한 외부성(=외부 효과)이 있고 거시 경제적 효과도 있다고 합니다.
* macro (거대한 ⇔ micro) + economic (경제적인) = macroeconomic - 거시 경제적인

(B) ② <u>**For instance**</u>, (at the aggregate level), improving the level of national energy efficiency / has / positive effects (on macroeconomic issues) (such as energy dependence, climate change, health, national competitiveness and reducing fuel poverty).

** aggregate: 집합의

구▸ 예를 들어, 집합적인 차원에서, 국가의 에너지 효율 수준을 높이는 것은 에너지 의존도, 기후 변화, 건강, 국가 경쟁력, 그리고 연료 빈곤을 줄이는 것과 같은 거시 경제적 문제에 긍정적인 영향을 미친다고 합니다.

독▸ 예시가 제시되었으니 앞 문장 중심 문장!

(C) ① <u>**However**</u>, the calculation (of such cost effectiveness) is not / easy: it / is not simply / a case (of looking at private costs and comparing them to the reductions achieved).

구▸ 'compare A to B'는 'A를 B와 비교하다'를 의미합니다.
 - 하지만 그러한 비용 효율성의 계산은 쉽지 않은데, 그것은 단순히 사적비용을 살펴보고 그것을 달성한 감소와 비교하는 것이 아니라고 합니다.

독▸ 'However'가 제시되었으므로 중심 문장!

주어진 글 다음에 이어질 글의 순서로 가장 적절한 것을 고르시오.

① Negotiation can be defined as an attempt to explore and reconcile conflicting positions in order to reach an acceptable outcome.

(A)

① Areas of difference can and do frequently remain, and will perhaps be the subject of future negotiations, or indeed remain irreconcilable.

② In those instances in which the parties have highly antagonistic or polarised relations, the process is likely to be dominated by the exposition, very often in public, of the areas of conflict.

(B)

① In these and sometimes other forms of negotiation, negotiation serves functions other than reconciling conflicting interests.

② These will include delay, publicity, diverting attention or seeking intelligence about the other party and its negotiating position.

(C)

① Whatever the nature of the outcome, which may actually favour one party more than another, the purpose of negotiation is the identification of areas of common interest and conflict.

② In this sense, depending on the intentions of the parties, the areas of common interest may be clarified, refined and given negotiated form and substance.

* reconcile: 화해시키다 ** antagonistic: 적대적인 *** exposition: 설명

해설 [정답 : ④]

주어진 문장에서는 'Negotiation can be defined as an attempt to explore and reconcile conflicting positions in order to reach an acceptable outcome.' 협상은 수용할 수 있는 결과에 도달하기 위해 상충하는 입장을 탐색하고 화해시키려는 시도라고 하며, 협상을 기본적으로 정의하고 있습니다.

(C)-①번 문장에서는 'Whatever the nature of the outcome' 그 결과의 성격이 무엇이든지라고 했는데, 이것은 주어진 문장의 협상의 정의로서 언급된 내용과 연결됩니다. 또한 'purpose of negotiation is the identification of areas of common interest and conflict' 협상의 목적은 공통의 이익과 갈등의 영역을 밝히는 것이라고 했는데, 이것은 '협상의 정의'에서 '협상의 목적'으로 주제를 전환하는 내용이므로 (C)는 주어진 문장 뒤에 와야 합니다.

(C)-②번 문장에서는 'depending on the intentions of the parties, the areas of common interest may be clarified, refined' 당사자들의 의도에 따라 공통의 영역은 명확해지고, 정제된다고 합니다.

(A)-①번 문장에서는 'Areas of difference can and do frequently remain …… indeed remain irreconcilable', 다른 영역은 남을 수 있고, 실제로 남으며, 화해할 수 없는 상태로 남게 될 것이라고 합니다. 이것은 (C)-②번 문장의 협상 당사자들의 공통 영역이 명확해지고 정제되는 것에 대한 예시 문장이 되므로 (A)는 (C) 뒤에 와야 합니다.

(A)-②번 문장에서는 'instances in which the parties have highly antagonistic or polarised relations', 당사자들이 매우 적대적이거나 양극화된 관계를 맺고 있는 사례가 언급됩니다. (B)-①번 문장에서는 'In these and sometimes other forms of negotiation, negotiation serves functions other than reconciling conflicting interests' 이러한 협상에서는 협상은 상충하는 이익을 화해시키는 것이 아닌 기능을 제공한다고 했는데, 이것은 협상 당사자들이 적대적인 (A)의 내용을 전제조건으로 전개하고 있으므로 (B)는 (A) 뒤에 와야 합니다. 그러므로 정답은 (C)-(A)-(B)가 됩니다.

주 ①. Negotiation / can be defined / as an attempt to explore and reconcile / conflicting positions (in order to reach an acceptable outcome).

* reconcile: 화해시키다

구▶ 협상은 수용할 수 있는 결과에 도달하기 위해 상충하는 입장을 탐색하고 화해시키려는 시도라고 정의될 수 있다고 합니다.

독▶ 협상을 정의하고 있습니다.

(A) ①. Areas (of difference) / can and do frequently remain, and will perhaps be / the subject of future negotiations, or indeed remain irreconcilable.

구▶ 이견이 있는 영역은 남을 수 있고, 실제로 자주 남으며, 아마도 향후 협상의 주제가 되거나 실제로 화해할 수 없는 상태로 남게 될 것이라고 합니다.

독▶ 협상 과정에서 존재하는 이견에 관한 설명 문장입니다.

(A) ②. In those instances / in which / the parties / have / highly antagonistic or polarised relations, the process / is likely to be dominated by the exposition, very often in public, of the areas of conflict.

** antagonistic: 적대적인 *** exposition: 설명

구▶ 당사자들이 매우 적대적이거나 양극화된 관계를 맺고 있는 그런 경우에, 그 과정은 갈등 영역에 대한 아주 흔히 공개적인 설명에 의해 지배될 가능성이 있다고 합니다.

독▶ 존재하는 협상의 성격 중 하나로 협상 당사자들이 매우 적대적인 관계에 있는 협상 사례가 언급됩니다.

(B) ①. In these and sometimes other forms of negotiation, negotiation / serves / functions other than reconciling conflicting interests.

구▶ 이러한 형태의 협상과 때로는 다른 형태의 협상에서, 협상은 상충하는 이익을 화해시키는 것이 아닌 기능을 제공한다고 합니다.

독▶ 주 ①번 문장의 정의가 적용되지 않는 협상에 대한 설명 문장입니다.

(B) ②. These / will include / delay, publicity, diverting attention or seeking intelligence (about the other party and its negotiating position).

구▶ 이러한 것들에는 지연, 홍보, 주의를 돌리거나 상대방과 그쪽의 협상 입장에 관한 정보를 구하는 것이 포함될 것이라고 합니다.

독▶ (B) ①번 문장에서 이어지는 화해 역할이 아닌 다른 기능을 하는 협상의 사례가 언급되고 있습니다.

(C) ①. Whatever the nature of the outcome, which / may actually favour / one party more than another, the purpose of negotiation / is / the identification of areas (of common interest and conflict).

구▶ 실제로 다른 당사자보다 한쪽 당사자에게 더 유리할 수도 있는, 그 결과의 성격이 무엇이든, 협상의 목적은 공통의 이익과 갈등의 영역을 밝히는 것이라고 합니다.

독▶ 당사자들의 형평성이 일치하지 않는 성격 역시 주 ①번 문장과는 다른 협상의 목적의 결과로서 설명되고 있습니다.

(C) ②. In this sense, depending on the intentions of the parties, the areas (of common interest) / may be clarified, refined and given negotiated form and substance.

구▶ 이러한 의미에서 당사자들의 의도에 따라 공통의 이익 영역은 명확해지고, 정제되며, 협의가 이뤄진 형식과 실체가 주어질 수 있다고 합니다.

독▶ (C) ①번 문장의 관점에서 협상에 접근하는 경우에 대해서 언급되고 있습니다.

주어진 글 다음에 이어질 글의 순서로 가장 적절한 것을 고르시오.

> ① A firm is deciding whether to invest in shipbuilding.
> ② If it can produce at sufficiently large scale, it knows the venture will be profitable.

(A)
① There is a **"good" outcome**, in which both types of investments are made, and both the shipyard and the steelmakers **end up** profitable and happy. Equilibrium is reached.
② Then there is a "bad" outcome, in which neither type of investment is made.
③ This second outcome also is an equilibrium **because** the decisions not to invest reinforce each other.

(B)
① Assume that shipyards are the only potential customers of steel.
② **Steel producers** figure they'll make money if there's a shipyard to buy their steel, **but** not **otherwise**.
③ Now we have two possible outcomes — what economists call "multiple equilibria."

(C)
① **But** one key input is low-cost steel, and it **must** be produced nearby.
② The company's decision boils down to this: if there is a steel factory close by, invest in shipbuilding; **otherwise**, don't invest.
③ Now consider the thinking of potential steel investors in the region.

* equilibrium: 균형

해설 [정답 : ⑤]

주어진 지문에서 한 회사가 조선업에 투자할 때, 충분한 규모로 생산된다면 수익성이 있다고 합니다.

(B)의 ①번, ②번 문장에서 조선업자가 제철업자의 유일한 소비자라고 고려했을 때 제철업자는 그들의 철을 조선업자가 산다면 수익이 생기고 그렇지 않다면 생기지 않는다고 합니다. (B)의 ③번 문장에서 그 때, 두 가지 결과가 생긴다고 합니다. (A) ①번, ②번 문장에서 (B)에서 제시된 두 가지 결과가 나열되어 제시되므로 (B) 다음에 (A)가 와야 합니다.

이제 (C)가 (B) 앞인지, (A) 뒤인지 판단해야 합니다. (C)의 ①, ②번 문장에서 제철 공장이 근처에 있다면 투자를 할 것이고 그것이 아니라면 투자를 하지 않는다고 합니다. (C)의 ③번 문장에서 제철업자를 고려하자고 하며 (B) ①번, ②번 문장에서 제철업자의 생각에 대해서 제시하므로 (C)는 (B) 앞에 와야합니다. 또한 주어진 지문에서 조선업에 투자하는 회사가 서술되고 주어진 지문 ②번 문장에서 충분한 규모로 생산된다면 수익성이 있다는 내용과 (C) ①번 문장에서 가장 중요한 고려사항은 낮은 철의 가격과 그 철이 근처에서 생산되어야 한다는 내용은 (C) ①번 문장의 'But'을 통해서 전환되므로 정답은 (C)-(B)-(A)가 됩니다.

주 ①. A firm / is deciding / whether to invest in shipbuilding.

> 구 ▶ 'whether to-V'는 'V할지 말지'를 의미합니다
> - 한 회사가 조선업에 투자할지 안할지 결정을 하고 있다고 합니다.

주 ②. If it / can produce (at sufficiently large scale), it / knows / the venture / will be / profitable.

> 구 ▶ 만약 충분히 대규모로 생산할 수 있다면, 그 모험이 (= 조선업에 투자하는 것이) 수익성 있을 것이라는 것을 알고 있다고 합니다.

> * profit (이익) + -able (가능한) = profitable - 이익이 가능한 ⇒ 수익성 있는

(A) ①. There / is / a "good" outcome, (in which both types of investments / are made), and both the shipyard and the steelmakers / **end up** / profitable and happy. Equilibrium / is reached.

* equilibrium: 균형

> 구 ▶ 'both A and B'는 'A와 B 둘 다'를 의미합니다.
> - '좋은' 결과가 있는데, 그것은 두 가지 투자 형태가 모두 이루어지고, 조선업자와 제철업자가 결국 수익성을 가지고 만족하게 되는 것이다. 균형이 이루어지는 것이라고 합니다.

> 독 ▶ 'end up V-ing'는 '결국 ~이 되다'를 의미하므로 결과를 제시해줍니다. 중심 문장
> - 두 가지 투자 형태가 모두 이루어지면 결국 조선업자와 제철업자 모두 만족한다고 합니다.

(A) ②. Then there / is / a "bad" outcome, (in which neither type of investment / is made).

> 구 ▶ '나쁜' 결과가 있는데, 그것은 투자가 모두 안 이루어진 것이라고 합니다.

(A) ③. This second outcome / also is / an equilibrium **because** the decisions (not to invest) / reinforce / each other.

> 구 ▶ 그러한 두 번째 결과 또한 균형을 이루는 것인데, 왜냐하면 투자하지 않는 결정이 서로를 강화하기 때문이라고 합니다.

> 독 ▶ 'because'가 제시되었으므로 중심 문장
> - 두 가지 투자 형태가 모두 이루어지지 않은 나쁜 결과 또한 서로를 강화하므로 균형을 이룬 것이라고 합니다.

(B) ①. Assume that shipyards / are / the only potential customers of steel.

> 구 ▶ 조선업이 철의 유일한 잠재적 소비자라고 가정하라고 합니다.

(B) ②. Steel producers / figure / they'll make / money / if there's a shipyard (to buy their steel), **but** not **otherwise**.

> 구 ▶ 제철업자는 그들의 철을 구매할 조선업자가 있다면 돈을 벌것이고 그렇지 않으면 벌지 못한다고 합니다.

> 독 ▶ 'but'과 'otherwise'가 제시되었으므로 중심 문장
- 유일한 철의 소비자가 조선업자이므로 그 조선업자가 제철업자의 철을 산다면 돈을 벌고 그렇지 않는다면 돈을 벌지 못한다고 합니다.

(B) ③. Now we / have / two possible outcomes — what economists / call / "multiple equilibria."

> 구 ▶ 그때, 경제학자들이 '복수 균형'이라고 부르는 두 가지 결과를 가지게 된다고 합니다.

(C) ①. **But** one key input / is / low-cost steel, / and it / **must be produced** nearby.

> 구 ▶ 하지만, 한 가지 핵심 투자는 낮은 비용의 철이고, 그것은 (= 철은) 반드시 근처에서 생산되어야 한다고 합니다.

> 독 ▶ 'but'이 제시되었으므로 중심 문장
- 낮은 비용의 철이 있어야 하며 그 철이 근처에서 생산되어야 한다고 합니다.

(C) ②. The company's decision / boils down to / this: if there / is / a steel factory / close by, invest in shipbuilding; **otherwise**, don't invest.

> 구 ▶ 그 회사의 결정은 다음과 같이 요약되는데, 만약 제철 공장이 근처에 있다면, 조선업에 투자하고 그렇지 않다면, 투자하지 않는다고 합니다.

> 독 ▶ 'otherwise'가 제시되었으므로 중심 문장
- (C) ①번 문장에서 그 철이 근처에서 생산되어야만 한다고 했으므로 근처에 제철 공장이 있다면 투자하고 그렇지 않는다면 투자하지 않는다고 합니다.

* boil down to - 요약하다

(C) ③. Now consider / the thinking of potential steel investors (in the region).

> 구 ▶ 그 지역에 있는 잠재적 철 투자자의 (= 제철업자의) 생각을 고려해보자고 합니다.

주어진 글 다음에 이어질 글의 순서로 가장 적절한 것을 고르시오.

> ① The fruit ripening process **brings about** the softening of cell walls, sweetening and the production of chemicals that give colour and flavour.
> ② The process is induced by the production of a plant hormone called ethylene.

(A)

① If ripening could be slowed down by interfering with ethylene production or with the processes that respond to ethylene, fruit could be left on the plant until it was ripe and full of flavour but would still be in good condition when it arrived at the supermarket shelf.

(B)

① In some countries **they** are **then** sprayed with ethylene before sale to the consumer to induce ripening.

② **However**, fruit picked before it is ripe has less flavour than fruit picked ripe from the plant.

③ Biotechnologists **therefore** saw an opportunity in delaying the ripening and softening process in fruit.

(C)

① The problem for growers and retailers is that ripening is followed sometimes quite rapidly by deterioration and decay and the product becomes worthless.

② Tomatoes and other fruits are, **therefore**, usually picked and transported when they are unripe.

* deterioration: (품질의) 저하

해설 [정답 : ⑤]

주어진 지문에서 과일 숙성 과정은 화학 물질의 생산을 야기하며 에틸렌이라는 식물 호르몬의 생산에 의해 유도된다고 합니다. (B)의 ①번 문장은 몇몇의 나라에서 'they'는 판매되기 전에 숙성을 유도하기 위해서 에틸렌이 뿌려진다고 합니다. 또한 ①번 문장의 'then' 통해서 판매되기 전 과정이 (B) 앞에 제시되어야 함을 알 수 있습니다.

(C)의 ②번 문장에서 숙성이 품질 저하와 부패를 따라오게 하므로 토마토와 다른 과일들은 익지 않을 때 수확하고 운송한다고 하고 'they'가 (C) ②번 문장의 'Tomatoes and other fruits'를 지칭하므로 (B)가 (C) 뒤에 와야 합니다.

(B)의 ②번 문장에서 'However'로 전환되어 익기 전에 수확하는 방식의 문제점을 제시합니다. 그 후 ③번 문장에서 생명공학자들이 숙성을 늦추는 것에 있어서 기회를 엿보고 있다고 합니다. 이는 (A)의 ①번 문장에서 구체화되어 (B)의 ②번 문장에서 제기된 문제점을 해결하는 해결책으로 에틸렌의 생산이나 에틸렌에 반응하는 과정을 방해하는 것이 제시됩니다. 그러므로 (B) 뒤에는 (A)가 와야 합니다. 그래서 정답은 (C)-(B)-(A)가 됩니다.

주 ①. The fruit ripening process / brings about / the softening of cell walls, sweetening and
the production of chemicals (that give / colour and flavour).

구 ‘bring’은 ‘가져오다’, ‘about’은 ‘~에 대해서’, ‘bring about’은 ‘~에 대해서 가져오다’ ⇒ ‘야기하다’가
됩니다.
- 과일 숙성 과정은 세포벽의 연화, 감미, 색과 맛을 주는 화학 물질의 생산을 야기한다고 합니다.

독 ‘bring about’을 통해서 인과관계를 제시하므로 중심 문장!
- 과일 숙성 ⇒ 세포벽 연화, 감미, 화학 물질 생산으로 이해하시면 됩니다.

주 ②. The process / is induced / by the production of a plant hormone (called ethylene).

구 그 과정은 에틸렌이라는 식물 호르몬의 생선으로부터 유도된다고 합니다.

(A) ①. If ripening / could be slowed down (by interfering with ethylene production or
with the processes that respond to / ethylene), / fruit / could be left (on the plant) / until it /
was / ripe and full of flavour / **but** would still be (in good condition) / when it / arrived (at
the supermarket shelf).

구 ‘by V-ing’는 ‘V함으로써’를 의미합니다.
- ‘interfere with A’는 ‘A를 방해하다’를 뜻합니다.
- 만약 에틸렌 생산을 방해하거나, 에틸렌에 반응하는 과정을 방해함으로써 숙성을 늦출 수 있다면,
과일은 익어서 맛이 가득 찰 때까지 식물에 남아 있을 수 있지만, 슈퍼마켓 선반에 도착했을 때,
여전히 좋은 상태를 유지할 것이라고 합니다.

독 ‘but’이 제시되었으므로 중심 문장
- 과일에 숙성을 늦춘다면 과일은 완전히 익을 때까지 식물에 붙어있을 수 있고 슈퍼마켓에 도착했을
때에도 상태가 좋을 것이라고 합니다.

(B) ①. (In some countries) they / are then sprayed (with ethylene) (before sale to the consumer) (to
induce ripening).

구 몇몇의 나라에서, 그 다음에 숙성을 유도하기 위해 소비자에게 판매하기 전에 에틸렌을 뿌린다고
합니다.

(B) ②. **However**, fruit (picked before it is ripe) has / less flavour than fruit (picked ripe from the
plant).

구 하지만 익기 전에 수확한 과일은 식물에서 익은 상태로 수확된 과일보다 맛이 덜하다고 합니다.

독 ‘However’가 제시되었으므로 중심 문장
- 과일을 익기 전에 수확하고 스프레이를 뿌리는 방법은 맛이 덜하다고 합니다.

(B) ③. Biotechnologists **therefore** / saw / an opportunity (in delaying /

the ripening and softening process) in fruit.

> 구 ▶ 'in V-ing'는 'V함으로써'를 의미합니다.
> - 그러므로 생명공학자들은 과일에서 숙성과 연화과정을 지연시킴으로써 기회를 보고 있다고 합니다.

> 독 ▶ 'therefore'이 제시되었으므로 중심 문장!
> - 과일을 익기 전에 수확하고 스프레이를 뿌리는 방법이 맛이 덜한 문제점에 대해서 생명공학자들이 기회를 엿보고 있다고 합니다.

(C) ①. The problem (for growers and retailers) is / that ripening / is followed sometimes quite rapidly

(by deterioration and decay) / and the product / becomes / worthless.

* deterioration: (품질의) 저하

> 구 ▶ 재배자와 소매업자의 문제는 품질 저하와 부패가 때때로 빠르게 숙성을 따라오고 제품이 가치 없게 되는 것이라고 합니다.

(C) ②. Tomatoes and other fruits / are, **therefore**, usually picked and transported / when they / are /

unripe.

> 구 ▶ 그러므로, 토마토와 다른 과일들은 종종 익지 않았을 때 수확되고 운송된다고 합니다.

> 독 ▶ 'therefore'이 제시되었으므로 중심 문장!
> - 숙성이 되면 부패와 품질 악화가 따라오니 익지 않은 채로 수확하여 운송한다고 합니다.

주어진 글 다음에 이어질 글의 순서로 가장 적절한 것을 고르시오.

> ⓪ Green products involve, in many cases, higher ingredient costs than those of mainstream products.

(A)

① They'd rather put money and time into known, profitable, high-volume products that serve populous customer segments than into risky, less-profitable, low-volume products that may serve current noncustomers.

② Given that choice, these companies may choose to leave the green segment of the market to small niche competitors.

(B)

① **Even if** the green product succeeds, it may cannibalize the company's higher-profit mainstream offerings.

② Given such downsides, companies serving mainstream consumers with successful mainstream products face what seems like an obvious investment decision.

(C)

① Furthermore, the restrictive ingredient lists and design criteria that are typical of such products may make green products inferior to mainstream products on core performance dimensions (e.g., less effective cleansers).

② **In turn**, the higher costs and lower performance of some products attract only a small portion of the customer base, **leading to** lower economies of scale in procurement, manufacturing, and distribution.

* segment: 조각 ** cannibalize: 잡아먹다 *** procurement: 조달

해설 [정답 : ⑤]

주어진 문장에서는 친환경 제품은 주류 제품보다 더 높은 원료비를 포함한다고 합니다.

(C)-①에서는 게다가 그런 제품에서 제한적인 원료 목록과 디자인 기준이 친환경 제품을 주류 제품보다 더 열등하게 만들 수 있다고 합니다. 주어진 문장과 (C) 모두 주류 제품과 비교한 친환경 제품의 단점들이 언급되었고, 'Furthermore'을 통해 단점이 나열되고 있다는 것을 알 수 있으므로 (C)는 주어진 문장 뒤에 와야 합니다.

(C)-②에서는 친환경 제품의 단점으로 인한 부정적인 결과로 더 낮은 규모의 경제를 언급했는데 (B)-①의 'cannibalize the company's high-profit mainstream offerings', 고수익 주류 제품을 잡아먹는다는 단점을 재진술하는 (B)가 (C) 뒤에 와야 합니다.

B-②에서는 소비자들이 요구를 충족하는 기업들은 명백한 투자 결정처럼 보이는 것에 직면한다고 합니다. (A)-①에서는 그들은 고객의 요구를 이미 알고 있고 수익성이 있는 다량의 제품에 돈과 시간을 투자하고 싶다고 합니다. 문맥상 (A)-①을 지칭하는 것은 (B)-②의 'companies'밖에 없으므로 (A)는 (B) 뒤에 와야 합니다.

* 내용추론, 접속사, 대명사를 모두 이용해 풀 수 있으면서도 난이도가 높은 좋은 문제입니다. 꼭 다시 한 번 풀어보고 연습해보는 것을 추천 드립니다.

주 ①. Green products / involve, (in many cases), higher ingredient costs / than those of mainstream products.

구▶ 많은 경우, 친환경 제품은 주류 제품보다 더 높은 원료비를 수반한다고 합니다.

(A) ①. They'd rather put / money and time (into known, profitable, high-volume products) / that serve / populous customer segments / than into risky, less-profitable, low-volume products / that may serve / current noncustomers.

* segment: 조각

구▶ 그들은 현재 고객이 아닌 사람들의 요구를 충족할 수 있는 위험하고 수익성이 더 낮은 소량의 제품보다는, 다수의 고객 계층의 요구를 충족하는, 이미 알고 있고 수익성이 있는 다량의 제품에 돈과 시간을 투자하고 싶어 한다고 합니다.

(A) ②. Given that choice, these companies / may choose / to leave the green segment (of the market) (to small niche competitors).

구▶ 그런 선택을 고려하면, 이들 기업은 소규모 틈새 경쟁업체들에게 시장의 친환경 부문을 남겨두는 선택을 할 수 있다고 합니다.

독▶ 친환경 제품이 주류 제품보다 기업에 도움이 되지 않기 때문에 주류 제품을 파는 기업이 소규모 경쟁 업체들에게 친환경 제품을 넘긴다는 것입니다.

* niche - 틈새시장

(B) ①. Even if the green product / succeeds, it / may cannibalize / the company's higher-profit mainstream offerings.

** cannibalize: 잡아먹다

구▶ 친환경 제품이 성공하더라도 기업의 고수익 주류 제품을 잡아먹을 수 있다고 합니다.

독▶ 'Even if'가 제시되었으므로 중심 문장
- 그것이 성공하더라도, 고수익 주류 제품을 잡아먹는다는 단점이 있다고 합니다.

(B) ②. Given such downsides, companies (serving mainstream consumers / with successful mainstream products) face / what seems like / an obvious investment decision.

구▶ 이런 부정적인 면을 고려하면, 성공적인 주류 제품으로 주류 소비자들의 요구를 충족하는 기업들은 마치 명백한 투자 결정처럼 보이는 것에 직면한다고 합니다.

독▶ 부정적인 면으로 인해 친환경 제품이 아닌 주류 제품을 파는 기업들이 겪는 문제점이 언급됩니다.

(C) ①. <u>Furthermore</u>, the restrictive ingredient lists and design criteria (that are / typical of such products) may make / green products / inferior to mainstream products (on core performance dimensions) (e.g., less effective cleansers).

구 ▶ 'make + O + O.C'는 'O를 O.C하게 만들다'를 의미합니다.
- 게다가 그런 제품에서 일반적인 제한 성분 목록과 디자인 기준이 친환경 제품을 주류 제품보다 핵심 성능 측면(예를 들어, 덜 효과적인 세척제)에서 더 열등하게 만들 수 있다고 합니다.

독 ▶ 핵심 성능 측면에서 주류 제품보다 열등하다는 친환경 제품의 단점이 나열되고 있습니다.

(C) ②. <u>In turn</u>, the higher costs and lower performance (of some products) / attract / only a small portion (of the customer base), <u>leading to</u> / lower economies of scale / in procurement, manufacturing, and distribution.

*** procurement: 조달

구 ▶ 결과적으로, 일부 제품의 더 높은 비용과 더 낮은 성능은 고객층의 오직 적은 부분만 유인해서, 조달, 제조, 유통에서 더 낮은 규모의 경제를 초래한다고 합니다.

독 ▶ 'In turn'이 언급되므로 중심 문장
- 더 높은 비용은 더 높은 원료비, 더 낮은 성능은 열등한 성능으로 인해 친환경 제품이 더 낮은 규모의 경제를 초래한다고 합니다.

22 25학년도 수능 37번 (정답률 34%)

주어진 글 다음에 이어질 글의 순서로 가장 적절한 것을 고르시오.

---

① Watch the birds in your backyard.
② If one bird startles and flies off, others will follow, not waiting around to assess whether the threat is real.
③ They have been infected by emotional contagion.

(A)
① Marc wondered whether the birds in line were more fearful **because** they didn't know what their flockmates were doing.
② Emotional contagion would have been impossible for individual grosbeaks in the linear array except with their nearest neighbors.

(B)
① In a long-term research project that Marc did with some of his students on patterns of antipredatory scanning by western evening grosbeaks, they found that birds in a circle showed more coordination in scanning than did birds who were feeding in a line.

(C)
① The birds in a line, who could only see their nearest neighbor, not only were less coordinated when scanning, **but** also were more nervous, changing their body and head positions significantly more than grosbeaks in a circle, where it was possible for each grosbeak to see every other grosbeak.

* grosbeak: 콩새류(類) ** array: 정렬

해설 [정답 : ③]

주어진 지문에서는 감정 전염에 대해서 소개하고 있습니다. (A)-①번 문장에서는 Marc가 선에 있는 새들에 대해 궁금했던 점과 (A)-②번 문장에서 감정 전염이 선에 있는 새들에게 불가능하다고 합니다. (B)에서는 Marc의 연구가 소개되며 Marc의 연구에서 원을 그리는 새들이 선을 그리는 새들보다 더욱 조화를 이루었다고 합니다. (C)에서는 선을 이루는 새들이 관찰을 할 때 덜 조화를 이루었고 원형에 있는 새들보다 더욱 긴장해 있었다고 합니다.

우리는 Chapter 5-1에 재진술 부분을 통해서 같은 말을 하는 내용끼리는 붙어 있어야 한다는 것을 배웠습니다. 재진술된 내용들이 붙어 있어야 평가원이 제시한 글의 통일성, 응집성, 일관성이 지켜지기 때문입니다. 비록 재진술의 표현이 제시되지는 않았지만 (B)의 마지막 부분에서 원을 그리는 새들이 선을 그리는 새들보다 더욱 조화를 이루었다는 내용과 (C)의 앞부분인 선을 이루는 새들이 관찰을 할 때 덜 조화를 이루었다는 내용이 동일하므로 재진술임을 알 수 있습니다. 그러므로 우리는 (B)-(C)의 연결을 확정지을 수 있습니다.

그러면 (A)-(B)-(C) 이거나 (B)-(C)-(A)가 될 것입니다. 물론 (A)-(B)-(C)는 선지에 없어서 자동 (B)-(C)-(A)가 되긴하지만 우리는 공부하는 입장이므로 (A)가 왜 주어진 지문 뒤로는 갈 수 없고 (C) 뒤로 가야만 하는지를 알아야 합니다. 독해력이 좋은 학생들은 (B)에서 Marc의 연구가 한 연구에 대해 소개하므로 (B)가 가장 먼저 와야하고 (A)에서는 연구를 통해 Marc가 궁금했던 점을 (A)-②번 문장에서 감정 전염을 느낄 수 없다는 결론을 통해 (A)가 마지막에 와야함을 알 수 있습니다. 또한 (C)에 중간 부분에서 일렬로 선 새들은 더욱 긴장한다고 합니다. 이는 (A)-①번 문장에서 일렬로 있는 새는 더욱 공포를 느낀다로 재진술됩니다. 그러므로 (C)-(A)가 되어 정답은 (B)-(C)-(A)가 됩니다.

주 ①. Watch / the birds (in your backyard).

구 뒷마당의 새를 관찰해보라고 합니다.

주 ②. If one bird / startles and flies off, others / will follow, (not waiting around to assess whether the threat / is / real).

구 만약 새 한 마리가 놀라 날아오르면 다른 새들도 위협이 진짜인지 아닌지 판단하기 위한 기다림이 없이 다른 새들도 따라간다고 합니다.

독 만약 새 한 마리가 날아오르면 다른 새들도 다른 판단없이 따라 날아오른다고 합니다.

주 ③. They / have been infected (by emotional contagion).

구 그들은 (= 따라 날아오른 새들은) 감정 전염에 감염되었다고 합니다.

독 따라 날아오른 새들은 먼저 날아오른 새의 감정에 전염되어 따라 날아오른 것이라고 합니다.

(A) ①. Marc / wondered / whether the birds (in line) / were / more fearful **because** they / didn't know / what their flockmates / were doing.

구 Marc는 줄을 선 새들이 그들의 (= 새들의) 무리가 무엇을 하는지 모르기 때문에 더욱 공포를 느끼는지 아닌지 궁금해 했다고 합니다.

독 'because'가 제시되었으므로 중심 문장
 - Marc가 줄은 선 새들은 그들의 무리가 무엇을 하는지 모르기 때문에 다른 새들보다 더욱 공포를 느낄지 아닌지가 궁금했다고 합니다.

(A) ②. Emotional contagion / would have been / impossible (for individual grosbeaks in the linear array) (except with their nearest neighbors).

* grosbeak: 콩새류(類) ** array: 정렬

구 감정 전염은 가장 가까운 곳에 있는 이웃을 제외하고 선으로 정렬한 하나의 콩새류에게는 불가능했을 것이라고 합니다.

독 주어진 지문에서 제시된 감정 전염은 가장 가까이에 있는 새들이 아니면 선으로 정렬한 개인 콩새류에게는 불가능하다고 합니다.

(B) ①. In a long-term research project (that Marc / did with some of his students (on patterns of antipredatory scanning by western evening grosbeaks)), they / found / that birds (in a circle) / showed / more coordination in scanning than did birds (who were feeding in a line).

* grosbeak: 콩새류(類)

구▶ 'in V-ing'는 'V-ing함에 있어서'로 해석하시면 됩니다.

- Marc가 자신의 학생 몇 명과 함께 진행한 서양 콩새류의 포식자 회피 관찰의 패턴에 관한 연구에서, 그들은 원을 그리고 있는 새들이 일렬로 먹이를 먹고 있는 새들보다 더 많은 관찰에 있어서 더 많은 조화를 보인다는 것을 발견했다고 합니다.

독▶ Marc가 시행한 연구에서 원 모양으로 나는 새들이 일렬로 나는 새들보다 더 조화를 보였다고 합니다.

* anti (반대) + predatory (포식자의) = antipredatory - 포식자를 회피하는

* coordination - 조화, 협동, 조정

(C) ①. The birds (in a line), (who could only see / their nearest neighbor), not only were less coordinated when scanning, **but** also were more nervous, (changing their body and head positions significantly more than grosbeaks in a circle), where it / was possible / for each grosbeak / to see every other grosbeak.

* grosbeak: 콩새류(類)

구▶ 'not only A but also B'는 'A뿐만 아니라 B도'를 뜻합니다.

- 'it is (was) + 형용사 + to-V'는 가주어/진주어를 의미합니다.
- 'to-V'의 앞 'for N'는 의미상 주어를 뜻하며 'N이 V하다'로 해석하시면 됩니다.
- 일렬로 있는 새들은 가장 가까운 이웃만 볼 수 있는데, 관찰할 때 조화가 떨어질뿐만 아니라 더욱 긴장하고 있었고 각각의 콩새가 다른 모든 콩새를 보는 것이 가능한 원형의 콩새들보다 몸과 머리의 위치를 더욱 많이 바꿨다고 합니다.

독▶ 일렬로 나열한 새들은 원형의 새들보다 조화가 안되었고 더욱 불안해 했다고 하며 일렬로 나열한 새들에 대한 부연 설명이 이어지고 있습니다.

주어진 글 다음에 이어질 글의 순서로 가장 적절한 것을 고르시오.

> ① The most commonly known form of results-based pricing is a practice called *contingency pricing*, used by lawyers.

(A)
① **Therefore**, only an outcome in the client's favor is compensated.
② From the client's point of view, the pricing makes sense in part **because** most clients in these cases are unfamiliar with and possibly intimidated by law firms.
③ Their biggest fears are high fees for a case that may take years to settle.

(B)
① By using contingency pricing, clients are ensured that they pay no fees until they receive a settlement.
② In these and other instances of contingency pricing, the economic value of the service is hard to determine before the service, and providers develop a price that allows them to share the risks and rewards of delivering value to the buyer.

(C)
① Contingency pricing is the major way that personal injury and certain consumer cases are billed.
② In this approach, lawyers do not receive fees or payment until the case is settled, when they are paid a percentage of the money that the client receives.

* intimidate: 위협하다

해설 [정답 : ④]

주어진 지문에서 가장 흔하게 알려진 결과 기반 가격 책정은 변호사들이 사용하고 'contingency pricing'이라고 불리는 관행이라고 합니다. (A)의 ①번 문장에서 따라서, 오직 의뢰인이 선호하는 결과에 대해서만 보상받는다고 합니다. 이에 대한 이유가 주어진 지문에 제시되지 않았으므로 (A)는 주어진 지문 뒤에 올 수 없습니다. (B)의 ①번 문장은 contingency pricing을 사용함으로써 의뢰인들은 판결을 받을 때까지 수수료를 지불하지 않아도 된다고 합니다. (C)의 ①번 문장에서는 Contingency pricing에 대한 설명이 제시되어 있습니다. (B)와 (C) 모두 주어진 지문 뒤에 올 수 있으므로 (A), (B), (C) 간의 관계를 파악해야 합니다.

(C)의 ②번 문장에서 변호사들이 재판이 끝날 때까지 수수료를 받지 않고 의뢰인이 받는 돈의 일부분을 받는 것은 의뢰인이 재판에서 이겼을 시 받는 돈의 일부를 받는다는 뜻입니다. 이는 (A)의 ①번 문장에서 의뢰인이 선호하는 결과, 즉, 승소시에만 수수료를 받을 수 있다는 내용의 원인이 되므로 (C)는 (A) 앞에 와야 합니다. 또한 (B)의 ②번 문장에서 재판에 대한 예시뿐만 아니라 contingency pricing이 사용되는 다른 예시에 대해서도 언급하고 있으므로 재판에 대한 예시인 (B)가 (A) 뒤에 와야 합니다.

(C) 다음에 (A)가 와야하고 (B)의 ②번 문장에서 재판에 대한 예시뿐만 아니라 다른 예시에 대한 포괄적인 설명을 하므로 (B)는 (C) - (A) 앞에 올 수 없습니다. 그러므로 정답은 (C)-(A)-(B)가 됩니다.

주 ①. The most commonly known form of results-based pricing / is / a practice (called *contingency pricing*, used by lawyers).

구▶ 가장 흔하게 알려진 결과 기반 가격 책정은 변호사들이 사용하고 'contingency pricing'이라고 불리는 관행이라고 합니다.

(A) ①. **Therefore**, only an outcome (in the client's favor) / is compensated.

구▶ 그러므로 오직 의뢰인의 선호내에 있는 (= 의뢰인이 원하는) 결과에 대해서만 보상받는다고 합니다.

독▶ 'Therefore'이 제시되었으므로 중심 문장
  - 의뢰인이 원하는 결과에 대해서만 돈을 받는다고 합니다.

(A) ②. (From the client's point of view), the pricing / makes sense (in part) **because** most clients (in these cases) / are unfamiliar with and possibly intimidated (by law firms).

* intimidate: 위협하다

구▶ 의뢰인의 관점에서 가격 책정은 부분적으로 이해할 수 있는데, 왜냐하면 그러한 소송에서 대부분의 의뢰인들은 법률 사무소에 익숙하지 않고 위협받을 수도 있기 때문이라고 합니다.

독▶ 'because'가 제시되었으므로 중심 문장
  - 의뢰인이 법률 사무소에 익숙하지 않고 법률 사무소가 재판에 대해서 의뢰인에게 협박할 수도 있기 때문에 의뢰인이 원하는 결과에 대해서만 법률 사무소에 돈을 지급하는 것이 의뢰인에게 합리적일 수 있다고 합니다.

(A) ③. Their biggest fears / are / high fees (for a case (that may take years to settle)).

구▶ 그들의 (= 의뢰인들의) 가장 큰 공포는 판결을 받는데 수 십년이 걸릴 수 있는 재판에 대한 높은 비용이라고 합니다.

독▶ 의뢰인들은 판결까지 오래 걸리는 재판에 대한 높은 수수료가 제일 큰 걱정이라고 합니다.

(B) ①. By using contingency pricing, clients / are ensured / that they / pay / no fees (until they / receive / a settlement).

구▶ 'By V-ing'는 'V하므로써'를 의미합니다.
  - contingency pricing을 사용함으로써, 의뢰인들은 그들이 판결을 받을 때까지 수수료를 지불하지 않아도 된다는 것을 보장받는다고 합니다.

독▶ contingency pricing에서 의뢰인들은 그들이 판결을 받기 전에 수수료를 지불하지 않아도 된다고 합니다.

(B) ②. In these and other instances (of contingency pricing), the economic value of the service / is hard to determine (before the service), and providers / develop / a price (that allows / them / to share / the risks and rewards of delivering value to the buyer).

구 ‘allow A to-V’는 ‘A가 to-V하는 것을 허락하다’를 의미합니다.
- contingency pricing에 대한 다른 예시들에서 서비스의 경제적 가치는 서비스를 받기 전에 결정되기 어렵고, 공급자들은 그들이 (= 공급자들이) 구매자들에게 가치를 전달하는 위험과 가치를 공유하는 것을 허락하는 가격을 전개한다고 (= 전달한다고) 합니다.

독 재판에서뿐만 아니라 다른 예시에서 적용되는 contingency pricing은 공급자들이 구매자에게 서비스를 제공하는 위험과 보상을 나누는 방식으로 가격을 설정한다고 합니다.

(C) ①. Contingency pricing / is / the major way (that personal injury and certain consumer cases / are billed).

구 Contingency pricing은 개인 부상과 특정한 소비자 소송에서 비용이 청구되는 주요한 방식이라고 합니다.

독 Contingency pricing이 이용되는 사례를 제시하고 있습니다.

(C) ②. In this approach, lawyers / do not receive / fees or payment (until the case is settled), when they / are paid / a percentage of the money (that the client receives).

구 그러한 접근에서 (= Contingency pricing이 사용될 때) 변호사는 재판이 끝날 때까지 수수료나 급료를 받지 않는데, 그들은 의뢰인이 받는 돈의 일부분을 지불받는다고 합니다.

독 Contingency pricing에서 변호사들은 재판이 끝날 때까지 수수료를 받지 않고 재판이 끝난 후 의뢰인이 받는 돈의 일부분을 수수료로 받는다고 합니다.

주어진 글 다음에 이어질 글의 순서로 가장 적절한 것을 고르시오.

> ① Spatial reference points are larger than themselves.
> ② This isn't really a paradox: landmarks are themselves, **but** they also define neighborhoods around themselves.

(A)

① In a paradigm that has been repeated on many campuses, **researchers** first collect a list of campus landmarks from students.

② Then they ask another group of students to estimate the distances between pairs of locations, some to landmarks, some to ordinary buildings on campus.

(B)

① **This asymmetry of distance estimates** violates the most elementary principles of Euclidean distance, that the distance from A to B **must** be the same as the distance from B to A.

② Judgments of distance, then, are not necessarily coherent.

(C)

① The remarkable finding is that distances from an ordinary location to a landmark are judged shorter than distances from a landmark to an ordinary location.

② **So**, people would judge the distance from Pierre's house to the Eiffel Tower to be shorter than the distance from the Eiffel Tower to Pierre's house.

③ Like black holes, landmarks seem to pull ordinary locations toward themselves, **but** ordinary places do not.

* asymmetry: 비대칭

해설 [**정답** : ①]

주어진 지문에서 랜드마크는 그들 스스로를 정의하기도 하지만 주변 지역을 정의하므로 스스로보다 더 크다고 합니다.

(A) ①번, ②번 문장에서 연구자들은 학생들에게 랜드마크에서부터 일반 장소까지의 거리와 일반 장소에서 랜드마크까지의 거리를 추정하라는 실험을 진행함을 알 수 있습니다. 이러한 실험의 결과는 (C) ①번 문장의 결과로 이어지며, 주목할 만한 결과는 일반 장소에서 랜드마크까지의 거리가 랜드마크에서 일반 장소까지의 거리보다 짧게 판단되었다는 것이라고 합니다. (C)의 ①번 문장이 실험의 결과에 해당하므로 (A) 다음에는 (C)가 와야 합니다.

(Chapter 1-1에서 실험은 예시이기 때문에 중요하다고 했습니다. 또한 파급 영어 (상), (하)편에서 다양한 실험 지문을 보았기 때문에 (A)에서 (C)로의 연결이 어색하시면 안됩니다.)

(C)의 ②번, ③번 문장에서 (C) ①번 문장에서 제시된 일반 장소에서 랜드마크까지의 거리가 랜드마크에서 일반 장소까지의 거리보다 짧게 판단되었다는 결과를 예시와 비유를 통해서 재진술하고 있습니다. 이러한 결과는 (B)의 'This asymmetry of distance estimates', '거리 추정에서의 비대칭'이 지칭하는 대상이 되므로 (C) 다음에는 (B)가 와야 합니다. 그러므로 정답은 (A)-(C)-(B)가 됩니다.

주 ①. Spatial reference points / are / larger than themselves.

구▶ 공간적 기준점은 그들 스스로보다 크다고 합니다.

*   spatial - 공간의
**   reference (언급, 참조) + point (점) = reference point - 언급점, 참조점 ⇒ 기준점

주 ②. This / isn't really / a paradox: landmarks / are / themselves, **but** they / also define / neighborhoods (around themselves).

구▶ 그것은 랜드마크는 그 자체이기도 하지만, 또한 자기 주변 지역을 규정한다는 점에서 역설적이지 않다고 합니다.

독▶ 'but'이 제시되었으므로 중심 문장
- 공간 기준점이 자신 스스로보다 크다는 관점은 공간 기준점이 그들 스스로를 정의하기도 하지만 이웃한 공간도 정의한다는 점에서 적절하다고 합니다.

(A) ①. In a paradigm (that / has been repeated / on many campuses), / **researchers** / first collect / a list of campus landmarks (from students).

구▶ 많은 캠퍼스에서 반복되어 왔던 패러다임에서, 연구자들은 첫 번째로 학생들로부터 캠퍼스의 랜드마크 목록을 수집했다고 합니다.

독▶ 실험이 제시되고 있으므로 중심 문장

(A) ②. Then they / ask / another group of students / to estimate / the distances (between pairs of locations), (some to landmarks, some to ordinary buildings on campus).

구▶ 'ask + I.O + D.O'는 'I.O에게 D.O를 물어보다'를 의미합니다.
- 그들은 (= 연구자들은) 다른 그룹의 학생들에게 쌍으로 이루어진 장소 사이의 거리, 즉 캠퍼스에 있는 어떤 장소에서 랜드마크까지, 어떤 장소에서 평범한 건물까지의 거리를 측정하는 것을 물어봤다고 합니다.

독▶ 랜드마크를 추천해준 학생들이 아닌 다른 학생들에게 랜드마크까지의 거리와, 평범한 장소까지의 거리를 물어봤다고 합니다.

(B) ①. This asymmetry of distance estimates / violates / the most elementary principles of Euclidean distance, / that the distance (from A to B) / **must** be / the same (as the distance from B to A).

* asymmetry: 비대칭

구▶ 'from A to B'는 'A부터 B까지'를 의미합니다.
- 그러한 비대칭적인 거리 측정은 A부터 B까지의 거리는 반드시 B부터 A까지의 거리와 같아야 한다는 가장 기본적인 Euclidean 거리 법칙을 위반한다고 합니다.

독▶ 'must'가 제시되었으므로 중심 문장
- 'This asymmetry of distance estimates'는 A부터 B까지의 거리와 B부터 A까지의 거리가 같다는 법칙을 위반한다고 합니다. 즉, 'This asymmetry of distance estimates'는 A부터 B까지의 거리와 B부터 A까지의 거리가 다르다는 것을 알 수 있습니다.

(B) ②. Judgments of distance, then, / are not necessarily / coherent.

구▶ 그러면, 거리에 대한 판단은 반드시 일관성 있는 것은 아니라고 합니다.

* coherent - 일관적인

(C) ①. The remarkable finding / is / that distances (from an ordinary location to a landmark) / are judged shorter than distances (from a landmark to an ordinary location).

구▶ 주목할 만한 결과는 평범한 장소에서 랜드마크까지의 거리가 랜드마크에서 평범한 장소까지의 거리보다 더 짧다고 판단된 것이라고 합니다.

(C) ②. **So**, people / would judge / the distance (from Pierre's house to the Eiffel Tower) to be shorter / than the distance (from the Eiffel Tower to Pierre's house).

구▶ 그래서 사람들은 Pierre의 집에서 에펠탑까지의 거리가 에펠탑에서 Pierre의 집까지 거리보다 더 짧다고 판단할 것이라고 합니다.

독▶ 'So'가 제시되었으므로 중심 문장
　- (C) ①번 문장에서 제시된 내용에 대한 예시에 해당합니다. 일반적인 장소는 Pierre의 집과 대응되고 랜드마크는 에펠탑과 대응됩니다.

(C) ③. (Like black holes), landmarks / seem to pull / ordinary locations (toward themselves), **but** ordinary places / do not.

구▶ 블랙홀처럼, 랜드마크는 평범한 장소를 그들 방향으로 끌고 오는 것처럼 보이지만 평범한 장소는 그렇지 않다고 합니다.

독▶ 'but'이 제시되었으므로 중심 문장
　- 평범한 장소에서 랜드마크까지의 거리가 랜드마크에서 평범한 장소까지의 거리보다 짧다는 것을 비유적으로 표현하고 있습니다.

주어진 글 다음에 이어질 글의 순서로 가장 적절한 것을 고르시오.

> ① There are a number of <u>human resource management practices</u> that are necessary to support organizational learning.

(A)

① <u>**Their**</u> role <u>**should**</u> be to assist, consult, and advise teams on how best to approach learning.

② They <u>**must**</u> be able to develop new mechanisms for cross-training peers — team members — and new systems for capturing and sharing information.

③ To do this, human resource development professionals <u>**must**</u> be able to think systematically and understand how to promote learning within groups and across the organization.

(B)

① <u>**For example**</u>, <u>performance evaluation and reward systems</u> that reinforce long-term performance and the development and sharing of new skills and knowledge are particularly important.

② <u>**In addition**</u>, the human resource development function may be dramatically changed to keep the emphasis on continuous learning.

(C)

① In a learning organization, every employee <u>**must**</u> take the responsibility for acquiring and transferring knowledge.

② Formal training programs, developed in advance and delivered according to a preset schedule, are insufficient to address shifting training needs and encourage timely information sharing.

③ Rather, <u>human resource development professionals</u> <u>**must**</u> become learning facilitators.

해설 [정답 : ③]

주어진 문장에서는 'human resource management practices that are necessary to support organizational learning' 조직 학습을 지원하는 데 필요한 인적 자원 관리 관행이 있다고 합니다.

(B)-①번 문장에서는 예시로 'performance evaluation and reward systems', 업무 평가 그리고 보상 시스템이 언급됩니다. 이 시스템들의 역할이 'reinforce long-term performance' 장기적 성과 강화, 'development and sharing of new skills and knowledge' 그리고 새로운 기술과 지식의 개발 및 공유라는 점을 고려해 보면, (B)-①번 문장의 예시는 주어진 문장의 인적 자원 관리 관행의 사례가 되어야 하므로 (B)는 주어진 문장 뒤에 와야 합니다.

계속해서 (B)-②번 문장에서는 'human resource development function may be dramatically changed to keep the emphasis on continuous learning' 지속적인 학습에 중점을 두도록 인적 자원 개발 기능을 변경할 수도 있다고 하며 인적 자원 관리에 대한 설명이 이어지고 있습니다. (C)-①번 문장에서는 'learning organization, every employee must take the responsibility for acquiring and transferring knowledge' 학습 조직에서 모든 직원은 지식 습득과 전수에 대한 책임을 져야 한다고 했습니다. 이것은 (B)의 관행이 조직원들의 책임으로 확대되는 내용으로 이어질 수 있으므로 (C)는 (B) 뒤에 와야 합니다.

(C)-②번 문장에서는 'Formal training programs, …… information sharing', 형식적인 교육 프로그램은 교육적 요구에 대응하기에 충분하지 않고, 정보 공유 촉진에도 충분하지 않다고 합니다. 이어서 (C)-③번 문장에서는 'human resource development professionals must become learning facilitators' 인적 자원 개발 전문가들은 학습의 촉진자가 되어야 한다고 하며 형식적 교육 프로그램의 한계와 인적 자원 개발전문가들의 역할을 (C)에서 언급하고 있습니다. (A)-①번 문장에서는 'Their role should be to assist, consult, and advise teams on how best to approach learning', 그들의 역할은 학습에 가장 잘 접근하는 방법에 대해 팀을 지원하고, 상담하고 조언하는 것이라고 했는데, 여기서 그들은 (C)의 인적 자원 관리 전문가들을 지칭하고, 그들의 역할을 구체적으로 설명하는 내용이므로 (A)는 (C) 뒤에 와야 합니다. 그러므로 정답은 (B)-(C)-(A)가 되므로 정답은 ③번이 됩니다.

주 ①. There / are / a number of human resource management practices (that are / necessary / to support / organizational learning).

구▶ 조직의 학습을 지원하는 데 필요한 여러 가지 인적 자원 관리 관행이 있다고 합니다.

(A) ①. Their role / **should** be / to assist, consult, and advise teams / on how best to approach learning.

구▶ 그들의 역할은 학습에 가장 잘 접근하는 방법에 대해 팀을 지원하고, 상담하고, 조언하는 것이어야 한다고 합니다.

독▶ 'should'가 제시되었으므로 중심 문장
- 그들 (= (C)-③번 문장의 인적 자원 개발 전문가들)의 역할이 언급됩니다.

(A) ②. They / **must** be able to develop / new mechanisms / for cross-training peers — team members — and new systems / for capturing and sharing information.

구▶ 그들은 동료, 즉 팀원을 두 가지 이상의 일이 가능하도록 훈련시키기 위한 새로운 기법과 정보를 수집하고 공유하기 위한 새로운 시스템을 개발할 수 있어야 한다고 합니다.

독▶ 'must'가 제시되었으므로 중심 문장
- 그들이 시스템적으로 해야 하는 역할이 이어서 언급됩니다.

(A) ③. To do / this, human resource development professionals / **must** be able to think systematically / and understand / how to promote learning (within groups and across the organization).

구▶ 이를 이행하기 위해, 인적 자원 개발 전문가들은 체계적으로 사고하고 집단 내 및 조직 전체에서 학습을 촉진하는 방법을 이해할 수 있어야 한다고 합니다.

독▶ 'must'가 제시되었으므로 중심 문장
- 역할 수행을 위해 인적 자원 개발 전문가가 가지고 있어야 하는 능력이 언급되며, 이를 통해 (A)-①, ②번 문장의 그들이 전문가들을 지칭한다는 것을 정확히 알 수 있습니다.

(B) ①. <u>**For example**</u>, performance evaluation and reward systems (that / reinforce / long-term performance) and the development and sharing (of new skills and knowledge) / are particularly important.

> 구 예를 들어, 장기적인 성과를 강화하는 업무 평가 및 보상 시스템, 그리고 새로운 기술과 지식의 개발 및 공유가 특히 중요하다고 합니다.

> 독 예시로 언급된 시스템과 공유는 조직의 학습을 지원하는 역할을 하는 관행들이므로 주어진 문장의 예시가 되는 문장임을 알 수 있습니다.

(B) ②. <u>**In addition**</u>, the human resource development function / may be dramatically changed / to keep the emphasis / on continuous learning.

> 구 또한, 지속적인 학습에 계속 중점을 두도록 인적 자원 개발 기능을 획기적으로 변경할 수도 있다고 합니다.

> 독 'in addition'으로 추가적인 내용을 제시하므로 중심 문장

> - 인적 자원 관리 관행에 추가적으로 인적 자원 개발 기능을 변경하는 것에 대해 언급하고 있습니다.

(C) ①. In a learning organization, every employee / <u>**must**</u> take / the responsibility (for acquiring and transferring knowledge.)

> 구 학습 조직 내 모든 직원은 지식 습득과 전수에 대한 책임을 져야 한다고 합니다.

> 독 'must'가 제시되었으므로 중심 문장

> - 학습 조직 내 직원들이 가져야 하는 책임에 대해 설명하고 있습니다.

(C) ②. Formal training programs, (developed (in advance) and delivered according to a preset schedule), / are / insufficient / to address / shifting training needs and / encourage / timely information sharing.

> 구 사전에 개발되어 미리 정해진 일정에 따라 제공되는 형식적인 교육 프로그램은 변화하는 교육적 요구에 대응하기에 충분하지 않고, 시기적절한 정보 공유를 촉진하기에도 충분하지 않다고 합니다.

> 독 형식적 교육 프로그램은 (C)-①번 문장에서 지식 습득과 전수를 위해 기능하는 것인데, 이것의 단점을 언급하며, 변화된 방식의 교육 프로그램이 필요하다는 것을 암시하고 있습니다.

(C) ③. Rather, human resource development professionals / <u>**must**</u> become / learning facilitators.

> 구 오히려 인적 자원 개발 전문가들이 학습의 촉진자가 되어야 한다고 합니다.

> 독 'must'가 제시되었으므로 중심 문장

> - (C)-②번 문장에서 언급된 교육 프로그램의 한계를 해결하기 위한 방안이 언급되고 있습니다.

주어진 글 다음에 이어질 글의 순서로 가장 적절한 것을 고르시오.

> ① Wildfire is a natural phenomenon in many Australian environments.
>
> ② The intentional setting of fire to manage the landscape was practised by Aboriginal people for millennia.

(A)

① **However**, the pattern of burning that stockmen introduced was unlike previous regimes.

② When conditions allowed, they would set fire to the landscape as they moved their animals out for the winter.

③ This functioned to clear woody vegetation and also stimulated new plant growth in the following spring.

(B)

① **Although** grasses were the first kinds of plants to recolonize the burnt areas they were soon succeeded by further woody plants and shrubs.

② About the only strategy to prevent such regrowth was further burning — essentially using fire to control the consequences of using fire.

(C)

① The young shoots were a ready food source for their animals when they returned.

② **However**, the practice also tended to reinforce the scrubby growth it was intended to control.

* regime: 양식 ** scrubby: 관목이 우거진

해설 [정답 : ①]

주어진 글 ①번 문장에서는 'Wildfire is a natural phenomenon in many Australian environments' 산불은 호주 환경에서 자연스러운 현상이라고 말하며 산불을 처음 언급하고, 다음 ②번 문장에서는 'fire to manage the landscape was practised by Aboriginal people for millennia' 경관 관리를 위해 불을 지르는 행위는 원주민들에 의해 수천년 동안 행해졌다고 하며 호주에서 원주민들이 산불을 활용한 사례가 언급되고 있습니다. (A)-①번 문장에서는 'burning that stockmen introduced was unlike previous regimes' 목축업자들이 도입한 불을 지르는 방식은 이전의 양식과는 달랐다고 하며 겨울에 가축들을 외부로 이동시켜 불을 지르는 새로운 불 지르기 방식을 언급하는데, 여기서 이전 양식은 주어진 글 ②번 문장의 원주민들의 불 지르는 방식을 지칭하고, 이것과는 대조되는 새로운 불 지르기 사례로 목축업자의 사례가 언급되는 (A)가 주어진 글 뒤에 와야 합니다.

(A)-③번 문장에서는 'This functioned to clear woody vegetation and also stimulated new plant growth' 이러한 불이 숲이 우거진 초목을 없애고, 새로운 식물의 성장을 촉진했다고 하며 목축업자들의 불 지르는 방식의 효과가 언급됩니다. (C)-①번 문장에서는 'The young shoots were a ready food source for their animals when they returned', 어린 새싹은 그들의 동물들이 돌아왔을 때, 준비된 식량원이라고 했습니다. 여기서 young shoots는 (A)-③번 문장의 'new plant' 새로운 식물, their animals와 they는 (A)-②번 문장의 불을 지르면서 이동시켰던 동물들을 지칭합니다. 이것은 1. 동물 이동(A-②) - 2. 불 지르기(A-②) - 3. 식물 성장(A-③) - 4. 동물 귀환(C-①) - 동물의 식물 섭취(C-①)로 이어지는 일련의 과정으로 구성되어야 하므로 (C)는 (A) 뒤에 와야 합니다.

(C)-②번 문장에서는 'practice also tended to reinforce the scrubby growth', 그 관행(불 지르는 행위)이 통제하고자 했던 관목의 성장을 강화하는 경향도 있었다고 합니다. 이것은 식물의 성장을 통제하는 불의 역기능으로 내용이 전환되는 내용입니다. (B)-①번 문장에서는 'they were soon succeeded by further woody plants and shrubs' 맨 처음 대량 서식한 풀에 이어 목본성 식물과 관목이 뒤를 이었다고 했습니다. 이것은 (C)의 통제하고자 했던 관목이 성장한 구체적인 사례에서 이어지는 내용이 되므로 (B)는 (C) 뒤에 와야 합니다. 그러므로 정답은 (A)-(C)-(B)가 됩니다.

* 원래 순서 문제에서 정답이 ①번으로 나오게 되면 지문의 난이도와 관계 없이 오답률이 치솟는 경향이 있습니다. 하지만 절대평가 전환 이후 최고 오답률을 찍었던 이 문제는 그저 '정답이 ①번이기 때문이구나' 라고 쉽게 생각하고 넘어갈 문제는 절대 아닙니다. (A)의 위치를 모호하게 하기 위한 장치들이 덕지덕지 발라져 있었기 때문에 지문의 어려운 난이도와 ①번을 정답 범주에 넣지 않는 수험생들의 풀이 경향이 합쳐져 이러한 결과물이 나왔다고 볼 수 있습니다.

주 ①. **Wildfire** / **is** / a natural phenomenon (in many Australian environments.)

구 산불은 호주의 많은 환경에서 자연스러운 현상이라고 합니다.

주 ②. The intentional setting (of fire) / to manage / the landscape / was practised / by Aboriginal people / for millennia.

구 경관을 관리하기 위해 의도적으로 불을 지르는 일은 수천 년 동안 호주 원주민들에 의해 행해졌다고 합니다.

독 산불의 사례 중 하나로 원주민들이 의도적으로 불을 질렀던 사례가 언급됩니다.

(A) ①. **However**, the pattern (of burning (that stockmen / introduced)) / was / unlike previous regimes.

* regime: 양식

구 하지만 목축업자들이 도입한 불 지르기 방식은 이전 양식과는 달랐다고 합니다.

독 'However'가 제시되었으므로 중심 문장
  - 또 다른 산불 사례로 목축업자들이 불을 지르는 방식이 언급되며, 이전의 양식은 주어진 글 ②번 문장의 원주민들의 불 지르기 방식을 지칭합니다.

* (live)stock (가축) + man (남자) = stockman - 목축업자

(A) ②. When conditions / allowed, they / would set / fire to the landscape / as they / moved / their animals (out for the winter).

구 여건이 허락되면, 그들은 겨울에 자신들의 가축을 외부로 이동시켜, 경관에 불을 지르곤 했다고 합니다.

독 목축업자들이 불을 지르는 방식을 설명하고 있습니다.

(A) ③. This / functioned / to clear woody vegetation / and also stimulated / new plant growth (in the following spring.)

구▶ 이는 숲이 우거진 초목을 없애는 역할을 했고, 또한 이듬해 봄에 새로운 식물의 성장을 촉진했다고 합니다.

독▶ 이러한 불 지르기 방식의 효과를 언급하고 있습니다.

(B) ①. **Although** / grasses / were / the first kinds of plants / to recolonize / the burnt areas / they / were soon succeeded / by further woody plants and shrubs.

구▶ 불에 탄 지역에 다시 대량 서식한 첫 번째 식물류는 풀이었지만, 목본성 식물과 관목이 곧 그것들의 뒤를 이었다고 합니다.

독▶ ‘Although’가 제시되었으므로 중심 문장

  - 불에 탄 지역에서 어떤 식물이 성장하는지를 설명하고 있습니다.

* succeed - ① 성공하다 ② 뒤를 잇다

(B) ②. About the only strategy (to prevent / such regrowth) / was / further burning — essentially using / fire (to control / the consequences of using fire).

구▶ 그러한 재성장을 막기 위한 거의 유일한 전략은 불을 더 지르는 것이었는데, 본질적으로는 불을 사용하여 불을 사용한 결과를 통제하는 것이있다고 합니다.

독▶ (B)-①번 문장에서 언급된 식물들의 성장을 불을 질러서 방해하는 내용이 언급되고 있습니다.

(C) ①. The young shoots / were / a ready food source for their animals when / they / returned.

구▶ 어린 새싹은 그들의 동물들이 돌아왔을 때 준비된 먹을 수 있는 식량원이었다고 합니다.

독▶ 동물들이 돌아왔다는 것은 (A)-②번 문장에서 목축업자들이 외부로 이동시킨 동물들이 돌아온 것을 지칭하며, 그때 불을 지른 후 자라난 새싹들을 동물들이 먹었다는 것을 알 수 있습니다.

* shoot - 순(싹)

(C) ②. **However**, the practice / also tended to reinforce / the scrubby growth (it / was intended to control).

** scrubby: 관목이 우거진

구▶ 하지만, 그 관행은 또한 통제하고자 했던 우거진 관목의 성장을 강화하는 경향도 있었다고 합니다.

독▶ ‘However’가 제시되었으므로 앞 뒷 문장 중심 문장

  - 관행은 불을 지르는 행위를 의미하며, 이것이 (A)-③번 문장에서 언급된 초목을 없애는 식물의 통제와 다르게, 관목의 성장을 강화하는 역효과로 이어지기도 했다는 내용이 언급됩니다.

01 25학년도 9월 평가원 39번 (정답률 72%)

글의 흐름으로 보아, 주어진 문장이 들어가기에 가장 적절한 곳을 고르시오.

> Unfortunately, at the scales, accuracy, and precision most useful to protected area management, the future not only promises to be unprecedented, **but** it also promises to be unpredictable.

To decide whether and how to intervene in ecosystems, protected area managers normally need a reasonably clear idea of what future ecosystems would be like if they did not intervene. (①) Management practices usually involve defining a more desirable future condition and implementing management actions designed to push or guide ecosystems toward that condition. (②) Managers need confidence in the likely outcomes of their interventions. (③) This traditional and inherently logical approach requires a high degree of predictive ability, and predictions **must** be developed at appropriate spatial and temporal scales, often localized and near-term. (④) To illustrate this, consider the uncertainties involved in predicting climatic changes, how ecosystems are likely to respond to climatic changes, and the likely efficacy of actions that might be taken to counter adverse effects of climatic changes. (⑤) Comparable uncertainties surround the nature and magnitude of future changes in other ecosystem stressors.

* adverse: 해로운 ** magnitude: 크기

해설 [정답 : ④]

Ⅰ. 주어진 문장에서 불행하게도 보호 지역 관리에 가장 유용한 규모, 정확성 그리고 정밀도에서 미래는 전례가 없을 뿐만 아니라 예측할 수 없는 것이 될 것이라고 합니다. 주어진 문장 뒤에서는 보호 지역 관리에 대해서 예측할 수 없다는 내용이 제시되어야 합니다.

Ⅱ. ④번 앞 문장에서는 그러한 전통적이고 본질적으로 논리적인 접근 방식은 높은 수준의 예측 능력을 요구하고, 예측은 반드시 적절한 공간적, 시간적 규모에서 종종 국지적이고 단기적인 규모로 이루어져야만 한다고 합니다. 즉, 생태계에 개입하기 위해서는 높은 수준의 예측이 필요하다고 합니다. 하지만 ④번 뒷 문장에서는 이를 설명하기 위해서, 기후 변화를 예측함에 있어서 불확실성, 생태계가 기후 변화에 어떻게 반응할 가능성이 있는지, 그리고 기후 변화의 해로운 영향에 대응하기 위해 취할 수도 있는 행동의 가능한 효율을 고려해 보라고 합니다. 즉, 예측에 불확실성이 있다는 내용입니다. ④번 앞 문장의 높은 예측 수준이 필요하다와 ④번 뒷 문장의 예측의 불확정성이 크다는 내용은 역접의 내용없이 연결될 수 없습니다. 그러므로 ④번에서 내용 단절이 발생합니다.

Ⅲ. 주어진 문장에서 'Unfortunately'와 예측할 수 없다는 내용을 통해 역접의 내용이 제시되었고 ④번 뒷 문장에서 예측의 불확정성에 대해서 제시되고 있습니다. 그러므로 정답은 ④번이 됩니다.

주. Unfortunately, (at the scales, accuracy, and precision most useful to protected area management), the
future / not only promises to be unprecedented, **but** it also promises to be unpredictable.

> 구▶ 'not only A but also B'는 'A뿐만 아니라 B도'를 의미합니다.
> - 불행하게도 보호 지역 관리에 가장 유용한 규모, 정확성 그리고 정밀도에서 미래는 전례가 없을 뿐만
> 아니라 예측할 수 없는 것이 될 것이라고 합니다.

> 독▶ 'but'이 제시되었으므로 중심 문장
> - 보호 지역 관리와 관련된 미래에 대해 전례가 없을 뿐만 아니라 예측할 수 없다고 합니다.

* un (부정) + precedented (전례가 있는, 선례가 있는) = unprecedented – 전례가 없는

Ⅰ. To decide / whether and how to intervene in / ecosystems, protected area managers / normally
need / a reasonably clear idea of what future ecosystems / would be like (if they did not
intervene).

> 구▶ 생태계에 개입할지 여부와 어떻게 개입할지 결정하기 위해, 보호 지역 관리자는 그들이 (= 보호 지역
> 관리자들이) 개입하지 않을 경우 미래의 생태계가 무엇과 비슷할지에 대해 논리적으로 확실한 생각을
> 일반적으로 필요로 한다고 합니다.

> 독▶ 생태계에 개입할지 여부와 방법에 대해 결정할 때, 관리자들은 그들이 개입하지 않는다면 미래의
> 생태계가 어떻게 될지를 생각해야 한다고 합니다.

Ⅱ. Management practices / usually involve / defining a more desirable future condition and
implementing management actions (designed to push or guide ecosystems toward that condition).

> 구▶ 관리 관행은 일반적으로 너 바람직한 미래 상태를 정의하고 생태계를 그 상태 쪽으로 (= 더 바람직한
> 미래 상태로) 밀고 가거나 이끌도록 설계된 관리 조치를 실행하는 것을 포함한다고 합니다.

> 독▶ 생태계 관리는 바람직한 미래의 생태계 상태를 설정하고 바람직한 생태계로 이끌기 위해 관리 행동을
> 실행한다고 합니다.

Ⅲ. Managers / need / confidence (in the likely outcomes of their interventions).

> 구▶ 관리자들은 그들의 (= 관리자들의) 개입의 결과에 대해서 자신감을 필요로 한다고 합니다.

> 독▶ 관리자는 생태계에 개입했을 때의 결과에 대해서 자신감을 가져야 한다고 합니다.

Ⅳ. This traditional and inherently logical approach / requires / a high degree of predictive ability, and predictions / **must** be developed (at appropriate spatial and temporal scales, often localized and near-term).

구▶ 그러한 전통적이고 본질적으로 논리적인 접근 방식은 높은 수준의 예측 능력을 요구하고, 예측은 반드시 적절한 공간적, 시간적 규모에서 종종 국지적이고 단기적인 규모로 이루어져야만 한다고 합니다.

독▶ 'must'가 제시되었으므로 중심 문장
- Ⅱ번 문장에서 바람직한 미래 생태계 상태를 정의하고 이를 위해 행동하는 접근은 높은 미래 예측 가능성이 필요하다고 합니다.

Ⅴ. To illustrate this, consider / the uncertainties (involved in predicting climatic changes), how ecosystems / are likely to respond to / climatic changes, and the likely efficacy of actions (that might be taken to counter / adverse effects of climatic changes).

* adverse: 해로운

구▶ 'in V-ing'는 'V-ing 함에 있어서'를 의미합니다.
- 이를 설명하기 위해서, 기후 변화는 예측함에 있어서 불확실성, 생태계가 기후 변화에 어떻게 반응할 가능성이 있는지, 그리고 기후 변화의 해로운 영향에 대응하기 위해 취할 수도 있는 행동의 가능한 효율을 고려해 보라고 합니다.

독▶ 기후 변화 예측이 불확실성으로 인해 매우 어렵다고 합니다.

Ⅵ. Comparable uncertainties / surround / the nature and magnitude of future changes in other ecosystem stressors.

** magnitude: 크기

구▶ 다른 생태계 스트레스 요인에서 미래의 변화 규모와 성격에서도 상대적인 불확실성이 존재한다고 합니다.

독▶ 기후 변화뿐만 아니라 다른 생태계 요인들의 변화 규모와 성격도 예측하기 어렵다고 합니다.

글의 흐름으로 보아, 주어진 문장이 들어가기에 가장 적절한 곳을 고르시오.

Note that copyright covers the expression of an idea and not the idea itself.

Designers draw on their experience of design when approaching a new project. This includes the use of previous designs that they know work-both designs that they have created themselves and those that others have created. (①) Others' creations often spark inspiration that also **leads to** new ideas and innovation. (②) This is wellknown and understood. (③) **However**, the expression of an idea is protected by copyright, and people who infringe on that copyright can be taken to court and prosecuted. (④) **This** means, **for example**, that **while** there are numerous smartphones all with similar functionality, this does not represent an infringement of copyright as the idea has been expressed in different ways and it is the expression that has been copyrighted. (⑤) Copyright is free and is automatically invested in the author, **for instance**, the writer of a book or a programmer who develops a program, unless they sign the copyright over to someone else.

* infringe: 침해하다 ** prosecute: 기소하다

해설 [정답 : ④]

Ⅰ. 주어진 문장에서 저작권은 아이디어의 표현을 보호하지 아이디어 그 자체를 보호하지 않는 것에 주목하라고 합니다. 이를 통해 주어진 문장 뒤에서는 아이디어의 표현을 보호하고 아이디어 그 자체를 보호하지 않는 저작권과 관련된 내용이 제시될 것임을 알 수 있습니다.

Ⅱ. ④번 앞 문장에서 아이디이의 표현은 저작권으로 보호된나고 합니다. 하지만 ④번 뒷 문장에서 아이디어가 다양하게 표현되면 저작권 침해가 아니라고 합니다. 저작권 보호가 된다는 내용과 저작권 침해가 아니라는 내용은 역접의 표현 없이 제시될 수 없으므로 ④번 뒷 문장의 'This'는 ④번 앞 문장을 지칭하지 않습니다. 그래서 ④번에서 내용 단절이 발생합니다.

Ⅲ. ④번 뒷 문장에서 저작권의 보호를 받는 것은 표현이고 다양한 아이디어의 표현은 저작권 침해가 아니라는 내용이 전개되고 ④번에서 단절이 발생하므로 정답은 ④번이 됩니다.

주. Note / that copyright / covers / the expression of an idea and not the idea itself.

> 구 ▶ 저작권은 아이디어의 표현을 보호하지 아이디어 그 자체를 보호하지 않는 것에 주목하라고 합니다.

Ⅰ. Designers / draw on / their experience of design / when approaching a new project.

> 구 ▶ 디자이너들은 새로운 프로젝트에 접근할 때, 그들의 디자인 경험에 의존한다고 합니다.

* draw on – 의존하다.

Ⅱ. This / includes / the use of previous designs / that they / know / work-both designs (that they have created themselves) and those (that others have created).

> 구 ▶ 'both A and B'는 'A와 B 둘 다'를 의미합니다.
> - 그것은 그들이 아는 그들 스스로 만든 디자인들과 다른 사람들이 만든 디자인 둘 다인 이전의 디자인의 사용을 포함한다고 합니다.

Ⅲ. Others' creations / often spark / inspiration (that also **leads to** / new ideas and innovation).

> 구 ▶ 다른 사람들의 창조물은 흔히 새로운 아이디어와 혁신을 야기하는 영감을 불러일으킨다고 합니다.

> 독 ▶ 'lead to'가 제시되었으므로 중심 문장!
> - 다른 사람의 창조물 ⇒ 영감 ⇒ 새로운 아이디어와 혁신으로 이해하시면 됩니다.

Ⅳ. This / is / wellknown and understood.

> 구 ▶ 그것은 잘 알려져 있고 이해된다고 합니다.

Ⅴ. **However**, the expression (of an idea) / is protected (by copyright), and people (who infringe on / that copyright) / can be taken (to court) and prosecuted.

* infringe: 침해하다 ** prosecute: 기소하다

> 구 ▶ 하지만, 아이디어의 표현은 저작권에 의해 보호되며 그 저작권을 침해한 사람은 법정에 가고 기소될 수 있다고 합니다.

> 독 ▶ 'However'이 제시되었으므로 앞 뒷 문장 중심 문장!
> - 다른 사람의 창조물이 영감을 불러일으키지만 아이디어의 표현은 저작권으로 보호된다고 합니다.

VI. This means, (**for example**), that **while** there are / numerous smartphones all (with similar functionality), this / does not represent / an infringement of copyright / **as** the idea / has been expressed (in different ways) and it is / the expression / that has been copyrighted.

> 구 ‘different + 복수명사’는 ‘다양한 복수명사’를 의미합니다.
> - ‘copyright’은 ‘저작권’을 의미하지만 동사로 사용되었으므로 ‘저작권하다’ = ‘저작권을 보호하다’를 의미합니다.
> - ‘it be동사 + 명사 + that’은 ‘it that 강조 구문’을 의심해야 합니다.
> - ‘it’이 지칭하는 대상이 없으므로 강조 구문입니다.
> - 예를 들어, 유사한 기능을 가진 많은 스마트폰이 있지만, 그 아이디어가 다양한 방식으로 표현되었고, 표현이 저작권 보호를 받기 때문에 그것은 저작권의 침해가 아니라고 합니다.

> 독 ‘while’이 ‘반면에’로 해석되고 ‘as’가 ‘~때문에’로 해석되므로 중심 문장!
> - 아이디어가 다양한 방식으로 표현되면 저작권 침해가 아니라고 합니다.

VII. Copyright / is / free / and is automatically invested (in the author), **for instance**, the writer (of a book or a programmer) (who develops / a program), (unless they / sign / the copyright over to someone else).

> 구 ‘unless’는 ‘if not’으로 해석하시면 됩니다.
> - ‘sign A over to B’는 ‘A를 B에게 넘기는 계약을 하다, 양도하다’를 의미합니다.
> - 저작권은 무료이며 저작자, 예를 들어, 어떤 책의 저자나 프로그램을 개발한 프로그래머가 저작권을 다른 누군가에게 양도하지 않는 한 그 저작자에게 자동으로 부여된다고 합니다.

글의 흐름으로 보아, 주어진 문장이 들어가기에 가장 적절한 곳을 고르시오

> **Rather**, it evolved naturally as certain devices were found in practice to be both workable and useful.

 Film has no grammar. (①) There are, **however**, some vaguely defined rules of usage in cinematic language, and the syntax of film — its systematic arrangement — orders these rules and indicates relationships among them. (②) As with written and spoken languages, it is important to remember that the syntax of film is a **result** of its usage, not a determinant of it. (③) There is nothing preordained about film syntax. (④) Like the syntax of written and spoken language, the syntax of film is an organic development, descriptive rather than prescriptive, and it has changed considerably over the years. (⑤) "Hollywood Grammar" may sound laughable now, **but** during the thirties, forties, and early fifties it was an accurate model of the way Hollywood films were constructed.

* preordained: 미리 정해진

해설 [정답 : ④]

Ⅰ. 주어진 문장에서 오히려 '그것'은 특정한 방법이 실질적으로 운영될 수 있고 유용하다는 것이 밝혀지면서 자연스럽게 발달되었다고 합니다. 주어진 문장의 'Rather'을 통해서 주어진 문장 앞에서는 '그것'에 대한 부정어를 포함한 내용이 제시 되어야함을 알 수 있습니다.

Ⅱ. ①번 앞 문장에서 영화에 문법은 없지만 ①번 뒷 문장에서 모호하게 정의된 규칙이 있다는 내용이 'however'로 전환되는 것에 논리적 결함이 없습니다. 또한 ②번 뒷 문장에서 사용의 결과이지 결정 요인이 아니라는 내용이므로 논리적 결함이 없으며 ③번 뒷 문장에서 영화에 미리 정해진 것은 없다는 내용은 ②번 뒷 문장과 같은 맥락을 제시합니다. ④번 뒷 문장부터 영화 문법의 발전 양상으로 소재가 전환되나 논리적 결함이 존재한다고 보기 어렵습니다. ⑤번 뒷 문장에서는 영화의 문법은 없지만 모호한 규칙이 남아있다는 글 전체의 내용에 대한 예시를 제시하므로 논리적 결함이 없습니다. 즉 단절이 없습니다.

Ⅲ. 단절이 없으므로 주어진 문장의 근거를 통해서 정답을 찾아야 합니다. 주어진 문장의 '그것'은 영화를 지칭하며, 주어진 문장에서 제시된 영화의 자연스러운 발전에 대한 내용이 ④번 뒷 문장에서 진술되고 있고 ④번 앞 문장에서 '그것'에 해당하는 영화가 미리 정해진 것이 없다는 부정의 내용이 제시되므로 정답은 ④번이 됩니다.

주. **Rather**, it / evolved naturally / as certain devices / were found (in practice) to be / both workable and useful.

> 구 ‘both A and B’는 ‘A와 B 둘 다’를 의미합니다.
> - 오히려, ‘그것’은 특정한 방법이 실질적으로 운영될 수 있고 유용하다는 것이 밝혀지면서 자연스럽게 발전했다고 합니다.

> 독 ‘Rather’이 제시되었으므로 중심 문장!
> - ‘Rather’과 ‘Instead’는 앞에 부정적인 내용이 제시되어야 하므로 주어진 문장 앞에서 ‘그것’에 대한 부정적인 내용이 제시되어야 합니다.

Ⅰ. Film / has / no grammar.

> 구 영화는 문법이 없다고 합니다.

Ⅱ. There are, **however**, / some vaguely defined rules of usage (in cinematic language), / and the syntax of film — (its systematic arrangement) — / orders / these rules and indicates / relationships (among them).

> 구 그러나, 영화 언어 사용에 관한 모호하게 정의된 규칙들이 있고, 영화의 문법, - 체계적인 방식 - 은 이러한 규칙들을 정리하고 그것들 사이의 관계를 나타낸다고 합니다.

> 독 ‘however’가 제시되었으므로 중심 문장!
> - 영화에 문법은 없지만 모호하게 정의된 규칙들이 있다고 합니다.

* syntax - 구문, 문법

Ⅲ. (As with written and spoken languages), it / is / important / to remember / that the syntax of film / is / a **result** of its usage, / not a determinant of it.

> 구 ‘it be동사 + 형용사 + to-V’는 가주어/진주어 의심!
> - ‘it’이 지칭하는 대상이 없으므로 가주어/진주어
> - 쓰는 언어와 말하는 언어에서 마찬가지로, 영화의 문법은 그것의 사용 결과이지, 결정요인은 아니라는 것을 기억하는 것이 중요하다고 합니다.

> 독 ‘result’ 결과가 제시되었으므로 중심 문장!
> - 사용의 결과이지 결정요인이 아니라는 것은
>   영화의 사용 ⇒ 영화의 문법, 영화의 문법 ≠ 영화로 이해하시면 됩니다.

Ⅳ. There / is / nothing preordained (about film syntax).

* preordained: 미리 정해진

> 구 영화의 문법에 대하여 미리 정해진 것은 아무 것도 없다고 합니다.

Ⅴ. (Like the syntax of written and spoken language), the syntax of film / is / an organic development, (descriptive (rather than prescriptive)), / and it / has changed considerably (over the years).

> **구** 쓰는 언어와 말하는 언어의 문법처럼, 영화의 문법은 유기농의 (자연스러운) 발전이고, 규범적이기보다는 묘사적이며, 그리고 이것은 수년동안 상당히 변화해왔다고 합니다.

* de (down - 아래) + script (적다) + -ive (형용사형 접사) = descriptive - 묘사적인, 서술적인
** pre (미리) + script (적다) + -ive (형용사형 접사) = prescriptive - 규정적인

Ⅵ. "Hollywood Grammar" / may sound / laughable now, **but** (during the thirties, forties, and early fifties) it / was / an accurate model of the way / Hollywood films / were constructed.

> **구** 'Hollywood Grammar'은 지금은 웃기는 소리로 들릴지도 모르지만, 30년대, 40년대, 50년대 초반에는 할리우드 영화의 제작 방식의 정확한 모델이었다고 합니다.

> **독** 'but'이 제시되었으므로 중심 문장!
> - 영화의 문법이라는 것이 말이 안되는 것 같지만 영화의 문법이 존재했었다는 것을 제시하고 있습니다.

글의 흐름으로 보아, 주어진 문장이 들어가기에 가장 적절한 곳을 고르시오.

> It may be easier to reach an agreement when settlement terms don't **have to** be implemented until months in the future.

 Negotiators **should** try to find ways to slice a large issue into smaller pieces, known as using *salami tactics*. (①) Issues that can be expressed in quantitative, measurable units are easy to slice. (②) **For example**, compensation demands can be divided into cents-per-hour increments or lease rates can be quoted as dollars per square foot. (③) When working to fractionate issues of principle or precedent, parties may use the time horizon (when the principle goes into effect or how long it will last) as a way to fractionate the issue. (④) Another approach is to vary the number of ways that the principle may be applied. (⑤) **For example**, a company may devise a family emergency leave plan that allows employees the opportunity to be away from the company for a period of no longer than three hours, and no more than once a month, for illness in the employee's immediate family.

* increment: 증가 ** fractionate: 세분하다

해설 [정답 : ④]

Ⅰ. 주어진 문장에서 합의 조건이 미래에 몇 개월까지 실행될 필요가 없을 때 합의에 도달하는 것이 더 쉽다고 합니다. 주어진 문장 앞 뒤에 합의 조건이 몇 개월 동안 실행될 필요가 없는 것과 관련된 내용이 제시되어야 합니다.

Ⅱ. 지문에서 단절이 존재하지 않습니다. ⑤빈을 고른 학생이 23% 존재합니다. ⑤번을 고른 학생 중 대부분은 단절이 없기 때문에 찍은 것으로 보입니다. ⑤번 앞 문장에서 원칙을 적용하는 방법의 수를 다양하게 하는 것이 다른 관점이라고 합니다. ⑤번 뒷 문장에서 원칙의 예시로 가족 응급 휴가 계획이 제시되고 있고 이러한 원칙이 적용하는 방법으로는 3시간 이내, 한 달에 한 번 이내로 다양한 조건이 제시되고 있습니다. 그러므로 ⑤번에서 단절이 빌생하지 않습니다.

Ⅲ. 단절이 존재하지 않으므로 주어진 문장의 내용을 통해서 판단해야 합니다. 주어진 문장에서 합의 조건이 미래에 몇 개월까지 실행될 필요가 없을 때 합의에 도달하는 것이 더 쉽다고 합니다. 즉, 합의 조건을 시간상 미루는 것이 이득이 된다는 내용입니다. 이는 합의 조건이란 원칙을 몇 개월까지 이행할 필요가 없다는 시간의 조정을 통해 합의에 도달하는 것으로 ④번 앞 문장에서 원칙이 효과가 있을 때와 원칙을 얼마나 지속시킬 지에 대한 시간 지평선을 이용한다는 내용의 예시에 해당합니다. 그러므로 정답은 ④번이 됩니다.

주. It / may be / easier / to reach an agreement (when settlement terms / don't **have to** be implemented (until months in the future)).

> 구 ▸ 'It + be동사 + 형용사 + to-V'는 진주어/가주어입니다.
> - 정착 조건이 (= 합의 조건이) 미래에 몇 개월까지 실행될 필요가 없을 때 합의에 도달하는 것이 더 쉽다고 합니다.

> 독 ▸ 'have to'가 제시되었으므로 중심 문장
> - 미래에 몇 개월동안 합의가 이행될 필요가 없으면 합의에 도달하기 쉽다고 합니다.

Ⅰ. Negotiators / **should** try to find / ways (to slice a large issue into smaller pieces), (known as using *salami tactics*).

> 구 ▸ 'slice A into B'는 'A를 B로 쪼개다'를 의미합니다.
> - 협상가들은 반드시 'salami tactics'를 사용하는 것으로 알려진 큰 이슈를 작은 조각들로 쪼개는 방법을 찾으려고 노력해야 한다고 합니다.

> 독 ▸ 'should'가 제시되었으므로 중심 문장
> - 협상가들은 큰 이슈를 작은 조각들로 쪼개는 방법을 생각해야만 한다고 합니다.

Ⅱ. Issues (that can be expressed in quantitative, measurable units) / are easy to slice.

> 구 ▸ 양적이고 측정가능한 단위로 표현될 수 있는 이슈들은 쪼개기 쉽다고 합니다.

> 독 ▸ 숫자로 표현될 수 있는 이슈들은 쪼개기 쉽다고 합니다.

Ⅲ. **For example**, compensation demands / can be divided into / cents-per-hour increments or lease rates / can be quoted (as dollars per square foot).

* increment: 증가

> 구 ▸ 예를 들어, 보상 요구는 시간당 센트 증가로 쪼갤 수 있고, 임대료는 평당 달러로써 인용될 수 있다고 (= 값을 매길 수 있다고) 합니다.

> 독 ▸ 'For example'이 제시되었으므로 앞 문장 중심 문장
> - Ⅱ번 문장에서 숫자로 표현될 수 있는 이슈들이 나누어지는 것에 대한 예시를 보여주고 있습니다.

* lease rates - 임대료

Ⅳ. When working to fractionate / issues of principle or precedent, parties / may use / the time horizon (when the principle / goes into effect or how long it / will last) (as a way to fractionate the issue).

** fractionate: 세분하다

[구] 원칙이나 관례의 이슈들을 세분화하는 작업을 할 때, 집단들은 시간 지평선을 (원칙이 효과가 있을 때 혹은 그것이 (= 원칙이) 얼마나 지속될지) 이슈를 세분화하는 방법으로써 사용할 수 있다고 합니다.

[독] 집단들은 원칙이 언제 효과가 있을 지와 언제까지 효과가 지속될지를 통해서 이슈들을 세분화할 수 있다고 합니다.

Ⅴ. Another approach / is to vary / the number of ways (that the principle / may be applied).

[구] 다른 접근은 원칙이 적용될 수 있는 방법의 수를 다양하게 하는 것이라고 합니다.

[독] 시간 지평선을 이용하는 것 말고 이슈를 세분화하는 다른 방법은 원칙을 적용하는 방식을 다양하게 하는 것이라고 합니다.

Ⅵ. **For example**, a company / may devise / a family emergency leave plan (that allows / employees / the opportunity (to be away from the company) (for a period of no longer than three hours, and no more than once a month), (for illness in the employee's immediate family)).

[구] 'allow + I.O + D.O'는 'I.O에게 D.O를 허락하다'를 의미합니다.
- 예를 들어, 회사는 직원의 직계 가족의 질병에 대해 직원에게 3시간 이내, 한 달에 한 번 이내의 기간 동안 회사를 떠날 수 있는 기회를 허락하는 가족 응급 휴가 계획을 고안할 수 있다고 합니다.

[독] 'For example'이 제시되었으므로 앞 문장 중심 문장
- 직원 가족의 질병에 대해 3시간 이내, 한 달에 한 번 이내 동안 회사를 비울 수 있는 응급 휴가 계획처럼 적용될 수 있는 방법의 수를 다양하게 할 수 있다고 합니다.

글의 흐름으로 보아, 주어진 문장이 들어가기에 가장 적절한 곳을 고르시오.

> At the next step in the argument, **however,** the analogy breaks down.

  Misprints in a book or in any written message usually have a negative impact on the content, sometimes (literally) fatally. (①) The displacement of a comma, **for instance**, may be a matter of life and death. (②) Similarly, most mutations have harmful consequences for the organism in which they occur, meaning that they reduce its reproductive fitness. (③) Occasionally, **however**, a mutation may occur that increases the fitness of the organism, just as an accidental failure to reproduce the text of the first edition might provide more accurate or updated information. (④) A favorable mutation is going to be more heavily represented in the next generation, since the organism in which it occurred will have more offspring and mutations are transmitted to the offspring. (⑤) **By contrast**, there is no mechanism by which a book that accidentally corrects the mistakes of the first edition will tend to sell better.

* analogy: 유사 ** mutation: 돌연변이

해설 [정답 : ④]

Ⅰ. 주어진 문장에서는 그러나 논거의 다음 단계에서는 그 유사성이 깨진다고 합니다. 주어진 문장 앞에는 유사성이 적용되는 논거에 대한 설명이 나올 가능성이 높습니다.

Ⅱ. 지문은 책에서 오류가 발생하는 것을 돌연변이에 비유하여 설명하고 있습니다. ④번 앞 문장에서는 'however, a mutation may occur that increases the fitness of the organism', 하지만 유기체의 적합성을 상승시키는 돌연변이가 발생할 수 있다고 했는데, 이것은 같은 문장의 'accidental failure to reproduce the text of the first edition might provide more accurate' 초판의 텍스트를 복사하지 못한 것이 더 정확하다는 것과 같다고 말하며 이를 책에 발생하는 오류에 비유합니다.
그런데 ④번 뒷 문장에서는 'favorable mutation is going to be more heavily represented in the next generation' 유리한 돌연변이는 다음 세대에 더 많이 나타나고 더 많은 돌연변이가 자손에게 전달된다고 했습니다. ⑤번 뒷 문장에서는 'no mechanism by which a book that accidentally corrects the mistakes of the first edition will tend to sell better' 대조적으로 초판의 오류를 바로잡은 책이 더 팔리는 경향이 있는 매커니즘은 없다고 말합니다.
여기서 내용의 단절이 발생합니다.
돌연변이=책 초판의 오류 (③번 앞 문장)
적합성이 높은 돌연변이=책 초판 텍스트의 오류를 수정하지 않은 것이 더 정확한 경우 (③번 뒷 문장)
적합성이 높은 돌연변이가 더 많은 자손에게 전달≠초판의 오류를 바로잡은 책이 더 잘 팔리지 않는다 (④번 뒷 문장)는 것은 내용적으로 같은 비유라고 볼 수 없기 때문입니다.

Ⅲ. 이 내용의 단절은 적합성이 높은 돌연변이가 더 많은 자손에게 전달된다는 ④번 뒷 문장에서부터 시작합니다. 여기서, 뒤에 나오는 서로 맞지 않는 두 비유가 주어진 문장의 유사성이 깨지는 것을 의미하고, 주어진 문장의 논거는 ④번 앞 문장의 적합성이 높은 돌연변이를 책 초판의 오류를 수정하지 않은 것이 더 정확하다는 비유를 의미하므로 주어진 문장은 ④번에 들어가야 합니다.

주. (At the next step in the argument), <u>**however**</u>, the analogy / breaks down.

* analogy: 유사

구▶ 그러나 논거의 다음 단계에서는 그 유사성은 깨진다고 합니다.

독▶ 'however'가 제시되었으므로 중심 문장
  - 유사성이 어긋나는 주제로 전환되는 문장입니다.

Ⅰ. Misprints (in a book or in any written message) / usually have / a negative impact on the content, sometimes (literally) fatally.

구▶ 책이나 어떤 서면 메시지에서 오타가 발생하면 일반적으로 내용에 부정적인 영향을 미치며 때로는 (문자 그대로) 치명적이기도 하다고 합니다.

독▶ 책이나 메시지에서 발생하는 오타는 내용에 치명적 악영향을 준다고 합니다.

Ⅱ. The displacement of a comma, <u>**for instance**</u>, / may be / a matter of life and death.

구▶ 예를 들어, 쉼표의 위치가 잘못 찍히는 것은 생사가 걸린 문제일 수 있다고 합니다.

독▶ 'for instance'가 제시되었으므로 앞 문장이 중심 문장
  - Ⅱ번 문장의 예시 문장이며, 쉼표의 위치가 잘못된 것은 오타의 구체적인 사례가 됩니다.

Ⅲ. Similarly most mutations / have / harmful consequences for the organism / in which / they / occur, meaning / that / they / reduce / its reproductive fitness.

** mutation: 돌연변이

구▶ 마찬가지로 대부분의 돌연변이는 그것이 발생하는 유기체에 해로운 결과를 가져오는데 이는 그것들이 생식 적합성을 감소시킨다는 것을 뜻한다고 합니다.

독▶ 책에서 발생하는 오타를 돌연변이로 바꿔서 설명하므로 각각
  책 - 유기체
  오타 - 돌연변이
  치명적 악영향 - 생식 적합성을 감소시킨다
  는 내용으로 비유를 정리할 수 있습니다.

Ⅳ. Occasionally, <u>**however**</u>, a mutation / may occur / that / increases / the fitness of the organism, just as an accidental failure (to reproduce the text of the first edition) / might provide / more accurate or updated information.

구▶ 그러나 때때로 유기체의 적합성을 상승시키는 돌연변이가 발생할 수 있는데, 이는 우연히 초판의 텍스트를 복사하지 못한 것이 더 정확하거나 최신의 정보를 제공할 수도 있는 것과 마찬가지라고 합니다.

독▶ 'however'가 제시되었으므로 중심 문장
  - 돌연변이에 관한 새로운 주장이 언급됩니다. 돌연변이(초판의 텍스트를 복사하지 못한 것)가 악영향이 아닌, 긍정적인 효과(더 정확하거나 최신 정보를 제공한다)를 만들어낼 수도 있다고 합니다.

Ⅴ. A favorable mutation / is going to be more heavily represented (in the next generation), since / the organism (in which / it / occurred) / will have / more offspring and mutations / are transmitted to the offspring.

구▶ 유리한 돌연변이는 다음 세대에 더 많이 나타날 것인데 그 돌연변이가 발생한 유기체는 더 많은 자손을 낳을 것이고 돌연변이가 자손에게 전달되기 때문이라고 합니다.

독▶ 돌연변이가 자손을 많이 낳으며 전달되는 것은 Ⅴ번 문장에서 적합성이 증가한 돌연변이가 증가하게 되는 것으로 볼 수 있습니다.

Ⅵ. **By contrast**, there / is / no mechanism / by which / a book (that / accidentally corrects / the mistakes (of the first edition)) / will tend to sell better.

구▶ 대조적으로, 우연히 초판의 오류를 바로잡은 책이 더 잘 팔리는 경향이 있을 메커니즘은 없다고 합니다.

독▶ ‘by contrast’로 앞 뒷 문장을 대조하므로 중심 문장
- 돌연변이가 적합성이 상승해 후대에 이어지는 것과는 다르게, 오류를 고친 책은 더 잘 팔리지 않는다고 합니다. 책의 오타와 생물 돌연변이가 모두 같지는 않음을 보여주는 내용이라 볼 수 있습니다.

글의 흐름으로 보아, 주어진 문장이 들어가기에 가장 적절한 곳을 고르시오.

> A problem, **however**, is that supervisors often work in locations apart from their employees and **therefore** are not able to observe their subordinates' performance.

In most organizations, the employee's immediate supervisor evaluates the employee's performance. (①) This is **because** the supervisor is responsible for the employee's performance, providing supervision, handing out assignments, and developing the employee. (②) **Should** supervisors rate employees on performance dimensions they cannot observe? (③) To eliminate this dilemma, more and more organizations are implementing assessments referred to as 360-degree evaluations. (④) Employees are rated not only by their supervisors **but** by coworkers, clients or citizens, professionals in other agencies with whom they work, and subordinates. (⑤) **The reason** for this approach is that often coworkers and clients or citizens have a greater opportunity to observe an employee's performance and are in a better position to evaluate many performance dimensions.

* subordinate: 부하 직원

해설 [정답 : ②]

Ⅰ. 주어진 문장에서 그러나, 문제는 감독관이 종종 그들의 직원과 떨어진 장소에서 일하므로, 부하 직원들의 수행을 관찰할 수 없다는 것이라고 합니다. 주어진 문장의 'however'을 통해서 주어진 문장 앞에서는 이와 반대되는 내용이 제시되며, 주어진 문장 뒤에서는 감독관이 직원들을 관찰할 수 없다는 문제점에 대해서 제시되어야 합니다.

Ⅱ. ②번 앞 문장에서 감독관이 감독을 제공하고, 업무를 주며, 직원을 개발하면서 그 직원의 성과를 책임지기 때문에 감독관이 직원의 수행을 평가한다고 합니다. 하지만 ②번 뒷 문장에서 감독관이 관찰할 수 없는 수행 측면에서 직원을 평가하는 것이 마땅한지에 대한 의문을 제기하고 있습니다. 즉 ②번 앞 문장에서는 감독관이 직원을 평가하는 이유에 대해서 설명하지만 ②번 뒷 문장에서는 감독관이 직원을 평가하는 것에 대한 의문을 제기하므로 ②번에서 반대 내용으로 3. 내용 단절이 발생합니다.

Ⅲ. ②번 앞 문장에서 감독관이 직원들을 평가하는 것은 주어진 문장에서 감독관이 직원들을 평가하는 것에 대한 문제점과 'however'을 통해서 전환되고 ②번 뒷 문장에서 감독관이 관찰하지 못하는 직원들의 수행에 대해서 제시되므로 정답은 ②번이 됩니다.

주. A problem, / **however**, is / that supervisors / often work (in locations) (apart from their employees) and **therefore** are not able to observe / their subordinates' performance.

* subordinate: 부하 직원

구 그러나, 문제는 감독관이 종종 그들의 직원과 떨어진 장소에서 일하므로, 부하 직원들의 수행을 관찰할 수 없다는 것이라고 합니다.

독 'however'과 'therefore'이 제시되었으므로 중심 문장
- 문제점은 감독관이 일하는 장소가 직원들과 멀리 떨어져 있어서 직원들의 수행을 관찰할 수 없다는 것이라고 합니다.

Ⅰ. In most organizations, the employee's immediate supervisor / evaluates / the employee's performance.

구 대부분의 조직에서, 직원의 즉각적인 감독관이 직원들의 수행을 평가한다고 합니다.

Ⅱ. This / is / **because** the supervisor / is responsible for / the employee's performance, (providing supervision, handing out assignments, / **and** (providing, handing과 developing을 연결) developing the employee).

구 그것은 (= 감독관이 직원들의 수행을 평가하는 것은) 감독을 제공하고, 과업을 주며, 그리고 직원들을 발전시키면서, 그 직원의 성과를 책임지기 때문이라고 합니다.

독 'because'가 제시되었으므로 중심 문장
- 감독관이 감독하고, 업무를 매정하고, 직원들을 발전시키면서 직원들의 수행을 책임지므로 감독관이 직원들의 수행을 평가한다고 합니다.

Ⅲ. **Should** supervisors / rate / employees (on performance dimensions) (they / cannot observe)?

구 감독관이 그들이 관찰할 수 없는 수행 차원에서 직원들을 평가해야만 할까?라며 묻고 있습니다.

독 'Should'가 제시되었으므로 중심 문장
- 감독관이 직원의 수행을 관찰할 수 없는 부분까지 평가해야하냐는 당위성을 묻고 있습니다.

Ⅳ. To eliminate / this dilemma, / more and more organizations / are implementing / assessments (referred to as 360-degree evaluations).

구 'refer A as B'는 'A를 B라고 언급하다, 부르다'를 의미합니다.
- 그러한 딜레마를 (= Ⅱ번 문장의 질문을) 제거하기 위해서, 더욱더 많은 조직들이 360도 평가라고 불리는 평가를 시행하고 있다고 합니다.

Ⅴ. Employees / are rated / not only by their supervisors **but** by coworkers, clients or citizens, professionals (in other agencies) (with whom they work), and subordinates.

구▶ 'not only A but also B'는 'A뿐만 아니라 B도'를 의미합니다.
- 직원들은 자신의 관리자에 의해서 뿐만 아니라 동료, 고객이나 시민, 함께 일하는 다른 대행사의 전문가들, 그리고 부하 직원들에게 평가받는다고 합니다.

독▶ 'but'이 제시되었으므로 중심 문장
- 감독관이 볼 수 없는 수행은 감독관이 평가할 수 없으므로 동료, 고객 등 다양한 사람들에게 평가받는 360도 평가에 대해서 제시하고 있습니다.

Ⅵ. **The reason** (for this approach) / is / that often coworkers and clients or citizens / have / a greater opportunity (to observe / an employee's performance) / and are in a better position (to evaluate / many performance dimensions).

구▶ 그러한 접근의 (= 360도 평가의) 이유는 동료와 고객이나 시민들이 흔히 어떤 직원의 성과를 관찰할 더 많은 기회를 가지고, 많은 평가 영역을 평가할 수 있는 더 낳은 위치에 있기 때문이라고 합니다.

독▶ 'reason'이 제시되었으므로 중심 문장
- 동료나 고객이 감독관보다 더 직원들의 수행을 관찰할 수 있으므로 360도 평가를 시행한다고 합니다.

글의 흐름으로 보아, 주어진 문장이 들어가기에 가장 적절한 곳을 고르시오.

> There's **a reason** for that: traditionally, park designers attempted to create **such a feeling** by planting tall trees at park boundaries, building stone walls, and constructing other means of partition.

Parks take the shape demanded by the cultural concerns of their time. Once parks are in place, they are no inert stage — their purposes and meanings are made and remade by planners and by park users. Moments of park creation are particularly telling, **however**, for they reveal and actualize ideas about nature and its relationship to urban society. (①) **Indeed**, what distinguishes a park from the broader category of public space is the representation of nature that parks are meant to embody. (②) Public spaces include parks, concrete plazas, sidewalks, even indoor atriums. (③) Parks typically have trees, grass, and other plants as their central features. (④) When entering a city park, people often imagine <u>a sharp separation from streets, cars, and buildings</u>. (⑤) What's behind **this idea** is not only landscape architects' desire to design aesthetically suggestive park spaces, **but** a much longer history of Western thought that envisions cities and nature as antithetical spaces and oppositional forces.

* aesthetically: 미적으로 ** antithetical: 대조적인

해설 [정답 : ⑤]

Ⅰ. 주어진 문장에서 그것에는 이유가 있는데, 전통적으로 공원 디자이너들은 공원 가장자리에 키가 큰 나무를 심고, 돌담을 쌓고, 다른 칸막이 수단을 세움으로써 그러한 느낌을 만들려고 시도한다고 합니다. 공원 가장자리에 키가 큰 나무를 심고, 돌담을 쌓는 등 칸막이 수단을 세우는 이유와 디자이너들이 이를 통해 만들려고 하는 느낌을 찾으면 됩니다.

Ⅱ. ⑤번 뒷 문장에서 '그 생각' 뒤에 있는 것은 풍경 건축가들의 욕망 뿐만 아니라 오래된 서양의 사고 방식이라고 합니다. 이를 통해 '그 생각'은 건축가들과 디자이너의 생각임을 알 수 있고, ⑤번 앞 부분에서 디자이너나 건축가들의 생각이 제시되지 않았으므로 지시사 단절이 있음을 알 수 있습니다. 만약, ⑤번에서의 단절이 느껴지지 않았다면 단절이 없는 지문으로 풀어야 합니다. 단절이 느껴지지 않으니 주어진 문장에서 제시된 'such feeling'이 지칭하는 대상을 찾아야 합니다.

Ⅲ. ⑤번 앞 문장에서 사람들이 도로, 차, 그리고 건물들과 분리된 것을 공원에서 상상한다고 합니다. 이는 주어진 문장에서 'such feeling'에 해당하며 주어진 문장은 디자이너들이 그러한 느낌인 도로, 차, 그리고 건물들과 분리된 느낌을 만들도록 시도한다는 내용으로 ⑤번 뒷 문장에서 'this idea'인 디자이너들이나 건축가들의 생각에 해당합니다. 그러므로 정답은 ⑤번입니다.

주. There's / **a reason** for that: traditionally, park designers / attempted to create / such a feeling (by planting tall trees at park boundaries, building stone walls, and constructing other means of partition).

구 'by V-ing'는 'V하므로써'를 의미합니다.
- 그것에는 이유가 있는데, 전통적으로 공원 디자이너들은 공원 가장자리에 키가 큰 나무를 심고, 돌담을 쌓고, 다른 칸막이 수단을 세움으로써 그러한 느낌을 만들려고 시도한다고 합니다.

독 'reason'이 제시되었으므로 중심 문장
- 공원 디자이너들이 공원 가장자리에 나무를 심고 돌담을 쌓는 등 칸막이 수단을 세움으로써 만들고자 하는 느낌이 있다고 합니다.

Ⅰ. Parks / take / the shape (demanded by the cultural concerns of their time).

구 공원은 그것이 속한 시간대의 문화적 관심사를 요구하는 형태를 취한다고 합니다.

독 공원은 공원이 만들어진 시기의 문화적 관심사를 반영한다고 합니다.

Ⅱ. Once parks / are in place, they / are / no inert stage — their purposes and meanings / are made and remade (by planners and by park users).

구 공원이 만들어질 때, 그들은 (= 공원들은) 비활성화 단계가 아닌데, 그들의 (= 공원들의) 목적과 의미는 계획자나 공원 사용자들에 의해 만들어지고 재창조된다고 합니다.

독 공원의 목적과 의미는 계획자와 공원 사용자들에 의해 만들어진다고 합니다.

Ⅲ. Moments of park creation / are particularly telling, **however**, (for they / reveal and actualize / ideas about nature and its relationship to urban society.

구 'for S V'는 'S가 V하기 때문이다'로 해석하시면 됩니다.
- 그러나 특히 공원이 만들어지는 순간 말하는데 (= 의미가 있는데), 그들이 자연에 대한 생각과 도시 사회와의 연관성을 드러내고 실제화하기 때문이라고 합니다.

독 'however'가 제시되었으므로 앞 뒷 문장 중심 문장
- 공원을 조성할 때 그 당시 자연에 대한 생각과 도시 사회와 공원과의 관계가 드러난다고 합니다.

Ⅳ. **Indeed**, what distinguishes a park from the broader category of public space / is / the representation of nature (that parks / are meant to embody).

구 'distinguish A from B'는 'A를 B로부터 구별하다'로 해석하시면 됩니다.
- 사실상, 공원을 공공장소의 분류로부터 구별하는 것은 공원이 구체화하는 자연의 표현이라고 합니다.

독 'Indeed'가 제시되었으므로 중심 문장
- 다른 공공장소들과 구별되는 공원의 특징은 자연을 표현한다는 것이라고 합니다.

Ⅴ. Public spaces / include / parks, concrete plazas, sidewalks, even indoor atriums.

> 구 공공 장소는 공원, 콘크리트 광장, 보도, 심지어 실내 아트리움들을 포함한다고 합니다.

Ⅵ. Parks / typically have / trees, grass, and other plants (as their central features).

> 구 공원들은 전형적으로 중심적 특징들로써 나무, 풀, 다른 식물들을 가지고 있다고 합니다.

Ⅶ. When entering a city park, people / often imagine / a sharp separation (from streets, cars, and buildings).

> 구 도시 공원으로 들어갈 때, 사람들은 도로, 차 그리고 건물들로부터 뚜렷한 분리를 종종 상상한다고 합니다.

Ⅷ. What's (behind this idea) / is / not only landscape architects' desire (to design aesthetically suggestive park spaces), **but** a much longer history of Western thought (that envisions / cities and nature (as antithetical spaces and oppositional forces)).

* aesthetically: 미적으로 ** antithetical: 대조적인

> 구 'not only A but (also) B'는 'A뿐만 아니라 B'로 해석하시면 됩니다.
> - 그러한 생각 뒤에 있는 것은 미적으로 제시되는 공원 공간은 디자인하는 풍경 건축가들의 욕망뿐만 아니라 대조적인 공간과 반대적인 힘으로써 도시와 자연을 바라보는 오래된 역사적인 서양의 사고 방식이 있다고 합니다.

> 독 'but'이 제시되었으므로 중심 문장
> - 공원과 도시가 분리되었다는 생각은 건축가와 디자이너들의 욕망뿐만 아니라 도시와 자연을 대조적인 공간으로 보는 오래된 사상에서부터 비롯되었다고 합니다.

글의 흐름으로 보아, 주어진 문장이 들어가기에 가장 적절한 곳을 고르시오.

> Continuous emissions measurement can be costly, particularly where there are many separate sources of emissions, and for many pollution problems this may be a major disincentive to direct taxation of emissions.

Environmental taxes based directly on measured emissions can, in principle, be very precisely targeted to the policy's environmental objectives. (①) If a firm pollutes more, it pays additional tax directly in proportion to the rise in emissions. (②) The polluter thus has an incentive to reduce emissions in any manner that is less costly per unit of abatement than the tax on each unit of residual emissions. (③) The great attraction of basing the tax directly on measured emissions is that the actions the polluter can take to reduce tax liability are actions that also reduce emissions. (④) **Nevertheless**, the technologies available for monitoring the concentrations and flows of particular substances in waste discharges have been developing rapidly. (⑤) In the future, it may be possible to think of taxing measured emissions in a wider range of applications.

* abatement: 감소 ** liability: 부담액

해설 [정답 : ④]

Ⅰ. 주어진 문장에서는 지속적인 배출물 측정은 특히 개별 배출원이 많은 경우 비용이 많이 들 수 있으며, 많은 오염 문제에 있어 이는 배출물에 직접적으로 과세하는 것에 주요한 지해 요소가 될 수 있나고 합니다.

Ⅱ. 지문은 환경세, 그중에서도 측정된 배출물에 직접 과세히는 것을 주제로 잡고 있습니다. 그 중 ④번 앞 문장에서 'The great attraction of basing the tax directly on measured emissions' 세금을 측정된 배출물에 직접 기반으로 하는 것의 매력으로 'actions the polluter can take to reduce tax liability are actions that also reduce emissions' 기업이 세금 부담액을 줄이기 위해 취할 수 있는 조치가 배출물을 줄이는 조치일 수 있다는 점을 언급하고 있습니다. 이 문장은 분명히 측정된 배출물에 과세하는 것의 장점을 언급하고 있는데, 다음 ④번 뒷 문장에서는 'technologies available for monitoring the concentrations and flows of particular substances in waste discharges have been developing rapidly' 폐기물 배출에서 특정 물질의 농도와 흐름을 관찰하는 데 이용될 수 있는 기술은 빠르게 발전하고 있다고 합니다.
여기서 두 문장을 비교한다면, ④번 앞 문장은 배출물에 과세하는 것의 장점에 관한 내용이며, ④번 뒷 문장은 폐기물 배출에 이용되는 기술의 발전에 관한 내용입니다. 문제는 ④번 뒷 문장의 'Nevertheless'로, 두 문장이 내용상 역접의 의미로 이어질 수 없으므로 단절이 발생하게 됩니다.

Ⅲ. 주어진 문장은 배출물에 대한 직접 과세가 비용이 많이 든다는 점을 지적하며, 이것이 오염 문제에 있어 과세의 저해 요소가 된다고 말하고 있습니다. 이 직접적인 과세를 어렵게 할 수 있는 요인을 설명하고 있는 주어진 문장의 내용이 ④번에 들어가야 직접적인 과세의 장점 (= ④번 앞 문장)-직접적 과세를 어렵게 하는 점(주어진 문장)-해결책으로 기술의 발전을 언급하는 내용 (= ④번 뒷 문장) 으로 자연스럽게 이어질 수 있습니다. 그러므로 정답은 ④번이 됩니다.

주. Continuous emissions measurement / can be / costly, particularly where there / are / many separate sources of emissions, and (for many pollution problems) this / may be / a major disincentive / to direct taxation of emissions.

구▶ 지속적인 배출물 측정은 특히 개별 배출원이 많은 경우 비용이 많이 들 수 있으며, 많은 오염 문제에 있어 이는 배출물에 직접적으로 과세하는 것에 주요한 저해 요소가 될 수 있다고 합니다.

독▶ 지속적인 배출물 측정의 단점으로 비용이 많이 든다는 점이 언급되고, 배출물을 측정하는 것이 배출물에 직접적으로 과세하는 것을 저해한다고 말하고 있습니다.

* dis (반의어) + incentive (자극 요소) = disincentive – 저해 요소

Ⅰ. Environmental taxes (based directly on measured emissions) / can, in principle, be very precisely targeted / to the policy's environmental objectives.

구▶ 측정된 배출물에 직접적으로 기반한 환경세는 원칙적으로 그 정책의 환경적 목표를 매우 정확하게 겨냥할 수 있다고 합니다.

독▶ 배출물에 기반한 환경세의 장점이 언급되는 문장입니다.

Ⅱ. If / a firm / pollutes more, it / pays / additional tax (directly in proportion to the rise in emissions).

구▶ 어떤 기업이 더 많이 오염시키면 그 기업은 배출물 증가에 직접적으로 비례한 추가 세금을 낸다고 합니다.

독▶ Ⅰ번 문장에서 언급된 환경세를 어떻게 부과하는지에 관해 설명하고 있습니다.

Ⅲ. The polluter / **thus** has / an incentive / to reduce emissions / in any manner (that is / less costly per unit of abatement / than the tax on each unit of residual emissions).

* abatement: 감소

구▶ 따라서 공해 기업은 잔여 배출물의 단위당 세금보다 감소 단위당 비용이 덜 드는 어떤 방식으로든 배출량을 줄이려는 동기를 갖게 된다고 합니다.

독▶ 'thus'가 제시되었으므로 중심 문장
 - Ⅱ번 문장과 묶어서 이해해야 하는 내용으로, 기업이 더 많이 오염시킬수록 늘어난 배출물로 인해 세금이 늘어나기 때문에, 배출물을 줄여 내는 세금을 감소시키려는 동기를 갖게 된다고 말하고 있습니다.

* residual - 남은

IV. The great attraction (of basing the tax directly on measured emissions) / is that the actions (the polluter / can take / to reduce / tax liability) are / actions (that also reduce / emissions).

** liability: 부담액

구▶ 세금을 측정된 배출물에 직접 기반하는 것의 매우 큰 매력은 공해 기업이 세금 부담액을 줄이기 위해 취할 수 있는 조치가 배출물을 줄이는 조치이기도 하다는 점이라고 합니다.

독▶ Ⅰ, Ⅱ, Ⅲ번 문장을 정리하는 내용으로, 기업이 배출물이 늘어나면 세금도 비례하여 늘어난다(Ⅱ번 문장)-그래서 기업은 내는 세금을 줄이기 위해 배출물을 줄인다(Ⅲ번 문장)-그 결과 배출물이 줄어들기 때문에 배출물의 감소라는 환경적 목표에 도달한다(Ⅰ번 문장)

V. **Nevertheless**, the technologies (available for monitoring the concentrations) and flows of particular substances (in waste discharges) / have been developing rapidly.

구▶ 그럼에도 불구하고, 흐름을 관찰하는 데 이용할 수 있는 기술과 폐기물 배출에서 특정 물질의 농도는 빠르게 발전해 오고 있다고 합니다.

독▶ 'Nevertheless'가 제시되었으므로 중심 문장

- 물질의 농도와 흐름을 관찰하는 기술은 폐기물 방출을 측정하는 데 있어서 발생하는 문제점을 해결하는 요소로 볼 수 있습니다.

* concentrate (집중하다) + -tion (명사형 접사) = concentration - 농도 (성분이 얼마나 집중되어 있는가)

VI. In the future, it / may be / possible / to think / of taxing measured emissions (in a wider range of applications.)

구▶ 미래에는 더 광범위한 적용으로 측정된 배출물에 대한 세금 부과를 생각하는 것이 가능할 수도 있다고 합니다.

독▶ 세금을 더 광범위하게 측정된 배출물로 부과하는 것은 Ⅴ번 문장에서 언급된 기술을 통해 문제점을 해결하게 된 경우를 의미합니다.

글의 흐름으로 보아, 주어진 문장이 들어가기에 가장 적절한 곳을 고르시오.

> Also, it has become difficult for companies to develop new pesticides, even those that can have major beneficial effects and few negative effects.

  Simply maintaining yields at current levels often requires new cultivars and management methods, **since** pests and diseases continue to evolve, and aspects of the chemical, physical, and social environment can change over several decades. (①) In the 1960s, many people considered pesticides to be mainly beneficial to mankind. (②) Developing new, broadly effective, and persistent pesticides often was considered to be the best way to control pests on crop plants. (③) Since that time, it has become apparent that broadly effective pesticides can have harmful effects on beneficial insects, which can negate their effects in controlling pests, and that persistent pesticides can damage non-target organisms in the ecosystem, such as birds and people. (④) Very high costs are involved in following all of the procedures **needed to** gain government approval for new pesticides. (⑤) **Consequently**, more consideration is being given to other ways to manage pests, such as incorporating greater resistance to pests into cultivars by breeding and using other biological control methods.

* pesticide: 살충제 ** cultivar: 품종 *** breed: 개량하다

해설 [정답 : ④]

Ⅰ. 주어진 문장에서 또한 회사가 새로운 살충제를 개발하는 것은 심지어 그것들이 주요한 이익적인 효과와 적은 부정적인 효과를 가지고 있다고 하더라도 어려워졌다고 합니다. 'Also'를 통한 나열이 제시되었으므로 소재가 바뀌거나 같은 소재더라도 내용이 바뀌는 나열 단절이 지문에 있음을 추론할 수 있습니다.

Ⅱ. ④번 앞 문장까지는 살충제들이 1960년대에는 해충들을 관리하는 가장 좋은 방식으로 생각되었으나 1960년대 이후에 다른 개체에 대한 부작용이 밝혀졌다고 합니다.
반면 ④번 뒷 문장에서는 새로운 살충제들을 정부에 허가받는데 있어서 많은 비용이 들어간다고 합니다.
④번 앞 문장에서는 살충제들의 부작용에 대해 제시되었지만 ④번 뒷 문장에서는 살충제라는 같은 소재이지만 새로운 살충제들을 허가받는 데에 있어 어려움을 제시하고 있습니다.
즉, ④번에서 나열 단절이 발생합니다.

Ⅲ. ④번 앞 문장까지의 살충제들의 부작용에 대한 내용이 주어진 문장의 'Also'로 나열되어, 새로운 살충제에 대한 어려움이 제시됩니다. 또한 ④번 뒷 문장에서 새로운 살충제들에 대한 어려움의 이유로 정부의 허가를 받기 위한 높은 비용이 제시되고 있으므로 정답은 ④번이 됩니다.

주. Also, it / has become / difficult / for companies / to develop / new pesticides, even those (that can have / major beneficial effects and few negative effects).

* pesticide: 살충제

구▶ 'It + become + 형용사 + to-V'는 가주어/진주어입니다.
- 'to-V' 앞에 제시된 'for N'은 의미상 주어입니다.
- 또한 회사가 새로운 살충제를 개발하는 것은 심지어 그것들이 (= 새로운 살충제들이) 주요한 이익적인 효과와 적은 부정적인 효과를 가지고 있다고 하더라도 어려워졌다고 합니다.

Ⅰ. Simply maintaining yields (at current levels) / often requires / new cultivars and management methods, since pests and diseases / continue to evolve, and aspects of the chemical, physical, and social environment / can change (over several decades).

** cultivar: 품종

구▶ 단순히 수확량을 현재의 수준으로 유지하는 것은 종종 새로운 품종들과 새로운 관리 방법을 요구하는데, 해충들과 질병들이 계속 진화하고 있고 화학적, 물리적, 사회적 환경의 측면에서 수십 년 동안 변화가 가능하기 때문이라고 합니다.

독▶ 'since'가 '~때문에'로 제시되었으므로 중심 문장입니다.
- 수확량을 현재의 수준으로 유지하기 위해서는 새로운 품종들과 새로운 관리 방법이 필요하다고 합니다.

Ⅱ. In the 1960s, many people / considered / pesticides / to be mainly beneficial (to mankind).

구▶ 'consider A to-V'는 'A가 V하다고 생각하다'를 의미합니다.
- 1960년대에는, 많은 사람들이 살충제들이 인류에 주로 이로울 것이고 생각했다고 합니다.

Ⅲ. Developing new, broadly effective, and persistent pesticides / often was considered / to be the best way (to control / pests on crop plants).

구▶ 'consider A to-V'가 수동태 형태로 사용되어 'A be considered to-V'의 형태로 제시되고 있습니다.
- 새롭고, 광범위하게 효율적이며 지속적인 살충제들을 개발하는 것이 종종 작물에 있는 해충들을 통제하기 위한 최선의 방법으로 생각되어졌다고 합니다.

Ⅳ. Since that time, it / has become / apparent that broadly effective pesticides / can have /

harmful effects (on beneficial insects), which can negate / their effects in controlling pests,

and that persistent pesticides / can damage / non-target organisms (in the ecosystem, such as birds

and people).

> 구 ▶ 'It + become + 형용사 + to-V'는 가주어/진주어입니다.
> - ',' 뒤에 제시된 'which'는 계속적 용법으로 사용될 수 있습니다. '그래서 ~하다'로 해석하시면
>   됩니다.
> - 'in V-ing'는 'V함에 있어서'를 뜻합니다.
> - 그때 (= 1960년대) 이래로 광범위하게 효율적인 살충제들은 유익한 곤충들에게 해로운 영향을 줄 수
>   있고, 그래서 해충들을 통제함에 있어서 그것들의 효과들을 (= 살충제들의 해충을 통제하는 효과들을)
>   무효화 할 수 있으며, 지속적인 살충제들은 생태계에서 목표로 하지 않는 생물체인 새들과 사람들에게
>   손상을 입힐 수도 있다는 것이 분명해졌다고 합니다.

> 독 ▶ 광범위하게 효과적이고 지속적인 살충제들이 가장 좋은 방법으로 여겨졌던 1960년대와 달리 그 이후
>   광범위하게 효과적이고 지속적인 살충제들이 다른 생물체에도 부정적인 영향을 끼치는 것이 밝혀졌다고
>   합니다.

* negate – 무효화하다

Ⅴ. Very high costs / are involved (in following / all of the procedures (**needed to** gain /

government approval for new pesticides)).

> 구 ▶ 'in V-ing'는 'V함에 있어서'를 의미합니다.
> - 새로운 살충제들에 대한 정부의 허가를 얻는데 필요한 모든 과정을 따름에 있어서 매우 높은 비용이
>   포함된다고 합니다.

> 독 ▶ 'need to'가 제시되었으므로 중심 문장
> - 새로운 살충제들에 대한 정부의 허가를 받는데 많은 비용이 든다고 합니다.

Ⅵ. **Consequently**, more consideration / is being given to / other ways (to manage pests),

(such as incorporating greater resistance to pests into cultivars (by breeding and using /

other biological control methods)).

*** breed: 개량하다

> 구 ▶ 'by V-ing'는 'V함으로써'를 의미합니다.
> - 결과적으로, 다른 생물학적 통제 방법을 개량하고 이용함으로써 품종에 더 강한 해충 저항력을
>   포함하는 것과 같은 해충을 관리하는 다른 방법들이 더 많이 고려되고 있다고 합니다.

> 독 ▶ 'Consequently'가 제시되었으므로 중심 문장
> - 새로운 살충제들을 허가받는데 들어가는 비싼 비용들로 인해 해충을 관리하는 데 있어서 살충제가 아닌
>   다른 방법들이 고려되고 있다고 합니다.

글의 흐름으로 보아, 주어진 문장이 들어가기에 가장 적절한 곳을 고르시오.

> Without any special legal protection for trade secrets, **however**, the secretive inventor risks that an employee or contractor will disclose <u>the proprietary information</u>.

Trade secret law aims to promote innovation, although it accomplishes this objective in a very different manner than patent protection. (①) Notwithstanding the advantages of obtaining a patent, many innovators prefer to protect their innovation through secrecy. (②) They may believe that the cost and delay of seeking a patent are too great or that secrecy better protects their investment and increases their profit. (③) They might also believe that the invention can best be utilized over a longer period of time than a patent would allow. (④) Once <u>the idea</u> is released, it will be "free as the air" under the background norms of a free market economy. (⑤) Such a predicament would **lead** any inventor seeking to rely upon secrecy to spend an inordinate amount of resources building high and impassable fences around their research facilities and greatly limiting the number of people with access to the proprietary information.

* patent: 특허 ** predicament: 곤경

해설 [정답 : ④]

Ⅰ. 주어진 문장에서 그러나, 영업 비밀에 대한 어떤 특별한 법적 보호 없이, 비밀주의 발명가는 직원이나 계약자가 독점적인 정보를 드러낼 위험을 감수하게 된다고 합니다. 'however'가 제시되었으므로 주어진 문장의 앞에는 주어진 문장의 내용과 반댓밀이 제시뇌어야 합니다. 즉, 주어진 문장은 비밀주의 발명가에 대한 부정적인 내용이므로 주어진 문장 앞에는 비밀주의 발명가에 대한 긍정적인 내용이 제시되어야 합니다.

Ⅱ. ③번 앞 문장과 ④번 앞 문장에서는 발명가들은 비밀이 그들에게 더 잘 투자를 보호하고 더 많은 수익을 가져다 줄 것이며, 그들의 발명품들이 특허 기간보다 더 오래 잘 활용될 것이라고 생각한다고 합니다. 하지만 ④번 뒷 문장에서는 그 아이디어가 공개되면 '공기처럼 자유롭게' 유출된다고 하므로 부정적인 내용이 제시됩니다. 즉 ④번에서 서로 반대되는 내용이 역접의 접속사 없이 이어지고 있으므로 ④번에서 내용 단절이 발생합니다. 또한 ④번 뒷 문장의 'the idea'는 공개되는 'idea'인데 이는 ④번 앞 문장에 제시되지 않았으므로 지시사 단절에도 해당합니다.

Ⅲ. ④번에서 발생한 내용 단절은 주어진 문장의 'however'를 통해서 해소가 되며, 'the idea'는 주어진 문장의 'disclose the proprietary information'을 지칭하므로 지시사 단절 역시 해소가 됩니다. 그러므로 주어진 문장이 들어가야할 위치는 ④번이 됩니다.

주. (Without any special legal protection for trade secrets), **however**, the secretive inventor / risks / that an employee or contractor / will disclose / the proprietary information.

> 구 그러나, 영업 비밀에 대한 어떤 특별한 법적 보호 없이, 비밀주의 발명가는 직원이나 계약자가 독점적인 정보를 드러낼 위험을 감수하게 된다고 합니다.

> 독 'however'이 제시되었으므로 중심 문장
> - 법적 보호가 없다면 독점적인 정보들이 직원이나 계약자에 의해서 유출될 위험이 있다고 합니다.

* dis (반의어) + close (닫다) = disclose - 열다, 드러내다

* proprietary - 독점적인

Ⅰ. Trade secret law / aims to promote / innovation, although it / accomplishes / this objective (in a very different manner than patent protection).

* patent: 특허

> 구 영업 비밀에 관한 법률은 혁신을 촉진하는 것을 목표로 하지만, 그것은 (= 영업 비밀에 관한 법률은) 특허 보호와는 매우 다른 방식으로 그러한 목표를 (= 혁신을 촉진하는 것을) 이룬다고 합니다.

> 독 영업 비밀에 관한 법률은 특허 보호와는 다른 방법으로 혁신을 추구한다고 합니다.

Ⅱ. (Notwithstanding the advantages of obtaining a patent), many innovators / prefer to protect / their innovation through secrecy.

> 구 특허를 얻는 이점에도 불구하고, 많은 혁신가들은 비밀을 통해서 그들의 혁신을 보호하는 것을 선호한다고 합니다.

> 독 특허가 있음에도 불구하고, 많은 혁신가들은 특허가 아닌 비밀을 통해 혁신을 보호하고자 한다고 합니다.

Ⅲ. They / may believe / that the cost and delay of seeking a patent / are / too great or that secrecy / better protects / their investment and increases / their profit.

> 구 그들은 (= 혁신가들은) 특허를 추구함에 있어서 비용과 시간 지연이 너무 크거나 비밀이 그들의 투자를 더 잘 보호하고 그들의 이익을 더 잘 증가시킬 것이라고 믿는다고 합니다.

> 독 혁신가들은 특허는 시간과 돈이 너무 많이 든다고 생각하며, 비밀이 그들의 투자 보호와 이익 창출에 더 좋다고 생각한다고 합니다.

Ⅳ. They / might also believe / that the invention / can best be utilized (over a longer period of time than a patent would allow).

> 구 그들은 (= 혁신가들은) 또한 발명품이 특허가 허용할 기간보다 더욱 오랜 기간 최고로 활용될 수 있다고 믿을 수도 있다고 합니다.

> 독 혁신가들은 특허로 보호되는 기간보다 자신들의 발명품이 더욱 오래 활용된다고 생각한다고 합니다.

Ⅴ. Once the idea / is released, it / will be / "free as the air" (under the background norms of a free

market economy).

구▸ 그 아이디어가 공개되면, 그것은 자유 시장 경제의 기반 규범에 따라 '공기처럼 자유롭게' 될 것이다.
(= 유출될 것이다.)

독▸ 아이디어가 공개되면 유출 정도가 심하다고 합니다.

Ⅵ. Such a predicament / would **lead** / any inventor seeking to rely upon secrecy / **to** spend an

inordinate amount of resources building high and impassable fences (around their research facilities)

and greatly limiting the number of people (with access to the proprietary information).

** predicament: 곤경

구▸ 'lead A to-V'는 'A가 V하도록 야기하다'를 의미합니다.

- 'spend A V-ing'는 'A를 V-ing하는 데 소비하다'를 뜻합니다.
- 그러한 곤경은 비밀에 의존하는 것을 추구하는 발명가가 그들의 연구 시설 주변에 높고 통과할 수 없는
울타리를 치고 독점 정보에 접근할 권리를 가진 사람의 수를 크게 제한하는 데 과도한 양의 자원을
소비하게 될 것이라고 합니다.

독▸ 'lead to'가 제시되었으므로 중심 문장

- 비밀을 추구하는 발명가들은 정보 공개시 Ⅴ번 문장에서 제시되었듯이 '공기처럼 자유롭게' 유출되기
때문에 발명가들의 연구 시설에 대한 보호와 정보에 접근할 수 있는 사람을 줄이는 것에 대해 더 많은
노력을 하게 된다고 합니다. 즉, 비밀유지를 위해서 더 많은 투자를 해야하고 주의를 기울여야 한다고
합니다.

글의 흐름으로 보아, 주어진 문장이 들어가기에 가장 적절한 곳을 고르시오.

> As long as the irrealism of the silent black and white film predominated, one could not take filmic fantasies for representations of reality.

Cinema is valuable not for its ability to make visible the hidden outlines of our reality, **but** for its ability to reveal what reality itself veils — the dimension of fantasy. (①) **This is why**, to a person, the first great theorists of film decried the introduction of sound and other technical innovations (such as color) that pushed film in the direction of realism. (②) **Since** cinema was an entirely fantasmatic art, these innovations were completely unnecessary. (③) And what's worse, they could do nothing **but** turn filmmakers and audiences away from the fantasmatic dimension of cinema, potentially transforming film into a mere delivery device for representations of reality. (④) **But** sound and color threatened to create just such an illusion, **thereby** destroying the very essence of film art. (⑤) As Rudolf Arnheim puts it, "The creative power of the artist can only come into play where reality and the medium of representation do not coincide."

* decry: 공공연히 비난하다 ** fantasmatic: 환상의

해설 [정답 : ④]

Ⅰ. 주어진 문장에서 무성 흑백 영화의 비현실주의가 지배하는 한, 누구든 영화적 환상을 현실의 표현으로 생각하지 않을 것이라고 합니다. 또한 주어진 문장 뒤에서는 무성 흑백 영화의 비현실주의와 관련된 내용이 제시되어야 합니다.

Ⅱ. ④번 앞 문장에서는 소리와 같은 기술적 혁신들이 영화를 현실의 묘사를 위한 전달 장치로 변형시킴으로써, 영화의 본질인 환상적 차원에서 영화를 멀어지게 했다고 합니다. ④번 뒷 문장에서는 소리와 색채같은 기술적 혁신들이 영화를 망쳤다고 합니다. 이 두 내용은 기술적 혁신들이 영화에게 안 좋은 영향을 끼친다는 같은 내용을 제시합니다. 그러므로 ④번 뒷 문장에서는 'But'을 통해서 역접의 관계를 이루지 못합니다. 그래서 ④번에서 단절이 발생합니다.

Ⅲ. ④번 뒷 문장이 흑백 무성 영화와 역접을 이루며, 소리와 색깔에 대한 내용을 제시합니다. 또한 흑백 무성 영화가 영화적 환상을 현실에 대한 묘사로 착각하지 않는, 즉 영화적 본질을 잘 추구한 반면, ④번 뒷 문장에서 소리와 색채가 영화를 망치고 있다는 내용은 역접을 이룰 수 있습니다. 그러므로 정답은 ④번이 됩니다.

주. As long as the irrealism of the silent black and white film predominated, / one / could not take / filmic fantasies (for representations of reality).

> 구 ▶ 'As long as S V'는 'S가 V하는 한'으로 해석하시면 됩니다.
> - 무성 흑백 영화의 비현실주의가 지배하는 한, 누구든 영화적 환상을 현실의 표현으로 취하지
>   (= 생각하지) 않을 것이라고 합니다.

Ⅰ. Cinema / is / valuable / not for its ability (to make / visible / the hidden outlines of our reality), but for its ability (to reveal / what reality / (itself) veils — the dimension of fantasy.

> 구 ▶ 'make + O + O.C'는 'O를 O.C하게 만들다'를 뜻합니다. 이 문장에서는 O와 O.C가 도치되었습니다.
> - 'not A but B'는 'A가 아니라 B'로 해석하시면 됩니다.
> - 영화는 우리 현실의 숨겨진 윤곽을 보이게 만드는 능력이 가치가 있는 것이 아니라, 현실 그 자체가
>   가리고 있는 것, 즉 환사의 차원이 드러나는 능력이 가치가 있다고 합니다.

> 독 ▶ 'but'이 제시되었으므로 중심 문장
> - 영화는 현실을 보여주는 것이 아닌 현실에 가려져 있는 환상의 측면을 드러내기 때문에 가치가 있다고
>   합니다.

> * veil - 숨기다

Ⅱ. **This is why**, (to a person), the first great theorists (of film) / decried / the introduction (of sound and other technical innovations) (such as color) that pushed / film (in the direction of realism).

* decry: 공공연히 비난하다

> 구 ▶ 그것은 최초의 위대한 영화 이론가가 영화를 현실의 방향으로 밀어내는 소리와 다른 기술적인
>   혁신들의 도입을 공공연히 비난한 이유라고 합니다.

> 독 ▶ 'This is why'를 통해서 인과 관계를 제시하므로 중심 문장
> - 영화는 환상의 측면을 드러냄으로써 가치를 가지기 때문에 현실을 반영하는 소리와 다른 기술적
>   혁신이 영화에 도입되는 것은 비난 받았다고 합니다.

Ⅲ. **Since** cinema / was / an entirely fantasmatic art, these innovations / were / completely unnecessary.

** fantasmatic: 환상의

> 구 ▶ 영화는 전체적으로 환상의 예술이기 때문에, 그러한 혁신들은 (= 소리와 기술적인 혁신들은) 완전히
>   불필요하다고 합니다.

> 독 ▶ 'Since'를 통해서 인과 관계를 제시하므로 중심 문장

Ⅳ. And what's worse, they / could do / nothing **but** turn / filmmakers and audiences / away (from the
fantasmatic dimension of cinema), potentially transforming / film / into a mere delivery device (for
representations of reality).

> 구 'do nothing but A'는 'A만 할뿐이다'로 이해하시면 됩니다.
> - 'turn + A + away from + B'는 'A를 B로부터 멀어지게 하다'로 해석하시면 됩니다.
> - 'transform + A + into + B'는 'A를 B로 변형시키다'를 뜻합니다.
> - 그리고 설상가상으로, 그것들은 (= 혁신들은) 잠재적으로 영화를 현실의 표현을 단순히 전달하는
>   장치로 변형시키면서, 영화 제작자와 관객을 영화의 환상적인 차원에서 멀어지게 하는 것만 할
>   뿐이였다고 합니다.

> 독 'but'이 제시되었으므로 중심 문장
> - 소리와 같은 혁신들이 현실을 표현함으로써 영화 제작자들과 관객들을 영화를 가치있게 하는
>   환상으로부터 멀어지게 했다고 합니다.

Ⅴ. **But** sound and color / threatened to create / just such an illusion, **thereby** destroying /
the very essence of film art.

> 구 소리와 색깔은 그러한 환상들을 만들겠다고 위협하여, 그러므로 영화 예술의 본질을 파괴한다고 합니다.

> 독 'but'이 제시되었으므로 중심 문장
> - 소리와 색깔과 같은 기술적인 혁신들이 혁신들로 만들 수 없는 영화적 환상을 만드는데 이용됨으로써
>   영화의 본질이 파괴되고 있다고 합니다.

Ⅵ. As Rudolf Arnheim / puts / it, "The creative power of the artist / can only come into play /
where reality and the medium of representation / do not coincide."

> 구 Rudolf Arnheim이 말한 것처럼, "예술가의 창의적 힘은 현실과 표현의 매체가 일치하지 않는
>   곳에서만 발휘할 수 있다"고 합니다.

> 독 현실과 표현의 매체가 (= 영화가) 일치하지 않는, 즉 영화가 현실을 표현하지 않는 곳에서 예술가인
>   영화 제작자의 창의적인 힘이 발휘될 수 있다고 합니다.

글의 흐름으로 보아, 주어진 문장이 들어가기에 가장 적절한 곳을 고르시오.

> It was not until relatively recent times that scientists came to <u>understand the relationships between the structural elements of materials and their properties.</u>

   The earliest humans had access to only a very limited number of materials, those that occur naturally: stone, wood, clay, skins, and so on. (①) With time, they discovered techniques for producing materials that had properties superior to those of the natural ones; these new materials included pottery and various metals. (②) Furthermore, it was discovered that the properties of a material could be altered by heat treatments and by the addition of other substances. (③) At this point, materials utilization was totally a selection process that involved deciding from a given, rather limited set of materials, the one best suited for an application based on its characteristics. (④) <u>This knowledge</u>, acquired over approximately the past 100 years, has empowered them to fashion, to a large degree, the characteristics of materials. (⑤) **Thus**, tens of thousands of different materials have evolved with rather specialized characteristics that meet the needs of our modern and complex society, including metals, plastics, glasses, and fibers.

해설 [정답 : ④]

Ⅰ. 주어진 문장에서는 과학자들이 물질의 구조적 요소와 물질 특성의 관계를 이해하게 된 것은 비교적 최근이었다고 합니다. 그러므로 물질의 요소와 물질 특성의 관계와 관련된 내용이 뒷 문장에 나올 가능성이 높음을 염두에 두고 글을 읽어야 합니다.

Ⅱ. ④번 앞 문장에서는 물질의 이용이 제한된 물질의 집합 속에 물질의 특성에 근거하여 가장 적합한 물질을 결정하는 것을 포함하는 선택의 과정이었다고 했습니다. 그런데 ④번 뒷 문장에서는 지난 100년 동안 획득된 이 지식으로 그들은 상당한 물질의 특성을 형성할 수 있게 되었다고 했습니다. ④번 앞 문장에서는 물질의 특성에 근거하여 적합한 물질을 결정한다고 했는데, 이 지식으로 물질의 특성을 형성할 수 있게 되었다는 ④번 뒷 문장의 내용은 서로 연결될 수 없으므로 단절이 발생합니다.

Ⅲ. 주어진 문장의 'relationships between the structural elements of materials and their properties', 구조적 요소와 물질의 특성의 관계가 ④번 뒷 문장의 'This knowledge'를 지칭합니다. 또한 ④번 앞 문장에서의 이전 시기의 물질 이용, 그리고 주어진 문장의 과학자들이 관계를 파악한 것이 비교적 최근이었다는 내용으로 볼 때, 'past 100 years', 100년이라는 시간은 두 문장 사이의 기간을 의미하고 있음을 알 수 있습니다. 그러므로 정답은 ④번이 됩니다.

주. It was not until relatively recent times / that scientist / came to understand / the relationships / between the structural elements (of materials) and their properties.

구 'It is not until A that S V'는 'A하고나서야 비로소 S가 V하다'를 의미합니다.
- 비로소 과학자들이 물질의 구조적 요소와 물질 특성의 관계를 이해하게 된 것은 비교적 최근에 이르러서였다고 합니다.

독 물질의 구조적 요소와 물질 특성의 관계에 대해 지문에서 파악해야 합니다.

Ⅰ. The earliest humans / had / access (to only a very limited number of materials), those that occur naturally: stone, wood, clay, skins, and so on.

> 구 ▶ 초기 인류는 매우 제한된 수의 물질, 즉 돌, 나무, 찰흙, 가죽 등 자연적으로 존재하는 물질에만 접근할 수 있었다고 합니다.

Ⅱ. With time, they / discovered / techniques (for producing materials) that had / properties / superior (to those of the natural ones); these new materials / included / pottery and various metals

> 구 ▶ 시간이 흐르면서 그들은 자연적인 특성의 물질보다 더 우수한 특성을 가진 물질을 만들어 내는 기술을 발견했는데, 이 새로운 물질에는 도자기와 다양한 금속이 포함되었다.

> 독 ▶ 글이 시간 순으로 전개되고 있음을 알 수 있으며, 시간이 흐르면서 자연적인 물질 접근에서, 물질을 만들어내기 시작했다고 합니다.

Ⅲ. Furthermore, it was discovered / that the properties of a material / could be altered (by heat treatments / and by the addition of other substances).

> 구 ▶ 게다가, 물질의 특성이 열처리와 여타 다른 물질의 첨가로 바뀔 수 있다는 것이 발견되었다고 합니다.

Ⅳ. At this point, materials utilization / was totally / a selection process / that involved deciding from a given, (rather limited set of materials), the one best (suited / for an application / based on its characteristics).

> 구 ▶ 이 시기에, 물질 이용은 주어진 상당히 제한된 물질 집합 중에서 물질의 특성에 근거하여 용도에 가장 적합한 물질을 결정하는 것을 수반하는 전적으로 선택의 과정이었다고 합니다.

Ⅴ. This knowledge, acquired over approximately the past 100 years, / has empowered them / to fashion, to a large degree, the characteristics of materials.

> 구 ▶ 대략 지난 100년 동안 획득된 이 지식으로 그들은 상당한 정도로 물질의 특성을 형성할 수 있게 되었다고 합니다.

> 독 ▶ 'This knowledge'는 주어진 문장의 물질의 구조적 요소와 물질 특성의 관계에 관한 과학자들의 이해를 지칭합니다. 그 지식을 통해 제한된 물질 중 선택을 하던 예전과 다르게 많은 물질의 특성을 형성할 수 있었다는 것입니다.

Ⅵ. **Thus**, tens of thousands of different materials / have evolved / with rather specialized characteristics / that meet / the needs of our modern and complex society, (including metals, plastics, glasses, and fibers).

> 구 ▶ 따라서 금속, 플라스틱, 유리, 섬유를 포함하여, 현대적이고 복잡한 우리 사회의 요구를 충족하는 상당히 특화된 특성을 가진 수만 가지의 다양한 물질이 생성되었다고 합니다.

> 독 ▶ 'Thus'가 언급되므로 중심 문장
> - Ⅵ번 문장과 연결되는 문장입니다.

글의 흐름으로 보아, 주어진 문장이 들어가기에 가장 적절한 곳을 고르시오.

> Yes, some contests are seen as world class, such as identification of the Higgs particle or the development of high temperature superconductors.

Science is sometimes described as a winner-take-all contest, meaning that there are no rewards for being second or third. This is an extreme view of the nature of scientific contests. (①) Even those who describe scientific contests in such a way note that it is a somewhat inaccurate description, given that replication and verification have social value and are common in science. (②) It is also inaccurate to the extent that it suggests that only a handful of contests exist. (③) **But** many other contests have multiple parts, and the number of such contests may be increasing. (④) By way of example, for many years it was thought that there would be "one" cure for cancer, **but** it is now realized that cancer takes multiple forms and that multiple approaches are needed to provide a cure. (⑤) There won't be one winner — there will be many.

* replication: 반복 ** verification: 입증

해설 [**정답** : ③]

Ⅰ. 주어진 문장에서는 물론, 힉스 입자의 확인 또는 고온 초전도체 개발과 같은 몇몇 대회는 세계적인 수준으로 여겨진다고 합니다.

Ⅱ. ③번 앞 문장에서 'It is also inaccurate to the extent that it suggests that only a handful of contests exist' 그것은 단지 소수의 대회만 존재한다는 것을 보여 줄 경우에 또한 부정확하다고 했습니다. ③번 뒷 문장에서는 'But many other contests have multiple parts, and the number of such contests may be increasing', 많은 대회에는 다양한 부분이 있고, 그런 대회의 수는 증가하고 있다고 합니다. 이것은 ③번 앞 문장의 소수의 대회를 뒤집는 내용이므로 내용상의 단절이 존재한다고 보기에는 어렵습니다.

Ⅲ. 그렇다면 주어진 문장과 비교하여 내용을 확인해야 합니다. 먼저 주어진 문장의 힉스 입자의 확인과 같은 몇몇 대회는 ③번 앞 문장의 소수의 대회의 예시가 되며, 주어진 문장의 세계적인 수준의 대회는 ③번 앞 문장의 부정확한 경우가 아닌 예시로 예외적인 예시를 설명하고 있습니다.
또한 ③번 뒷 문장에 증가하고 있고, 다양한 부분이 있는 많은 대회는 주어진 문장의 세계적인 수준의 대회와 대조적인 내용이 되므로 주어진 문장은 ③번에 들어가야 합니다.

주. Yes, some contests / are seen as world class, such as identification (of the Higgs particle) or the development (of high temperature superconductors).

구▶ 물론, 힉스 입자의 확인 또는 고온 초전도체 개발과 같은 몇몇 대회는 세계적인 수준으로 여겨진다고 합니다.

독▶ 세계적인 수준으로 여겨지는 대회에 관한 사례가 등장합니다.

Ⅰ. Science / is sometimes described as a winner-take-all contest, meaning / that / there / are no / rewards (for being second or third).

구▶ 과학은 때때로 승자독식 대회로 묘사되는데, 이는 2등이나 3등인 것에 대한 보상이 없다는 뜻이라고 합니다.

독▶ 과학의 특징으로 승자독식이라는 점이 언급됩니다.

Ⅱ. This / is / an extreme view of the nature (of scientific contests).

구▶ 이는 과학대회의 본질에 대한 극단적인 견해라고 합니다.

독▶ 이 승자독식이라는 특징은 과학대회에 대해 극단적인 견해라는 점을 말하고 있습니다.

Ⅲ. Even those (who / describe scientific contests (in such a way)) / note / that / it / is a somewhat inaccurate description, given that replication and verification / have / social value / and are / common in science.

* replication: 반복 ** verification: 입증

구▶ 과학대회를 그렇게 설명하는 사람들조차도 그것이 다소 부정확한 설명이라고 말하는데, 반복과 입증이 사회적 가치를 지니고 있으며 과학에서는 일반적이라는 것을 감안할 때 그렇다고 합니다.

독▶ 과학대회가 승자독식이라고 보는 것도 부정확하다고 말하며, 그 원인으로 과학이 지닌 사회적 가치와 일반성을 언급하고 있습니다.

Ⅳ. It / is / also inaccurate to the extent / that / it / suggests / that only a handful of contests / exist.

구▶ 또한 그것은 단지 소수의 대회만 존재한다는 것을 보여 줄 경우에 또한 부정확하다고 합니다.

독▶ Ⅳ번 문장에서 더 나아가 소수의 대회에서 역시 설명이 부정확하다고 말하며 승자독식이라는 주제가 적용되는 범위를 제한하고 있습니다.

Ⅴ. **But** / many other contests / have / multiple parts, and the number (of such contests) / may be increasing.

구▶ 하지만 다른 많은 대회에는 다양한 부분이 있고, 그런 대회의 수는 증가하고 있을 것이라고 합니다.

독▶ 'but'이 제시되었으므로 중심 문장
　 - Ⅴ번 문장에서 소수의 대회가 아닌 대회의 경우로 다시 그 범위를 바꾸고 있습니다.

Ⅵ. By way of example, for many years / it / was thought / that / there / would be / "one" cure for cancer, **but** it / is now realized / that / cancer / takes multiple forms and that multiple approaches / are needed to provide a cure.

구▶ 'It'이 지칭하는 대상이 없으므로 가주어/진주어
- 예를 들어, 여러 해 동안 암에 대해 '하나'의 치료법만 있다고 생각되었지만, 암은 여러 가지 형태를 띠고 치료를 제공하기 위해 다양한 접근 방식이 필요하다고 이제 인식된다고 합니다.

독▶ 'but'이 제시되었으므로 중심 문장
- 암의 치료를 위해 다양한 접근 방식이 필요하다고 인식되는 것은 Ⅵ번 문장의 다양한 부분의 구체적 사례가 됩니다.
암의 첫 치료법 개발자 – 승자
차후 다른 치료법을 개발한 사람 – 패자
라는 것이 승자독식의 견해라면,
오늘날에는 모든 치료법이 필요하다고 말하는 것은 과학이 더 이상 승자독식의 견해를 띠고 있지 않다는 것을 보여 주고 있습니다.

Ⅶ. There / won't be / one winner — there / will be / many.

구▶ 승자는 한 명이 아니라 여러 명이 있을 것이라고 합니다.

독▶ 승자가 여러 명이 존재하는 것은 승자독식과 반대되는 내용이며, 과학이 승자독식이라는 주장을 반박하고 있는 필자의 주장 문장이라고 볼 수 있습니다.

글의 흐름으로 보아, 주어진 문장이 들어가기에 가장 적절한 곳을 고르시오.

I have still not exactly pinpointed Maddy's character **since** wickedness takes many forms.

Imagine I tell you that Maddy is bad. Perhaps you infer from my intonation, or the context in which we are talking, that I mean morally bad. Additionally, you will probably infer that I am disapproving of Maddy, or saying that I think you **should** disapprove of her, or similar, given typical linguistic conventions and assuming I am sincere. (①) **However**, you might not get a more detailed sense of the particular sorts of way in which Maddy is bad, her typical character traits, and the like, since people can be bad in many ways. (②) **In contrast**, if I say that Maddy is wicked, then you get more of a sense of her typical actions and attitudes to others. (③) The word 'wicked' is more specific than 'bad'. (④) **But** there is more detail **nevertheless,** perhaps a stronger connotation of the sort of person Maddy is. (⑤) In addition, and again assuming typical linguistic conventions, you **should** also get a sense that I am disapproving of Maddy, or saying that you should disapprove of her, or similar, assuming that we are still discussing her moral character.

* connotation: 함축

해설 [정답 : ④]

Ⅰ. 주어진 문장에서 나는 여전히 Maddy의 성격을 지적하지 않았는데, 왜냐하면 사악함은 여러 가지 형태를 가지기 때문이라고 합니다. 주어진 문장 뒤에서는 사악함과 관련된 내용이 제시되어야 합니다.

Ⅱ. ④번 앞 문장에서 '사악함'이라는 단어는 '나쁘다'라는 단어보다 더 구체적이라고 합니다. ④번 뒷 문장에서는 그러나 그럼에도 불구하고 더 많은 세부 사항과 Maddy라는 사람의 종류에 대한 강한 함축이 있다고 합니다. 위 두 문장은 구체적이라는 같은 맥락을 가지고 있으므로 ④번 뒷 문장의 'But'으로 전환될 수 없습니다. 그러므로 접속사 단절이 발생합니다.

Ⅲ. ④번에서 단절이 발생하며, 주어진 문장에서 사악함이 여러 형태를 가지기 때문에 Maddy의 성격을 정확하게 지적하지 않았다는 내용은 ④번 뒷 문장에서 더 많은 세부 사항이 있다는 내용과 'But'을 통해서 역접을 이룰 수 있으며, ②번 뒷 문장 이후부터 사악함에 대해서 제시하므로 정답은 ④번이 됩니다.

주. I / have still not exactly pinpointed / Maddy's character (**since** wickedness / takes / many forms).

구▶ 나는 여전히 Maddy의 성격을 정확하게 지적하지 않았는데, 왜냐하면 사악함은 여러 가지 형태를 가지기 때문이라고 합니다.

독▶ 'since'가 '~때문에'로 해석되므로 중심 문장
- 사악함이 여러 가지 형태를 가진다 ⇒ Maddy의 성격을 지적하지 않는다고 이해하시면 됩니다.

* pinpoint - 지적하다

Ⅰ. Imagine / I / tell / you / that Maddy is bad.

구▶ 'tell + I.O + D.O'는 'I.O에게 D.O를 말하다'를 의미합니다.
- 내가 너에게 Maddy가 나쁘다고 말하는 것을 상상해보라고 합니다.

Ⅱ. Perhaps you / infer (from my intonation, or the context (in which we are talking)), that I / mean / morally bad.

구▶ 아마도 너는 나의 억양 혹은 우리가 이야기하는 상황으로부터 내 뜻이 도덕적으로 나쁘다는 것이라고 추론한다고 합니다.

* intonation - 억양

Ⅲ. Additionally, you / will probably infer / that I / am disapproving of / Maddy, / or saying / that (I think) you / **should** disapprove of / her, or similar, / given typical linguistic conventions / and assuming / I am sincere.

구▶ 'that S V S' V' '에서 'S V'는 삽입절입니다. 'S가 V하기에'로 해석하시면 됩니다.
- 'given'이 단독으로 제시될 경우 '~를 고려하면'을 뜻합니다/
- 추가적으로 전형적인 언어적 관습과 내가 진실되다고 가정한다면, 너는 아마도 내가 Maddy를 싫어하고 내가 생각하기에 너는 그녀를 싫어해야만 하거나 혹은 나와 비슷해야 한다고 추론할 것이라고 합니다,

독▶ 'should'가 제시되었으므로 중심 문장!
- 내가 Maddy가 나쁘다고 하면 내가 Maddy를 싫어하고 너도 Maddy를 싫어해야만 한다고 추론한다고 합니다.

Ⅳ. **In contrast**, if I / say / that Maddy is wicked, / then you / get / more of a sense (of her typical actions and attitudes to others).

구▶ 대조적으로, 내가 Maddy가 사악하다고 이야기 한다면, 너는 그녀의 다른 사람에 대한 전형적인 행동과 태도들에 대한 더 많은 인식을 가지게 된다고 합니다.

독▶ 'In contrast'가 제시되었으므로 중심 문장!
- '나쁘다'고 이야기할 때와는 달리 사악하다고 이야기 한다면 더 많은 인식을 하게 된다고 합니다.

Ⅴ. The word 'wicked' / is / more specific than 'bad'.

> 구 '사악하다'는 단어는 '나쁘다'는 단어보다 더 구체적이라고 합니다.

Ⅵ. **But** there is / more detail **nevertheless**, / perhaps a stronger connotation of the sort of person Maddy / is.

* connotation: 함축

> 구 그러나 그럼에도 불구하고 더 많은 세부 사항이 있고, 아마도 Maddy라는 사람 유형에 대한
> 더 강한 함축이 있다고 합니다.

> 독 'But'과 'nevertheless'가 제시되었으므로 중심 문장
> - 더 많은 세부 사항과 더 강한 함축이 있다고 합니다.

Ⅶ. In addition, and again assuming / typical linguistic conventions, / you / **should** also get / a sense / that I / am disapproving of / Maddy, or saying / that you / **should** disapprove of / her, or similar, assuming / that we / are still discussing / her moral character.

> 구 게다가, 다시 전형적인 언어 관심을 상정하면, 우리가 그녀의 도덕적 성격에 대해서 상정하면서 너는
> 내가 Maddy를 싫어하거나 혹은 네가 그녀를 나와 비슷하게 싫어해야만 한다는 감각을 얻게 돼야만
> 한다고 합니다.

> 독 'should'가 제시되었으므로 중심 문장!
> - 더 많은 세부사항과 더 많은 인지와 함께 '나쁘다'고 이야기 했을 때와 동일한 인식을 얻게 된다고
> 합니다.

15 21학년도 9월 평가원 38번

(정답률 43%)

글의 흐름으로 보아, 주어진 문장이 들어가기에 가장 적절한 곳을 고르시오.

> As long as you do not run out of copies before completing **this process**, you will know that you have a sufficient number to go around.

We sometimes solve number problems almost without realizing it. (①) **For example**, suppose you are conducting a meeting and you want to ensure that everyone there has a copy of the agenda. (②) You can deal with this by labelling each copy of the handout in turn with the initials of each of those present. (③) You have then solved this problem without resorting to arithmetic and without explicit counting. (④) There are numbers at work for us here all the same and they allow precise comparison of one collection with another, **even though** the members that make up the collections could have entirely different characters, as is the case here, where one set is a collection of people, while the other consists of pieces of paper. (⑤) What numbers allow us to do is to compare the relative size of one set with another.

* arithmetic: 산수

해설 [**정답 : ③**]

Ⅰ. 주어진 문장에서 '그 과정'을 완료하기 전에 복사본이 떨어지지 않는 한, 너는 네가 돌리는 충분한 수의 복사본이 있다는 것을 알 것이라고 합니다. 주어진 문장 앞에서는 '그 과정'에 대하여 제시되어야 하며, 주어진 문장 뒤에서는 충분한 수의 복사본이 있다는 것과 관련된 내용이 제시되어야 합니다.

Ⅱ. ③번 앞 문장에서 참석한 사람들 이름의 첫 글자를 순서대로 복사본에 적음으로써 그것을 다룬다고 합니다. ③번 뒤 문장에서 그러면 산수에 의존하지 않고 명백한 숫자 세기 없이 그 문제를 해결한다고 합니다. 첫 글자를 순서대로 복사본에 적는 것이 모두에게 복사본이 전달된다는 것을 보증하며 산수와 숫자 세기 없이 문제를 해결한다는 것은 인과관계가 성립하지 않아 ③번에서 내용 단절이 발생합니다. 하지만 이를 발견하기 어려울 것이라고 생각합니다. 단절을 발견하지 못했다면 단절이 없다고 생각하고 주어진 문장을 통해서 풀이하시면 됩니다.

Ⅲ. 주어진 문장의 'this process'는 ③번 앞 문장의 참석한 사람들의 이름 첫 글자를 복사본에 적는 것을 지칭합니다. 또한 주어진 문장에서 충분한 수의 복사본이 있다는 것을 아는 것은 ③번 뒤 문장에서는 참석한 모두에게 복사본을 줄 수 있다는 것을 암으로써 산수와 숫자 세기 없이 문제를 해결한 것과 인과관계가 성립하므로 정답은 ③번이 됩니다.

* 단절이 존재해도 보이지 않을 때, Ⅰ번 과정에서 생각한 것을 통해서 답을 찾으면 됩니다.

주. As long as you / do not run (out of copies) (before completing this process), / you / will know / that you / have / a sufficient number (to go around).

구▶ 'As long as'는 '~하는 한'을 의미합니다.

- '그 과정'을 완료하기 전에 복사본이 떨어지지 않는 한, 너는 네가 돌리는 충분한 수의 복사본이 있다는 것을 알 것이라고 합니다.

Ⅰ. We / sometimes solve / number problems almost (without realizing it).

구▶ 우리는 때때로 거의 깨닫지 못한 채 숫자 문제를 풀기도 한다고 합니다.

Ⅱ. **For example**, suppose you / are conducting / a meeting and you / want to ensure / that everyone there / has / a copy of the agenda.

구▶ 예를 들어, 네가 회의를 하고 있고 네가 그 곳에 있는 모두이 안건의 복사본을 확실히 갖게 하고 싶어 한다고 가정해 보라고 합니다.

독▶ ‘For example’이 제시되었으므로 앞 문장 중심 문장

Ⅲ. You / can deal with / this / by labelling / each copy of the handout (in turn with the initials of each of those present).

구▶ ‘by V-ing’는 ‘V함으로써’를 의미합니다.
- 너는 그것을 참석한 각각의 사람들의 이름 첫 글자를 순서대로 복사본에 적음으로써 다룰 수 있다고 합니다.

* present - 현재 ⇒ 현재 있는 ⇒ 참석한
** initial - 처음의 ⇒ 이름 첫 글자

Ⅳ. You / have then solved / this problem (without resorting to arithmetic and without explicit counting).

* arithmetic: 산수

구▶ 그러면 너는 그 문제를 산수에 의존하지 않고 명백한 숫자 세기 없이 해결한 것이라고 합니다.

Ⅴ. There are numbers (at work) (for us here) all the same and they / allow / precise comparison of one collection (with another), **even though** the members (that make up / the collections) / could have / entirely different characters, (as is the case here), (where one set / is / a collection of people), (while the other consists of pieces of paper).

구▶ ‘comparison of A with B’는 ‘A와 B를 비교하다’를 의미합니다.
- 비록 그 집합을 구성하는 것들이 한 세트는 사람들의 집합이고 다른 세트는 종이로 구성된 경우처럼 완전히 다른 특징을 가질 수 있음에도 불구하고 여기에 우리에게 영향을 미치고 있는 숫자가 있고 그들은 하나의 집단을 다른 집단과 정확한 비교를 할 수 있게 한다고 합니다.

독▶ ‘even though’가 제시되었으므로 중심 문장
- 계산이나 숫자세기 없이 비록 각각의 집합의 성격이 다르지만 비교할 수 있다고 합니다.

Ⅵ. What numbers allow / us / to do / is to compare / the relative size of one set / with another.

구▶ ‘allow A to-V’는 ‘A가 V하는 것을 허락하다’를 뜻합니다.
- ‘compare A with B’는 ‘A와 B를 비교하다’를 의미합니다.
- 숫자가 우리에게 허락하는 것은 한 세트의 상대적인 크기를 다른 세트와 비교하는 것이라고 합니다.

글의 흐름으로 보아, 주어진 문장이 들어가기에 가장 적절한 곳을 고르시오.

In the case of specialists such as art critics, **a deeper familiarity** with materials and techniques is often useful in reaching an informed judgement about a work.

Acknowledging the making of artworks does not require a detailed, technical knowledge of, say, how painters mix different kinds of paint, or how an image editing tool works. (①) All that is required is a *general sense* of a significant difference between working with paints and working with an imaging application. (②) **This sense** might involve a basic familiarity with paints and paintbrushes as well as a basic familiarity with how we use computers, perhaps including how we use consumer imaging apps. (③) **This** is because every kind of artistic material or tool comes with its own challenges and affordances for artistic creation. (④) Critics are often interested in the ways artists exploit different kinds of materials and tools for particular artistic effect. (⑤) They are also interested in the success of an artist's attempt — embodied in the artwork itself — to push the limits of what can be achieved with certain materials and tools.

* affordance: 행위유발성 ** exploit: 활용하다

해설 [정답 : ③]

Ⅰ. 주어진 문장에서는 예술 비평가와 같은 전문가의 경우, 재료와 기법에 대한 깊은 친숙함이 작품에 대한 충분한 정보에 기반한 판단에 도달하는 데 흔히 유용하다고 합니다. 이것은 재료와 기법에 대한 친숙함이라는 개념을 예술 비평가의 예시로 확대하는 문장이므로, 주어진 문장 앞에는 친숙함과 관련된 설명이, 뒤에는 예술 비평가에게 적용한 보충 설명이 언급될 가능성이 높습니다.

Ⅱ. Ⅰ번 문장에서는 예술 작품을 만드는 것을 인정하는 것이 나왔고, 이에 대한 요구 조건으로 세세한 기술적인 지식을 요구하지는 않는다는 내용이 나왔습니다. 그럼 요구하는 조건은 무엇일까요? Ⅱ번 문장에서 직접 페인트로 칠하는 행위와 디지털 기기로 하는 이미지 어플을 사용하는 차이 정도를 요구한다고 합니다. Ⅲ번 문장에서 'this sense'로 Ⅱ번 문장에서 언급한 내용을 연결하고 있습니다. Ⅳ번 문장에서 '이는 모든 종류의 예술적 재료나 도구가 예술 창작을 위한 고유한 어려움과 행위 유발성을 가지고 있기 때문이다'라는 내용이 나오는데, Ⅲ번 문장과 Ⅳ번 문장 사이에서 단절이 일어납니다.

Ⅲ. 주어진 문장을 보면 '예술 비평가와 같은 전문가의 경우, 재료와 기술에 대한 더 깊은 친숙함은 종종 작품에 대한 깊이 있는 판단을 내리는 데 유용하다'라는 내용이 나오는데, 재료와 기술에 대한 더 깊은 친숙함은 Ⅳ번 문장에서 언급된 '예술적 재료나 도구가 예술 창작을 위한 고유한 어려움과 행위 유발성을 가지고 있다'의 결과적인 내용입니다. 그러므로 ③번에 주어진 문장이 위치해야 합니다.

주. (In the case of specialists such as art critics), a deeper familiarity (with materials and techniques) /
is often / useful (in reaching / an informed judgement (about a work)).

> 구 ▶ 예술 비평가와 같은 전문가의 경우, 재료와 기술에 대한 더 깊은 친숙함은 종종 작품에 대한 깊이 있는 판단을 내리는 데 유용하다고 합니다.

> 독 ▶ 재료와 기술에 대한 더 깊은 친숙함이 이끌어 내는 작품에 대한 깊이 있는 판단을 '인과관계'의 논리로 설명하고 있습니다. '인과관계' 또한 글의 내용을 설명하는 방식이므로 어느 문장의 뒤에서 주어진 문장이 설명으로 쓰일 것인가를 판단하는 것이 핵심입니다.

Ⅰ. Acknowledging the making of artworks / does not require / a detailed, technical knowledge (of,
say, (how painters / mix / different kinds of paint, or how an image editing tool / works)).

> 구 ▶ 예술 작품의 제작을 인정하는 것은, 예를 들어 화가들이 어떻게 다양한 종류의 페인트를 섞는지, 또는 이미지 편집 도구가 어떻게 작동하는지에 대한 상세한 기술적 지식을 필수로 하지 않는다고 합니다.

> 독 ▶ 예술 작품의 제작에 상세한 기술적 지식이 필수가 아니라는 내용이기에 글을 읽는 독자에게 예술 작품의 제작에 필수적인 것이 무엇인가에 대한 의문을 낳게 합니다.

Ⅱ. All (that / is / required) / is / a general sense (of a significant difference) (between working with
paints and working with an imaging application).

> 구 ▶ 필요한 것은 페인트로 작업하는 것과 이미지화를 만들어주는 애플리케이션으로 작업하는 것 사이의 중요한 차이에 대한 일반적인 감각이라고 합니다.

> 독 ▶ 즉, 예술 작품의 제작에 필수적인 것은 '이미지화 애플리케이션(적용)'이라고 합니다. Ⅰ번 문장에서 생긴 의문인 무엇이 필수인가에 대한 설명입니다.

Ⅲ. This sense / might / involve / a basic familiarity (with paints and paintbrushes as well as a basic
familiarity) (with (how we / use / computers)), perhaps (including (how we / use /
consumer imaging apps)).

> 구 ▶ 이러한 감각은 페인트와 붓에 대한 기본적인 친숙함뿐만 아니라 컴퓨터를 어떻게 사용하는지, 아마도 소비자용 이미지화 앱을 어떻게 사용하는지에 대한 기본적인 친숙함을 포함할 수 있다고 합니다.

> 독 ▶ '이미지화 애플리케이션'의 범주에 포함되는 요소들을 설명합니다. 예술 작품의 제작에 필수적인 내용의 구체적 설명입니다.

Ⅳ. This / is / (because every kind of artistic material or tool / comes (with its own challenges and affordances for artistic creation)).

* affordance: 행위유발성

구▸ 이는 모든 종류의 예술적 재료나 도구가 예술 창작을 위한 고유한 어려움과 행위 유발성을 가지고 있기 때문이라고 합니다.

독▸ Ⅲ번 문장에서 나온 내용은 예술 작품 제작에 필수적인 것들을 설명했는데, 이 필수적인 것들에 대한 이유로 재료나 도구가 고유한 어려움과 행위 유발성이라는 문제를 유발한다는 설명은 의미의 단절이 있습니다. Ⅳ번 문장은 주어진 문장의 '재료와 기술에 대한 더 깊은 친숙함이 이끌어 내는 작품에 대한 깊이 있는 판단'의 이유로 적절합니다.

Ⅴ. Critics / are / often interested (in the ways (how artists / exploit / different kinds of materials and tools (for particular artistic effect)).

** exploit: 활용하다

구▸ 비평가들은 종종 예술가들이 특정한 예술적 효과를 위해 다양한 종류의 재료와 도구를 어떻게 활용하는지에 관심을 가진다고 합니다.

Ⅵ. They / are / also interested (in the success of an artist's attempt — embodied in the artwork itself — to push the limits) (of (what / can be / achieved (with certain materials and tools)).

구▸ 그들은 또한 예술가의 시도의 성공에도 흥미가 있는데 -예술 작품 내에서 그 자체로 구현된- 이 시도는 특정한 물질과 도구를 이용해서 성취될 수 있는 것의 한계를 넘어보려는 것이라고 합니다.

17 21학년도 6월 평가원 39번

(정답률 42%)

글의 흐름으로 보아, 주어진 문장이 들어가기에 가장 적절한 곳을 고르시오.

> When the team painted fireflies' light organs dark, a new set of bats took twice as long to learn to avoid them.

Fireflies don't just light up their behinds to attract mates, they also glow to tell bats not to eat them. This twist in the tale of the trait that gives fireflies their name was discovered by Jesse Barber and his colleagues. The glow's warning role benefits both fireflies and bats, **because** these insects taste disgusting to the mammals. (①) When swallowed, chemicals released by fireflies **cause** bats to throw them back up. (②) The team placed eight bats in a dark room with three or four fireflies plus three times as many tasty insects, including beetles and moths, for four days. (③) During the first night, all the bats captured at least one firefly. (④) **But** by the fourth night, most bats had learned to avoid fireflies and catch all the other prey instead. (⑤) It had long been thought that firefly bioluminescence mainly acted as a mating signal, **but** the new finding explains why firefly larvae also glow despite being immature for mating.

* bioluminescence: 생물 발광(發光) ** larvae: larva(애벌레)의 복수형

해설 [정답 : ⑤]

Ⅰ. 그 팀이 반딧불이에서 빛이 나는 기관을 어둡게 칠했을 때, 새로운 한 무리의 박쥐는 그것을 피하는 법을 배우는 데 2배의 시간이 걸렸다고 합니다. 2배의 시간이 걸렸다는 비교를 통해서 주어진 문장 앞에서 박쥐가 반딧불이를 피하는 것과 관련된 내용이 제시되어야 합니다.

Ⅱ. 단절이 존재하지 않습니다.

Ⅲ. 단절이 존재하지 않으므로 우리가 Ⅰ에서 추측한 내용을 근거로 판단해야 합니다. 박쥐가 반딧불이를 피하는 것에 대한 첫 번째 실험은 ⑤번 전 문장에서 네 번째 밤에 대부분의 박쥐들은 반딧불이를 피하는 법을 배웠다고 마무리 됩니다. 즉 그 후에 주어진 문장이 들어가야 하므로 정답은 ⑤번이 됩니다.

주. When the team / painted / fireflies' light organs / dark, / a new set of bats / took / twice (as long to learn to avoid / them).

> 구▶ 그 팀이 반딧불이에서 빛이 나는 기관을 어둡게 칠했을 때, 새로운 한 무리의 박쥐는 그것을 피하는 법을 배우는데 2배의 시간이 걸렸다고 합니다.

Ⅰ. Fireflies / don't just light up / their behinds (to attract / mates), they / also glow to tell / bats / not to eat them.

> 구▶ 'not just A, (but) also B'는 'A뿐만 아니라 B이다'를 의미합니다.
> - 'tell + I.O + D.O'는 'I.O에게 D.O를 말하다'를 뜻합니다.
> - 반딧불이는 짝의 주의를 끌기 위해서 뒤에 불을 밝히는 것만이 아니라, 그들이 박쥐에게
>   그들을 먹지 말라고 빛을 내기도 한다고 합니다.

* glow - 빛나다.

Ⅱ. This twist (in the tale of the trait) (that gives / fireflies / their name) / was discovered (by Jesse Barber and his colleagues).

> 구▶ 'give + I.O + D.O'는 'I.O에게 D.O를 주다'를 의미합니다.
> - 반딧불이에게 이름을 준 특성 이야기의 꼬임은 'Jesse Barber'와 그의 동료들에 의해서 발견되었다고
>   합니다.

Ⅲ. The glow's warning role / benefits / both fireflies and bats, **because** these insects / taste / disgusting (to the mammals).

> 구▶ 'both A and B'는 'A와 B 둘 다'를 의미합니다.
> - 빛이 나는 경고의 역할은 반딧불이와 박쥐 둘 다에게 이익이 되는데, 그 곤충이 그 포유동물에게는
>   역겨운 맛이 나기 때문이라고 합니다.

> 독▶ 'because'를 통해서 인과관계를 제시하므로 중심 문장!
> - 반딧불이가 역겨운 맛이 남 ⇒ 불빛을 통해서 박쥐가 반딧불이를 먹지 않는 것이 이득으로
>   이해하시면 됩니다.

* disgusting - 역겨운

Ⅳ. When swallowed, / chemicals (released by fireflies) / cause / bats / to throw them back up.

> 구▶ 'cause A to-V'는 'A가 V하는 것을 야기하다'를 의미합니다.
> - 삼켰을 때, 반딧불이에서 방출된 화학 물질은 박쥐를 다시 뱉어내게 야기한다고 합니다.

> 독▶ 'cause'를 통해서 인과관계가 제시되므로 중심 문장!
> - 반딧불이의 화학 물질 ⇒ 박쥐가 반딧불이를 뱉어냄으로 이해하시면 됩니다.

Ⅴ. The team / placed / eight bats (in a dark room) (with three or four fireflies) (plus three times as many tasty insects), (including beetles and moths), (for four days).

구 그 팀은 8마리의 박쥐를 서너 마리의 반딧불이와 그보다 세배 많은 딱정벌레와 나방을 포함한 맛있는 벌레들을 어두운 방에 나흘 동안 두었다고 합니다.

Ⅵ. During the first night, all the bats / captured / (at least) one firefly.

구 첫 번째 밤동안 모든 박쥐들은 적어도 한 마리의 반딧불이를 잡았다고 합니다.

Ⅶ. **But** (by the fourth night), most bats / had learned / to avoid / fireflies / and catch / all the other prey instead.

구 그러나 네 번째 밤에는, 대부분의 박쥐는 반딧불이를 피하고 대신에 다른 먹이를 잡는 법을 배웠다고 합니다.

독 'But'이 제시되었으므로 중심 문장!
- 첫 번째 밤에는 반딧불이를 잡았지만 마지막 밤에는 잡지 않았다고 합니다.

Ⅷ. It / had long been thought / that firefly bioluminescence / mainly acted (as a mating signal), **but** the new finding / explains / why firefly larvae / also glow (despite being immature for mating).

* bioluminescence: 생물 발광 (發光) ** larvae: larva(애벌레)의 복수형

구 오랫동안 반딧불이의 생물 발광은 주로 짝짓기의 신호 역할을 한다고 생각되었지만, 그 새로운 발견은 왜 반딧불이 애벌레들도 미숙함에도 불구하고 빛이 나는 지를 설명해줬다고 합니다.

독 'but'이 제시되었으므로 중심 문장!
- 새로운 발견이 왜 애벌레들도 미숙함에도 빛이 나는지를 알려줬다
⇒ 박쥐에게 본인이 맛이 역겨움을 알려주는 신호로 이해하시면 됩니다.

글의 흐름으로 보아, 주어진 문장이 들어가기에 가장 적절한 곳을 고르시오.

> **As a result**, they are fit and grow better, **but** they aren't particularly long-lived.

When trees grow together, nutrients and water can be optimally divided among them all so that each tree can grow into the best tree it can be. If you "help" individual trees by getting rid of their supposed competition, the remaining trees are bereft. They send messages out to their neighbors unsuccessfully, **because** nothing remains but stumps. Every tree now grows on its own, giving rise to great differences in productivity. (①) Some individuals photosynthesize like mad until sugar positively bubbles along their trunk. (②) This is **because** a tree can be only as strong as the forest that surrounds it. (③) And there are now a lot of losers in the forest. (④) Weaker members, who would once have been supported by the stronger ones, suddenly fall behind. (⑤) Whether the reason for their decline is their location and lack of nutrients, a passing sickness, or genetic makeup, they now fall prey to insects and fungi.

* bereft: 잃은 ** stamp: 그루터기 *** photosynthesize: 광합성하다

해설 [정답 : ②]

Ⅰ. 주어진 문장에서는 결과적으로, 그것들은 건강하고 더 잘 자라지만 특별히 더 오래 살지는 못한다고 합니다. 접속사가 많이 언급되며, 대명사 'they'를 파악하는 것도 중요합니다.

Ⅱ. ①번 뒷 문장에서는 어떤 개체들은 미친 듯이 광합성을 한다고 했습니다. 그런데 ②번 뒷 문장에서는 나무는 자신을 둘러싼 숲만큼만 강하기 때문이라고 했는데, 이것은 오히려 나무의 활동 범위가 제한되는 내용이므로 광합성의 원인 문장으로 보기 어렵습니다. 그러므로 내용 단절이 발생합니다.

Ⅲ. 주어진 문장에서는 그것들은 건강하고 더 잘 자라지만 오래 살지는 못한다고 했는데, 이것은 ①번 뒷 문장의 'individuals photosynthesize like mad' 광합성을 미친 듯이 하는 것에 대한 부정적인 결과로 이어져야 합니다. 또한 ②번 뒷 문장의 'a tree can be only as strong as the forest that surrounds it', 나무가 자신을 둘러싸고 있는 숲만큼만 강한 것은 주어진 문장의 나무들이 오래 살지 못하는 것에 대한 원인이 되어야 하므로 주어진 문장은 ②번에 들어가야 합니다.

주. **As a result**, they / are fit / and grow better, but they / aren't particularly long-lived.

> 구 그 결과, 그것들은 건강하고 더 잘 자라지만 특별히 오래 살지는 못한다고 합니다.

> 독 'as a result', 'but'이 언급되므로 중심 문장

Ⅰ. When trees / grow together, nutrients and water / can be optimally divided among them all / so that each tree / can grow into the best tree / it / can be.

> 구 'so that'은 '~를 위해서'를 의미합니다.
>   - 나무가 함께 자랄 때는 각 나무가 가능한 최고의 나무로 성장할 수 있도록 영양분과 물이 그것들 모두 사이에서 최적으로 분배된다고 합니다.

> 독 영양분과 물이 최적으로 분배되는 것이 나무의 공동 성장의 조건임을 알 수 있습니다.

Ⅱ. If you / "help" / individual trees (by getting rid of their supposed competition), the remaining trees / are bereft.

* bereft: 잃은

> 구 'by V-ing'는 'V함으로써'를 의미합니다.
>   - 만약 네가 경쟁자로 여겨지는 나무를 제거하여 개별 나무를 '도와주면' 나머지 나무를 잃게 된다고 합니다.

> 독 나무가 함께 자라는 조건에 어긋났기 때문에 발생하는 결과입니다.

Ⅲ. They / send / messages out to their neighbors unsuccessfully, **because** nothing / remains but stumps.

** stamp: 그루터기

> 구 그것들은 그루터기 외에는 무엇도 남아있지 않기 때문에 이웃 나무들에 메시지를 보내지만, 소용이 없다고 합니다.

> 독 제거된 식물들의 행동을 의미합니다.

Ⅳ. Every tree / now grows on its own, giving rise to great differences in productivity.

> 구 이제 모든 나무가 그것 나름대로 자라 생산성에 큰 차이가 생긴다고 합니다.

Ⅴ. Some individuals / photosynthesize like mad until sugar / positively bubbles along their trunk.

*** photosynthesize: 광합성하다

> 구 어떤 개체들은 당분이 줄기를 따라 확연히 흘러넘칠 때까지 미친 듯이 광합성을 한다고 합니다.

> 독 Ⅴ번 문장의 예시로 언급된 나무 중 하나입니다.

Ⅵ. This / is / **because** a tree / can be only as strong as the forest / that / surrounds / it.

구 이는 나무는 자신을 둘러싸고 있는 숲만큼만 강할 수 있기 때문이라고 합니다.

독 'because'가 제시되었으므로 중심 문장

- Ⅵ번 문장에서는 어떤 나무들이 당분이 흘러넘칠 정도로 광합성을 한다고 했는데, 나무가 자신을 둘러싸는 숲만큼만 강해지는 것은 그 숲의 범위를 넘어서면 약해진다는 것을 의미하므로 나무들의 지나친 광합성에 대한 원인이라고 보기 어렵습니다.

Ⅶ. And there / are / now a lot of losers (in the forest).

구 그리고 지금 숲에는 많은 패자가 있다고 합니다.

독 여기서 패자는, Ⅴ번 문장의 둘러싸고 있는 숲에서도 다른 나무에 비해 제대로 성장하지 못해 생산성이 뒤떨어진 나무들을 지칭합니다.

Ⅷ. Weaker members, who / would once have been supported (by the stronger ones), suddenly fall behind.

구 한때는 강한 구성원들의 지원을 받았을 약한 구성원들이 갑자기 뒤처진다고 합니다.

독 'weaker members' 역시 Ⅷ번 문장의 'losers'를 지칭합니다.

Ⅸ. Whether the reason (for their decline) / is / their location and lack of nutrients, a passing sickness, or genetic makeup, they / now fall prey to insects and fungi.

구 'whether'은 '~이던지 아니던지'를 의미합니다.

- 그것들의 쇠락 원인이 위치와 영양분 부족이든, 일시적인 질병이든, 혹은 유전적 구성이든, 이제 그것들은 곤충과 균류의 먹이가 된다고 합니다.

글의 흐름으로 보아, 주어진 문장이 들어가기에 가장 적절한 곳을 고르시오.

> On top of the <u>hurdles introduced</u> in accessing his or her money, if a suspected fraud is detected, the account holder **has to** deal with <u>the phone call</u> asking if he or she made the suspicious transactions.

Each new wave of technology is intended to enhance user convenience, as well as improve security, **but** sometimes these do not necessarily go hand-in-hand. **For example**, the transition from magnetic stripe to embedded chip slightly slowed down transactions, sometimes frustrating customers in a hurry. (①) **Make** a service too burdensome, and the potential customer will go elsewhere. (②) This obstacle applies at several levels. (③) Passwords, double-key identification, and biometrics such as fingerprint-, iris-, and voice recognition are all ways of keeping the account details hidden from potential fraudsters, of keeping your data dark. (④) **But** they all inevitably add a burden to the use of the account. (⑤) This is all useful at some level — indeed, it can be reassuring knowing that your bank is keeping alert to protect you — **but** it becomes tiresome if too many such calls are received.

* fraud: 사기

해설 [정답 : ⑤]

I. 주어진 문장에서는 자기 돈에 접근하는 데 도입된 난관들에 더해, 만약 의심스러운 사기가 감지되면 예금주는 의심스러운 거래를 했는지 묻는 내용의 전화 통화를 해야만 한다고 합니다.

II. ③번 뒷 문장에서 비밀번호, 이중 키 확인, 지문, 홍채, 음성 인식과 같은 생체 인식들이 사기꾼으로부터 계정 세부 정보를 숨겨준다고 합니다. ④번 뒷 문장에서 그것들은 모두 계좌 사용에 부담을 가중한다고 합니다. 그런데 ⑤번 뒷 문장에서는 이것이 모두 어느 정도 유용하다고 했는데, 'This'가 지칭하는 것이 ⑤번 앞 문장에 의미상으로 존재하지 않으므로 대명사 단절이 발생합니다.

III. ⑤번 앞 문장의 'they'는 사용자의 부담을 가중시키므로, 주어진 문장의 hurdles로 이어집니다. 또한 주어진 문장의 전화를 받는 것은 의미상 ⑤번 뒷 문장의 'This'라는 대명사로 전환되어야 하므로 정답은 ⑤번이 됩니다.

주. On top (of the hurdles introduced / in accessing / his or her money), if / a suspected fraud / is detected, the account holder / **has to deal** with / the phone call / asking / if / he or she / made / the suspicious transactions.

* fraud: 사기

구▶ 자신의 돈에 접근하는 데 도입된 난관에 더해, 만약 의심스러운 사기가 감지되면, 예금주는 본인이 그 의심스러운 거래를 했는지 묻는 내용의 전화 통화를 응대해야만 한다고 합니다.

독▶ 'has to'가 제시되었으므로 중심 문장

Ⅰ. Each new wave (of technology) / is intended / to enhance / user convenience, as well as improve / security, **but** sometimes / these / do not necessarily go / hand-in-hand.

> 구 ▶ 각각의 새로운 기술의 물결은 보안을 향상할 뿐만 아니라, 사용자 편의성을 향상하려는 의도이지만, 때때로 이것들이 반드시 함께 진행되지는 않는다고 합니다.

> 독 ▶ 'but'이 제시되었으므로 중심 문장
> - 보안 향상과 편의성 향상이라는 기술의 장점과 이것이 그대로 진행되지는 않는다는 기술의 단점이 나열되고 있는 문장입니다.

Ⅱ. **For example**, the transition (from magnetic stripe to embedded chip) slightly slowed down / transactions, sometimes / frustrating / customers (in a hurry).

> 구 ▶ 예를 들어 마그네틱 띠에서 내장형 칩으로의 전환은 거래(의 속도)를 약간 늦췄는데, 때로 바쁜 고객을 좌절시켰다고 합니다.

> 독 ▶ 'For example'이 제시되었으므로 앞 문장 중심 문장
> - 내장형 칩으로의 전환은 Ⅰ번 문장의 기술의 물결에 대한 예시이며, 이것이 고객들을 좌절시킨 것은 편의성 부분을 향상시키지 못한 기술의 단점에 대한 예시가 됩니다. 마그네틱 띠에서 내장형 칩으로의 전환은 신용 카드에서의 변화를 의미합니다.

Ⅲ. **Make** / a service / too burdensome, and the potential customer / will go / elsewhere.

> 구 ▶ 서비스를 너무 부담스럽게 만들면, 잠재 고객은 다른 곳으로 갈 것이라고 합니다.

> 독 ▶ 명령문이 제시되었으므로 중심 문장

Ⅳ. This obstacle / applies (at several levels).

> 구 ▶ 이런 장벽은 여러 수준에서 적용된다고 합니다.

> 독 ▶ 여러 수준에서 적용되는 것에 대한 예시가 뒷 문장에서 언급될 가능성이 높습니다.

Ⅴ. Passwords, double-key identification, and biometrics (such as fingerprint-, iris-, and voice recognition) / are / all ways (of keeping / the account details / hidden / from potential fraudsters, of keeping / your data / dark).

> 구 ▶ 'keep A from B'는 'A를 B로부터 막다'를 의미합니다.
> - 비밀번호, 이중 키 확인, 지문, 홍채 및 음성 인식과 같은 생체 인식은 모두 잠재적인 사기꾼으로 부터 계정 세부 정보를 숨겨 주는, 즉 여러분의 데이터를 비밀로 유지하는 방법이라고 합니다.

> 독 ▶ 문장에서 언급된 모든 기술들은 전부 기술의 물결로 인하여 발생되었고, 보안 향상에 기여하므로 기술 물결의 장점에 대한 예시가 됩니다.

Ⅵ. **But** they / all inevitably add / a burden / to the use (of the account).

> 구 ▶ 'add A to B'는 'A를 B에 더하다'를 의미합니다.
> - 하지만 그것들은 모두 불가피하게 계좌 사용에 부담을 가중한다고 합니다.

> 독 ▶ 'But'이 제시되었으므로 앞 뒷 문장 중심 문장
> - 반면 소비자의 계좌 사용 부담을 늘린다고 하는 것은 편의성 향상에 기여하지 못한 기술의 단점에 해당하는 내용입니다.

Ⅶ. This / is / all useful / at some level — indeed, it / can be / reassuring / knowing / that / your bank / is keeping / alert / to protect you — **but** it / becomes / tiresome / if / too many such calls / are received.

> 구 ▶ 'It + be 동사 + 동명사'는 가주어/진주어입니다.
> - 이것은 모두 어느 정도 도움이 되며, 실제로, 여러분의 은행이 너를 보호하기 위해 경계를 늦추지 않고 있다는 것을 알게 되어 안심이 될 수 있지만, 그러한 전화를 너무 많이 받게 되면 귀찮은 일이 된다고 합니다.

> 독 ▶ 'but'이 제시되었으므로 중심 문장
> - 이러한 기술들은 모두 도움이 된다고 했으므로 Ⅰ번 문장의 보안 향상에 대한 예시가 되지만, 이러한 기술의 산물인 전화를 받는 것은 우리를 귀찮게 하므로 사용자의 편의성을 향상시키지 못한 것이 됩니다.

20 22학년도 6월 평가원 39번 (정답률 37%)

글의 흐름으로 보아, 주어진 문장이 들어가기에 가장 적절한 곳을 고르시오.

> This is particularly true **since** one aspect of sleep is decreased responsiveness to the environment.

The role that sleep plays in evolution is still under study. (①) One possibility is that it is an advantageous adaptive state of decreased metabolism for an animal when there are no more pressing activities. (②) This seems true for deeper states of inactivity such as hibernation during the winter when there are few food supplies, and a high metabolic cost to maintaining adequate temperature. (③) It may be true in daily situations as well, **for instance** for a prey species to avoid predators after dark. (④) **On the other hand**, the apparent universality of sleep, and the observation that mammals such as cetaceans have developed such highly complex mechanisms to preserve sleep on at least one side of the brain at a time, suggests that sleep additionally provides some vital service(s) for the organism. (⑤) If sleep is universal even when this potential price must be paid, the implication may be that it has important functions that cannot be obtained just by quiet, wakeful resting.

* metabolism: 신진대사 ** mammal: 포유동물

해설 [정답 : ⑤]

Ⅰ. 주어진 문장에서 그것은 특히 사실인데, 잠의 한가지 측면은 환경에 대한 반응성이 감소하는 것이기 때문이라고 합니다. 주어진 문장의 'This'가 지칭하는 대상이 주어진 문장 앞에서 제시되어야 하며 주어진 문장 뒤에서는 환경에 대한 반응성이 감소하는 것과 관련된 내용이 제시되어야 합니다.

Ⅱ. ⑤번 앞 문장에서 잠이 가지는 보편성과 잠에 대한 관찰을 통해서 잠이 생명체에게 생명 유지와 관련된 다른 도움들을 추가적으로 제공한다고 합니다. ⑤번 뒷 문장에서는 'this potential price'가 지불됨에도 불구하고 잠이 보편성을 가진다면 잠은 깨어있을 때 얻을 수 없는 중요한 기능을 (= 도움을) 가진다는 것을 알 수 있다고 합니다. 하지만 ⑤번 앞 문장에서는 'this potential price'가 지칭하는 비용에 대한 내용이 제시되어 있지 않으므로 ⑤번에서 지시사 단절이 발생합니다.

Ⅲ. ⑤번에서 단절이 발생하며 주어진 문장의 'This'가 지칭하는 내용은 ⑤번 앞 문장에서 잠이 동물에게 추가적인 도움을 제공한다는 내용입니다. 또한 ⑤번 뒷 문장의 'this potential price'가 주어진 문장의 잠으로 인해 환경에 대한 반응성이 감소하는 것을 지칭하므로 정답은 ⑤번이 됩니다.

주. This / is / particularly true since one aspect of sleep / is / decreased responsiveness (to the environment).

구▶ 그것은 특히 사실인데, 잠의 한가지 측면은 환경에 대한 반응성이 감소하는 것이기 때문이라고 합니다.

독▶ 'since'가 제시되었으므로 중심 문장
- 잠이 환경에 대한 반응성을 감소시키기 때문에 'This'가 사실이라고 합니다.

Ⅰ. The role (that sleep plays in evolution) / is still under study.

구▶ 진화에 있어서 잠이 하는 역할은 여전히 연구 중이라고 합니다.

Ⅱ. One possibility / is / that it / is / an advantageous adaptive state (of decreased metabolism) (for an animal) / when there / are / no more pressing activities.

* metabolism: 신진대사

구▶ 한 가지 가능성은 그것이 (= 잠이) 더 이상 긴급한 활동이 없을 때, 동물에게 신진대사를 줄이는 유리한 적응적 상태라는 것이라고 합니다.

Ⅲ. This / seems true for / deeper states (of inactivity) (such as hibernation during the winter) (when there / are / few food supplies, / and a high metabolic cost (to maintaining adequate temperature)).

구▶ 그것은 (= 잠이 유리한 적응적 상태라는 가능성은) 먹을 것이 거의 없고 적절한 체온을 유지하는 데 높은 신진대사 비용이 발생하는 겨울 동안 겨울잠과 같은 깊은 비활동 상태에 적절한 것처럼 보인다고 합니다.

* hibernation - 겨울잠

Ⅳ. It / may be / true (in daily situations as well), / (**for instance**) for a prey species (to avoid predators after dark).

구▶ 'to-V' 앞에 존재하는 'for N'은 'to-V'의 의미상 주어에 해당합니다.
- 그것은 (= 잠이 유리한 적응 상태라는 가능성은) 예를 들어, 먹이가 되는 종들이 밤 이후에 포식자를 피하기 위한 것처럼 일상 상황에서 또한 사실이라고 합니다.

독▶ 'for instance'가 제시되었으므로 중심 문장

Ⅴ. **On the other hand,** the apparent universality (of sleep), / and the observation (that mammals / (such as cetaceans) have developed / such highly complex mechanisms (to preserve / sleep on at least one side of the brain at a time), suggests / that sleep / additionally provides / some vital service(s) (for the organism).

** mammal: 포유동물

구▶ 반면에, 잠의 분명한 보편성, 그리고 'cetaceans'와 같은 포유동물들이 한 번에 적어도 뇌 한쪽에서는 잠을 유지하는 매우 고도로 복잡한 메커니즘을 발전시켰다는 관찰은 잠이 생명체에게 생명 유지와 관련된 도움을 추가적으로 제공한다는 것을 제시한다고 합니다.

독▶ 'On the other hand'가 제시되었으므로 앞 뒷 문장 중심 문장
- 겨울잠을 자는 동물이나 혹은 먹이가 되는 피식 동물들 뿐만 아니라 포식자와 같은 다른 유형의 동물들에게도 잠이 나타나는 보편성과 'cetaceans'와 같은 포유동물은 적어도 뇌 한쪽에서는 잠을 유지하는 경향이 있다는 것은 낮은 신진대사를 통한 이득 뿐만 아니라 다른 이득이 있음을 알려준다고 합니다.

Ⅵ. If sleep / is / universal / even when this potential price **must** be paid, / the implication / may be / that it / has / important functions that cannot be obtained just (by quiet, wakeful resting).

구▶ 만약 잠이 그러한 잠재적인 비용이 반드시 지불될 때에도 보편성을 가진다면, 그 설명은 그것이 (= 잠이) 조용한, 깨어있는 상태의 휴식으로부터 얻을 수 없는 중요한 기능을 가지고 있다는 것이라고 합니다.

독▶ 'must'가 제시되었으므로 중심 문장
- 그러한 잠재적 비용이 지불될 때도 잠을 자는 것은 잠에 다른 중요한 기능이 있다는 것을 의미한다고 합니다.

글의 흐름으로 보아, 주어진 문장이 들어가기에 가장 적절한 곳을 고르시오.

> This makes sense from the perspective of information reliability.

The dynamics of collective detection have an interesting feature. Which cue(s) do individuals use as evidence of predator attack? In some cases, when an individual detects a predator, its best response is to seek shelter. (①) Departure from the group may signal danger to nonvigilant animals and **cause** what appears to be a coordinated flushing of prey from the area. (②) Studies on dark-eyed juncos (a type of bird) support the view that nonvigilant animals attend to departures of individual group mates **but** that the departure of multiple individuals **causes** a greater escape response in the nonvigilant individuals. (③) If one group member departs, it might have done so for a number of reasons that have little to do with predation threat. (④) If nonvigilant animals escaped each time a single member left the group, they would frequently respond when there was no predator (a false alarm). (⑤) **On the other hand**, when several individuals depart the group at the same time, a true threat is much more likely to be present.

* predator: 포식자 ** vigilant: 경계하는 *** flushing: 날아오름

해설 [정답 : ③]

Ⅰ. 주어진 문장에서 그것은 정보 신뢰성의 관점에서 이해가 된다고 합니다. 주어진 문장의 'This'가 지칭하는 대상이 주어진 문장 앞에서 제시되어야 하며 주어진 문장 뒤에서는 정보의 신뢰성과 관련된 내용이 제시되어야 합니다.

Ⅱ. 지문에서 단절이 존재하지 않습니다. ④번을 고른 27%의 수험생들이 있습니다. 하지만 ④번 앞 문장의 한 무리 동료가 무리에서 이탈하는 것은 포식자의 위협이 아닌 다른 이유를 가지고 있을 것이라는 내용은 ④번 뒷 문장에서 하나의 무리 동료가 이탈할 때마다 도망간다면 포식자가 없음에도 불구하고 도망가게 되는 가짜 경보일 것이라는 내용의 이유가 되므로 ④번에서도 단절이 존재하지 않습니다.

Ⅲ. 단절이 존재하지 않으므로 주어진 문장의 내용을 통해서 판단해야 합니다. 주어진 문장의 'This'는 정보의 신뢰성의 관점에서 이해된다고 합니다. 이 지문에서 제시된 정보는 무리에서 한 개체가 이탈할 때와 무리에서 다수의 개체가 한 번에 이탈할 때를 지칭한다는 것을 알 수 있습니다. ④번 문장 뒷 문장과 ⑤번 문장 뒷 문장을 통해 한 개체가 이탈할 때보다 무리에서 다수의 개체가 한 번에 이탈할 때 정보의 신뢰성이 더 높음을 알 수 있습니다. 즉 'This'는 무리에서 한 개체가 이탈할 때보다 무리에서 다수의 개체가 한 번에 이탈할 때 더 예민하게 반응하는 것이고 이는 ③번 앞 문장에서 제시되고 있습니다. 또한 정보의 신뢰성에 대한 구체적인 내용이 ③번 뒷 부분에서 제시됩니다. 그러므로 정답은 ③번이 됩니다.

주. This / makes sense (from the perspective of information reliability).

구▸ 그것은 정보 신뢰성의 관점에서 이해가 된다고 합니다.

Ⅰ. The dynamics of collective detection / have / an interesting feature.

구▸ 집단적 탐지의 역학은 흥미로운 특징이 있다고 합니다.

Ⅱ. Which cue(s) do individuals / use (as evidence of predator attack)?

* predator: 포식자

구▸ 개체들은 포식자의 공격의 증거로써 어떤 신호를 사용할까?라며 질문하고 있습니다.

Ⅲ. In some cases, when an individual / detects / a predator, its best response / is to seek / shelter.

구▸ 때때로, 한 개체가 포식자를 탐지했을 때, 가장 좋은 반응은 안식처를 찾는 것이라고 합니다.

Ⅳ. Departure (from the group) / may signal / danger (to nonvigilant animals) and **cause** what appears to be / a coordinated flushing of prey (from the area).

** vigilant: 경계하는 *** flushing: 날아오름

구▸ 무리로부터의 이탈은 경계하지 않는 동물들에게 위험의 신호를 줄 수 있고, 그 구역으로부터 먹잇감들의 협동적인 날아오름인 것처럼 보이는 것을 야기할 수 있다고 합니다.

독▸ 'cause'가 제시되었으므로 중심 문장
- 무리에서 이탈하는 것은 경계하지 않는 다른 동물들에게 위험 신호를 줄 수 있고 다 같이 도망가는 것을 야기할 수도 있다고 합니다.

Ⅴ. Studies (on dark-eyed juncos (a type of bird)) / support / the view that nonvigilant animals / attend to / departures of individual group mates **but** that the departure (of multiple individuals) / **causes** / a greater escape response (in the nonvigilant individuals).

구▸ (새의 한 종류인) 검은 눈 'juncos'에 대한 연구는 경계하지 않는 동물들이 무리 동료들의 개별적 이탈에 주목하지만 다수 무리 동료들의 이탈은 경계하지 않는 동물들에게 더 큰 도망 반응을 야기할 수 있다는 견해를 지지한다고 합니다.

독▸ 'but'과 'cause'가 제시되었으므로 중심 문장
- 무리의 동료들이 하나씩 개별적으로 이탈하는 것에도 주목하긴 하지만, 무리 동료들이 한꺼번에 무리에서 이탈하는 것은 더 큰 도망 반응을 일으킬 수 있다고 합니다.

Ⅵ. If one group member / departs, it / might have done (so for a number of reasons) (that

have little to do with / predation threat).

구▶ 만약 하나의 무리 동료가 이탈한다면, 그것은 (= 하나의 무리 동료의 이탈은) 포식 위험과 관련이 없는
여러 이유로 일어날 수 있다고 합니다.

독▶ 무리 동료 중 한 개체만 이탈했다면 포식자의 위험이 아닌 물을 마시러 가거나, 먹이를 찾으러 가는 등
여러 이유로 이탈했을 수도 있다고 합니다.

Ⅶ. If nonvigilant animals / escaped each time (a single member / left / the group), they /

would frequently respond (when there was / no predator) (a false alarm).

구▶ 만약 경계하지 않는 동물들이 한 무리 동료가 무리에서 떠날 때마다 도망간다면, 그들은 (= 경계하지
않는 동물들은) 포식자가 없을 때에도 종종 반응할 것이라고 (= 도망갈 것이라고) 합니다. 또한 이를
가짜 경보라고 합니다.

독▶ 무리 동료 중 한 개체만 이탈했을 때마다 도망간다면 포식자가 없음에도 불구하고 도망가게 된다고
합니다.

Ⅷ. **On the other hand**, when several individuals / depart / the group (at the same time), a true threat /

is much more likely to be / present.

구▶ 반면에, 여러 개체가 동시에 무리를 이탈할 때, 진짜 위험이 존재할 가능성이 높다고 합니다.

독▶ 'On the other hand'가 제시되었으므로 앞 뒷 문장 중심 문장
- 무리 동료들이 하나씩 무리에서 이탈할 때는 가짜 경보일 가능성이 있지만 여러 무리 동료들이 동시에
이탈한다면 진짜 포식자의 위험이 있을 가능성이 높다고 합니다.

글의 흐름으로 보아, 주어진 문장이 들어가기에 가장 적절한 곳을 고르시오.

> In particular, they define a group as two or more people who interact with, and exert mutual influences on, each other.

In everyday life, we tend to see any collection of people as a group. (①) **However**, social psychologists use this term more precisely. (②) It is this sense of mutual interaction or inter-dependence for a common purpose which distinguishes the members of a group from a mere aggregation of individuals. (③) **For example**, as Kenneth Hodge observed, a collection of people who happen to go for a swim after work on the same day each week does not, strictly speaking, constitute a group **because** these swimmers do not interact with each other in a structured manner. (④) **By contrast**, a squad of young competitive swimmers who train every morning before going to school is a group **because** they not only share a common objective (training for competition) **but** also interact with each other in formal ways (e.g., by warming up together beforehand). (⑤) It is this sense of people coming together to achieve a common objective that defines a "team".

* exert: 발휘하다 ** aggregation: 집합

해설 [정답 : ②]

Ⅰ. 주어진 문장에서는 특히, 그들은 집단을 서로에게 상호 작용을 하고, 상호 영향력을 발휘하는 둘 이상의 사람들로 정의한다고 합니다. 즉 주어진 문장은 집단에 대한 정의를 제시하며, 대명사인 'they'와 같은 단서를 이용해야 할 필요가 있습니다.

Ⅱ. ①번 앞 문장에서 group이 언급되며, ②번 앞 문장에서 사회 심리학자들은 이 용어를 더 정확하게 사용한다고 했습니다. ②번 뒷 문장에서는 집단의 구성원을 단순한 개인들의 집합으로부터 구별하는 것은 상호 작용 또는 상호 의존감이라고 했습니다. 'It is this sense of ~' 표현은 '이것이 바로 ~다'로 해석되어 앞에 언급된 내용을 강조하는 숙어 표현인데, 강조되는 'mutual interaction or inter-dependence', 상호 작용과 상호 의존성이 ②번 앞 문장에서 언급되지 않으므로 단절이 발생합니다.

Ⅲ. ②번 앞 문장에서 social psychologist는 주어진 문장의 they를 지칭하고, 사회 심리학자들이 집단이라는 용어를 더 정확하게 사용하는 것에 대한 예시가 바로 주어진 문장의 집단에 대한 정의를 설명합니다. 또한 주어진 문장의 상호 작용하는 사람들, 그리고 상호 영향력을 발휘하는 집단의 대한 정의는 ②번 뒷 문장의 상호 작용과 상호 의존성으로 연결되므로 정답은 ②번이 됩니다.

주. In particular, they / define / a group as two or more people (who / interact with, and exert / mutual influences on, each other).

* exert: 발휘하다

> 구 ‘define A as B’는 ‘A를 B로 정의하다’를 의미합니다.
> - 특히, 그들은 서로에게 상호작용하고, 상호 영향력을 발휘하는 둘 이상의 사람들로 집단을 정의한다고 합니다.
> 독 집단의 정의에 대한 설명 문장입니다.

Ⅰ. In everyday life, we / tend / to see any collection (of people) (as a group).

> 구 일상생활에서 우리는 어떤 사람들의 무리라도 하나의 집단으로 보는 경향이 있다고 합니다.
> 독 집단에 대한 언급이 처음 등장하는 문장입니다.

Ⅱ. **However**, social psychologists / use / this term / more precisely.

> 구 그러나 사회 심리학자들은 이 용어를 더 정확하게 사용한다고 합니다.
> 독 ‘However’가 제시되었으므로 앞 뒷 문장 중심 문장
> - ‘this term’은 Ⅰ번 문장의 ‘group’, 집단을 말하며, 이것을 사회 심리학자들이 사용하는 예시에 대한 설명이 뒤에 언급되어야 합니다.

Ⅲ. It / is / this sense (of mutual interaction or inter-dependence) (for a common purpose) which / distinguishes / the members of a group / (from a mere aggregation of individuals).

** aggregation: 집합

> 구 ‘It + be 동사 + 명사 + 관계대명사’는 It 강조 구문입니다.
> - ‘distinguish A from B’는 ‘A를 B와 구별하다’를 의미합니다.
> - 집단의 구성원들을 단순한 개인들의 집합으로부터 구별하는 것은 바로 공동의 목적을 위한 서로의 상호 작용 또는 상호 의존감이라고 합니다.
> 독 집단의 구성원과 개인의 집합의 차이점은 상호 작용 또는 상호 의존감이라는 설명입니다.

Ⅳ. **For example**, as Kenneth Hodge / observed, a collection (of people) (who / happen / to go for a swim / after work / on the same day / each week) does not, strictly speaking, constitute / a group (**because** / these swimmers / do not interact with each other (in a structured manner)).

> 구 예를 들어, Kenneth Hodge가 진술한 바와 같이, 매주 같은 날에 일을 마치고 우연히 수영을 하러 가는 사람들의 무리는 엄밀히 말하면 집단을 구성하지 않는데, 이러한 수영하는 사람들은 구조적인 방식으로 상호 작용하지 않기 때문이라고 합니다.
> 독 ‘For example’이 제시되었으므로 앞 문장 중심 문장, ‘because’가 제시되었으므로 중심 문장
> - 수영을 하러 가는 사람들의 무리가 상호 작용하지 않았음으로 집단으로 볼 수 없다는 예시 문장입니다.

Ⅴ. **By contrast**, a squad (of young competitive swimmers (who / train / every morning) (before / going to school)) is / a group / **because** / they / not only share / a common objective (training / for competition) **but** also / interact with each other (in formal ways) (e.g., by warming up together beforehand).

> **구** 대조적으로, 매일 아침 학교에 가기 전에 훈련을 하는, 경쟁을 하는 어린 수영 선수들은 공동의 목표(경기를 위한 훈련)를 공유할 뿐만 아니라 공식적인 방식(예를 들면, 미리 함께 워밍업을 함)으로 상호 작용하기 때문에 집단이라고 합니다.

> **독** 'By contrast'를 통해 대조하므로 앞 뒷 문장 중심 문장, 'because'와 'but'이 제시되었으므로 중심 문장
> - 반면 서로 경쟁하는 수영 선수들은 목표와 상호 작용이 존재하므로 집단이라고 볼 수 있다는 내용으로 대조되고 있습니다.

Ⅵ. It / is / this sense (of people / coming together (to achieve / a common objective)) that / defines / a "team".

> **구** 'It + be 동사 + 명사 + that'는 it that 강조 구문입니다.
> - '팀'을 정의하는 것은 바로 공동의 목표를 달성하기 위해 사람들이 함께 모이는 이러한 생각이라고 합니다.

> **독** Ⅴ번 문장의 예시를 다시 개념으로 정리한 문장입니다.

글의 흐름으로 보아, 주어진 문장이 들어가기에 가장 적절한 곳을 고르시오.

> Compounding the difficulty, now more than ever, is what ergonomists call information overload, where a leader is overrun with inputs—via e-mails, meetings, and phone calls—that only distract and confuse her thinking.

　Clarity is often a difficult thing for a leader to obtain. Concerns of the present tend to seem larger than potentially greater concerns that lie farther away. (①) Some decisions by their nature present great complexity, whose many variables **must** come together a certain way for the leader to succeed. (②) **Alternatively**, the leader's information might be only fragmentary, which might **cause** her to fill in the gaps with assumptions—sometimes without recognizing them as such. (③) And the merits of a leader's most important decisions, by their nature, typically are not clear-cut. (④) **Instead** those decisions involve a process of assigning weights to competing interests, and then determining, based upon some criterion, which one predominates. (⑤) **The result** is one of judgment, of shades of gray; like saying that Beethoven is a better composer than Brahms.

* ergonomist: 인간 공학자　** fragmentary: 단편적인

해설 [정답 : ②]

Ⅰ. 주어진 문장에서 어려움을 더하는 것은 지도자가 정보 과부화를 겪는 것으로, 자신의 생각을 흐트러뜨리고 혼란스럽게 할 뿐인 매체를 통한 주입에 압도당하는 것이라고 합니다. 우리는 이를 통해 주어진 문장 뒤에는 어려움이 제시되어야 하는 것을 알 수 있습니다.

Ⅱ. ②번 앞 문장에서 몇몇 결정들은 본질상 엄청난 복잡성을 나타내고 지도자들을 이를 합쳐야만 한다고 합니다. ②번 뒷 문장에서 'Alternatively'를 제시하며, 지도자의 정보가 단편적인 경우를 제시하고 있습니다. 'Alternatively'는 정보를 나열할 때 사용하는 접속사로 ②번 뒷 문장 앞에는 단편적인 경우와 나열될 수 있는 내용이 제시되어야 합니다. 하지만 결정들이 복잡성을 나타내고 지도자들이 이를 합쳐야만 하는 것은 ②번 뒷 문장에서 제시하는 지도자의 정보에 대한 어려움과 나열될 수 없습니다. 그러므로 2.접속사 단절로 인해 ②번에서 단절이 발생합니다.

Ⅲ. 주어진 문장이 정보의 과부하라는 지도자의 정보 처리의 어려움을 제시하고 있고 ②번 뒷 문장이 정보가 단편적일 경우의 문제점을 제시하므로 정답은 ②번이 됩니다.

주. Compounding the difficulty, (now more than ever), is / what ergonomists / call / information overload, / where a leader / is overrun with / inputs—(via e-mails, meetings, and phone calls)—(that only distract and confuse / her thinking).

* ergonomist: 인간 공학자

구▶ 'call + O + O.C'는 'O를 O.C라고 부르다'를 의미합니다.
- 'via'는 '~를 통해서'를 뜻합니다.
- 지금 그 어느 때보다도 어려움을 더하는 것은 인간 공학자들이 정보 과부하라고 부르는 것으로, 지도자는 자신의 생각을 흐트러뜨리고 혼란스럽게 할 뿐인 이메일, 회의, 통화를 통한 주입에 압도당한다고 합니다.

Ⅰ. Clarity / is often / a difficult thing (for a leader / to obtain).

구▶ 'for N to-V'는 'N이 V하는 것'을 뜻합니다.
- 명료함은 지도자가 얻기 어려운 것이라고 합니다.

Ⅱ. Concerns (of the present) / tend to seem / larger than potentially greater concerns (that lie farther away).

구▶ 'tend to-V'는 'V하는 경향이 있다'를 의미합니다.
- 현재의 걱정은 더 멀리 떨어져 있는 잠재적으로 더 큰 우려보다 더 커보이는 경향이 있다고 합니다.

Ⅲ. Some decisions by their nature / present / great complexity, whose many variables / **must** come together / a certain way (for the leader to succeed).

구▶ 몇몇의 그들의 결정은 본질상 엄청난 복잡성을 나타내는데, 그 수 많은 변수들은 지도자가 성공하기 위해서 특정한 방식으로 합쳐져야만 한다고 합니다.

독▶ 'must'가 제시되었으므로 중심 문장!
- 지도자가 성공하기 위해서는 복잡한 변수들을 특정한 방식으로 합쳐야만 한다고 합니다.

Ⅳ. **Alternatively**, the leader's information / might be / only fragmentary, which might cause / her / to fill in / the gaps (with assumptions)—sometimes (without recognizing them as such).

** fragmentary: 단편적인

구▶ 그 대신에, 지도자의 정보는 오직 단편적일 수 있는데, 그것은 지도자가 공백을 추정으로 채우게 하는데, 때때로는 그것을 인식하지 못하고 할 수 있다고 합니다.

독▶ 'cause'를 통해서 인과관계를 제시하므로 중심 문장!
- 만약 정보가 단편적이라면 추정을 통해서 공백을 채워야 한다고 합니다.

Ⅴ. And the merits of a leader's most important decisions, (by their nature), typically / are not / clear-cut.

구▶ 그리고 지도자의 가장 중요한 결정의 장점은 본질상 명확하지 않다고 합니다.

Ⅵ. __Instead__ those decisions / involve / a process of assigning / weights / to competing interests, and then determining, (based upon some criterion), (which one predominates).

구▶ 'assign A to B'는 'A를 B에 배정하다'를 의미합니다.
- 대신에 그 결정은 상충되는 이익에 무게 (=중요성)을 배정하고 어떤 기준에 따라 어떤 것이 우위를 점하는 지를 결정하는 과정을 포함한다고 합니다.

독▶ 'Instead'를 통해서 전환이 제시되었으므로 중심 문장!
- 지도자들의 결정은 분명하지 않고 어떤 것에 중요성을 배정하고 어떤 것이 우위를 점하게 할지 결정하는 것이라고 합니다.

* pre (미리) + dominate (지배하다) = predominate - 미리 지배하다 ⇒ 선취하다, 우위를 점하다.

Ⅶ. __The result__ / is / one of judgment, (of shades of gray); (like saying that Beethoven / is / a better composer than Brahms).

구▶ 그 결과는 베토벤이 브람스보다 훌륭한 작곡가라고 말하는 것과 같은 판단의 하나, 회색의 색조 (= 미묘한 차이) 중 하나라고 합니다.

독▶ 'The result'로 결과를 제시하므로 중심 문장!

24 22학년도 수능 38번 (정답률 30%)

글의 흐름으로 보아, 주어진 문장이 들어가기에 가장 적절한 곳을 고르시오.

> Retraining current employees for new positions within the company will also greatly reduce their fear of being laid off.

Introduction of robots into factories, while employment of human workers is being reduced, creates worry and fear. (①) It is the responsibility of management to prevent or, at least, to ease these fears. (②) **For example**, robots could be introduced only in new plants rather than replacing humans in existing assembly lines. (③) Workers **should** be included in the planning for new factories or the introduction of robots into existing plants, **so** they can participate in the process. (④) It may be that robots **are needed to** reduce manufacturing costs **so that** the company remains competitive, **but** planning for such cost reductions **should** be done jointly by labor and management. (⑤) **Since** robots are particularly good at highly repetitive simple motions, the replaced human workers **should** be moved to positions where judgment and decisions beyond the abilities of robots are required.

해설 [정답 : ⑤]

Ⅰ. 주어진 문장에서 회사 안에서 현재 직원에게 새로운 직책을 위한 재교육을 하는 것 또한 해고될 공포를 줄일 수 있다고 합니다. 또한 주어진 문장 뒤에서는 새로운 직책을 위한 재교육에 대해서 제시되어야 합니다.

Ⅱ. 단절이 보이지 않습니다. ④번의 경우 (31% 선택), ④번 앞 문장에서 노동자들이 새로운 공장을 짓거나 현재 공상에서 로봇이 도입되는 로봇에 대한 계획에 있어서 참여헤야만 한다고 합니다. ④번 뒷 문장에서도 역시 로봇을 통해 제조 비용을 낮출 수 있지만 제조 비용을 낮추기 위해 로봇을 도입하는 계획에 노동자와 회사가 함께 해야 한다고 합니다. 즉, 로봇을 도입하는 계획에 노동자가 참여해야 한다는 내용으로 ④번 뒷 문장은 ④번 앞 문장을 재진술합니다. 그러므로 ④번 역시 단절이 존재하지 않습니다.

Ⅲ. 단절이 존재하지 않으므로 Ⅰ에서 판단한 내용을 근거로 들어갈 곳을 찾아야 합니다. 새로운 직책을 위한 재교육과 관련된 내용은 ⑤번 뒷 문장에서 로봇으로 대체된 노동자들은 로봇의 능력을 넘어서는 판단과 결정이 필요한 직책으로, 즉 새로운 직책으로 옮겨져야만 한다고 제시되었습니다. 이는 주어진 문장의 새로운 직책에 대한 내용과 같은 내용을 제시하므로 정답은 ⑤번이 됩니다.

주. Retraining current employees (for new positions) (within the company) / will also greatly reduce / their fear of being laid off.

> 구▶ 회사 안에서 새로운 직책을 위해 현재 직원을 재교육하는 것은 또한 해고될 공포를 크게 줄어들게 할 것이라고 합니다.

Ⅰ. Introduction (of robots into factories), / while employment of human workers / is being reduced, / creates / worry and fear.

> 구▶ 공장에서 로봇의 도입은, 인간 노동자의 고용을 감소시키며, 걱정과 공포를 만든다고 합니다.
> 독▶ 공장에 로봇을 도입하는 것은 인간에게 걱정과 공포를 준다고 합니다.

Ⅱ. It / is / the responsibility of management / to prevent or, (at least), to ease / these fears.

> 구▶ 'It + be 동사 + N + to-V'는 '가주어/진주어'입니다.
> - 그러한 공포들을 막고 적어도, 지우는 것은 경영의 책임감이라고 합니다.
> 독▶ 공장에 로봇을 도입하는 것으로 인한 공포를 지우고 막는 것이 경영의 책임이라고 합니다.

Ⅲ. **For example**, robots / could be introduced / only (in new plants) (rather than replacing / humans (in existing assembly lines)).

> 구▶ 예를 들어, 로봇은 기존 조립 라인에서 인간을 대체하는 대신에, 오직 새로운 공장에 도입될 수 있다고 합니다.
> 독▶ 'For example'이 제시되었으므로 앞 문장 중심 문장
> - 로봇 도입으로 인한 걱정과 공포를 줄이는 방법 중 하나는 로봇을 새로운 공장에만 도입하는 것과 같이 일부에만 도입하는 것이라고 합니다.

Ⅳ. Workers / **should** be included in / the planning (for new factories) or the introduction (of robots) (into existing plants), / **so** they / can participate in / the process.

> 구▶ 노동자들은 새로운 공장을 계획하거나 기존 공장에 로봇을 도입하는 계획에서 포함되어야만 하는데, 그래서 그들은 (= 노동자들은) 과정에 참여할 수 있다고 합니다.
> 독▶ 'should'가 제시되었으므로 중심 문장
> - 노동자들이 새로운 공장이나 로봇 도입의 계획에 포함되어야만 로봇이 도입되는 과정에 참여할 수 있다고 합니다.

Ⅴ. It / may be / that robots / **are needed to reduce** / manufacturing costs / **so that** the company /

remains / competitive, **but** planning (for such cost reductions) **should be done** jointly / by labor and

management.

구 회사가 경쟁력을 유지하기 위해서 로봇들은 제조 비용을 낮추는 데 필요하지만, 그러한 비용 감소를
계획하는 것은 반드시 노동자와 회사가 함께 해야만 한다고 합니다.

독 'need to', 'so that', 'but', 'should'가 제시되었으므로 중심 문장
- Ⅳ번 문장을 재진술하여 제조 비용을 감소시키는 로봇을 도입하는 것에 대한 계획에 회사와 노동자
모두 참가해야만 한다고 합니다.

Ⅵ. **Since** robots / are particularly good at / highly repetitive simple motions, / the replaced human workers

/ **should** be moved (to positions) (where judgment and decisions (beyond the abilities of robots) /

are required).

구 'be good at A'는 'A를 잘하다'를 의미합니다.
- 로봇들은 특히 매우 반복적이고 간단한 동작을 잘하기 때문에, 교체된 인간 노동자들은 로봇의 능력을
넘어선 판단과 결정이 필요한 위치로 옮겨져야만 한다고 합니다.

독 'Since', 'should'가 제시되었으므로 중심 문장
- 로봇이 도입으로 인해 로봇으로 대체된 노동자들은 로봇이 하지 못하는 판단과 결정이 필요한 직책으로
옮겨져야만 한다고 합니다.

글의 흐름으로 보아, 주어진 문장이 들어가기에 가장 적절한 곳을 고르시오.

> Personal stories connect with larger narratives to generate new identities.

The growing complexity of the social dynamics determining food choices makes the job of marketers and advertisers increasingly more difficult. (①) In the past, mass production allowed for accessibility and affordability of products, as well as their wide distribution, and was accepted as a sign of progress. (②) Nowadays it is increasingly replaced by the fragmentation of consumers among smaller and smaller segments that are supposed to reflect personal preferences. (③) Everybody feels different and special and expects products serving his or her inclinations. (④) In reality, these supposedly individual preferences **end up** overlapping with emerging, temporary, always changing, almost tribal formations solidifying around cultural sensibilities, social identifications, political sensibilities, and dietary and health concerns. (⑤) **These consumer communities** go beyond national boundaries, feeding on global and widely shared repositories of ideas, images, and practices.

* fragmentation: 파편화 ** repository: 저장소

해설 [정답 : ⑤]

Ⅰ. 주어진 문장에서는 개인적인 이야기가 새로운 정체성을 형성하며 더 큰 이야기와 연결된다고 합니다. 그러므로 주어진 문장 뒤에는 새로운 정체성을 형성하는 것에 대한 내용이 나올 가능성이 높습니다.

Ⅱ. ⑤번 앞 문장에서는 개인적 선호라고 생각되는 이런 것들은 결국 문화적 감성, 사회 정체성, 정치적 감성, 식생활과 건강에 관한 관심을 중심으로 확고해지는, 최근에 생겨나고, 일시적이며, 항상 바뀌고, 부족적인 형성물과 겹쳐지게 된다고 합니다. ⑤번 뒷 문장에서는 이들 소비자 집단이 국경을 넘어 개념, 이미지, 관습의 전 세계에 넓게 공유된 저장소로 더 강화된다고 합니다. ⑤번 앞 문장에서는 소비자 집단에 대한 언급이 없으며, 개인적 선호가 부족적인 형성물과 겹친다는 것이 국경을 넘어 확대된다고 볼 수도 없으므로 단절이 발생합니다.

Ⅲ. 주어진 문장의 개인의 이야기는 ⑤번 앞 문장의 개인적인 선호와 연결됩니다. 이것이 더 큰 이야기로 확대된다고 했으므로 이것은 또한 ⑤번 앞 문장의 문화, 사회, 정치 등과 같은 관심을 중심으로 겹쳐지게 된다는 내용 뒤에 이어져야 합니다. ⑤번 뒷 문장에서 국경을 넘어 전 세계의 저장소로 인해 더 강화된다는 내용은 주어진 문장의 대한 보충 설명으로 연결되는 것이 적절합니다. 그러므로 주어진 문장은 ⑤번에 들어가야 합니다.

주. Personal stories connect with larger narratives to generate new identities.

> 구 개인의 이야기는 새로운 정체성을 생성하며 더 큰 이야기와 연결된다고 합니다.

I. The growing complexity / of the social dynamics / determining food choices / makes the job of marketers and advertisers / increasingly more difficult.

> 구 'make + O + O.C'는 'O가 O.C하도록 만들다'를 의미합니다.
>   - 식품 선택을 결정하는 사회적 역학이 점점 복잡해지면서 마케팅 담당자와 광고주의 업무가 점점 더 어려워지고 있다고 합니다.

II. In the past, mass production / allowed for / accessibility and affordability (of products), as well as / their wide distribution, and was accepted / as a sign of progress.

> 구 과거에 대량 생산은 제품을 광범위하게 유통하게 할 뿐만 아니라 제품을 입수하고 구매 비용을 감당할 수 있게 했으며, 발전의 신호로 받아들여졌다고 합니다.

> 독 과거의 생산 구조였던 대량 생산에 관한 설명입니다.

III. Nowadays it / is increasingly replaced (by the fragmentation (of consumers (among smaller and smaller segments) (that are supposed to reflect / personal preferences))).

* fragmentation: 파편화

> 구 요즘 그것은 개인의 선호를 반영해야 하는 점점 더 작은 규모의 부문사이에서 소비자 단편화에 의해 점점 더 대체되고 있다고 합니다.

> 독 오늘날에는 대량 생산이 아니라 더 작은 규모의 생산을 실행하고 있다는 내용으로 전환되고 있습니다. 이것은 II번 문장과 대조가 됩니다.

IV. Everybody / feels / different and special / and expects / products / serving his or her inclinations.

> 구 모든 사람은 각기 다르고 특별하다고 느끼고, 자신의 기호를 만족시키는 제품을 기대한다고 합니다.

> 독 IV번 문장의 소비자 단편화가 진행된 이유에 대해 설명하고 있습니다.

V. In reality, these supposedly individual preferences / **end up** / overlapping with emerging, temporary, always changing, almost tribal formations (solidifying around cultural sensibilities, social identifications, political sensibilities, and dietary and health concerns).

> 구 현실에서, 개인적 선호라고 생각되는 이런 것들은 결국 문화적 감성, 사회 정체성, 정치적 감성, 식생활과 건강에 관한 관심을 중심으로 확고해지는, 최근에 생겨나고, 일시적이며, 항상 바뀌고, 거의 부족적인 형성물과 겹쳐지게 된다고 합니다.

> 독 'end up'은 '결국 ~가 되다'를 의미하므로 결과를 제시하는 중심 문장
>   - IV번 문장의 사람마다 다른 기호와 선호 제품을 'individual preferences'로 지칭하고 있고, 이것은 문화, 사회 등을 중심으로 다른 형성물과 맞물린다는 것입니다.

Ⅵ. These consumer communities / go (beyond national boundaries), feeding on / global and widely
shared repositories (of ideas, images, and practices).

** repository: 저장소

구▶ 이들 소비자 집단은 국경을 넘어 개념, 이미지, 관습의 전 세계의 널리 공유된 저장소로 인해 더 강화된다고 합니다.

독▶ 주어진 문장과 연결 지어 추론해본다면, 주어진 문장의 개인의 이야기는 Ⅴ번 문장의 개인적 선호를 의미하고, 이 개인적 선호가 더 큰 이야기로 연결되어, 국경을 넘어 전 세계의 개념, 이미지 등을 통해 더 강화되는 것입니다.

26 25학년도 6월 평가원 39번 (정답률 23%)

글의 흐름으로 보아, 주어진 문장이 들어가기에 가장 적절한 곳을 고르시오.

> <u>This active involvement</u> provides a basis for depth of aesthetic processing and reflection on the meaning of the work.

There are interesting trade-offs in the relative importance of subject matter (i.e., figure) and style (i.e., background). (①) In highly representational paintings, plays, or stories, the focus is on subject matter that resembles everyday life and the role of background style is to facilitate the construction of mental models. (②) Feelings of pleasure and uncertainty carry the viewer along to the conclusion of the piece. (③) In highly expressionist works, novel stylistic devices work in an inharmonious manner against the subject matter **thereby** creating a disquieting atmosphere. (④) **Thus**, when the work is less "readable" (or easily interpreted), its departure from conventional forms reminds the viewer or reader that an "aesthetic attitude" is needed to appreciate the whole episode. (⑤) An ability to switch between the "pragmatic attitude" of everyday life and an "aesthetic attitude" is fundamental to a balanced life.

* aesthetic: 미학의 ** pragmatic: 실용주의의

해설 [정답 : ⑤]

Ⅰ. 주어진 문장에서는 이러한 적극적인 관여는 미학적 처리와 작품 의미 성찰의 깊이에 대한 기반을 제공한다고 했습니다. 적극적인 관여가 대명사로 언급되었기 때문에 주어진 문장 앞에는 적극적인 관여가 무엇인지에 대한 내용이 나와야 합니다.

Ⅱ. ①번 앞 문장에서는 'subject matter' 주제와 'style' 스타일을 처음 언급합니다. ①번 뒷 문장에서는 'focus is on subject matter that resembles everyday life' 초점을 일상생활과 비슷한 주제에 맞춘다고 했고, 'role of background style is to facilitate the construction of mental models' 스타일의 역할은 심성 모형의 구성을 촉진하는 것이라고 말하며 주제와 스타일의 역할을 정리하고 있습니다. 지문은 계속해서 예술 관찰 시 주제와 스타일 간의 조화와 관련된 내용을 나열합니다.
스타일의 역할인 심성 모형 구성의 사례로 'Feelings of pleasure and uncertainty' 즐거움과 불확실성을 언급하는 ②번 뒷 문장,
'work in an inharmonious manner against the subject matter thereby creating a disquieting atmosphere' 표현주의 작품에서는 조화롭지 않은 스타일과 주제로 불안한 분위기를 조성한다는 ③번 뒷 문장,
그로 인해 'departure from conventional forms reminds the viewer or reader that an "aesthetic attitude"' 작품이 전통적 방식에서 벗어났을 때, 독자에게 "미학적 태도"가 필요하다는 새로운 주제가 언급되는 ④번 뒷 문장,
'switch between the "pragmatic attitude" of everyday life and an "aesthetic attitude"' "실용주의적 태도"와 "미학적 태도" 사이의 균형을 유지하는 것에 관한 ⑤번 뒷 문장 모두 유기적으로 연결되어 예술을 관찰하기 위한 두 태도를 설명하는 글의 주제를 설명하고 있기 때문에 단절을 잘 파악하기 어렵습니다.

Ⅲ. 그렇다면 주어진 문장의 단서인 대명사 'This active involvement' 이러한 적극적인 관여가 무엇인지를 지문에서 파악해야 합니다. 이 적극적인 관여로 인해 주어진 문장에서는 미학적 처리와 의미 성찰에 기반을 제공받는다고 했고, 이는 내용상 ⑤번 앞 문장의 미학적 태도를 사용하는 것을 의미합니다. 전체적 내용을 감상하기 위해 미학적 태도를 사용하는 것은 작품에 적극적으로 관여하는 것과 비슷하며, 그로 인해 미학적 처리와 작품 의미 성찰을 더 깊게 할 수 있는 것은 미학적 태도를 작품 감상에 사용하는 것에 대한 결과가 될 수 있습니다. 그러므로 주어진 문장은 ⑤번에 들어가야 합니다.

주. This active involvement / provides / a basis (for depth of aesthetic processing) / and reflection (on the meaning of the work.)

* aesthetic: 미학의

구▶ 이러한 적극적인 관여는 미학적 처리와 작품 의미 성찰의 깊이에 대한 기반을 제공한다고 합니다.

독▶ 적극적인 관여를 통해 가능한 효과로 미학적 처리와 의미 성찰 기반을 제공받는다는 것을 언급하고 있습니다.

Ⅰ. There / are / interesting trade-offs / in the relative importance / of subject matter (i.e., figure) / and style (i.e., background).

구▶ 주제(즉, 형상)와 스타일(즉, 배경)의 상대적 중요성에는 흥미로운 균형이 있다고 합니다.

독▶ 주제는 형상, 스타일은 배경과 같고, 둘 사이에는 중요성의 측면에서 균형이 있다고 말하고 있습니다.

Ⅱ. In highly representational paintings, plays, or stories, the focus / is / on subject matter (that / resembles / everyday life) and the role (of background style) / is / to facilitate / the construction of mental models.

구▶ 고도로 구상주의적인 그림, 연극 또는 이야기에서는 초점이 일상생활과 유사한 주제에 있고, 배경 스타일의 역할은 심성 모형의 구성을 용이하게 하는 것이라고 합니다.

독▶ Ⅰ번의 내용을 구상주의적인 사례에 적용하여 설명하고 있는 문장입니다. 일상생활과 유사한 주제에 초점을 맞춘다는 점, 배경 스타일의 역할로 정신적 모델의 구성을 촉진한다는 것이 언급됩니다.

Ⅲ. Feelings (of pleasure and uncertainty) / carry / the viewer (along to the conclusion of the piece).

구▶ 즐거움과 불확실성의 감정은 관객을 작품의 결말까지 함께 이끌고 간다고 합니다.

독▶ 언급되는 감정들은 Ⅱ번 문장의 배경 스타일로 인해 촉진된 정신적 모형의 구성이라고 볼 수 있습니다.

IV. In highly expressionist works, novel stylistic devices / work (in an inharmonious manner against the subject matter) / **thereby** / creating / a disquieting atmosphere.

구▶ 고도로 표현주의적인 작품에서는 새로운 스타일 장치가 주제와 조화롭지 않은 방식으로 작용하여, 그럼으로써 불안한 분위기를 조성한다고 합니다.

독▶ 'thereby'가 제시되었으므로 중심 문장
- Ⅱ번 문장과는 다른 사례로 표현주의적인 작품이 언급되고 있습니다. 표현주의 작품에서는 스타일과 주제가 조화롭지 않게 작용하여 불안한 분위기를 조성한다고 했습니다. 두 사례를 정리하면 다음과 같습니다.
Ⅱ번 문장-구상주의적 작품: 초점이 일상생활과 유사한 주제에 있다. 스타일-정신적 모형의 구성을 촉진한다.
Ⅳ번 문장-표현주의적 작품: 주제-새로운 스타일의 장치, 둘이 조화롭지 않게 작용하여 불안한 분위기를 조성한다.

* atmosphere - ① 대기 ② 분위기

V. **Thus**, when / the work / is / less "readable" (or easily interpreted), its departure (from conventional forms) / reminds / the viewer or reader / that / an "aesthetic attitude" / is needed / to appreciate / the whole episode.

구▶ 'remind A B'는 'A에게 B를 상기시키다.'를 의미합니다.

따라서 작품이 덜 '읽기 쉬운'(혹은 쉽게 해석되는) 상태일 때, 그것이 전통적인 방식에서 벗어났다는 것은 보는 사람이나 독자에게 작품의 전체내용을 제대로 감상하기 위해 '미학적 태도'가 필요하다는 것을 상기시킨다고 합니다.

독▶ 'Thus'가 제시되었으므로 중심 문장
- 내용적으로 중요한 문장이며 글의 주제와 가깝습니다. 작품이 읽기 덜 쉬운(=어려운) 상태라는 것, 전통적인 방식에서 벗어난 이유는 Ⅳ번 문장에서 언급된 스타일과 주제가 조화롭지 않게 작용해 불안한 분위기를 조성하기 때문입니다. 이에 대한 해결책으로 내용을 제대로 감상하기 위해 지문은 미학적 태도에 관해서 설명하고 있습니다.

* conventional - 전통적인, 관습적인

VI. An ability / to switch / between / the "pragmatic attitude" of everyday life / and an "aesthetic attitude" / is / fundamental / to a balanced life.

** pragmatic: 실용주의의

구▶ 'switch between A and B'는 'A와 B 사이에서 전환하다'를 의미합니다.

- 일상생활의 '실용주의적 태도'와 '미학적 태도' 사이를 전환하는 능력은 균형 잡힌 삶에 핵심적이라고 합니다.

독▶ 미학적 태도는 Ⅴ번 문장에서 언급된 읽기 어려운 표현주의적인 작품을 제대로 감상하는 데 필요한 태도를 의미합니다. 반면 실용주의적 태도는 Ⅱ, Ⅲ번 문장에서 언급된 구상주의적인 작품을 관람할 때 일상생활과 유사한 주제, 스타일로 인한 느낌 등으로 관객들이 작품을 관람할 때 사용하는 태도와 같은 의미라고 볼 수 있으며, 작품에 따라 두 태도를 전환해야 한다는 것이 중요하다는 것을 알 수 있습니다.

memo

Chapter

06

문법

01 20학년도 수능

다음 글의 밑줄 친 부분 중 어법상 **틀린** 것은?

해설 [정답 : ④]

주절의 술어동사인 becomes가 뒤에 있으므로 the nonhuman creatures를 수식하는 분사구가 이어져야 하는데, 뒤에 분사의 목적어인 their world가 있으므로 inhabited를 능동의 의미를 나타내는 현재분사인 inhabiting으로 고쳐야 합니다.

02 18학년도 수능

다음 글의 밑줄 친 부분 중 어법상 **틀린** 것은?

해설 [정답 : ②]

뒤에 핵심 요소를 모두 갖춘 절이 이어지고 있으므로 what은 올 수 없습니다. 문맥상 '~인지'의 의미가 되어야 하므로 what을 whether로 고쳐야 합니다. ②번 앞에 접속사 and, 그리고 제대로 된 what절이 나오지만, 병렬구조를 묻는 선지가 아닙니다.

03 19학년도 9월 평가원

다음 글의 밑줄 친 부분 중 어법상 **틀린** 것은?

해설 [정답 : ⑤]

What 뒤에 필수적인 구성 성분을 모두 갖춘 완전한 절이 왔으므로 관계대명사 what은 쓸 수 없습니다. '~라는 것'이라는 뜻을 표현하려면 명사절을 이끄는 접속사 that을 써야 합니다.

04 20학년도 6월 평가원

다음 글의 밑줄 친 부분 중 어법상 틀린 것은?

해설 [정답 : ⑤]

'~가 ~하는데 (시간)이 걸리다'라는 의미의 'it takes 시간 for ~ to do'에서 시간에 해당하는 표현인 long이 앞으로 나가 'the 비교급, the 비교급'의 일부를 이룬 문장입니다 즉, to reveal all of its subtleties to us가 의미상의 주어, 진주어이므로, that이 아니라 가주어의 역할을 하는 it으로 바꿔야 합니다.

05 22학년도 6월 평가원

다음 글의 밑줄 친 부분 중 어법상 틀린 것은?

해설 [정답 : ⑤]

'both A and B' 표현으로 연결되는 구조에서 and에 의해 see와 함께 to에 연결되어 the ability of the human mind를 수식해야 하므로, discovers를 discover로 고쳐야 합니다.

06 18학년도 6월 평가원

다음 글의 밑줄 친 부분 중 어법상 틀린 것은?

해설 [정답 : ③]

두 개의 동사구인 lay an egg in the nest of another bird와 leaves it for that bird to raise가 and로 연결되어 관계사 which(선행사 cuckoo birds)의 술어 역할을 해야 합니다. 관계사 which의 선행사가 복수이므로, leaves를 leave로 바꿔야 합니다.

07 21학년도 6월 평가원

다음 글의 밑줄 친 부분 중 어법상 틀린 것은?

해설 [정답 : ②]

the belief를 설명하는 that이 이끄는 동격절(the belief = that 이하 문장)에서 주어인 individual successes 다음에 동사가 이어져야 하므로, depending을 depend로 고쳐야 합니다.

08 18학년도 9월 평가원

다음 글의 밑줄 친 부분 중 어법상 <u>틀린</u> 것은?

해설 [**정답 : ②**]

문장 앞에 이미 문장의 술어동사인 is가 존재하므로, 동사의 역할을 하지 않으면서 the nature right outside their doors를 수식하는 현재분사 waiting으로 고쳐야 합니다.

09 21학년도 9월 평가원

다음 글의 밑줄 친 부분 중 어법상 <u>틀린</u> 것은?

해설 [**정답 : ①**]

밑줄 친 부분 다음에 the best is recognized와 the rest are overlooked가 and에 의해 연결되어 있는데, 둘 다 주어와 수동태의 구조를 가진 완전한 형태의 절이므로, 관계대명사 which를 관계부사 where로 고쳐야 합니다. where는 performance showcases를 수식합니다.

10 20학년도 9월 평가원

다음 글의 밑줄 친 부분 중 어법상 <u>틀린</u> 것은?

해설 [**정답 : ④**]

that feeling of superiority를 선행사로 하는 관계대명사 that이 이끄는 관계사절의 동사가 나와야 하기 때문에, actualizing을 actualizes로 고쳐야 합니다.

11 19학년도 6월 평가원

다음 글의 밑줄 친 부분 중 어법상 <u>틀린</u> 것은?

해설 [**정답 : ④**]

문맥상 or을 기준으로 동사 원형 take와 병렬 관계를 이루어 조동사 can과 이어져야 하므로 refuse로 고쳐야 합니다.

12 19학년도 수능

다음 글의 밑줄 친 부분 중 어법상 **틀린** 것은?

해설 [정답 : ②]

it은 the quality of monumentality를 가리키고 문맥상 그것이 성취되었다는 의미로 was achieved를 대신할 수 있도록 did를 was로 고쳐야 합니다.

13 20학년도 3월 교육청

다음 글의 밑줄 친 부분 중 어법상 **틀린** 것은?

해설 [정답 : ⑤]

두 개의 절을 연결해야 하므로 대명사 it은 적절하지 않습니다. 두 절을 연결하는 역할을 할 수 있는 관계대명사 which나, 접속사를 포함한 and it과 같은 경우로 고쳐야 합니다.

14 20학년도 7월 교육청

다음 글의 밑줄 친 부분 중 어법상 **틀린** 것은?

해설 [정답 : ④]

접속사 that절 이하 문장은 완전한 문장이 와야 하므로 lacking을 술어 동사인 lack으로 고쳐야 합니다.

15 20학년도 10월 교육청

다음 글의 밑줄 친 부분 중 어법상 **틀린** 것은?

해설 [정답 : ③]

that이 선행사가 incorporating culturally relevant pedagogy and consideration of nonacademic factors인 주격 관계대명사로 쓰였으므로, that절 뒤에는 주어가 빠진 상태인 술어 동사가 와야 합니다. 그러므로 promoting을 promote로 고쳐야 합니다.

16 20학년도 4월 교육청

다음 글의 밑줄 친 부분 중 어법상 <u>틀린</u> 것은?

해설 [정답 : ④]

문장에서 are의 보어가 와야 하므로 보어 역할을 할 수 있는 형용사가 와야 합니다. 그러므로 부사인 closely를 형용사인 close로 고쳐야 합니다.

17 19학년도 4월 교육청

다음 글의 밑줄 친 부분 중 어법상 <u>틀린</u> 것은?

해설 [정답 : ④]

is의 보어가 와야 하므로 보어 역할을 할 수 있는 형용사가 와야 합니다. 그러므로 부사인 naturally를 형용사인 natural로 고쳐야 합니다.

* 생략이 된 경우가 아니라면 문법 문제에서 'is' 뒤에는 '명사' 혹은 '형용사 (전치사 명사구 포함)'와 같은 '보어'가 와야 합니다. 하지만 ④번 문장에서는 보어가 존재하지 않으므로 'S+ is + C'의 구조가 'C + S + is'로 도치된 것을 파악할 수 있어야 합니다.

18 19학년도 10월 교육청

다음 글의 밑줄 친 부분 중 어법상 <u>틀린</u> 것은?

해설 [정답 : ③]

주어가 An individual neuron인 문장에서 술어 동사로 이미 uses가 나왔으므로 sends는 술어 동사로 쓸 수 없습니다. An individual neuron을 수식하는 현재분사 sending으로 고쳐야 합니다.

19 19학년도 7월 교육청

다음 글의 밑줄 친 부분 중 어법상 <u>틀린</u> 것은?

해설 [정답 : ③]

관계대명사 that절의 선행사는 people's beliefs입니다. 선행사가 복수 동사이므로 동사 역시 복수 동사가 와야 하므로 leads를 lead로 고쳐야 합니다.

20 19학년도 3월 교육청

다음 글의 밑줄 친 부분 중 어법상 틀린 것은?

해설 [**정답** : ⑤]

that 앞에 선행사가 없으므로 that은 접속사 역할을 하며, that절 이하에 완전한 문장이 와야 합니다. 즉 writing down future tasks의 술어 동사가 와야 하므로 unloading을 unloads로 고쳐야 합니다.

21 18학년도 4월 교육청

다음 글의 밑줄 친 부분 중 어법상 틀린 것은?

해설 [**정답** : ④]

문장에서 know의 목적어, 즉 that의 선행사가 없으므로 접속사 that이 되어야 하는데, that 뒷 문장이 주어가 없는 불완전한 문장이므로 that절로 볼 수 없습니다. 그러므로 that은 어법상 잘못되었으며, 문맥상 간접의문문의 문장이므로 의문사 which로 고쳐야 합니다.

22 18학년도 7월 교육청

다음 글의 밑줄 친 부분 중 어법상 틀린 것은?

해설 [**정답** : ③]

which 이하 문장인 we are to make the decisions has exploded가 완전한 문장이므로 관계대명사 which는 올 수 없습니다. from which와 같은 관계부사로 고쳐야 합니다.

23 18학년도 10월 교육청

다음 글의 밑줄 친 부분 중 어법상 틀린 것은?

해설 [**정답** : ④]

humiliate의 주체는 it(This data)인데, 수동의 의미인 humiliated는 문맥상 적절치 않으므로 능동의 의미를 가진 humiliating으로 고쳐야 합니다.

24 18학년도 3월 교육청

다음 (A), (B), (C)에 들어갈 말로 알맞은 것을 고르시오.

해설 [**정답 : ②**]

(A) '명령문, and ~' ~하면 ~할 것이다라는 의미의 구문이므로 명령문 문장이 나와야 합니다. 그러므로 Adopt가 적절합니다.

(B) deprive의 동작 주체와 대상이 같으므로 대상을 지칭하는 재귀대명사 themselves를 써야 합니다.

(C) 뒤에 오는 절이 문장의 요소를 모두 갖춘 완전한 형태이므로 관계부사 where을 써야 합니다.

25 17학년도 7월 교육청

다음 글의 밑줄 친 부분 중 어법상 틀린 것은?

해설 [**정답 : ④**]

접속사 While이 나오기 때문에 밑줄 친 부분은 주어가 both civilizations, 술어 동사로 구성된 완전한 문장이 와야 하며, 현재분사 having를 had로 바꿔야 합니다.

26 17학년도 10월 교육청

다음 글의 밑줄 친 부분 중 어법상 틀린 것은?

해설 [**정답 : ①**]

문장의 핵심 성분인 주어(the latter), 동사(will not disclose), 목적어(the information provided)가 모두 있는 완전한 문장이므로 관계대명사 which가 올 수 없습니다. 접속사인 that과 같은 것으로 고쳐야 합니다.

27 17학년도 4월 교육청

다음 글의 밑줄 친 부분 중 어법상 틀린 것은?

해설 [**정답 : ⑤**]

주어가 the traditional link이므로 단수 동사가 와야 하며, were을 was로 바꿔야 합니다.

28   17학년도 3월 교육청

다음 글의 밑줄 친 부분 중 어법상 **틀린** 것은?

해설 [정답 : ④]

문장의 주어인 The effects가 동사 damage의 주체이므로 능동의 의미를 가진 damaging으로 고쳐야 합니다.

29   22학년도 수능

다음 글의 밑줄 친 부분 중 어법상 **틀린** 것은?

해설 [정답 : ④]

What이 관계대명사가 된다면 뒤에 나온 절이 불완전해야 하는데, 뒤의 절이 주어 (cell metabolism and structure), 동사 (should be), 보어 (complex)로 이루어진 완전한 문장이 오므로 관계대명사 what이 쓰일 수가 없습니다. What을 That과 같은 단어로 바꿔야 합니다.

30   22학년도 10월 교육청

다음 글의 밑줄 친 부분 중 어법상 **틀린** 것은?

해설 [정답 : ②]

approached가 앞의 something을 수식하므로 분사구문이라는 것을 알 수 있습니다. 해석상 something approached a local form, 지역의 예술 형태에 접근하는 어떤 것, 능동태의 역할을 하는 현재분사가 쓰여야 하므로 approached를 approaching으로 바꿔야 합니다.

31   22학년도 9월 평가원

다음 글의 밑줄 친 부분 중 어법상 **틀린** 것은?

해설 [정답 : ③]

관계대명사 which 뒤의 절이 주어 (those), 동사 (will be), 보어 (better ~)으로 이루어진 완전한 문장이 오므로 뒷 문장이 불완전해야 하는 which가 올 수 없습니다. 해석상 선행사 guarantees와 관계사절 뒤의 문장이 같은 내용이므로 동격의 that으로 바꿔야 합니다.

32 21학년도 7월 교육청

다음 글의 밑줄 친 부분 중 어법상 <u>틀린</u> 것은?

해설 [정답 : ⑤]

전치사 with 뒤에 주어 (each) 동사 (believes)로 완전한 문장이 오므로 잘못되었습니다. with + N + V-ing 분사구문으로 'N이 V하면서'로 해석되어야 하므로 believes를 believing으로 바꿔야 합니다.

33 21학년도 4월 교육청

다음 글의 밑줄 친 부분 중 어법상 <u>틀린</u> 것은?

해설 [정답 : ⑤]

So uniformly를 강조하기 위해 문장의 앞으로 나가면서 주어 (this expectation)와 동사 (is)가 도치된 문장입니다. 원래 문장은 this expectation is so uniform that the ~, so that 강조 구문이며, is의 보어 역할을 하는 형용사가 와야 하므로 uniformly를 uniform으로 바꿔야 합니다.

* uniform은 제복이라는 뜻의 명사로도 쓰이지만, 획일적인이라는 뜻의 형용사로도 쓰입니다.

34 23학년도 9월 평가원

다음 글의 밑줄 친 부분 중 어법상 <u>틀린</u> 것은?

해설 [정답 : ②]

②번 문장에서 의문사 + to 부정사인 'how to choose from alternatives and make a decision'은 복수 명사이므로 requires의 주어가 될 수 없으며, 일반동사인 Learn 역시 술어 동사 requires의 주어 역할을 할 수 없으므로 주어 역할을 할 수 있는 준동사인 동명사 Learning이나 to 부정사 To learn으로 고쳐야 합니다.

35 23학년도 6월 평가원

다음 글의 밑줄 친 부분 중 어법상 틀린 것은?

해설 [정답 : ③]

③번 문장에서 관계대명사 which 뒷 문장이 주어, 동사가 존재하는 문장이 오므로 주어 또는 목적어가 빠진 불완전한 문장이 와야 하는 which는 올 수가 없습니다. 이 경우, 뒷 문장의 주어 rhythmic time이 선행사 others의 소유격이 되므로 선행사인 others를 수식하는 관계절을 이끌면서 뒤에 있는 rhythmic time을 수식할 수 있는 소유격 관계대명사가 필요합니다. 그러므로 which를 whose로 고쳐야 합니다.

36 23학년도 수능

다음 글의 밑줄 친 부분 중 어법상 틀린 것은?

해설 [정답 : ②]

②번 문장 일부분을 해석하면 다음과 같습니다. '옷은 사람들이 자신을 세상에 보여주는 방식의 일부이다'
여기서 how 절의 주어인 people이 스스로를 보여주는 것이므로 주어와 목적어가 같다는 것을 알수 있습니다. 그러므로 them은 재귀대명사인 themselves로 바꿔야 합니다.